THE SCHIZOPHRENIC SYNDROME

An Annual Review
1971

The Schizophrenic Syndrome:

An Annual Review
1971

Edited by

ROBERT CANCRO, M.D.

Professor, Department of Psychiatry
University of Connecticut Health Center (Hartford)

BRUNNER/MAZEL • New York
BUTTERWORTHS • London

FOREWORD

The fact that Doctor Cancro and his distinguished International Advisory Board have decided to publish a collection of the latest outstanding articles on the schizophrenic syndrome will be applauded by psychiatrists everywhere. As it is made up, the work presents rather a complete overview of the latest thinking about this great enigma which still challenges clinicians and researchers alike and which is the source of so much distress to families of victims of the illness.

As the editor of several publications, this writer is struck by the need for works of this kind. He is aware of the fact that they must be uneven as compendiums are wont to be. But there is a unity in the unevenness and that is worthwhile. When one considers the amount of material that comes over an editor's desk that is of the "me too" and "I can do it better" variety, one can appreciate unity and practicality.

The value of an expert overview, a collection of authoritative articles by men known to be expert in the field, is therefore apparent. Clinicians, researchers, teachers, and writers will be appreciative of a compendium gathered in one volume, written by men expert in the field, and selected by men aware of the overall picture and aware, too, of the needs of the readers.

About the only thing we can all agree on in regard to schizophrenia at the moment is that we are dealing with a multiform disorder, and progress in understanding it is moving as does progress in general—not in a straight line but in a spiral. We pass the same point after a time, but it is on a higher plane, and now there is justification for believing that we are closer to the goal which we so earnestly seek. There is renewed interest in the study of genetic factors in schizophrenia. When heredity was emphasized in the illness at the end of the last century, it resulted in the loss of interest and some despair by the clinicians. They felt they were dealing with illnesses beyond redemption and they gave up their interest in "moral treatment." It was then that the large hospitals became "warehouses."

Presently, however, the situation is different. Approach to this segment of the problem is on a much higher plane. There is good evidence that genetic factors are necessary but by no means sufficient for the development of the disorder. Then, too, the science of genetics has advanced markedly, mayhaps too fast, for the world may not be ready for it, as it is not ready for weather control, and was not ready for nuclear fission. It is obvious, therefore, that the present volume will fulfill a need, it will locate us in space and indicate to us what we know and what we do not know, and we can move on from there.

It will be hard to find a more knowledgeable group of writers on the schizophrenias than the ones included herein. "The cast of characters" is studded with well-known names and interlarded with new ones with fresh viewpoints, both of which are necessary. The amount of material already written on the subject is incalculable and there is danger that the clinician, already surfeited with material, might become jaded and depend upon material he learned in his residency years. This contemporary volume has been carefully selected and weeded and is available for perusal as time permits. That the offering will be of value to the residents preparing for the "Boards" goes without saying.

Though I am tempted as an older clinician to point out some of the names which adorn the table of contents, I shall resist that temptation and simply say that in presenting this contemporary overview of a most difficult subject, the editors perform a valuable service to the specialty.

FRANCIS J. BRACELAND, M.D.
Hartford, Connecticut

CONTENTS

SECTION V
GENETIC STUDIES

SECTION VI
COGNITIVE AND PERCEPTUAL STUDIES

SECTION VII
PROGNOSIS

PREFACE

Some time ago Mr. Bernard Mazel suggested that there was a real need for an annual review of the literature on the schizophrenic syndrome. My first reaction was rather negative but this failed to dissuade him from his advocacy of the idea. Shortly thereafter his suggestion was presented by me to a group of residents who responded to it very positively. Being of a scientific bent of mind (and not liking to be proven wrong), I then presented the idea to a second group of residents. They were equally supportive. It was easier to concede defeat at this point vis-à-vis residents than to continue to seek out more samples. Since it was obvious that generalizing from residents to more senior psychiatrists was methodologically unsound, I discussed the idea with several older colleagues who were also enthusiastic. Gradually I came to realize that there is a need among interested professionals for some guidance through the everexpanding literature on the schizophrenic reactions.

The goal of the project is to identify and collect in one source the outstanding contributions during a specified period of time. In order to achieve this goal it is necessary to review the European and Asian literature as well as the American. The selection of our International Advisory Board was in response to the recognition of this need. The Board is an exceedingly distinguished one and I am grateful for their willingness to participate in making the selections. The members of the board are Manfred Bleuler, L. T. Doi, Robert G. Heath, Gabriel Langfeldt, David Rosenthal, David Shakow, John K. Wing, and Lyman C. Wynne.

It was decided to emphasize primarily the journal literature but not to exclude individual chapters that were published in a book. The value of this effort is in part the listing of recommendations which have *not* been included in the volume for a variety of administrative reasons; e.g., untranslated, permission to reprint not obtained, space, etc. There were several chapters and articles in the English literature which were recommended. These included Leopold Bellak's *Research on Ego Func-*

tion Patterns: *A Progress Report* which appeared in *The Schizophrenic Syndrome* edited by Leopold Bellak and Laurence Loeb, published by Grune & Stratton in 1969. Also recommended but not included were: *Clinical Prediction of Outcome in Schizophrenia* by Robert Cancro which appeared in *Comprehensive Psychiatry*, 349, 10, 1969; *A Report on a Pair of Male Monozygotic Twins Discordant for Schizophrenia* by David A. MacSweeney which appeared in *The British Journal of Psychiatry*, 315, 116, 1970; *Genetic Research in the Schizophrenic Syndrome* by David Rosenthal which appeared in *The Schizophrenic Reactions: A Critique of the Concept, Hospital Treatment, and Current Research* edited by Robert Cancro and published by Brunner/Mazel in 1970; *Twin Studies in Schizophrenia and Neuroses* by James R. Stabenau, William Pollin, and Martin G. Allen which appeared in *Seminars in Psychiatry*, 65, 2, 1970; and, *Hallucinations and Delusions as Points on Continua Function* by John S. Strauss which appeared in the *Archives of General Psychiatry*, 581, 21, 1969. For a Russian viewpoint of clinical psychiatry, *Symptom, Syndrome, Disease: A Clinical Method in Psychiatry* by A. V. Snezhnevsky was recommended. It appeared in Sylvano Arieti's *World Biennial of Psychiatry and Psychotherapy* which was published by Basic Books in 1970.

For the German-reading public the following articles were recommended: *Über Familienforschung und Therapie bei Schizophrenen* by L. Kaufmann and C. Muller which appeared in *Der Nervenarzt*, 302, 40, 1969; *Die Gesellschaft und ihre psychish Kranken*, by J.-E. Meyer which appeared in *Universitas*, 24. *Jahrgang*, Nov. 1969, 1167; *Die Katatonie* by B. Pauleikhoff which appeared in *Fortschritte der Neurologie und Psychiatrie*, 461, 37, 1969; *Verhaltensbiologische Hypothesen zur Entstehung endogener Psychosen* by D. Ploog which appeared in Gerd Huber's *Schizophrenie und Zyklothymie* published by Thieme in 1969; and, *Zur nosologischen Umgrenzung der kindlichen und präpuberalen Schizophrenie aus katamnestischer Sicht* by C. Eggers & H. Stutte which appeared in *Fortschritte der Neurologie und Psychiatrie*, 305, 37, 1969.

Also untranslated into English are two selections from the Japanese literature. The first is *My Approach to Schizophrenics* by Yoichi Eguma, which appeared in *Seihin Igaku*, 235, 11, 1969. The second is a chapter on Shunen which appeared in *Seishinbunseki to Seishinbyori* by L. T. Doi published by Igakushoin in 1970.

The selections included in this volume were taken from the literature of January 1969 through June of 1970, inclusive. Future volumes will cover only a twelve month period. We are not confining the selection to a fixed number nor are we seeking fixed numbers in any particular category. The articles represent the most important contributions in terms of original research, original ideas, or reviews of a topic. The eight categories into which this present volume is divided are not permanent. As the emphasis in the literature fluctuates, so will our categories and the number of articles within those categories.

An effort such as this one involves an obligation to many people. First I would like to thank the authors, editors, and publishers who have permitted us to reprint their work. I am also deeply grateful to the International Advisory Board for making the selections. Mrs. Beatrice Cherlin, my secretary, and Mrs. Gloria Cancro, my wife, have borne up remarkably well under the vicissitudes of bringing this volume into existence. My list of thanks would be incomplete without acknowledging their efforts.

ROBERT CANCRO, M.D.
June, 1971

Section I

HISTORICAL DEVELOPMENT, CLASSIFICATION, AND THEORETICAL CONSIDERATIONS

1

SOME RESULTS OF RESEARCH IN SCHIZOPHRENIA

Manfred Bleuler

The Dean Research Award was established by the Fund for the Behavioral Sciences and is presented jointly with the American College of Psychiatrists to emphasize the importance of basic research toward an understanding of schizophrenia; each year, a scientist who has made an important contribution in this area is honored.

Following is the text of a lecture delivered by Dr. Manfred Bleuler on the occasion of his receiving the eighth annual award of $2,500 at a seminar held in Atlanta, Georgia, February 14, 1970, by the American College of Psychiatrists. Dr. Bleuler is a member of a distinguished family which has for many decades been associated with the Burghölzli Clinic in Zürich, Switzerland, and is the son of Eugen Bleuler, the originator of the term "schizophrenia." In his own right, Dr. Bleuler has developed an international reputation as a result of his clinical investigations of schizophrenia. He has devoted himself to long-term followup studies of large populations of patients with this illness and has made statistical analyses which not only have advanced our knowledge of schizophrenia as an illness, but have also thrown light on its genesis, diagnosis, and therapy.

It would be quite inappropriate for me to give you an over-all presentation of the problems of schizophrenia on such an occasion. Rather, I should like to discuss some of the results of the research carried out by myself and others at Burghölzli.

RESEARCH AIMS

Our research has been directed towards three important areas. We have followed the history of the psychosis and the life-history of patients as well as the life histories of their close relatives over long periods, mainly, decades. We have tested various influences on the course of the psychosis, particularly that of the therapy, but also the effect from other

Reprinted from *Behavioral Science*, Volume 15, No. 3, 1970, by permission of James G. Miller, M.D., Ph.D., Editor, and the American College of Psychiatrists, sponsors of the Stanley R. Dean Research Award. Copyright 1970, *Behavioral Science*.

sources, such as the loss of relatives, long periods of hospitalization, and so on. The main work within these boundaries has been a study of 208 schizophrenics who were admitted to the Burghölzli Clinic in 1942-43. All of these patients, as well as their parents, siblings, spouses, and off-spring, were followed until 1963-64, or until death.

We have investigated how essential a role physical damage plays in the genesis of schizophrenia. Because I wanted to know how frequently and to what degree schizophrenic or similar complications arose in somatic patients, I examined the sequelae of the most varying physical disturb-ances. If somatic damage is important in the genesis of schizophrenia, then schizophrenic or similar psychoses could be expected to occur among physical patients. I have been particularly interested in the psycho-pathology of all kinds of endocrine illnesses.

SPECIFIC STUDIES

Throughout my career, I have felt that one knows the patient he has personally treated best, and so the great majority of schizophrenics in my research have been my own personal patients. From these, I have selected a few who I think merit attention here. These consist mainly of the 208 schizophrenics and their families mentioned above. I shall discuss schizophrenic psychoses which endured for decades, their therapy, research on their etiology, and the fate of the schizophrenic's offspring. But I shall not here document these with specific figures: all the correla-tions and exact citations appear in my writings and I refer the interested to those sources.[1]

Diagnosis

We should not speak of the course of schizophrenia without com-menting on diagnosis. As you are well aware, the term "schizophrenia" is frequently misused: there are still some who use this diagnosis only for the most severe, incurable, and deteriorating psychoses. Others use it in such a wide sense that almost all of us could be called schizophrenic. In Europe, at least, it is becoming more and more usual to call a poli-tician schizophrenic when one does not agree with him.

The diagnosis of schizophrenia must be reserved for real psychoses. It entails an extremely severe alteration of the personality, at least tem-porarily. If we judge from our own everyday experience and that of our healthy fellowmen, we cannot understand the thoughts, feelings, and

---

[1] A selected bibliography of Dr. Bleuler's research may be found at the end of this article.

behavior of a psychotic. This does not exclude the possibility of an understanding during careful psychiatric treatment. People who are well-characterized, so-called originals, schizoids, psychopaths, nervous subjects, and so on are not included in my diagnosis of schizophrenia.

Criteria. What kinds of psychoses do we then acknowledge as being schizophrenias? Most important for diagnosis is the double life in the schizophrenic: behind or beside psychotic phenomena, signs of a normal intellectual and emotional life can be discovered. Furthermore, I have made the diagnosis of schizophrenia only if at least three of the following signs were present: (*a*) typical schizophrenic dissociation of thought; (*b*) typical alterations of emotional expressions; (*c*) catatonic symptoms; and (*d*) delusions or hallucinations of the sort usual in schizophrenia. Psychoses with amnesic symptoms, with thought disorders of the organic type, or with somnolence are never considered to be schizophrenic. Conjectures as to the course and prognosis should not be considered when the diagnosis is being made. Much more could be said with regard to diagnosis. It is sufficient to state here that, with the above mentioned diagnostic criteria in mind, a large majority of psychiatrists agree concerning the diagnosis "schizophrenia" in a large proportion of patients.

Course

Schizophrenia used to be considered a disease that was, generally speaking, progressive in nature. However, such an assumption was based mainly on the observation of hospitalized, chronic patients. My own investigations give quite another picture. They have been carried out on unselected patients, and they have also included all the patients who were discharged after hospitalization. *On an average the psychosis shows no change for the worse after a duration of five years.* Twenty, 25, and more years after the onset of psychosis, the proportion of recovered to improved and to unimproved patients remains the same as five years after onset. This statement is just as valid if we take hospitalization, earning capacity, or general psychiatric findings as a criterion. After the fifth year of the psychosis, about one-fourth of the schizophrenics are always still hospitalized and three-fourths are not. It is important to add that the one-fourth who remain hospitalized does not always consist of the same patients. Many patients are hospitalized for a certain time, discharged, and later readmitted. What remains stable is only the proportion of hospitalized as compared to nonhospitalized patients.

I shall select only two figures from my statistics in regard to the social condition of schizophrenics decades after the onset of the disease: after the fifth year, about half the former patients live outside the hospital without special care or treatment; only about 10 percent live permanently in hospital wards for severe and moderately severe cases. It is not always the same patients who are hospitalized. These figures are valid at least for Switzerland in the middle of this century.

Of more general value is the evaluation of the course on the basis of an over-all psychiatric assessment. More than a quarter of the patients still develop acute episodes 20 to 40 years after the onset of the psychosis, and they improve or again recover from these. Such patients never attain any long-standing stable condition; however, more than half —perhaps even three-quarters—do attain stability some years after onset: between a fourth and a third of these are definite recoveries. It should be added, however, that no chronic schizophrenic conditions are entirely stable. If we observe old schizophrenics carefully, we always see fluctuations of their conditions. What is surprising and unexpected is a further observation: late changes in the condition of old schizophrenics are more frequently improvements than deteriorations. Improvements in chronic schizophrenics 20, 30, and more years after onset of the psychosis are frequent, and in rare cases we even see late recoveries.

Careful observation also shows that even decades after onset schizophrenics quite frequently show reactions to environmental changes which make psychological sense. I shall mention only one pertinent example which impressed me very much. After the death of a near relative, the psychotic condition of a schizophrenic is often altered. Whether the condition is improved or impaired depends upon the type of relationship the patient had to the deceased: if the patient was dependent upon the deceased in an infantile manner and if he did not fight against his dependence, the death of the protective person is usually followed by impairment. This is not the case if the patient had a highly ambivalent and painful relationship to the deceased, if he fought against his dependence, if he sought protection and at the same time hated the protection and the protector. In such a case, the death of a relative can be followed by the improvement of a chronic schizophrenic.

All these findings together give us the modern picture of schizophrenic psychoses. The general, average course of the disease during decades is not toward progressive deterioration, not toward petrification, not toward dementia, not toward the loss of all human qualities and a mere vegetative existence. On the contrary, whereas it was formerly thought that the outcome of real schizophrenia would always be complete deterioration if the patient lived long enough, today we have reason to hope, rather, that all schizophrenics could recover if they lived long enough. Research on the clinical course of the illness confirms what clinicians realized long ago: in the schizophrenic, the healthy human is hidden and remains hidden, even if the psychosis lasts long. The healthy life of schizophrenics is never extinguished. How different such an observation is from what we see in patients with chronic brain diseases!

Therapy

If we survey the successes and the failures of most therapies, not only some months or years afterwards, but also two and more decades later, we can no longer believe that one specific therapeutic procedure is the correct one. We rather see that any procedure may either succeed or fail. Each therapeutic technique may be successful if it accomplishes one or more of the following results: (*a*) helps to introduce the patient to an active community; (*b*) confronts him suddenly with new responsibilities or severe dangers; or (*c*) helps him to quiet down and relax. These aims must be striven for. It is of secondary importance what technique in the service of these aims is chosen.

> (*a*) An active community may be built up in very different ways: in many cases, initially during the personal psychotherapy, and then later in group psychotherapy with a physician or an occupational therapist as leader. Life in a ward of the hospital should in itself be group therapy. Sometimes the family of the patient can be a good therapeutic community, for instance if the members work together in agriculture or in a family business. In other cases, a first contact between the patient, his nurses, and his doctors might best be initiated during somatic therapy.
>
> (*b*) Confrontation with a new and threatening situation even in the healthy mobilizes emotional and somatic defensive forces. The effects of electroshock and of other shock therapies probably arise mainly from such a mobilization. Even more important than somatic shock is sudden confrontation with a new and surprising social situation demanding action: giving the patient unexpected responsibilities, early discharge from the hospital, sudden change of hospitals, and so on. Surprising and appropriate interpretation in direct psychotherapeutic analysis can have the same effect.
>
> (*c*) Quiet and orderly surroundings as well as regularity in the day's schedule have a tranquilizing influence. The way in which physicians, nurses, and relatives speak with the patient and react to his morbid behavior is of great importance. They have to be natural and must behave as they actually are and as they feel, but at the same time, they must feel and must show a stable and mature kind of sympathy. Their personalities must enable them to remain calm and benevolent when confronted with wild outbursts and resistance.

Every measure which results in introducing a schizophrenic to an active community, in shaking him out of his autism, or in calming down his excitation may be helpful. Choice of special therapeutic techniques and of their sequence has to be adapted to the most personal needs and to the momentary condition of the patient.

RESULTS

I have compared the outcome of the 208 schizophrenic patients from my main studies to the outcome of other patients who had fallen ill some decades earlier. The resultant statistics enable us to compare the efficiencies of former and more recent treatments. The result of such a comparison corresponds to the impression of most clinicians. It seems certain that:

1. The most severe forms of schizophrenia can be prevented by appropriate therapy. I refer to the psychoses which start early in life with an acute episode, followed without improvement by a life-long chronic condition. This form of psychosis, which used to be frequent at the beginning of the century, is less common now.

2. All schizophrenic conditions can at least be improved and alleviated by therapy.

3. With the help of therapy, episodic courses with good intermissions are becoming more frequent, and chronic psychoses with constant hospitalization, rarer.

These are encouraging statements. Two further statements are less so:

4. My statistics do not indicate that the number of permanent, full recoveries has increased since the improvement of therapeutic methods.

5. The statistics do not show that the number of severe chronic psychoses is diminished by therapy.

Such a lack of statistical evidence does not exclude the possibility that in some cases therapy results in permanent full recovery of otherwise chronic patients. These fortunate results, however, are not frequent enough to be visible in statistics.

Nobody denies that the introduction of neuroleptic drugs was an important step in the progress of schizophrenic therapy. Reliable statistics demonstrate that the prognosis of the disease some months or even some years after its onset is best if the patients have been put on neuroleptics after admission to hospital. On the other hand I should like to point out that none of my 208 patients took neuroleptics for long periods. Despite the lack of longstanding medication, the percentage of steady recoveries is great. If we consider such an observation and if we also consider the many dangers of neuroleptic medication for long periods, we shall be cautious in its application. We can dispense with permanent administration of drugs more frequently than usual. However, there are some patients in whom new acute attacks can be prevented only by medication lasting many years. In other instances a chronic psychosis can be kept under a certain control only with permanent medication.

THE GENESIS AND NATURE OF SCHIZOPHRENIA

A good deal of my clinical work has been devoted to investigating the conditions under which schizophrenia develops. Like most clinicians, I have abandoned the idea that one single cause of the disease can be discovered. There must be a combination of many different conditions in the background of schizophrenia.

Clinical experience compels me first to make a negative statement: I have studied very carefully the endocrinological functions of schizophrenics and the psychopathology of endocrine patients. Clinical experience can easily be summarized in the statement: Endocrine patients are not schizophrenics and schizophrenics are not endocrine patients. We studied not only the psychopathology of endocrine patients but also the psychopathology of many other severe acute somatic patients in general hospital practice. If they became mentally disturbed, it was not, as a rule, in the same way schizophrenics did.

Genesis

One of the most profound experiences a physician can have is to plunge into the study of the lives of schizophrenics and their relatives. He feels as if he were caught up in a fatal destiny, in a tragedy which follows logical lines. Frequently, the person who later became a patient was a problem child of problem parents. We can follow step-by-step how the child influenced his parents, and how the parents affected their child, in unhealthy ways. As he grows, the child becomes more difficult, more afflicted, more dependent, and more insecure. Growing up as a harmonious personality becomes more and more impossible for the child, and being a good parent becomes more and more impossible for the parents. If new demands are made on the unity and harmony of the personality, on the constancy and harmony of the ego, the psychosis breaks out in a way that seems to be fatal. Many clinicians have had the same impression. It has frequently and carefully been described in the psychoanalytical and phenomenological literature.

I suffer doubts when I consider critically my impression that the disease develops clearly as the consequence of the actions and reactions of the patient's personality to his human environment. Can we explain such a tremendous disaster as becoming schizophrenic by simple psychological conclusions, just as we explain everyday experiences with our healthy acquaintances? Similar doubts lead many physicians to refuse to consider that schizophrenia could be psychogenic. Jaspers comes to the conclusion that it is not from philosophic considerations. I know that these same doubts do not play the same dominant role in American psychiatry.

As the physician of a schizophrenic whom I have studied carefully, I am tormented again and again with this great question: Have I discovered the actual etiology or have I imagined it? Can I deduce the causes of the psychosis from psychological principles? Is an apparent psychodynamic explanation the right one? Confronted with these questions, I feel myself compelled to look for answers in every possible way.

Statistical considerations are important to the study of the problem. I investigated the frequencies of many kinds of psychological stress in the life histories of schizophrenics and compared them to their frequencies in the life histories of other patients and of healthy people. I could not find an outstanding specific stress situation in the history of all schizophrenics which was not also common in the history of many other people. Certainly misery of any kind is more frequent in the premorbid lives of schizophrenics than in the general population, but not more frequent than in the lives of patients with neurotic or psychopathic development, or with drug or alcohol problems. Widespread inquiries, including the questioning of 3,355 persons, showed, for instance, that a broken home is on the average not more common in the histories of schizophrenics than in the population as a whole.

In spite of all this, the search for statistical correlations with possible psychogenic bases for the illness has not been useless. If the correlations failed to explain schizophrenia clearly and simply as a psychological problem, they have confirmed, nevertheless, that at least some psychological reactions in many cases have some significance for its etiology. My statistics showed, for instance, that many types of worry about a loved person have different incidences in schizophrenic men than in schizophrenic women. Early loss of a parent which increased tension in the relationship with the remaining parent during childhood, and education by schizophrenic parents or by foster parents are more frequent in female than in male schizophrenics. The pathogenic significance of emotional stresses in the parental family is further demonstrated by another observation: among schizophrenics who have schizophrenic siblings, there are more women than men. We must conclude that familial worries during childhood are more important for the genesis of the psychosis in girls than in boys (or only important in girls). A similar observation can be made after onset of the disease: dramatic alterations of the psychotic condition after the death of the father, the mother, the husband, or a loved one are more frequent in women than in men.

All this seems to indicate that disturbed relationships with the family members are significant for the development of schizophrenia in women. Statistics demonstrate that causal relationships do exist. In schizophrenic men the relationships to other men, to managers, and to subordinates probably play a similar role.

Statistics up to now do not prove that schizophrenia is a psychogenetic disease. They only suggest that some psychological developments participate in the genesis of the psychosis. This is not much, but it is an encouragement when we are meditating and pondering over a life history and when we are trying to identify ourselves with our schizophrenic patient.

Hereditary Predisposition

It is not possible in all cases to trace a convincing story of psychological dynamics. Most resistant to any psychological explanation are the benign, acute, phasic forms of schizophrenia. We are frequently quite perplexed when we try to discover the psychodynamics of a sudden acute new episode which arises in a seemingly recovered patient. These phasic schizophrenic psychoses frequently lack a convincing psychological background which often characterizes manic-depressive psychoses. There are also reasons to assume that hereditary predispositions are more decisive for these forms of illness.

It is impossible to find in the life history of schizophrenics any psychotraumatic situation to which only schizophrenics and not also many non-schizophrenic people were exposed. Nobody has been successful in discovering a specific psychotraumatic situation in the background of schizophrenia. Psychological and environmental reasons and psychodynamics are, therefore, not sufficient in themselves to explain schizophrenia. We must postulate other dispositions and we cannot find any others but personal sensibilities due to hereditary predispositions.

I cannot discuss here in detail the hereditary background of schizophrenia but should only like to point out that it should be considered differently from the way it was viewed during the last half century. The view that schizophrenia is transmitted from one generation to the next through a pathogenic gene, according to Mendel's law, has become quite improbable. Family histories and the number of schizophrenics among relatives of schizophrenics do not support such an assumption. A further important argument against the Mendelian theory of schizophrenia is found in the fact that schizophrenics are much less fertile in comparison to the general population. I was able to confirm this finding of earlier authors. Diminished fertility in a disease of the frequency of schizophrenia, if it resulted from one or two pathogenic genes, would presuppose a much higher mutation rate than has ever been observed. We can exclude the possibility that the essential background of schizophrenia consists in one or a few pathogenic genes which influence the brain by an error of metabolism.

On the contrary, however, there is much evidence for the assumption that the hereditary background of schizophrenia is given by many genes. These might not be pathogenic in themselves. The hereditary predisposition might rather consist of a lack of harmony among different inborn dispositions, an incompatibility of certain constellations of genes.

On the basis of what we know and leaving out speculations, we can summarize our present knowledge about the nature and genesis of schizophrenia: the background of schizophrenia consists in both dysharmonic, contradictory inborn dispositions in the development of the personality, and dysharmonic, contradictory human relationships. An unsound human environment reinforces the contradictions in the personality and the unsound personality creates contradictory attitudes towards the later patient. He gets sick when confronted with severe demands. Therapeutic experience confirms this theory that the same influences which help the schizophrenic also develop a strong and resistant personality in the healthy: being a member of a community, in which we can use hands and brains, at times confrontation with difficulties and dangers and enough time to calm down and relax.

THE CHILDREN OF SCHIZOPHRENICS

An important part of my interest and of my research has been devoted to the children of schizophrenics. Their expectation of health and happiness, according to other authors, is poor. Kallman, for instance, found that 15 percent of them were destined to become schizophrenic, many of them schizoid, and psychopathic, while only about one-third could be expected to be normal.

In my own experience, 9 percent of the children of schizophrenics themselves become schizophrenic, if they grow to maturity. Some other authors agree. On the other hand, I found many more healthy children and fewer psychopathic children than did most other authors. Nearly three-quarters of the children of my schizophrenics are healthy. It is interesting to look for the reasons behind such a tremendous difference between the findings of most other authors and myself. The main reason is to be found, I believe, in the way I became acquainted with these children, which was quite different from that of the other authors. I was the physician responsible for treating the schizophrenics and often also their children. I knew the life history and the living conditions of these children. Other authors who have investigated the children of schizophrenics have carefully collected information with regard to unsound personality traits. The result of the two types of observation must be different: a collection of unhappy personality types easily gives the picture of a psychopathic personality—if one does not consider the terrible living conditions to which these personality types were a reaction. A timid, retiring, and moody child might be called a psychopath, but not if one knows that his paranoid mother has isolated this child from any contact with other children and other people, that she even keeps him away from school, and warns him all day long against delusional persecutors. I admire the love of these children for their sick mothers and fathers, their endeavors to help them, and their fight for a suitable position in life in spite of the tremendous restraints and sufferings conferred upon them by their parents' psychoses. Compared to these healthy aspects of their personality, the unhealthy ones have often seemed to me to be insignificant.

The further life history of these children frequently demonstrates that, when the immediate influence of the schizophrenic parent had ceased, they developed into healthy and able adults. They had not been psychopathic, but had shown a quite natural reaction to a terrifying stress situation, and were able after it was over to overcome their difficulties.

We must esteem the great energy with which most children of schizophrenics fight their way toward a good social position in life, in spite of tremendous difficulties. The large majority of the children of my schizophrenics who have grown up have achieved what can be expected from their schooling and professional training, and have reached the social standard of their parents or have even surpassed it. Some of them seem to have been hardened and to have developed strong personalities because of the hardships of their childhood.

Until recently, the interest in the children of schizophrenics has been concentrated upon their mental health. Their suffering in itself, however, has not been described and considered enough. Their care and education are often neglected to an unbelievable degree. It is true that many schizophrenic parents can love their children and be very kind to them, but it is also true that many others maltreat their children, both physically and morally. The children suffer even more from the ambivalent attitude of their parents than from their constant cruelty. Many healthy parents are not able to protect their children from illtreatment at the hands of psychotics. The children of schizophrenics are also frequently cared for by foster parents who are not equal to the task. As a rule the grief of these children remains concealed. They do not complain themselves. Their parents have distorted memories of what they have done to their children and they deny maltreating them. The foster parents remain silent on the subject of their incompetence.

If one considers the sad childhood of many children of schizophrenics, one is astonished that many more than half of them are healthy personalities. However, the grief even of many of the healthy children exists, and it is never quite extinguished. It overshadows their life. They feel humiliated by misery and inferior to happier people. I have heard many of them say: "If anybody has suffered as I have because of my mother, he can never laugh and be happy as anyone else." They often feel uncertain in erotic partnership. They feel that a happier boy or girl would not want to have anything to do with them. They are also afraid of the danger that they or their children could become psychotic. Some of them do not marry. Others feel that they only deserve an inferior partner—a dangerous attitude for the prognosis of marriage. Social care for children is well organized in Switzerland. However, many children of schizophrenics do not get the help they are in need of. I have collected similar reports from six different countries with different welfare organizations. Nowhere is sufficient assistance given to children of schizophrenics. So many times they would need psychiatric advice, consolation and friendship, and they do not get it.

As we all know, schizophrenics themselves need much more help than is given to them in many hospitals all over the world. But we should also bear in mind the grief of the children of our patients. It is great enough for us to do everything we can do to allay it.

So I've summarized in the short time available to me the major findings in various aspects of schizophrenia of the lifetime of research of myself and my colleagues who were closely associated with me. Given an opportunity for a longer presentation I would be able to provide both qualitative and quantitative observations to document them.

MANFRED BLEULER: SELECTED BIBLIOGRAPHY

Vererbungsprobleme bei Schizophrenen. *Z. ges. Neurol. Psychiat.* 127, 321-388, 1930; Eng. trans. in *J. nerv. ment. Dis.* 74, 1931.

Schizophrenia. Review of the work of Prof. Eugen Bleuler. *Arch. Neurol. Psychiat.* 26, 610-627, 1931.

Psychotische Belastung von körperlich Kranken. *Z. ges. Neurol. Psychiat.* 146, 780-810, 1932.

Der Rorschach-Vejrsuch als Unterscheidungsmittel von Konstitution und Prozess. *Z. ges. Neurol. Psychiat.* 151, 571-578, 1934.

Erblichkeit und Erbprognose: Durchschnittsbevölkerung, Schizophrenie, manisch-depressives Irresein, Epilepsie, 1933-1936. *Fortschr. Neurol. Psychiat.* 9, 250-664, 1937.

Erblichkeit und Erbprognose: Schizophrenie, manisch-depressives Irresein, Epilepsie, Durchschnittsbevölkerung. *Fortschr. Neurol. Psychiat.* 10, 392-403, 1938.

Erblichkeit und Erbprognose: Schizophrenie, manisch-depressives Irresein, Epilepsie, Durchschnittsbevölkerung. *Fortschr. Neurol. Psychiat.* 11, 287-302, 1939.

Erblichkeit und Erbprognose: Schizophrenie, manisch-depressives Irresein, Epilepsie, Durchschnittsbevölkerung (1939-1940). *Fortschr. Neurol. Psychiat.* 13, 49-63, 1941.

Krankheitsverlauf, Persönlichkeit und Verwandtschaft Schizophrener und ihre gegenseitigen Beziehungen. Leipzig: Thieme, 1941.

Das Wesen der Schizophrenieremission nach Schockbehandlung. *Z. gen. Neurol. Psychiat.* 173, 553-597, 1941.

Die spätschizophrenen Krankheitsbilder. *Fortschr. Neurol. Psychiat.* 15, 259, 1943.

Schizophrenes und endokrines Krankheitsgeschehen. *Arch. Klaus-Stift. Vereb.-Forsch.* 18, 403, 1943.

Die Prognose der Psychosen, insbesondere der Schizophrenie. *Periodische Mitteilungen der Schweiz. Lebensversicherungs-Ges.* 1946, 175-186.

Forschungen zur Schizophreniefrage. *Wien. Z. Nervenheilk.* 1, 129-148, 1948.

Bedingte Einheitlichkeit im Erbgang—eine überwundene Schwierigkeit in der Konstitutionsforschung am Menschen. *Arch. Klaus-Stift. Vererb.-Forsch.* 24, 355-364, 1949.

Endokrinologie in Beziehung zur Psychiatrie (Uebersichtsreferat). *Zbl. ges. Neurol. Psychiat.* 110, 225, 1950.

Forschungen und Begriffswandlungen in der Schizophrenielehre 1941-1950. *Fortschr. Neurol. Psychiat.* 19, 385-456, 1951.

Biologie und Entwicklungslehre der Personlichkeit. *Verh. schweiz. naturforsch. Ges. Bern,* 1956, 36-43.

Gedanken zur heutigen Schizophrenielehre—am Beispiel der Konstitutionspathologie erläutert. *Wien. Z. Nervenheilk.* 7, 255-270, 1953.

Endokrinologische Psychiatrie. Stuttgart: Thieme, 1954.

Zur Psychotherapie der Schizophrenie. *Dtsch. med. Wschr.* 79, 841-842, 1954.

Das Wesen der Serpasil-Behandlung an Schizophrenen. In: Das zweite Serpasil-Symposium der psychiatrischen Universitätsklinik Burghölzli, Zürich. *Schweiz. med. Wschr.* 85, 439-444, 1955.

Familial and personal background of chronic alcoholics. In: O. Dietheim: *Etiology of chronic alcoholism.* Springfield, Ill.: Charles C Thomas 1955, Pp. 110-166.

A comparative study of the constitution of Swiss and American alcoholic patients. In: O. Diethelm: *Etiology of chronic alcoholism.* Springfield, Ill.: Charles C Thomas, 1955, Pp. 167-178.

Research and changes in concepts in the study of schizophrenia, 1941-1950. *Bull. Isaac Ray Med. Lib.,* 3, 1-132, 1955.

Psychiatrische Irrtümer in der Serotoninforschung. *Dtsch. med. Wschr.* 81, 1078-1081, 1956.

Comparaison entre les effets de la Chlorpromazine et de la Réserpine en psychiatrie. *Encéphale*, 45, 334-338, 1956.

Eugen Bleuler. Die Begründung der Schizophrenielehre. In: *Gestalter unserer Zeit. Bd. 4: Erforscher des Lebens.* Oldenburg: Gerhard Stalling Verlag, 1956.

Aspects secrets de la psychiatrie. *Evolut. Psychiatr.* 1956/I, 45-50.

Die Problematik der Schizophrenien als Arbeitsprogramm des II. Internationalen Kongresses für Psychiatrie. *Nervenarzt* 28, 529-533, 1957.

Scopo e tema del nostro congresso. *Pisani* 71/3, 481-491, 1957.

Aims and topic of our congress. Hamdard, *Medical Digest* (Karachi), May 1958.

International cooperation in research on schizophrenia. *Bull. Menninger Clinic* 22, 43-49, 1958.

Endokrinologische Behandlungsverfahren bei psychischen Störungen. In: *Therapeutische Fortschritte in der Neurologie und Psychiatrie,* hgg. v. H. Hoff; Urban und Schwarzenberg, Wien-Innsbruck 1960, Pp. 294-305.

Entwicklungslinien psychiatrischer Praxis und Forschung. *Schweiz. med. Wschr.* 91, 1549, 1961.

Early Swiss sources of Adolf Meyer's concepts. *Amer. J. Psychiat.* 119, 193-196, 1962.

Schizophrenieartige Psychosen und Aetiologie der Schizophrenie. *Schweiz. med. Wschr.* 92, 1641-1647, 1962.

Conception of schizophrenia within the last fifty years and today. *Proc. Roy. Soc. Med.* 56, 945-952, 1963.

Endokrinologische Psychiatrie. In: *Psychiatrie der Gegenwart—Forschung und Praxis.* Band I/Ib; Teil B, S. 161-252. Springer, Berlin-Gottingen-Heidelberg 1964.

Ursache und Wesen der schizophrenen Geistesstörungen. *Dtsch. med. Wschr.* 89, 40 & 41, 1865-1870 und 1947-1952, 1964.

Neue Therapiemöglichkeiten im Vergleich zu alten in der Psychiatrie. *Dtsch. med. Wschr.* 89, 501-505, 1964.

Significato della ricerca psicoterapeutica per la teoria sulla schizofrenia e per il paziente schizofrenico. *Arch. Psicol. Neurol. Psichiat.* 27/4-5, 353-368, 1966.

Neue Entwicklung des Schizophrenieproblems. *Praxis* (Bern) 56/10, 326-331, 1967.

A 23-year longitudinal study of 208 schizophrenics and impressions in regard to the nature of schizophrenia. In: *The transmission of schizophrenia,* D. Rosenthal & S. S. Kety, (Eds.) Pergamon Press, Oxford 1968, Pp. 3-12.

2

DRIVE THEORIES OF SCHIZOPHRENIA

Seymour Epstein and Margaret Coleman

A number of drive or arousal theories of schizophrenia are critically reviewed. All assume that the basic defect in schizophrenia consists of a
low threshold for disorganization under increasing stimulus input. The
arousal that results is broader than anxiety, in the usual sense of the
term, as it is contributed to by all sources of stimulation, including positive and negative affect, as well as external stimulation. The theories differ
in the mechanisms they postulate to account for the relationship between
stimulation and disorganization, in the range of phenomena they attempt
to explain, and in the level of their conceptual units. While lacking in a
firm data base, the theories were considered to be promising because of
their heuristic value and their ability to integrate physiological and psychological aspects of the disorder within a single framework.

There have recently appeared in psychological literature a number
of activation or drive theories of schizophrenia. These theories have the
virtue of parsimoniously accounting for a variety of symptoms and of
reducing a complex disorder to a basic defect in a psychophysiological
system. They thus provide a basis for an integration of biologic and
psychologic views on the nature of schizophrenia.

It should be noted that drive is used here in the sense of its meaning
in behavior theories, such as Hull's (16), where it is a theoretical
construct that refers to the energetic aspects of behavior independent
of directional tendencies. For purposes of this paper, concepts of arousal
and activation, divested of specific physiological referents, can be considered as equivalents. Drive, so defined, is obviously a far cry from its

From the Psychology Department, University of Massachusetts, Amherst, and Rad-
cliffe College, Cambridge, Mass.

Supported in part by Research Grant MH 01293 from the National Institute of
Mental Health, US Public Health Service.

Based on an honors paper written by the second author under the supervision of
the first, when the latter was a Visiting Professor at Harvard University.

Reprinted, by permission of author and editor, from: *Psychosomatic Medicine,* 32:
113-140, 1970.

use in psychoanalytic and other systems, where it refers to directed or motivated behavioral tendencies, impulses, or instincts.

It is noteworthy that a variety of theorists of different persuasion, including Freud (9, 10), Pavlov (40, 41, 42), and Hull (16), have all arrived at the position that organisms must deal with the quantitative aspects of the total amount of effective stimulation to which they are exposed, and that the mechanisms for doing so have widespread implications for complex functioning. None of these theorists deals with the concept of drive in physiological terms, although Pavlov makes an appearance of doing so by inventing quasiphysiological terms. Ultimately, of course, the validity of the concept of drive will depend upon the discovery of a functional, if not an anatomically localized, equivalent. Yet, at this point, there is some advantage in examining the explanatory possibilities of the concept without attempting to tie it to questionable, physiological correlates.

The present paper presents a synopsis and critique of a number of recently proposed drive theories of schizophrenia. Included, as well, is Pavlov's theory of schizophrenia, for, although not new, it has much in common with the other theories, and is unknown to many Western psychologists and psychiatrists. Freud's theory and psychoanalytic variants are not included, for they are drive theories in a different sense of the term than its use here.

It should be noted that the term "theory" is used in its loosest sense. None of the viewpoints presented contain the degree of internal consistency, comprehensiveness, explicitness, and the data base required of an elegant theory. All are highly speculative. The aim of this paper is not to present a list of theories that can be evaluated as right or wrong, but to present some variations in thinking about a theme that has intrigued a number of students of schizophrenia. It is our hope to provide concepts and speculations that will stimulate new thinking, particularly with regard to perspectives in research.

MEDNICK: RECIPROCAL AUGMENTATION OF ANXIETY AND STIMULUS GENERALIZATION

The Theory

According to Mednick (34), the primary symptoms of schizophrenia are produced by a state of heightened drive. Following Hull's theory, he assumes that the effect of an increase in drive is to raise the response strength of all habit tendencies aroused in a situation. From this, it is deduced that schizophrenics should show anomalies in conditioning, in stimulus generalization, in complex learning, and in thinking.

According to Hull (16), in the absence of response competition, there is a direct relationship between drive and response strength. It follows that the greater the drive, the more rapidly simple conditioning should take place. Mednick therefore hypothesizes that schizophrenics, who are presumed to have high drive, condition more rapidly than normals.

From Hull's assumption that the strength of a response tendency is a multiplicative function of habit strength and drive, it follows that increases in drive raise the strength of competing responses as well as dominant responses. Given a sufficient increase in drive, weak response tendencies, normally below threshold, should be raised above threshold. By raising subthreshold tendencies above threshold, an increase in drive should broaden the gradient of stimulus generalization—i.e., response tendencies should be elicited by increasingly less relevant stimuli. This produces deficit in performance on complex tasks, as the new, inappropriate response tendencies compete with the older, correct ones. It follows that schizophrenics should exhibit excessively broad generalization gradients and demonstrate increasing deficit due to the interference of competing response as learning becomes more complex. The same process is said to account for the intrusion of inappropriate elements in schizophrenic thinking.

A key concept for Mednick is "the reciprocal augmentation of anxiety and stimulus generalization." That is, as drive mounts, stimulus generalization presumably increases, and, as stimulus generalization increases, an increasing number of stimuli become capable of evoking anxiety, thereby increasing the overall level of drive, which further increases stimulus generalization, and so on. This self-perpetuating spiral is said to terminate in a state of acute schizophrenic disorganization.

It is assumed that the preschizophrenic is an individual who, for reasons of either heredity or environment, or both, has an excessively high drive level. If the preschizophrenic is fortunate enough to be exposed to only limited anxiety-provoking situations, it is possible for him to lead his life as a schizoid individual and not experience schizophrenic breakdown. However, should a sufficiently anxiety-arousing situation arise, the spiral of reciprocal augmentation of anxiety and generalized fear is set into motion, and precipitates acute schizophrenic disorganization. Why does everyone not become schizophrenic? Mednick notes (34) that the schizophrenic-prone individual must be high on three predisposing characteristics which are highly correlated: drive level, a slow rate of recovery from anxiety, and a broad range of reactivity to anxiety-producing cues.

A transition from acute to chronic schizophrenia is said to occur when the fragmented, remote thoughts brought above threshold by the heightened drive become dominant because they are reinforced as a result of their ability to reduce anxiety. That is, they are retained because they are less anxiety-provoking than more direct thoughts. The low level of drive that is achieved through this avoidance learning of anxiety-producing thoughts is said to characterize the state of chronic schizophrenia.

Evaluation

Mednick's theory is able to account for a variety of symptoms of schizophrenia with relatively few assumptions, within the context of Hull's broad theoretical system, which has received considerable support in the laboratory. The hypotheses generated from the theory are open to direct experimental verification, and point the way to important experiments on the relationship of drive level to performance in schizophrenics and normals, and on response interference in simple and complex tasks. No matter what the outcome of such research, it should provide information of some importance. The theory has thus far stimulated a number of studies, mainly in Mednick's laboratory, on generalization, association, and simple and complex learning in schizophrenics and normal persons (14, 31, 32, 33, 34, 35, 37, 58). It has also provided the framework for a promising longitudinal study, in progress, on preschizophrenic children (36).

As to the validity of the theory, it must be concluded that, to date, empirical support is, at best, equivocal. While Mednick (34) asserts that his four fundamental hypotheses have been generally supported, Lang and Buss (21) disagree. The lack of agreement stems in part from differences in procedures and in subject populations in different studies. To the extent that this is so, it indicates that the hypotheses are of limited generality, and important qualifications are missing. While some of Mednick's preliminary data in his longitudinal study on preschizophrenia have failed to support the theory, it is too early to pass judgment on the basis of this study.

It is difficult to know exactly what Mednick means by drive. At times he clearly appears to be referring to the drive of Hull's system. For Hull, drive is an intervening variable, i.e., a conceptual term developed for the theoretical purpose of accounting for certain stimulus-response relationships. It is anchored at the stimulus end to variables of need deprivation and stimulus intensity, and at the response end to measures of performance. However, Mednick gives the term a different operational significance when he equates it with anxiety, and, in the studies that he cites, assumes that it can be measured directly by indexes of physiological arousal. This approach, unless adequately qualified, introduces difficulties, as it is well known that different physiologic systems are not directly covariant (18, 19, 52). Moreover, as we have noted elsewhere (6), anxiety, which can be viewed as an avoidance motive, is different from nonspecific physiological arousal, the nondirectional component of all states of motivation and stimulation. That is, arousal is a more fundamental concept, as, while all anxiety involves arousal, not all arousal involves anxiety. Which variable is it that the schizophrenic presumably cannot cope with? Within a Hullian framework it should appear that Mednick believes it is general arousal, yet he repeatedly refers to anxiety. Furthermore, while Mednick apparently assumes that there is a direct relationship between physiological arousal and strength of response tendency, there is evidence for an inverse relationship under certain circumstances (6, 18, 19, 40, 41, 42, 56). Mednick assumes that because the chronic schizophrenic is not reactive, his level of physiological arousal is low. He fails to consider that the chronic schizophrenic, while manifestly low in behavioral, and even physiological reactivity to stimulation, may nevertheless have a high resting level of physiological arousal (54).

Mednick assumes that high drive produces disorganization by raising subthreshold response tendencies above threshold. He fails to consider that attention is a relative matter, and to the extent that some responses become dominant, others necessarily become less so. Given a multiplicative relationship between habit strength and drive, an increase in drive must increase the separation between suprathreshold strong and weak responses. Only for a limited time, and in the exceptional circumstance where the dominant response is barely above, and the competing response barely below threshold, should response competition become a problem as the result of increasing drive. With further increases in drive, responses that are slightly dominant should become increasingly more so.

Mednick fails to consider that fixation in thought and behavior, and not only disorganization, are observed under high states of stress and drive. From Mednick's theoretical position, it would have to be predicted that integrated, fixated responses, such as occur in obsessions and delusions, should, with increasing anxiety, give way to disorganized responses because of the intrusion of competing responses. Yet, clinical observation supports the opposite view—i.e., the more anxiety increases, the more tenaciously fixated responses are adhered to.

Perhaps the most serious weakness in Mednick's theory is the concept of reciprocal augmentation of anxiety and stimulus generalization, which he uses as a causal explanation of schizophrenia. As Lang and Buss have pointed out (21), if anxiety invariably produces an increase in stimulus generalization and if stimulus generalization invariably produces an increase in anxiety, what is to prevent everyone from becoming schizophrenic? Mednick's argument that the schizophrenic-prone individual must be high in three disposing characteristics does not provide an adequate answer, since if the three are highly correlated, as Mednick maintains, it follows that an increase in one should invariably set off the invidious spiral. The preschizophrenic individual who is high on the three factors to begin with should simply be ahead in the race to schizophrenia. Apparently a critical factor has been omitted which is necessary to account for why reciprocal augmentation produces schizophrenia in some, but not other individuals.

The theory deals almost exclusively with cognitive symptoms of schizophrenia. It has little to say about impulse control, motivation, perceptual anomalies, and emotional aberrations, and thus cannot be considered a general theory of schizophrenia.

BROEN AND STORMS' CONCEPT OF A RESPONSE STRENGTH CEILING

The Theory

Broen and Storms indicate (4) that they do not mean to present a complete theory of schizophrenia, but only "a possible explanation for the clustering of some schizophrenic behaviors." Like Mednick, they are primarily interested in the effects of general arousal upon cognitive performance, and, like Mednick, they follow Hull in assuming that response strength is a multiplicative function of habit tendencies and drive strength. However, unlike Mednick, they attempt to account for disorganization by utilizing a concept of a response strength ceiling rather than a threshold. They assume that, as drive mounts, an increasing number of responses are brought to a ceiling, and thereby acquire increasingly similar response probabilities. As a result, normal response hierarchies are destroyed, behavior becomes randomized, and disorganization follows.

The following factors are said to determine how readily disorganization will take place: (1) the relative initial strengths of dominant and competing habit tendencies, (2) the arousal level of the individual, and (3) the height of the ceilings of response strength for different response tendencies. It is evident that given a high arousal level or a low ceiling, the ceiling will be reached more quickly than if such is not the case. This leads to the inference that schizophrenics, who are prone to disorganization, must either be in a state of heightened arousal or have unusually low ceilings for response strength, or both.

Broen and Storms make it clear that they mean to equate physiological arousal with Hull's concept of generalized drive. They assume that arousal can be measured by any of a number of physiological reactions. They state (4) "The term arousal is used to indicate a dimension of relatively diffuse cortical and physiological activation, which may be measured by changes in peripheral physiological indicants such as increases in heart rate, blood pressure, and respiration rate."

The concept of a ceiling for response strength and Hull's postulate that response strength is a multiplicative function of drive and habit strength, i.e., the strength of a response tendency, are used to account for a variety of symptoms, including disturbances in association and concept formation, delusions, hallucinations, and regression.

Associative disturbance in schizophrenics is said to be produced by response tendencies that are related to appropriate responses, but "thrown into one pot, mixed, and subsequently picked out at random" (Bleuler in Broen and Storms (4)). This phenomenon is accounted for by a high level of drive bringing appropriate and inappropriate response tendencies to similar ceilings, and therefore to nearly equal probabilities of occurrence. Evidence is cited that schizophrenics have unstable associative responses (48, 50), do poorly on tasks with words that have more than one meaning (7), and do poorly with proverbs that encourage competing responses (2).

Deficit in concept formation is said to be produced by a high drive level raising correct and incorrect associations to ceiling so that incorrect responses are as likely to be evoked by a common label as correct responses. Overinclusion occurs when incorrect responses and similar correct responses within a category are raised to similar ceilings. Underinclusion occurs when responses that should be included in a category are similar to those that should be excluded, and both are brought to similar ceilings for exclusion.

Delusions are produced when inappropriate thoughts are raised to similar ceilings as appropriate thoughts. At first, the delusions tend to be fragmented and disorganized because of the randomization of equally probable thoughts. Through learning, certain thoughts which happen to be more anxiety reducing than others become stabilized. As a result, thought fragmentation is reduced and a stable delusional system develops, which, because of a reduction in anxiety or drive level, is not interfered with by competing responses. Such a state characterizes the chronic schizophrenic, who is considered to be in a state of reduced arousal.

Broen has recently introduced (3) a refinement into the theory by considering individual differences in defensive style. The refinement represents an integration of the views of Silverman (46) and Venables (54) on breadth of attention with Broen and Storms' views on response disorganization. Broen states that while response disorganization is basic to all schizophrenics, chronic schizophrenics are able to reduce disorganization by narrowing their range of awareness. When the chronic schiophrenic is presented with a situation in which he cannot avoid dealing with multiple cues, he, like the acute schizophrenic, demonstrates overinclusion and excessive distractibility. It is therefore suggested that the discrepant findings in the literature on overinclusive thinking in chronic schizophrenics may be resolved by taking into account the nature of the experimental task with respect to its demand characteristics for broad relative to narrow attention.

Evaluation

In evaluating the views of Broen and Storms, it is necessary to consider that they do not mean to provide an inclusive theory of schizophrenia. They make no attempt to account for affective, volitional, and interpersonal disturbances, nor does the theory concern itself with the etiology of schizophrenia, other than to imply that whatever conditions cause an individual to have a high level of arousal or low response strength ceilings make him prone to develop schizophrenia.

Like Mednick, Broen and Storms attempt to account for a variety of aberrant behaviors with a few basic concepts. While their concept of response strength ceiling provides a more satisfactory explanation of drive-induced disorganization than Mednick's threshold concept, there are nevertheless difficulties with the concept and with the explanations derived from it.

One unsatisfactory aspect of the theory is that it offers no rationale for why there should be similar ceilings for different response tendencies. If this is a fundamental condition of the human organism, one might expect it to serve some function. The argument might have been made, following Pavlov (41) and Freud (10), that the organism can withstand only a limited amount of stimulation. This is at least a biologically significant assumption consistent with evidence of homeostatic regulation in other systems. However, Broen and Storms do not refer to a ceiling for arousal, but to ceilings for response strength. Why should the organism have a response system which, with increasing drive, causes response tendencies to reach a similar level? To the extent that the concept cannot be fitted into a broader system, the empirical burden of proof for its support is that much greater.

While evidence is cited to the effect that schizophrenic associations are more variable than normal associations, that schizophrenic thinking is disrupted by response competition to a greater extent than normal thinking, and that an increase in arousal produces response disorganization both in schizophrenics and normals, these findings are not specific to the theory. There is hardly a theory that would not predict that schizophrenics are more disorganized than normals and that greater disorganization occurs as situations become more complex. To state that there are response strength ceilings for individual responses without indicating the nature of the responses that have low and high ceilings is to have a hypothesis of such generality that it is difficult to confirm or refute. This would not be the case if the limiting assumption were made that response tendencies were ultimately raised to the *same* ceiling, as this would yield a highly testable and interesting deduction, namely, with increasing drive, an increasing number of responses should become *identical* in probability of occurrence. This would correspond to the "ideas of a certain category thrown into one pot, mixed, and subsequently picked out at random," that Broen and Storms refer to. They imply, but do not explicitly state, that they may have a common ceiling in mind. In any event, the data they cite do not provide an adequate test for a common ceiling. In the absence of such a limiting assumption, it does not follow that an increase in drive will necessarily produce randomization of responses, as it is possible for ceilings of different responses to differ drastically, which would produce a change in response hierarchies with increasing drive, but not necessarily disorganization, other than for the brief interval during which competing response tendencies bypassed each other on their way to different ceilings.

Like Mednick, Broen and Storms fail to consider that fixation as well as disorganization can be produced by high levels of arousal. To be internally consistent, they would have to argue that fixation occurs at high drive levels only in the absence of response competition. That this is clearly not the case is indicated by research on animals in the laboratory (25) and by observation of humans in the clinic. With regard to the former, fixations occur despite prior practice in having made appropriate responses. Increasing the level of stress tends to strengthen the fixations, rather than to cause them to break down because of interference from competing responses. Feldman and Green (8) have demonstrated that fixated responses occur despite evidence of correct perceptual discrimination indicative of correct response tendencies. Their animals under high arousal apparently failed to use correct response tendencies that were there. Clinical observation of certain schizophrenic symptoms, such as obsessions, compulsions, fixed delusions, and stereotyped movements, likewise suggests that complex fixated responses tend to become exaggerated, rather than replaced by randomized behavior, under mounting stress. Nor can the argument be made that when stress becomes *sufficiently* high, disorganization eventually prevails, as fixations have been maintained until death, often contributing to it, despite the availability of adaptive competing responses.

The theory cannot account for the paradoxical responses reported by Pavlov (40, 41, 42) in simple conditioning experiments where competing responses are not an issue. Pavlov noted that as the intensity of a conditioned stimulus increases, the magnitude of the conditioned response increases up to a point, after which it decreases. He found a similar curvilinear relationship with the strength of the conditioned stimulus held constant, and the strength of motivation varied. Pavlov attributed the decrease in the magnitude of the response to an over-compensatory inhibitory process which serves to control level of excitation.

The same criticism of Mednick's identification of physiological arousal with Hull's concept of drive applies to Broen and Storms' use of the term. They, like Mednick, fail to take into account the lack of a strong, direct relationship among different physiological systems. They also fail to distinguish between resting arousal level, tonic reactivity, and phasic reactivity. Thus, they use induced muscle tension in their experiments as an index of "diffuse arousal," apparently unaware that motor output may exert a far different influence upon physiological activity than stimulus input (52). They fail to consider that there is a confounding of distraction and arousal in any task that requires the maintenance of a constant pressure on a dynamometer. As a result, what they attribute to the influence of arousal upon response competition may be a consequence of a direct influence by response competition itself.

The theory is at its best when accounting for cognitive disorganization produced by high levels of arousal and response competition. It presents a less convincing case when it attempts to account for other symptoms of schizophrenia. As an example, regression is described as disorganized and primitive thinking, and attributed to the intrusion of competing responses as a result of high drive level. The explanation fails to consider that there is also regression that is an integrated reinstatement of earlier patterns of behavior, also produced by high levels of stress.

The Theory

According to Venables (54), schizophrenics suffer from an "input dysfunction." Following Weckowicz (55), he concludes that acute schizophrenics exhibit parasympathetic dominance, and have excessively low levels of resting arousal. Consistent with Wilder's law of initial value (56), he assumes that individuals with a low resting arousal level have an excessively high level of reactivity to stimulation. This accounts for self-reports by schizophrenics of a "flooding with stimulation," as indicated in the following case cited by Venables from McGhie and Chapman (27): "Everything seems to grip my attention although I am not particularly interested in anything. I am speaking to you just now, but I can hear noises going on next door and in the corridor. I find it difficult to shut these out and it makes it more difficult to concentrate on what I am saying to you. . . . Things are coming in too fast. I lose my grip of it and get lost. I am attending to everything at once and as a result I do not really attend to anything" (54).

A transition from parasympathetic to sympathetic dominance is said to mark the onset of the chronic stage. The chronic schizophrenic is described as having a high resting level of arousal and a low level of reactivity to stimulation. Such an adjustment is consistent with Wilder's law and serves the adaptive function of preventing an already highly aroused organism from becoming further aroused, thereby serving a homeostatic function. In an attempt to reduce his high level of arousal, the chronic schizophrenic presumably withdraws from stimulation, which further contributes to his lack of responsivity and produces the flat effect characteristic of the disorder.

Venables notes that while the view that acute schizophrenics are hypoaroused and chronic schizophrenics are hyperaroused appears contradictory to superficial observation and to the theoretical formulations of others, it is supported by the available evidence. He reports that depressant drugs, such as sodium amytal, often produce temporary improvement in chronic schizophrenics (12, 22), and amobarbital, which decreases cortical and autonomic activity, produces remissions from catatonic stupor (49). Also, he notes that chronic schizophrenics have a higher, and acute schizophrenics a lower, sedation threshold than normal persons (45). Chronic schizophrenics have been reported to have higher basal levels of skin conductance, pulse rate, and respiration rate than normal persons (26, 57). Gromoll (13) compared process and reactive patients (assumed to parallel chronic and acute schizophrenics) on percentage time alpha rhythm, expecting to find that the reactive schizophrenics had higher levels of cortical arousal, but found the opposite to be the case.

A major hypothesis for Venables is that acute schizophrenics have excessively broad, and chronic schizophrenics excessively narrow, attention. This follows from a presumed relationship between arousal and attention, such that the higher the arousal level, the narrower the attention. Narrowing of attention is assumed to be adaptive for the chronic schizophrenic in that it reduces the range of stimulation for an individual already excessively aroused. In support of his position, Venables cites studies which report a breakdown in size constancy following stress or the administration of sympathetic excitants. Size constancy is assumed to be dependent upon peripheral cues, which, if there is narrowing of attention, are ignored. Venables notes that excitatory drugs and stress have been found to reduce interference from competing cues on the Stroop tests, as well as to reduce interference from early upon later trials in binary guessing games. These effects are presumed to illustrate narrowed attention produced by high levels of arousal. Evidence from Kinsey *et al* (17) is cited to the effect that there is a rise in tactual and pain threshold, and a decrease in peripheral perception as the result of increasing arousal during sexual orgasm. While considerable evidence is cited to support the view that high arousal and presumed sympathetic dominance are associated with narrowed attention, relatively little evidence is provided to support the position that parasympathetic dominance and low arousal are associated with broadened attention. Those studies which are cited in support of the latter view mainly concern the effect of drugs presumed to decrease EEG arousal upon performance on tasks such as the Gottschaldt test, the Luchin's water jar problems, and the Stroop test, all of which are assumed to be indicators of breadth of attention.

Having presented some evidence that arousal in normal persons is related to breadth of attention, Venables attempts to support the thesis that schizophrenics, who presumably have deviant levels of arousal, suffer from an attention defect. He therefore hypothesizes that acute schizophrenics have excessively broad, and chronic schizophrenics excessively narrow, attention. Venables notes that chronic schizophrenics sometimes report living in a "flatter world" than the normal person, that nonparanoid schizophrenics underestimate and paranoid schizophrenics overestimate distance, and that acute schizophrenics tend to overinclude. Studies of incidental learning are said to indicate narrowed attention in non-paranoid chronic schizophrenics. Dunn's finding of selective perceptual errors in chronic schizophrenics (5) is reinterpreted as indicating the presence of narrowed attention produced by a content-induced increase in arousal. Narrowing of attention in reference to cues of space and time presumably causes chronic schizophrenics to be relatively uninfluenced by anchoring cues in tasks requiring estimations of time, weight, and length. Acute schizophrenics, on the other hand, are said to be excessively influenced by such cues.

In addition to a defect in breadth of attention, Venables notes other input dysfunctions in schizophrenia. He cites evidence that reaction time in normals and nonchronic schizophrenics is less for visual than for auditory stimuli, while the reverse is true for chronic schizophrenics. Deteriorated schizophrenics are reported to have unusually high two-click separation thresholds. Such findings are said to reveal a selective impairment in the auditory mode. While normal persons demonstrate a consistent decrease in reaction time as a function of increasing intensity of light flashes, nonparanoid chronic schizophrenics show paradoxical effects at high intensity levels, indicating that they have a problem in coping with the intensity component of stimulation.

Evaluation

The theory is more sophisticated than the preceding theories with respect to its use of the concepts of arousal and reactivity. The evidence presented makes a convincing case for what Venables refers to as "an input dysfunction" in schizophrenia. It is to the theory's credit that it takes seriously differences among schizophrenic subtypes, and proposes for evaluation new ones based on ratings of behavior. Weaknesses are (1) the evidence cited in support of the proposed basic defect in breadth of attention is highly inferential, (2) the studies cited on arousal level in acute and chronic schizophrenics are highly selective, and (3) support for most hypotheses is post hoc rather than based on studies designed to test the hypotheses.

A key set of assumptions is that chronic schizophrenics are high in basal arousal level and low in reactivity to stimulation, and acute schizophrenics are low in basal arousal level and high in reactivity to stimulation. While reduced reactivity to stimulation in chronic schizophrenics is well documented, the other three conclusions are not. Venables cites a number of studies that report high arousal levels in chronic schizophrenics. However, there are several that he does not cite, including one of his own, that report no difference between chronic schizophrenics and normals (11, 43, 53), and a number that report chronic schizophrenics to have lower arousal levels than the normal person (15, 44, 51). When the final picture on "arousal" in chronic schizophrenics is in, it will not be surprising if the results are found to vary with subject variables other than chronicity, with the particular physiological system under consideration, and with the nature of the experimental situation during which measures were obtained. For example, in a recently completed study by Smith (47), it was found that high "arousal" could be indicated by one system and low arousal by another.

Evidence on reactivity and arousal level in acute schizophrenia, adequately defined, is meager, very likely because acute schizophrenics are difficult to test. It would be useful to obtain psychophysiological measures on acute schizophrenics and examine correlates of the reported state of being "flooded with stimulation" and incapable of screening out incidental stimuli. It is to the credit of Venables' theory that it points to the need for such investigation.

In the absence of adequate descriptive data, Venables infers the existence of acute and chronic states on the basis of length of hospitalization. Such a procedure introduces considerable error as (1) not all patients go through acute stages, (2) the acute stage may precede hospitalization, and (3) reoccurrence of an acute reaction is possible after a period of chronicity. What is attributed to a difference between acute, excitable patients and chronic, stabilized ones may thus be a consequence of other factors that happen to be correlated with length of institutionalization. Further error is introduced by making comparisons between studies on chronic schizophrenics in a particular hospital using a specific procedure with acute schizophrenics in another hospital using a different procedure. Few studies are cited in which direct comparisons were made on arousal levels or reactivity to stimulation among chronic schizophrenics, acute schizophrenics, and normals, within a single investigation. Another source of weakness lies in the inference that if a relationship between two variables can be demonstrated in normals, then a difference between schizophrenics and normal persons on one of the variables can be assumed to have been caused by the other. This is, of course, only one of a number of possibilities. It is conceivable, for example, that Wilder's law of initial value does not hold in the same manner for schizophrenics as for normal persons, so that low reactivity in chronic schizophrenia need not be a result of high arousal levels, even if it is established that there is an inverse relationship in normals. Such a discrepancy would be consistent

with the view that schizophrenics have difficulty in maintaining homeostatic control of arousal.

On a logical basis, divisions of schizophrenia according to acute excitability versus chronic stability, paranoid organization versus disorganization, and degree of withdrawal, are promising within the framework of
theories that emphasize arousal, reactivity, and stimulus input dysfunctions. Venables provides scales for measuring such variables. It should be
noted, however, that he has used such divisions mainly in a post hoc
manner to account for unexpected data. It remains to be seen whether
the divisions will withstand cross-validation. It might be noted, paren-
thetically, that if basal arousal level is as fundamental in determining
schizophrenic behavior as Venables believes it to be, it should provide
a particularly useful subdivision of schizophrenia in investigations of a
variety of dependent variables, including physiological reactivity to
stimulation.

One difficulty with the evidence cited in support of the position that
chronic schizophrenics suffer from excessively narrow, and acute schizophrenics, from excessively broad attention, is that it can be subsumed
under a broader hypothesis concerning general reactivity to stimulation.
Thus, an attention defect may be less basic than Venables assumes. It is
interesting, in this respect, that Venables argues that high sympathetic
arousal induces compensatory adjustive reactions which limit further
increases in arousal. Such a view has implications which go far beyond
an attention defect in schizophrenia, and suggests that schizophrenics
have difficulty in regulating reactivity to the intensity component of all
stimulation.

Like the other theories thus far reviewed, Venables' theory is limited in
scope, concentrating primarily upon the cognitive aspects of schizophrenic
symptomatology, and offering little in the way of explaining other symptoms, or contributing to an understanding of etiology. Thus, while the
theory postulates parasympathetic dominance in acute schizophrenia, it
does not indicate why this should be the case. Is so-called "parasympathetic dominance" a basic biological defect that produces schizophrenia,
or does a prolonged period of psychological stress produce excessive sympathetic activity which is followed by a compensatory state of parasympathetic dominance, and it is the decompensation which ushers in the
acute stage of schizophrenia?

Limitations notwithstanding, the theory performs a useful function in
drawing attention to a largely neglected aspect of schizophrenia, namely
that no matter what else schizophrenia is, it involves a defect in the regulation of stimulus inputs.

The Theory

In this section an attempt is made to present an integrated view of Pavlov's ideas on schizophrenia based on several of his translated works (40, 41, 42).

For Pavlov, there are two fundamental processes, excitation and inhibition, the interaction of which accounts for all behavior. Given a stimulus of sufficient strength, an excitatory impulse is said to be conducted through the nervous system, causing an excitatory wave to spread over the cortex. The excitatory wave induces an inhibitory wave (negative induction), which serves to limit its spread. According to the law of reciprocal induction, excitatory reactions induce inhibitory reactions, and inhibitory reactions induce excitatory reactions (positive induction). Inhibition is assumed to be less stable than excitation. By interacting with excitation at all levels of organization, a complex system of inhibition and disinhibition throughout the nervous system is produced.

The three basic forms of inhibition are internal, external, and transmarginal. Internal inhibition is confined to the cerebral cortex, while the others occur at subcortical levels, as well. Internal inhibition is considered to be an active form of inhibition in that it develops with experience. It is responsible for conditioning, discrimination, generalization, extinction, and delay of response tendencies. That is, it imparts control and precision to learning, memory, and behavior. External inhibition occurs immediately upon the presentation of a new stimulus, and is therefore considered to be passive, or unconditioned. External inhibition interrupts ongoing activity, and, in so doing, frees the organism to attend to new stimulation. It is responsible for the orienting, or "what-is-it" reflex, taking precedence over the conditioned reflex. In general, it directs the organism's attention away from old and toward new stimulation. By inhibiting internal inhibition, external inhibition can interfere with conditioning, learned discrimination, and conditioned delay, and release previously suppressed responses. Transmarginal inhibition is similar to external inhibition in that it is reflexive, passive, and unconditioned, and reduces reactivity to ongoing stimulation. It is a diffuse emergency form of inhibition whose function is to protect the organism from excessive excitation from the combined effects of all sources of stimulation, internal and external. It can inhibit internal and external inhibition as well as excitation, thereby producing various levels of disinhibition, depending upon its intensity.

A phenomenon of particular importance for pathological behavior is the occurrence of "paradoxical phases." Following a heightened level of excitation, such as produced by intense stimulation, insoluble conflict, or rapid alternation between excitatory and inhibitory stimuli, Pavlov noted a peculiar and highly orderly change in hierarchies of response strength. The first stage consisted of what appeared to be a state of total inhibition, during which the animal failed to manifest any conditioned responses to stimuli arranged along previously established dimensions of response strength. The next stage, which he called the "ultraparadoxical phase," consisted of a complete reversal of the normal hierarchy; stimuli that had previously elicited the strongest responses produced the weakest responses, while stimuli that had previously elicited the weakest responses produced the strongest responses. The ultraparadoxical phase was followed by a series of paradoxical phases in which stimuli of intermediate strength produced the strongest responses, with the point of strongest response shifting toward stronger stimuli, until the original gradient was restored. Between paradoxical phases, a "stage of equivalence" was observed, during which all stimuli evoked similar and large responses. With repeated exposure to the same source of stress, the stages were repeated, but each time more rapidly, until the stress could be withstood without disruption of the normal hierarchy.

Pavlov explained the sequence of paradoxical phases by assuming the dissipation of transmarginal inhibition. The transmarginal inhibition was presumed to be so extensive at first as to inhibit all conditioned responses. With the passage of time, and the gradual lifting of transmarginal inhibition, first weak excitation was disinhibited, followed by the disinhibition of increasingly stronger excitation—i.e., as the organism recovered, and was able to tolerate increasing levels of stimulation, increasingly stronger excitation was released from inhibitory control. (A more complete discussion of paradoxical phases is presented elsewhere (6).) In support of the view that paradoxical phases are produced by the dissipation of transmarginal inhibition, Pavlov demonstrated that the developmental sequence could be reversed by procedures designed to increase inhibition, such as by the administration of certain drugs, and by testing under conditions of increasing sleepiness, which Pavlov viewed as a form of protective inhibition.

Pavlov assumed that the amount of stimulation that an organism can tolerate before transmarginal inhibition is evoked is a function of its resting level of excitation and its ceiling for tolerating excitation. Thus, transmarginal inhibition can be evoked by raising excitation, by lowering tolerance for excitation, or by a combination of the two. Among the external conditions said to favor evocation of transmarginal inhibition are (1) an overwhelming amount of stimulation in terms of intensity or rate of stimulation, (2) a "strain on the inhibitory capacities of the animal," such as can be produced by long delays and difficult discrimination, (3) conflict between excitatory and inhibitory response tendencies, and (4) rapid alternation between excitatory and inhibitory stimuli. Among the internal conditions are old age, illness, mental and physical fatigue, hypnosis, and drowsiness.

Pavlov assumed that there are marked individual differences in resting level of excitation and in ceilings for tolerating excitation as a consequence of heredity and early experience. He described two pathological extremes, a "strong, excitable type," and a "weak, inhibitory type." Under stress, the inhibitory type develops symptoms of excessive inhibition, and the excitatory type symptoms of impulsivity and disinhibition. The former is apt to exhibit signs of depression, suggestibility, withdrawal, reduced reactivity to stimulation, and paradoxical effects. The latter is apt to manifest symptoms of impulsivity, a breakdown in discrimination and ability to delay, and a delay in the extinction of unreinforced responses.

Pavlov noted that while, on some occasions, excessive arousal produces paradoxical responses and disorganization, on others it accomplishes the opposite, and produces fixations. Unfortunately, he did not describe the conditions that determine which of the two is apt to occur. However, some reasonable inferences can be made from concepts within his theory. Given a highly focused source of excitation and a strong, momentary response tendency, fixation should be favored because of negative induction. Pavlov stated that fixations are caused by "pathological inertness of the cortex." This corresponds to his view that given a source of strong, focalized excitation, negative induction encapsulates the excitation, thereby protecting the cortex from widespread over-excitation. The result is that a part of the cortex is isolated from the rest of the cortex, and associations and response tendencies governed by it are removed from the influence of the remainder of the cortex. The development of paradoxical phases, and the consequent disorganization of response hierarchies should be favored by a diffuse source of excitation and the existence of competing response tendencies of differential strength established through the development of internal inhibition. Disruption of response hierarchies by stress would then occur as the result of transmarginal inhibition inhibiting the internal inhibition.

Pavlov did not believe in a single arousal system that is uniformly reflected in the activity of all component systems. He attributed special significance to cortical excitation and its control, and referred to interactions between and within systems. He assumed that subcortical centers energize the cortex, which, in turn, imposes inhibitory regulation upon the subcortical centers. He believed that a stimulus, depending upon its intensity and other factors that influence the excitatory level of the organism, could induce a complex chain of inhibitory and disinhibitory reactions. For example, he noted that a moderately strong stimulus can produce cortical inhibition and a consequent disinhibition of autonomic activity, while a yet stronger stimulus can produce inhibition at both levels.

Having reviewed some of the basic principles of Pavlov's theory, his views on schizophrenia can be considered. The symptoms of schizophrenia, in one form or another, are attributed to transmarginal inhibition. Schizophrenia is considered to be an adaptive reaction when the organism is stimulated beyond its normal adaptive capacities. As individuals with a weak nervous system are considered to be excessively prone toward inhibitory reactions and to have a low threshold for transmarginal inhibition when stimulated by physical, social, and developmental crises of everyday life, they are assumed to be the ones most susceptible to schizophrenia. The nature of the symptoms and the course of the disorder are determined by the depth and breadth of the transmarginal inhibition.

Some symptoms, such as cognitive disorganization, withdrawal, flatness of affect, and unreactivity to stimulation, are a direct consequence of the inhibitory state. Cognitive disorganization is attributed to cortical inhibition—i.e., the schizophrenic is viewed as a partially functionally decorticated organism. Emotional outbursts, lack of impulse control, and primitive behavior are attributed to the disinhibition of subcortical centers following cortical inhibition. The inhibition of internal inhibition by transmarginal inhibition accounts for regression, inability to delay, inability to maintain a set, a breakdown in discrimination, and a delay in extinction of conditioned responses and in habituation following the repeated presentation of the same stimulus. Pathological inertness of the cortex is said to account for obsessions and stable delusions.

The paradoxical phase explains why schizophrenics sometimes overreact to trivial events and under-react to significant ones. As an illustration of the paradoxical phase, Pavlov cites the case of a schizophrenic who failed to respond to a question asked in a loud voice but responded when the question was whispered. Negativism and certain delusions are said to be manifestations of the ultraparadoxical phase. In the ultraparadoxical phase, a fear can be substituted for a wish, and vice versa. Thus, a person with a strong desire for independence may imagine himself as enslaved, and one who wishes to be liked imagines that he is hated.

Echolalia, echopraxia, catalepsy, and catatonia are considered to be hypnotic-like symptoms, and therefore attributable to transmarginal inhibition, which Pavlov considered to provide the explanation of hypnosis.

Evaluation

Pavlov's concept of a threshold for transmarginal inhibition is similar, in some respects, to Broen and Storms' (4) concept of a response strength ceiling. This is particularly true for Pavlov's equivalence stage, which generates identical predictions to Broen and Storms' response-strength ceiling hypothesis, both assuming that a variety of response tendencies are brought to similar levels of strength. For Pavlov, the equivalence stage is but one of a number of stages. Assuming that the experimental data that Pavlov cites on paradoxical phases are valid, it must be concluded that Pavlov's theory can account for Broen and Storms' data, but the reverse is not true. Pavlov's concepts have a further advantage in that they describe a system of broad adaptive significance to the organism, rather than providing a post hoc explanation of some specific phenomena.

Pavlov's views on subsystems of arousal are clearly more in keeping with the psychophysiological facts than the views of theorists who assume the existence of a single arousal system in which the components vary in unison. With regard to the symptoms of schizophrenia, Pavlov stresses the importance of *cortical* excitation and inhibition, rather than general autonomic arousal and its inhibition.

An obvious weakness in Pavlov's theorizing is his tendency to "neurologize," for which he has been considerably criticized by Western psychologists. Pavlov believed that a science of behavior must be anchored in physiology, and he did not hesitate to construct physiological terms to account for essentially behavioral data. This produced the unfortunate consequence that many Western psychologists who found the physiology unacceptable rejected the overall theory. What remained for them were limited aspects of the theory that could readily be integrated into an American behavioristic psychology. A preferable solution would have been to recognize Pavlov's neurological speculations were merely hypothetical constructs, despite his protestations otherwise, and that they need only be represented by functional equivalents somewhere in the nervous system, and not necessarily in the anatomic locations specified by Pavlov.

A more serious criticism is that Pavlov's explanations of symptoms are often too general to be definitively tested. Although the theory is high in internal consistency and is able to account for a wide variety of data with few constructs, its details have not yet been adequately worked out. Thus, while concepts such as positive and negative induction, and different levels of inhibition interacting at different levels of the nervous system give the theory flexibility and post hoc explanatory power, the qualifying assumptions that are necessary for specific predictions are often lacking. On the other hand, it should be noted that the concept of paradoxical phases, which has extremely important implications, is testable, but has received surprisingly little research interest in the West.

The theory, in general, has stimulated much research in Russia (23). That it has not in this country is very likely due to lack of familiarity with it. It is interesting to observe that recent research relevant to the theory is being undertaken within the framework of other drive theories by researchers apparently unaware of Pavlov's views.

EPSTEIN: SCHIZOPHRENIA AS A DISORDER OF EXCITATORY MODULATION

The Theory

Epstein's theory of schizophrenia is a direct outgrowth of a more general theory of anxiety (6). For purposes of the present paper it will suffice to list the following basic propositions of the anxiety theory that are relevant to the theory of schizophrenia:

1. The organism must defend itself against high levels of stimulation, and respond to lower levels of stimulation in order to survive.

2. Anxiety and nonspecific arousal are related but differentiable concepts. Anxiety can be classified as an avoidance motive, while arousal is the nonspecific component of all states of motivation and stimulation. Arousal is the broader and more fundamental concept, as all anxiety involves arousal, while not all arousal is produced by anxiety. It follows that defenses against arousal are more fundamental than defenses against anxiety.

3. There exists a fundamental psycho-physiological system for coping with the intensity component of stimulation through inhibition. The development of this system has implications for the development of reality awareness and emotional and impulse control.

4. Within this system, the relationship between excitation and inhibition is described by the Law of Excitatory Modulation (LEM), which in simplified form states that the gradient of inhibition is steeper than the gradient of excitation. As a result, the organism can respond to rapid rates and high magnitudes of stimulation at relatively efficient levels of

arousal—i.e., without being overwhelmed. It can be deduced, without further assumptions, that the expansion of both gradients as the result of appropriate experience produces an expansion of awareness without a corresponding increase in excitability.

5. An effective control system is a "fine-tuned" inhibitory system in which small increments in inhibition balance small increments in excitation. This can be contrasted with an inadequate, or abnormal, inhibitory system which has an "all-or-none" character, so that excitation tends to be blocked completely or experienced with overwhelming intensity.

6. Inhibition is organized in depth and breadth. Thus, an increase in inhibition at one level can produce disinhibition at another. The LEM is presumed to hold at all levels. As a result of the interaction of inhibition at different levels, it is possible for inhibition to both modulate excitation and be modulated by higher forms of inhibition. It is through such a hierarchy of inhibitory control that refined discrimination is achieved. In general, the greater the stress, the more inhibition shifts from a fine-tuned process to one that diffusely shuts out or fails to shut out stimulation in general—i.e., the more it takes on an "all-or-none" characteristic.

7. The most fundamental experience through which "excitatory modulation"—i.e., the ability to dampen excitation in small degrees through inhibition—develops is the repetitive occurrence of an appropriately arousing stimulus. The phenomenon that occurs is habituation, which has greater implications for expansion of awareness and control of emotions than has generally been recognized.

Given the assumption that the defective regulation of arousal has far more serious consequences than the defective regulation of anxiety, the question may be raised as to what the nature of a disorder in the former system would be like. Considering some of the propositions listed above, schizophrenia would appear to be a likely consequence. In comparing schizophrenia to neurosis, which is considered to be a disorder of anxiety, it is assumed that while both involve crudely modulated defenses of the all-or-none type, the defenses of the neurotic are confined to specific areas of threat. When the neurotic is exposed to strong stimulation in one of these areas, he must either shut off reactivity to the stimulation or be overwhelmed. Because of his inability to react at intermediate levels of anxiety or arousal, he does not learn to cope with the situation, and it remains an encapsulated area of sensitivity to which he continues to respond in an all-or-none manner. For the schizophrenic, on the other hand, the problem is more general, as it is assumed to involve excessive sensitivity to all stimulation. Thus, emotions, which are associated with strong inner stimulation, are particularly apt to induce disorganization.

To protect himself from being overstimulated, the schizophrenic generally attempts to restrict his subjective and objective world of experience. The only alternative, given an all-or-none defense system, is to be overstimulated. In either event, he fails to obtain experiences in dealing with the repetition of stimulation at appropriate levels of arousal that is necessary for the development of an adequately modulated inhibitory system. Thus, like the neurotic, the schizophrenic's all-or-none defense system is self-maintaining.

In sum, the basic defect in schizophrenia is assumed to consist of an inadequately modulated inhibitory system for controlling excitation. Because of a crude all-or-none system, the schizophrenic is unable to vary his inner and outer reactions to correspond closely to the requirements of variations in internal and external stimulation. This defect is considered to involve all spheres of functioning, including sensation, perception, attention, cognition, and emotional control. As the problem concerns the modulation of stimulus-produced excitation, it is most apt to be manifested at the higher magnitudes of stimulation. Put otherwise, the more serious the underlying disorder, the lower the level of stimulation necessary to produce symptoms.

Assuming that the basic defect in schizophrenia is an inadequately modulated inhibitory system for controlling excitation, all the major symptoms of the disorder can be accounted for, including a tendency to over- and under-respond, poor contact with reality, anhedonia, poor impulse control, a defect in attention, cognitive deficit, and hallucinations.

The tendency to over- or under-respond, which follows most directly from the assumption of an inadequately modulated inhibitory system, is one of the most dramatic and widely observed symptoms of schizophrenia. Some schizophrenics are generally withdrawn and unresponsive, while others are excessively reactive and become excited by the most trivial events. Cases are reported of schizophrenics who have seriously mutilated themselves without giving evidence of having felt pain, and of patients who, to their own surprise, found they could look directly at the sun without discomfort (20). At the opposite extreme are schizophrenics who report that the slightest stimulation is excessive and that even pleasurable feelings are experienced with an intensity that makes them difficult to bear. Not only do schizophrenics have states of being under- or over-reactive, but the same schizophrenic may suddenly shift from one extreme to the other.

Poor contact with reality can be deduced from the relationship between excitatory modulation and reality awareness. If an individual cannot react at efficient levels of arousal to stimulation, but must protect himself from excessive arousal, it can be expected that he will learn to avoid stimulating experiences, either directly or by interpreting situations in a manner so as to reduce their arousal value. The alternative is to be over-stimulated. In either event, the ability to learn from experience and to expand awareness, which requires expansion of the total range of stimulation, is impaired. It could be said that the schizophrenic is more concerned with protecting himself from the intensity aspects of stimulation than in increasing his awareness of the cue aspects, as the latter adds a new source of stimulation. That is, to the extent that the signal or cue aspects of stimuli are ignored, a major source of stimulation is removed. It is true that avoidance of awareness exposes the schizophrenic to potentially overwhelming stimulation, as without attending realistically to the signal function of cues his ability to defend himself is reduced, but this is the price that he pays for the use of an all-or-none system against excitation.

Anhedonia, "a marked, widespread, and refractory defect in pleasure capacity," is listed by Meehl (38) as a primary symptom of schizophrenia. According to Epstein's anxiety theory, arousal level and the capacity for pleasurable reactions to stimulation are closely related. Given excessive and possibly an insufficient arousal level to begin with, further stimulation is experienced as aversive. As a result of abnormal arousal levels during an early formative period, it is presumed that the preschizophrenic learned to fear and therefore avoid normal increments in stimulation, including departures from expectancies that are often the basis of humor in normal individuals. To the extent that increments in stimulation are experienced as aversive, it is evident that pleasure capacity must be reduced.

As to impulse control, it is noted that schizophrenics tend to be over-controlled or undercontrolled, and that the same schizophrenic can vary from one extreme to the other. No new assumptions are required here, since what has been said about over- and under-responsiveness to external stimulation applies equally well to the control of impulses and other sources of inner stimulation. Opler reports (39) that Irish schizophrenics tend to be withdrawn, inhibited, and to have a complex fantasy life, while Italian schizophrenics are impulsive, and exhibit predominantly overt behavioral symptoms, with a minimal development of fantasy life. While cultural influences apparently reversed the manifestation of the disorder, what remained constant was the unmodulated nature of the control system.

Given a crude, or all-or-none inhibitory system for reacting to stimulus inputs, it follows that schizophrenics must suffer from an attention defect.

Effective atention requires a fine-tuned inhibitory net, which simultaneously allows excitation from certain stimulus sources to pass through while screening out excitation from other sources. In an autobiographical account, a schizophrenic patient notes the following: "I can almost feel the filter breaking down, the old soreness pulling and tightening at my brain. Soon every stimulus will have to be interpreted at once" (24). In an all-or-none system, the only alternative to an absence of selective inhibition, as in the above case, is excessively broad inhibition, which means a loss in sensitivity and the blunting of awareness. This is the state of adjustment that is often reached by patients classified as "in remission," in which a compromise is reached, such that attention is restricted to stimuli that are minimally arousing and maximally necessary to attend to in order to lead a minimal existence.

Cognitive deficit in schizophrenia can be deduced from an attention defect, and, at a more fundamental level, from the inability to adequately modulate excitation, and therefore to cope with the intensity component of stimulation which must be modulated if the cue component is to be effectively dealt with. The schizophrenic is considered to be more interested in protecting himself from the immediate arousal consequences of stimuli than in comprehending their meaning otherwise. Thinking itself involves sustained attention and the possibility for frustration and criticism, both tending to be tension producing. The excessive arousal that results can be expected to be dealt with defensively by avoiding a continuation of the thinking. The alternative is that a high level of arousal will be experienced which will directly interfere with cognitive functioning and induce all-or-none inhibitory reactions, making fine discrimination impossible.

There are two sources of psychogenic hallucinations. One is the self-induced sensory isolation that results from the schizophrenic broadly inhibiting reactivity to external stimulation. It is assumed that there is a tendency to maintain stimulation within limits, and that, to the extent that the schizophrenic avoids attending to external stimuli, his attention automatically focuses upon internal stimuli. As a result of the subjective intensity of the latter, he becomes incapable of distinguishing internal from external stimulation. A second form of hallucination, observed in acute agitated schizophrenics (20), is attributed to a breakdown in cortical functioning due to excessive stimulation. The view that excessive and insufficient stimulation can both lead to a breakdown in cortical functioning is consistent with the assumption that total excitation must be maintained within homeostatic limits.

The question might be raised as to why drugs that reduce tension and excitability should not invariably cure schizophrenia if the disorder is due to excessive stimulation which induces a shift to an all-or-none inhibitory system. It should be considered that the schizophrenic has developed habits and styles of behavior that are maintained when the conditions that gave rise to them are no longer present. Moreover, the ability to modulate excitation, which failed to develop because of excessive arousal at an early formative stage, has to be learned through experience in dealing with appropriate stimulation at appropriate arousal levels by means other than avoidance. Finally, crude inhibitory controls may succeed in maintaining arousal under most circumstances within normal limits, and in such cases, tranquilizing drugs can make no further contribution. That is, there is a well stabilized adjustment to a primary deficiency.

The predisposition to schizophrenia is held to reside in the factors that interfere with mastery of the intensity component of stimulation, which include insufficient stimulation, excessive stimulation, insufficiently stable stimulation, and an excessively high or low resting level of arousal at a formative period. These factors either cause stimulation not to be attended to or to be experienced as excessive, and therefore to be avoided. In either event, the individual fails to obtain experience in the process of habituation, which is presumed to be necessary for the development of excitatory modulation and the expansion of reality awareness at a rudimentary level. A variety of situations, biological and psychological, presumably foster the development of schizophrenia. An infant may be genetically constituted to have an excessively high or low resting level of arousal to begin with. Such an infant would require unusually sensitive care in order to be exposed to appropriate levels of stimulation which would allow him to develop the capacity to respond with appropriate increments in arousal to stimulation. Illnesses and injuries that make the individual sensitive to stimulation during critical developmental periods may also play a decisive role. Regarding psychological factors, a mother-child relationship that is regarded as particularly conducive to schizophrenia is one in which the mother has strong, unconscious feelings of hostility toward the child. Such a relationship is apt to produce a state of prolonged high arousal in the child. "An effective way to produce such a state would be to repeatedly arouse expectancies and appetites only to frustrate them. This could be accomplished within the context of a mother-child relationship which is positive enough to have the child seek more of it, and negative enough to leave strong needs unfulfilled. To maintain arousal at a sufficiently high pitch requires a delicate art of providing sufficient gratification at just the right moment so that the need is not abandoned. It is necessary to keep the carrot always in sight, making it available when interest flags, and removing it before the need is satisfied. Such an art can readily be achieved without practice by an ambivalent mother who consciously means to love a child she unconsciously hates, and can neither reject it nor allow it to be happy" (6).

An implication of the theory for psychotherapy is that it is important to recognize that it is the control of arousal from all sources, and not merely fear and anxiety, that is the basic problem for the schizophrenic. Thus, he must learn to develop modulated controls with regard to experiencing and expressing emotions, and this can be accomplished only by repeated experience in small degrees. The schizophrenic should be helped to recognize his tendency to react to stimulation in an all-or-none manner, and that this is necessarily a self-defeating process which prevents learning from occurring. At the same time he should recognize that he cannot force himself to behave effectively when excessively aroused, and that at such times withdrawal is in order. In like manner, it can be helpful to the schizophrenic to recognize that his motivation can stand in his way. In other words, the more highly motivated the schizophrenic is, the more he will be aroused, and the more he is aroused, the more he will experience disorganization and failure. Such a state is apt to be particularly discouraging and to induce further withdrawal.

The major research implication of the theory is that it is necessary to consider *absolute* deviations from appropriate responses, and not to simply examine mean differences in direction of response, as is the customary procedure. To the extent that the fundamental defect in schizophrenia is an inadequately modulated inhibitory system, the only prediction that can safely be made is that the individual schizophrenic will either over- or under-respond. On any measure it can be anticipated that some schizophrenic groups will be found who obtain a higher mean response than normals, others who obtain a lower mean response, and yet others who show no mean difference, with the individuals overresponding balancing those who under-respond. Of course, should it be found that a particular subgroup uniformly under- or over-responds, an analysis in terms of directional and absolute differences will produce the same results. Among the variables of stimulus input that require investigation are intensity, rate, frequency, duration, time since stimulus presentation, and mode of stimulus presentation. All of these should be investigated at different intensity levels, with resting level of arousal treated as a parameter, as, according to the theory, the greater the sensory load of combined inner and outer stimulation that the individual must cope with, the more apt he is to exhibit a breakdown in excitatory modulation.

Evaluation

On the positive side, the theory of schizophrenia is embedded within a broader, empirically based theory of anxiety that has direct implications for the development of emotional control and the expansion of reality awareness, both of which are critical with regard to the symptomatology of schizophrenia. The theory of schizophrenia is reasonably parsimonious, internally consistent, and extensive in that it is able to relate symptoms of sensation, perception, cognition, and emotion to one underlying cause.

On the negative side, the theory of schizophrenia, at this point, is highly speculative, and lacks an adequate data base. While its flexibility allows it to explain diverse findings by others, the explanations, as post hoc ones, do not provide a true test of the theory, but indicate only that it is promising. This, of course, is to be expected, since it is a new theory. Two studies, both recent doctoral dissertations (1, 47), have been completed within its framework. In one (1), stimulus intensity was varied at three levels, once by increasing the intensity of pure tones, and once by varying the emotional significance of words in a word association test. Chronic schizophrenics were found to exhibit deficient autonomic reactivity to both classes of stimuli, and more important, the deficit increased as a direct function of increasing stimulus intensity. Both findings held for schizophrenic groups subdivided according to whether premorbid adjustment was relatively good or poor. The second study investigated habituation (47), with stimulus intensity treated as a parameter in chronic schizophrenics divided into low and high withdrawn groups. Again it was found that schizophrenics were relatively unreactive to stimulation, and that the differences from normal controls increased at the upper intensity levels. Both effects were exhibited to a greater extent by the high than by the low withdrawn group. Of particular interest, there was evidence in both studies of sudden increases in autonomic reactivity, consistent with an all-or-none inhibitory system. While these two studies are promising with respect to supporting aspects of the theory, they represent a very small beginning, and it remains to be seen whether the promise will hold up in further work.

At this point, the theory can best be regarded as a logical tour de force, whose value is largely heuristic. It also has value in suggesting new vantage points for evaluating data.

MCREYNOLDS' THEORY OF UNASSIMILATED PERCEPTS

The Theory

Unlike the other theories thus far reviewed, which are primarily arousal theories with secondary implications for cognition, McReynolds' theory (28, 29, 30) is primarily a cognitive theory with secondary implications for arousal. Anxiety is attributed to a cognitive failure in assimilating percepts, and schizophrenia to a high level of anxiety produced by a high level of unassimilated percepts. A percept is defined as a conceptual unit "used to refer to that which one is, or is assumed to be, aware of, regardless of whether this is related directly to sensory input or whether it results from the individual's re-examination and reorganization of older percepts and memories" (28). It is assumed that there is an inherent tendency to obtain new percepts, exhibited in a continuous seeking of new experiences. It is further assumed that "man has an inherent tendency to assimilate percepts into perceptual systems." The combined process of obtaining and assimilating new percepts constitutes "perceptualization." Perceptualization has an optimum rate; if it is too low, it produces boredom; if it is too high, excitement. Normally, the functions of obtaining new percepts and of assimilating them keep abreast of each other. Should assimilation not keep pace with intake, a surplus of unassimilated percepts accumulates, generating anxiety, defined as "the feeling tone concomitant with a large mass of unassimilated percepts."

There are at least four factors which make assimilation difficult (29). These are: (1) a high rate of perceptual intake, (2) extreme novelty of perceptual intake, (3) uncertainty about the future, making it impossible to assimilate percepts whose significance depends upon unavailable information, and (4) incongruencies between the content of percepts and the systems available for assimilating them. While the first three factors tend to disappear in time, incongruency does not, and therefore is considered to be the major source of enduring anxiety. The higher an individual's anxiety, the more he attempts to avoid new percepts, to assimilate incongruent percepts, and to maintain schemata which have assimilated percepts in the past.

Schizophrenic symptoms are a consequence of excessive anxiety and of the defenses mobilized against this anxiety. Two defenses which the schizophrenic relies heavily upon are avoidance of new percepts and inappropriate assimilation of old percepts. The former keeps anxiety from increasing, and the latter reduces the current anxiety level. Avoidance of new percepts is manifested directly in symptoms of selective avoidance, withdrawal, and apathy. Inappropriate assimilation of old percepts is exhibited in delusions and thought disorder. A variety of secondary defenses and symptoms derive from elaboration of the two major defenses.

In an attempt to selectively avoid percepts which are unassimilable, the individual with selective avoidances is forced to attend to other, often inappropriate percepts in order to maintain an adequate rate of perceptualization. As a result, thought and behavior become idiosyncratic, and peculiar activities are engaged in, such as making odd collections, developing peculiar hobbies, and being generally eccentric.

A high level of unassimilable percepts reduces the tendency to seek novel percepts. Not only does this produce apathy and boredom, but it also produces a state of self-induced sensory deprivation which causes hallucinations. Support for this interpretation is provided by laboratory evidence that sensory deprivation can, under certain circumstances, produce hallucinations in normal persons.

Delusions represent attempts at assimilating otherwise unassimilable percepts. All individuals stabilize their world of experience by organizing perceptual data into conceptual schemata. The greater the quantity of unassimilable percepts, the greater the pressure to organize percepts into schemata. When experience for some reason cannot be assimilated into reasonable conceptual schemata, it tends to be assimilated into idiosyncratic ones. The strengths of the delusions that result are a direct function of the number of percepts they assimilate. Once formulated, a delusion is maintained because the individual avoids percepts incongruent with it, and seeks out percepts which confirm it.

Disordered thinking, other than that associated with delusions, arises partly because the schizophrenic has idiosyncratic patterns of perception as a result of selective avoidance reactions, and partly because his low rate of perceptualization is insufficient for maintaining adequate cortical functioning. As a result, he suffers from a defect in sustaining attention and logical thought. A high quantity of unassimilated percepts results in a loosening of conceptual boundaries. The diffuseness of the boundaries, in turn, increases the rate of assimilation of percepts, thereby reducing anxiety. Overinclusive thinking is attributed to the schizophrenic relaxing of his categorical standards in order to increase his rate of assimilation. The influence upon cognition of certain physiological states, drugs, dreams, and lobotomies is said to relate to their ability to loosen categorical boundaries and thereby reduce anxiety.

Schizophrenia and neurosis differ quantitatively only, the former being associated with a greater quantity of unassimilable percepts, which fosters more desperate measures to avoid new percepts and to assimilate old ones.

There are two main implications of the theory for psychotherapy. One is that schizophrenics require exposure to novelty at a rate they can assimilate. The other is that schizophrenics require help in cognitive restructuring to permit them to assimilate percepts in socially acceptable ways. The emphasis in therapy is thus upon cognitive factors.

Evaluation

Both the strengths and the weaknesses of the theory lie in its treatment of anxiety at a cognitive level. As a result, the theory has a dimension of complexity that the other theories lack, but is unable to deal adequately with certain lower order phenomena.

The assumptions that anxiety is produced when experiences cannot be integrated into conceptual schemata, and that the schizophrenic suffers from unassimilated percepts are supported by autobiographical accounts of schizophrenics (20). In these accounts, the individuals report having made a reasonably satisfactory adjustment to life until something happened that undermined their basic assumptions about the nature of themselves or their world. This was followed by anxiety of "nightmare" proportions and a fragmentation of sensory experience.

McReynolds' explanation of delusions as an extension of the normal process of perceptual organization follows directly from the basic assumptions of his theory. Learning theories, such as Mednick's and Broen and Storms', have difficulty in accounting for stable delusions that are themselves anxiety-producing, such as delusions of persecution. The argument that the delusion is less disturbing than an alternative one is not convincing, since the delusion can be distressing to suicidal dimensions. Learning theories obviously fare better with delusions of grandeur, which are at least manifestly rewarding. McReynolds, by assuming that anxiety produced by unassimilated percepts is more distressing than specific fears, has no problem in accounting for disturbing delusions, as they assimilate material that cannot be otherwise assimilated.

Unfortunately McReynolds does not sufficiently elaborate his interesting use of the concept of schemata as a means of imposing stability upon an anxiety-provoking, erratic world of experience. A weak point lies in the assumption that the capacity of a conceptual schema to reduce anxiety is solely a function of the *quantity* of percepts it assimilates. That is, any one unassimilated percept is considered to be equivalent to any other unassimilated percept in its ability to elicit anxiety, the magnitude of which is assumed to vary only with the total number of percepts that remain unassimilated. That this assumption is untenable is immediately apparent when one considers specific examples, such as the large number of difficult-to-assimilate percepts produced by a magician's performance in comparison to the single item of information that a loved one is dead. It is self-evident that the significance of a percept, as well as the number of percepts, must be taken into consideration.

By selecting cognitive schemata as a beginning point and treating anxiety as a derivative, the theory is in the awkward position of having to derive the simple from the more complex. While McReynolds is justified in noting that cognition exerts an influence upon emotion, by failing to note the reverse relationship, he replaces one limited viewpoint with another. He takes to task learning theorists for defining anxiety as anticipatory, conditioned fear, noting that such a position fails to account for the anxiety produced by unassimilated percepts. Yet, by defining anxiety in terms of unassimilated percepts, he is unable to account for the anxiety noted by the learning theorists.

While some explanations of derived symptoms follow directly from the theory, others have a contrived quality. Thus, the view that hallucinations are produced by insufficient rate of perceptualization is reasonable in view of reports that sensory deprivation in the laboratory can produce hallucinations, but explanations of conceptual deficit, overinclusion, volitional anomalies, and the influence of certain drugs and physiological conditions are less convincing. For example, conceptual deficit is attributed to an overinclusive tendency that is resorted to in an attempt to increase the rate of assimilation of percepts. Presumably by weakening categorical boundaries, percepts are assimilated and anxiety is reduced. If this is correct, it follows that the highly disorganized schizophrenic is in a state of reduced anxiety. Yet observation fails to support such a conclusion, as most disorganized schizophrenics are often manifestly anxious. While such patients may exhibit overinclusive tendencies as indicated by excessive reactivity to incidental stimulation (27), the overinclusion apparently does not increase assimilation, but, if any thing, represents a failure in assimilation and a new source of anxiety.

In conclusion, McReynolds' concept of unassimilated percepts as a source of anxiety is a promising one that provides a new vantage point for viewing certain symptoms of schizophrenia. Also, it adds a direct means for dealing with certain complex symptoms that the other drive-theories lack. However, unassimilated percepts are clearly not the only source of anxiety, and the concept should be considered as an important supplement to other concepts, and not as a substitute.

FINAL SUMMARY AND CONCLUSIONS

A number of drive or arousal theories of schizophrenia were reviewed These theories share in common the assumption that a basic defect in schizophrenia consists of a low threshold for disorganization under increasing stimulus input. The arousal that results is broader than fear or anxiety in the usual sense of these terms, as it involves a reaction to the combined stimulation from all sources, including positive and negative emotions and impulses, as well as external stimuli. The theories differ in the mechanisms they postulate to account for the relationship between stimulation and disorganization, in the range of phenomena they attempt to account for, and in the complexity of their basic conceptual unit. Thus, Venables and most of the other theorists believe that the schizophrenic cannot adequately assimilate the most simple sensory stimulation, while McReynolds believes that the fundamental difficulty involves the assimilation of meaningful material. The theorists who assume that the basic defect is at a sensory level attempt to derive cognitive dysfunction from dysfunction at the sensory level. Although it is appealing to derive the complex from the simple, and this is generally the preferred method, it should be recognized that the relationship does not necessarily have to proceed in this direction. It is possible for a disturbance in a complex perceptual-cognitive system to produce simple physical and sensory disturbances, as the whole field of psychosomatic medicine testifies. An adequate theory of schizophrenia should be able to deal at a fundamental level with breakdowns in both simple levels of functioning, and in complex perceptual-cognitive integrative systems, such as self- and world-concepts. Most important, such a theory should indicate the mechanisms by which breakdown at one level produces breakdown at another, and what the differential implications are for breakdown proceeding in one direction rather than the other. While no such theory has yet been proposed, one could proceed from an incorporation of some of the features of the theories that have been reviewed.

All the above theories were highly speculative, and all have a relatively weak data base. Their major contribution lies in their heuristic value. Further support will have to come from findings that relate the concept of nonspecific arousal to a demonstrable anatomical or physiological equivalent, and from behavioral studies that are better controlled than those in the past, particularly with respect to the selection and description of patient samples.

REFERENCES

1. BERGERON, J. A. *Psychological Reactivity of Schizophrenic and Control Subjects to Dimensions of Primary Intensity of Pure Tones and of Socioemotional Significance of Words.* Unpublished doctoral dissertation, University of Massachusetts, 1967.

2. BLAUFARB, H. A demonstration of verbal abstracting ability in chronic schizophrenics under enriched stimulus and instructional conditions. *J Consult Psychol* 26:471, 1962.

3. BROEN, W. E., JR. Response disorganization and breadth of observation in schizophrenia. *Psychol Rev* 73:579, 1966.

4. BROEN, W. E., & STORMS, L. H. Lawful disorganization: The process underlying a schizophrenic syndrome. *Psychol Rev* 73:265, 1966.

5. DUNN, W. L. Visual discrimination of schizophrenic subjects as a function of stimulus meaning. *J Personality* 23:48, 1954.

6. EPSTEIN, S. "Toward a Unified Theory of Anxiety." In *Progress in Experimental Personality Research* (ed. 4). Maher, B. A., Ed., Acad. Press, New York, 1967.

7. FAIBISH, G. M. Schizophrenic response to words of multiple meaning. *J Personality* 29:414, 1961.

8. FELDMAN, R. S., and GREEN, K. F. Antecedents to behavior fixations. *Psychol Rev* 74:250, 1967.

9. FREUD, S. *The Problem of Anxiety.* Norton, New York, 1936.

10. FREUD, S. *Beyond the Pleasure Principle.* Bantam, New York, 1959.

11. FRIEDMAN, M. *Perceptual and Psychogalvanic Responses of Schizophrenic and Normal Subjects to Cues of Nurturance and Rejection in Interactions with Mother, Father, and Peer Figures.* Unpublished doctoral dissertation, University of Massachusetts, 1966.

12. FULCHER, J. H., GALLAGHER, W. J., and PFEIFFER, C. C. Comparative lucid intervals after amobarbital CO_2 and arecoline in chronic schizophrenics. *Arch Neurol Psychiat* 78:392, 1957.

13. GROMOLL, H. E. *The Process-Reactive Dimension of Schizophrenia in Relation to Cortical Activation and Arousal.* Unpublished doctoral thesis, University of Illinois, Urbana, 1961.

14. HIGGINS, J., and MEDNICK, S. A. Reminiscence and stage of illness in schizophrenia. *J Abnorm Psychol* 66:314, 1963.

15. HOWE, E. S. GSR conditioning in anxiety states, normals, and chronic schizophrenic subjects. *J Abnorm Psychol* 56:183, 1958.

16. HULL, C. L. *Principles of Behavior.* Appleton, New York, 1943.

17. KINSEY, A. C., POMEROY, W. B., MARTIN, C. E., and GEBBARD, P. H. *Sexual Behavior of the Human Female.* Saunders, Philadelphia, 1953.

18. LACEY, J. I. The evaluation of autonomic responses: Toward a general solution. *Ann NY Acad Sci* 67:123, 1956.

19. LACEY, J. I. Somatic response patterning and stress: Some revisions of activation theory. In *Psychological Stress.* Appley, M. H., and Trumball, R., Eds., Appleton, New York, 1967.

20. LANDIS, C. *Varieties of Psychopathological Experience.* Rinehart, New York, 1964.

21. LANG, P., and BUSS, A. Psychological deficit in schizophrenia: II. Interference and activation. *J Abnorm Psychol* 70:77, 1965.

22. LINDEMANN, E. Psychological changes in normal and abnormal individuals under the influence of sodium amytal. *Amer J Psychiat* 11:1083, 1932.

23. LYNN, R. Russian theory and research in schizophrenia. *Psychol Bull* 60:486, 1963.

24. MACDONALD, N. "Living with Schizophrenia." In *The Inner World of Mental Illness.* Kaplan, B., Ed., Harper, New York, 1964, p. 173.

25. MAIER, N. R. F. *Frustration.* McGraw-Hill, New York, 1949.

26. MALMO, R. B., SHAGASS, C., and SMITH, A. A. Responsiveness in chronic schizophrenia. *J Personality* 19:359, 1951.

27. McGHIE, A., and CHAPMAN, J. S. Disorders of attention and perception in early schizophrenia. *Brit J Med Psychol* 34:103, 1961.

28. McREYNOLDS, P. A restricted conceptualization of human anxiety and motivation. *Psychol Rep 2 (Suppl.)*:293, 1956.

29. McREYNOLDS, P. "Anxiety, Perception, and Schizophrenia." In *The Etiology of Schizophrenia*. Jackson, D., Ed., Basic Books, New York, 1960, p. 248.

30. McREYNOLDS, P. Toward an understanding of schizophrenic behaviors. Report No. 30, Behavioral Research Laboratory, Palo Alto Veterans Administration Hospital, 1964.

31. MEDNICK, M. T. Mediated generalization and the incubation effect as a function of manifest anxiety. *J Abnorm Psychol* 55:315, 1957.

32. MEDNICK, S. A. Distortions in the gradient of stimulus generalization related to cortical brain damage and schizophrenia. *J Abnorm Psychol* 51:536, 1955.

33. MEDNICK, S. A. Generalization as a function of manifest anxiety and adaptation to psychological experiments. *J Consult Psychol* 21:491, 1957.

34. MEDNICK, S. A. A learning theory approach to research in schizophrenia. *Psychol Bull* 55:316, 1958.

35. *Current Research in Schizophrenia*. Mednick, S. A., and Higgins, J., Eds., Edwards, Ann Arbor, 1961.

36. MEDNICK, S. A., and SCHULSINGER, F. *The Preschizophrenic*. Report of Study at the Psykologisk Institut, Kommunehospitalet, Copenhagen, Denmark, 1965.

37. MEDNICK, S. A., and WILD, C. Reciprocal augmentation of generalization and anxiety. *J Exp Psychol* 63:621, 1962.

38. MEEHL, P. E. Schizotaxia, schizotypy, schizophrenia. *Amer Psychol* 17:827, 1962.

39. OPLER, M. K. Schizophrenia and culture. *Sci Amer* 197:103, 1957.

40. PAVLOV, I. P. *Conditioned Reflexes*. Translated by G. V. Anrep, Oxford, London, 1927.

41. PAVLOV, I. P. *Lectures on Conditioned Reflexes*. Translated by W. H. Gantt, Internat Univ Press, New York, 1928.

42. PAVLOV, I. P. *Conditioned Reflexes and Psychiatry*. Translated by W. H. Gantt, Internat Univ Press, New York, 1941.

43. PISHKIN, V., and HERSHISER, D. Respiration and GSR as functions of white sound in schizophrenia. *J Consult Psychol* 27:330, 1963.

44. RICHTER, C. P. The electrical skin resistance: Diurnal and daily variations in psychopathic and in normal persons. *Amer Med Ass Arch Neurol Psychiat* 19:488, 1928.

45. SHAGASS, C. "Drug Thresholds as Indicators of Personality and Affect." In *Drugs and Behavior*. Uhr, L., and Miller, J. G., Eds., Wiley, New York, 1960.

46. SILVERMAN, J. The problem of attention in research and theory in schizophrenia. *Psychol Rev* 71:352, 1964.

47. SMITH, B. D. *Habituation and Spontaneous Recovery of Skin Conductance and Heart Rate in Schizophrenics and Controls as a Function of Repeated Tone Presentations*. Unpublished doctoral dissertation, University of Massachusetts, 1967.

48. SOMMER, R., DEWAR, R., and OSMOND, H. Is there a schizophrenic language? *Arch Gen Psychiat* (Chicago) 3:665, 1960.

49. STEVENS, J. M., and DERBYSHIRE, A. J. Shifts along the alert-repose continuum during remission of catatonic stupor with amorbarbital. *Psychosom Med* 20:99, 1958.

50. STORMS, L. M., and BROEN, W. E., JR. Verbal associative stability and appropriateness in schizophrenics, neurotics, and normals as a function of time pressure. *Amer Psychol* 19:460, 1964.

51. Syz, H. C., and Kinder, E. F. Electrical skin resistance in normal and in psychotic subjects. *Arch Neurol* 19:1026, 1928.
52. Taylor, S., and Epstein, S. The measurement of autonomic arousal: Some basic issues illustrated by the covariation of heart rate and skin conductance. *Psychosom Med* 29:514, 1967.
53. Venables, P. H. The effect of auditory and visual stimulation on the skin potential response of schizophrenics. *Brain* 83:77, 1960.
54. Venables, P. H. "Input Dysfunction in Schizophrenia." In *Progress in Experimental Personality Research* (Vol. 1). Maher, B. A., Ed., Acad. Press, New York, 1964, p. 1.
55. Weckowicz, T. E. Autonomic activity as measured by the mecholyl test and size constancy in schizophrenic patients. *Psychosom Med* 20:66, 1958.
56. Wilder, J. The law of initial value in neurology and psychiatry. *J Nerv Ment Dis* 125:73, 1957.
57. Williams, M. Psychophysiological responsiveness to psychological stress in early chronic schizophrenic reactions. *Psychosom Med* 15:456, 1953.
58. Woods, P. J. A test of Mednick's analysis of the thinking disorder in schizophrenia. *Psychol Rep* 9:441, 1961.

3

AN ESSAY ON SCHIZOPHRENIA AND SCIENCE

Roy R. Grinker, Sr.

Schizophrenia, most dreaded of all mental illness, has plagued mankind for countless years without abatement. Although it reached significance as a discrete clinical entity under the rubric of dementia praecox only in 1860, approximately 7,000 papers on the subject by Bellak's (1) count have been published between 1936 and 1956. It is likely that in the last 100 years more investigators have spent more time, money, and energy, and written more on schizophrenia than on all other psychiatric problems combined. Yet our ignorance concerning its definition, causes, course, treatments, and outcome is still abysmal. The most we can say is that several theories have been developed which are competitive, each one promising resolution of all the problems of etiology.

We gain little satisfaction from the fact that psychiatry in its investigations of schizophrenia is no more backward than oncology in its researches on cancer. Even worse, its victims crowd our institutions because it does not produce an early death. Thus it costs more in suffering and money than any other disease. Where have our researches failed? Are current paradigms inadequate? Must we await a breakthrough or a scientific revolution to be developed by a future genius?

We should harken to the classical philosophers who served many roles in ancient society, but primarily were concerned with the meanings of human existence. Thus their influence was closely linked to, and was one of the several precursors of, the scientific method. Philosophers did not always aim to discover ultimate or immutable "truths," but catalyzed serious thinking in depth by devising searching questions posed in dia-

From the Institute for Psychosomatic and Psychiatric Research and Training of the Michael Reese Hospital and Medical Center, Chicago.

Reprinted, by permission of author and editor, from: *Archives of General Psychiatry,* 20: 1-24, 1969.

logues with students and peer scholars. To ask significant questions facilitated answers that at least had temporary validity.

Perhaps apocryphal is the story that on Gertrude Stein's death-bed her life-long companion Alice Toklas beseeched the friend who lay between life and death: "What's the answer, Gertrude, What's the answer?" Miss Stein at last stirred and said, "What's the question?" This is the problem of all science—to ask the right questions. I believe that the main obstacles to our understanding of schizophrenia have been that most of us have not known the significant questions and then how to get the answers.

In this essay I intend to approach the problem of posing questions of schizophrenia by a circuitous route. First, I shall review selections of a lifetime of research in psychiatry in summary form to demonstrate the evolution of approaches to the kinds of questions that I think are appropriate for the solution of various clinical problems.* Second, I shall review the prototypic literature on schizophrenia to determine the theoretical position, often implicit, of the authors. Third, I shall attempt to integrate the various theoretical positions. Fourth, I shall suggest what questions should be raised for which research strategies are possible.

A NEUROLOGICAL FRAME OF REFERENCE

During the 1920's many American physicians were becoming interested in the neurological and psychiatric specialties. Although psychiatrists or alienists had staffed the governmental mental institutions, albeit meagrely, private psychiatric practice was sparse, academic positions scarce, and training programs were virtually nonexistent. Those who could, studied abroad to become neuropsychiatrists, a combination of what are now differentiated specialties. Their basic training was in neuropathology, a branch of pathology developed by Nissl and Alzheimer in Germany. General pathology was the model "Queen of the sciences."

Neuropathology actually originated in laboratories attached to psychiatric hospitals with the discovery of "equivalent to normal" techniques for staining discrete elements of the neurones, their fibers and the glia cells. The *fundamental question* concerned the morphological changes in the ganglion cells specific to various psychiatric entities. Nissl described a wide variety of observable microscopic alterations upon which

---

* This essay was written to clarify my own thinking about schizophrenia preparatory to embarking on a new research program. It was not intended to be an autobiography, but rather to piece together my previous concepts and investigations in order to make my own position explicit to myself. When one indulges in this often disagreeable exercise it is amazing how straight, albeit interrupted, the cognitive line often is.

he imposed a complicated classification. Unfortunately the specificity of these changes, in fact even their acuteness or chronicity, could not be substantiated, much less their correlation with clinical symptoms or syndromes. A later more sophisticated histochemistry suffered the same fate.

A *secondary question* inquired into the site of the lesions of the central nervous system related to specific psychiatric diseases. Location of brain tumors and large focal lesions corresponded fairly well with neurological symptoms. Where was the lesion in schizophrenia responsible for the cognitive disorder? Some neuropathologists described specific alterations in one or the other of the cell layers of the neocortex. Others described changes in the cells of the hypothalamus to account for the emotional disturbances. But these have long since been buried in the Potter's Field of abandoned hypotheses. Even when psychological disturbances are associated with neurological conditions such as tumors, aphasias, and infections they cannot be explained by the site of the central process.

My personal research followed this same general pattern of intense interest in cell changes and localization of lesions in carbon monoxide poisoning, toxic encephalitis, encephalomyelitis, and various degenerative diseases of the nervous system. My transition to physiology began with studies on central nervous regulation of sugar metabolism in experimental animals (2) and on regeneration of the central nervous system. Finally in 1934 with Louis Leiter (3) I experimented with hypothalamic stimulation of the cat. We could not confirm the presence of a regulatory vasomotor center because of the muscle movements also associated with stimulation. However I became interested in the relationship between the functions of the hypothalamus and the higher cortical centers and decided to continue this work on intact humans.

In 1938 I developed a nasal electrode which could be inserted into the sphenoid bone under the hypothalamus from the nasopharynx in the intact human subject without harm (4). Stimulation in that area enabled me to pick up poststimulatory slow waves plus muscle twitching. Subsequently in 1939 I stimulated the hypothalamic nasal lead and demonstrated *secondary* excitatory cortical effects picked up from surface electrodes both of which occurred in bursts for sometime after the stimulation (5). The hypothalamus acted as a condenser giving off repeated bursts of excitation firing the cortical neurones. This led me to the following speculative statements about schizophrenia.

> In schizophrenia, deficiencies in the autonomic nervous system are less under basal conditions or conditions of ordinary maintenance, than under *stress* during which normal reactive processes fail. The biological data resulting from studies of schizophrenia suggest

strongly a deficiency in some central coordinating process, mirrored clinically in defective homeostasis. There is also evidence from the psychological side that schizophrenics are incapable of adequately solving, with their psychosomatic constitution, the problems of frustration and separation that the bare act of living within a restricting society creates. Their visceral cravings are of such strength that inhibitions are over-ridden, compromise rejected and autonomic drives overwhelm the cortex, destroying ego functions (5).

In the same paper I speculated that the olfactory cortex (hippocampus) may be concerned in more evolved, perhaps higher, autonomic regulatory functions. Its evolution from an olfactory center affording the organism cognizance of real danger ahead, to one preparing for symbolic danger signaled by anxiety, seems logical.

In 1939, I wrote an essay on the similarity between jacksonian concepts of neurological inhibition and freudian concepts of psychological repression (6). As one would expect if these theories were significant, they would be virtually identical.

> The two terms include two dynamic factors: (1) the abandonment of a figurative level of activity (negative aspect) and (2) the adoption of a new level of activity (positive aspect). Thus regression and devolution are synonomous.

I discussed at great length the inadequacy of utilizing diseases of the brain as causative factors for mental symptoms. They are *permitted* by loss of control accompanying a process of dissolution which need not be due to an anatomical lesion. Hypotheses of morphological localizations of psychic functions (consciousness in the cortex or id in the hypothalamus) are dangerously satisfying and tend to obliterate all important considerations of content (7). Nevertheless in 1941 utilizing the hypothalamic lead, Serota and I demonstrated the deficient reactivity of the schizophrenic to stimulation and hypothesized this as a basic biological defect (8). Due to a failure of autonomic homeostatic mechanisms, the more devastating are the effects of frustration, rejection, and trauma and the more the schizophrenic is forced into motor acts of adaptation, either to attack the noxious environment or withdraw from it.

In summary, some of us who had acquired neuropathological techniques and became psychiatrists moved rapidly into neurophysiology making experimental lesions controlled by histological examinations. Still we could not answer questions concerning psychopathology since our experimental animals could not imitate depression or schizophrenia. We recognized that our questions concerning psychopathology could only be posed to man himself.

The holocaust of war and its effect on men under stress seem, on initial consideration, to have little meaning for the advancement of psychiatry or little influence on the study of schizophrenia. My colleague John Spiegel (9) and I found to the contrary that we gained much knowledge and considerable shaping of our future thinking. For American psychiatry, World War II was a great stimulus to many young physicians who turned to psychiatry as a specialty. More important, without evaluation of its ultimate effect, war experiences taught many medical men and psychiatrists the importance of anxiety, its defenses, and results, and the meanings of unconscious forces. As a sequel, psychoanalysis burgeoned after the war as the specialty of "first-class citizens" in psychiatry.

The study of war neuroses, as it is said of schizophrenia, encompasses the entire field of psychiatry. The entire range of factors from the biological to the sociological were sharply etched in miniature and required only a magnified view for understanding. Likewise time was compressed so that in rapid succession we could view predisposition, precipitation, breakdown, and recovery. War neuroses helped us understand ego-functions in action within a large field of life experiences.

Both overseas and in the United States we found that in the background of many soldiers were factors that seemed to prepare them or act as predispositions for neurotic breakdowns. Among these were broken homes, excessive dependency, and a wide range of neurotic personality characteristics (10). The men who survived the rigors of combat with only a few emotional disturbances were, prior to Army life, more aggressive, alert, slightly faster learners, more independent, came from more stable homes, were more capable of group identifications, and displayed fewer neurotic traits. These plus a high quality of motivation and confidence in leaders seemed to protect the ego from disastrous regression.

Complicating matters still more, we learned that the quality and meaning of the stress situations were equally important so that actually the only valid operational test for endurance was performance on the job. This clearly indicated that selection is only a partial professional responsibility. The subjects needed, in addition, assistance in maintaining ego-integrity in the stress situation. Actually the group unit was extremely important in that cohesiveness and confidence in leadership were superb protections against anxiety.

We realized as never before the potency of anxiety in initiating dynamic processes leading to defensive struggles, symptom formation, and regressions ranging from the temporary and benign "syndrome of ego depletion" to psychotic breakdowns. The struggles of the ego against anxiety could lead to phobias, hysterical symptoms, physiological disturbances or depressions. The ego-depletions were temporary bankruptcies into dependency. But the ego breaks with reality were dramatic phenomena. These men often looked like the most regressed schizophrenics on the back wards of our still existent "snake pits." They were soiled, gibbering, drooling, frightened animal-like creatures who usually showed concomitant physiological regression. Some crawled on all fours or stood bent over in a simian posture. Others were rigid and tremulous like a parkinsonian. These temporary regressions were most dramatic, because while imitating schizophrenia they were completely reversible with appropriate therapy.

There can be no question that war neuroses and their concomitants represent ego struggles with overwhelming anxiety. Differing from the schizophrenic, the anxiety had to be endured by men only temporarily and the defensive structures were not crystallized or made permanent. Yet basically there was little to differentiate the most severe effects from the schizophrenic reactions seen in civilian life.

AN EARLY INVESTIGATION OF SCHIZOPHRENIA

In 1947 Beck began an attempt to correlate the responses of the Rorschach test with the clinical phenomena of schizophrenia. The investigation developed into one of the first multidisciplinary research programs in psychiatry culminating in a number of publications. The first was entitled "The Six Schizophrenias" (11) and was published in 1954. I was responsible for the clinical psychiatric aspects of the research and wrote the introductory chapter for the first monograph in which my early theoretical position on clinical research in general and specifically on schizophrenia is outlined.

We tried to emphasize the current behavior elicited by social service reports of patterns in work, school, and home and from verbal and nonverbal performance in interviews avoiding references to previous psychotic episodes. This experience, which has influenced my subsequent work with various categories of illness, led me to suggest, in 1951, that psychiatry should become and be called a behavioral science.

According to our design we attempted to elicit what constitutional or developmental factors (genetic) produce a type of personality (premorbid) and what challenges with a particular psychological meaning to the patient act to precipitate a schizophrenic illness.

We were interested in detailed analysis of the psychodynamics of the current illness and tried to make a careful formulation in terms of several factors.

1. What functions of the ego were lost and to what degree? Under this heading we wanted to know how much of the ego's capacity to synthesize conflicting emotions, to delay and control motor activity, to test external perceptions of reality, etc., were still intact or were lost.

2. We strove for an accurate formulation of the emotional life in an effort to determine at what level the organization of feelings and drives was currently effective. We were not interested in such psychoanalytic classifications as oral, anal, and phallic phases, but in the degree of infantilism or maturity of the emotional organization.

3. We wanted to know what emotional and ego organization was concerned with defense against the process of dissolution in the progression of the illness.

4. We asked what means were being used to attempt a restitution of emotional organization and ego functions.

I think that our outline in which the internal processes, the life situations, the premorbid personality, and the precipitating factors were factored in terms of the various traits attributed to schizophrenia clearly indicated that our concept of personality in relation to life situations was transactional. This is the current model with which we work in all our clinical activities. To bring the Rorschach test into coincidence with this type of analysis of social functioning in health and sickness required a new formulation of the various processes at work within the psychological system.

We chose to utilize the dynamic neurology and psychiatry of Hughlings Jackson and Freud. Thus we have talked about regression from the result of serious and impossible life situations. Any process that affects the ego's functions causing it to regress or to return to a more primitive functioning must by its very action so alter the affective life of the individual that it becomes dedifferentiated or organized at a more primitive level. Ego and affective processes are not independent variables. Primitive processes have always been present but with the maturation of a healthy ego its primitiveness is held in abeyance, ready however to spring forth again when the ego's functions are weakened. When the differentiated ego reaches the capacity to react to reality with delay, synthesis, and control, then primitive affect is no longer possible. This then becomes damped down, inhibited, repressed but remains latent. When the ego becomes weakened, affect reappears in much but not all of its primitive, alogical, and infantile forms. However, as in all processes that represent transactions, there are facets of the personality which have a compensatory function when some part of the personality becomes weakened. These attempt to deal with interpersonal situations as substitutes for what has been lost. Furthermore, even though many of the ego's functions have disappeared or those that are more primitive have returned there are still attempts to reconstruct old relationships by the weakened still active forces of the ego's activities. In addition, there are attempts to reconstitute new forms of adjustment through fantasy, although these are rarely successful.

STRESS RESEARCH

During World War II and ever since I have been working consistently on the problems of human stress responses with a number of co-investigators. We have published many contributions concerned with the psychophysiological aspects of anxiety and of anger and depression. These have been summarized recently with a partial but extensive bibliography of our work in a chapter in Spielberger's (12) collection. Here I shall briefly indicate the significance of our study on anxiety to schizophrenia, because as in most psychiatric syndromes unbearable anxiety is the central focus from which devastating defenses radiate.

In part, our extensive research program was undertaken because we felt there was a need for a methodological model applicable to general problems of psychosomatic research. If such a model were fruitful in the study of a single affective state, it might be utilized in studies of other affects and perhaps eventually lead to the formulation of general laws. In our research we chose to study anxiety because of its great importance in the economy of human existence (13).

> Anxiety has a special role in the adjustive processes of the human organism, both as an indicator of stress and as a precursor of further stress response. We believe that anxiety is a signal to the self and others portending that organismic adjustments are being made to current or expected stress in the dynamically interrelated somatic, psychological, and behavioral processes. At higher levels of anxiety, as in the holocaust of war or unexpected catastrophes, equilibrium becomes so disorganized that adequate behavior, psychological efficiency, and somatic functions are profoundly disturbed. However, milder anxiety is of great significance as a signal of threat to the organism, for it precedes or accompanies active preparation for adjustment and hence may lead to facilitation of functioning at all levels.

Psychologically, the defense responses may be seen in such maneuvers as counterphobic activity, magical, ritualistic behavior or thought, *withdrawal,* or character alteration. Thus, anxiety in some past time may be responsible for the development of psychiatric syndromes and personality deformations. Threatening recrudescence in the present, it may intensify the previous defenses or evoke new types of defenses, for free anxiety is one of the most unendurable afflictions of man. As a signal of danger, anxiety is accompanied by a host of interrelated somatic processes which are in the nature of activities preparatory to emergency action. Often these are patterned in individual ways which derive from the subject's early learning. Whatever the later stimulus, the personal pattern is evoked and recognized. With decrease in psychological defenses and lessened control, anxiety mounts and the somatic responses tend to become less discrete and patterned, and more diffuse, global, and undifferentiated. Similarly, the same differentiation of function can be seen in cognitive, conative, and behavioral processes as the defensive utilization of the anxiety signal breaks down.

Our theoretical position encompassed the assumption that anxiety could be viewed as a system composed of many parts—biological, psychological, social—all related to the principles of organization. Each part of the system, the subsystems, transact according to different time-scales after the appropriate stimulus. Like all systems anxiety may be viewed as having constitutional, integrative and systemic determinants. The first concerns the *what,* the second the *how,* and the third the *why* questions.

Only when stressors evoked responses could they be termed stressful so that our first task was to develop methods for quantifying anxiety with precision corresponding to measurements of other variables (14). It became clear that stress stimuli did not evoke specific affects but general emotional arousals to which the endocrine responses were activated to some degree, no matter what affect seemed to dominate. The ultimate conclusion was that the hypothesis of "response-specificity" was more fruitful than "stimulus-specificity." No matter what the stress-stimulus, the responses are mostly but not exclusively within the autonomic or voluntary nervous system and for each, within specific organ or organs or selective muscle groups.

These responses as well as the type and degree of defenses against arousal are probably built into the organism either by constitutional factors or as the result of early experiences. Patterns of response although varying to some degree can give rise to the development of general laws of responsiveness (nomothetic) in relation to critical periods of the human life-cycle. It is likely that personality patterns can be correlated with somatic response patterns since both develop from an early common matrix (15).

Inevitably in any serious discussion of schizophrenia we will have to ask the question: *What* is this disease, reaction, or way of life? No longer can we be satisfied to utilize the kraepelinian (16) classification or Bleuler's (17) differentiation of primary and secondary symptoms. A new look at the definition of the syndrome as a whole and its subcategories is imperative. As a clinician, I had realized some time ago that the problem of redefinition in our classifications of illness would be necessary if we were successfully to correlate physiological, chemical, and endocrine processes with behavioral phenomena. In 1954, I began with some of my colleagues to take a fresh look at depressions (18) ; later we moved on to the borderline syndrome which will be described in the next section.

We decided to conduct a clinical study of depression, hoping that an orderly representation of various components of the syndrome could further our knowledge and enable us to classify subgroups. But the amount of information we acquired from our pilot studies interfered with our scanning attempts and forced us reluctantly to deal with our data statistically. Despite our qualms, the statistical methods were effective without sacrificing the "living" quality of our case material. We found that the methods used, namely, the preparation of a protocol for investigation; careful interviews of a large sample of patients; conversion of this "case material" to a form that could be analyzed statistically by means of a Q-sort, and factor-analysing the resulting data, provided meaningful conclusions.

Our experience during the pilot phase of the study, after careful psychiatric diagnostic interviews were discussed in conference, was that rarely did a depression emerge from a single, clear-cut, precipitating event or experience. We found almost invariably a series of events that led up to the clinical illness. We also found that it was rare for the research group to reach a consensus on a formulation of the patients' psychodynamics.

Although we were unable to determine why a particular person became depressed (premorbid personality, precipitating factors, and psychodynamics), we were able to subdivide the syndrome into subcategories. Included in our findings was a factor which seemed basic to depressions in general (factor I with despair and hopelessness). Factor IV (anxiety), seemed to indicate activity, either regressive or progressive. The remaining factors probably indicate types of syndromes characterized by modes of defense against, and resolution of, the depressive affect.

Recently the hypothesis that real, anticipated, or imagined object-loss precedes the onset of a wide variety of physical illnesses has been proposed. Yet none of our depressed patients was plagued by more than transient symptoms, such as constipation, dry mouth, decreased sebum secretion, etc. Even the patients who were purest in the psychosomatic factor showed no evidence of somatic disease. Does the depressive affect substitute for or protect against physical illness, or are long-term follow-up studies necessary to establish a relationship if any?

Our research has developed a number of factors: Five factors of "feelings and concerns," ten factors of "current behaviors," and, combining the two sets, four "factor patterns." These are now available for correlations with demographic data, variations in premorbid personality, type of onset, precipitating factors, physical disease, course of illness, amenability to psychotherapy, shock therapy, pharmacotherapy, milieu therapy, etc.; prognosis, relapses, and accurate physiological, endocrinological, biochemical, and EEG measurements.

The results of our research, which should stimulate efforts for improvement in methodology, indicated the difficulty experienced by psychiatrists in observing, recording, and conceptualizing behavior patterns in the mentally ill; the elusiveness, when faced by unbiased inquiry, of definitive premorbid personality, precipitating factors, and unstereotyped psychodynamics; the pathetically inadequate routine hospital records, which in no way can be entrusted for use in clinical research, necessitating the development of new sources of information for each clinical problem; and the apparent nonrelatedness of clinical depression with physical disease.

Though aware of the existing clinical vacuum before embarking on this research program, we feel that our results further emphasize the tremendous need for improving and extending clinical psychiatric research, without which meaningful psychodynamic and biological correlations are impossible.

A report from our Institute by Lichtenberg, et al (19) demonstrated the depressed patients' repetitiveness in behavior and rejection of information. In the occupational therapy department depressed patients occupied in small tasks requiring the rational use of information relied on preferred action patterns and resisted the influence of information. They experienced hopelessness regarding the attainment of goals when the responsibility was attributed to personal defects. Information in the form of assurance, granting of dependency wishes, or punishment simply increased their responsibility and feeling of personal defect. Regression involved some return to an early level of an orientation of expectancy related to a particular situation, a particular behavioral style, or a generalized goal independent of any person. All of these primitive patterns resulted in behavior for which some aspect of information was excluded.

This leads to the suggestion that the various dynamic formulations derived from psychoanalytic investigations of depressives are not representative of causes except as stressors long before the onset and that later they are augmented as the results of the depressive process (20). I postulated the following circle of events: (1) through a series of variable precipitating events the inner conflicts and unresolved problems or unrealistic techniques of problem-solving weaken a susceptible ego. This internal conflict as a stressor is as weakening to the ego as is external combat to soldiers; (2) the ego-depletion weakens the ego's problem-solving functions, still further narrows its span of control, and exposes the conflicts which were intensified by external problems and which contributed in the first place to weakening a susceptible ego; (3) the ego depletion and regression are documented by the loss of esteem, the felt hopelessness regarding the attainment of goals, and the acceptance of personal defect as the responsibility for failure. Secondarily the use of stereotyped tasks and the blocking out of change are defenses adopted to avoid greater responsibility, more failure and hopelessness. These defenses are facilitated by the nonacceptance of communication and information.

Ego depletion, lack of self-esteem, regressed behavior, and felt hopelessness, and the concomitant exposure of severe intrapsychic conflicts require time for restitution. It seems possible that time is the essential element in all so-called specific psychotherapeutic, milieu, and somatotherapeutic remedies for depression.

In sum, we have focused on an observable phenomenon of disturbed reception of communications in depressive patients (rather than their communications and their contents) and speculated about its meaning. As a phenomenon considered within the framework of ego-psychology, techniques of the behavioral sciences are suitable for its investigation. Fatigue from internal conflict, regression to previous modes of communication, and transactional processes among several causes, effects, and defenses are apparent. For a better understanding of this complicated process more information is necessary regarding psychological processes involving time.

These researches on depression utilized the patients' symptoms as traits that are essentially repetitive and common to all depressions. The goal was relatively simple in that factoring enabled us to combine symptoms into groupings that differentiated subcategories, especially those clearly dominated by behaviors. The hitches in the research lay: (1) in the absence of many different behaviors and (2) the overemphasis of observers on inferences about feelings. Unfortunately, feelings and behavior were not clearly correlated so that patterns containing both had to be constructed. It became obvious that the methods used in the depression research were not adequate for our next program of clinical investigation.

RESEARCH ON THE BORDERLINE

In 1960 we began a programmatic study that was closer to the problems of schizophrenia than any previous research, culminating in a single publication entitled the "Borderline Syndrome" (21) with my colleagues Werble and Drye in 1968. In retrospect the logic and the methods of the research were directly related to a long line of previous research.

The term borderline had been used for several decades without clear definition. In fact, about a dozen synonyms are used depending on local taste, the most common of which is chronic undifferentiated schizophrenia. Most clinicians consider the borderline as a latent, ambulatory, not-quite-schizophrenic. We were not satisfied that this was a correct appraisal of a peculiar behavioral pattern and therefore asked whether a borderline syndrome sui generis exists and if so, what are its attributes and secondarily does it have subcategories and how can these be defined? The question was: "What is the borderline?"

Sifting through the literature and the various pronouncements made on the basis of cherished theories, the positive statements seemed to indicate a syndrome characteristic of failure in the development of certain ego functions giving rise to a syndrome of "stable instability." By studying the borderline we hoped to separate part of the confused and confusing waste-land of schizophrenia into a well-defined area. To do this we had to develop new approaches based on the hitches that plagued us in our previous work.

1. We could not use symptoms as in the depression research because these were not well defined and consisted in a wide range of behaviors.

2. We could not use psychiatrists as observers and describers since most of them prefer to infer and speculate. Instead we used those persons among nurses, aides, occupational and recreational therapists who serve, observe, and transact with patient-subjects.

3. Raw data obtained from a large number of observers to wipe out

biases were translated into well-defined rating scales utilizing a framework of ego-psychology based on psychoanalytic theory. Ego functions were redefined clearly and precisely into behavioral variables.

4. Statistical analysis was basically a clustering procedure the results of which were subjected to a multiple-discriminant function analysis. Ten components accurately identified membership in one of four groups for 51 of 59 patients; 20 variables predicted group membership for all subjects.

Our research identified the characteristics of the borderline syndrome as a whole and specified four component types or subcategories none of which need to be described here except to state that the results corresponded well when subsequently tested against individual patient studies in depth. The classification enabled us to correlate the groups with family type and follow-up results and to set the basis for the search for etiological agents ranging from heredity to culture.

We believe that the clinician should now be able to diagnose the borderline syndrome and/or its four groups and know something about their life histories and effectiveness of various therapies. We believe that the theory of ego functions translated into operational strategies enables the investigator, by studying these final-common-pathways, to assess validly and objectively the quality and quantity of internal psychological functions. Internal dynamics and external behavior need not be fractionated. Finally, procedures for the study of other obscure symptom complexes, like schizophrenia, can be approached with modification from the framework of ego functions, proposals that I shall discuss later.

TOWARD UNIFIED THEORY

After World War II John Spiegel and I, dissatisfied with the overall conceptual approach to psychiatry and unhappy about the available texts, attempted by means of dialogues over a period of three years to develop a generalized theory. We learned a great deal which we carried with us continually in our separate fields but not enough for the edification of others, so that we abandoned the project. We were convinced, however, that overarching theories had to embrace the entire field from biology to sociology and more, and that specific aspects of the field as foci could only be viewed in transactional processes with other foci. We used the concept of transaction in psychiatry for the first time, borrowed from the philosopher Dewey, as different from interaction.

In 1950 with several kindred spirits we organized a continuous multi-disciplinary conference of several distinguished investigators to work

"Toward a Unified Theory of Human Behavior." Our first and only report was published in 1956 (22) although we included in this volume only four of our nine conferences. The summary of the monograph indicates how we oriented ourselves in fields and systems and defined them, how we dealt with principles of stability and growth, transactional relationships, systems of communication, and levels of generalization in relation to empirical phenomena.

I shall continue with the "unified theory" discussion only because of its importance for theories of schizophrenia. In its second edition of our monograph published in 1967 Jurgen Ruesch made the following statement.

> Until a generation or two ago the life sciences considered organisms to be so complex that unified theory of behavior was out of the question. This position led to the establishment of separate disciplines, departments and associations. Each homogeneous profession has dealt with some aspects of behavior in its own way. But with the rapid advances in data processing and the development of the team approach, behavioral scientists were able to focus upon larger segments of behavior and take on bigger and more time-consuming tasks. The cooperation of neighboring disciplines in large-scale investigations yielded heterogeneous data that traditional theories could not encompass. The inclusion of anthropological, social, psychological, economic and biological data all within the same enterprise necessitated the development of new models. To cope with the organized complexities of the events under study, system theories were developed, whereby the term "system" was used to refer to a cluster of components or units engaged in mutual interaction. Scientifically, the evidence for interaction is found in the fact that measurements within such a system are in some ways correlated. In closed systems no particle, energy or information is added from the outside, while in open systems exchange of particles, energy or information from the outside is needed. In brief, open systems engage in transactions with the surroundings, while closed systems do not. Systems then are verbal or digital entities upon which theories are based.

In my introduction to the second edition of the same book I asked the question: "Does this kind of thinking (general systems theory) have a more practical application to our understanding of psychopathology and sociopathology?" It is becoming clearer that severe stressors or strains in later life evoke, in addition to various specific stress-responses or defensive maneuvers, partial regression or disintegration of system-attributes. Then the total system begins to break down into its parts which have been important in the development of the more organized integrative states. It is then that the various parts reveal in their own way the impact of the earliest experiences which have impinged upon the organism while still undifferentiated.

The use of pathology (here psychopathology) for the understanding of structure, function, and relationships is the traditional medical model of research on "experiments of nature." The study of maturation and development is more difficult and takes longer. Recently, I have attempted to interest investigators in the study of healthy or normal persons. I called these mentally healthy male subjects "homoclites" because of their tendency to conform or follow the common path (23-25). How humans get to be healthy should help us understand how and when they deviate into sickness.

It is a reasonable postulate that there is no one positive mental health but a variety of healthy, adaptive states depending on heredity, constitution, and physical and emotional experience during maturation and development, resulting in psychodynamic and behavioral characteristics of the sociocultural matrix within which development occurred.

As a result of the permutations of many variables a variety of personalities ensue. Some are deficient in adaptability in one way or another, and some closely approach the profile of what we call categories of psychiatric illness with anxieties, depressions, compulsions, etc. Others come even closer to illness, temporarily, under stressful conditions but they are still healthy if we are not confused by what their psychodynamics may be, or what their psychological test reports may reveal. They are healthy if they behave in accordance with the lowest common denominator of environmental expectations. In this there is still room for deviance, for creativity, and for directional change influencing the environment.

The healthiest person has the largest repertoire of internalized roles, so that his adaptation is effective in a wide range of transactions. The homoclite is thus limited, the borderline restricted; yet even they can adapt within a protected environment. The adaptive capacity of the normal is not unlimited from this frame of reference, either. Although we still do not have frontiers or hill and valley societies, we do have a variety of environments into which even the limited person can fit. Preventive psychiatry, like military reclassification, may operate well by finding the fit.

Under resting conditions or, to use the metaphor of the machine, while idling, the capacity for adaptation or problem-solving cannot be ascertained. Psychophysiological studies on schizophrenics do not clearly reveal deviances unless these subjects are exposed to stress stimuli. During stress or change the kind of integration, the adaptive capacity, the reservoir of social roles become clearer. Homoclites were successful within their particular environment at a special school while performing a particular job. This environment was simply an extension of life-long cultural influences preparing them to do as well as they could, to help others, and to avoid ambitions for wealth and prestige.

Probably as important, perhaps more so than capacity for a variety of social roles or flexibility within a number of rapidly changing situations, is the ability to develop and maintain affectional relations with one or more other persons. For example, some borderline patients have the ability to adapt and conform to a protective environment, to behave "as if," and to relate by means of complementarity. Yet their capacity to form or maintain affectional relations is damaged so that they greatly fear and avoid personal closeness. As a corollary to this deficiency, they cannot neutralize their aggressive drives and are easily aroused to anger.

Normality and illness are polarities of a wide range of integrations; and without any strains, an unlikely hypothetical condition, there is only normality. When strained, the organismic systems respond according to the processes by which the many subvariances have become integrated. There are few new defenses or coping devices—they have already been built into the organism. Thus, the degree of health or illness in the stress responses reveals the quality and quantity of integration.

The stages or phases of development or the life cycle may be viewed from a variety of theoretical positions: biogenetic, psychosexual, epigenetic, behavioral, or learning theories. They all have in common the concept of primary undifferentiation, gradually passing through critical periods of differentiation which are age-specific. All include concepts of process not only in differentiation, but in the phenomenon of dedifferentiation, as for example the overburdened businessman demanding infantile attention when physically ill or the regressive dependency of the men with "combat fatigue." For each phase there are specific scientific disciplines concerned with creating and storing knowledge, specific medical specialties for diagnosis and therapy, and specific psychotherapeutic strategies, as well as corresponding social institutions.

The stages can be enumerated as follows (26) : (1) the relatively undifferentiated neonate; (2) the phases of differentiation or learning through imprinting, reinforcement, imitation, identification with other human objects, etc.; (3) the phase of specific personality, psychosomatic differentiation, and coping development; (4) the phase of health, including proneness to disease; (5) the phase of disease; (6) the phase of chronic illness; and (7) the phase of dying and death. Each phase has its genic, environmental, and experiential components, and to a degree not yet clearly understood, spontaneous movement and shifts due to intervention may occur.

I now come to the discussion of the essence of theories about schizophrenia. It may seem that I have taken a round-about path but of all psychiatric conditions, schizophrenia more than any represents how psychiatry has developed as a professional discipline and as a scientific approach to mental illness, and therefore epitomizes its theoretical sophistication or lack of it. The researches of various investigators may be discussed under the heading of a specific category of theory within which they operate. Some are relatively simple, others immensely complicated. Operationally, consistent systematic procedures with adequate controls are frequently lacking. Theoretically there is a tendency for either reductionistic or humanistic concepts with few attempts at integration within an overarching or global theory. In brief, schizophrenic research in general exposes more "splitting" than synthesis.

1. *The Organic Concepts.*—Although this theoretical approach has been maintained for over 100 years its emphasis has shifted considerably. The early neuropathologists searched for specific cellular changes or specific localizations of cellular loss or agenesis. Kraepelin (16) attributed the loss of inner unity to a disease of the brain. Jung (27) postulated a hypothetical psychotoxin. Manfred Sakel (28) speculated on an intensified tonus of the parasympathetic nervous system blockading the nerve cell and fostering anabolic forces at a central site, the hypothalamus. Others thought that they could demonstrate an aplasia of the endocrine sex glands, of the circulatory system as well as of the thyroid and adrenals. Osmond (29) postulated a faulty metabolic breakdown of epinephrine. More popular are new concepts of aberrations in the area of amine metabolism such as serotonin and norepinephrine or in general, a disturbance in transmethylation. All of these trends toward explaining schizophrenia in physical or reductionistic terms have been severely and objectively criticized by Kety (30) as highly subjective and incompletely controlled experimentally.

Heath (31) has persisted in identifying a biochemical manifestation of a genetic defect in schizophrenia (taraxein) producing or correlated with aberrant spike-like electrical potentials in the septal region of the brain. Lately he has developed evidence that could indicate an auto-immune allergic process. Others have indicated that lactate and lactate-pyruvic acid ratio is higher in schizophrenics than in normals, but if so this indicates a permeability of red blood cells and is not necessarily related to energic defects.

A few more organic concepts may be mentioned. Some authors have utilized the idea that corticothalamic physiology is disturbed. Others believe that there is an internal structural defect—i.e., a failure of development of the central nervous system in schizophrenic children. The idea that the "model psychosis" produced by LSD can further our knowledge of schizophrenia is related to the opportunity to study how biochemical factors can produce psychotic behavior.

Among the organic theories the concept of hereditary transmission of a faulty gene (s) has been emphasized by Kallman (32). Some of his figures are startling. He found 86% concordance in monozygotic twins against' 14% in dizygotic twins, both much more frequent than in other siblings. Reports have indicated that nonschizophrenic members of the family of schizophrenic patients may show some manifestations of the disturbance. Recently a reworking of Kallman's figures indicate that his conclusions may not be so clear-cut. However, of adults who were raised in orphanages or adoptive homes, those who came from schizophrenic mothers had a higher rate of schizophrenia and antisocial behavior, indicating a probable genetic rather than psychosocial origin (Heston (33)).

I shall not consider further details of the organic concepts since they have been repetitively affirmed in countless papers and on the other hand, criticized by many authors. In sum, this theoretical approach postulates a hereditary genic or acquired proclivity to a disturbance in metabolic or endocrine functions secondarily affecting brain physiology, or perhaps a primary disturbance of cerebral metabolism. All other manifestation of symptoms, course, and outcome are secondary. In modern-day organic theory, a morphological basis cause has been superceded by a chemical one. The search continues.

2. *Developmental Concepts.*—In the previous section I have briefly alluded to the hereditary genetic failures of maturation affecting brain function because of some inherent defects. Even though these were not present in the processes of development many things may go wrong about which we know little. These are certainly important influences which may affect the organism's methods of adaptation. What went wrong, we ask, when the individual becomes schizophrenic in later life: reception of stimuli (8), perception, integration of various perceptions or central synthesis?

What satisfactions and/or dissatisfactions does the developing infant or child experience, what traumatic experiences does it suffer, what degrees and quality of information are imparted to it, what are the sources of conditioning, reinforcement, and object-identifications all leading to learning, and finally what conflicts and traumas does it experience, all or any of which may later culminate in schizophrenia?

These compound questions, in total and in part, are at present impossible to answer. More serious than this is the fact that few investigators have been or are oriented to their resolution. Most of the prominent theoretical propositions are derived from experiences during therapy. Let me make my own position clear. Clinical propositions in the form of testable hypotheses require considerable research but this does not consist of techniques employed during the course of any form of therapy. Reconstructions of childhood processes from treatment of adults is not satisfactory etiological research.

Psychoses demonstrate disturbances between the ego and reality, a statement with which everyone should agree without knowing why. The schizophrenic is incapable of cathecting his own bodily boundaries so that reality is not experienced as stable and constant. There is then no reality standard by which to measure thoughts and feelings.

The developmental field is moving away from inferences based on psychoanalytic reconstructions and work with experimental animals into a new discipline of *child development* based on observations and descriptions of learning during its processes. Information theory has given impetus to the study of information overloading, underloading, and confusion (34). All this is an auspicious beginning but still a far cry from explanation of schizophrenia. However there is a beginning interest in prospective studies of development in high risk populations of children (with schizophrenic mothers). These predisposed children living in unkind environments often gradually withdraw into a lonely existence.

3. *Interpersonal Theory Including Family, Society, and Culture.*—Although Adolf Meyer's name is linked to the general thesis that mental illnesses are reactions to interpersonal and situational problems, it was Sullivan (35) who developed interpersonal theory as explanatory for the development of schizophrenia. The basic problem of all human development and maladjustment is related to anxiety which becomes malignant in early phases of the life-cycle. The subject's concepts of self (the self-system) and of others begin in childhood but are constantly exposed to the vicissitudes of life experiences. In a real sense Sullivan's theoretical concepts are retrospective reconstructions on which descriptions of child

development are based. For him mental illness is an expression of disturbed interpersonal relations in which distortions are due to secondary security operations. This theoretical model like others depends on reconstructions and can only be considered fruitful if studies of childhood development indicate evidence that the influence of the human environment produces psychological distortions. Nevertheless Sullivan's theories have had a profound effect on psychotherapy.

Returning specifically to schizophrenia, there is an increasing number of contributions relating the condition to distorted forms or overloading of information. Artiss (34) for example considers schizophrenia a special system of communication. Beck (36) states that the symptoms or symptom-complexes of schizophrenia do not constitute a disease but represent a special language, a medium of communication, an idiom.

The *family* has attracted increased interest as a focus of study on the etiology of various psychiatric syndromes. Goldfarb (37) has pointed out how necessary the family is for the child not only for nurturance and protection but also for learning how to adapt and survive. This seems self-evident. Currently there is interest in the family as an etiological agent producing distortions and deviances in the susceptible child. What is most important is the turning of attention from an individual parent (i.e., the so-called schizophrenogenic mother) to the family as a whole—a system with its own structure, function, and transactions.

Within the family Bateson has described as characteristic of schizophrenia a form of disturbed communication and behavior in its victims which he calls double-bind. Few people including Bateson consider that this one aspect of family communications is in itself etiological. Lidz (38) views the members of the family more individually according to psychoanalytic theory. The schizophrenic evolves from a dominant mother ("skewed" pattern), or from a seductive father ("schism" pattern). Wynne and Singer (39-41) use sociological theory, considering the family one whose roles are ambiguously structured under a facade of "pseudo-mutuality" with "rubber-fence" protective devices against the extended social environment. In general, the schizophrenic is considered a scapegoat whose continued sickness is necessary for the family's stability. According to Wynne and Singer, the schizophrenic internalizes the ways of thinking, meanings, anxieties, irrationalities, confusions, and ambiguities of the family social organization. Thus family patterns can be linked to the personality organization of its offsprings. As Beck puts it: the individual, family, and culture are interadaptive.

In our study of the families of the borderline patients we utilized some new concepts and found that we could differentiate three types of families but none was specific for the syndrome or its individual groupings. Nevertheless all families were unhealthy. This was the most we could conclude, and in addition the patients in their own families carried on the sick behavior.

Schizophrenics seem to appear, or at least are more frequently diagnosed, in lower-class populations and seem to drift to or at least to concentrate in slum and skid-row areas. The sociocultural matrix of the family of origin seems to be different. Although schizophrenia differs in various cultures in content, its processes are reported to be the same in every country in the world. Rapid social change and upward or downward movement seem to be predispositions (42). Transcultural studies suffer because of the use of analogical instead of causative propositions. At present we cannot articulate the propositions relating to society and culture with personality processes in health and sickness in spite of much creative transcultural studies and renewed approaches to "mankind" as an overarching concept.

4. *Psychological Theory.*—Hundreds if not thousands of articles have been published by psychologists reporting the results of experiments and tests applied to schizophrenic patients (1). In fact what psychoanalysts call ego-psychology has been considered the domain of psychology for a long time. Studies on impairment of intelligence, perceptual difficulties, personality difficulties, and psychometric results abound in the psychological literature. Yet it is difficult to extrapolate the theoretical basis for most of the psychological studies.

Hanfmann and Kasanin (43) noted the need to formulate hypotheses in terms of general psychological theory. They based their research on Vigotsky's findings of loss of ability to think in abstract concepts and regression to primitive level of "thinking in complexes." Objects are seen not as classes of objects but as individuals which together form concrete complexes. Utilizing the Vigotsky test the authors showed that there was a reduction in conceptual thinking in schizophrenics when compared with normals of the same educational level.

Kurt Goldstein (44) also found an impairment of attitudes toward the abstract in the schizophrenic resulting therefore in concrete behavior similar to that of patients with brain disease. The abstract attitude of which Goldstein writes consists of: abilities to assume a mental set voluntarily, to shift voluntarily from one aspect of the situation to another, to keep in mind several aspects, to grasp the essentials of a whole, to break these up into parts and isolate them, to abstract common properties, to plan ahead, to assume an attitude of the possible, to think and act symbolically, to detach the ego from the outer world.

Shakow (45-47) worked for many years with schizophrenics and has not only presented important empirical data but has also developed new theory. He has developed a five-stage model in the context of need/tension/gratification/tension reduction: (1) The schizophrenic is weak in curiosity and in search for stimulation. (2) The schizophrenic is extremely sensitive to irrelevancies. (3) He has unrealistic perceptions, over or under scans and articulates. (4) Centrally he shows variability, inappropriateness, poor thinking, inappropriate personalities. (5) Output in behavior is perseverative, slow, variable, and anomalous and he habituates slowly. "There is little doubt that the schizophrenic's is an inefficient, unmodulated system, full of affective *noise* and undeterminant figure-ground relationships."

In another discussion of segmentalization and "set" Shakow (46) points out the schizophrenic's preoccupation with the past, which breaks up his relationship with the current environment. He develops minor sets because he cannot maintain a generalized set. In terms of set the schizophrenic reacts to the old as new and perseverates the new. His anxiety creates an aversion of the new—a "neophobia." It is as if in reacting with too much or too little he is controlled by invisible forces indicating a disturbed integration of central control systems. I quote his theoretical views on the origin of schizophrenia because I consider them to be the most significant of our current positions.

> The schizophrenic falls down in that very important aspect of adaptation, the ability to maintain a generalized set. Actually this inability to keep a major set may perhaps be the secondary result of an underlying trend to establish minor sets, of a positive tendency to segmentalize both the external and the internal environments. The schizophrenic patient appears to be doing this in part as an indirect effort to attain the satisfaction of early fundamental needs which, in contrast with the normal person, have never been adequately satisfied in the ordinary course of events, particularly in the familial setting. This ordinary course of events includes the thousands, nay millions, of appropriate effective reinforcements of behaviors which over the years lay the ground for what we call normal development.
>
> These archaic needs now have to be satisfied in an organism which has outstripped these needs because of the automatic physical and intellectual development that has come with age. This is even more complicated by the fact that with the chronological growth of the developing organism, the schizophrenic finds himself in an environment which has changed concomitantly as well. It has changed

in the sense of being organized to provide fewer and fewer outlets for his infantile or childish needs. Further, the environment presses upon him with demands of its own for acting his chronological age, demands which he has at least to make a stab at meeting. I remember a patient with whom I worked who would periodically reiterate: "I have to socialize!" Then he would on occasion make desultory efforts in this direction by going to parties where triangular cut sandwiches were being served—the criterion he believed his mother had always set for parties of high social level.

It is because of this discrepancy between maturity and chronology that regression cannot be thought of as literally as some theorists have. These segmental cravings cannot be satisfied while total integrated control, the structure which is indispensable to the maintenance of major sets, is effective. Almost inevitably, there results a perverted use of the naturally developed devices to satisfy these needs. We then see preoccupation with ordinarily unconscious bodily processes, with the mechanics of processes rather than with their ends, the use of the thinking process in peculiar ways, etc., etc.— the immense variety of schizophrenic symptoms which can in a sense be viewed as difficult expressions of only partial integration, or individuation, or breakdown of major sets: in other words, of segmentalization. There is an increased awareness of, and preoccupation with, the ordinarily disregarded details of existence—the details which normal people spontaneously forget, train themselves, or get trained, rigorously to disregard. These, rather than the biologically adaptive functional aspects of the situation, appear to take on a primary role (46).

Shakow points out that the schizophrenic's poor adaptation, especially when behaving voluntarily, is poor; he chooses superficial tasks and has difficulty in getting "involved." *Variability* which is considered a handicap to research with schizophrenics should be considered an expected characteristic trait. As a consequence repeated tests or stimuli are necessary and longitudinal studies should be the most productive. Psychological tests applied to schizophrenia are ingenious but controls of variability and cooperation as well as research designs have been oriented toward the secondary effects rather than toward elucidating the primary processes.

5. *Anxiety Theory.*—Up to this point I have delayed discussing the difficult problem of anxiety in schizophrenic patients. The *Diagnostic and Statistical Manual* (DSM II) contains little reference to anxiety in schizophrenics and in fact describes simple schizophrenics as being apathetic. In diagnostic conferences all around the country the descriptions of schizophrenics frequently include the statement "flattening of affect." Just what reference does this have to anxiety? Is it absent? Any one who works intensively with these patients knows full well the unique depth and

severity of their nameless dreads even to the point of fear of possible annihilation, though these may not be apparent on the surface due to the strength of psychological defenses.

Psychoanalytic psychiatry has contributed to our understanding of anxiety as a powerful destroyer of cognitive functions as well as an initiator of vigorous defensive maneuvers. The theory postulates that psychiatric symptomatology for the most part is an evidence of kinds of defense. Thus our nosology is based on the ultimate patterned defenses against anxieties derived from various conflictual and experimental processes.

Otto Will (48-49) expressed the role of anxiety in schizophrenics clearly. He states that anxiety reflecting a fear of loss of object relations is destructive of the ordinary processes of development and influences self-concepts, communication skills, close ties with persons needed for survival, and self-esteem. Such anxiety is associated with the attitude that love hurts. As a general result the mental processes are disorganized, social estrangement occurs, and there is retreat from the surrounding world. The severity of the schizophrenic's anxiety when uncovered is tremendous and the loneliness (sometimes misconstrued as depression) when he withdraws is abysmal.

The question for us here is how do we view the basic anxiety of the schizophrenic, whether free, repressed, associated with defenses or restitutional processes. Anxiety is the variable on which the clinician and theoretician must focus since all that we know about the dynamic psychology and behavior of the schizophrenic may be signals of anxiety.

Anxiety in itself cannot be innate yet we may postulate a basic central nervous irritability which quantitatively is so great that when psychological content is acquired it takes the form of anxiety. Are the genetic abnormalities (50) that influence central nervous system functions directly or indirectly the basis for lack of adaptation to hurting experiences or the cause of increased sensitivity to the usual frustrations? Does the location of central disturbances of function in the diencephalic midline have significance for the schizophrenic's overreaction? Are the developmental experiences within the family or in the larger human environment so traumatic that excessive anxiety is produced? Finally is the anxiety of the schizophrenic qualitatively and/or quantitatively different from the neurotic anxiety?

I have enumerated only a few of the multiple possibilities of anxiety as a causative, intervening, or secondary variable in the schizophrenic process. We could speculate endlessly about the position of anxiety in the large cause-and-effect chain which is not linear in that anxiety is apparent both as one of the causes and one of the results. In fact the position of anxiety could well be the basis of a whole new classifiication system for schizophrenia since anxiety is in itself a biopsychosocial phenomenon.

6. *Psychoanalysis.*—Despite the fact that in his early days Freud was engaged in treating patients some of whom were later found to be schizophrenics, he stated that these "narcissistic neuroses" could not be treated by means of psychoanalysis. Subsequently later generations of analysts have been treating schizophrenics by modifying the classical techniques, and many psychoanalytically oriented psychiatrists have attempted to utilize insight or uncovering psychotherapy for these patients. Since psychoanalytic theory, knowledge, and techniques are inextricably interwoven, those who specialize in the treatment of schizophrenics have attempted to contribute to theoretical knowledge of the disorder within the framework of so-called structural psychoanalytic theory.

Frieda Fromm-Reichmann (51) believed that schizophrenics suffer from the intense anxiety of being abondoned and therefore withdraw and are unable to ask for acceptance. Intense anxiety is due to the outcome of the universal conflict between dependency and hostility magnified overwhelmingly in schizophrenics. The symptoms are then attempts to ward off anxiety. Erikson in his delineation of epigenetic stages indicated that early experiences leading to basic mistrust instead of trust leave enduring and tragically disturbing patterns of behavior. Similarly Bergman et al. (52) repeated the concept that the schizophrenic has intense conflicts about unsatisfied early oral needs. "The psychotic lives under the shadow of the breast."

Otto Will (48-49) became the most skilled and articulate representative of the Fromm-Reichmann school. He states:

> Schizophrenia gains meaning as we consider the uniqueness of the patient (whose behavior is schizophrenic), his associations (those with whom he is more or less schizophrenic), the people of his past (with whom he has learned to live and begin to manifest schizophrenic behavior), his expectations of the future (which may seem to require perpetuation of psychosis), and situations in which variations of the disorder appear. In brief, the term may be used to describe a complex of operations in a social field (49).

Otto Will believes that maturation depends on matching available ability with experience suitable for further development leading to success or failure. In childhood especially, mutual adaptation of child and parent begins the development of object relations necessary for survival. The behavior of the child calls for adequate responses of the mother, more important even than gratifying simple biological needs such as hunger.

> Inappropriate, insufficient, or excessive responses from the environment may lead to the appearance of behavioral distortion or lacks. Such deviations may be revealed in the human as defects in personality described as weakness of ego boundaries, imperfections of self- and body-image, difficulties in need-recognition, inability to conceptualize social roles, etc. (49) .

The disorder involves all levels of behavior from endocrine functions to thought and speech; the total organism is involved.

The classical psychoanalysts may not agree with the above postulates although in practice they are similarly applied in therapy. To the contrary such analysts (Fenichel (53)) convert their empirical experiences into terms embodying instinct theory, oral fixation of libido, and introjection and identification, not much different than the general psychoanalytic theory of neuroses. Nevertheless, no matter at what point psychoanalytic theory is utilized, the ultimate outcome is a recognition that schizophrenia is a disturbance of some if not all ego functions observable in deviant behavior. It is the source of such disturbances about which little consensus is reached.

A major contribution of psychoanalysis has been its focus on anxiety as a central problem of mankind resulting in defensive maneuvers or coping devices to avoid this unendurable feeling. Arieti (54) for example states:

> Schizophrenia is a specific reaction to a severe state of anxiety, originating in childhood, re-experienced and increased in some later period of life. The specificity of this reaction consists in the teleological or motivational use of a more or less advanced impairment of the abstract attitude.

By teleological use Arieti means avoidance of anxiety and the development of uniqueness leading to asocial or desocial states. The impairment of ability to abstract is associated with paleological thinking, desymbolization, desocialization, and retreat from emotion. He does not answer what causes this fundamental devastating anxiety or whether it is qualitatively and/or quantitatively unique.

CLASSIFICATION OF SCHIZOPHRENIAS

All existing theoretical concepts dealing with schizophrenia are severely crippled by the lack of answers to the question *what* is it? Investigators have been struggling with etiological and teleological questions applied to empirical studies without being able to define the class or classes of subjects observed. The lacunae in our knowledge of what is schizophrenia are evidenced by the difficulties clinical psychiatrists and psychologists have in making diagnoses by means of interviews or psychological tests. Cross-cultural reliability is pitifully low. Witness also the use of the terms pseudolatent and borderline as indications of uncertainty.

Although the term dementia praecox was coined by Morel, Kraepelin continued to use it. By 1919 he concluded that neither terminal dementia nor precocity was an essential element since many patients completely recover. He also raised the question whether the same morbid process could be the cause of divergent forms. Kraepelin's theoretical formulation postulated a weakening of the higher psychic levels which check oscillations of feelings and weaken emotional activities which form the mainsprings of volition. The results are disintegration and injury of psychic development.

Kraepelin classified the syndrome into: (1) simple insidious dementia, (2) hebephrenia or silly dementia, (3) depression or stupor, (4) depression with delusions, (5) agitation and excitement, (6) catatonia; excitement and stupor, (7) paranoia with dementia, and (8) paranoia with hallucinations.

Little has been added to our knowledge of classes of schizophrenia since the time of Kraepelin who considered that there was a distinct disease with hereditary disposition, familial incidence based on recessive genetic characteristic, and preceded by character disturbances in childhood.

The classification in the current *Diagnostic and Statistical Manual* (DSM-II) is little different than Kraepelin's original one. It includes simple, hebephrenic, catatonic-excited, catatonic-withdrawn, paranoid, acute schizophrenic episode, latent, residual, schizoaffective-excited, schizoaffective-depressed, childhood, chronic undifferentiated, other. It is evident that over these many years there has been little change in our knowledge of what is schizophrenia.

In 1909 Jung (27) made the first attempt in dealing with the individual psychological processes in schizophrenia as contrasted with the kraepelinian classification. He demonstrated the applicability of freudian analysis to the meaning of psychic processes. During subsequent years freudians have increasingly ignored classification and diagnosis, following Freud's example. More and more psychoanalysts urged consideration of the individual's problems and became less interested in diagnosis and classification which is the basic foundation of a scientific psychiatry.

In recent times schizophrenia has been considered as a group or, pejoratively speaking, diagnostic wastebasket. There is question as to whether it implied a disease or way of life or perhaps even a terminal point of regression within an hierarchical series of faults in "vital balance" (55), what Adolf Meyer called progressive maladaptation to the environment. Redlich and Freedman (56) state that there is great diagnostic uncertainty and little knowledge about incidence, prevalance, or natural history; dynamic descriptions and explanations are intermixed; the meaning of behavior does not explain the causes, disciplines work in isolation, and to every finding is attributed the whole story.

Confusion often exists between the labels of psychosis and schizophrenia despite the fact that they have different meanings. The term psychosis indicates a *behavioral* deviation concomitant with a variety of internal psychological processes. Once a schizophrenic always a schizophrenic, but psychotic behavior may disappear or become ameliorated because of the strength of coping devices or unconscious defenses. Some great and creative historical persons or even average adolescents were at one time psychotic, but through processes of growth and change, or by learning how to live with their schizophrenia, they recover their balance

Some authors like Bellak (1) wrote that schizophrenia was not a single disease with a single cause. He stated that the symptoms of this syndrome were the final common pathway of a number of conditions manifested by severe disturbances of ego functions (multifactorial or psychosomatic).

Bleuler (17) devised the term schizophrenia and avoided classification except to separate primary or constant symptoms from changing accessory symptoms that contribute to the variability of the external picture. The fundamental symptoms according to Bleuler are disturbances of the associations, disturbances in affect, ambivalence, loosening of ties with reality, and recourse to fantasy living or autism.

Under the influence of Adolf Meyer in the United States the concept of schizophrenia as a reaction became widespread but the concept of endogenous or process schizophrenia is still maintained with postulated differences in causes, course, and outcome. As Garmezy (57) states, the basis for this differentiation was the concern with prognosis. The poorly integrated premorbid personality, social isolation, and poor emotional responses to others and no apparent precipitatory cause, fulminating course presumably characterize the process form derived from an organic base.

Other systems of classification have been recently reported. Katz (58) developed a phenomenological typology. Beck (59) using process terms described adult reaction patterns as the core, dream, sanctuary, and transitional types, although all showed defects in intellectual functioning, emotional disturbances, and high fantasy activity which Bleuler had stated were fundamental to the schizophrenic process. The recent interest in typologies and attempts to separate out the parts of a vast nosological mixture are extremely important because classification is a basic prerequisite of science. At present the vast accumulations of repetitive clinical observations in thousands of publications represent a "wilderness without a theory" (59).

SYNTHESES OF THEORIES

Theories of psychopathology in general have been zealously defended and considered to be contradictory to each other. Millon (60) and Grinker (11) have clearly stated that theories of psychopathology should be considered as complementary, differing according to their areas of focus. They may be enumerated as biophysical, intrapsychic, behavioral, and phenomenological, all specifying hypotheses concerning etiology, pathology, and treatment. Classification of theories is, however, still a matter of personal choice. Each is associated with specific levels of organization and is associated with a certain amount of dogma. As Millon states, theories should be evaluated on the grounds of simplicity and parsimony, generality of application, empirical precision, and derivable consequences. A pure psychogenetic theory is as untenable as a pure genetic theory (61). There should be complementarity.

The numerous theoretical approaches to the problem of schizophrenia are vigorously adhered to by their various proponents. In accordance their hypotheses, research designs, and in general their paradigms seem quite different but they all can be subsumed under several general categories.

The theories have not been developed a priori but are usually based on observational phenomena of which cognitive and emotional disturbances of function are apparently central. Bleuler's outstanding contribution has been the separation of primary invariant psychological disturbances from secondary symptoms. Psychoanalysts on the basis of empirical evidence have further refined the distinction between basic anxiety and defensive and restitutive processes. Shakow has outlined his thinking concerning psychopathological theory in general. First, the phenomena are defined via objective empirical studies from which inferences and categorization can be made and theory constructed. These are the contributions to the *what* question. Second, further theory may be developed concerning etiology, the *why* question. Unfortunately, cycles of overemphasis on meaning at the expense of rigor alternate with rigorous measurements devoid of meaning.

Jackson (31) attempted to categorize current theories as follows: (1) organic, (2) biological vulnerability, (3) predisposition plus stress, (4) psychosomatic, (5) early trauma revivified, (6) maladaption of the family group, and (7) purely psychogenetic. There are several other similar summaries. I would like to propose another scheme of general theories each one of which interdigitates with and complements the other.

1. *The organic theories* which postulate disturbances of structure-function of the central nervous system. These may be inherited or acquired and act directly on the nervous system, or indirectly through abnormalities of the endocrine system (adrenals, thyroid, etc.), or through disordered metabolism.

2. *The psychological theories* concerned with functional disturbances of mentation and feelings as end process of ontogenetic experiences.

3. *The social theories* concerned with the direct influences of the human environment at various levels on the learning processes during maturation (59).

The overlapping and the multiplicity of factors place theory of schizophrenia in the currently acknowledged broad *biopsychosocial* field. Among the terms used to incorporate all the approaches are *psychosomatic, multifactorial, field theory, general systems theory,* etc. These are much more sophisticated than the usual oversimplified two-system correlations, or the hope-inspiring concept of difficulty in central control, or deficiencies in organizational processes, or the pessimistic statement that schizophrenia is an attempt to adapt to a problem that is insoluble.

Bleuler's theory was based on the proposition of primary psychological symptoms. Since then considerable evidence has accumulated to indicate that there are somatic symptoms as well and certainly there are multiple behavioral deviations. Since we cannot fractionate the symptomatic field, so too the theoretical approach requires a generalized field theory (63, 64). The question therefore is how do we deal with the extended field conceptually as well as operationally (65).

I should like now to restate the theoretical concepts applicable to schizophrenia temporarily breaking the *biopsychosocial* unity into its parts in an attempt at achieving a schematic chronological order. In order, they are as follows.

1. *Altered Biogenic or Hereditary Background.*—Some genic devia-

tions, probably recessive, predispose the individual to adaptive difficulties because of disordered structure-function of the central nervous system or disorders of the endocrine or metabolic systems indirectly affecting the central nervous system. These do not, however, make a schizophrenic.

2. *Developmental Experiences.*—Early inputs by virtue of satisfactions vs. dissatisfactions, trauma vs. safety, security vs. threats of annihilation, information of various quantities, and consistency furnished by mother and/or family and other members of the human environment prepare the individual for living in a stressful world and create a life style of varying degrees of stability. These experiences acting on a prepared soil (heredity) within critical periods are more or less unsuccessful.

3. *Anxiety.*—In the explanation of neurotic symptoms we usually view them as defenses against anxiety which is the resultant of conflict. Thresholds of anxiety are attributed to interactions between biological predispositions and developmental experiences. These are the significant foundations on which later cues (internal or external stimuli) act to evoke coping, integrative or disintegrative behaviors depending on quantitative factors. Clinical observations on schizophrenics, however, indicate that their anxieties may be *qualitatively* different from the neurotic anxiety. It is for this reason that I have discussed anxiety theory separately from psychological and psychoanalytical theories and indicated that it may represent a crucial difference from the neuroses. The phenomena of anxiety must be included in any theory of schizophrenia concerned with the chronology of etiological factors.

4. *Challenges.*—These constitute the meaningful precipitating factors acting on a prepared organism. They may be overwhelming or mild, overt or covert, consistent or inconsistent. Yet they expose the characteristic psychological set of the schizophrenic's neophobia, perseverations or weakening of central control. When present in lesser degrees these interactions may be exposed only by psychological test situations; in greater degree they may be observable in overt behavior in social situations.

5. *Primary Symptoms.*—These include disturbances of psychological associations, disturbances in affect, ambivalence, loosening of ties with reality, and recourse to fantasy life. Permutations of these and their individualized expressions have been utilized in the current system of classification of types of symptoms.

6. *Secondary Symptoms.*—These include coping devices or defenses which mask the schizophrenic's integrative weakness, compensations, hallucinatory and delusional attempts at restitution of stability as well as reactions to primary symptoms and to anxiety. Among the latter are

aggressive attacks on the disturbers who attempt to permeate defenses, this in spite of terrifying loneliness after withdrawal.

The chronological ordering of these processes is artificial because all elements are active at all subsequent times after their initial apperance. They are usually reinforced and positive feedback mechanisms accentuate prior elements. The cycle generates intensification of the disorder since there is no evidence of control or negative feedback mechanisms. Correspondingly schizophrenia is never cured. It may spontaneously come to a halt or it may spontaneously, or through various interventions in some way, be alleviated. Thus psychotherapy may accomplish a more realistic evaluation of challenges or a detachment of voluntary movement by isolation away from known stimuli to which the individual is vulnerable. Drugs may decrease central excitability or behavioral therapy may ameliorate responses to anxiety. Some psychotherapy may open outlets for unsatisfied childhood needs and family therapy may decrease the demands on voluntary behavior. At any rate as theories in general postulate factors responsible for any disease (the host, the provocative agents and the environment), so therapy may act on any one of this triad. But because the process is established before "critical" periods, rarely do any therapies "cure."

Because the process begins so early (undermining the validity of a purely "reactive" schizophrenia) and is based on primary biological foundations which, even though latent, are probably always part of various transactions during the developmental phases and even later, field concepts require specific chronological ordering of the included parts. The systems within the schizophrenic field are not equipotential and there is a progressive movement of parts, each one being dependent on its precursor, toward ultimate regression.

One of the mysteries embodies the universality of the primary symptom complex (thought disturbance) and the common subcategories of secondary symptoms giving rise to the existing classifications (Kraepelin's or Beck's Six Schizophrenias, etc.). Are these phenomena related to the degree of anxiety? Great anxiety has an effect on cognition as does intense depression. Or is the source (quality) of anxiety the reason for the cognitive disturbance—i.e., the unmanageable world as perceived during developmental periods? Is anxiety unmanageable because of genetic factors or because it is actually too stressful, or because object relations and ego boundaries are constitutionally so weak?

There is sufficient consistency in the classical schizophrenia symptomatologies to warrant the establishment of a syndrome with subtypes. It must be admitted that the boundaries of each category are weak and imperfect for any degree of reliability. Yet we need to ask whether any of the schizophrenic phenomena are specific and unique in themselves. Cognitive disturbances, regressions, withdrawals, and anxieties are present in neuroses, in depressions and to some degree in the so-called healthy. If the flow of events does not include genic or constitutional factors then regression is a natural psychological phenomena which anyone can utilize under certain circumstances beyond thresholds of endurance. The splitting of the ego occurs even in healthy (normal) development. The fact is that the ego is originally split and in development is synthesized resulting in a specific self-system and a life-style. Everyone needs to withdraw into isolation from time to time.

Each set of theories, and I have certainly now illustrated only their prototypes, and each combination of theories evoke specific hypotheses and questions. Even more important than specific questions is the need now to bring the multiple theories into an understandable and fruitful synthesis. This is needed to alleviate the competitive spirit interfering with significant multidisciplinary research. To view the theories, stated precisely, in complementary form may enable good multidisciplinary research to develop.

WHAT ARE THE QUESTIONS?

Based on my own previous work, the results of empirical studies on schizophrenics, and theoretical propositions, certain specific questions may be raised:

1. Are there better methods by which to determine the genic predisposition? How does the gene(s) act—directly or indirectly? Where does the effect take place? Are there specific endocrine, metabolic, or other biochemical disturbances in the central nervous system; are they focal or general processes?

2. Can we improve epidemiological studies of schizophrenia? Can extensive prospective longitudinal studies of high-risk populations of children (66) be made?

3. Can we attribute phases of the development of the syndrome to stresses associated with various phases of the human life-cycle?

4. If we distinguish schizophrenia as a condition that is associated with vulnerability to various perceptual inputs and minor stimuli (67), are ego functions congenitally weak and unstable, predisposing to overreactions, or do particular family and other environments weaken ego functions?

5. Is anxiety of specific quality and quantity an etiological factor for schizophrenia or is it the schizophrenic's response pattern?

6. Are the phenomena of withdrawal and/or aggression attributes of schizophrenia or are these defenses against the unbearable and perhaps unclear anxiety and aggression?

7. Are the schizophrenic response patterns specific or are they exaggerations of common human responses to stress as in war neuroses, or in anxiety states or in other regressive, dedifferentiating processes?

8. Shakow points out the poor generalized preparation for input (lack of curiosity and search for stimulation), the poor preparation for specific input (extreme sensitivity for irrelevancies), the disturbance of actual input (unrealistic perceptions), the defect in central control involving thinking, affect, variability, etc., and the inadequacy of the output stage giving rise to deficient and disorganized performances. Is this the primary gestalt that differentiates the schizophrenic from the healthy?

9. Can we, on the basis of better observational and descriptive techniques, improve the classification of schizophrenia (the *what* question)?

10. Can we avoid simple correlational methods and instead use multivariate analyses?

11. Can we view the separate theories (biological, psychological, and social) as system-determinants and thereby operationally approach problems transactionally?

12. Finally, can we unify our theoretical concepts into a single comprehensive theory that encompasses all levels of disturbed behavior?

I am sure that many more questions about the *what, how,* and *why* of schizophrenia could be raised. I would urge that small circumscribed research projects, even though associated with good scientific rigor, be abandoned for designs oriented toward answering larger more significant questions. These are hard, lengthy, and give no easy answers.

I have recounted several examples of clinical research that I have pursued over a span of several decades. Each focus required a different set of operations, a special strategy. The depressions could be studied through their symptoms. The borderlines could be observed in a relatively free field for their natural but crippled behaviors. The schizophrenic requires special challenges to determine his vulnerabilities and his responses. I have tried to link these investigations with the problems of research on schizophrenia.

Having asked a number of questions and given no answers, the reader and myself are naturally still unsatisfied. We have hesitated in the past to ask the basic questions because they are difficult, life-time consuming, and frustrating. Gertrude instead of asking, "What's the question" might have told dear Alice, "The question is how do you go about getting the answers?"

WHERE ARE THE ANSWERS?

A study of the literature concerned with schizophrenia reveals repetitive statements of theory and of empirical observations whose relevance is obscure, producing in fact, many "little answers" which are difficult to integrate. The student soon arrives at a point of redundancy of information or "noise." The levels of complexity are so many that theories emphasizing simplicity and parsimony are too limited and those emphasizing generalities are too global. What we call theories are collections of related propositions, not "facts." Unfortunately as yet "facts" or empirical observations on schizophrenia lack adequate precision and definition.

The problems associated with schizophrenia demonstrate clearly that there is no single cause and that multiple factors enter into every aspect of cause, course, and outcome. As a result many theories have been constructed appropriate to various specific foci of observation or levels of interest. These necessitate different techniques of study for which expertise in various scientific disciplines is required. Each requires concentration, technology, and language specific for its purposes. Yet each is dependent on others especially on clinical or empirical investigations to define *what* is being studied. The geneticist, biochemist, or physiologist, etc., requires firm and accurate diagnoses to be sure he is studying processes of schizophrenics, their subcategories and the state or phase of the everchanging disturbance.

What are these many scientists studying? What is schizophrenia? These are *first* questions still not answered. For example, the combined experiences and study of the literature by several psychologists and psychiatrists (11) years ago forced us into an artificial consensus to develop a *Michael Reese* definition of schizophrenia as a temporary working hypothesis. What is needed now is a well-conceived program of study in continuity to define clinical schizophrenia and its categories that can be useful for *all* scientific studies. Briefly stated I believe that this requires a study of verbal and gross behaviors in relatively free fields where opportunities are present for many kinds of relations with a variety of people. The focus then would be on what challenges, well defined, excite or ameliorate equally well-defined categories of responses. What psychological tests represent these challenges in brief or miniature encounters?

When we know more about what schizophrenia and/or its categories are, then geneticists, physiologists, chemists, psychologists, and sociologists will be studying the same process. Certainly all systems, but some more than others (genetics), require behavioral referents for their correlations. Yet today we know that simple correlations artificially disregard different units of measurement and different temporal dimensions. Modern multivariate analyses require clinical phenomena and classification as the scientific backbone on which the flesh of a host of other variables may be properly positioned.

We have become increasingly aware that correlations between brain structure-function and behavior, between emotional effective responses and internal feelings and concerns, between deficient logical structures and capacities for abstract thinking, between limited emotional and cognitive means and adaptation to reality are indeed not simple. As a result more interest in bridging theories and models has developed.

It is not that we should discard theories appropriate to various levels of organization and experience, nor abolish specific methods of investigation. To put each in an appropriate position within a total field, so that the transactions among its parts may be defined in process-terms by observations from specific frames of reference, permits a larger more correct view of any biopsychosocial system. At the same time, it does not sacrifice the hard sciences of experimentation nor the softer sciences of behavioral observations.

Drs. David Shakow, Jurgen Ruesch, Daniel Offer, Daniel X. Freedman, David Hamburg, Beatrice Werble, and Roy R. Grinker, Jr., gave comments and suggestions and encouraged me to publish this essay.

REFERENCES

1. BELLAK, L. (ed.): *Schizophrenia,* New York: Logos Press, 1958.
2. HILLER, F., and GRINKER, R. R., SR.: The Nervous Regulation of Sugar Metabolism: II., *Arch Neurol Psychiat* 22:919-925 (Nov.) 1929.
3. LEITER, L., and GRINKER, R. R., SR.: Role of the Hypothalamus in Regulation of Experimental Studies With Observations on Respiration, *Arch Neurol Psychiat* 31:54-86 (Jan.) 1934.
4. GRINKER, R. R., SR.: A Method for Studying and Influencing Corticohypothalamic Relations, *Science* 87:73-74 (Jan. 21) 1938.
5. GRINKER, R. R., SR.: Hypothalamic Functions in Psychosomatic Interrelations, *Psychosom Med* 1:19-47 (Jan.) 1939.
6. GRINKER, R. R., SR.: A Comparison of Psychological "Repression" and Neurological "Inhibition," *J Nerv Ment Dis* 89:765-781 (June) 1939.
7. GRINKER, R. R. SR.: Interrelations of Psychiatry, Psychoanalysis and Neurology, *JAMA* 116:2236-2241 (May 17) 1941.
8. GRINKER, R. R., SR., and SEROTA, H. M.: Electroencephalographic Studies of Corticohypothalamic Relations in Schizophrenia, *Amer J Psychiat* 98:385-392 (Nov.) 1941.

9. GRINKER, R. R., SR., and SPIEGEL, J. P.: *Men Under Stress*, Philadelphia: Blakiston, 1945.

10. GRINKER, R. R., SR., et al: A Study of Psychological Predisposition to the Development of Operational Fatigue: I. In Officer Flying Personnel, *Amer J Orthopsychiat* 16:191-206 (April) 1946; and II. In Enlisted Flying Personnel, pp. 207-214 (April) 1946.

11. GRINKER, R. R., SR.: In Beck, S. J.: *The Six Schizophrenias*, Research Monograph No. 6, New York: American Orthopsychiatric Association, 1954, chap. 1.

12. GRINKER, R. R., SR.: "The Psychosomatic Aspects of Anxiety," in Spielberger, C. D. (ed.): *Anxiety and Behavior*, New York: Academic Press, Inc., 1966.

13. GRINKER, R. R., SR., et al: A Theoretical Approach to Problems of Anxiety, *Arch Neurol Psychiat* 76:420-432 (Oct.) 1956.

14. GRINKER, R. R., SR.: Anxiety as a Significant Variable for a Unified Theory of Human Behavior. *Arch Gen Psychiat* 1:537-546 (Nov.) 1959.

15. GRINKER, R. R., SR.: *Psychosomatic Research*, New York: W. W. Norton, 1953.

16. KRAEPELIN, E.: *Dementia Praecox and Paraphrenia*, R. Mary Barclay (trans.-ed.), Edinburgh: E. S. Livingston, 1919.

17. BLEULER, E.: *Dementia Praecox or the Group of Schizophrenias*, J. Zinkin (trans.-ed.), New York: International Universities Press, 1950.

18. GRINKER, R. R., SR., et al: *The Phenomena of Depression*, New York: Paul B. Hoeber, Inc., 1961.

19. LICHTENBERG, P.: Definition and Analysis of Depression, *Arch Neurol Psychiat* 77:519-528 (May) 1957.

20. GRINKER, R. R., SR.: Reception of Communications by Patients in Depression, *Arch Gen Psychiat* 10:576-580 (June) 1964.

21. GRINKER, R. R., SR., WERBLE, B., and DRYE, R.: *The Borderline Syndrome*, New York: Basic Books Inc., 1968.

22. GRINKER, R. R., SR. (ed.): *Toward a Unified Theory of Human Behavior*, New York: Basic Books Inc., 1956 (second edition, 1967).

23. GRINKER, R. R., SR.: "Mentally Healthy" Young Males (Homoclites), *Arch Gen Psychiat* 1:405-453 (June) 1962.

24. GRINKER, R. R., SR.: "A Dynamic Story of the 'Homoclite,'" in Masserman, J. (ed.): *Science and Psychoanalysis*, New York: Grune & Stratton, Inc., 1963, pp. 115-133, vol. 6.

25. GRINKER, R. R., SR.: Normality Viewed as a System, *Arch Gen Psychiat* 17:320-325 (Sept.) 1967.

26. GRINKER, R. R., SR.: *Psychiatry and Our Dangerous World*, address read at McGill University, Oct. 3, 1968, Amsterdam: Excerpta Medica Foundation, to be published.

27. JUNG, C.: *The Psychology of Dementia Praecox*, A. A. Brill (trans.-ed.), New York: Journal of Nervous and Mental Disease Publishing Co., 1909.

28. SAKEL, M.: *Schizophrenia*, New York: Philosophical Library, 1958.

29. OSMOND, H., and SMYTHIES, M. B.: Schizophrenia: A New Approach, *J Ment Sci* 98:309 (May) 1952.

30. KETY, S. S.: Biochemical Theories of Schizophrenia, *Int J Psychiat* 1:179-200 (Jan.) 1967; and in Romano, J.: *The Origins of Schizophrenia*, Amsterdam: Excerpta Medica Foundation, 1967.

31. HEATH, R., in JACKSON, D. D. (ed.): *The Etiology of Schizophrenia*, New York: Basic Books Inc., 1960.

32. KALLMANN, F. J.: *Heredity in Health and Mental Disorder*, New York: W. W. Norton, 1953.

33. HESTON, L. L.: Psychiatric Disorders in Foster Home Reared Children of Schizophrenic Mothers, *Brit J Psychiat* 112:489 (April) 1966.

34. ARTISS, K. L. (ed.): *The Symptom as Communication in Schizophrenia*, New York: Grune & Stratton, Inc., 1959.

35. SULLIVAN, H. S.: *Schizophrenia as a Human Process,* New York: W. W. Norton, 1962.
36. BECK, S. J.: *Psychological Processes in the Schizophrenic Adaptation,* New York: Grune & Stratton, Inc., 1965.
37. GOLDFARB, W.: "Emotional and Intellectual Consequences of Psychological Deprivation in Infancy," in Hoch, P. H., and Zubin, J. (eds.): *Psychopathology of Childhood,* New York: Grune & Stratton, Inc., 1955.
38. MISCHLER, E. G., and HERTZIG: "Family Interaction Patterns and Schizophrenia" in Romano, J. (ed.): *The Origins of Schizophrenia,* Amsterdam: Excerpta Medica Press, 1967, pp. 121-131.
39. WYNNE, L. C.: "Family Transactions and Schizophrenia: II. Conceptual Considerations for a Research Strategy," in Romano, J. (ed.): *The Origins of Schizophrenia,* Amsterdam: Excerpta Medica Press, 1967, pp. 165-179.
40. WYNNE, L., and SINGER, M. T.: Thought Disorder and Family Relations of Schizophrenics, *Arch Gen Psychiat* 9:191-198 (Sept.) 1963.
41. SINGER, M.: "Family Transactions and Schizophrenia: I. Recent Research Findings," in Romano, J. (ed.): *The Origins of Schizophrenia,* Amsterdam: Excerpta Medica Press, 1967.
42. CLAUSEN, J. A., and KOHN, M. L.: "Social Relations and Schizophrenia," in Jackson, D. D. (ed.): *The Etiology of Schizophrenia,* New York: Basic Books, Inc., 1960.
43. HANFMANN, E., and KASANIN, J.: *Conceptual Thinking in Schizophrenia,* New York: Nervous and Mental Diseases Monographs, 1942.
44. SIMMEL, M. L. (ed.): *The Reach of the Mind:* Essays in Memory of Kurt Goldstein, New York: Springer Verlag, 1968.
45. SHAKOW, D.: Segmental Set: A Theory of the Formal Psychological Deficit in Schizophrenia, *Arch Gen Psychiat* 6:1-17 (Jan) 1962.
46. SHAKOW, D.: Understanding Normal Psychological Function: Contributions From Schizophrenia, *Arch Gen Psychiat* 17:306-319 (Sept.) 1967.
47. SHAKOW, D.: In Simmel, M. (ed.): *The Reach of Mind: Essays in Memory of Kurt Goldstein,* New York: Springer Verlag, 1968.
48. WILL. O. A.: "Schizophrenia and the Psychotherapeutic Field, *Contemporary Psychoanal* 1:1-29 (Oct.) 1964.
49. WILL, O. A.: "Schizophrenia: The Problem of Origin," in Romano, J. (ed.): *The Origins of Schizophrenia,* Amsterdam: Excerpta Medica Press, 1967, pp. 214-228.
50. ROSENTHAL, D.: "An Historical and Methodological Review of Genetic Studies of Schizophrenia," in Romano, J. (ed.): *The Origins of Schizophrenia,* Amsterdam: Excerpta Medica Press, 1967.
51. FROMM-REICHMAN, F.: *Principles of Intensive Psychotherapy,* Chicago: University of Chicago Press, 1950.
52. BERGMAN, P., MALESKY, C., and ZAHN, T. B. Oral Functions in Schizophrenia, *J Nerv Ment Dis* 146:351-359 (May) 1968.
53. FENICHEL, O.: *The Psychoanalytic Theory of the Neuroses,* New York: W. W. Norton & Co., Inc., 1945.
54. ARIETI, S.: *Interpretation of Schizophrenia,* New York: Brunner, 1955.
55. MENNINGER, K., MAYMAN, M., and PRUYSER, P.: *The Vital Balance,* New York: Viking Press, 1963.
56. REDLICH, F. C., and FREEDMAN, D. X.: *The Theory and Practice of Psychiatry,* New York: Basic Books Inc., 1966.
57. GARMEZY, N.: "Process and Reactive Schizophrenia," in Jackson, D. D. (ed.): *The Etiology of Schizophrenia,* New York: Basic Books Inc., 1960.
58. KATZ, M., COLE, J. O., and BARTON, W. E. (eds.): *The Role and Methodology of Classification in Psychiatry and Psychopathology,* Chevy Chase, Md., US Department of Health, Education and Welfare, Public Health Service, 1967.
59. BECK, S. J.: *The Six Schizophrenias,* New York: Grune & Stratton, Inc., 1955.

60. MILLON, T. (ed.): *Theories of Psychopathology,* Philadelphia: W. B. Saunders Co., 1967.
61. KIND, H.: The Psychogenesis of Schizophrenia, *Int J Psychiat* 3:383-403 (May) 1967.
62. MISCHLER, E. G., and SCOTCH, N. A.: Sociocultural Factors in the Epidemiology of Schizophrenia, *Int J Psychiat* 1:62-109 (Jan.) 1967.
63. GRINKER, R. R., SR.: "Open-System" Psychiatry, *Amer J Psychoanal* 26:115-128 (Aug.) 1966.
64. VON BERTALANFFY, L.: "General Systems Theory in Psychiatry," in Arieti, S. (ed.): *American Handbook of Psychiatry,* New York: Basic Books Inc., 1966, vol. 3.
65. AUERBACH, A. (ed.): *Schizophrenia, an Integrated Approach,* New York: The Ronald Press, 1959.
66. MEDNICK, S. A.: "The Children of Schizophrenics (High Risk Group Method)," in Romano, J. (ed.): *The Origins of Schizophrenia,* Amsterdam: Excerpta Medica Press, 1967, pp. 179-201.
67. CALLAWAY, E., JONES, R. T., and LAYNE, R. S.: Evoked Responses and Segmental Set of Schizophrenics, *Arch Gen Psychiat* 12:83-89 (Jan.) 1965.

4

CROSS-NATIONAL STUDY OF DIAG-
NOSIS OF MENTAL DISORDERS:
Hospital Diagnoses and Hospital Patients
in New York and London

Barry J. Gurland, Joseph L. Fleiss, John E. Cooper,
Lawrence Sharpe, Robert E. Kendell, and
Pamela Roberts

Statistical reports based on diagnoses submitted by public psychiatric hospitals in the United States and the United Kingdom show wide cross-national differences in the ratios of newly admitted patients given diagnoses of schizophrenia or affective disorder (1, 2). This contrast between the two countries could be explained by cross-national differences in either the clinical condition of patients admitted to public psychiatric hospitals or the relationship between the patients' clinical condition and the hospital diagnoses.

We have already examined the effects of these two factors for a single New York State mental hospital (Brooklyn) and a single London area mental hospital (Netherne). We found both factors to be present, with the second factor far more important than the first (3, 4). In this paper we will report on results from a wider survey of New York and London

This work was supported by Public Health Service Grant MH-09191 from the National Institute of Mental Health.

B. J. Gurland, M.B., M.R.C.P., D.P.M.; J. L. Fleiss, Ph.D.; L. Sharpe, M.B., D.P.M., and P. Roberts: Biometrics Research, New York State Department of Mental Hygiene, New York, N.Y. J. E. Cooper, B.M., M.R.C.P., D.P.M.; and R. E. Kendell, M.D., M.R.C.P., D.P.M.: Institute of Psychiatry, University of London, and the Royal Bethlem and Maudsley Hospitals.

Reprinted, by permission of author and publisher, from: *Comprehensive Psychiatry*, 11:18-25, 1970.

public mental hospitals and explore the relationship between the clinical condition of patients and their hospital diagnoses.

Sample Selection

We determined that about 180 patients from each city would give a sufficiently large sample for statistical precision. This number is close to half the number of patients expected to be admitted in any week to all nine state mental hospitals that serve the metropolitan area of New York City, based on admission statistics for 1967. Therefore, the number of patients selected from each New York hospital was taken to be equal to half of that hospital's average number of weekly admissions. Selection was at random, was spread over seven consecutive days at each hospital, and yielded 192 patients.

The sampling problem in London was more complicated, since fully 23 area mental hospitals serve the Greater London area. As a first step, five of the 23 hospitals were excluded because they had less than half of their catchment population living within the boundary of Greater London. Each of the 18 remaining hospitals was assigned to one of three types, depending on whether the catchment area it served was peripheral or central to the city, or both. Three hospitals were randomly selected from each of the three types, with the probability of a hospital's selection being roughly proportional to its number of admissions in 1967. At each of the nine selected hospitals, a series of consecutive admissions approximately equal to the average number of weekly admissions in the preceding year was studied. A total of 174 patients was studied in London.

The only criteria for inclusion in the study were that the patient's age be in the interval 20-59 years, and that he be newly admitted (though not necessarily a first admission) to the hospital (not be a transfer from another state or area mental hospital or a return from leave).

Method of Study

As soon as possible after admission, every selected patient was interviewed by a project psychiatrist using a standardized mental state interview schedule (5, 6) and a standardized psychiatric history schedule. In the majority of cases, the interview was conducted within 48 hours of admission. The project psychiatrist made precoded ratings of psychopathology during the mental state interview. The ratings were combined into summary scores measuring various dimensions of psychopathology. Descriptions of these measures and evidence for their reliability are given by Kendell et al (7).

Following each interview, the project psychiatrist made a diagnosis using the eighth revision of the International Classification of Diseases in conjunction with the glossary of terms compiled in the U.K. by the Registrar General (8). The final project diagnosis given a patient was arrived at by consensus after the interviewing psychiatrist discussed his choice with at least one other project psychiatrist. Evidence for the reliability of the project psychiatrists' diagnoses is given by Cooper et al (3).

The hospital diagnosis given a patient is the one finally emerging from the New York State Department of Mental Hygiene for the New York sample and from the Ministry of Health for the London sample, after the routine procedures beginning at the hospital are gone through. The project psychiatrist had no access to the patient's clinical record, nor did the hospital personnel have access to the project psychiatrist's judgments.

Two broad categories of diagnoses are of especial interest, schizophrenia and affective disorder. Within the category of schizophrenia we include the schizophrenias, schizoaffective psychosis and the paranoid states. Within the category of affective disorder we include both the depressed and manic types of manic-depressive psychosis, involutional melancholia, reactive depressive psychosis and depressive neurosis.

Characterizing Clinical Condition

In this paper we restrict the characterization of a patient's clinical condition to the project's ratings of mental state psychopathology, because we have more confidence in these than in the ratings of the patient's psychiatric history. We found the ratings of psychopathology to be more reliable (median intraclass correlation coefficient $= .85$) than the items of psychiatric history (median coefficient $= .60$) (9).

In our previous work (4) we were able to identify the fourteen dimensions of psychopathology, as rated by the project, which best discriminated the hospital diagnosis of schizophrenia from that of affective disorder at both Brooklyn State Hospital in New York and Netherne Hospital in London. These dimensions, each scored as the sum of the ratings made on the items from the standard mental state interview which refer to a circumscribed area of psychopathology, are as follows: general anxiety, specific anxiety, retardation, depressed mood, and apathy; hypomania; depersonalization, lack of insight, delusions of control, delusions of persecution, delusions of grandeur, somatic delusions, blunting, and incomprehensibility.* For ease of reference only, we designate the first five dimensions as the scales of "mood disturbance"; the next dimension stands by itself as the scale "hypomania"; and the last eight dimensions we designate as the scales of conceptual or perceptual "disorganization."

The most powerful method of comparing our two current samples of psychiatric patients from New York and London would be to cluster all patients into homogeneous groups, and then to determine whether these groups are represented in different proportions in the two samples and whether patients from the same group tend to be diagnosed differently by the two sets of hospitals. All of the existing methods of numerical typology, which purport to cluster subjects on the basis of how similar they are, suffer from one defect or another, not the least of which is the requirement for very large sample sizes (10). In the absence of a sound method which is purely empirical, we rely instead on the ad hoc approach described below.

We developed methods for clustering patients into groups within which psychopathology was fairly homogeneous in the light of the following results from our earlier study at Brooklyn and Netherne. Patients who had high scores on the scales of disorganization were most often diagnosed schizophrenic by the staff at both hospitals. Patients who scored high on the scale for hypomania were called schizophrenic in a majority of cases by both hospitals, but a sizable minority was diagnosed manic-depressive, manic by the Netherne hospital staff. Patients who had high scores on the scales of mood disturbance were more likely to be diagnosed as a depressive disorder by both hospitals than were patients who scored high in the other areas. At Netherne, the diagnosis of a depressive disorder was the majority diagnosis for such patients. At Brooklyn, on the other hand, only a minority of such patients were given a diagnosis of depression, the majority being called schizophrenic.

These three areas of psychopathology are thus seen to be associated to a greater or lesser degree with hospital diagnoses at both Brooklyn and Netherne. Their use as the basis for constituting homogeneous groups of patients in the current replication sample is therefore indicated because we are again especially interested in the association between psychopathology and hospital diagnoses.

Since a patient can have either a high or a low score in any of the three areas of mood disturbance, hypomania, and disorganization, it is possible to define a total of eight relatively homogeneous groups of pa-

---

* Certain dimensions, such as auditory hallucinations, were omitted because they added little to the discriminations achieved with the fourteen dimensions above, and were much less frequently noted as present.

tients, each group having a characteristic pattern of high and/or low scores in the three areas. Because few patients fulfilled the criteria for two of the groups (one group with low scores in all three areas, and a second with a high score only on hypomania), these two groups had to be merged into a single one, leaving seven groups instead of eight.

Figure 1 illustrates the rules we adopted for assigning patients to groups. The exact rules may be obtained from the authors; here, we will deal only with the main principles. The scale used for measuring each

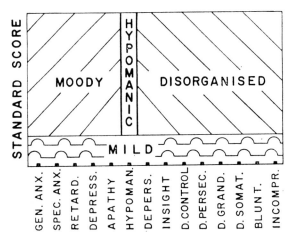

Fig. 1.—Schema for assigning patients to behavioral categories.

of the fourteen dimensions had been standardized to a mean of 50 and a standard deviation of 10 across all patients in our first study at Brooklyn and Netherne hosptials. A high standard score for a patient would be represented in the figure by a point high along the vertical scale for that dimension of psychopathology.

Patients are grouped into seven kinds on the basis of our ratings of their psychopathology. Patients who score high, i.e. above a stipulated point near the mean, only on conceptual or perceptual disorganization are called "disorganized." Patients who score high only on mood disturbance are called "moody." Patients who score high on both the scales of mood disturbance and the scales of disorganization are called "bipolar."

All those patients who score high on the hypomania scale we call hypomanic, but there are three varieties. Those with high scores on disorganization as well as on hypomania are "hypomanic-disorganized." Those with high scores on mood disturbance as well as on hypomania are "hypomanic-moody." Those with high scores in all three areas, namely mood disturbance, disorganization, and hypomania, are "hypomanic-bipolar." Finally, there is a kind of patient who scores low on all the scales; we call this kind the "mild" group. The mild group also contains a very small number of patients who score high only on hypomania but not on any other dimension.

In our earlier study we had observed, both at Brooklyn and Netherne Hospitals, that the disorganized, hypomanic-disorganized and hypomanic-bipolar groups of patients were more likely to receive a hospital diagnosis of schizophrenia than were the moody, hypomanic-moody and mild groups of patients. Conversely, the latter three groups were more likely to be called affective disorder than were the former three groups.

RESULTS

In the samples of patients studied in this survey of New York and London hospitals, the difference in ratios of schizophrenia to affective disorders, as diagnosed by the hospital staffs, is in the same direction as previously reported. In the New York sample this ratio was over nine to one (119 schizophrenics to 13 affectives), and in the London sample about even (59 schizophrenics to 68 affectives). This difference has been studied using the project diagnoses* as a basis of comparison by Cooper et al (11). Here we study it using, for the most part, behavioral categories as a basis of comparison.

Comparison of the Patients' Clinical Conditions

For purposes of this comparison, patients were excluded from analysis if the hospital and project diagnoses concurred that the patient was neither schizophrenic nor affectively ill. This restriction eliminated a number of clearcut alcoholics, drug addicts and patients with organic disorders. Table 1 compares the distribution of the seven groups of patients in the London and New York samples. The total frequencies for the three groups of patients expected on the basis of our previous work to have the highest proportions of schizophrenics as diagnosed by the hospitals (namely the disorganized, hypomanic-disorganized, and the hypo-

---

* The project diagnoses showed a ratio of schizophrenia to affective disorder equal to 0.9:1 (56 schizophrenics to 62 affectives) in the New York hospitals and 0.8:1 (61 schizophrenics to 76 affectives) in the London hospitals.

TABLE 1

PERCENTAGE DISTRIBUTION OF GROUPS OF PATIENTS FOR NEW YORK AND
LONDON SAMPLES (OMITTING PATIENTS AGREED BY HOSPITAL AND
PROJECT TO BE NEITHER SCHIZOPHRENIC NOR AFFECTIVE)

Group	New York	(N = 147)	London	(N = 153)
Disorganized	22.4		15.7	
Hypomanic-Disorganized	21.8		17.6	
Hypomanic-Bipolar	11.6		15.0	
"Highest probability of being called schizophrenia"		55.8		48.3
Bipolar	19.0	19.0	21.6	21.6
Hypomanic-Moody	3.4		9.8	
Mild	9.5		3.3	
Moody	12.2		17.0	
"Highest probability of being called affective"		25.1		30.1
Total		99.9		100.0

manic-bipolar groups) are shown on the line labeled "Highest probability of being called schizophrenia." The total frequencies for the three groups of patients expected to have the highest proportion of affective disorders as diagnosed by the hospitals (namely the moody, hypomanic-moody, and the mild kinds) are shown on the line labeled "Highest probability of being called affective."

The ratio of patients in the groups expected to have the highest proportions of schizophrenics to those in groups expected to have the highest proportions of affective disorders is somewhat greater in New York (55.8:25.1 or 2.2:1) than in London 48.3:30.1 or 1.6:1). This difference in ratios is in the same direction as the previously mentioned difference in the ratios of hospital diagnoses of schizophrenia and affective disorder, 9.1:1 in New York and 0.9:1 in London, but is of a much smaller order of magnitude. Thus, only a small part of this latter difference could be attributed to a difference between New York and London hospitals in the kinds of patients who are candidates for a diagnosis of schizophrenia or affective illness.

Comparison of Relationship Between Hospital Diagnosis and Patients' Clinical Condition

We now proceed to examine the relationship between kinds of patient and the hospital diagnosis in the New York and London samples. For purposes of this comparison, only those patients are included whom the hospitals diagnosed as either schizophrenic or affectively ill. The differences between the New York and London hospital staffs in the way they diagnose patients whose psychopathology is similar is shown in Fig. 2.

Each pair of horizontal bars represents one of the seven groups of patients. In each pair of bars the upper represents the patients in the

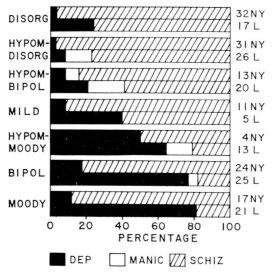

FIG. 2.—New York Hospitals versus London Hospitals.

New York sample who belonged to that category of psychopathology, while the lower represents the corresponding group in the London sample. Within each bar, the solid area represents the proportion of patients diagnosed depressive; the open area, the proportion diagnosed manic-depressive, manic; and the cross-hatched area, the proportion diagnosed schizophrenic. The first two categories together form the affective disorders.

In every one of the seven groups of patients shown here, the New York hospitals diagnose a higher proportion of patients as schizophrenic than do the London hosptials. Thus, even when patients are placed in groups within which there is relative homogeneity of ratings of psychopathology (i.e., similarity in clinical condition), the New York hospital diagnoses show a higher ratio of schizophrenia to affective disorder in every group than do the London hospital diagnoses.

The disparity in the ratios of schizophrenic to affective disorders, as diagnosed by the New York and London hospitals, is greatest in the moody and bipolar groups and much less in the other groups, suggesting at first sight that there are only a few groups of patients which give rise to substantial disagreement in the New York and London hospital diagnoses, and that there are other groups upon which there is substantial agreement. However, this inference is largely spurious and arises mainly because the New York hospitals diagnose a high percentage of all patients as schizophrenic. In those groups where London hospitals also diagnose a high percentage of patients as schizophrenic, apparent agreement is obtained with New York, but where London diagnoses a high percentage of patients as affectively ill, a striking contrast emerges between the hospital diagnoses.

Only in the hypomanic-moody group do the New York hospitals diagnose a depressive disorder as often as schizophrenia, but this is only a small group of four patients. Only one patient was given a hospital diagnosis of manic-depressive, manic in the entire New York sample: he was a member of a hypomanic-bipolar group. In short, the association between the diagnoses of the New York hospitals and the various kinds of patients as defined by their ratings of psychopathology is weak, and is statistically significant only at the 10% level ($x^2 = 12.2$, $df = 6$, for schizophrenia versus affective disorders).

Diagnoses by the London hospital staffs, on the other hand, tell a different story. For example, the disorganized patients are diagnosed mostly as schizophrenic, whereas the moody patients are diagnosed mostly as depressive. The London hospitals diagnose manic-depressive, manic disorders more frequently than do the New York hospitals, and do so mostly for patients in the groups with a hypomanic element. The association between the various kinds of patients and the diagnoses in the London hospitals is far stronger than in New York, and is statistically significant beyond the 0.1 per cent level ($x^2 = 36.2$, $df = 6$, for schizophrenia versus affective disorders).

One way of summarizing this comparison is that the diagnoses in the New York hospitals are heavily weighted in favor of schizophrenia and do not distinguish among these various kinds of patients with nearly as much sensitivity as do the diagnoses by the London hospitals.

DISCUSSION

We have assumed that the ratings of psychopathology made by our team, and the kinds of patients defined by these ratings, have, for the analyses reported here, adequately characterized the patients' clinical condition in both New York and London. There remains the possibility that other associations would have emerged between the patients' clinical condition and the hospital diagnoses if the patients' psychopathology had been rated by other methods or by interviewers of a different background; or if reliable items in the patients' psychiatric and socio-cultural history had been included in characterizing the patients' clinical condition. This possibility is being examined, but does not seem likely to alter our overall conclusions.

CONCLUSION

The differences between New York and London in the ratio of schizophrenia to affective disorder, as reported in hospital diagnoses, appear to be primarily a result of differences in the way the two groups of hospital psychiatrists diagnose patients, and only slightly a result of differences in the actual psychopathology exhibited by patients eligible for these diagnoses. New York hospital staffs tend to give a diagnosis of schizophrenia to the major proportion of every kind of patient group (from which the alcoholics, drug addicts and patients with organic disorder have been excluded), whereas the London hospital staffs tend to diagnose schizophrenia only in certain kinds of patient groups and affective disorder in other kinds of patient groups.

SUMMARY

Samples of patients from New York and London public mental hospitals were examined to investigate the sources of the reported cross-national difference in the ratio of schizophrenia to affective disorder among hospital admissions. The primary source of this difference was that the hospital staffs in New York tend to diagnose all kinds of patients (excluding alcoholics, drug addicts and patients with organic disorders) as schizophrenic, whereas in London some kinds of patients are diagnosed mainly as schizophrenic and others mainly as affective disorder.

ACKNOWLEDGMENTS

The authors wish to thank Dr. J. Zubin, the director of the project, and Dr. M. Kramer for their advice and help; Dr. W. Edwards Deming for developing the sampling methods; and Dr. Tibor Farkas who acted as an interviewer. They appreciate the cooperation extended by the directors and staffs of the hospitals surveyed.

REFERENCES

1. KRAMER, M.: Some problems for international research suggested by observations on differences in first admission rates to mental hospitals of England and Wales and of the United States. *In:* Proceedings of the Third World Congress of Psychiatry, Vol. 3. Toronto, University of Toronto Press/McGill University Press, 1961, pp. 153-160.

2. KRAMER, M.: Cross-national study of diagnosis of the mental disorders: Origin of the problem. *Amer. J. Psychiat.* 125:1-11, 1969.

3. COOPER, J. E., KENDELL, R. E., GURLAND, B. J., SARTORIUS, N., and FARKAS, T.: Cross-national study of diagnosis of the mental disorders: Some results from the first comparative investigation. *Amer. J. Psychiat.* 125:21-29, 1969.

4. GURLAND, B. J., FLEISS, J. L., COOPER, J. E., KENDELL, R. E., and SIMON, R.: Cross-national study of diagnosis of the mental disorders: Some comparisons of diagnostic criteria from the first investigation. *Amer. J. Psychiat.* 125:30-39 1969.

5. SPITZER, R. L., FLEISS, J. L., BURDOCK, E. I., and HARDESTY, A. S.: The mental status schedule: Rationale, reliability and validity. *Compr. Psychiat.* 5:384-395, 1964.

6. WING, J. K.. BIRLEY, J. L. T., COOPER, J. E., GRAHAM, P., and ISAACS, A. D.: Reliability of a procedure for measuring and classifying "present psychiatric state." *Brit. J. Psychiat.* 113:499-515, 1967.

7. KENDELL, R. E., EVERITT, B., COOPER, J. E., SARTORIUS, N., and DAVID, M. E.: The reliability of the "present state examination." *Int. J. Soc. Psychiat.* 3:123-129, 1968.

8. General Register Office: A Glossary of Mental Disorders (Studies on Medical and Population Subjects, No. 22). London, H. M. Stationery Office, 1968.

9. ZUBIN, J.: Cross-national study of diagnosis of the mental disorders: Methodology and planning. *Amer. J. Psychiat.* 125:12-20, 1969.

10. FLEISS, J. L.. and ZUBIN, J.: On the methods and theory of clustering. *Multivar. Behav. Res.* 4:235-250, 1969.

11. COOPER, J. E., KENDELL, R. E., GURLAND, B., SHARPE, L., COPELAND, J. R. M., and SIMON, R.: Survey of state hospitals in New York and area mental hospitals in London. Read at Annual APA Meeting, Miami Beach, Florida, May 1969.

5

PROCESS-REACTIVE SCHIZOPHRENIA
RECENT DEVELOPMENTS

Jerry Higgins[1]

A review is presented of recent research in the area of process-reactive schizophrenia, including research on the criteria commonly used to determine process-reactive status; personality characteristics of process *vs.* reactive schizophrenics; autonomic arousal and responsiveness; conceptual functioning; linguistic and associative processes; learning and performance; censure sensitivity; parent perception; and family dynamics. Despite problems surrounding the process-reactive concept, it continues to permit reduction of heterogeneity in schizophrenia with sufficient frequency to ensure its continued and broadened application.

Since the appearance in the Journal of a review of early studies involving the process-reactive distinction in schizophrenia (85), the concept has attracted considerable attention in the area of psychopathology (166). In addition to papers emphasizing the general fruitfulness of the process-reactive concept for reducing heterogeneity in schizophrenia (37, 71, 74) and for providing a link between diverse foci of research in schizophrenia (160), a number of writers have appraised its efficacy in such areas as psychophysiological functioning (114, 196), information processing (36, 150, 174, 195), motivation and emotion (19), avoidance behavior and hypersensitivity to noxious stimulation, both physical and social (70, 72, 173), perceptual and cognitive processes (107, 161, 172), developmental theory (152, 162), familial factors (5, 63, 122, 135, 139-141), socio-environmental orientation (86), and therapeutic intervention with patient (12, 32, 60) and family (87). Attention has further been

Reprinted, by permission of author and editor, from: *The Journal of Nervous and Mental Diseases,* 149:450-472, 1969. Copyright 1969, The Williams & Wilkins Co.

[1] Department of Psychology, University of California, Santa Barbara, California 93106. Preparation of this review was facilitated by a Faculty Research Grant from the University of California. The author wishes to thank Judith C. Peterson and Jo Anne Hewitt for their assistance.

directed to several conceptual and methodological issues surrounding the process-reactive concept (73, 91, 154). The concept has also found a place in recent texts on psychopathology (18, 125, 130) as well as in at least one introductory text in psychology (110). As final evidence of its fertility, the concept has even spawned a book of its very own (108).

The purpose of the present paper is to review research generated by the process-reactive distinction from December 1962 (the concluding date of the last survey [85]) to the present,[2] relating such research, where appropriate, to previous work.[3]

CRITERIA

Of the four major sets of criteria previously used to determine process-reactive status, all but the Phillips scale have suffered a decline in popularity. In the case of the Elgin and Kantor and associates scales this subsidence is probably due to the relatively ambiguous and abstruse nature of their items as compared to the greater simplicity and specificity of the Phillips. As for the mecholyl test, inherent difficulties in administration in combination with questionable reliability (92) have doubtlessly contributed to its demise. Recent evidence further indicates that the mecholyl test is not an effective predictor of long term outcome and consequently "should not be employed to defend the concept of 'reactive' and 'process' schizophrenia" (194, p. 251). Studies attesting the prognostic power of the Phillips scale continue to appear, dealing with both short (23, 69, 183, 190) and long term (22, 23, 41, 142, 148, 149) outcome. Cicchetti and Ornston (30) have also "found that the more *inadequate* the patient's premorbid sexual and social adjustment [as measured by the Phillips], the *lower* his level of premorbid occupational adjustment, the *earlier* his first neuropsychiatric hospitalization, the *less adequate* his level of hospital work adjustment, and the *greater* percentage of time hospitalized for mental illness since his first admission" (30, p. 160). Nuttall and Solomon (149) also reported that the Phillips was related to age at first admission (process younger), and Cancro and Sugerman (23) have found the Phillips to be related to rate of onset (process insidious). While not gainsaying its prognostic efficacy in the sense of assessing ability to get out and stay out of the hospital, some evidence has emerged that Phillips scores may be related less to *improvement* than to *initial level* of functioning (121).

---

[2] January, 1969.

[3] In the interest of space, specific references to previous work will not be cited but may be readily obtained from the earlier review (85).

Regardless of its merits, one inescapable drawback of any rating scale such as the Phillips lies in the potential distorting influence of the rater. Although high interjudge reliability has been reported in the past by a number of investigators, at least one study reported a less impressive interrater r of .65 (199). The recently developed Ullmann-Giovannoni (193) self-report inventory obviates this problem, while at the same time providing a rapid, easy means of process-reactive assessment which may be readily introduced into research procedures. The Ullmann-Giovannoni inventory consists of 24 true-false items "dealing with behavior evidencing interaction with the environment . . ." (193, p. 41) and yields scores with ordinal properties. Meichenbaum found that the Ullmann-Giovannoni predicted both short (136) and long term (137) outcome. Johnson and Ries (102) have also developed a 35-item sociosexual self-report inventory, but attempts to derive such an inventory from the Minnesota Multiphasic Personality Inventory have been unsuccessful (100, 164).

Global clinical judgment of process-reactive status based upon case histories has also proven predictive of short and long term outcome, as well as continued improvement (or lack thereof) following discharge (24, 179, 180). In contrast, however, Cancro and Sugerman (23) reported that clinical classification, while related to rate of onset, was not predictive of either short or long term outcome. These discrepant findings may be due to the fact that different judgmental frames of reference were employed in the different studies.

Recent years have seen a number of welcome studies evaluating the comparability of the various process-reactive criteria which, of course, is prerequisite to any meaningful comparison of investigations utilizing different criteria. Moderate to high correlations have been obtained between the Phillips on the one hand and the Elgin (69, 177), the Kantor and associates (69, 98), and Social Competence (83) criteria on the other. In what might be taken as evidence of concurrent validity of the newer Ullmann-Giovannoni self-report measure, similarly substantial relationships have also been reported between it and the Phillips (83, 102, 103), the Elgin (115), and Social Competence (83). An exception to this rule is Magaro's (129) failure to obtain a significant correlation between Ullmann-Giovannoni and Phillips scores. However, Magaro's patients were considerably more chronic than those of any other study. Since chronicity is related to propensity to "fake sick" in self-report (65), it is possible that the Ullmann-Giovannoni responses in Magaro's study were so distorted by his chronic sample, whereas the Phillips scores were determined by raters working mainly with case histories.[4] Aside from the general inadvisability of employing chronic samples in process-reactive research (91), Magaro's findings warrant particular caution with respect to the use of a self-report process-reactive index with chronic subjects.

In other studies of intercriteria comparability, reasonably robust correlations were obtained between the Johnson-Ries self-report measure and the Phillips (102), between the Elgin and Kantor and associates criteria (69), and between clinical impression and the Phillips (23). Further testimony of the inadequacy of the mecholyl test comes from Judson and Katahn (105), who obtained a negligible and nonsignificant relationship between mecholyl response and Elgin scores. In sum, the more widely used process-reactive criteria, with the exception of the mecholyl test, are comparable when confined to relatively acute populations.

PERSONALITY

The conclusion that process schizophrenics function at a lower level of personality organization, as inferred from Rorschach responses, than do reactives continues to receive some support (9, 118, 192) with two dissenting studies (77, 106). Achenbach and Zigler (1) found that process patients displayed greater self-acceptance than reactives, concluding that "Rather than being ominous in nature, high self-image disparity would invariably appear to accompany the attainment of higher levels of development since the greater cognitive differentiation found at such levels must invariably lead to a greater capacity for self-derogation, guilt, and anxiety" (1, p. 204). However, Feder (59) was recently unable to reproduce this finding, possibly owing to her use of a different measure of self-acceptance. Pugh and Ray (153) found process patients to exhibit both hostile, acting out and withdrawn, apathetic behavior, with reactives showing more socially appropriate behavior. Reactives have been found to score higher than process patients on Barron's ego strength scale in one study (61), with no process-reactive difference appearing in another (164). The greater preference for ambiguity in a tachistoscopic recognition task shown by process schizophrenics was also interpreted as indicative of a more pronounced deficiency in ego strength (203). Reactives describe themselves on a Q sort as more energetic and jealous than process schizophrenics (101) and less controlled and indifferent (104). However, reactives also show greater gains

---

[4] Magaro himself arrived at essentially the same interpretation of his results.

in control during treatment as reflected in handwriting size decrement (49).

Ries, Johnson, Armstrong, and Holmes (159) could not discriminate between the Draw-A-Person Test protocols of process and reactive schizophrenics over "80 diagnostic signs culled from the literature" (159, p. 184). Supporting the conclusions of previous work, however, Figetakis (61) found reactives to show superior sexual differentiation on the Draw-A-Person Test. Reactives also display greater heterosexual interest, whereas process schizophrenics are more narcissistic (and oral) on the Blacky Picture Test (61). This differential love object cathexis (process-self *vs.* reactive-opposite sex) received corroboration from process-reactive performance on a perceptual task (145). Although differential process-reactive parental identification was not revealed by means of rating techniques (101, 133), the Blacky indicated greater identification with the mother on the part of process schizophrenics (145). Many of the roles assumed by reactive schizophrenics, as determined from Q sorts, also appear to be lacking in social validity (81).

There seems to be a tendency for process patients to score more highly on the schizophrenia (Sc) scale of the Minnesota Multiphasic Personality Inventory (26, 88, 164), although the strength of this relationship appears to fluctuate depending upon whether or not the Sc scores are corrected for defensiveness (K). Process schizophrenics have further been found to be less extraverted on the Maudsley Personality Inventory (3),[5] less cooperative (116, 204), and less susceptible to hypnosis (204), although no less attentive (204), achievement-oriented (175), or delusional (52) than reactives. E. B. Klein and Solomon (112) also observed a nearly significant tendency for process patients to be less submissive than reactives in a game-playing situation.

AROUSAL AND RESPONSIVENESS

A number of studies, employing both physiological and behavioral indices of autonomic arousal, suggest that reactive schizophrenics are characterized by higher resting levels of autonomic activity than process schizophrenics. Thus, Crider, Grinspoon, and Maher (34) obtained

---

[5] Although the authors "predicted that process schizophrenics would achieve higher scores on the Maudsley Personality Inventory scale of extraversion than would reactive schizophrenics" (p. 69), the theoretical rationale for such a prediction is not altogether clear, especially since their introduction states that "Schizophrenic patients showing a history of extraverted behavior trends tend to be judged as 'reactive' (good prognosis), whereas those revealing a history of more introverted trends tend to be judged as 'process' (poor prognosis)" (p. 69).

higher skin potential and faster simple reaction time from their reactive group. This same team of investigators also observed that, as intensity and rate of auditory stimulation (noise) increased, the reaction time of their process group decreased and approached that of the reactives, further suggesting that the resting level of arousal is lower for process schizophrenics inasmuch as their performance can be enhanced by augmented sensory input (35). The work of Crider and his colleagues receives support from Donoghue (47), who obtained similar results and reached similar conclusions regarding process-reactive levels of arousal using a concept formation task with varying intensity of an unpleasant tone as auditory stimulation. Moreover, the results of studies on classical conditioning (187) and associative interference (2, 90) and generalization (89) suggest that, following Hullian notions concerning the relationship between performance and total effective drive (16), reactive schizophrenics function at a higher level of arousal than do process schizophrenics. However, a study by Irwin and Renner (96) involving associative interference did not support this position, providing some evidence to the contrary.

Contradictory results were also reported by Bergeron (10), who found reactives to have a lower arousal level than process patients as indexed by skin conductance. To further cloud the issue, some studies have not obtained a process-reactive arousal difference in either direction. As in previous research, Vollenweider (197) could not distinguish between the critical flicker frequency thresholds[6] of process and reactive patients. D. J. Reynolds (155), too, was unable to detect process-reactive resting level differences over a number of physiological measures, although all of his subjects were quite chronic, none having been hospitalized less than 3 years, thereby reducing the likelihood of more positive results (91). Unlike Crider et al. (35) and Donoghue (47), neither E. B. Klein, Cicchetti, and Spohn (111) nor Schweid (170) found either differential process-reactive reaction times (111, 170) or differential improvement in reaction time with increased auditory input (noise) (170). With regard to the latter result, however, it must be noted that Schweid's procedure included a preparatory interval prior to stimulus onset which brought reaction times near ceiling even without noise; further, the reactive end of the process-reactive continuum was not well represented in Schweid's sample. M. Friedman (66), Rice (157), and Ward and Carlson (198) also failed to obtain a process-reactive difference in resting skin resistance.

---

[6] Critical flicker frequency threshold has been reported to vary directly with arousal level (131).

The picture for autonomic responsiveness is not a great deal clearer. Reactives have been found to display greater autonomic responses as measured by various physiological indices to neutral sound and light stimuli (181), a visual discrimination task (198), and verbal censure (4), the last finding receiving corroboration from the subjective reports of greater anxiety following censure on the part of the reactive subjects. Altshuler (2) also found that reactives scored more highly on the Taylor Manifest Anxiety Scale, which is best interpreted as an index of responsiveness to anxiety-evoking stimuli (134). Exceptions are M. Friedman's (66) and Rice's (157) investigations wherein process and reactive schizophrenics did not display differential skin resistance responses to pictures of nurturant and rejecting parents and peers (66) or an auditory stimulus (157). D. J. Reynold's study (155) also failed to reveal a process-reactive difference in responsiveness to exercise, a cold pressor test, and a mental arithmetic task failure followed by verbal censure, but this may well be ascribed to the aforementioned chronicity of his sample. Bergeron (10), too, did not detect differential process-reactive responsiveness to stimulation. However, since "reactivity to stimulation was found to vary directly in strength with Initial Basal Conductance" (10, p. 102), which was lower for reactives, Bergeron's results are difficult to interpret; it might be argued that his reactives were actually showing greater relative responsiveness. In any event, it is noteworthy that no study of responsiveness has produced contradictory results, i.e., greater responsiveness on the part of process schizophrenics. Thus, while the data concerning arousal level remain highly equivocal, there does seem to be slightly less ambiguity with regard to the proposition that reactive schizophrenics are more autonomically responsive than process schizophrenics, a conclusion that is generally consonant with previous research.

Not only are quantitative differences in responsiveness to stimuli of interest, but process and reactive schizophrenics may also process stimulus input in qualitatively distinctive ways. For example, drawing from a carefully formulated series of studies in perceptual functioning (e.g., 38, 144), Cromwell (36) has predicted and found that reactives perceive stimulus displays in a less redundant, richer fashion than do process patients.[7] While the reactive's ability to integrate stimuli (such as common human and mechanical sounds, musical phrases, Thematic Apperception Test cards, parent-child interaction pictures) is superior at low levels of affectivity (51, 95), the process schizophrenic's integrative functions rise

---

[7] The supporting data were obtained from paranoid reactives and nonparanoid process patients only, although it is likely that a strict process-reactive classification would yield similar data (38).

to the reactive's level as stimuli become more emotionally arousing (51). This finding is analogous to those of Crider et al. (35) and Donoghue (47) described above. A related notion, that process schizophrenics experience greater difficulty in disregarding trivial or meaningless input, as measured by evoked electroencephalographic responses to tones, failed to receive support (20), although results lay in the predicted direction and, as in Schweid's (170) study, "relatively few of our patients represented extreme examples of the reactive . . . groups (170, p. 87). Similarly, neither Deckner (39) nor Rice (157) obtained differential process-reactive processing of weak vs. strong meaning responses.

CONCEPTUAL FUNCTIONING

Several investigators have hypothesized that process schizophrenics are more concrete or overexclusive in conceptualization than reactives. The preponderance of studies, involving a variety of measures—proverbs (22, 105, 106,[8] 169), metaphors (53), similarities (117), Epstein's inclusion test (11, 54, 169), sorting behavior (138, 169), stimulus generalization (138), a word identity task (138), and a battery of seven conceptual tests (163)—failed to support such a hypothesis. Indeed, Lewinsohn (121) found that process schizophrenics displayed superior abstraction ability on Gorham proverbs and the abstraction subtest of the Shipley-Hartford test. More supportive results were obtained by Johnson (99), Little (two studies) (123), and Meichenbaum (136), with reactives performing in a more abstract fashion than process patients. It may be of some import that all of these investigators employed a proverbs test as their measure of abstraction.[9] In a study of more complex design, Gregg and Frank (80), using proverbs, the Goldstein Object Sorts, and similarities (WAIS), found that the conceptual responses of process schizophrenics were concrete but socially meaningful, whereas the conceptual responses of reactives were abstract but autistic. Similar work by M. L. Schwartz, Hunt, and Walker (168) and Sturm (188, 189), however, does not corroborate Gregg and Frank's findings. Notwithstanding the problem of subject chronicity which entered into some of the studies yielding negative results (53, 54), the findings regarding the hypothesis of greater concreteness in process schizophrenia are much more confusing than was the case in earlier process-reactive research. The varying definitions of abstract-concrete thought and the concomitant proliferation of assessment

---

8 There appears to have been considerable (85 per cent) overlap in the composition of the samples employed in these two (105, 106) studies.

9 Meichenbaum also included the Similarities subtest from the Wechsler Adult Intelligence Scale (WAIS).

devices have contributed to this confusion. For example, there was no appreciable correlation between Miller's (138) three conceptualization tasks.

With respect to general intellectual deficit, Belmont, Birch, D. F. Klein, and Pollack (9) found that process schizophrenics scored 16 IQ points lower on the Wechsler-Bellevue Intelligence Scale (Form 1) and displayed inferior recall of Rorschach responses. Similarly, Digiondomenico's (42) process schizophrenics were inferior on the Full-Range Picture Vocabulary Test. Berman (11), Brodsky (15), Donoghue (47), and Strain (185) all found reactives to display superior performance on concept formation tasks, with Johannsen, S. H. Friedman, Leitschuh, and Ammons (98) dissenting. From stories told to Thematic Apperception Test-type pictorial stimuli, Cohen (31) concluded that process patients are lower in "general cognitive ability." Gancherov (68) found that process schizophrenics showed less "problem-solving ability" than reactives over a battery of tests. Stier (183) also noted that reactives were superior in analytic (Picture Completion, Block Design, and Object Assembly subtests of the WAIS) and logical (Piaget Logical Puzzles Test) abilities, and Belmont et al. (9) found greater evidence of irrational thinking in the Rorschach protocols of process patients. On the basis of Kuhlmann-Anderson Group Intelligence Test scores obtained in the second grade, Health, Albee, and Lane (82) have suggested that even in childhood process schizophrenics demonstrated greater intellectual deficit than did reactives; further, process patients showed greater childhood deficit than their siblings whereas reactives did not, and were more likely to be the most deficient in the family. On the other hand, Sizemore (175) was unable to find a process-reactive difference in previous "school performance." Neither Cancro (22) nor Rice (157) obtained a relationship between the process-reactive dimension and performance on the vocabulary subtest of the WAIS,[10] nor did M. L. Schwartz et al. (168) obtain a process-reactive difference in either current intelligence as measured by the CVS Intelligence Scale or premorbid intelligence as estimated by five clinical psychologists from CVS vocabulary responses. S. Schwartz (169), too, failed to find any relationship between process-reactive schizophrenia and cognitive deficit over a number of simple timed perceptual and motor tasks as well as those requiring abstract thought. However, Schwartz' schizophrenics were rather homogeneous; they "all had in common general cooperativeness, residence on an open ward, the expectation that they would soon leave the hospital, and, in most cases, a medical

---

[10] The vocabulary subtest correlates highly with full scale IQ (200).

judgment of absence of serious or disruptive psychiatric symptoms in their day-to-day functioning in the hospital" (169, p. 446). Moreover, on a process-reactive scale range of 8 points, the standard deviation of Schwartz' schizophrenics was only 1.96.

In broader diagnostic terms, when CVS Intelligence Scale protocols were presented to 45 clinical psychologists for evaluation (167), "Retardates were . . . judged as process more than reactive schizophrenic. Reactives were called normal more often than organic or retardate" (167, p. 150). While the tendency for organics to be classified as process more than reactive schizophrenic did not reach statistical significance, it was "clearly in the predicted direction" (167, p. 152), which is consonant with previous research.

LANGUAGE AND ASSOCIATIVE PROCESSES

Process schizophrenics have been observed to be less coherent (95) and to evince more severe thought disorder (22) in their verbalization. There has also been some suggestion that process schizophrenics are less able to utilize the information available in the structure, redundancy, and context of language commonly used by others, including reactives (39, 151). Such an inability could well contribute to faulty communication. However, a very recent investigation (124) found reactives to be less adept at utilizing contextual constraints (although the experimental tasks employed in the conflicting studies were quite different, the former using Taylor's Cloze Procedure (39) and Shannon's guessing game technique (151), the latter (124) modified Williams' word strings). Further neither Hunt, M. L. Schwartz, and Walker (93) nor M. L. Schwartz et al. (168) found confusion in thinking on the Similarities subtest of the Wechsler-Bellevue Intelligence Scale (Form 1) (93) or the vocabulary section of the CVS Intelligence Scale (168) to be related to process-reactive schizophrenia. Similarly, Rice (157) did not find thought disorganization to be any more pronounced in the essays of process than of reactive schizophrenics. It is unfortunate that it is so difficult to assess the degree of overlap between these various measures of "schizophrenicity," or to compare the frameworks within which these judgments were made.

A group of studies has been concerned with the problem of associative commonality in process-reactive schizophrenia as reflected in word association tasks. Studies by Dokecki and his colleagues (44, 45) and Foley (62) have indicated that process schizophrenics show less associative commonality than reactives. However, this finding did not receive confirmation in studies by Deckner,[11] Dockecki,[12] Higgins (85), Rodnick,[13] Schweid (170),[14] and Ries and Johnson (158). Although the last mentioned invetigators did obtain the commonality difference in a subsample of chronic (over 5 years of hospitalization) patients, this finding, too, could not be reproduced by either Deckner[11] or Dokecki.[12] Methodological differences between studies may account for some of the discrepancy in results (85). Process schizophrenics have been found to prefer more child to adult responses than reactives on Gottesman's Forced-Choice Word Association Test (183), perhaps indicative of a less mature level of associative functioning on the part of these patients. While a "less mature" level of associative behavior would seem to some extent isomorphic with "lower commonality," it is difficult to generalize from "forced" to "free" associative behavior. Process schizophrenics have also displayed a dearth of associations when required to name acquaintances (106, 109), possibly reflecting greater environmental withdrawal in general and social withdrawal in particular.

In disagreement with previous research, process schizophrenics have been observed to be less stable than reactives in their word associations over time (44, 45). Again, methodological differences may explain these contradictory results, inasmuch as the word association task in the earlier study was administered under a "speed" set, while a "relaxed" set was used in the later research.

LEARNING AND PERFORMANCE

In agreement with prior research on size estimation in process-reactive schizophrenia, Davis, Cromwell, and Held (38) found that process schizophrenics overestimate while reactives tend to underestimate. In terms of time estimation, process schizophrenics are apparently less accurate and more variable than reactives, although direction of error was not reported (146, 147). Also in accord with previous research, Gibeau (77) found the perception of process schizophrenics to be characterized by greater field dependency than reactives on the embedded figures test (but not on the rod and frame test). Cancro and Sugerman (21, 190), on the other hand, have obtained a curvilinear relationship between the process-reactive dimension and rod and frame performance, with process schizophrenics being both more field-dependent and more field-independent than

---

[11] Deckner, C. W. Personal communication, 1968.
[12] Cromwell, R. L. Personal communication, 1968.
[13] Rodnick, E. H. Personal communication, 1965.
[14] The reactive end of the process-reactive continuum was under-represented in Schweid's sample.

reactives, suggesting that reactives "are less firmly committed to a particular [perceptual-cognitive] style . . ." (21, p. 11) . Process schizophrenics have also been found to be more susceptible than reactives to the autokinetic effect (64) . Using a visual recognition task, M. Friedman (66) found process schizophrenics to have higher perceptual thresholds than reactives, and to make more misperceptions.

Katahn, Harris, and Swanson (109) required process and reactive schizophrenics to recall a "list of 60 words which contained animal names, persons' first names, vegetables, and professions" (109, p. 104) . Although as good as or better than reactives in recall of animals, vegetables, and professions, process schizophrenics were inferior in their recall of persons' first names, i.e., items with interpersonal implications. Process schizophrenics also report fewer socially determined (popular) responses on the Rorschach (9) . Further, reactives have been reported to perform better on the Insight-Emotional test (67) , a test designed "to replicate some of the parameters of the learning process involved in psychotherapy" (p. 7377) . When reinforcement was withheld in a four-way lever-pressing task, process schizophrenics were more likely than reactives to revert rapidly to responses dominant to other stimuli (165) , "reacting quickly and often inappropriately to cues of impending change . . ." (165, p. 4081) .

Process-reactive differences have not emerged in finger tapping (117) or motor impersistence (46) .

REINFORCEMENT EFFECTS

A number of studies have continued to explore the hypothesis that process schizophrenics are more sensitive to certain types of reinforcement than reactives. The weight of the evidence suggests that process and reactive schizophrenics are not differentially sensitive to nonsocial, concrete forms of reinforcement such as candy, cigarettes, poker chips worth money, etc., at least as they affect such behaviors as paired associate (171) and probability (132) learning, although R. D. Reynolds (156) did find that candy and cigarettes were more effective in increasing the operant response rate (pulling a plunger) of reactive than of process schizophrenic males; the reinforcers had no differential effect upon process and reactive female patients. Similarly, several studies have failed to reveal differential process-reactive response to social reinforcement (i.e., censure or praise) in a variety of rote (67, 76, 165) and conceptual (40, 67, 185) learning tasks, as well as simple (111) and complex (29, 64) performance tests. However, some investigations have obtained more positive results with social reinforcement which are congruent with the bulk of previous research. Barry (4), Meichenbaum (136), and Young (205) found that the abstract and conceptual functioning of process schizophrenics declined following censure, while the performance of reactives was either less affected (205), unaltered (4), or improved (136). Praise was not differentially effective (136). Both Sherman (171) and Irwin and Renner (96) found that praise improved performance on a complex verbal learning task for process and reactive schizophrenics alike. The reactives also improved under censure, but censure suppressed improvement in the process group. In striking contrast, when a simple, two-alternative learning task was presented, *wherein a readily apparent means of avoiding censure* constituted the correct response (i.e., the noncensured alternative), process schizophrenics demonstrated superior performance under censure, while reactives continued to respond to praise (96). Further, Webb, Davis, and Cromwell (202) obtained greater process-reactive differences in size estimation in response to scenes depicting maternal rejection and dominance than to less censorious scenes. Magaro (128) was unable to reproduce this finding, at least for the dominance scene; however, even though the same pictorial stimuli were employed in the two studies, the size estimation tasks were quite different. Finally, Hunting (94) has recently reported the results of a tachistoscopic recognition task which indicate that process schizophrenics may be hypersensitive to a broad class of anxiety-arousing stimuli of which censure is but a subset.[15]

Some writers have commented on the apparent paradox involved in postulating that process schizophrenics are hypersensitive to noxious social stimulation but hyporesponsive at the autonomic level. Barry (4) and Rodnick (161) have cogently, and independently, argued that the process schizophrenic's avoidance responses (which usually interfere with adaptive behavior) in the face of noxious stimuli are learned defenses inasmuch as they reduce or prevent anxiety, thereby maintaining the individual's autonomic equilibrium. Additional support for the notion that process schizophrenics, perhaps by means of some mechanism such as Silverman's (173) "sensory input processing-ideational gating," cope with yet remain unaware of disturbing events derives from studies of the ability of process and reactive schizophrenics to detect stimulus-condition differences. Gancherov (68) found that process schizophrenics were unable to discriminate on an adjective check list between an "authori-

---

[15] While Webb (201) did not obtain differential process recognition thresholds for words rated as "good" or "bad" on Osgood's evaluative dimension of the Semantic Differential (reactives had a lower threshold for "good" words), whether the "bad" words were also "anxiety" words is moot.

tarian" and an "understanding" experimenter, although they showed superior performance on nontimed verbal problem-solving tasks under the "authoritarian" experimenter. In contrast, the reactives, who did not display differential performance, were able to describe the experimenters' behavior accurately. Similarly, Nathanson (143) found that process schizophrenics "had considerably greater difficulty in discriminating the warm and loving from the censorious and rejecting parent figures on two [Semantic Differential] dimensions" (143, p. 280). Sowards' (178) results were less clear. Although her process group was somewhat better, both process and reactive schizophrenics experienced difficulty discriminating between praise and censure or between levels of intensity of these.

Other than Gancherov's, there have been a few studies of the effect of "atmosphere" upon process-reactive schizophrenics. In one study, the results of which seem somewhat at odds with Gancherov's, DeLuca (40) recorded greater increments in performance for process schizophrenics than for reactives over equivalent forms of cognitive tasks under encouragement and information on how to improve, and greater decrements in the absence of such a set to improve. Little (123) did not obtain differential process-reactive proverb performance under either a "positive, sympathetic, encouraging, permissive, accepting, warm, friendly, helpful, and interested" examiner or a "businesslike, brusque, clipped, challenging, and sarcastic" examiner. Blumenthal (13) observed that process schizophrenics suffered greater speech disruption (stuttering, tongue slips, intruding incoherencies, etc.) than reactives when shifted from a supportive interview and interviewer to a more stressful interviewless supportive interviewer combination. These studies on the effects of general atmosphere and experimenter quality are exceedingly difficult to compare meaningfully inasmuch as the degree of similarity of these relatively global conditions across studies is not readily ascertained.

PERSON PERCEPTION

Much previous work had suggested that process and reactive schizophrenics are differentially sensitized to parental figures, the process patient being more threatened by maternal cues, and the reactive by paternal cues. Many investigators have focused on this proposition with mixed results. One approach has involved taping the process and reactive schizophrenics' perceptions of their parents. Using various questionnaires designed to assess parental child-rearing attitudes and practices, Becker and Siefkes (8), Bradford (14), Cicchetti (27), Cicchetti, E. B. Klein, Fontana, and Spohn (29), Craig (33), Farina and Holzberg (56), Fontana, E. B. Klein, and Cicchetti (64), E. B. Klein et al. (111), and McKinley (133) generally found little support for the hypothesis of differential mother-father perception in process-reactive schizophrenia, with the exceptions that process patients cited their mother as the parent who made the decisions affecting them most, while reactives named the father (64) and reactive females reported their mothers to be more over-protective relative to their fathers than did process females (33). Female process patients also ascribed greater dominance and punitiveness to their parents than did reactives, and were more disposed to view their parents as more punitive than their parents viewed themselves (8).

On the basis of Q sort ratings, however, Johnson and Meadow (101) found that "reactives tend to perceive their fathers as aggressive and overtly rejecting, whereas process patients tend to perceive their fathers as more passive and covert in their behavior. Reactive fathers were gen-erally described in more negative terms than were process fathers" (101, p. 307). Jackson (97) had process and reactive schizophrenics rate their fathers and mothers on Osgood's Semantic Differential: "Reactive Ss rated their fathers as more leading, strong, hard and cruel . . . [and] dominant than their mothers, but the Process Schizophrenics did not rate their mothers as more dominant than their fathers" (97, p. 51). However, unlike reactives, the process schizophrenics did rate their mothers as more "talkative" than their fathers.

Another approach to assessing process-reactive differences in parent perception consists of exposing patients to graphic material emphasizing maternal or paternal figures and recording their reactions. For example, Nathanson (143) employed the Semantic Differential to obtain ratings on pictures of a mother or a father rejecting, scolding, handing food to, and reading to a child; no rating differences appeared between process and reactive schizophrenics in response to mother vs. father cues. Sim-ilarly, M. Friedman (66) did not detect process-reactive differences in ability to identify and describe blurred pictures of nurturance and rejection interactions between a mother or a father and a child. Three studies required patients to discriminate between variations of pictures of a mother or father scolding a child. Magaro (127) found process schizo-phrenics to suffer maximum impairment on the mother-scolding scene, with reactives showing poorer discrimination on the father-scolding scene. Cicchetti et al. (29) were unable to reproduce these results. Farina and Dunham (55), however, concurred with Magaro in concluding that "there is a slight association between the subjects' premorbid adjustment [proc-ess-reactive status] and performance for the mother relative to the father pictures. The Good [reactive] group patients have more difficulty discriminating the father in comparison to the mother pictures than the Poors [process schizophrenics]. . . . This trend is consistent with previous findings and suggests that Poor [process] group patients are more disturbed by mother than father cues whereas Good [reactive] subjects show greater sensitivity to father content" (55, p. 71). Digiondomenico (42) exposed process and reactive schizophrenics to a "severe-censure" scene depicting "a mother standing over a boy, with mother's arm raised in a striking position, and boy's arm in a defensive position" between administrations of the WAIS Arithmetic and Digit Symbol subtests. No differential process-reactive change in performance appeared following exposure. I. Z. Goodman (79) used photographs of maternal and paternal figures in an attempt to influence the preferences of process and reactive schizophrenics for various items. No differential process-reactive response to the parental influence was evident.

Other investigators have employed tape recordings of bogus parents as stimuli. For instance, D. Goodman (78) had process and reactive schizophrenics listen to a simulated mother or father censuring or praising a child during an interval between successive administrations of the WAIS Digit Symbol subtest. Process schizophrenics showed maximum interference in performance following exposure to the maternal censure tape, while reactives showed maximum interference following exposure to paternal censure. Craig (33) replicated D. Goodman's procedure with female subjects but did not obtain process-reactive differences. Both Cicchetti (27) and Geisinger (75) used tapes simulating parental interaction in which the dominance-submission roles were varied. Process-reactive differences in response to these tapes were not manifested in either accuracy of recall of the content of the contrived interactions and in attitudes toward the parent figures (27) or in WAIS Digit Symbol performance (75). In sharp contrast, Jackson (97), using similar dominance-submission tapes to influence choice between identical geometric designs, concluded: "In support of prior research . . . the maternally dominant cues were more influential to Process Ss while the paternally dominant cues had greater effect upon Reactive Ss" (97, p. 38). Bradford (14) exposed process and reactive schizophrenics to "a tape recorded pseudo-interview in which one mother subscribed to domineering, subtly rejecting, and overprotective child rearing practices . . . whereas the other assumed the role of a warmly supportive, democratic mother." The subjects then rated their reactions to these "mothers" on a number of descriptive scales. "Much of the data related to the hypothesis of differential responsiveness to the experimental figures proved to be nonsignificant" (14, p. 5545). Finally, in a study which combined visual with audio representation, Donovan and Webb (48) had their subjects listen to successive presentations of words spoken by a male or female voice while viewing an appropriate accompanying photograph of a father or mother figure. The words were masked by decreasing amounts of noise until recognition thresholds were established. While the thresholds of reactives did not vary, process schizophrenics had a higher threshold for female- than for male-spoken words, suggesting avoidance of maternal contextual cues on the part of the process patient.

Still others have introduced parental surrogates. Sterne (182) had trained "mother figure" experimenters administer paired associate learning tasks to process and reactive schizophrenics under praise following a correct response or censure following an error; no process-reactive learning differences appeared. More usual has been the practice of using experimenters of different sex, as in a study by E. B. Klein et al. (111) which failed to reveal a differential process-reactive response to male and female experimenters on a simple reaction time task. Similarly, DiMauro (43) had male and female "authority figures" administer censure during conceptual tasks (proverbs and similarities); differential process-reactive performance was not obtained. The same strategy was employed with somewhat greater success by Lefcourt and his associates. These investigators have found that process schizophrenics rejected more Holtzman Inkblot cards (116), displayed better WAIS Digit Span performance (115), and more frequently avoided eye contact (115) with a female than with a male examiner, while reactives evinced more rapid finger tapping in the presence of a male than a female experimenter (117). However, these workers caution that "In general, results do not provide much support for previously reported differential sensitivity of process and reactive schizophrenics to the sex of their examiner" (117, p. 93). In a highly imaginative study, Fontana et al. (64) enlisted a 55-year-old man and a 57-year-old woman as parent surrogates. Following introduction to the subject, they would comment, "You know, you remind me a lot of my son." Nevertheless, the process and reactive schizophrenics were not differentially influenced by the surrogates in an autokinetic situation. Finally, Stoller (184) required process and reactive schizophrenics to perform a visual discrimination task in the presence of *their own mothers.* The mother predicted the correctness of each response within the hearing of her child. Although the mothers of process patients predicted fewer errors than their children actually committed (while the mothers of reactives were relatively accurate), the process schizophrenics were more likely than reactives to respond erroneously following their mother's prediction of an error. "Despite more predictions of 'right,' her [process] children seem to respond more readily to 'wrong' . . ." (p. 170).

A few studies have been addressed to broader forms of person perception. In contrast with previous research, Berman (11) did not obtain differential process-reactive conceptual performance on tests involving social-interpersonal materials as compared to nonsocial-noninterpersonal items. However, more recently Levenson (120) found that process schizophrenics display a "reluctance to engage in direct confrontation with any stimuli [verbal or pictorial] which could be interpreted as having interpersonal implications" (p. 1201). Dunn's (50) results are consonant with Levenson's. Dunn assessed process and reactive schizophrenics' reactions to display of their products (mosaics) to groups vs. individuals. While reactives preferred to have their work evaluated by groups, process schizophrenics eschewed group evaluation, suggesting avoidance of involvement with others on the part of process schizophrenics, particularly involvement which includes evaluation. Buck and Kates (17) had process and reactive schizophrenics view and rate films of rectangles moving in ways which connoted love or anger. The groups did not differ in their ratings of the anger film, but the process schizophrenics rated the love film as less indicative of love than did the reactives, suggesting that process schizophrenics "may not have developed the appropriate categories to which stimulus inputs of high love can be referred for adequate coding . . ." (p. 488). Similarly, Farina, Holzberg, and Kimura (58) stated that "it is our impression that Poors [process schizophrenics] perceive others in a less differentiated way than do Goods [reactive schizophrenics] . . ." (p. 444); however, the number of differences in description between liked and disliked acquaintances did not reach conventional levels of statistical significance ($\chi^2 = 1.82$; corrected for continuity $= 0.81$, 1 df, $p > .05$).

FAMILY FACTORS

The organization of the families of process and reactive schizophrenics has received attention. For instance, Solomon and Nuttall (176) reported some suggestion of birth order being related to process-reactive schizophrenia, with process schizophrenics being later-born and reactives earlier-born.

Researchers have also employed the parents of process and reactive schizophrenics as subjects in an attempt to delineate differences in child-rearing practices. These investigations have frequently explored the notion generated by previous family research and indirectly supported by some of the person perception work that process schizophrenics have been exposed to deviant maternal behavior, while reactives have experienced aberrant paternal behavior. Baxter, Williams, and Zerof (7) found that the fathers of reactive schizophrenics, relative to mothers, subscribed to more deviant child-rearing attitudes on a modified version of the Child-Rearing Attitude Scale. Although the parents of process schizophrenics tended to report more deviant attitudes than the parents of reactives, this difference did not reach statistical significance. Neither Farina and Holzberg (56) nor Cicchetti and Farina (28) found the parents of process and reactive schizophrenics to hold differential attitudes on the Child-Rearing Attitude Scale (56) or the Parental Attitude Research Instrument (28).

On a task which assessed the type of child discipline a parent might employ in a variety of hypothetical problem situations, Baxter et al. (7) observed that "The fathers of the Goods [reactive schizophrenics] tend to respond to the crisis situations with more verbal censure than the mothers of Goods [reactives], while the mothers of Poors [process schizophrenics] tend to report more verbal censure than do the fathers of Poors [process schizophrenics]" (p. 575). The mothers of process schizophrenics also more frequently resorted to physical-material discipline than did the fathers. "The father of the Goods [reactives] is clearly more punitive and authoritarian than the mother, while the reverse tends to occur in families of Poors [process schizophrenics]" (p. 577). However, there was no evidence to suggest that the parents of process schizophrenics employed more discipline than the parents of reactives. In consonance with previous work, Baxter et al. (7) also concluded from rating behavior that the parents of process schizophrenics (especially fathers) were less mature in their cognitive functioning than the parents of reactives.

Farina and Holzberg (56) have noted that the relationship between expressed dominance (as measured by a questionnaire) and behavioral dominance (as displayed in a structured situational test) varied for the parents of process and reactive schizophrenics. While there was a direct relationship between attitude and behavior among the mothers of process patients, the mothers of reactives tended to express less domineering attitudes the more domination they actually exercised. A similar, but nonsignificant, trend was also apparent for fathers. Farina and Holzberg ascribed these results to greater social alertness and defensiveness on the part of the parents of reactives. However, Cicchetti and Farina (28), in a similar study, did not reproduce Farina and Holzberg's results, nor did Baxter et al. (7) obtain a significant difference between groups of parents of process and reactive schizophrenics on an abbreviated form of the Marlowe-Crowne Social Desirability Scale.

Other studies have also employed direct observation in the effort to unravel interaction processes in the families of process and reactive schizophrenics. Farina and Dunham (55) replicated an earlier study in which the parents of process and reactive schizophrenics were required to solve a series of hypothetical problems involving their child, with the modification that the patient was also included in the interaction. "In accord with prior investigations, families of Poors [process schizophrenics] displayed significantly more conflict in interacting than families of Goods [reactive schizophrenics]; and fathers, relative to mothers, were more dominant in Good [reactive] than Poor [process] families" (p. 72). This finding parallels that of Baxter et al. (7) using attitude scales. In addition, reactive schizophrenics appeared to be more active and assertive within their families than did their process counterparts. None of these results was reproduced, however, in subsequent replication by Farina and Holzberg (57). On the other hand, in a similar study Lerner (119) did find the patterns of maternal dominance in the families of process schizophrenics and paternal dominance in the families of reactives. Further, the parents of process patients evinced greater conflict and simultaneously distorted or masked the fact of their conflict.[16] Finally Becker and Siefkes (8) obtained "quite limited support" for their hypothesis that, in a structured situational test involving child problem solving, the families of female process schizophrenics would be characterized by paternal dominance, and the families of female reactives by maternal dominance; no differences in amount of conflict appeared.

CONFOUNDING VARIABLES

A number of methodologically oriented studies point to several factors which may be sources of unwanted variance in process-reactive research which require control. One group of investigations has dealt with the issue of the confusion of severity of illness with process-reactive concept. Blumenthal (13) and Strain (185, 186) have presented evidence that severity of illness as measured by the Montrose Mental Health Scale (13) and Overall and Gorham's Brief Psychiatric Rating Scale (symptom severity) (185, 186) is essentially unrelated to the process-reactive continuum. However, both Cicchetti (27) and Lewisohn (121), using the L-M Fergus Falls Behavior Rating Scale (adequacy of ward behavior)

---

16 It may be noted that Cicchetti (27) did not obtain differential process-reactive response to tapes simulating parental interactions of varying levels of conflict.

(27) and Lorr's Multidimensional Scale for Rating Psychiatric Patients (also symptom severity) (121) found definite severity of illness relationships, with the process schizophrenic being more severely ill. It would seem that whether or not severity of illness is considered to be a contaminating variable in process-reactive research depends upon the assessment technique employed to measure severity. Nevertheless, in view of the positive findings which have emerged, it might behoove the cautious investigator to take severity of illness into account, preferably by means of an assessment device which has yielded relationships with process-reactive schizophrenia.

Several studies have reinforced the conclusion of previous research that socio-cultural factors are interwoven with current usage of the process-reactive concept. Both Nuttall and Solomon (149) and Chapman and Baxter (two samples) (25) have found the Phillips scale to be correlated with social class. However, while Nuttall and Solomon's data indicated that process schizophrenics are more likely to come from the lower classes, Chapman and Baxter concluded that it is reactive schizophrenics that come from lower class homes. To confuse the matter further, D. Goodman (78) and Chapman and Baxter (in a third sample) (25) found no significant relationship between the Phillips and social class. The explanation for these contradictory results is not readily apparent. Baxter and Arthur (6) noted that interparental conflict as revealed during an interview varied jointly with the process-reactive status of the schizophrenic child and the socioeconomic status of the family. Magaro's (127) work on perceptual discrimination "also indicates that the social-class variable should be controlled when using the premorbid-adjustment [process-reactive] dimension" (p. 420). Race has also been found to be related to process-reactive ratings, with Negro schizophrenics more likely to be rated as process than Caucasian schizophrenics (113).

Chronicity, as indexed by duration of hospitalization, has also proven a confounding factor. For example, Tyrell, Struve, and M. L. Schwartz (191) reported that "Our results offer confirmation for the conclusion that total length of lifetime hospitalization is a major variable accounting for the tendency of process schizophrenics to be diagnosed as brain-injured and reactive schizophrenics to be diagnosed as nonbrain-injured on the Yacorzynski Battery" (p. 256). While results were not reported for length of current hospitalization, it must also be noted that no subject in the Tyrell et al. study had a current hospitalization of greater than 1 year.

Finally, Bradford (14) found that process schizophrenics receiving tranquilizers were unable to differentiate between simulated "negative" and "positive" mothers, while nontranquilized process patients (and both drug and nondrug reactives) differentiated clearly. Bradford concluded: "Tranquilizing medication appears to reduce the Poor Premorbids' [process schizophrenics'] affective arousal to potentially aversive stimuli, but has a negligible effect on Good Premorbids [reactive schizophrenics]" (p. 5546).

CONCLUSIONS

The previous review (85) concluded on the optimistic note that "Although the evidence to date is far from unequivocal, it would seem . . . that process-reactive schizophrenia is a justifiable classificatory principle . . ." (p. 22). At this date the writer is somewhat less certain of the future of the concept. It sometimes seems that for every study supporting the efficacy of the concept two nonsupportive ones can be cited. Notwithstanding this less than ideal state of affairs, it should be noted that while nonsupportive studies are many, *contradictory* studies are few. An old, but occasionally forgotten, admonition is that the null hypothesis cannot be accepted. Given the host of sources of error variance which continue to plague process-reactive research (91)—including small samples, under-representation of ends of the continuum, chronicity, drugs, sociocultural contamination, and careless selection of dependent variables, to mention but a few—it is not particularly surprising that many investigators have been unable to reject the null. Although this criticism does not apply with equal force to all the investigations reviewed, the will-o'-the-wisp quality of much process-reactive research may often be traced to a failure to control these extraneous sources of variance adequately.

Despite the problems surrounding the concept, it continues to permit reduction of schizophrenic heterogeneity with sufficient frequency to ensure its continued and broadened application.[17]

---

[17] As an example of the latter trend, process and reactive schizophrenics have even been examined for differences in haptoglobin subtypes (126)—with negative results.

REFERENCES

1. ACHENBACH, T. and ZIGLER, E. Social competence and self-image disparity in psychiatric and nonpsychiatric patients. *J. Abnorm. Soc. Psychol.*, 67:197-205, 1963.
2. ALTSHULER, H. Competitional and Non-Competitional Paired Associates Learning in Process and Reactive Schizophrenics. Doctoral dissertation, Illinois Institute of Technology, No. 65-8878. University Microfilms, Ann Arbor, Mich., 1966.
3. ARMSTRONG, H. E., JR., JOHNSON, M. H., RIES, H. A. and HOLMES, D. S. Extraversion-introversion and process-reactive schizophrenia. *Brit. J. Soc. Clin. Psychol.*, 6:69, 1967.

4. BARRY, R. R. The Effects of a Stress Condition on Process and Reactive Schizophrenics. Doctoral dissertation, Fordham University, No. 68-3677. University Microfilms, Ann Arbor, Mich., 1968.

5. BAXTER, J. C. Family relationship variables in schizophrenia. *Acta Psychiat. Scand.*, 42:362-391, 1966.

6. BAXTER, J. C. and ARTHUR, S. C. Conflict in families of schizophrenics as a function of premorbid adjustment and social class. *Family Process*, 3:273-279, 1964.

7. BAXTER, J. C., WILLIAMS, J. and ZEROF, S. Child-rearing attitudes and disciplinary fantasies of parents of schizophrenics and controls. *J. Nerv. Ment. Dis.*, 141:567-579, 1965.

8. BECKER, J. and SIEFKES, H. Parental dominance, conflict, and disciplinary coerciveness in families of female schizophrenics. *J. Abnorm. Psychol.*, 74:193-198, 1969.

9. BELMONT, J., BIRCH, H. G., KLEIN, D. F. and POLLACK, M. Perceptual evidence of CNS dysfunction in schizophrenia. *Arch. Gen. Psychiat.*, 10:395-408, 1964.

10. BERGERON, J. A. Physiological Reactivity of Schizophrenic and Control Subjects to Dimensions of Primary Intensity of Pure Tones and of Socioemotional Significance of Words. Doctoral dissertation, University of Massachusetts, No. 67-12,537. University Microfilms, Ann Arbor, Mich., 1967.

11. BERMAN, G. Conceptual Functioning of Schizophrenics Classified along the Process-Reactive Continuum. Doctoral dissertation, Stanford University, No. 63-4583. University Microfilms, Ann Arbor, Mich.,1963.

12. BETZ, B. J. Differential success rates of psychotherapists with "process" and "nonprocess" schizophrenic patients. *Amer. J. Psychiat.*, 119:1090-1091, 1963.

13. BLUMENTHAL, R. The effects of level of mental health, premorbid history and interpersonal stress upon the speech disruption of chronic schizophrenics. *J. Nerv. Ment. Dis.*, 139:313-323, 1964.

14. BRADFORD, N. H. Comparative Perceptions of Mothers and Maternal Roles by Schizophrenic Patients and their Normal Siblings. Doctoral dissertation, University of Minnesota, No. 65-15,244. University Microfilms, Ann Arbor, Mich., 1966.

15. BRODSKY, M. Sorting decrement in schizophrenia as a function of social climate. *J. Clin. Psychol.*, 24:162-165, 1968.

16. BROEN, W. E., JR. and STORMS, L. H. Lawful disorganization: The process underlying a schizophrenic syndrome. *Psychol. Rev.*, 73:265-279, 1966.

17. BUCK, L. and KATES, S. L. Perceptual categorizations of love and anger cues in schizophrenics. *J. Abnorm. Soc. Psychol.*, 67:480-490, 1963.

18. BUSS, A. H. *Psychopathology*. Wiley, New York, 1966.

19. BUSS, A. H. and LANG, P. J. Psychological deficit in schizophrenia: I. Affect, reinforcement, and concept attainment. *J. Abnorm. Psychol.*, 70:2-24, 1965.

20. CALLAWAY, E., III, JONES, R. T. and LAYNE, R. S. Evoked responses and segmental set of schizophrenia. *Arch. Gen. Psychiat.*, 12:83-89, 1965.

21. CANCRO, R., and SUGERMAN, A. A. Psychological differentiation and process-reactive schizophrenia. *J. Abnorm. Psychol.*, 74:415-419, 1969.

22. CANCRO, R. The relationship between premorbid adjustment, presenting picture, and outcome in schizophrenia. Proceedings of the 76th Annual Convention of the Amer. Psychol. Ass., 3:495-496, 1968.

23. CANCRO, R. and SUGERMAN, A. A. Classification and outcome in process-reactive schizophrenia. *Compr. Psychiat.*, 9:227-232, 1968.

24. CENTOR, A. A Comparison of Prognosis and Improvement Rate of Two Differentiated Groups of Schizophrenics. Doctoral dissertation, New York University, No. 65-7287. University Microfilms, Ann Arbor, Mich., 1966.

25. CHAPMAN, L. J. and BAXTER, J. C. The process-reactive distinction and patients' subculture. *J. Nerv. Ment. Dis.*, 136:352-359, 1963.

26. CHURCH, J. C. Relationship between Premorbid History and MMPI Profiles of Schizophrenics. Unpublished master's thesis, University of North Carolina, Chapel Hill. 1963.

27. CICCHETTI, D. V. Reported family dynamics and psychopathology: I. The reactions of schizophrenics and normals to parental dialogues. *J. Abnorm. Psychol.*, 72:282-289, 1967.

28. CICCHETTI, D. V. and FARINA, A. Relationship between reported and observed dominance and conflict among parents of schizophrenics. *J. Consult. Psychol.*, 31:223, 1967.

29. CICCHETTI, D. V., KLEIN, E. B., FONTANA, A. F. and SPOHN, H. E. A test of the censure-deficit model in schizophrenia, employing the Rodnick-Garmezy visual-discrimination task. *J. Abnorm. Psychol.*, 72:326-334, 1967.

30. CICCHETTI, D. V. and ORNSTON, P. S. Reported family dynamics and psychopathology: II. The reactions of mental patients to a disturbed family in psychotherapy. *J. Abnorm. Psychol.*, 73:156-161, 1968.

31. COHEN, R. M. The Emotional Effect of Conflictual Material upon Process and Reactive Schizophrenic Patients. Paper read at the 38th Annual Convention of the Eastern Psychological Association, Boston, April, 1967.

32. COYLE, F. A., JR. and COYLE, G. F. An operant explanation of the process-reactive differentiation. *J. Psychol.*, 61:39-45, 1965.

33. CRAIG, J. E. Perceived Parental Attitudes and the Effects of Maternal versus Paternal Censure and Approval in Good and Poor Premorbid Hospitalized Female Schizophrenics. Doctoral dissertation, University of Wisconsin, No. 66-7641. University Microfilms, Ann Arbor, Mich., 1966.

34. CRIDER, A. B., GRINSPOON, L. and MAHER, B. A. Autonomic and psychomotor correlates of premorbid adjustment in schizophrenia. *Psychosom. Med.*, 27:201-206, 1965.

35. CRIDER, A., MAHER, B. and GRINSPOON, L. The effect of sensory input on the reaction time of schizophrenic patients of good and poor premorbid history. *Psychonom. Sci.*, 2:47-48, 1965.

36. CROMWELL, R. L. Stimulus redundancy and schizophrenia. *J. Nerv. Ment. Dis.*, 146:360-375, 1968.

37. CROMWELL, R. L. and DOKECKI, P. R. Schizophrenic language: A disattention interpretation. In Rosenberg, S. and Koplin, J. H., eds. *Developments in Applied Psycholinguistics Research*, pp. 209-260. Macmillan, New York, 1968.

38. DAVIS, D., CROMWELL, R. L. and HELD, J. M. Size estimation in emotionally disturbed children and schizophrenic adults. *J. Abnorm. Psychol.*, 72:395-401, 1967.

39. DECKNER, C. W. and BLANTON, R. L. Effect of context and strength of association on schizophrenic verbal behavior. *J. Abnorm. Psychol.*, 74:348-351, 1969.

40. DELUCA, J. N. Motivation and performance in chronic schizophrenia. *Psychol. Rep.*, 22:1261-1269, 1968.

41. DEWOLFE, A. S. Self-reports and case histories of schizophrneic patients: Reliability and validity of Phillips Scale ratings. *J. Clin. Psychol.*, 24:415-418, 1968.

42. DIGIONDOMENICO, P. A. Variables Associated with Maternal-Censure Induced Performance Interference in Schizophrenia. Doctoral dissertation, Pennsylvania State University, No. 66-8711. University Microfilms. Ann Arbor, Mich., 1966.

43. DIMAURO, J. T. The Effects of Verbal Censure on the Concpetual Ability of Process and Reactive Schizophrenics. Doctoral dissertation, Temple University, No. 65-1404. University Microfilms, Ann Arbor, Mich., 1965.

44. DOKECKI, P. R., CROMWELL, R. L. and POLIDORO, L. G. The chronicity and premorbid adjustment dimensions as they relate to commonality and stability of word association responses in schizophrenics. *J. Nerv. Ment. Dis.*, 146:310-311, 1968.

45. DOKECKI, P. R., POLIDORO, L. G. and CROMWELL, R. L. Commonality and stability

of word association responses in good and poor premorbid schizophrenics. *J. Abnorm. Psychol.*, 70:312-316, 1965.

46. DOMRATH, R. P. Motor impersistence in schizophrenia. *Cortex.* 2:474-483, 1966.

47. DONOGHUE, J. R. Motivation and Conceptualization in Process and Reactive Schizophrenia. Doctoral dissertation, University of Nebraska, No. 64-8875. University Microfilms, Ann Arbor, Mich., 1964.

48. DONOVAN, M. J. and WEBB, W. W. Meaning dimensions and male-female voice perception in schizophrenics with good and poor premorbid adjustment. *J. Abnorm. Psychol.*, 70:426-431, 1965.

49. DOWNING, R. W., EBERT, J. N., BORUCHOW, J. K. and VALENTINE, J. H. Temporal changes in handwriting size, level of premorbid social functioning and intellectual level during treatment in acute schizophrenics. *J. Nerv. Ment. Dis.*, 142:526-533, 1966.

50. DUNN, R. E. Schizophrenia, Socio-Sexual Adjustment, Evaluation, and Involvement with People. Doctoral dissertation, University of Washington, No. 65-5417. University Microfilms, Ann Arbor, Mich., 1965.

51. DWARSHUIS, L. The Affect-Arousing Value of the Stimuli as a Determiner of Affective Complexity in Schizophrenics and Normal Subjects. Paper read at the 72nd Annual Convention of the American Psychological Association, Los Angeles, September, 1964.

52. ELISEO, T. S. Delusions in process and reactive schizophrenia. *J. Clin. Psychol.*, 20: 352, 1964.

53. ELISEO, T. S. Figurative and literal misinterpretations of words by process and reactive schizophrenics. *Psychol. Rep.*, 13:871-877, 1963.

54. ELISEO, T. S. Overinclusive thinking in process and reactive schizophrenics. *J. Consult. Psychol.*, 27:447-449, 1963.

55. FARINA, A. and DUNHAM, R. M. Measurement of family relationships and their effects. *Arch. Gen. Psychiat.*, 9:64-73, 1963.

56. FARINA, A. and HOLZBERG, J. D. Attitudes and behaviors of fathers and mothers of male schizophrenic patients. *J. Abnorm. Psychol.*, 72:381-387, 1967.

57. FARINA, A. and HOLZBERG, J. D. Interaction patterns of parents and hospitalized sons diagnosed as schizophrenic or nonschizophrenic. *J. Abnorm. Psychol.*, 73: 114-118, 1968.

58. FARINA, A., HOLZBERG, J. D. and KIMURA, D. S. A study of the interpersonal relationships of female schizophrenic patients. *J. Nerv. Ment. Dis.*, 142:441-444, 1966.

59. FEDER, C. Z. Relationship between self-acceptance and adjustment, repression-sensitization and social competence. *J. Abnorm. Psychol.*, 73:317-322, 1968.

60. FIELD, T. and MILLER, G. A. Prognostic implications with process-reactive schizophrenics in rehabilitation counseling. *Penn. Psychiat. Quart.*, 7:43-46, 1967.

61. FIGETAKIS, N. Process-Reactive Schizophrenia: Ego-Strength and Selected Psychosexual Dimensions. Doctoral dissertation, Michigan State University, No. 64-7504. University Microfilms, Ann Arbor, Mich., 1964.

62. FOLEY, L. J. A Study of the Word Associations of Schizophrenic Dimensions with Varied Instructions. Doctoral dissertation, Rutgers—The State University, No. 67-9248. University Microfilms, Ann Arbor, Mich., 1968.

63. FONTANA, A. F. Familial etiology of schizophrenia: Is a scientific methodology possible? *Psychol. Bull.*, 66:214-227, 1966.

64. FONTANA, A. F., KLEIN, E. B. and Cicchetti, D. V. Censure sensitivity in schizophrenia. *J. Abnorm. Psychol.*, 72:294-302, 1967.

65. FONTANA, A. F., KLEIN, E. B., LEWIS, E. and LEVINE, L. Presentation of self in mental illness. *J. Consult. Psychol.*, 32:110-119, 1968.

66. FRIEDMAN, M. Perceptual and Psychogalvanic Responses of Schizophrenic and Normal Subjects to Cues of Nurturance and Rejection in Interaction with

Mother, Father, and Peer Figures. Doctoral dissertation, University of Massachusetts, No. 66-7628. University Microfilms, Ann Arbor, Mich., 1966.

67. FULK, R. H. Premorbid Variables and Learning Parameters in Schizophrenia. Doctoral dissertation. The Ohio State University, No. 65-3856. University Microfilms, Ann Arbor, Mich., 1965.

68. GANCHEROV, B. S. "Authoritarian" and "Understanding" Test Administration in Relation to Problem-Solving Ability and Inter-Personal Discrimination in Process and Reactive Schizophrenics and Non-Schizophrenics. Doctoral dissertation, University of Southern California, No. 62-6055. University Microfilms, Ann Arbor, Mich., 1963.

69. GARFIELD, S. L. and SUNDLAND, D. M. Prognostic scales in schizophrenia. *J. Consult. Psychol.*, 30:18-24, 1966.

70. GARMEZY, N. Adaptive mechanisms in schizophrenia. *Bull. Menninger Clin.*, 29: 24-36, 1965.

71. GARMEZY, N. Contributions of Experimental Psychology to Understanding the Origins of Schizophrenia. Paper read at the First Rochester International Conference on the Origins of Schizophrenia, Rochester, N. Y., March, 1967.

72. GARMEZY, N. The prediction of performance in schizophrenia. In Hoch, P. H. and Zubin, J., eds. *Psychopathology of Schizophrenia*, pp. 129-181. Grune & Stratton, New York, 1966.

73. GARMEZY, N. Process and reactive schizophrenia: Some conceptions and issues. In Katz, M. M., Cole, J. O. and Barton, W. E., eds. *The Role and Methodology of Classification in Psychiatry and Psychopathology*, pp. 419-466. Public Health Service Publication No. 1584, Washington, D. C., 1968.

74. GARMEZY, N. Some determiners and characteristics of learning research in schizophrenia. *Amer. J. Orthopsychiat.*, 34:643-651, 1964.

75. GEISINGER, D. L. The Effect of Maternal versus Paternal Dominance on the Performance of Good and Poor Premorbid Schizophrenics. Doctoral dissertation, Syracuse University, No. 66-9847. University Microfilms, Ann Arbor, Mich., 1966.

76. GERSTON, A. N. An Experimental Investigation of the Task Efficiency of Schizophrenics under Varying Conditions of Social Need and Social Support. Doctoral dissertation, New York University, No. 68-10,059. University Microfilms, Ann Arbor, Mich., 1968.

77. GIBEAU, P. J. Field Dependency and the Process-Reactive Dimension in Schizophrenia. Doctoral dissertation, Purdue University, No. 65-8603. University Microfilms, Ann Arbor, Mich., 1965.

78. GOODMAN, D. Performance of good and poor premorbid male schizophrenics as a function of paternal versus maternal censure. *J. Abnorm. Soc. Psychol.*, 69: 550-555, 1964.

79. GOODMAN, I. Z. The influence of parental figures on schizophrenic patients. *J. Abnorm. Psychol.*, 73:503-512, 1968.

80. GREGG, A. H. and FRANK, G. H. An analysis of conceptual thinking in process and reactive schizophrenics. Proceedings of the 74th Annual Convention of the American Psychological Association, 1:183-184, 1966.

81. GUTHRIE, D. M. Role Structure in Schizophrenic and Normal Adult Males. Doctoral dissertation, University of Southern California, No. 65-7231. University Microfilms, Ann Arbor, Mich., 1965.

82. HEATH, E. B., ALBEE, G. W. and LANE, E. A. Predisorder intelligence of process and reactive schizophrenics and their siblings. Proceedings of the 73rd Annual Convention of the American Psychological Association, 223-224, 1965.

83. HELD, J. M. and CROMWELL, R. L. Premorbid adjustment in schizophrenia: The evaluation of a method and some general comments. *J. Nerv. Ment. Dis.*, 146: 264-272, 1968.

84. HIGGINS, J. Commonality of word association responses in schizophrenia as a function of chronicity and adjustment: A response to Dokecki, Cromwell and Polidoro. *J. Nerv. Ment. Dis.*, 146:312-313, 1968.

85. HIGGINS, J. The concept of process-reactive schizophrenia: Criteria and related research. *J. Nerv. Ment. Dis.*, 138:9-25, 1964.

86. HIGGINS, J. Process-reactive schizophrenia and environmental orientation. *J. Schizophrenia*, 2:72-80, 1968.

87. HIGGINS, J. The schizophrenogenic mother revisited. *Brit. J. Psychiat. Soc. Wk.*, 9:205-208, 1968.

88. HIGGINS, J., MEDNICK, S. A. and PHILIP, F. J. The schizophrenia scale of the MMPI and life adjustment in schizophrenia. *Psychology*, 2 (4):26-27, 1965.

89. HIGGINS, J., MEDNICK, S. A., PHILIP, F. J. and THOMPSON, R. E. Associative responses to evaluative and sexual verbal stimuli by process and reactive schizophrenics. *J. Nerv. Ment. Dis.*, 142:223-227, 1966.

90. HIGGINS, J., MEDNICK, S. A. and THOMPSON, R. E. Acquisition and retention of remote associates in process-reactive schizophrenia. *J. Nerv. Ment. Dis.*, 142: 418-423, 1966.

91. HIGGINS, J. and PETERSON, J. C. Concept of process-reactive schizophrenia: A critique. *Psychol. Bull.*, 66:201-206, 1966.

92. HIGGINS, J. and PETERSON, J. C. The mecholyl test in schizophrenia. *Amer. J. Psychiat.*, 123:979-985, 1967.

93. HUNT, W. A., SCHWARTZ, M. L. and Walker, R. E. Judgmental bias in the differentiation of process and reactive schizophrenia. *J. Clin. Psychol.*, 21:172, 1965.

94. HUNTING, W. H. Differences in the Perceptual Recognition Responses of Good and Poor Premorbid Schizophrenics to Anxiety and Neutral Words. Doctoral dissertation, University of California, Los Angeles, No. 66-11,955. University Microfilms, Ann Arbor, Mich., 1966.

95. HUSNI-PALACIOS, M., PALACIOS, J. R. and GIBEAU, P. J. Auditory perceptual patterns of process and reactive schizophrenics. *J. Project. Techn.*, 31:86-91, 1967.

96. IRWIN, L. and RENNER, K. E. Effect of parise and censure on the performance of schizophrenics. *J. Abnorm. Psychol.*, 74:221-226, 1969.

97. JACKSON, N. L. P., JR. Sex and dominance cues in good-poor premorbid schizophrenia. *J. Abnorm. Psychol.* In press.

98. JOHANNSEN, W. J., FRIEDMAN, S. H., LEITSCHUH, T. H. and AMMONS, H. A study of certain schizophrenic dimensions and their relationship to double alternation learning. *J. Consult. Psychol.*, 27:375-382, 1963.

99. JOHNSON, M. H. Verbal abstracting ability and schizophrenia. *J. Consult. Psychol.*, 30:275-277, 1966.

100. JOHNSON. M. H. and HOLMES, D. S. An attempt to develop a process-reactive scale for the MMPI. *J. Clin. Psychol.*, 23:191, 1967.

101. JOHNSON, M. H. and MEADOW, A. Parental identification among male schizophrenics. *J. Personality*, 34:300-309, 1966.

102. JOHNSON, M. H. and RIES, H. A. A self-report scale for process-reactive schizophrenia. *J. Nerv. Ment. Dis.*, 143:481-483, 1966.

103. JOHNSON, M. H. and RIES, H. A. Validational study of the self-report scale for process-reactive schizophrenia. *J. Consult. Psychol.*, 31:321-322, 1967.

104. JOHNSON, M. H. and ROZYNKO, V. A factorial study of parental and self perceptions of schizophrenics and normals. *Calif. Ment. Hlth Res. Dig.*, 5:122-124, 1967.

105. JUDSON, A. J. and KATAHN, M. The relationship of autonomic responsiveness to process-reactive schizophrenia and abstract thinking. *Psychiat. Quart.*, 37:19-24, 1963.

106. JUDSON, A. J. and KATAHN, M. Levels of personality organization and production

of associative sequences in process-reactive schizophrenia. *J. Consult. Psychol.*, 28:208-213, 1964.

107. KANTOR, R. E. and HERRON, W. G. Perceptual learning in the reactive-process schizophrenias. *J. Project. Techn.*, 29:58-70, 1965.

108. KANTOR, R. E. and HERRON, W. G. *Reactive and Process Schizophrenia.* Science and Behavior Books, Palo Alto, Calif., 1966.

109. KATAHN, M., HARRIS, J. H. and SWANSON, R. T. Production of associative sequences in process-reactive schizophrenic and nonschizophrenic groups. *J. Consult. Psychol.*, 31:104, 1967.

110. KENDLER, H. H. *Basic Psychology*, 2nd ed. Appleton-Century-Crofts, New York, 1968.

111. KLEIN, E. B., CICCHETTI, D. and SPOHN, H. A test of the censure-deficit model and its relation to premorbidity in the performance of schizophrenics. *J. Abnorm. Psychol.*, 72:174-181, 1967.

112. KLEIN, E. B. and SOLOMON, L. Agreement response tendency and behavioral submission in schizophrenia. *Psychol. Rep.*, 18:499-509, 1966.

113. LANE, E. A. The influence of sex and race on process-reactive ratings of schizophrenics. *J. Psychol.*, 68:15-20, 1968.

114. LANG, P. J. and BUSS, A. H. Psychological deficit in schizophrenia: II. Interference and activation. *J. Abnorm. Psychol.*, 70:77-106, 1965.

115. LEFCOURT, H. M., ROTENBERG, F., BUCKSPAN, B. and STEFFY, R. A. Visual interaction and performance of process and reactive shizophrenics as a function of examiner's sex. *J. Personality*, 35:535-546, 1967.

116. LEFCOURT, H. M. and STEFFY, R. A. Sex-linked censure expectancies in process and reactive schizophrenics. *J. Personality*, 34:366-380, 1966.

117. LEFCOURT, H. M., STEFFY, R. A., BUCKSPAN, B. and ROTENBERG, F. Avoidance of censure by process and reactive schizophrenics as a function of examiner's sex and type of task. *J. Gen. Psychol.*, 79:87-96, 1968.

118. LERNER, P. M. Correlation of social competence and level of cognitive perceptual functioning in male schizophrenics. *J. Nerv. Ment. Dis.*, 146:412-416, 1968.

119. LERNER, P. M. Resolution of intrafamilial role conflict in families of schizophrenic patients. II. Social maturity. *J. Nerv. Ment. Dis.*, 145:336-341, 1967.

120. LEVENSON, R. L. Some Variables Influencing Selective Attention in Schizophrenia. Doctoral dissertation, Yeshiva University, No. 67-9666. University Microfilms, Ann Arbor, Mich., 1967.

121. LEWINSOHN, P. M. Does the Phillips Scale of Premorbid Adjustment predict improvement or initial status? Proceedings of the 75th Annual Convention of the American Psychological Association, 2:225-226, 1967.

122. LIDZ, T., FLECK, S. and CORNELISON, A. R. *Schizophrenia and the Family.* International Universities Press, New York, 1965.

123. LITTLE, L. K. Effects of the interpersonal interaction on abstract thinking performance in schizophrenics. *J. Consult. Psychol.*, 30:158-164, 1966.

124. LIVINGSTON, P. B. and BLUM, R. A. Attention and speech in acute schizophrenia: An experimental study. *Arch. Gen. Psychiat.*, 18:373-381, 1968.

125. LONDON, P. and ROSENHAN, D., eds. *Foundations of Abnormal Psychology.* Holt, Rinehart and Winston, New York, 1968.

126. LOVEGROVE, T. D. and NICHOLLS, D. M. Haptoglobin subtypes in a schizophrenic and control population. *J. Nerv. Ment. Dis.*, 141:195-196, 1965.

127. MAGARO, P. A. Perceptual discrimination performance of schizophrenics as a function of censure, social class, and premorbid adjustment. *J. Abnorm. Psychol.*, 72:415-420, 1967.

128. MAGARO, P. A. Size estimation in schizophrenia as a function of censure, diagnosis, premorbid adjustment and chronicity. *J. Abnorm. Psychol.*, 74:306-313, 1969.

129. MAGARO, P. A. A validity and reliability study of the process-reactive self-report scale. *J. Consult. Clin. Psychol.*, 32:482-485, 1968.

130. MAHER, B. A. *Principles of Psychopathology: An Experimental Approach.* McGraw-Hill, New York, 1966.

131. MALEY, M. J. Two-flash threshold, flicker-fusion threshold, and skin conductance. *Psychonom. Sci.*, 9:633-634, 1967.

132. McINNIS, T. L. and ULLMANN, L. P. Positive and negative reinforcement with short- and long-term hospitalized schizophrenics in a probability learning situation. *J. Abnorm. Psychol.*, 72:157-162, 1967.

133. McKINLEY, R. A. Perceived Parental Attributes of Schizophrenics as a Function of Premorbid Social Adjustment. Doctoral dissertation, State University of Iowa, No. 64-3408. University Microfilms, Ann Arbor, Mich., 1964.

134. McREYNOLDS, P. Relations between psychological and physiological indices of anxiety. In McReynolds, P., chm. The concept of anxiety: A reexamination. Symposium presented at the 47th Annual Convention of the Western Psychological Association, San Francisco, May, 1967.

135. MEDNICK, S. A. and SCHULSINGER, F. A longitudinal study of children with a high risk for schizophrenia: A preliminary report. In Vandenberg, S. G., ed. *Methods and Goals in Human Behavior Genetics*, pp. 255-295. Academic Press, New York, 1965.

136. MEICHENBAUM, D. H. Effects of social reinforcement on the level of abstraction in schizophrenics. *J. Abnorm. Psychol.*, 71:354-362, 1966.

137. MEICHENBAUM, D. H. Validational study of marital status and the self-report scale for process-reactive schizophrenia. *J. Consult. Clin. Psychol.*, 33:351-356, 1969.

138. MILLER, H. J. Reliability of Verbal and Motor Measures of Degree of Inclusion with Comparisons of Normal, Reactive and Process Schizophrenic, and Organic Subjects. Doctoral dissertation, Indiana University, No. 66-14,861. University Microfilms, Ann Arbor, Mich., 1967.

139. MISHLER, E. G. and WAXLER, N. E. Family interaction processes and schizophrenia: A review of current theories. *Merrill-Palmer Quart.*, 11:269-315, 1965.

140. MISHLER, E. G. and WAXLER, N. E. Family interaction and schizophrenia: An approach to the experimental study of family interaction and schizophrenia. *Arch. Gen. Psychiat.*, 15:64-74, 1966.

141. MISHLER, E. G. and WAXLER, N. E. Family Interaction Patterns and Schizophrenia: A Multi-level Analysis. Paper read at the First Rochester International Conference on the Origins of Schizophrenia, Rochester, N. Y., March, 1967.

142. NAMECHE, G., WARING, M. and RICKS, D. Early indicators of outcome in schizophrenia. *J. Nerv. Ment. Dis.*, 139:232-240, 1964.

143. NATHANSON, J. A. A semantic differential analysis of parent-son relationships in schizophrenia. *J. Abnorm. Psychol.*, 72:277-281, 1967.

144. NEALE, J. M. and CROMWELL, R. L. Size estimation in schizophrenics as a function of stimulus-presentation time. *J. Abnorm. Psychol.*, 73:44-48, 1968.

145. NORMINGTON, C. J. Some Aspects of Psychosexual Development in Process-Reactive Schizophrenia. Doctoral dissertation, Michigan State University, No. 65-711. University Microfilms, Ann Arbor, Mich., 1965.

146. NORMINGTON, C. J. Extended report: Time-estimation in process-reactive schizophrenia. Unpublished manuscript, Colorado State University, Fort Collins, 1967.

147. NORMINGTON, C. J. Time-estimation in process-reactive schizophrenia. *J. Consult. Psychol.*, 31:222, 1967.

148. NUTTALL, R. L. and SOLOMON, L. F. Factorial structure and prognostic significance of premorbid adjustment in schizophrenia. *J. Consult. Psychol.*, 29:362-372, 1965.

149. NUTTALL, R. L. and SOLOMON, L. F. Prognosis in schizophrenia: The role of premorbid, social class, and demographic factors. Unpublished manuscript, Boston College, Boston, no date.

150. PEARL, D. Stimulus input and overload in relation to classifications of schizophrenia. *Newsltr Res. Psychol.*, 4:44-56, 1962.

151. PEARL, D. Language processing ability of process and reactive schizophrenics. *J. Psychol.*, 55:419-425, 1963.

152. PHILLIPS, L. Social competence, the process-reactive distinction and the nature of mental disorder. In Hoch, P. H. and Zubin, J., eds. *Psychopathology of Schizophrenia*, pp. 471-481. Grune & Stratton, New York, 1966.

153. PUGH, L. A. and RAY, T. S. Behavior style categories of chronic schizophrenic women. *Arch. Gen. Psychiat.*, 13:457-463, 1965.

154. RASKIN, A. Unresolved Issues in the Process-Reactive Classification. Paper read at the 71st Annual Convention of the American Psychological Association, Philadelphia, August, 1963.

155. REYNOLDS, D. J. An Investigation of the Somatic Response System in Chronic Schizophrenia. Doctoral dissertation, University of Pittsburgh, No. 63-2442. University Microfilms, Ann Arbor, Mich., 1963.

156. REYNOLDS, R. D. Operant Response as a Function of the Premorbid Adjustment of Schizophrenic Subjects. Doctoral dissertation, Purdue University, No. 65-5040. University Microfilms, Ann Arbor, Mich., 1965.

157. RICE, J. K. Disordered Language as Related to Autonomic Arousal and the Process-Reactive Distinction. Doctoral dissertation, University of Wisconsin, No. 67-12,467. University Microfilms, Ann Arbor, Mich., 1968.

158. RIES, H. A. and JOHNSON, M. H. Commonality of word association and good and poor premorbid schizophrenia. *J. Abnorm. Psychol.*, 72:487-488, 1967.

159. RIES, H. A., JOHNSON, M. H., ARMSTRONG, H. E., JR. and HOLMES, D. S. The Draw-A-Person Test and process-reactive schizophrenia. *J. Project. Techn.*, 30:184-186, 1966.

160. RODNICK, E. H. Clinical psychology, psychopathology, and research in schizophrenia. In Koch, S., ed. *Psychology: A Study of a Science*. vol. 5. *The Process Areas, the Person, and Some Applied Fields: Their Place in Psychology and in Science*, pp. 738-779. McGraw-Hill, New York, 1963.

161. RODNICK, E. H. Cognitive and perceptual response set in schizophrenics. In Jessor, R. and Feshbach, S., eds. *Cognition, Personality, & Clinical Psychology*, pp. 173-209. Jossey-Bass, San Francisco, 1967.

162. RODNICK, E. H. The psychopathology of development: Investigating the etiology of schizophrenia. *Amer. J. Orthopsychiat.*, 38:784-798, 1968.

163. SACKS, S. Concreteness, Overinclusion, and Symptomatology in Schizophrenia. Doctoral dissertation. University of Houston, No. 67-16,145. University Microfilms, Ann Arbor, Mich., 1968.

164. SCHAEFER, S. M. J. MMPI profiles of good and poor premorbid schizophrenics. Unpublished thesis, University of Minnesota, Minneapolis, 1965.

165. SCHENCK, H. U. Regression in Schizophrenics as a Function of Censure, Reinforcement Cues. and Habit Hierarchies. Doctoral dissertation, University of California, Los Angeles, No. 65-13,095. University Microfilms, Ann Arbor, Mich., 1966.

166. SCHOOLER, C. and FELDMAN, S. E. *Experimental Studies of Schizophrenia*. Psychonomic Press, Goleta, Calif., 1967.

167. SCHWARTZ, M. L. Diagnostic judgmental confusion and process-reactive schizophrenia. *J. Abnorm. Psychol.*, 73:150-153, 1968.

168. SCHWARTZ, M. L., HUNT, W. A. and WALKER, R. E. Clinical judgment of vocabulary responses in process and reactive schizophrenia. *J. Clin. Psychol.*, 19:488-494, 1963.

169. SCHWARTZ, S. Diagnosis, level of social adjustment, and cognitive deficits. *J. Abnorm. Psychol.*, 72:446-450, 1967.

170. SCHWEID, E. I. Verbal Reaction Times of Schizophrenics under Varying Conditions of Noxious Stimulation. Doctoral dissertation, University of Washington, No. 66-12,045. University Microfilms, Ann Arbor, Mich., 1966.

171. SHERMAN, M. The Responsiveness of Chronic Schizophrenics to Social Reinforcement as a Function of Subject Variables, Situation, and Performance Criterion. Doctoral dissertation, Stanford University, No. 64-7683. University Microfilms, Ann Arbor, Mich., 1964.

172. SILVERMAN, J. The problem of attention in research and theory in schizophrenia. *Psychol. Rev.*, 71:352-379, 1964.

173. SILVERMAN, J. Psychological deficit reduction in schizophrenia through response-contingent noxious reinforcement. *Psychol. Rep.*, 13:187-210, 1963 [Monogr. Suppl. 2-V13].

174. SILVERMAN, J. Variations in cognitive control and psychophysiological defense in the schizophrenias. *Psychosom. Med.*, 29:225-251, 1967.

175. SIZEMORE, F. H. A Study of the Educational Problems and Potentials of Good and Poor Premorbid Schizophrenics. Doctoral dissertation, University of Mississippi, No. 68-2146. University Microfilms, Ann Arbor, Mich., 1968.

176. SOLOMON, L. and NUTTALL, R. Sibling order, premorbid adjustment and remission in schizophrenia. *J. Nerv. Ment. Dis.*, 144:37-46, 1967.

177. SOLOMON, L. and ZLOTOWSKI, M. The relationship between the Elgin and the Phillips measures of process-reactive schizophrenia. *J. Nerv. Ment. Dis.*, 138: 32-37, 1964.

178. SOWARDS, B. A. Reinforcement Values and Discrimination of Reinforcement Levels in Normal and Schizophrenic Groups. Doctoral dissertation, Indiana University, No. 64-5498. University Microfilms, Ann Arbor, Mich., 1964.

179. STEPHENS, J. H. and ASTRUP, C. Prognosis in "process" and "non-process" schizophrenia. *Amer. J. Psychiat.*, 119:945-953, 1963.

180. STEPHENS, J. H. and ASTRUP, C. Treatment outcome in "process" and "non-process" schizophrenics treated by "A" and "B" types of therapists. *J. Nerv. Ment. Dis.*, 140:449-456, 1965.

181. STEPHENS, J. H., BROWN, C., FORSTER, J. W. and KLEIN, H. G. Orienting responses in "process" and "non-process" schizophrenics. *Cond. Reflex*, 2:166, 1967 (abstr.).

182. STERNE, A. L., III. Paired-Associate Learning by Hospitalized Schizophrenics under Conditions of Response-Specific Verbal Censure and Approval. Doctoral dissertation, Vanderbilt University, No. 67-7463. University Microfilms, Ann Arbor, Mich., 1967.

183. STIER, S. A. Developmental Attainment, Outcome and Symbolic Performance in Schizophrenia. Doctoral dissertation, University of California, Los Angeles, No. 68-7486. University Microfilms, Ann Arbor, Mich., 1968.

184. STOLLER, F. H. Relationship between mothers' predictions and the performance of schizophrenics and their siblings. Proceedings of the 74th Annual Convention of the American Psychological Association, 1:169-170, 1966.

185. STRAIN, G. S. Perofrmance of Process and Reactive Schizophrenic Subjects in an Extended Learning Situation. Paper read at the 13th Annual Convention of the Southeastern Psychological Association, Atlanta, April, 1967.

186. STRAIN, G. S. Severity of Behavioral Symptoms in Schizophrenia. Paper read at the 15th Annual Convention of the Southwestern Psychological Association, New Orleans, April, 1968.

187. STRUVE, F. A., III. Classical Cardiac Conditioning with Process and Reactive Schizophrenics and Normals. Doctoral dissertation, Northwestern University, No. 65-12,170. University Microfilms, Ann Arbor, Mich., 1966.

188. STURM, I. E. "Conceptual area" among pathological groups: A failure to replicate. *J. Abnorm. Psychol.*, 69:216-223, 1964.
189. STURM, I. E. Overinclusion and concreteness among pathological groups. *J. Consult. Psychol.*, 29:9-18, 1965.
190. SUGERMAN, A. A. and CANCRO, R. Field independence and outcome in schizophrenia: A U-shaped relationship. *Percept. Motor Skills*, 27:1007-1013, 1968.
191. TYRELL, D. J., STRUVE, F. A. and SCHWARTZ, M. L. A methodological consideration in the performance of process and reactive schizophrenics on a test for organic brain pathology. *J. Clin. Psychol.*, 21:254-256, 1965.
192. ULLMANN, L. P. and ECK, R. A. Inkblot perception and the process-reactive distinction. *J. Clin. Psychol.*, 21:311-313, 1965.
193. ULLMANN, L. P. and GIOVANNONI, J. M. The development of a self-report measure of the process-reactive continuum. *J. Nerv. Ment. Dis.*, 138:38-42, 1964.
194. VAILLANT, G. E. and FUNKENSTEIN, D. H. Long-term follow-up (10-15 years) of schizophrenic patients with Funkenstein (adrenalinmechoyl) tests. In Hoch, P. H. and Zubin, J., eds. *Psychopathology of Schizophrenia*, pp. 244-251. Grune & Stratton, New York, 1966.
195. VENABLES, P. H. Input dysfunction in schizophrenia. In Maher, B. A., ed. *Progress in Experimental Personality Research*, vol. 1, pp. 1-47. Academic Press, New York, 1964.
196. VENABLES, P. H. Psychophysiological aspects of schizophrenia. *Brit. J. Med. Psychol.*, 39:289-297, 1966.
197. VOLLENWEIDER, J. A. Differences in Critical Flicker Frequency in Process and Reactive Schizophrenics Treated with Thorazine and Compazine. Doctoral dissertation, Fordham University, No. 63-5609. University Microfilms, Ann Arbor, Mich., 1963.
198. Ward, W. D. and CARLSON, W. A. Autonomic responsivity to variable input rates among schizophrenics classified on the process-reactive dimension. *J. Abnorm. Psychol.*, 71:10-16, 1966.
199. WATSON, C. G. and LOGUE, P. E. A note on the interjudge reliability of Phillips and Elgin scale ratings. *J. Clin. Psychol.*, 24:64-66, 1968.
200. WECHSLER, D. *Manual for the Wechsler Adult Intelligence Scale.* Psychological Corporation, New York, 1955.
201. WEBB, W. W. Premorbid adjustment and the perception of meaning. *Percept. Motor Skills*, 17:762, 1963.
202. WEBB, W. W., DAVIS, D. and CROMWELL, R. L. Size estimation in schizophrenics as a function of thematic content of stimuli. *J. Nerv. Ment. Dis.*, 143:252-255, 1966.
203. WILTON, M. M. Differential Preference for Ambiguity in Process and Reactive Schizophrenics. Doctoral dissertation, Boston University Graduate School, No. 66-11,327. University Microfilms, Ann Arbor, Mich., 1966.
204. YOSPE, L. P. The Hypnotic Susceptibility of Acute and Chronic Schizophrenics. Doctoral dissertation, University of Missouri, No. 68-3669. University Microfilms, Ann Arbor, Mich., 1968.
205. YOUNG, H. D. The Effects of Oral Censure on the Conceptual Performance of Chronic Schizophrenics as a Function of Premorbid Adjustment and Current Mental Health. Doctoral dissertation, Columbia University, No. 62-3708. University Microfilms, Ann Arbor, Mich., 1962.

6

THE IMPACT OF THE THERAPEUTIC
REVOLUTION ON NOSOLOGY

Heinz E. Lehmann

*The wit of man has rarely been more exercised than in the
attempt to classify the morbid mental phenomena covered by
the term "insanity." The result has been disappointing.*

D. H. TUKE

Psychiatry on the North American continent has long been haunted by
a strange epidemiological phenomenon. Since the 1950's, the first admission rate for schizophrenia in U.S. mental hospitals has been about 33%
higher and that of manic-depressive reaction about 800% lower than in
corresponding hospitals in England (Kramer, 1968). Large sums of
research money are now being spent on solving the problem of whether
this consistent discrepancy reflects a real difference of incidence of these
diseases or only different diagnostic habit patterns in the two countries.
Particularly puzzling to scientists and clinicians has been the low incidence of manic-depressive disorder in the U.S.

Being to some extent actively involved in this research, I was startled
at a recent psychiatric meeting to hear a U.S. participant remark casually that in his part of the country the incidence of manic-depressive
disease had about tripled in the last two years; more precisely, since
the treatment of manic states with lithium salts and the prescription
of lithium for the prevention of recurrent manic and depressive episodes
had gained wide publicity and proved its clinical value.

Was there really a causal relationship between the introduction of a
new treatment and the incidence of the disease for which the treatment
was being used?

Reprinted, by permission of author and publisher, from: *Problématique de la psy-
chose,* Pierre Doucet and Camille Laurin (Eds.) New York: Excerpta Medica Foundation, 1969.

The general rule in medicine is that diagnosis determines treatment. In the example I just mentioned, this rule was reversed: treatment determined diagnosis. Such reversal of ordinary medical logic is known as "therapeutic testing" and is occasionally used when other, more rational methods of making a diagnosis are not available.

Sometimes, taking a shortcut, a physician uses a therapeutic test for diagnosis as an expedient, to save time and trouble. In other cases, a therapeutic test may be the only possible way of establishing a diagnosis, e.g., if more direct and specific criteria are not known. This is frequently true in psychiatry, but is rare in other branches of medicine.

In our example, the psychiatrists who diagnosed manic-depressive diseases more frequently because there was now a new treatment for this disorder did so primarily for another reason. Because the generally applied diagnostic criteria for manic-depressive disorder are complex, questionable, not fully objective and, because of these shortcomings, ambiguous and equivocal, psychiatrists find that it is not difficult to fashion their diagnosis according to their personal attitudes and expectations.

This is unfortunately the present state of the art of diagnosis in most psychiatric conditions. Psychiatric diagnosis, with the exception of psychopathological states which are due to organic, toxic or metabolic factors, is not a science—in the strict positivistic meaning of the science concept—because psychiatric diagnosis cannot refer to external criteria. Without external criteria, it is impossible to describe specific procedures by which—given a certain psychopathological condition—anyone would necessarily arrive at the same diagnosis. This means that most psychiatric diagnoses, in contrast to most medical diagnoses, are not operationally defined concepts, but nosological constructs.

HISTORY OF NOSOLOGY

At this point, I should like to engage in a brief discussion of the term nosology and its historical background.

The first recorded use of the term nosology can be found in the Medical Dictionary by Robert James which was published in London in 1742. In his Dictionary, James defined nosology as the explanation of diseases, rather in the sense of modern pathology. However, a French contemporary of James, Boissier de Sauvages, who was Professor at the Medical Faculty of Montpellier, was fascinated by the new concept of nosology and—also being a botanist—had the ambition to become the Linnaeus of human diseases. Following in his tracks, the great Pinel, in 1798, published a *Nosographic Philosophique* which was a classification of mental diseases. And so, today, we use the term nosology, less in the original sense of being synonymous with pathology, but more in the sense of a methodology of diagnosis, of a classification of diseases.

But if the meaning of the term nosology as a special scientific discipline has changed in the two centuries since it was first conceived, the meaning of its subject matter, i.e., of the disease concept itself, has undergone even greater transformations during that time. In fact, the disease concept, today, is still a very controversial and fluid issue.

Sydenham, a contemporary of Newton, is usually regarded as the father of the modern concept of diseases as entities with causes, morbid manifestations and outcomes which are similar or specific for each type of disease. Sydenham was the first to stress the importance of the "natural history" approach to pathology. It took, however, almost another 100 years before Morgagni completed the modern concept of disease by introducing the study of morbid anatomy into medicine.

In the second half of the 19th century, Virchow's cellular pathology soon swept nosology clear of all vestiges of romantic speculation which had crept into it. Soon after, with the advent of bacteriology, the first decisive breakthrough was made toward achieving the nosological ideal of linking etiological factors with symptoms and course, to obtain an integrated picture of each specific disease entity. Rapid progress of the physical sciences led to the discovery of X-rays, the invention of the electrocardiograph and the development of numerous biochemical and endocrinological methods of diagnosis. These and many other new medical techniques, as well as automation, have come close to transforming the intuitive, clinical art of diagnosis into a hard science, based almost entirely on objective procedures.

SPECIAL PROBLEMS OF PSYCHIATRIC NOSOLOGY

In psychiatry, the growth of nosology was much less spectacular than in the rest of medicine. Psychiatry kept pace as long as the observation of symptoms and course of the disease provided all basic data for diagnosis, but when objective methods were discovered which furnished diagnostic criteria and specific causes for many somatic diseases, psychiatry started to trail behind.

The causes of the major psychiatric diseases, e.g., the functional psychoses, are still unknown or, e.g., in the neuroses, are multifactorial, complex and non-specific. There are no objective methods for the diagnosis of functional psychiatric diseases. Optimism ran high when Wassermann's test in 1910 made it possible to establish the diagnosis of dementia paralytica in individual patients beyond any doubt and when, at about the same time, Noguchi demonstrated the presence of spirochetes in the brains of patients who had died from dementia paralytica, thus proving syphilis as the specific cause of the disease. Again in the early 1930's, there was great enthusiasm with Berger's discovery of the electroencephalogram. Here seemed to be the royal road to an objective diagnosis of mental disease. However, the case of dementia paralytica remained an isolated model and the electroencephalogram has actually not been very helpful in the diagnosis of psychiatric diseases.

An ideal nosology would have to be based on etiology. Sydenham, too, had felt that a classification of specific causes would be the best way to classify diseases, but had realized that this was impossible in practice and concentrated on morbid manifestations and course of the diseases. The early explorers of psychiatric nosology, men like Pinel and his pupil Esquirol, were mainly describing symptoms and syndromes. By the middle of the 19th century, for the first time in medical history, distinct and wide-spread interest in the nosology of mental diseases had crystallized, and with it had developed an open controversy between those who wanted a classification according to causes and those who wanted a classification according to symptoms. There was also a violent controversy between psychiatrists who, like Griesinger, saw all mental diseases caused by physical brain diseases and other psychiatrists who, like Heinroth, conceived of mental diseases as the results of dynamic, psychological and spiritual struggles. Reacting to this confusion, Heinrich Neuman, in 1860, declared that psychiatry would only be able to progress if it decided to "throw over-board the whole business of classifications. . . ."

But nosological classification continued in psychiatry and Morel, Hecker and Kahlbaum described their classical syndromes of démence précoce, hebephrenia and catatonia. Falret introduced the time factor into psychiatric nosology and prepared the way for Kraepelin, whose system of psychiatric diseases combined a careful description of symptoms and syndromes with their course and outcome as well as their etiological factors, to the extent to which these were known.

PSYCHIATRIC NOSOLOGY OF THE 20TH CENTURY

Kraepelin's nosology seemed to fill the need which had existed for almost a century and his classification was soon accepted throughout the world. However, Jaspers (1959) pointed out that etiological factors were definitely known in only one group of psychiatric disorders, i.e., those comprising the organic brain syndromes and those psychiatric conditions which are caused by somatic disorders and intoxications. In another group, which included the important functional psychoses, we can be certain that we are dealing with diseases, but their causes are unknown and the diagnostic limits frequently blurred. In a third group, which Jaspers characterized as psychopathies, i.e., the neuroses, character and behavior disorders, we can no longer even be sure that we are dealing with diseases. Schneider (1950) refers to this group of psychiatric disorders as "abnormal variations of sane mental life" and concludes: "there are no neuroses but only neurotics." The concept of neurosis as a nosological entity remains a highly controversial issue in German psychiatry even today.

Adolf Meyer's (1958) psychobiological nosology—like modern psychosomatics—does not recognize clearly defined psychiatric disease entities, but only reaction types which are the results of complex habit patterns of non-adaptive responses in the life history of an individual.

Kleist (1953), following Griesinger's conviction, considers every mental disorder as the direct result of a cerebral, structural or functional lesion. His nosological ideology is impressive in its monolithic consistency and single-minded concentration on physical causes as factors determining his classification scheme. Unfortunately, his evidence has not kept pace with his theoretical aspirations and has not been convincing enough for many others to accept his nosological system, although Leonhard's (1960) classification, which recently has aroused a good deal of interest in psychiatric circles, has a similar neurological bias with an emphasis on genetic factors.

Ey's (1954) nosological system attempts to integrate a clinical, psychopathological approach with a psychophysiological basis and an existential philosophy. He views all psychiatric disorders as disturbed interactions of levels of awareness and functioning of the personality. The temporal factor tends to disappear in Ey's nosology. For example, acuteness of an illness becomes crisis, and chronicity becomes organization of symptomatic disturbances. Instead of autonomous disease entities, Ey sees a hierarchy of different degrees and levels of Jacksonian dissolution and release phenomena—from schizophrenia over manic-depressive disorder to neurosis. The normal individual for Ey is one who is free to master his development; the abnormal is the restrained, the unfree.

Psychoanalysts have not proposed a comprehensive classification of mental disorders, but the psychoanalytic-psychodynamic theory is their frame of reference for all psychiatric disturbances, with comparatively little scope left for clinical observations and physical evidence.

THREE NOSOLOGICAL CONTROVERSIES

The old controversies of the "symptomatologists" *versus* the "etiologists," and of the "organicists" *versus* the "dynamicists" have survived a century and are still very much part of our ongoing discussions in modern psychiatry which has added one other fundamental controversy. Stengel (1960) calls it a controversy between the "separatists" and the "gradualists" in psychiatry. The separatists conceive of the psychoses as autonomous disease entities which are qualitatively different from the neuroses and character disorders. The gradualists, led by Menninger and Ey, advocate a unitary concept of mental diseases, and see mental pathology distributed on a continuum from the normal to the psychotic, which is, according to this school, only quantitatively different from the neurotic, i.e., sicker.

COMPROMISE OUT OF COMPLEXITY

All official classifications today continue in the Kraepelinian tradition and combine symptomatological with etiological criteria, in spite of Jasper's early warnings against this kind of conceptual glibness. In 1947, Essen-Möller and Wohlfahrt made a specific attack on the thoughtless mixture of the two principles of classification. They recommend continuation of the tradition of Morel who, in 1860, was the first to use the "double voie" of syndromes and causes to classify mental diseases, but they ask to do it explicitly, in the sense of Birnbaum's (1928) "structural analysis," which distinguishes lucidly between pathogenic (etiological) and pathoplastic (symptomatological) factors. In addition to *syndrome* description and *etiology*, Essen-Möller and Wohlfahrt proposed a third dimension of psychiatric diagnoses, i.e., the *intensity* of the disturbance. In a recent publication, Fernandes (1967) has suggested to add a fourth dimension which refers to the specific *pattern* of a mental illness, which he calls the "syndromatic melody."

Langfeldt's system (1956) classifies psychotic disorders according to main diagnosis, personality type and situational background. The old American Standard Classification provided for the reporting of premorbid personality, precipitating factors and degree of psychiatric impairment. The latest International Classification of Diseases (1969) allows for multiple diagnoses and, like all generally adopted diagnostic systems in psychiatry, compromises by mixing etiological criteria with symptom and syndrome observations.

At the present state of our knowledge, it would be unrealistic to insist on absolute consistency of scientific classification in psychiatry. The result of the existing conceptual imperfection is what Marchais (1966) has called nosological polymorphism and Fernandes (1967) the aporia of psychiatry—a situation which Minkowski (1967) accepts by comparing it to the different languages of different cultures.

DIAGNOSIS—ITS MEANING, FUNCTION AND IMPLEMENTATION

Translated literally, the word diagnosis means "through-and-through knowledge" of a disease, including all causes, symptoms and time-related factors which interact to produce a consistent picture of the disease.

Because medicine has, at least partially, a solid scientific foundation, and because there can be no science without a system and no system without an orderly arrangement of its factors, diagnosis is necessary in all of medicine, including psychiatry. Scientists must reduce the number of factors in their systems. Usually, such reduction is achieved by clustering and classifying the factors. When the physician reduces the manifold factors with which he must deal by making diagnoses, he creates a nosology.

A medical diagnosis serves to choose a special treatment, to predict the likely future course of the disease, to establish the etiology of the disease, when it is known, and to provide material for statistical, biometric and epidemiological studies. Furthermore, diagnosis is the symbolic, shorthand language which physicians use for rapid communication. Finally, a diagnosis satisfies the clinician's need for conceptual security, for the closure of an open gestalt—it removes the magic from the treatment of the sick by making codified concepts out of nameless phenomena and subjective impressions.

There are three ways in which physicians may obtain information enabling them to make a diagnosis. In order of decreasing objectivity, they are:

1. *Laboratory tests.* These may be of a physical or chemical nature, but they always can be reduced to objective pointer readings, whether in the form of structural detail in an electron microscope picture, an EEG record, the write-out of an isotope scanner or the fluorescence of a chromatogram spot.

2. *History.* In any history of an individual disease there remain always many subjective components, due to the reporter's bias, inaccuracies of memory and observation, etc.

3. *Clinical observations.* These observations depend mainly on the diagnostician's special training in evaluating pathological factors, on the amount of his clinical experience and practice, on his general edu-

cation and cultural background and on his personal, theoretical or emotional biases.

In psychiatric diagnosis, a fourth way of obtaining important information is empathy. Empathy is an entirely subjective diagnostic tool. It may be defined as the immediate sensing of another person's emotional state within the context of an interpersonal relationship. Using one's own emotional responses to the patient in establishing a diagnosis is a legitimate procedure in psychiatry, because this branch of medicine must deal with phenomena which transgress the biological aspects of the system the psychiatrist seeks to evaluate.

THE SEARCH FOR PRECISION

If the concept of an ideal nosology is that of a system of disease entities based entirely on etiological factors, the concept of the best compromise would be a nosology based, at least, on entirely objective diagnoses. In the physical sciences, the persistent search for standards of absolute, immutable objectivity and precision has finally resulted in such unquestionable perfection as is represented in the latest official definition of the meter as 1,650,763.73 wave lengths, in vacuum, of a particular emission line of krypton-86 at —210° C, and the definition of the second as 9,192,631,770 cycles of the frequency associated with the transition between two energy levels of the isotope cesium-133. (The former time standard had been based on the rotation of the earth which had been found to be too erratic—Astin, 1968.)

Compared to such measuring devices, the methods of psychiatric diagnosis appear to be pitifully primitive. In a bid for greater objectivity precision of psychiatric diagnosis, tremendous emphasis has been placed during the last decade on behavior rating scales and their evaluation by computer-based high-powered statistical methods. Pichot (1966), after stating that the ideal of Kraepelin has not been achieved, points out that psychiatric nosology has always been exposed to two dangers, i.e., pseudo-classifications and obscure terminology. He sees a solution of the nosological dilemma in the application of mathematical methods, e.g., multivariate analysis. The data to be analyzed in this fashion would be the scores of commonly used rating scales.

The consistent use of well standardized rating scales and expert statistical treatment of the results, it is hoped, will save psychiatric nosology from the confusion created by such rapidly developing new "syndromes" as schizomania, phasophrenia, schizonoia (Marchais, 1966), eliminate the uncertainty of "whichophrenia" (Altschule, 1967), correct the

American tendency to overdiagnose schizophrenia (a tendency to which British psychiatrists have referred as schizophrenomania) and reduce the hugely swollen numbers of classifications which, in a recent "thesaurus" of psychiatric diagnoses, amount to 340 (Pörksen, 1967).

LIMITATIONS OF PSYCHIATRIC DIAGNOSIS

No doubt, standardized rating scales and mathematical methods of analysis are important steps towards greater objectivity—but only if one can assume that the data resulting from the rating scale scores are valid. However, there is some evidence that this is frequently not the case. We have presented this evidence and discussed the persisting problems in previous publications (Lehmann et al., 1965; Lehmann, 1967). Nevertheless, the preoccupation with more rigorous methods of gathering and evaluating psychiatric data for diagnostic purposes is so great that many investigators in this field do not stop to consider the self-evident fact that the best rating scales and the most sophisticated methods of evaluation are only as good as the competence of the person doing the rating. It is true that a structured interview is usually more reliable than an unstructured one, but greater reliability does not always mean that the information resulting from the structured interview is also more valid.

Even if one does not agree with Rümke (1957) that the final diagnosis of schizophrenia depends on the "praecox feeling" which the examiner must experience, one should ponder Minkowski's recollection (1967) of Bleuler's remark, that certain phenomena in psychiatric patients are better felt than seen or registered objectively. One might paraphrase this remark by saying that certain phenomena in psychiatric patients must be felt or seen correctly before they can be properly recorded and legitimately processed in the computer. The simple fact that we have no truly objective means of obtaining basic data for psychiatric diagnoses does not just go away if we refuse to look at it and busy ourselves with sophisticated statistics and computer hardware.

Psychiatric nosology has been ailing since its inception, 170 years ago. The lack of comparability between psychiatric diagnoses made in one country and those made in other countries has become ever more disturbing, as the worldwide increase of communication in all walks of life and all fields of science has fostered the growth of transcultural psychiatry, epidemiology and preventive mental health on an international level. Even within the confines of a single hospital sub-culture, psychiatric diagnoses are shaky.

Zubin (1967) has reviewed the agreement between different examiners for diagnostic categories and found that it ranged from 46% in the psychoneuroses to 84% for organic brain syndromes. He also reports that the consistency of diagnoses for a given patient over a period of time is relatively low, ranging from 24% for the neuroses, to 65% for organic psychoses and 74%, in one study, for personality disorders. Cooper (1967), in analyzing the reasons for such low consistency of psychiatric diagnoses over time, could show that it was mainly due to changes of doctors and that 81% of patients kept the same diagnosis during four admissions over a two-year period if the same doctor made a "standard diagnosis."

If we look with detachment at the recent enthusiastic efforts to give psychiatric nosology a new deal through more consistent use of structured interview schemata, behavior rating scales and multivariate analysis of the resulting data, we discover a new and rather disquieting nosological phenomenon to which I have referred as the "new syndrome explosion" (Lehmann, 1967). A growing multitude of new computer-made psychopathological syndromes, clusters and factors is constantly being added to those already in existence and no end is in sight. Nor does there seem to be any practical process by which one might eventually sift out those new syndromes which have truly clinical relevance.

FUTURE DEVELOPMENTS IN PSYCHIATRIC NOSOLOGY

On the other hand, a recent methodological exercise in psychiatric diagnosis, organized by the World Health Organization (Shepherd et al., 1968), suggests that the use of carefully written histories and *videotaped* interview material is invaluable for the delineation of basic issues in clinical diagnosis. Shepherd's group isolated three factors which account for most disagreement and difficulties of communication. They were: (1) variations at the level of clinical observation and perception; (2) variations in inferences drawn from observations; (3) variations in nosological schemata followed by individual clinicians.

The WHO group concluded that in the area of nosological schemata involving the teaching of diagnostic criteria, the need to establish general agreement is greatest. From personal experience, I would also stress the need for strengthened and improved training in clinical observation and perception, i.e., in psychopathology—at least on our continent.

Some invigorating influence on psychiatric nosology might also be expected from further research into the etiological factors of the functional psychiatric disorders.

And finally, there is the promising impact of developments in the field of psychiatric therapeutics. During the last 30 years, progress in the therapy of psychiatric disorders has outpaced progress in the fields of diagnosis and etiology, and now the interesting challenge of using new therapeutic discoveries in psychiatry to shore up its unstable nosology is presenting itself.

For instance, Dreger (1968), after reviewing the principles of classification used by Aristotle and Linnaeus and contrasting them to Galileo's principles of experiment and lawfulness, proposes to match therapeutic techniques to nosological groupings, before the ideal nosological criteria, i.e., the causes of behavioral disorders, will be available.

DRUGS OBSCURING DIAGNOSIS

One effect the advent of pharmacotherapy has had on clinical psychiatry may be considered to be detrimental to nosology, i.e., the immediate use of neuroleptic drugs in acute psychotic conditions, before an adequate diagnosis has been established. Fouks et al. (1966) have pointed out that the nice distinction between acute and chronic psychoses often disappears with modern pharmacotherapy which tends to inhibit the evolution of typical schizophrenic symptoms. In discussing Fouks' paper, Abély speaks of a mutilation, a decapitation of psychotic manifestations. The situation is not unlike that encountered in internal medicine, where the premature application of antibiotics in bacteremia or of morphine in acute abdominal pathology might obscure the precise diagnosis. At our hospital, we have a standing rule prohibiting the continued use of neuroleptic drugs in newly admitted patients until a definite diagnosis has been made.

SYMPTOM PROVOCATION BY DRUGS

An antitherapeutic effect of thymoleptic drugs in patients with latent or questionable schizophrenia has been proposed as a diagnostic test by Heinrich (1960), who showed that distinct schizophrenic symptoms can often be provoked with MAO inhibitors in patients in whom a diagnosis of schizophrenia was suspected, but could not be definitely established. In patients without schizophrenic process, this provocation test remains negative.

DIFFERENTIAL DIAGNOSIS AND DRUGS

In controlled therapeutic trials with antidepressant drugs, Wittenborn (1967) could demonstrate that imipramine was significantly more effective in patients suffering from reactive depression than in patients given the diagnosis manic-depressive disorder or involutional melancholia.

This differential therapeutic effect of drug therapy, according to nosological categories, must be distinguished from differences in the therapeutic action of drugs according to the presenting symptoms or syndromes. Examples of the latter are observations by Hollister and Overall (1965) that imipramine is more effective in retarded depressives and thioridazine in anxious depressives, or Sargant's claim (1962) that MAO inhibitors are particularly effective in atypical depressions. It should also be noted that none of these claims have been definitely confirmed.

A thorough statistical analysis of the results of drug therapy in two multi-hospital studies revealed two interesting findings:

1. Chlorpromazine proved to be the most effective phenothiazine for extremely apathetic, inert schizophrenics, in spite of the fact that—on single administration—this drug induces more apathy than other phenothiazines. Many psychiatrists, in line with the approach of treating target symptoms with specific counteracting drugs, hitherto have considered chlorpromazine to be contraindicated in syndromes characterized by apathy.

2. Schizophrenic patients with insight into their condition improved significantly on placebo and did not improve on two active drugs (Goldberg and Mattsson, 1968).

The latter observation suggests the possibility that schizophrenic manifestations in the presence of insight belong to a nosologically different category than schizophrenic manifestations without insight.

MODIFICATION OF SCHIZOPHRENIC PROCESS

One observation that has been shared by all who have treated schizophrenics with neuroleptic drugs is the modification of chronic and terminal stages of progressive schizophrenia. Vartanyan (1968) discussed this therapeutic pathomorphosis of terminal schizophrenia and observed in 35 patients in the end stages of schizophrenia a release of productive symptoms, after discontinuation of long-term drug therapy. These symptoms had only been masked previously, but prior to treatment it had been assumed that they were irreversibly extinguished.

Fouks et al. (1966) have pointed out that—contrary to Kraepelin's conceptions—pharmacotherapy is more effective in schizophrenia, where it frequently halts the natural course toward chronicity, than in manic-depressive disease, where maintenance treatment is less effective and sometimes even induces defect symptoms. However, this holds true only for neuroleptic drugs and antidepressants—the introduction of lithium as a preventive stabilizer in manic-depressive disease may have changed the situation.

On the other hand, there is also little doubt that prolonged drug therapy frequently tends to produce a pattern of retarded, aboulic behavior—"a reduction of energy potential"—which Huber (1964) thinks is due to a suppression of productive symptoms and a speeding up of the natural tendency of the schizophrenic process. Without drug therapy, this process is characterized by more gradual loss of active symptoms and the late appearance of a typical defect syndrome. Later, in the discussion following his paper, Huber also stated that with modern pharmacotherapy we are no longer justified in assuming that the schizophrenic defect is irreversible—on the contrary, it often responds favorably to a combination of pharmacotherapy and *social therapies.*

Follow-up studies of cohorts of schizophrenic patients in the pre-neuroleptic and postneuroleptic era have shown that schizophrenic patients treated with neuroleptics tended to show a definite increase of depressive symptomatology on re-admissions, in comparison to schizophrenics treated before the era of pharmacotherapy. Also noted were the well recognized facts that the periods of hospitalization were shortened and the number of rehospitalizations increased in the drug-treated patients. Another difference was a decrease of catatonic and an increase of paranoid syndromes in the drug-treatment sample; however, this shift in symptomatology may well have been the result of time-related and cultural factors, rather than due to the effects of pharmacotherapy (Battegay and Gehring, 1968; Achté, 1961; Bohaček, 1965).

DRUG RESPONSE AS DIAGNOSTIC CRITERION

Several investigators have made the interesting suggestion to introduce therapeutic responsiveness to specific psychotropic drugs as an external criterion for new diagnostic categories. The diagnosis of such psychiatric categories would then be operationally defined by an objective procedure: the observation of the therapeutic response to a given drug. (Thinking along similar lines Sutter et al. (1968) speak of the "personality" of different neuroleptic drugs.)

Overall and Hollister (1965) identified four different types of patients, each responding to a different type of drug. They think that patients who respond with exceptional improvement to treatment with specific drugs belong to fundamentally different psychopathological types and they believe that drug response, as a technique for identifying patient populations, has much to recommend it as a basis for further work in psychiatric typology.

Klein and Fink (1962) identified seven different response patterns to imipramine in a sample of patients, about evenly divided between depressive and schizophrenic patients. Six of these response patterns were associated with favorable therapeutic responses to imipramine. In a more recent paper, Klein (1968) has presented a "typology of clinical drug effects" and examined its interaction with psychiatric diagnoses. For example, in one group of patients with phobic anxiety, 100% responded to imipramine with a reduction of episodic anxiety, but the same group showed zero response to chlorpromazine. Although these patients could be sharply distinguished as a group on the basis of their drug responses, Klein states that various patients in this group may be referred to by different diagnosticians as obsessional, hysterical, atypical depressive pseudoneurotic schizophrenics, acute schizophrenics, alcoholics, etc.

TREATMENT-DECISION TYPES

Eschewing traditional diagnoses altogether, Brodsky et al. (1969) use a treatment-decision system which defines seven treatment types, e.g., a type characterized by action-proneness, disorganization of behavior and interference with interpersonal communication, or—another type—characterized by action-inhibition and withdrawal from interpersonal exchanges. Irrespective of formal diagnosis, their treatment program aims at rapid symptom suppression and an early end of hospitalization through the use of modern drugs and electroconvulsive therapy appropriate to each of the seven treatment types.

DRUGS AS PSYCHODYNAMIC SCALPELS

The observation that certain chronic schizophrenics will lose their apathy and inertia under neuroleptic therapy, while others will remain unchanged, suggests the use of a neuroleptic drug as a kind of psychodynamic scalpel, which permits us to separate the type of apathy serving as a reversible defense mechanism from the type of apathy which is the result of an irretrievable loss of primary drive and affect. Even the most experienced clinician is, as a rule, unable to make this distinction on purely clinical evidence, without pharmacotherapeutic intervention.

NEUROLEPTIC DRUGS AS ARBITERS OF A NOSOLOGICAL CONTROVERSY

The controversy of the "separatists" *versus* the "gradualists"—those who believe that psychoses are qualitatively different from neuroses and those who believe that all psychiatric disturbances are distributed over a continuum—may be empirically resolved by psychopharmacological evidence which is squarely in favor of the "separatist" school. Neuroleptic drugs (major tranquilizers) have a quasi specific antipsychotic action and anxiolytic sedatives (minor tranquilizers) are effective mainly in neurotic conditions, largely independent of dosage. If psychoses were only to be regarded as more intense disturbances than the neuroses, their treatment would simply call for larger doses of the same drugs which are effective in neurotic conditions, i.e., anxiolytic sedatives. This is not so. A relatively small dose of a neuroleptic is usually much more effective in the treatment of a psychotic condition than a very large dose of an anxiolytic sedative.

MOTIVATION AS A NOSOLOGICAL VARIABLE

The therapeutic revolution in psychiatry has, of course, found its expression not only in pharmacotherapy—the whole gamut of modern social therapies, from individual psychotherapy to the therapeutic community, has entered into every phase of this revolution. The patients who, today, present psychiatry with its greatest challenge are alcoholics, drug addicts and patients with behavior and character disorders. These are also the psychiatric conditions which are steadily increasing in almost every country—and they are the conditions which do not respond to drug therapy.

In many instances, the difference between success and failure, in the treatment of these patients with various methods of social therapy hinges on the presence or absence of motivation for treatment. Today, when we have a number of sophisticated and effective social therapies available, the motivational factor has become an important nosological variable. An addict or an aggressively acting-out patient who is motivated toward treatment has not only a different prognosis, but also a different psychodynamic background and a different interpersonal relationship pattern in comparison to his symptomatic counterpart, the patient without motivation.

The motivated and the non-motivated patients with character disorders seem to belong to different nosological categories and this difference must be recognized when evaluating such patients for therapy. One is reminded here of the apparent nosological difference between psychotic patients with and without insight and their differential response to drug and placebo therapy, which was discussed before.

FAILURE OF RESPONSE TO PSYCHOTHERAPY AS DIAGNOSTIC CRITERION

There is at least one condition where the failure to respond to psychotherapy is sometimes the decisive factor in making a diagnosis—

pseudoneurotic schizophrenia. As the name of this condition implies, its symptoms resemble closely those of a neurosis, but the fact that a patient presenting these symptoms may have received psychotherapy for several years without having received any therapeutic benefit tends to place the diagnosis of such a condition outside the nosological category of neuroses. A number of recent studies have established that from one to two-thirds of neurotic patients become symptom-free within two years, even without any treatment and very few, if any, neurotic patients fail to show at least some improvement when receiving psychotherapy (Malan et al., 1968; Weisker and DeBoor, 1968; Eysenck, 1952; Denker, 1946; Landis, 1938).

CONCLUSION

There is no doubt that the impact of the new therapeutic modalities on the whole of psychiatry has been very considerable. We have seen that secondary repercussions of this impact have also made themselves felt in psychiatric nosology. Sometimes they were the surprising results of accidental discoveries, at other times, of systematic observations, at still other times of experimental intervention and, occasionally, they were even the results of speculative inferences.

We admit that any impact that certain empirical achievements in treatment may have had on a theoretical construct like psychiatric nosology, is proof of the uncertain scientific structure of this nosology. But would we prefer to be in the position of those who, like our neurological colleagues, do not need any therapeutic advances to improve their almost flawless nosology? Perhaps our psychiatric patients benefit, at least in some small way, from our ignorance about the abstract foundations of our specialty. Perhaps we should continue for some more years to concentrate our energies on therapeutic advances and not worry over our scientific shortcomings in psychiatry. Who knows, perhaps there is such a thing as dynamic ignorance?

REFERENCES

ACHTÉ, K. A. (1961): Der Verlauf der Schizophrenie und der schizophrenieformen Psychosen. *Acta Psychiat. Scand.*, 36/*Suppl.* 155.

ALTSCHULE, M. D. (1967): Whichophrenia or the confused past, ambiguous present, and dubious future of the schizophrenia concept. *J. Schizophrenia*, 1, 8.

ASTIN, A. V. (1968): Standards of measurement. *Sci. Amer.*, 218, 50.

BATTEGAY, R. & GEHRING, A. (1968): Vergleichende Untersuchungen an Schizophrenen der präneuroleptischen und der postneuroleptischen Ära. *Pharmakopsychiat. Neuro-Psychopharm.*, 1, 107.

BIRNBAUM, K. (1928): *Handbuch der Geisteskrankheiten. Allgemeiner Teil* 1, p. 11. Berlin.

BOHACEK, N. (1965): Pharmakogene depressive Verschiebung bei schizophrenen Psychosen. *Z. Präv.-Med.,* 10, 511.

BRODSKY, C. M., FISCHER, A., & WILSON, G. C. (1969): Analysis of a treatment-decision system. *Dis. Nerv. Syst.,* 30, 17.

COOPER, J. E. (1967): Diagnostic change in a longitudinal study of psychiatric patients. *Brit. J. Psychiat.,* 113, 129.

DENKER, P. G. (1946): Results of the treatment of psychoneurosis by the general practitioner. *N. Y. St. J. Med.,* 46, 2164.

DREGER, R. M. (1968): Aristotle, Linnaeus, and Lewin, or the place of classification in the evaluative-therapeutic process. *J. Gen. Psychol.,* 78, 41.

ESSEN-MÖLLER, E. & WOHLFAHRT, S. (1947): Suggestions for amendment of official Swedish classification of mental disorders. *Acta Psychiat. (Kbh.), Suppl.* 47, 551.

EY, H. (1954): *Etudes Psychiatriques.* Desclée de Brouwer, Paris.

EYSENCK, H. J. (1952): The effects of psychotherapy, an evaluation. *J. Cons. Psychol.,* 16, 319.

FERNANDES, B. (1967): A propos de la classification des maladies mentales. *Ann. Méd.-Psychol.,* 125, 1.

FOUKS, L., PÉRIVIER, E., GILBERT, A., HOUSSAIT, A., & LERNO, M. (1966): Reflections of a chemotherapeutist on nosology. *Ann. Méd.-Psychol.,* 124, 503.

GOLDBERG, S. C. & MATTSSON, N. B. (1968): Schizophrenic subtypes defined by response to drugs and placebo. *Dis. Nerv. Syst.,* 29, 153.

HEINRICH, K. (1960): Die gezielte Symptomprovokation mit monoaminoxydrasehemmenden Substanzen in Diagnostik und Therapie schizophrener Psychosen. *Nervenarzt,* 2, 507.

HOLLISTER, L. E. & OVERALL, J. E. (1965): Reflections on the specificity of action of antidepressants. *Psychosomatics,* 6, 361.

HUBER, G. (1964): Grenzen der psychiatrischen Pharmakotherapie bei der Behandlung chronisch Schizophrener. In: *Begleitwirkungen und Misserfolge der psychiatrischen Pharmakotherapie,* p. 166. Editors: H. Kranz and K. Heinrich. Georg Thieme Verlag, Stuttgart.

International Classification of Diseases: Adapted for use in the United States. (Eighth Revision.)

JASPERS, K. (1959): *Allgemeine Psychopathologie.* Springer-Verlag, Berlin.

KLEIN, D. F. (1968): Psychiatric diagnosis and a typology of clinical drug effects. *Psychopharmacologia (Berl.)* 13, 359.

KLEIN, D. F. & FINK, M. (1962): Psychiatric reaction patterns to imipramine. *Amer. J. Psychiat.,* 119, 432.

KLEIST, K. (1953): Die Gliederung der neuropsychischen Erkrankungen. *Mschr. Psychiat. Neurol.,* 125, 526.

KRAMER, M. (1968): Cross-national study of diagnosis of the mental disorders: Origin of the study. *Presented at the Annual Meeting of the American Psychiatric Association, May 13th, Boston, Mass.*

LANDIS, C. (1938): Statistical evaluation of psychotherapeutic methods. In: *Concepts and Problems of Psychotherapy,* p. 155. Editor: S. E. Kinsie. Heinemann, London.

LANGFELDT, G. (1956): The prognosis in schizophrenia. *Acta Psychiat. Scand., Suppl.* 110.

LEHMANN, H. E. (1967): Empathy and perspective or consensus and automation? Implications of the new deal in psychiatric diagnosis. *Comprehens. Psychiat.,* 8, 265.

LEHMANN, H. E., BAN, T. A., & DONALD, M. (1965): Rating the rater. *Arch. Gen. Psychiat.,* 13, 67.

LEONHARD, K. (1960): Die atypischen Psychosen und Kleist's Lehre von den endogenen Psychosen. In: *Psychiatrie der Gegenwart,* 2. Springer-Verlag, Berlin.

MALAN, D. H., BACAL, H. A., HEATH, E. S. & BALFOUR, F. H. G. (1968): A study of psychodynamic changes in untreated neurotic patients. I. Improvements that are questionable on dynamic criteria. *Brit. J. Psychiat.,* 114, 525.

MARCHAIS, P. (1966): De quelques principes pour l'établissement d'une nosologie en psychiatrie. *Ann. Méd.-Psychol.,* 124, 512.

MEYER, A. (1958): *Psychobiology: A Science of Man.* Chas. C. Thomas, Springfield, Ill.

MINKOWSKI, E. (1967): A propos de la nosologie en psychiatrie. *Ann. Méd.-Psychol.,* 125, 67.

OVERALL, J. E. & HOLLISTER, L. E. (1965): Studies of quantitative approaches to psychiatric classification. In: *The Role and Methodology of Classification in Psychiatry and Psychopathology,* p. 277. Editors: M. M. Katz, J. O. Cole and W. E. Burton. Public Health Service Publication No. 1584, U.S. Government Printing Office, Washington, D.C.

PICHOT, P. (1966): Problèmes méthodologiques de la classification en psychiatrie. *Ann. Méd.-Psychol.,* 124, 486.

PÖRKSEN, N. (1967): Kritische Bemerkungen zu dem klinischen Diagnosenschlüssel von H. Immich. *Nervenarzt,* 38, 125.

RASKIN, A. (1968): The prediction of antidepressant drug effects: Review and critique. In: *Psychopharmacology: A Review of Progress* 1957-1967, p. 757. Editors: D. H. Efron, J. O. Cole, J. Levine and J. R. Wittenborn. Public Health Service Publication No. 1836, U.S. Government Printing Office, Washington, D.C.

RÜMKE, H. C. (1957): The clinical differentiation within the group of the schizophrenias. In: *Proceedings, II International Congress of Psychiatry, Vol.* 1, p. 302. Zurich.

SARGANT, W. (1962): The treatment of anxiety states and atypical depressions by the monoamine oxidase inhibitor drugs. *J. Neuropsychiat.,* 3/*Suppl.* 96.

SCHNEIDER, K. (1950): Systematic psychiatry. *Amer. J. Psychiat.,* 107, 334.

SHEPHERD, M., BROOKE, E. M., COOPER, J. E., & LIN, T. (1968): An experimental approach to psychiatric diagnosis. *Acta Psychiat. Scand.,* 44/*Suppl.* 201.

SUTTER, J. M., ALBARANES, R., & GUIN, P. (1968): Progrès en psychopharmacologie et adjustement individuel des conduites thérapeutiques. *Lyon Méd.,* 4, 37.

VARTANYAN, F. E. (1968): The change produced by treatment in the terminal stages of schizophrenia. *Zh. Nevropat. Psikhiat.,* 68, 250.

WEISKER, A. & DeBOOR, C. (1968): A follow-up study of the prognosis on spontaneous outcome of neurotic diseases. *Psyche (Heidelberg),* 22, 340.

WITTENBORN, J. R. (1967): Diagnostic classification and response to imipramine. *Folia Neuropsychiat. (Lecce),* 10, 69.

ZUBIN, J. (1967): Classification of the behavior disorders. *Ann. Rev. Psychol.,* 18, 373.

7

FLATTENING OF AFFECT AND PERSONAL CONSTRUCTS

F. M. McPherson, Valerie Barden, A. Joan Hay, D. W. Johnstone, and A. W. Kushner

Affective flattening is a disorder of emotional expression, of which a good definition is 'a gross lack of emotional response to the given situation' (Fish, 1962). It is a clinical sign whose assessment depends upon the clinician's interpretation of the patient's facial expression, tone of voice and content of talk (Harris & Metcalfe, 1956). Although these are subtle cues, it has been shown that experienced clinicians can assess the severity of affective flattening with a high level of inter-rater agreement (Miller *et al.*, 1953; Harris & Metcalfe, 1956; Wing, 1961; Dixon, 1968). The disorder is usually associated with a diagnosis of schizophrenia, although it may occur in other conditions, such as the organic psychoses (Bullock *et al.*, 1951).

There have been very few investigations of affective flattening (Herron & Kantor, 1968). Most authors have suggested that the disorder is merely one aspect of a more widespread deficit such as intellectual slowness (Harris & Metcalfe, 1956) or a generally reduced rate of responding (Salzinger & Portnoy, 1964).

Recently, however, Dixon (1968) has found a more specific abnormality associated with flattening of affect. She investigated the personal construct systems (Kelly, 1955; Bannister, 1965; Bannister & Mair, 1968) of schizophrenic patients with affective flattening. Whereas most previous studies of the construct systems of schizophrenics have been of the *structure* of their systems e.g. the relationships among constructs (Bannister, 1960, 1962; Bannister & Fransella, 1966), Dixon was concerned with the *content* of their systems i.e. with the types of constructs which they use

Reprinted, by permission of author and editor, from: *The British Journal of Psychiatry*, 116:39-43, 1970.

when differentiating between or among other people. Her method of eliciting constructs required the subject (S) to give what he considered to be the main differences between the people in pairs of photographs. In a very carefully controlled study of 37 schizophrenics, Dixon showed that those with affective flattening, when construing other people, made relatively little use of constructs descriptive of personality characteristics or current emotional state, whereas they used other types of construct as frequently as the other subjects.

The present study aims to confirm Dixon's findings. In schizophrenia research, because of difficulties associated with the selection of samples and with the reliability of diagnosis and assessment, it is important for replication studies to be conducted.

METHOD

Patients. 18 Ss were studied. Equal numbers of male and female, and paranoid and non-paranoid patients were selected randomly from among those in two wards who satisfied the following criteria: that they had had an unchanged diagnosis of schizophrenia for at least two years; that they were showing active, psychotic signs or symptoms (not necessarily flattening of affect) ; and that they were aged 17-60, inclusive.

The selected sample had the following characteristics:

Age: mean 31.2 years, S.D. 8.8 years, range 18-62 years.

Length of illness: mean time from first admission 5.8 years, S.D. 2.4 years, range 2-15 years.

Clinical assessment

Raters: The rating of flattening was made by two psychiatrists, both of whom were experienced in the assessment of schizophrenic patients, and knew the Ss well. They independently interviewed each S, and rated the amount of flattening shown. The ratings of each S were made within one day of each other.

Rating: The raters were instructed to use the term 'affective flattening' as they normally did: it was emphasized that it was 'affect' rather than 'mood,' and 'flattening' rather than 'incongruity,' that was to be rated. The assessment was recorded by the rater placing a mark at any point on a line 90 mm. long and labelled 'No flattening' at one end and 'Very considerable flattening' at the other.

Inter-rater agreement: Over the 18 Ss, the rank order correlation coefficient (Kendall's tau) between the two raters was $+0.44$ ($p<.005$, one-tailed test) . Because of this high inter-rater agreement, in subsequent calculations the mean of the two ratings was used as the criterion of the amount of flattening shown by each S.

Analysis of constructs

Experimental task: The procedure for eliciting constructs was that used, and described in detail, by Dixon (1968). The material comprised five pairs of photographs; each was of one or two adults or children who were engaged in activities such as carrying objects, fighting or reading. The people in each pair were usually similar in age, sex and apparent social and ethnic background, although these factors varied considerably between pairs. S was instructed to give the main differences between the people in each of the pairs; three minutes were allowed per pair. The instructions were repeated before each pair. The responses were tape-recorded and transcribed. The psychologist who administered the procedure had no knowledge of the clinical ratings. Testing took place within a day of the clinical ratings being made.

Content analysis: From each S, a series of bi-polar descriptive terms—constructs—had thus been elicited. Analysis of the content of these gives some indication of the characteristics to which S had attached greatest importance when differentiating among the people in the photographs. The use made of each of the following 12 categories of construct was analysed:

> *'Activity':* constructs which differentiated between or among the people according to what they were doing, e.g. 'the woman in this photo is carrying something, but the one in the other photo is not.'
>
> *'Stance':* constructs which referred to the stance or posture of the people, e.g. 'standing—sitting,' 'arms raised—arms by side.'
>
> *'Physique':* these described the physical characteristics or condition of the people, e.g. 'tall—short,' 'hungry-looking—well-fed.'
>
> *'Personality and emotional state':* these described the feelings, emotional state or more permanent personality traits of the people e.g. 'happy—sad,' 'looks angry—looks peaceful,' 'apprehensive—angry,' 'intelligent-looking—stupid-looking,' 'kind—cruel.'
>
> *'Age':* references to the age of the people in the photograph, e.g. 'older—younger,' 'about 35—about 50.'
>
> *'Nationality':* references to their nationality racial or ethnic characteristics.
>
> *'Occupation':* constructs which referred to their occupation, social class or status e.g. 'she is poor—she is better off.'

'*Clothes*': references to what the people were wearing.

'*Irrelevance*': occasionally, a patient would differentiate between the people in terms of constructs based on his own preoccupations or delusional system, e.g. 'he would try to harm me—she would like me.'

'*Background*': sometimes S ignored the people (and the instructions) entirely and referred to the background of the photograph or to its non-human features, e.g. 'It's sunny in this one but dull in that one' or 'there's a book here but not there.'

'*Photography*': sometimes all aspects of the content were ignored and S described the photograph itself, e.g. 'over-exposed—under-exposed.'

'*Denial*': this was scored when S said spontaneously that he could observe no (further) differences.

Detailed criteria are given in Dixon (1968).

Scorers: The content analysis of the transcribed descriptions was performed by two psychologists who worked independently and had no knowledge of the clinical ratings.

Scoring: The description of each pair of photographs by each S was scored separately. To simplify scoring, and to improve inter-scorer reliability, the scorers decided merely whether each category of construct had or had not been used by S. Each category was assigned a score of 0 (not used) or 1 (used). Over the five pairs, each category thus had a score ranging from 0 to 5. The score obtained in this way from each of the 12 categories was expressed as a percentage of the total category score obtained by summing the 12 individual scores. These percentage scores indicated the *relative* frequency with which S had used each category of construct. Percentage scores were used in order to control the effects of inter-S differences in the total number of constructs elicited.

Inter-scorer agreement: For each S, 60 scoring decisions had to be made, i.e. whether or not each of 12 categories had been used on each of 5 occasions. Therefore over the 18 Ss, 1,080 scoring decisions were made. The two scorers disagreed on only three of these. Because of this very high inter-scorer agreement—which had also been found by Dixon—the mean of the two scores was used as the measure of the frequency with which each S had used each category.

Comparison of construct use and rated flattening. Rank-order correlation coefficients (Kendall's tau) were calculated over the 18 Ss between each of the 12 individual category percentage scores and the clinical ratings.

RESULTS

The twelve correlation coefficients are shown in Table I.

TABLE I

CORRELATIONS BETWEEN RATINGS OF AFFECTIVE FLATTENING AND
RELATIVE (%) USE OF 12 CATEGORIES OF CONSTRUCT

Positive correlations show that the category of construct was
used *more* often by Ss with *high* amounts of rated flattening;
negative correlations show that the category was used *less* often
by Ss with *high* ratings of flattening. N = 18.

Category of construct	tau	Category of construct	tau
'Activity'	—.02	'Occupation'	+.06
'Stance'	+.26	'Clothes'	+.22
'Physique'	—.08	'Irrelevance'	+.12
'Personality and emotional state'	—.47*	'Background'	+.32
'Age'	+.02	'Photography'	+.08
'Nationality'	+.15	'Denial'	—.24

* $p < .01$ (two-tailed test)

Those Ss who had been rated as showing the most severe flattening
thus made least use of constructs describing the personality or current
emotional state of the people in the photographs, e.g. whether they
seemed kind, intelligent, happy, calm, etc. This confirmed Dixon's finding: in a sample of 37 schizophrenics, she had obtained a correlation of
—0.39 ($p < .01$, two-tailed test) between rated flattening and the use
of this category.

Dixon had also found a significant negative correlation between rated
flattening and the little-used Photography category, but this was not
confirmed by the present results. None of the other 10 correlations was
significant either in the present study or in Dixon's. One correlation
which was nearly significant was that in the present study between
flattening and the use of constructs referring to the background of the
photographs. Patients with severe flattening used this category *more*
frequently.

The use of the 'personality and emotional state' category was not related to the length of time for which the patient had been in hospital,
nor to drug dosage. There was no difference in the scores of male and
female patients. Differences related to sub-diagnosis will be considered
in a later article.

DISCUSSION

The present results have confirmed those of Dixon (1968) in showing that schizophrenic patients with flattening of affect are characterized by an abnormality in the content of their personal construct systems. When construing other people (or at any rate people in photographs), they make relatively little use of constructs referring to their personality traits or to their current emotional state. The frequency of use of other categories of construct, e.g. those describing other people's activities, physical characteristics or dress, is not significantly related to affective flattening.

It might be argued that an explanation of these results is that constructs in the 'personality and emotional state' category are more 'difficult' than other constructs and that their less frequent use by the more flattened schizophrenics may merely reflect the lower vocabulary level of these patients. However, this is not so. In a study of 47 schizophrenics, McPherson & Buckley (1969) found a non-significant correlation between the use of these constructs and scores on the Mill Hill Synonym Selection test. Moreover, Harris & Metcalfe (1956) found no difference in the Wechsler vocabulary scores of three groups of schizophrenics, clinically rated as showing 'gross,' 'moderate' and no affective flattening.

The correlations between the percentage use made of 'personality and emotional state' constructs and the ratings of each of the clinicians considered separately were $+0.44$ and $+0.53$, whereas that between the two ratings was $+0.44$. The present procedure can thus provide an estimate of the severity of a patient's affective flattening which agrees with the rating of an experienced rater at least as well as, and possibly better than, experienced raters agree with one another.

However, failure to use 'personality and emotional state' constructs is not what leads clinicians to regard a patient as being affectively flattened. Rather it is because the patient *does* use constructs of this type, but without concomitant affect, i.e. expression of emotion. The explanation of this apparent paradox is probably that there is an important difference between the normal clinical interview, which a clinician uses to assess whether affective flattening is present, and the method of eliciting constructs described in this study. In the latter situation the patient is free to attend to and emphasize, and conversely to ignore, any features of the people in the photographs: e.g. he can talk about their emotional state or he can choose not to. The procedure therefore assesses the patient's *spontaneous* use of constructs of different sorts. In the clinical interview situation, on the other hand, it is the clinician who usually determines what must be discussed. The patient will therefore often be *required* to refer to emotional topics and hence to use constructs in the 'personality and emotional state' category. Whether or not he expresses appropriate emotion when using them will determine whether he is assessed as showing affective flattening. The present results show that there is a close relationship between these abnormalities in the two situations, i.e. that it is those patients who spontaneously tend not to employ 'personality and emotional state' constructs who also, in an interview situation, use them without the concomitant expression of emotion, and are therefore assessed as showing flattening of affect.

Two points should be made regarding the method of content analysis used in the study. The first is that the 'personality and emotional state' category is obviously a very broad one, including as it does both constructs describing current emotional state, e.g. 'happy—sad,' 'apprehensive—calm' and those describing more permanent personality traits, e.g. 'honest—dishonest,' 'kind—cruel,' 'clever—stupid.' However, the category could not be defined more narrowly since inspection of the results of the content analysis showed that affectively flattened patients failed to use either type of construct.

Secondly, as described above, in the scoring method employed in this study and Dixon's, only the first use of each category of construct was scored for each pair of photographs. However, similar results would have been obtained even if the more time-consuming method had been used of counting every use made of each category during each three-minute period. If a sample of 18 schizophrenics, Buckley (1969) found a correlation of $+0.80$ between the two estimates of the percentage frequency of use of the 'personality and emotional state' category.

The present findings, along with those of Dixon, have implications both for personal construct theory and for theories of flattening of affect. For example, by demonstrating the existence of an abnormality confined to one aspect of the construct system, they do not support those theories which account for affective flattening in terms of some generalized deficit such as retardation or a general reduction in activity. On the other hand, they appear to be compatible with an explanation in terms of personal construct theory. These topics will be discussed in detail in subsequent articles.

SUMMARY

A content analysis of the constructs used by 18 schizophrenics to differentiate people in photographs confirmed Dixon's (1968) finding that affective flattening, as rated clinically, is significantly associated with a relative failure to use constructs descriptive of personality and emotional state. The use of other types of construct is not related to the severity of affective flattening.

ACKNOWLEDGMENTS

We are grateful to Dr. P. M. Dixon for assistance at all stages of the investigation and to Dr. A. D. Forrest for permission to see the patients. F. M. M. is supported by the Mental Health Research Fund, whose help he gladly acknowledges.

REFERENCES

BANNISTER, D. (1960). 'Conceptual structure in thought-disordered schizophrenics.' *J. ment. Sci.,* 106, 1230-49.
—— (1962). 'The nature and measurement of schizophrenic thought disorder.' *Ibid.,* 108, 825-42.
—— (1965). 'The rationale and clinical relevance of Repertory Grid Technique.' *Brit. J. Psychiat.,* 111, 977-82.
—— and FRANSELLA, F. (1966). 'A grid test of schizophrenic thought disorder.' *Brit. J. soc. clin. Psychol.,* 5, 95-102.
BANNISTER, D. (1960) and MAIR, J. M. M. (1968) *The Evaluation of Personal Constructs.* London: Academic Press.
BUCKLEY, F. (1969). *Flatness of Affect, Thought-Process. Disorder and Personal Constructs.* Unpubl. M.Sc Dissert., University of Edinburgh.
BULLOCK, F. N., CLANCEY, I. W., and FLEISCHHACKER, H. H. (1951). 'Studies in schizophrenia.' *J. ment. Sci.,* 97, 197-208.
DIXON, P. M. (1968). *Reduced Emotional Responsiveness in Schizophrenia.* Unpubl. Ph.D. Dissert., University of London.
FISH, F. J. (1962). *Schizophrenia.* Bristol: John Wright & Sons.
HARRIS, A., and METCALFE, M. (1956). 'Inappropriate affect.' *J. Neurol. Neurosurg. Psychiat.,* 19, 308-13.
HERRON, W. G., and KANTOR, R. E. (1968). 'Loss of affect.' *J. Psychol.,* 70, 35-49.
KELLY, G. A. (1955). *The Psychology of Personal Constructs.* New York: Norton.
McPHERSON, F. M., and BUCKLEY, F. (1969). 'Flattening of affect, personal constructs and vocabulary level.' (In preparation).
MILLER, D. H., CLANCY, J., and CUMMINGS, E. (1953). 'A method of evaluating progress in patients suffering from chronic schizophrenia.' *Psychiat. Quart.,* 27, 439-51.
SALZINGER, K., and PORTNOY, S. (1964). 'Verbal conditioning in interviews: application to chronic schizophrenics and relationship to prognosis for acute schizophrenics.' *J. psychiat. Res.* 2, 1-9.
WING, J. K. (1961). 'A simple and reliable sub-classification of chronic schizophrenia.' *J. ment. Sci.,* 107, 862-75.

8

ESTABLISHMENT OF DIAGNOSTIC VALIDITY IN PSYCHIATRIC ILLNESS:

Its Application to Schizophrenia

Eli Robins and Samuel B. Guze

A method for achieving diagnostic validity in psychiatric illness is described, consisting of five phases: clinical description, laboratory study, exclusion of other disorders, follow-up study, and family study. The method was applied in this paper to patients with the diagnosis of schizophrenia, and it was shown by follow-up and family studies that poor prognosis cases can be validly separated clinically from good prognosis cases. The authors conclude that good prognosis "schizophrenia" is not mild schizophrenia, but a different illness.

Since Bleuler (3), psychiatrists have recognized that the diagnosis of schizophrenia includes a number of different disorders. We are interested in distinguishing these various disorders as part of our long-standing concern with developing a valid classification for psychiatric illnesses (6, 7, 10, 11). We believe that a valid classification is an essential step in science. In medicine, and hence in psychiatry, classification is diagnosis.

One of the reasons that diagnostic classification has fallen into disrepute among some psychiatrists is that diagnostic schemes have been largely based upon a priori principles rather than upon systematic studies. Such systematic studies are necessary, although they may be based upon different approaches. We have found that the approach described

The authors are with the department of psychiatry, Washington University School of Medicine, 4940 Audubon Ave., St. Louis, Mo. 63110, where Dr. Robins is Wallace Renard professor and head of the department and Dr. Guze is professor. Dr. Robins is also psychiatrist-in-chief, Barnes and Renard Hospitals, and Dr. Guze is associate psychiatrist.

This work was supported in part by Public Health Service grants MH-13002 and MH-07081 from the National Institute of Mental Health.

here facilitates the development of a valid classification in psychiatry. This paper illustrates its usefulness in schizophrenia.

1. Clinical Description

In general, the first step is to describe the clinical picture of the disorder. This may be a single striking clinical feature or a combination of clinical features thought to be associated with one another. Race, sex, age at onset, precipitating factors, and other items may be used to define the clinical picture more precisely. The clinical picture thus does not include only symptoms.

2. Laboratory Studies

Included among laboratory studies are chemical, physiological, radiological, and anatomical (biopsy and autopsy) findings. Certain psychological tests, when shown to be reliable and reproducible, may also be considered laboratory studies in this context. Laboratory findings are generally more reliable, precise, and reproducible than are clinical descriptions. When consistent with a defined clinical picture they permit a more refined classification. Without such a defined clinical picture, their value may be considerably reduced. Unfortunately, consistent and reliable laboratory findings have not yet been demonstrated in the more common psychiatric disorders.

3. Delimitation from Other Disorders

Since similar clinical features and laboratory findings may be seen in patients suffering from different disorders (e.g., cough and blood in the sputum in lobar pneumonia, bronchiectasis, and bronchogenic carcinoma), it is necessary to specify exclusion criteria so that patients with other illnesses are not included in the group to be studied. These criteria should also permit exclusion of borderline cases and doubtful cases (an undiagnosed group) so that the index group may be as homogeneous as possible.

4. Follow-Up Study

The purpose of the follow-up study is to determine whether or not the original patients are suffering from some other defined disorder that could account for the original clinical picture. If they are suffering from another such illness, this finding suggests that the original patients did not comprise a homogeneous group and that it is necessary to modify the diagnostic criteria. In the absence of known etiology or pathogenesis, which is true of the more common psychiatric disorders, marked differences in outcome, such as between complete recovery and chronic illness, suggest that the group is not homogeneous. This latter point is not as compelling in suggesting diagnostic heterogeneity as is the finding of a change in diagnosis. The same illness may have a variable prognosis, but until we know more about the fundamental nature of the common psychiatric illnesses marked differences in outcome should be regarded as a challenge to the validity of the original diagnosis.

5. Family Study

Most psychiatric illnesses have been shown to run in families, whether the investigations were designed to study hereditary or environmental causes. Independent of the question of etiology, therefore, the finding of an increased prevalence of the same disorder among the close relatives of the original patients strongly indicates that one is dealing with a valid entity.

We hope it is apparent that these five phases interact with one another so that new findings in any one of the phases may lead to modifications in one or more of the other phases. The entire process is therefore one of continuing self-rectification and increasing refinement leading to more homogeneous diagnostic grouping. Such homogeneous diagnostic grouping provides the soundest base for studies of etiology, pathogenesis, and treatment. The roles of heredity, family interactions, intelligence, education, and sociological factors are most simply, directly, and reliably studied when the group studied is as homogeneous as possible.

We will demonstrate by examining certain studies that these principles concerning the validity of psychiatric diagnosis may be applied to schizophrenia. These studies show that it is possible to systematically divide cases of schizophrenia into a poor prognosis group and a good prognosis group. Further, these studies suggest that this differentiation is not simply a matter of severity of illness but that the two groups represent different illnesses.

NOMENCLATURE

Psychiatrists have recognized for many years that among patients given the diagnosis of schizophrenia there are two main groups—one with a poor prognosis and the other with a better prognosis. Different investigators have referred to these two groups by different diagnostic terms. The

TABLE 1

FOLLOW-UP STUDIES OF PATIENTS GIVEN THE DIAGNOSIS OF SCHIZOPHRENIA

Authors	Country	Number of Cases	Duration of Follow-up (Years)	Follow-up Results (In Percent)	
				Well	Symptoms + Incapacity
Cases Predicted to Have a Poor Outcome					
1 Clark and Mallett (4)	England	76	3	11	73
2 Eitinger and associates (5)	Norway	110	5-15	1	84
3 Stephens and Astrup (13)	U.S.A.	143	5-13	7	55
4 Astrup and associates (1)	Norway	435	6-22	15	68
5 Astrup and Noreik (2)	Norway	273	>5	6	66
6 Vaillant (14)	U.S.A.	35	2	14	—
7 Vaillant (15)	U.S.A.	48	8-15	13	74
		60	1-2	7	62
8 Johanson (8)	Sweden	100	10-18	<12	>88
9 Robins and Smith (12)	U.S.A.	35	6	9	91
Cases Predicted to Have a Good Outcome					
1 Eitinger and associates (5)	Norway	39	5-15	36	23
2 Stephens and Astrup (13)	U.S.A.	74	5-13	38	3
3 Astrup and associates (1)	Norway	398	6-22	—	26
4 Astrup and Noreik (2)	Norway	306	>5	—	17
5 Vaillant (14)	U.S.A.	30	2	83	—
6 Vaillant (15)	U.S.A.	24	8-15	83	17
		28	1-2	64	11

more common terms for poor prognosis cases are chronic schizophrenia, process schizophrenia, dementia praecox, and nuclear schizophrenia. For good prognosis cases, they are acute schizophrenia, reactive schizophrenia, schizo-affective psychosis, atypical psychosis, and schizophreniform psychosis.

DIAGNOSTIC VALIDATION BY FOLLOW-UP STUDIES

Table I summarizes those studies reported in English in which the authors attempted to define patients systematically into poor prognosis groups or good prognosis groups. These studies were prospective or retrospective. In the retrospective studies, the author, without knowledge of the outcome, made a prediction concerning prognosis based upon the original clinical manifestations in the clinical records. In the selection of patients for all of these studies, cases of organic brain syndrome (including delirium), mental deficiency, obsessional neurosis, and typical manic-depressive illness were excluded. It is worth noting that similar results were obtained in different countries. This implies that the findings probably have universal application.

Patients with the diagnosis of schizophrenia who were predicted to have a poor outcome did so in from 55 to 91 percent of cases, whereas they were well at follow-up in from one to 15 percent of cases only (table 1). Clinical features of the cases in these studies associated with a poor prognosis are summarized in table 2.

TABLE 2

Prognostic Features in Schizophrenia

Features Associated with a Poor Prognosis	Features Associated with a Good Prognosis
1. Insidious onset (more than six months of symptoms)	1. Prominent depressive symptoms
2. Hebephrenic clinical picture	2. Family history of affective disorders
3. "Massive" persecutory delusions	3. Absence of a family history of schizophrenia
4. Clear sensorium	4. Good premorbid adjustment
5. Schizoid personality	5. Confusion
6. Family history of schizophrenia	6. Acute onset (less than six months of symptoms)
7. Striking emotional blunting	7. Precipitating factors
	8. Concern with dying and guilt

Patients with the diagnosis of schizophrenia who were predicted to have a good outcome were found to have a poor prognosis in only three to 26 percent of cases, whereas they were well in 36 to 83 percent of cases (table 1). Clinical features associated with a good prognosis are summarized in table 2.

It is evident that in table 1, the figures do not add up to 100 percent except in three studies. This is because in the remaining studies, although the patients were not well, it was not possible to determine their incapacity. Therefore, we did not include them in the tables. It seems evident from the data in table 1 that, using the appropriate criteria, predicting a poor outcome is more likely to be correct than is predicting a good outcome.

The error in prediction for each group (poor outcome and good outcome) suggests two possibilities: either each group is not homogeneous, i.e., it includes patients with more than one illness, or each group represents a separate illness with a variable prognosis. The family studies described below permit, to a considerable extent, the resolution of these alternatives.

DIAGNOSTIC VALIDATION BY FAMILY STUDIES

There are many family studies of schizophrenia in the literature. We have limited ourselves for the present purpose to only two studies. We selected only studies in which the following three criteria were met: 1) There was a clinical differentiation made of poor prognosis from good prognosis index cases. 2) There was a follow-up of the index cases to establish the validity of the original differentiation. 3) There was a systematic study of schizophrenia and affective disorders among first-degree relatives. Since we believe that such family studies are very important in establishing diagnostic validity, we regret that there are so few to report.

TABLE 3

FAMILY STUDIES OF POOR PROGNOSIS VERSUS GOOD PROGNOSIS CASES

			Percent of Index Cases with Psychiatric Illness in First-Degree Relatives	
Author	Country	Number of Cases	Schizophrenia	Affective Disorder
Kant (9)	U.S.A.	50 good prognosis versus	8	38
		50 poor prognosis	32	6
Vaillant (14)	U.S.A.	30 good prognosis versus	20	50
		30 poor prognosis	23	7

The two pertinent studies are presented in table 3. The most striking finding in these studies is the great preponderance of affective disorders among the first-degree relatives of patients with a good prognosis. This indicates that many of the index cases with a good prognosis did not have schizophrenia but suffered from a different illness—an affective disorder. On the other hand, the finding of an increased prevalence of schizophrenia among the first-degree relatives of the good prognosis cases (eight percent in Kant's [9] series and 20 percent in Vaillant's [14] series) indicates that some of the good prognosis cases did, in fact, suffer from schizophrenia.

Another striking finding in these studies is the preponderance of schizophrenia among the first-degree relatives of patients with a poor prognosis (32 percent schizophrenia versus six percent effective disorder in Kant's [9] series, and 23 percent schizophrenia versus seven percent affective disorder in Vaillant's [14] series).

The only finding inconsistent with the two points just made is the similarity of the prevalence of schizophrenia among the relatives of good prognosis and poor prognosis index cases in Vaillant's (14) series. We have no explanation for this inconsistency. It suggests that Vaillant's (14) series of good prognosis cases included more patients with schizophrenia than did Kant's (9).

DISCUSSION

In this paper, we have reviewed selected studies written in English in which attempts were made to separate cases diagnosed as schizophrenia into two groups: one with a poor prognosis and the other with a good prognosis. These studies indicate that it is possible to achieve this separation with a high degree of success. The failure to achieve 100 percent success in predicting outcome and the overlap in the results of the family studies indicate that the criteria used for the separation need further refinement. The impressive results achieved, however, by using the method described in this paper for establishing diagnostic validity indicate that the method has great power.

The method shows its power not only by its ability to separate the two groups quite well but also by pointing up its failures, thus indicating where additional study is needed. This additional study may involve further refinement of clinical studies, of follow-up studies, or of family studies.

Even though at this time laboratory studies have not contributed reliably to the diagnosis of schizophrenia, without such reliable laboratory studies a completely satisfactory classification of schizophrenia may not be possible despite the refinements of clinical and family studies. Thus, as indicated earlier in the paper, a fully validated diagnostic classification will probably also require reliable laboratory studies. We hope we have demonstrated, however, that even in the absence of such laboratory studies, careful clinical, follow-up, and family studies have contributed importantly to our knowledge of schizophrenia. We believe that similar studies will accomplish as much in other psychiatric illnesses.

SUMMARY

A method for achieving a high degree of diagnostic validity for psychiatric illness was described. The method was applied to schizophrenia. It was shown that it is possible to separate poor prognosis from good prognosis cases of schizophrenia. Poor prognosis cases have a predominance of schizophrenia among their psychiatrically ill first-degree relatives.

Good prognosis cases have a predominance of affective disorder among their psychiatrically ill first-degree relatives. Therefore, apparent "schizophrenia" with a good prognosis is not a mild form of schizophrenia, but is a different illness. Research in schizophrenia, whether genetic, psychodynamic, clinical, sociological, chemical, physiological, or therapeutic, must take this differentiation into account.

REFERENCES

1. ASTRUP, C., FOSSUM, A., and HOLMBOE, R.: Prognosis in Functional Psychoses. Springfield, Ill.: Charles C. Thomas, 1962.
2. ASTRUP, C., and NOREIK, K.: Functional Psychoses: Diagnostic and Prognostic Models. Springfield, Ill.: Charles C Thomas, 1966.
3. BLEULER, E.: Dementia Praecox or the Group of Schizophrenias, trans. by J. Zinkin. New York: International Universities Press, 1950.
4. CLARK, J. A., and MALLETT, B. L.: A Follow-Up Study of Schizophrenia and Depression in Young Adults, Brit. J. Psychiat. 109: 491-499, 1963.
5. EITINGER, L., LAANE, C. V., and LANGFELDT, G.: The Prognostic Value of the Clinical Picture and the Therapeutic Value of Physical Treatment in Schizophrenia and the Schizophreniform States, Acta Psychiat. et Neurol. Scand. 33: 33-53, 1958.
6. GOODWIN, D. W., GUZE, S. B., and ROBINS, E.: Follow-up Studies in Obsessional Neurosis, Arch. Gen. Psychiat. 20: 182-187, 1969.
7. GUZE, S. B.: The Diagnosis of Hysteria: What Are We Trying To Do? Amer. J. Psychiat. 124: 491-498, 1967.
8. JOHANSON, E.: A Study of Schizophrenia in the Male: A Psychiatric and Social Study Based on 138 Cases with Follow-Up, Acta Psychiat. et Neurol. Scand. 33: supp. 125, 1958.
9. KANT, O.: The Incidence of Psychoses and Other Mental Abnormalities in the Families of Recovered and Deteriorated Schizophrenic Patients, Psychiat. Quart. 16: 176-186, 1942.
10. PURTELL, J., ROBINS, E., and COHEN, M.: Observations on Clinical Aspects of Hysteria: A Quantitative Study of 50 Hysteria Patients and 156 Control Subjects, J.A.M.A. 146: 902-909, 1951.
11. ROBINS, E.: "Antisocial and Dyssocial Personality Disorders," in Freedman, A. M., and Kaplan, H. I., eds.: Comprehensive Textbook of Psychiatry. Baltimore: Williams & Wilkins Co., 1967, pp. 951-958.
12. ROBINS, E., and SMITH, K.: unpublished data.
13. STEPHENS, J. H., and ASTRUP, C.: Prognosis in "Process" and "Non-process" Schizophrenia, Amer. J. Psychiat. 119: 945-953, 1963.
14. VAILLANT, G. E.: The Prediction of Recovery in Schizophrenia, J. Nerv. Ment. Dis. 135: 534-543, 1962.
15. VAILLANT, G. E.: Prospective Prediction of Schizophrenic Remission, Arch. Gen. Psychiat. 11: 509-518, 1964.

9

LAING'S MODELS OF MADNESS

Miriam Siegler, Humphrey Osmond,
and Harriet Mann

Bright young schizophrenics, like bright young people generally, are interested in reading about their condition. From the vast and varied selection of literature available to them, they appear to show a marked preference for R. D. Laing's *The Politics of Experience* (1967). The present authors, like other members of the "square" older generation, are of the opinion that they know what is best, and that this book is not good for these patients. It is an appealing book, and emotionally there is not a false note in it. This alone makes it important. But it contains treacherous confusions, and while we do not presume to make choices for our young friends we do feel that it is our duty to clarify the alternatives as presented in this book.

We have evolved a method for picking our way through the jungle of theories about schizophrenia: the construction of models (Siegler and Osmond, 1966). Briefly, our models are constructed by taking a single theory or point of view and asking its author or authors what schizophrenia is, how it might have come about, what is to be done about it, in what direction it is likely to alter over time, how the people involved with it ought to behave, and other such questions. We have labelled these questions "definition," "aetiology," "treatment," "prognosis," "the rights and duties of patients," and so forth, and they constitute the dimensions of the model. The answers to these questions make up the content of the model itself. The dimensions must be consistent with each other within any one model. When two or more such models have been constructed, they can be compared, dimension by dimension. In the physical sciences,

This work was made possible by funds from N.I.M.H. General Research Support Grant 1-SO1-FR-05558-01 and initiated by support from the American Schizophrenia Foundation, Inc.

Reprinted, by permission of author and editor, from: *The British Journal of Psychiatry*, 115:947-958, 1969.

workers are in the habit of comparing theories and showing in what way one is better than another, but in psychiatry, stemming as it does from empirical medicine, eclecticism prevails. Our models are an attempt to borrow from the physical sciences a certain orderliness which we find enviable. Thus far we have constructed six models of schizophrenia: medical, moral, psychoanalytic, family interaction, social, and conspiratorial. We now propose to apply our method to *The Politics of Experience*.

Most books and articles on schizophrenia are written either to express some point of view or theory about schizophrenia, or else to report some research on a problem that arises within a particular theory. In either case, it is usually evident from the start what model the author holds. In Laing's book, however, it is not immediately evident what kind of model will emerge from our process. In fact, it soon becomes apparent that the dimensions can be filled more than once, i.e. there is more than one model. The task, then, is to locate all of his statements which fit any of our dimensions, to put together all the dimensions which are compatible with each other, to see how many models result from this process, and to see what dimensions, if any, are missing from the identifiable models. Using this method, we find that Laing's book contains two more or less complete models, and a fragment of a third model. Of the three models, two have been described before (psychoanalytic, conspiratorial) and one is entirely new (psychedelic).

In the two models which are more or less complete, we have filled in the missing dimensions so that they are consistent with the existing ones. The dimensions which we have supplied in this way are bracketed, so that the reader may easily distinguish them from Laing's own statements.

We have filled some of the dimensions with Laing's own words, and in all these cases the quotation marks and page numbers are given. We have done this in order to convey the flavor of his argument, which might otherwise be lost. The method of model construction inevitably distorts the author's intentions, which are conveyed in part by the "mood" of the book, the order in which things are presented, the style of writing, and other means which lie outside of the argument itself. Arranging a theory as a model often destroys the uniqueness of the author's point of view, and yet it is precisely this uniqueness which prevents the comparison of one author's theory with another. We have, then, used the author's exact words whenever feasible in order to minimize this distortion without sacrificing the comparability which our method makes possible.

All statements in the dimensions which are not bracketed or in quotation marks are paraphrases of Laing's statements.

I. LAING'S CONSPIRATORIAL MODEL OF MADNESS

A. *The Model Described*

1. *Definition*

Schizophrenia is a *label* which some people pin on other people, under certain social circumstances. It is not an illness, like pneumonia. It is a form of alienation which is out of step with the prevailing state of alienation. It is a social fact and a political event.

2. *Aetiology*

Alienation, of which schizophrenia is one form, ". . . is achieved only by outrageous violence perpetrated by human beings on human beings." (p. xv) We are driving our children mad. We are intolerant of different fundamental structures of experience.

The social system, and not individuals, must be the object of study if we are to understand the aetiology of schizophrenia. The blame cannot be laid at anyone's door; "very seldom is it a question of contrived, deliberate cynical lies or a ruthless intention to drive someone crazy . . ." (p. 79).

3. *Behavior*

". . . Behavior that gets labelled schizophrenic is a special strategy that a person invents in order to live in an unliveable situation" (p. 79).

Transactional analyses are insufficient explanations of behavior. Electronic systems can play games which can be analyzed in this way, but human relations are transexperiential.

Psychiatrists have tended to pay more attention to the patient's behavior than to his experience.

4. *Treatment*

What is called "treatment" is really getting the patient to abandon his subjective experiential perspective for the therapist's objective one. The patient's experiences are interpreted away by the therapist, and said to mean something other than what the patient says they mean.

5. *Prognosis*

Once the label of "schizophrenic" is applied, it sticks, and treating someone in terms of this label reinforces the very behavior which caused the label to be applied in the first place. It is a vicious circle.

6. *Suicide*

(Suicide is a way out of the vicious circle.) *

---

* Suicide is discussed in another of Laing's books, *The Divided Self* (London: Tavistock Publications, 1959). The model in use in this book is the psychoanalytic model.

7. *Function of the hospital*

The hospital is a total institution which degrades and invalidates human beings. Once in the hospital, the patient hardly ever leaves, because he manifests more and more of the behavior for which he was hospitalized.

8. *Personnel*

The personnel for this model are all the people who come into contact with the person labelled as schizophrenic except the schizophrenic himself. "The person labelled is inaugurated not only into a role, but into a career of patient, by the concerted action of a coalition (a "conspiracy") of family, G.P., mental health officer, psychiatrists, nurses, psychiatric social workers, and often fellow patients." (p. 84) .

9. *Rights and duties of patients*

"The 'committed' person labelled as patient, and specifically as 'schizophrenic,' is degraded from full existential and legal status as human agent and responsible person to someone no longer in possession of his own definition of himself, unable to retain his own possessions, precluded from the exercise of his discretion as to whom he meets, what he does. His time is no longer his own, and the space he occupies is no longer of his own choosing. After being subjected to a degradation ceremonial known as psychiatric examination, he is bereft of his civil liberties in being imprisoned in a total institution known as a 'mental' hospital. More completely, more radically than anywhere else in our society, he is invalidated as a human being. In the mental hospital he must remain, until the label is rescinded or qualified by such terms as 'remitted' or 'readjusted.' " (p. 84) .
The schizophrenic has no rights and no duties.

10. *Rights and duties of families of patients*

(The family has driven the schizophrenic crazy, although they probably did not intend to do so, labelled him schizophrenic, and hospitalized him in a total institution. In doing so, they have forfeited the usual rights and duties of families toward one of their members.)

11. *Rights and duties of society*

(Society [i.e., all the members of a culture] seems to have the right to maintain the status quo, and in order to do so the status quo is represented as part of the natural order, or as a natural law. Society appears to have the right to lock people up in mental hospitals as a means of maintaining the status quo. It is not clear whether society has any duties toward its members in this model.)

12. *Goal of the model*

The goal of this model is to maintain the status quo by "treating" as medical patients certain individuals who, due to the strength of their inner perceptions and experiences, are exceptionally eloquent critics of the society.

B. *The Model Discussed*

We have identified this model as conspiratorial because it fits the description of that model given in our original paper (Siegler and Osmond, 1966). It has as its main concern the violation of the rights of the person labelled as schizophrenic. Since it is denied that the person so labelled has an illness, his incarceration in a building called a "hospital" is inexplicable. And so it is said that there is a conspiracy among those surrounding the "patient" to exile him to a total institution which is called a hospital but is really a kind of concentration camp.*

A conspiratorial model is a view of the fate of schizophrenics minus the medical context. We must now ask what it is about the medical context that disturbs Laing so much. First, Laing finds the practice of assigning diagnostic labels to patients unacceptable. He says: ". . . It is wrong to impute a hypothetical disease of unknown aetiology and undiscovered pathology to someone unless *he* can prove otherwise." (p. 71). Laing is certainly entitled to believe that this is wrong, but it is only fair to note that the practice of medicine consists to a great extent of imputing hypothetical diseases of unknown aetiology and undiscovered pathology to patients who are in no position to prove otherwise. All diseases are hypothetical, all are labels. There is no such thing as diabetes, there are only individuals who have certain experiences and physical symptoms which are said to have some relation to the hypothetical disease. Yet such a disease entity is an extremely powerful category, for all its philosophical inelegance. Without it, medical research would be unthinkable and practice chaotic. When doctors see "a case of pneumonia" or "a case of tuberculosis," they bring to bear on each case such knowledge as they and other doctors have accumulated about this hypothetical entity. Diagnosis is one of the principal functions of the physician. In the conspiratorial model, to label someone is to discriminate against him, but in the medical model to label someone is to bring the knowledge of medicine to bear upon him. It is an essential step which precedes and determines treatment. It may save his life.**

---

* Laing actually uses the word 'conspiracy' on page 84, but in parenthesis and with full quotation marks around it, which seems to suggest that he wishes to qualify the word somewhat.

** Diagnosis has another important function: it is a necessary step in conferring the sick role. Patients are anxious to have a diagnosis because without it their status as patient is dubious. They might otherwise be frauds, malingerers, or hypochondriacs.

Another aspect of medicine which seems to bother Laing is that when one removes the medical context from a medical interaction one is often left with an extraordinary situation. He describes a clinical examination, taken from Kraepelin's lectures, in which Kraepelin demonstrates a young girl's psychotic illness by noting her reactions when he attempts to stop her movements, forces a piece of bread out of her hands, sticks a needle into her forehead, and so forth (p. 73). Laing correctly notes that this is very peculiar behavior; but it is only so when taken out of the context as experienced and defined by Kraepelin, i.e. a clinical examination. The medical context permits people called doctors to perform all kinds of unusual actions on people called patients, and this enables them to treat illnesses. On the whole, people feel that the advantages of the medical model are such that the social fiction which is required to sustain it is worth preserving. But not everyone is of this opinion; some people, for example, Christian Scientists, feel that other values take precedence. As an individual, Laing is quite free to put forth any view on these matters that he chooses, but as a physician he is not free to put forth the view that the social fiction called medicine is more harmful than helpful.

In the dimension of "behavior," Laing correctly notes that psychiatrists tend to pay attention to behavior to the exclusion of experience. To the extent that they do so, they fail to behave like medical men, for a doctor does not simply observe his patient's behavior, but makes inquiries and, if possible, tests of what is going on "inside" the patient. The thermometer measures the inner experience of the patient, and is more accurate and useful than watching the patient mop his brow. Doctors ask their patients to tell them where it hurts, and they listen carefully to this information, in order to map out the nature and extent of the illness. Psychiatrists who no longer listen to the reports of their patients' experiences, or who interpret these experiences symbolically instead of using them as information, are not using the medical model.

One of the dimensions which is missing from Laing's model is suicide. Within the medical model, suicide is a medical risk in certain illnesses, especially in schizophrenia (Osmond and Hoffer, 1967). The doctor must be alert for signs of possible suicide, and he must use his clinical experience to avert it if possible. But in Laing's model, as in Goffman's (1961), suicide is conspicuous by its absence. Since the staff in this model seem to have rights in relation to the patient, but no duties toward him, it is not possible to say that it is the duty of the staff to prevent the patient from committing suicide. Laing and Goffman might have taken the stand that suicide is the patient's (or rather, "patient's") business, and that no one else has the right to interfere with it, but they do not do this; they prefer not to discuss it at all. Yet suicide is just the sort of moral dilemma which makes medicine the model of choice in the case of schizophrenia. The medical model is the only one which can simultaneously try to prevent death, and account for it if it occurs. In all other models of which we are aware, death must be seen as someone's fault. In medicine, as long as the doctor behaves like a doctor, he is not blamed for deaths which occur in his practice.

In addition to suicide, there are two other dimensions missing from Laing's model; the rights and duties of the patients' families, and the rights and duties of society. Since this model has as its central focus the rights of the person labelled as schizophrenic, it is not surprising that those of the other participants are ignored. Laing clearly wished to redress the balance in favor of the person labelled as schizophrenic. He appears to believe that the reason why the "patient" has lost so many rights is that we are "intolerant of different fundamental structures of experience" (p. 50). That is, he sees the family and community as repressive forces, unwilling to permit the schizophrenic to experience his unusual perceptions without interference. Because they fail to accept his experiences as authentic, Laing argues, they elicit frustrated and peculiar behavior from him, they then label it as schizophrenic, and extrude him from the family and community until he learns to see things their way. Given this picture of the "patient" as a victim of repressive forces, it is little wonder that Laing is not moved to consider the rights of the family and community.

We are in agreement with Laing's contention that most people cannot accept the fact that others experience the world in a radically different way from themselves (Mann, H., Siegler, M. and Osmond, H., 1968). On the whole people know very little about other experiential worlds. Many experiences are difficult to put into words, and some people are not as articulate as others, so most people do not guess how very different the experiences of others may be. However, we disagree with Laing's contention that it is in the area of experience that the schizophrenic comes to grief; his difficulties lie in the area of behavior. As long as a schizophrenic manages to behave normally, no one will show the slightest interest, kindly or otherwise, in his unusual experiences. A person may, with impunity, experience himself as walking down the street without clothes on; it is only when he actually does this that the community will take action. The community is generally indifferent to and ignorant of the inner experiences of its members, but it does deal with misbehavior by curtailing the rights that are contingent on acceptable behavior. Although the behavior required varies enormously from culture to culture, and from family to family, all cultures and all families exchange certain rights for certain behavioral conformities. When this breakdown of reciprocity occurs, the person in question loses his usual rights and moves into some new role, which has other rights. The possible roles for such a person of which we are aware are: bad, eccentric, prophetic, analysand, impaired, sick. Today, since there are schizophrenics in each of these roles, one might ask which of them is best off.*

Schizophrenics who occupy the "bad" role may be found in prisons; here they are offered the rights and duties of prisoners, including a determinate sentence for some specific infraction of the law. Some people believe that this is a kinder fate than the mental hospital, but unfortunately the advantages to the schizophrenic are often outweighted by the fact that the non-schizophrenic prisoners recognize that there is something wrong with him, and will not accept him into the highly normative sub-culture of the criminal. Foucault (1965) describes the situation which arose when, in eighteenth-century France, criminals, schizophrenics and the indigent were all locked up together: the schizophrenics quickly became highly visible, because they could not conform to the daily life of the prison. This situation is still reported today.

The role of eccentric is open to some schizophrenics. It has the great advantage of being an acceptable social role, but most communities cannot tolerate more than a few eccentrics, and there is no room for the enormous number of schizophrenics.

The role of prophet, like the eccentric role, is one which is open to very few people, whether they are schizophrenic or not. A schizophrenic who wished to occupy this role would find himself in competition with normal people whose temperament allowed them to excel in this way.

The role of analysand is open to a small number of schizophrenics who live in a few Western countries, and whose temperament permits them to engage in the psychoanalytic form of communication. In general, working class people are barred from this role both financially and culturally. Its main advantage is that a great deal of personal care and attention is lavished on the schizophrenic occupying this role. Among its disadvantages are that it may create financial and emotional strain in the analysand's family; the analysand feels guilty if his condition does not improve; and the analysand role is constantly being confused with the sick role.

---

* To our knowledge, no one has offered schizophrenics a choice of these roles, although some schizophrenics have moved or been moved from one role to another.

The impaired role is a kind of second-class citizenship, designed to offer support and protection to people who have disabilities. The blind, the deaf, the crippled, and the retarded are all examples of impaired people. These people are expected to behave as normally as possible in exchange for reduced demands upon them by others. Unlike that of sick people, their situation is not expected to change. Many schizophrenics, especially those in hospitals, occupy the impaired role, but unfortunately, it does not quite fit them, because most of them have fluctuating illnesses: they may be quite normal at some times, and very ill at others. In many countries there are mental hospitals which are really homes for the impaired and are neither equipped to give real medical care to the very ill, nor set up to allow normal living to those who are not ill at any given moment.

Some schizophrenics occupy the sick role. That is, they perceive themselves as having a major illness which, like many major illnesses, does not have an agreed-upon aetiology or a wholly successful treatment. They understand that they are not able to carry their full adult load of social responsibility because they are unfortunate enough to be very ill. They consult their physicians, take medication as directed (ideally), report changes in their condition when they occur, go into the hospital when their illness gets worse, follow the progress of medical research, talk with other patients with the same illness about their mutual difficulties, and ask their doctor if he thinks they will ever be really well again. Their lot is not an easy one, but they do occupy an ancient and respectable social role, that of the sick person. If they occupy the sick role fully, they do not blame themselves or their families for their condition. This relieves them of the additional burden of family strife, not a small matter for a young adult who may have to live with his family long past the time he would normally leave if he were well. The schizophrenic in the sick role may gain such comfort as he can from the knowledge that other major psychiatric diseases, such as general paresis and pellagra psychosis, have yielded to medical research.

II. LAING'S PSYCHOANALYTIC MODEL OF MADNESS

A. *The Model Described*

Only two dimensions of this model are present in Laing's book, aetiology and treatment.

1. *Aetiology*

". . . to the best of my knowledge, *no* schizophrenic has been studied whose disturbed pattern of communication has not been shown to be a reflection of, and reaction to, the disturbed and disturbing pattern characterizing his or her family of origin." (p. 78) *

2. Treatment

"Psychotherapy must remain an obstinate attempt of two people to recover the wholeness of being human through the relationship between them." (p. 32). "Psychotherapy consists in the paring away of all that stands between us, the props, masks, roles, lies, defences, anxieties, projections and interjections, in short, all the carry-overs from the past, transference and countertransference, that we use by habit and collusion, wittingly and unwittingly, as our currency for relationships." (p. 27).

B. The Model Discussed

We have identified this model as a psychoanalytic model, even though Laing is not an orthodox psychoanalyst, because it has the essential features of such a model: the source of the person's difficulties lies in the past, specifically in his disturbed family relationships, and the treatment consists of a special kind of corrective relationship between two people, patient and therapist. These features are not true of any other model.

It is interesting that only these two dimensions of the model are present, for these are the dimensions on which the strength of the psychoanalytic model rests. Diagnosis, for example, is of little concern in this model. Whereas the process of diagnosis is seen as prejudicial labelling in the conspiratorial model, and as an essential step toward determining treatment in the medical model, it is seen in the psychoanalytic model as a useless diversion. Why bother to determine what category a patient falls into, when the treatment is the same in any case, and every relationship between patient and therapist is unique?

The psychoanalytic model is opposed to the medical model at almost every point. Yet psychoanalysts are often medical doctors; in some coun-

---

* Although it may appear that Laing uses here a family interaction model, rather than a psychoanalytic one, this is not so. In the family interaction model as we have described it (Siegler and Osmond, 1966), the essential feature is that the disturbance is seen as lying *among* the members of the family, all of whom are, together, 'the patient.' Laing nowhere in this book shows the slightest concern for the experiences of the other members of the family. He simply uses the information provided by the family interaction model to reinforce his argument that the schizophrenic patient has been driven mad by his family, a statement which is meaningless in the other model. The purists among the family interactionists believe that only the analysis of the whole family together can alter the family pathology, whereas Laing maintains the psychoanalytic view that treatment occurs between two people, therapist and patient. In another book on schizophrenia (Laing, R. D. and Esterson, A., *Sanity, Madness and the Family*, Volume 1, Families of Schizophrenics). Laing also sees the function of the therapist to be the exploration of the patient's experience, rather than that of other family members.

tries, they must be. This has created the utmost confusion for schizophrenic patients, since they usually go to a doctor because they perceive themselves to be ill, and wish to be treated; they then discover that the treatment offered them carries with it a set of rights and duties, i.e. the role of analysand, which is incompatible with the sick role. The analyst uses the authority which derives from the fact that he is a physician to put forth an anti-medical view. It is almost as if a priest used the authority vested in him by the church to put forth a doctrine which was completely irreconcilable with that of the church. The difference between the two institutions is that the church strives to be overtly consistent, while medicine has a covert, unverbalized consistency, which is undisturbed by the peculiar and often outrageous opinions which doctors voice from time to time. The fact that doctors are not thrown out of medical societies for putting forth anti-medical views shows that the true consensus in medicine lies elsewhere than in verbalized doctrines. It is a tribute to the enduring qualities of the institution of medicine that doctors can advocate and even proselytize anti-medical views among patients without destroying the basic doctor-patient relationship between them.

But schizophrenic patients do not emerge unscathed from these encounters. The underlying assumption of psychoanalysis is that progress toward a "healthy" personality is possible, given hard work, good faith, enough time, and in most cases enough money. In medicine, there is no such contract; an illness may become suddenly worse, for no known reason, in spite of everyone's hard work and good faith. In the psychoanalytic model, these sudden reversals must be explained "dynamically," i.e., they are somebody's fault. Either the family does not really wish the patient to get well, or the patient has been damaged too severely to get well, or the patient is "afraid" to get well, or the analyst has not solved the countertransference problem. The fact that failure must be explained, either implicitly or explicitly, as someone's fault places a great additional burden on the schizophrenic and his family.

Laing's conspiratorial model is an account of how he thinks schizophrenics are treated at the present time; his psychedelic model (to follow) is an account of how he thinks schizophrenics ought to be treated. His psychoanalytic model, which seems to have crept into the book by mistake, is an account of what he actually does. He is a psychotherapist with a very deep regard for his patients, and he tells us, in these fragments of a model, that he forms meaningful and authentic relationships with them. Since it appears that the psychoanalytic model is the one which he actually uses, we feel it is incumbent upon him to inform his patients fully about it, so that they may compare it with the alternative models.

III. LAING'S PSYCHEDELIC MODEL OF MADNESS

A. *The Model Described*

1. *Definition*

Schizophrenia is "... itself a natural way of healing our own appalling state of alienation called normality ..." (p. 116). "Madness need not be all breakdown. . . . It may also be breakthrough. It is potentially liberation and renewal as well as enslavement and existential death." (p. 93). It is not an illness to be treated, but a "voyage." Socially, madness may be a form in which "... often through quite ordinary people, the light begins to break through the cracks in our all-too-closed minds." (p. 90).

2. *Aetiology*

"We have all been processed on procrustean beds. At least some of us have managed to hate what they made of us." (p. 47).

3. *Behavior*

"The madness that we encounter in 'patients' is a gross travesty, a mockery, a grotesque caricature of what that natural healing process of that estranged integration we call sanity might be." (p. 101). It is distorted by our misguided attempts to "treat" them. If we really understood our patients, we would see behavior which was a reflection of the natural healing process, a desire to explore the inner world.

4. *Treatment*

Instead of the degradation ceremonial of psychiatric examination, diagnosis and prognostication, we need, for those who are ready for it, "... an initiation ceremonial, through which the person will be guided with full social encouragement and sanction into inner space and time, by people who have been there and back." (p. 89).

5. *Prognosis*

(If a schizophrenic person were intelligently guided through his voyage into inner time and space, he would emerge a better person than he had been before; perhaps one might say that he would be "enlightened.")

6. *Suicide*

(If a schizophrenic person commits suicide while being guided on a voyage, that is just one of the risks—voyages are dangerous. There are no guarantees.)

7. *Function of the Hospital*

We need a place which has the right atmosphere for guided voyages into inner time and space. The schizophrenic person would leave this place when the voyage was over.

8. *Personnel*

The appropriate personnel for guiding these voyages are people who have been there and back, including ex-patients. "Among physicians and priests, there should be some who are guides. . . ." (p. 97).

9. *Rights and Duties of Schizophrenic Persons*

(The schizophrenic has the right to a well-guided voyage, in a setting that is conducive to inner exploration. He has the right to be spared psychiatric diagnosis and treatment which is designed to make him give up his own existential view. He has the duty to accept restraint if he is too much for the others.)

10. *Rights and Duties of Families*

(The family has the duty to let the schizophrenic person make his own choice about where and how to undergo an inner voyage. The family does not have the right to label a family member as "schizophrenic" and then hospitalize him for "treatment.")

11. *Rights and Duties of Society*

(Society has no rights in relation to schizophrenic persons, certainly not the right to label people and then send them to "hospitals." Society has the duty to organize itself in such a way that alienation is not "normal." Society has the duty to allow more "breakthrough.")

12. *Goal of the Model*

The goal of this model is to enable certain people, now called "schizophrenic," to develop their potentialities for inner exploration. If such people can be allowed and encouraged to move in this direction, all of us will benefit.

B. *The Model Discussed*

We have called this model "psychedelic," although Laing does not use the term in this book, because it is obvious that he thinks that schizophrenics may have, sometimes have, and ought to have the same kinds of experiences that normal individuals seek when they take mind-expanding drugs. From our point of view, Laing has failed to distinguish two very different kinds of experience, psychedelic and psychotic. We share his opinion that schizophrenics sometimes have psychedelic experiences, particularly at the beginning of their illnesses (Bowers and Freedman, 1966), and it is certainly true that some schizophrenics have been able to make creative use of their unusual experiences. It must be noted, however, that some creative individuals have always been able to make use of the experience of having a major illness to further their own self-development. During the era when well-to-do tubercular patients lived in "magic mountains," some were able to use this experience, with its enforced leisure and unusual physical sensations, to arrive at a different view of themselves than they might have otherwise achieved. Simply staying in bed for a long period may be a great boon to a contemplative individual. Even terminal cancer has brought out the best in some people, and in some family relationships.* But it is heartless to suggest, without the most exact explanation and qualification, to those suffering from tuberculosis, cancer, or schizophrenia that they should look on this as a rare opportunity for self-understanding. For most people and their families, a major disease means the end of hopes and plans, however modest. It almost always means a severe financial drain on the family, and families are sometimes destroyed by the disruption which a disease brings in its wake.

There is one dimension of this model which deserves mention, that of "personnel." Laing has suggested ex-patients, some physicians, and some priests as guides for the voyages of inner exploration. It is clear why he thinks that ex-patients and priests might be suitable, but we are at a loss to understand why physicians are considered for this role. Medicine is a dirty, rough business. It favors the thick-skinned person over the sensitive one, the practical person over the imaginative. Men of unsuitable temperament who chose medicine by mistake are often weeded out during medical training. Doctors who like their work enjoy coping with emergencies; they are cut from the same cloth as sailors and farmers, masons and carpenters. They see machinery and the human body in much the same way, and they are respectful and knowledgeable about the workings of both. They are accustomed to being obeyed, not because of their individual personalities, but because they are doctors, and they believe that they have been commissioned to deal with urgent matters of life and death. Making gurus out of doctors seems hardly worth the trouble when there are so many unemployed ex-patients about. Laing ought to make it clear what qualities of doctors he feels make them likely candidates for psychedelic guides.

* See, for example, John Gunther's *Death Be Not Proud* (1949) and Lael Tucker Wertenbaker's *Death of a Man* (1957).

Perhaps the most important point to be made about Laing's psychedelic model is its implication that schizophrenics will benefit from being seen as persons embarked on a voyage of self-discovery. It would be closer to the truth to see most of them as voyagers who have been shanghaied, for unknown reasons, on to a ship which never reaches port. Psychedelic voyages are usually voluntary, and the person usually knows what the agent of his changed perception is. Schizophrenia is involuntary, the person rarely knows the cause of his strange new perceptions, and he is unlikely to receive much helpful information about them. In a psychedelic experience, a "bad trip" can usually be avoided by surrounding oneself with known and trusted people, by choosing a setting that is secure and aesthetically pleasing, and by showing prudence and caution. In a psychotic experience, on the other hand, good people can be perceived as bad, so that it may be even worse to have beloved people around than those who are indifferent, for nothing is worse than to hate those one normally loves. Another critical difference between the two experiences is the absolute length of time that elapses. A psychedelic experience is necessarily short; it is usually counted in hours, not years.* But a psychosis may last ten or twenty years. A "bad trip" is an experience, whether drug-induced or naturally occurring, which is moving in the direction of being a psychosis but is still perceived as something that will end. Whether a "bad trip" will end or will turn into a psychosis depends in part on the benevolence of the surroundings, but much more on the continued presence in the body of the chemical substance which initiated the experience. People who "turn on" without drugs do not have "bad trips." They achieve altered states of consciousness with the aid of music, colored lights, meditation, deep breathing, and so forth, but are at liberty to interrupt or end the experience at any time, since the stimulus can be removed.

In addition to these differences in circumstances between the two states, there are many experiential differences. Some of these are listed below. We do not wish to imply by this that the two states are entirely comparable; even less, that they are at opposite ends of the same continuum. They can be seen as overlapping if one fails to take into account the length of time that the experience lasts and its place in the total life of the person involved. It is understandable that these states are often confused, since the "bad trip" lies between the psychedelic and the psychotic experiences. Confusion between these states can lead to someone on a "bad trip" being mistakenly hospitalized, when all that is required is the

---

* Those embarking on psychedelic voyages may make use of substances such as niacin to terminate the experience. They do not want interminable journeys.

guidance of a psychedelic adept. More tragic, even, is the fate of the psychotic individual whose anomalous experiences are seen as temporary, and who therefore is not promptly treated. We feel it is important to emphasize the differences between these states, in whatever dimensions they are observable.

PSYCHEDELIC EXPERIENCE	PSYCHOTIC EXPERIENCE
1. Time dimension Liberation from time. Expansion of time dimensions. Internal or external time may speed up, increasing possibility of quick and decisive action. Ability to modify past, present, future. The future is the realm of ambition and motivation.	Frozen in time: nothing will ever change. Shrinkage and collapse of time dimensions. Internal and external time may slow down, inhibiting action and creating despair. Inability to influence any of the temporal categories. The future is the realm of anxiety and danger.
2. Space dimension Expanded depth. Enhanced distance. Distance perception stable. Distances so vast that one feels liberated.	Reduced depth. Reduced distance. Distance perception highly variable. Distances so vast that one feels isolated and alienated.
3. Affect Feeling that everything is meaningful and exhilarating. Feelings of love, empathy, consideration, affection. Euphoria. Feeling of delight with oneself.	Feeling that everything contains hidden, threatening meanings. Feelings of isolation, fear, hatred, suspicion. Depression. Feeling of disgust with oneself.
4. Thought processes Thought changes are sought for, expected, valued. Seeing more possibilities that can be acted upon, which makes life exciting. Seeing beyond the usual categories. Seeing new connections which have always been possible. Ability to see things objectively. Ability to see things subjectively. Ability to explain thought changes.	Thought changes come unawares, are not welcome, are seen as accidental. Seeing so many possibilities that action is impossible. Seeing only fragments or parts of the usual categories. Seeing connections which are not possible. No objectivity, inability to disengage from total involvement. No subjectivity, estrangement from self. Desperate attempts (delusions) to explain thought changes.

PSYCHEDELIC EXPERIENCE	PSYCHOTIC EXPERIENCE
5. Perceptions	
Clear and distinct vision.	Blurred and distorted vision.
Augmentation of perception.	Diminution of perception.
Unusual perceptions seem to emanate from greater-than-human spirit or force.	Unusual perceptions seem to emanate from mechanical or sub-human forces.
Perceptual changes may be experienced as exhilarating, exciting, novel.	Perceptual changes may be experienced as frightening, threatening, dangerous.
6. Identity	
Feeling of unity with people and material objects.	Feeling of invasion by people and material objects.
Experience of the self.	Experience of the no-self, ego fragmentation.
Feeling of being at one with the world.	
	Feeling of being opposed to and in conflict with oneself and the world.
Feelings of humility and awe as one sees oneself as part of the universe.	Feelings of smallness and insignificance as one feels at the mercy of the universe.
Feelings of integrity and identity.	Loss of integrity and identity.
Pleasant, creative fantasies that one can control.	Nightmarish fantasies that one cannot control.
Feeling that one can join the company of other enlightened people.	Feeling that one is less and less human, more and more isolated.

Perhaps the best analogy from everyday life for these experiential states is the difference between good dreams, bad dreams, and nightmares. Dreams, whether good or bad, have always been of great interest, and much has been written about their interpretation. Far less interest has been shown in the interpretation of nightmares. When a person relates a nightmare, it is usually immediately after he has had it, when he wishes to be reassured that the nightmare is not real. People learn from both good dreams and bad dreams, but they seldom learn from nightmares. A good dream is one in which the symbols clearly manifest some aspect of the person's life or inner potentialities. A good dream is like a "good trip," a good psychedelic experience, or a naturally occurring experience of enlightenment. A bad dream is one which draws its symbols from the darker side of life; there may be feelings of sorrow, anger, fear or regret. But as with the good dream, the bad dream tells a meaningful story. It is like a chapter in a fairy story in which evil temporarily triumphs, but will eventually be overcome. A bad dream is like a "bad trip." Nightmares may or may not tell stories, but when they do the story only mounts in horror and never resolves itself. Most people have no desire to remember their nightmares, although they may wish to re-tell dreams years after they have had them. Nightmares are like psychotic states. People who have had psychotic illnesses do not usually want to talk about them or remember them; what they want most is just what the person wants who is coming out of a nightmare: to be told that the events in it did not really happen, that the "real" world is still there, and that it is over.

Another way to emphasize the difference between the psychedelic world and the psychotic world is to look at the accomplishments of both. The psychedelic world has provided new music, new fashions in clothing and the decorative arts, new vocabulary, new life-styles, and a new inter-generational dialogue. But not a single new art form has come out of the mental hospital. While individual schizophrenic patients may return to a creative life which they had before they became ill, or may, if they are very lucky, take up a new creative life when they leave the hospital, groups of schizophrenics cannot create any new style together, even in the small private psychiatric hospitals which house some of our most privileged young people. Even Dr. Laing's patients are not known to us for their contributions to music, poetry, or mysticism; we only know of them because Laing writes about them.

DISCUSSION

It is not surprising that *The Politics of Experience* appeals to bright young schizophrenics. Most of the possible roles open to them are of lower status than that enjoyed by normal people, and some roles, like the sick role, are of special status. But Laing has made a very bold move: he has offered them a status above that of normal people. They can hardly be expected to ignore this fine offer, especially when their daily lives are so miserable. Furthermore, Laing has cast his offer in a style that is very much in tune with the times. He is genuinely sympathetic with today's young people. His psychedelic model of schizophrenia is a timely one, and timeliness is a potent asset in a model. That is why we believe that his point of view must be scrutinized, in spite of its flaws and omissions.

Young schizophrenics are serious about Laing, and so we must be serious in examining his ideas. But how serious is Laing himself? This is a question which must be raised because he is a physician who uses the authority which derives from medicine to advocate a non-medical model. We wonder if Laing appreciates how much more serious he would seem if he gave up his medical identity.

Surely the young people who turn to Laing for help deserve to know what hat he is wearing, what role he offers them, what model he uses, what authority he speaks from. In this book, he offers three models which can be disentangled only with the greatest difficulty. None of them is the medical model, from which we believe he derives his authority. If Laing wishes to be a guru or a philosopher, there is no doubt a place for him, but young people who are suffering from schizophrenia may prefer to entrust themselves to a doctor who will treat their illness as best he can.

SUMMARY

In this paper, we have analyzed Laing's book, *The Politics of Experience,* using our method of constructing models. There appear to be three models of schizophrenia in this book, two which we have described before (psychoanalytic, conspiratorial) and one new one (psychedelic). We have discussed the shortcomings of each of these models, especially in relation to the medical model, which Laing does not describe, but which provides the source of his authority. We have also pointed out some of the differences between psychedelic and psychotic experiences, which we believe Laing has confused.

REFERENCES

BOWERS, MALCOLM B., and FREEDMAN, DANIEL X. (1966). 'Psychedelic experiences in acute psychosis.' *Arch. gen. Psychiat.,* 15, 240-8.

FOUCAULT, MICHAEL (1965). *Madness and Civilization.* Translated from the French by Richard Howard. New York: Random House, Inc.

GOFFMAN, ERVING (1961). 'On the characteristics of total institutions,' in *Asylums* (ed. Goffman). Garden City: Doubleday and Co., pp. 1-124; London: Pelican Books.

LAING, R. D. (1967). *The Politics of Experience.* London: Pelican Books; New York: Pantheon Books.

MANN, HARRIET, SIEGLER, MIRIAM, and OSMOND, HUMPHRY (1968). 'The many worlds of time.' *J. analyt. Psychol.,* 13, 33-56.

OSMOND, HUMPHRY, and HOFFER, ABRAM (1967). 'Schizophrenia and suicide.' *J. Schiz.,* 1, 54-64.

SIEGLER, MIRIAM, and OSMOND, HUMPHRY (1966). 'Models of madness.' *Brit. J. Psychiat.,* 112, 1193-203.

10

ON DOING RESEARCH IN SCHIZOPHRENIA

David Shakow

For many years I have been uncomfortably aware of the multitude of manifest and latent methodological problems facing the investigator who works with schizophrenics. One thing or another has, however, kept me from facing the facts straightforwardly and attempting, at least for myself, to delineate these as fully as I can. Knowing how often my colleagues and I have fallen short of achieving the "ideal" conditions we implicitly recognized as being needed, I am impressed with the desirability of making these conditions explicit. This explicitness would serve to keep the conditions constantly before one—at least clarifying the goal toward which to aspire.

But first permit me to indulge in a little self-analysis. In the course of this discussion, I expect to be shifting about in what may seem to be a somewhat harum-scarum fashion so that the points I make will probably appear to span the spectrum from the obscure to the obvious, the petty to the relatively important, the subjective to the objective. I trust you will bear with me in these apparent aberrancies. With so intricate a topic, a limited amount of such floundering is pardonable. And a further point: Sophisticated dynamicists, sensitive to possible symptoms of overdetermination, may also read into this "disorder" traces of rationalization. One must, of course, be assured that whatever overelaboration exists stems not from compulsivity, but rather from at least a moderate degree of clearsightedness—evidence of the ego's efforts to achieve stability. After

Submitted for publication Feb. 4, 1969.

From the National Institute of Mental Health, Public Health Service, US Department of Health, Education, and Welfare, Bethesda, Md.

Reprint requests to National Institute of Mental Health, Clinical Center, Bethesda, Md. 20014.

Reprinted, by permission of author and editor, from: *Archives of General Psychiatry*, 20: 618-642, 1969.

careful self-examination, I feel reasonably secure that what I shall present grows objectively out of actual experience and thinking about research with schizophrenics. I consider this essay a reflection of the wariness resulting from long experience with the difficulties encountered in actual research, the purpose of which is to serve as preparation for further research. I *do not* believe that it reflects the anticipatory anxieties which so often provide the dynamic base for avoiding potential research.

Carrying out research, even with normal human beings, is, as Gardner Murphy has said, "fiendishly complex." Research with disturbed human beings is even more so, particularly with those with whom it is difficult to communicate, among them schizophrenics. The marked range of schizophrenia, the marked variance within the range and within the individual, the variety of shapes that the psychosis takes, and both the expressive and compensatory behaviors that characterize it, all reflect this special complexity. Recent years have seen the complication further enhanced by the use of a great variety of therapeutic and other devices, such as drugs, that alter both the physiological and psychological nature of the organism. Research with schizophrenics, therefore, calls for awareness not only of the factors creating variance in normal human beings, but also of the many additional sources of variance this form of psychosis introduces.

The generalization that I am making about research with schizophrenics—that it differs quantitatively from ordinary behavioral research—is obvious. But the repeated differences in "degree" that I have found have, at times, lured me into entertaining the far-fetched notion that we may even be dealing with a difference that is more of the order of *quality* in the research relationship with the schizophrenic—a difference more akin to differences among species. Somebody has somewhere used the analogy of "Silly Putty" to illustrate the qualitative/quantitative paradox. Silly Putty can, when molded slowly, be worked into more or less the same kinds of shapes as ordinary putty. However, if Silly Putty is hit suddenly with a hammer, it shatters into myriad fragments. The minor quantitative difference from ordinary putty has now turned into qualitative one. Whether this kind of distinction really holds for schizophrenics will, of course, depend on the interpretations made of the differences found both in the nature of the problems encountered in investigative approaches and the results obtained from many studies. I do not really want to press this point, since it is still conjectural as far as I am concerned. I am just presenting the idea for its heuristic value, for what it may do to help maintain caution in dealing with schizophrenics. Tentatively, you might keep it in mind as we review the problems of doing research with schizophrenics.

The complexity I suggested would seem to call for investigators who know of the subtleties of the person they are working with; who, recognizing the many variables involved, are modest about the knowledge they achieve; who are as accurate as possible about making and reporting their observations; who check out these observations repeatedly for dependability; who have some appreciation of the meaning, as well as the factualness, of their observations; but who are still willing to stick their necks out. A tall order for all of us!

To put the problem succinctly, we may say that a consideration of the explicit and implicit factors involved in doing research in schizophrenia necessitates dealing successively with the full referents of each of the links of this deceptively simple chain of queries:

Why should *who* do *what* (*how, when* and *where*) to *whom*?

I shall suggest a few answers to each query in the chain.

GOALS OF RESEARCH (WHY?)

At first glance, the question "Why do research on schizophrenia?" seems to call for the obvious reply: "To understand the schizophrenic in order to heal or cure him (the choice of verbs depending on how ambitious one is!)." But even if we respond in this way we recognize that the answer carries much surplus meaning. We include in it not only the understanding of the schizophrenic as he is, but also the understanding of the *development* of conditions like his. We are, of course, interested in healing the present patient but, even more, in *preventing* schizophrenia, a goal which developmental knowledge, derived from studying many patients, will presumably help us to achieve.

In the broader context, however, we are counting on achieving much more. We are concerned with the implications of the knowledge gained from the study of schizophrenia for the understanding of the pathological process in general. Although we ordinarily use specific psychopathic symptomatology on a differential basis, we do it empirically, having no true understanding of either its generalized or "specificized" nature. We expect, however, that a deeper appreciation of the manifestations of pathology will emerge from systematic studies of schizophrenia, especially when these are done in comparative studies with other forms of disorder.

Perhaps the primary reason for studying schizophrenia is the faith that, by understanding this major pathological group, we will gain insights into the psychological and physiological process generally—normal as well as pathological. Indeed, for some of us working with this disorder, this is the major goal.

We must recognize, however, that this approach to the understanding of the normal through the abnormal is not a method generally accepted—particularly in psychology. As I have developed the argument in detail elsewhere (1), three factors may account for this neglect. The first is the psychologist's dual identity as human being and scientist. The second arises from a predilection for scientific purism—an attitude to which a field in the process of establishing itself as a science is particularly prone. Those in the field are likely to insist on a rigid and clear definition of its scope. A third factor, closely allied with purity, stems from an abhorrence for anything which smacks of the "applied." For persons with such abhorrence abnormal psychology appears by very definition to carry such implications.

We have therefore had to rely on paradigm-breakers and leaders in psychology such as Darwin, Galton, William James, Freud, and Goldstein to stress the importance of the abnormal for the understanding of the normal. Recently, Paul Weiss (2) has been an important trailblazer. Judging from today's broadening trends, the prospects for rapprochement are encouraging. Barriers between traditionally distinct areas are crumbling and hitherto alien territory is being explored. Sociologists and anthropologists on the one hand, biochemists and neurophysiologists on the other, have become interested in psychology, and psychologists, in turn, have been drawn to sociology, anthropology, biochemistry, and physiology. Psychiatrists have concerned themselves with normal process (both individual and group), and psychologists, with abnormal process. The special backgrounds and approaches that these disciplines bring to extend their own customary pursuits can result in nothing but gain for behavioral science as a whole.

INVESTIGATORS (WHO?)

We might begin defining the "natural" researchers in schizophrenia by making the obvious point that, given the marked shortage of competent investigators in all fields, the more investigators one can attract to this area the better. (I shall leave the question of who is "competent" to carry out such research for subsequent discussion.) Let us consider the individual investigators and disciplines involved.

Since schizophrenia research is so complex, it generally calls for attack by a group of investigators. The group approach to research may involve either persons from one discipline or persons representing several disciplines. Obviously the problems besetting the cooperation of individuals in a common enterprise in a single-discipline group are involved in the multidisciplined group as well. However, group enterprises of persons representing a variety of disciplines present special problems over and above those raised by undisciplined groups, and these call for special discussion. Luszki (3) considered many of these issues in detail, but I wish to stress a few additional aspects.

Aside from the fields professionally interested in the clinical aspects of schizophrenia, the research disciplines involved range from the physical-chemical sciences, through the behavioral, to the social sciences. Anybody acquainted with schizophrenia recognizes the breadth of possible relationships and the relevance of such an extensive attack.

The preferable research approach should be a cooperative one by members of various disciplines. Multidisciplined research has acquired a bad name in some quarters, and not unjustifiably, because it has suffered acutely from bandwagon tendencies. Frankfurter noted that the danger in a cross-disciplined activity is of "cross-sterilization" rather than cross-fertilization. As in so many human endeavors, because of our natural endowment for habituating, form gradually takes precedence over substance. In this context the mere establishment of a multidisciplinary activity is assumed at least to half-solve the problem. I trust that such naivete will not intrude on this discussion. If one is convinced, as I am, of the multifaceted nature of the problem of schizophrenia, only a multidisciplined attack appears feasible. (I say this without denying the value of the substantial achievements of independent researchers.)

A multidisciplined approach may, of course, be employed simultaneously on separate groups of subjects in unrelated (or at most, periodically compared) studies, whether in different parts of the globe or in the same institution. Here we are interested in multidisciplined research done not only under "one roof," but involving some communication during the various stages. Such research is essentially either (1) concurrent, (2) coordinated, or (3) integrated.

Concurrent research studies are those carried out by several disciplines on the same group of subjects, but in which no discipline has particular regard for the nature of the others' studies. No common theorizing occurs. The main concern is not to interfere with each other in scheduling the subjects. At most a modicum of communication may occur at joint meetings of the involved groups for presentation of independently arrived-at results.

In *coordinated* research there are more common concerns. The order in which separate studies are conducted is one concern. Consultations to arrange scheduling of patients may be held to minimize the stresses from one experimental area which may carry over to another. While no interchange of theoretical thinking is involved, exchanges of technical assistance or data among disciplines frequently occur. Occasionally, too, after individual studies are completed, efforts may be made to correlate findings among the different areas. As a consequence of this kind of multidisciplined activity, joint conferences for presentation of results are more likely to take place than with concurrent research.

Finally, there is the *integrated* type of study, the kind which may be viewed as truly interdisciplinary. Here the disciplines involved meet in advance to present their respective theoretical positions and hypotheses in order to organize their studies jointly. Such planning may facilitate mutually beneficial arrangements, such as conducting studies simultaneously to test hypotheses that have implications for two or more disciplines. If nothing else transpires, the disciplines may at least provide technical data for each other. In the main, however, they constantly scrutinize their hypotheses not only in the context of their own fields, but also in that of hypotheses from other fields which have interdisciplinary implications.

It follows naturally from what has been said that the recruitment of bidisciplined investigators—investigators who are expert in several areas—would be a great boon. But, since the stock of this highly desirable subgroup is likely to remain small, our discussion will focus on groups comprising varied, unidisciplinary persons.

The investigator must, of course, be competent and sufficiently experienced in his field. When several investigators from one discipline are participating, it is beneficial if they represent different theoretical outlooks. General experience with schizophrenia is of help in comprehending the dimensions of the disease and its many accessory problems, and familiarity with the particular patient population under investigation is also important. It is not unreasonable to question seriously the effectiveness of any aspect of a study carried on without regard for the specific patients involved. The effect on patients may conceivably be overlooked in biochemical studies, but decidedly not in those of a behavioral or social nature.

Besides these more general qualifications, in certain studies the investigator's personality traits, sex, and personal adjustment need attention as well, because of the possible influence of these factors on results.

WHAT?

Since it is not my intention here to propose a specific program of research on schizophrenia, but rather to consider in detail the *problems* of doing such research, I shall be brief in dealing with this question. I might point out that in some respects I have already dealt with an aspect of the *what* question in my attempt to answer the question of *who*. In the end, the problem boils down to the usual one faced by an investigator in any field: How does he discriminate between the essentially trivial and the significant questions? What are the most fruitful approaches to deal with the latter?

HOW?

Each link in the chain of queries which I have considered thus far is, of course, important. But the "How?" has perhaps the most relevance for research with schizophrenics since this group so markedly magnifies the already numerous difficulties inherent in ordinary, biopsychosocial research. Such difficulties appear mainly to fall under the *how* rubric.

In recent years questions on conditions under which research is carried out (mainly centering on what I am here designating as the "how") have gained great prominence. This is reflected particularly in the studies of Robert Rosenthal (4), and to some extent in the difficulties pointed out by other authors, such as Argyris (5). The emphasis is, on the whole, directed at the experimenter as source of error. (As you will see my own approach is somewhat more comprehensive. I see "ghosts" everywhere— in the subject and the setting as well as the experimenter!) Problems of this kind have, of course, been a constant source of concern to psychologists almost from the beginnings of psychology. My own serious involvement with these issues began in 1925-1926 as a member of Boring's seminar "On the Nature of Control in the Psychological Experiment." What I learned from that seminar and from my graduate program generally has stood me in good stead in my subsequent work with schizophrenics.

Like schizophrenia itself, the problem of *how* one approaches the schizophrenic in research is multifaceted. Four broad categories must be considered: (1) the *general* background with which the *investigator* approaches the study, (2) the *general* background with which the *subject* comes to the study, (3) the nature of the *specific* stimulus situation the *investigator* sets up, (4) the manner in which the *subject* responds to the *specific* stimulus situation.

In considering these four major headings, I shall present their details under ten subheadings.

A. GENERAL BACKGROUND FOR INVESTIGATOR'S APPROACH

1. *Investigator's General Approach—Time Scale.*—The first decision for an investigator to make relates to the broad organization of his study

in time. Is it to be a *cross-sectional* study (or several cross-sectional studies within a short period) or is it to extend over a considerable period—be *longitudinal* in character? Each approach obviously contributes significantly since each provides answers to different questions. My own experience has been that, for studies in schizophrenia (and in other fields), these general approaches tend to have their own natural, historical progression.

The investigator ordinarily begins with *cross-sectional group* studies intended to determine mean group levels of properly selected subjects on a variety of functions, for comparison with means from other selected groups. *Cross-sectional individual* studies on similar functions follow. Such studies enable one to establish individual profiles, from which *cross-sectional type* studies may devolve. The investigator can then go on to the development of the next stage, the *longitudinal individual* studies. Here he carries out repeated studies of the same person over time, studies which permit him to make predictions about that person. The final step in the process is the establishment of *longitudinal types* on the basis of the studies of persons representing a variety of conditions. Such generalized types permit predictions which go beyond the actuarial ones, the only kinds that can be derived from cross-sectional studies.

2. *Investigator's Methods of Approach.*—Having determined the nature of his general approach to the problem, the investigator can proceed to choose his particular *method* of approach. By method I mean the various ways one can go about describing the schizophrenic and his functioning. These range from a simplistic narrative recording of his behavior and feelings to rigorous control of variables. Each method in this range has its proper place in schizophrenia research, the choice of the most appropriate one depending on its relevance and the amount of control possible. The choice is frequently determined not only by the nature of the questions asked, but also by the investigator's discipline.

Four major methods may, for our purposes, be labelled naturalistic, seminaturalistic, free-laboratory, and controlled-laboratory.

(a) THE NATURALISTIC: In this approach the subject is studied where he happens to be—ordinarily on the hospital ward. Such situations obviously provide a wide range of stimuli and responses, for in such field settings no restrictions are placed on the subject's spontaneous responses to the stimuli—internal or external—he elects to respond to. The observer, himself, is *the* instrument. He records the patient's behavior as completely and accurately as he can subjectively, with little or no aid from instrumental controls.

(b) THE SEMINATURALISTIC: In this approach the stimuli are varied and the subject has practically unlimited freedom of response within the situation. His responses may be partial or total, depending on the goal of the study. A laboratory setting may frequently be used in seminaturalistic studies, but this is not essential. It may be a "natural habitat" set up under special conditions. The observations are usually selective, e.g., time samples. Controls are almost entirely of an observational nature (supported frequently by subsequent statistical analysis). For our present purposes, the clinical observational and interview approach ordinarily used by the psychiatrist may be included in this category. These techniques may be accepted as a variant of the seminaturalistic, although in some respects they also fall into the first category—the naturalistic. A study of susceptibility to environmental stimulation, where a wide range of stimuli are available to the subject under conditions where he is permitted to respond as selectively and freely as he wishes, is perhaps a more appropriate example. Projective tests belong with this approach.

(c) THE FREE-LABORATORY: Here the setting is more limited than with the previous approach, but the stimuli still remain varied. Responses may be total or only partially limited in the degree of freedom. The subjects may be permitted at least a choice among several alternatives. The study is invariably carried out in a laboratory setting, but actually falls between the seminaturalistic and the most rigorously controlled laboratory situation. The Luria conflict experiment, where the subjects respond to word stimuli while simultaneous recordings of several voluntary and physiological measures of emotion are made, exemplifies this approach. Most objective tests and questionnaires would be included in this category.

(d) THE CONTROLLED-LABORATORY: This approach calls for a fixed stimulus situation, generally segmental responses, with limited degrees of freedom available to the subject. The controls in these settings are likely, in large part, to be instrumental. Studies of reaction time and patellar tendon reflex latent time are behavioral examples of this group. Physiological and biochemical studies would ordinarily also fall into this group.

These methods of approach, of course, shade into each other, and for this reason the categories cannot be considered rigid. I have found it useful, however, to maintain these rough distinctions.

3. *Investigator's Modes of Approach.*—We must recognize, however, that built into the context just considered are underlying attitudes, goals, and predilections—which I call *modes*—that provide the framework for the investigator's approaches to the problems under study. The investigator needs not only to be aware of this apperceptive background, but also to understand the part it may play in the execution of specific studies.

Not infrequently we adopt postures based on these modes without being fully aware of how they determine our perspectives on a problem.

These modes can best be characterized in terms of dichotomies—either contrasting extremes of continuous distributions, or the bimodal, discontinuous, separated extremes of a parameter. The contrasting meanings in each pair of terms help to illuminate the nature of the particular parameter involved. A survey of these modes should help us in two ways: to recognize the complexities of the problems introduced, and to understand the variations interjected not only by the predilections of individual investigators, but also by the special affinities of their parent disciplines for particular modes of approach.

The first of these parameters may be designated the *descriptive-theoretical*. Since it ordinarily reflects a continuum which always involves some amount of description, the parameter might more accurately be labelled *descriptive atheoretical—descriptive theoretical*. The descriptions may range from those with no theoretical underpinning, consisting essentially of scavenged, desultory bits of observation (à la Magendie (6)), to descriptions which are systematically recorded in the context of well-formulated hypotheses or even a specific theory.

One aspect of the theoretical side of this parameter may be subsumed under a subparameter, *multisimple vs. single recondite*. The problem faced by the investigator is whether to approach the phenomena to be studied with a group of varied, relatively simple hypotheses, any of which can be displaced without affecting the others, or to try to subsume them under a highly complex single hypothesis (7-9).

The *direct-inferential* parameter also involves a continuum. The problem here is to decide whether to emphasize approaches that deal with direct description of the phenomena or with inferences of different degrees of remoteness. We indicate awareness of this parameter by use of such terms as "first-order inference" or "second-order inference." In psychiatry the extremes of this parameter are perhaps most commonly represented in the kraepelinian direct descriptive and the freudian dynamic interpretative approaches.

The *technique-subject* parameter indicates whether technique or subject is primary in the study. Is the investigation to be built around a particular technique which studies various kinds of subjects, or are the subjects to be made the central focus, to be studied by whatever techniques promise to provide the best answers to the questions being asked?

Closely related to the technique-subject parameter is the parameter for *method* or *problem*. In one aspect, the method ordinarily dictates the problem; in the other, the problem dictates the method.

The *qualitative-quantitative* parameter carries important consequences for the researcher. He has to consider whether he should yield to the usual pressures of science to put things in numbers—to bring "the mind within the compass of natural science," as Adrian has put it—or to emphasize instead, the qualitative approach. The investigator is usually aware of the fact that any particular study has to compromise between some level of precision and some degree of meaningfulness. At the extremes, he may even be faced with choosing between a high degree of exactness about the insignificant and meaningless profundities about the significant. In the behavioral sciences especially, the seasoned researcher recognizes that the degree of quantification attainable correlates roughly with both the stage of progress of his field of study and the level of development his method has achieved, and that premature overquantification can ultimately be a handicap rather than a help. The investigator is often judged as to his wisdom by how adequately he solves this problem.

The parameter we may designate as the *molecular-molar* or the *segmental-holistic*, also falls along a continuum. In general, the choice is discipline-associated. Ordinarily biochemistry and physiology seem to favor the molecular approach, while social psychology and sociology predominantly employ the molar. Witness, however, the type of holistic approach so strongly exemplified by the general physiologist, W. J. Crozier (10), who chose to work with total organisms in defined, controlled environments, rather than with the segmental preparations customarily used in physiology. Each approach is appropriate, of course, in its own setting.

A related parameter, that of *isolated study vs. systematic design,* deals with the total context of the experiment: whether isolated individual factors or interacting factors are to be placed simultaneously under study. If the former, single comparisons are possible; if the latter, a 2×2, 4×4 or even more elaborate design may be used, depending on the number of variables that can legitimately be studied simultaneously. These are obviously fewer in the biopsychosocial sphere than in the physicochemical. Here again, each kind of study has its appropriate setting.

With the *phenotypic-genotypic* parameter the investigator must determine whether he is primarily interested in end-results or in the factors that produce them. If he chooses a study concerned with effects, with surface phenomena that possibly arise from different origins, the problem he deals with is usually of a statistical or actuarial kind. A study of hostility, as evidenced in certain easily observed behaviors, for example, would be a phenotypic problem. More cryptic studies, such as that of the complex of factors that produces such effects, which themselves may vary widely, or of the underlying, dynamic explanation of the behavior, such as frustration, are genotypic problems.

Among the modes of approach one may also have to decide which aspect of the *nomothetic-ideographic* parameter to use. Choice of the former means an emphasis on laws generalized across persons, that is, laws applicable to a whole class of subjects. The latter deals with laws which refer only to particular individuals. The profitableness of employing each approach in its appropriate context, especially in schizophrenia, is obvious.

In choosing between the naturalistic and experimental methods (discussed previously in this section) we have in one sense also decided in a general way the related problem posed by the *contrived-spontaneous* parameter. The specific question faced here is whether to study a subject when he is found spontaneously to be in a special state—such as under a naturally occurring stress—or do we, as investigators, arrange situations which place him under such stress. Important ethical problems, such as the legitimacy of creating a sense of failure in the subject or of placing him in disturbingly stressful situations, are often integral to the choice of the contrived mode. "Spontaneous" situations may, of course, occur but are likely to arise so rarely that certain studies may not be possible unless conditions are deliberately manipulated.

Such are some of the underlying "biases" that determine the choices we make in approaching subjects. Hopefully, we make them with full awareness, so that the organization of our experiments will be appropriate to the questions we seek to answer.

B. BACKGROUND OF SUBJECT

4. *Factors in Subject.*—Having considered the methodological aspects of the general approach adopted by the *experimenter* in the context of his own pertinent apperceptive background, we now turn to what the subject brings to the experimental situation. We will then be able to evaluate the nature of the stimulus-response situation that develops against the respective backgrounds.

For one, the subject obviously brings to the experimental situation his patient status—he is not "normal," he is psychotic, the reason he was selected for study.

But, in addition to everything that this state implies, he is "modified" in other, more transient, respects as well, respects which may serve to alter the nature of his performance in the study.

ON DOING RESEARCH IN SCHIZOPHRENIA   201

These modifications may be the result of a great variety of causes: short-term or long-continuing drug administration or treatment, long-time hospitalization, one or more of a variety of specific psychosocial influences, ranging from brief visits by a family member, week-end visits home, temporary personal, interpersonal, or situational events on the ward, or long-term psychosocial therapy. If the investigator is to evaluate the subject's responses in a particular study, he must strive to become cognizant of these extra-experimental factors and attempt to assess their possible influence. At the very least, the description of the conditions of the study should include these potential modifiers. Indeed, these modifiers may be so important that, on occasion, special experiments may have to be conducted to measure their role more adequately.

C. CONDITIONS OF STIMULATIONS SET UP BY THE INVESTIGATOR

When the subject comes to an experimental situation the experimenter enters into a most difficult and subtle area affecting investigation in schizophrenia—the *relationship between schizophrenic and researcher.* To that general law of Murphy which has served researchers in all fields of science so effectively over the years, the investigator in schizophrenia must add its corollary: "The experimenter proposes, the schizophrenic disposes!" Unfortunately, these two persons frequently do not have the same goals in mind. Here occur all the explicit and implicit problems of what in psychology are called "instructions." It is an area where the importance of microscopic, latent, implied, accidental, and transient aspects is likely to play significant roles—roles frequently more substantial than those one is apt to accept automatically as the "verities" of personal intercourse: macroscopic, explicit, directed, and relatively permanent aspects.

Four major areas relating to the conditions of stimulation set up by the experimenter are involved: the *general* conditions of stimulation, the *specific* context of the particular stimuli, the *nature* of the stimuli themselves, and the *instructions* given to the subject.

5. *General Conditions—Levels of Stimulation/Contexts of Rest Set Up by Experimenter.*—The general conditions of stimulation involve a range of "levels," each ensconced in its associated context of one or another kind of preceding rest. The levels themselves are of six classes: (1) impersonal stimulation, (2) impersonal stimulation under stress, (3) impersonal affective stimulation, (4) impersonal affective stimulation under stress, (5) personal affective stimulation, (6) personal affective stimulation under stress. Each level occurs against a preceding experimental context of one of four states of "rest": (a) sensory deprivation, (b) basal

resting, (c) nonbasal resting, and (d) nonresting. Whichever level is involved, it ordinarily begins while the subject remains, for varying durations, in one of the four baseline "rest" states. For the last three, a natural gradual adaptational change in the character of the level occurs with time. Sensory deprivation, however, is a peculiar "rest" state such that, by definition, it cannot be invaded except in a most limited manner without its being destroyed.

As nearly as I can tell, these six classes and four levels of rest include the various kinds of situations dealt with in all the relevant disciplines— from biochemistry at one extreme to sociology at the other. These classes, of course, describe only baseline situations which may be subjected to further complications by many kinds of experimental modifiers, such as knowledge of the experiment and warning. I shall consider these shortly.

Each "rest" category and each class of stimulus level is described as follows:

(a) *Sensory deprivation* is a condition devoid of all experimenter-directed stimulation. In addition, the experimenter attempts deliberately to reduce the usual undirected background stimulation as much as he possibly can below the usual input level to create a situation where the input would inevitably come from within the subject. (b) In the *basal resting* condition a substantial period of physiological and psychological rest (defined as the minimization of both directed and undirected [casual] stimulation, although some external and internal undirected stimulation is unavoidable), which includes at least 12 hours of food abstinence, precedes the study. (c) Although food intake is not limited in the *nonbasal resting* condition, a substantial, carefully controlled rest period (of at least 30 minutes' duration) precedes the study. (d) In the *non-resting* condition, the subject is placed in the experimental situation almost immediately on reaching the experimental room, without any deliberately set preparatory rest period, except that unavoidably associated with the giving of instructions.

Whereas these four general situational settings emphasize the preparatory experimental background for rest (or nonrest) immediately preceding a study, the next six deal with the specific stimulus settings provided by the experimenter to elicit responses from the subject. (1) With *impersonal stimulation* the experimenter directs neutral stimuli at the subject. (2) With *impersonal stimulation under stress*, experimenter-directed neutral stimuli are presented under stress conditions (such as sudden loud noises) originating in the environment, stress situations which are obviously not the responsibility of the subject. (3) In the *impersonal affective stimulation* setting, the experimenter directs impersonal, emotional stimuli (such as affectively toned situations that are actually frightening, or their symbolic equivalents in the form of words like "fight" or "disgust") at the subject. (4) With *impersonal affective stimulation under stress,* the experimenter directs impersonal, emotional stimuli such as the above at the subject in a deliberately created stress context, such as startle. (5) In the *personal affective stimulation* situation, the experimenter directs personal, emotional stimuli (such as names of family members or rehearsals of traumatic incidents from childhood) at the subject. (6) With *personal affective stimulation under stress,* the experimenter directs personal, emotional stimuli, with the personal references emphasized (e.g., pointing up the subject's responsibility or blame), thus presumably creating a stress situation for the subject.

6. *Specific Conditions Set Up by Experimenter—Context of Stimuli.*— Aside from the "rest" background against which the experimenter chooses a level of stimulation for the subject, another important characteristic of the stimulus conditions is the *specific* context in which the actual stimuli are presented. I have in mind such contextual modifiers as experimental rest, knowledge about the experiment, warnings of coming stimulation, concurrent stimulation, frequency of stimulation, and the actual physical surroundings in which the stimulation occurs.

These pure manipulations of the experiment are, of course, "available" to the experimenter since he is the one responsible for introducing them. (The use of quotes around "available" is intentional, to convey my doubt as to whether experimenters are always aware of having introduced these factors, or, at least, of the part they may play in the subject's responses. Since even psychologists, who are constantly confronting such problems in their studies, frequently ignore them, we must be more tolerant of such oversights by researchers from other disciplines.)

Unless an experiment is deliberately designed to be of a continuous (nonstop) type, stimuli are usually presented in the context of intervening *rest* periods. Actually, the paradigm of the response process itself may be said to consist of a repetitive succession of "stimulus-response-rest-preparation for the next stimulus"—"stimulus-response-rest-etc.," sequences. Such interpolated rest periods—perhaps seen at their simplest in refractory phase—appear to be an important (probably essential) part of the ordinary stimulus-response processes that constitute the ordinary regime of living. In the experimental situation, if they are not provided by the experimenter as part of the procedure, the subject himself is likely to work them into the response process, whether openly, surreptitiously, or unawaredly. A basic organic need for such intervals of rest seems to be involved. The nature of these periods, their length, distribution in relation to the stimuli, and similar characteristics are all significant aspects of the total stimulus-response process.

Another contextual variable is *knowledge* of the nature and purpose of the experiment. On rare occasions such information is provided "fully" to the subject by the experimenter. Frequently it is done only in part, and sometimes not at all. (Occasionally even erroneous information may be provided, either implicitly or explicitly, to attain certain experimental ends. Such experimental manipulation is ordinarily revealed to the subject post-experimentally.) Even when the purpose of the experiment is not imparted intentionally by the experimenter, the subject may attain some degree of knowledge during the experiment. This knowledge is sometimes correct, at other times incorrect. And on occasion, the subject may ascribe a radically different purpose to the experiment, even when the experimenter has described it accurately to him. Whatever the case, the experimenter must recognize that different degrees of knowledge, lack of knowledge, or assumed knowledge may have varying effects on the results—from no effect at all to a considerable effect. The fanciful interpretations of an experiment's purpose conjured up by some schizophrenics may at times be responsible for very strange results.

Another aspect of experimental context, *warning* of an approaching stimulus, may also be important in determining results. Sometimes preparatory warning is given by the experimenter at the beginning of the experiment and sometimes before presentation of a group of stimuli or before each stimulus. The importance both of keeping conditions constant across subjects and of providing warnings at points appropriate for the purposes of the study needs to be emphasized.

The particular physical *surroundings* in which the stimulation takes place is another contextual variable. Experiments have shown that such specific environmental characteristics as the nature of the experimental room, the personality and sex of the experimenter, and similar variables may affect the results considerably.

A final contextual variable to which I should like to call attention is *concurrent stimulation*. This variable is at times experimenter-determined but usually arises unintentionally. I am, of course, not referring here to studies in disparate attention where the experimenter deliberately provides competing focal or focal/peripheral stimuli to determine the effects of dividing attention. I am concerned, rather, with the accidental, unintended stimuli originating in the environment, the extraexperimental stimuli provided by the subject himself, or on occasion, even if unwittingly, by the experimenter. All of these may have similar disturbing effects on the findings.

In dealing with schizophrenics, we must not forget the range of stimuli deriving from the intrinsic "pathology" of the subject, revealed most strikingly in his illusions, hallucinations, and delusions, states which may at times distort the experimental situation. (It is surprising, however, how far one can carry out dependable studies with very disturbed schizophrenics suffering markedly from such symptoms.) For the present our concern is with the more "normal" distortions of the experimental situation presented to the subject: reversals of figure and ground, making affective elements neutral, or the reverse, the exaggeration of extraneous stimuli, and the numerous other modifications that can be introduced, or that introduce themselves, into any situation. Such accessory stimulation may affect the outcome and therefore requires the investigator to exercise the greatest caution in analyzing the experimental situation, meticulously describing the procedure and judiciously evaluating the results.

7. *Stimuli Themselves.*—We now turn from the context of the stimulation to the intrinsic nature of the stimuli provided by the experimenter. It is important, especially when dealing with schizophrenics, to examine the stimuli carefully and microscopically, because what appear to us as simple "stimuli," to be taken at face value, can turn out to be highly complicated situations for such subjects. James once indicated (11) that the ordinary person has a great gift for coming to the point, for selecting the essential and disregarding the complex of concurrent stimulation that almost invariably surrounds it. In terms I have used previously, we would say that the average person distinguishes readily between figure and ground, between relevant and irrelevant content; he reacts to the former and neglects the latter. The schizophrenic frequently does not do this. It becomes necessary for us, then, through analysis of the nature of the various parameters of the stimulus, to become aware of the variety of ways in which the schizophrenic can go astray.

STIMULUS CHARACTERISTICS: Quality, intensity, and frequency are the three attributes that characterize the stimulus. The major *qualities* of the stimulus appear to fall into seven classes: how *focal or peripheral* it is; how *brief or extended* (duration) ; how *simple or complex;* how *discrete or continuous;* how *novel or old;* how *repetitive or varied;* and how *ambiguous or defined.* The experimenter must consciously and clearly structure the stimuli in these respects before presenting them to the subject. How the subject then structures the stimulus for himself is, of course, the crux of the problem.

The stimulus may also vary in *intensity*—its quantity—ranging from extreme mildness to marked strength. Variations in intensity may result in unusual and differential effects on the schizophrenic.

Finally, the stimulus may vary considerably in the *frequency* with which it is presented to the subject. By this attribute I do not mean the repetitive, as opposed to varied, succession of stimuli considered earlier (on pattern of stimulation), but, rather, the frequency with which either a specific stimulus or a pattern of varied stimuli is presented within a shorter or longer time.

8. *Instructions of the Investigator to the Subject.*—The response the experimenter calls for from the subject may be to do nothing, to provide a specific response, to react to a choice among several presented possibilities, or, in a fairly free situation, to leave it for the subject to determine on his own. It may be immediate or delayed, manual or verbal, simple or complex, requiring much or little effort. These instructions may vary in range of both explicitness and implicitness. All of these differential qualities are important for judging the adequacy of the response the schizophrenic subject actually makes.

D. RESPONSE PROCESS OF SUBJECT

The stimulus factors, the conditions set up by the experimenter, represent merely the front part of the stimulus-response paradigm. We still have to deal with the response portion, which, for our purposes, also includes the central process directly following stimulation and preceding the actual response. Two major factors are involved in the response process: the subject's perception of the specific task set for him by the experimenter, and his attitude toward the general experimental setting.

9. *Response of Subject—Reception of Instructions.*—When a stimulus situation is clearly set, we ordinarily assume that the normal subject's perception will be veridical and his response appropriate—in line with his own intention. In *aussage* (testimony) experiments, we realize that the subject may have perceived falsely (because of the deliberately introduced confusing and affective context), but expect his response, nevertheless, to remain congruous with the false perception and still in line with his own intention. The schizophrenic, however, may not only perceive falsely, but also respond inappropriately even to these erroneous perceptions. He may give responses not congruent with his actual perception, and even perhaps not in line with his own intention. What makes interpretation in specific instances with the schizophrenic so difficult is that his response may fall into any one of the categories of the perception/response complex: the perception may be veridical and the

response appropriate; the perception veridical, the response inappropriate; the perception false, the response appropriate; or the perception false, the response inappropriate.

James once deplored the fact that "it is the bane of psychology to suppose that where results are similar, processes must be the same" (12). To this we may add that it is equally specious for psychology (and other fields) to suppose that where situations appear similar to the experimenter they also appear similar to the subject. Since this is not so, the experimenter must scrupulously check both the accuracy of the subject's perception and the appropriateness of his response or report. He must not depend on his own suppositions.

In the process of forming his perception, the subject may substitute "self-instructions" for the instructions of the investigator, involving modifications that may be voluntary or involuntary, conscious or unconscious. These are capable of shifting the patient's response from one level of stimulation to another, without either experimenter or subject being aware of the change. These self-instructions may even be opposite to those of the investigator. In all studies—psychological, physiological, or even biochemical—instructions are given to the subject, usually explicitly, occasionally implicitly, to do, or not to do, something. The directive may be to lie still while a measurement is made or a reading taken, as in blood pressure, or it may be no more than the simple request to breathe in and out of a calorimeter. But if the subject instructs himself (involuntarily, of course!), while doing such breathing, to cast surreptitious glances at the disarray in the skirts of the metabolic technician (the actual basis for a discrepancy in some of our Worcester results), the likelihood of getting the "basal" reading sought is not great. Consider the multitude of similar incidents that can occur within the complex interactions of the ordinary experimental, to say nothing of the ordinary clinical, situation.

The peculiar nature of the schizophrenic (13, 14) makes him especially vulnerable to all varieties of stimulation. He is likely to make what is a simple, neutral situation for the normal person, into a highly stressful one for himself, or the reverse. In psychological studies this problem is met constantly. The schizophrenic may, for instance, not be "in" the experimental field at all (he may be either preoccupied or distracted); he may misinterpret the instructions (since communication is especially difficult with schizophrenics); or he may react with an idiosyncrasy that yields incongruous results. One of our patients refused to comply with the request of an examiner to repeat "digits backwards" on the Stanford-Binet, because "it wasn't right to do things backwards." Had he not disclosed the rigorous ethical principles which guided him and had he instead chosen to answer incorrectly, we would have been impressed by the "typical" high scatter some have held to be characteristic of schizophrenics!

10. *Response of Subject—Cooperation.*—In addition to his specific reactions to the investigator's instructions, the subject may manifest various degrees of compliance, depending on his spontaneous attitude toward the general setting. This attitude is labeled *cooperation.* It may range from active opposition, through various degrees of indifference, to active participation. The factors determining the patient's particular state are manifold: they arise from a combination of the motivating factors aroused by the immediate situation (which includes the particular study, the experimenter, the setting), but even more, from interfering factors, internal and external, which determine the subject's initial and continuing general receptivity. In the broadest sense, it reflects the subject's comparative receptivity to what is relevant and irrelevant in the environment.

The essence of the problem of cooperation in the schizophrenic is not fundamentally different from that in the normal subject. Dissimilarity arises from the considerably greater likelihood of obtaining poor cooperation from the schizophrenic, together with the lesser likelihood of knowing when such a state exists, because of the impaired communication between subject and experimenter. If for any reason the normal subject does not maintain the proper attitude, he is much more likely to reveal this fact to the experimenter. We frequently find in the schizophrenic not the unwillingness, but, rather, the inability to cooperate. This impediment stems mainly from his difficulty in separating the relevant from the irrelevant, especially when the latter comes from an internal source.

Although situations may exist where poor cooperation does not have any effect on the results, such instances are probably rare. This is true even for physiological studies, as Dunbar (15) has pointed out in her survey. The possible effects of active resistance are clear, the influence of indifferent response less so. The evidence presented by Dunbar indicates that, not only psychological, but practically all organic clinical and physiological studies, must take the attitude of the subject into account.

Although the validity of results obtained in any experimental situation or test is determined by the inextricably intertwined interrelationship of the condition of the subject and his attitude toward the tasks, the experimenter, and the general situation, it is important for anyone carrying through a study, to attempt to separate these factors and try to distinguish their relative importance for their effect on the results.

THE SCHIZOPHRENIC AS HUMAN BEING

The emphasis throughout this section on the *how* has centered so completely on the schizophrenic as "subject" that I hasten to add a corrective comment. I am afraid that I may have left the impression of having treated him too passively—in the extreme view, even as something to manipulate. I may appear to have lost sight of that major underlying principle of good research with persons—that of considering them as "human beings." (Laing (16) follows a long tradition of those who have been especially sensitive in this respect.) The brevity of this section does not accurately reflect my evaluation of the importance of the topic. Its obviousness, once mentioned, should sufficiently explain my succinctness.

In some ways I have already implied how significant I deem this issue to be. My detailed discussion of the psychological subtleties of the stimulus/response situation has revealed the importance I assign to the treatment of the schizophrenic as an *individual*. His ability to influence results, directly and indirectly, indicates how a disregard for personal characteristics may vitiate scientific findings.

Such considerations are, of course, fundamental; but here I am saying more. Schizophrenics are such special creatures that they require far more sensitive attention than does the normal person. Even in their most aggressive, reactive states, schizophrenics are in many ways much like timorous rabbits. The unpredictable quality of their behavior and affect appears to stem from an almost continuous state of anxiety and fright. It may be to freeze or flee, to dart suddenly here or dash suddenly there, overtly or covertly. When at all possible, one must be prepared to help them, at least to some extent, in circumventing such inconstancies in the nature of their response.

Schizophrenics cannot be pushed around: their prerogatives as persons have to be fully recognized and their qualities as human beings given special respect. "Control," in the sense of manipulation, has to be reduced to the minimum if one hopes to reduce their anxiety. Insofar as possible, they should be made partners in the study process, with the explicit and implicit superior-subordinate relationships that typify research projects made minimal. In short, the fundamental spirit inherent in therapy— what is called the "therapeutic attitude"—seems appropriate as well in research studies.

Throughout my own research career, I have been impressed by how experience, suitable personality, and fundamental liking for the patient, reflected in the behavior of persons dealing directly with schizophrenics, play a strongly positive role in promoting participation in studies. In similar situations I have found researchers without such qualities to be unsuccessful.

Further complicating this central, highly sensitive, area is the gamut of important related problems associated with doing research with human subjects, such as consent, violation of personality, and invasion of privacy. The fact that these are currently the subject of much controversy in both biomedical and behavioral research highlights the need for clarification of the issues underlying them.

WHEN?

Having dealt at such length with the "How?," I turn briefly to the "When?" and "Where?" before considering the final link of our chain-question, the "Whom." The period chosen for the conduct of a study assumes importance since, in dealing with human beings, the state of the organism is likely to be inconstant. Functions may be affected by diurnal, hebdomadal, menstrual, or seasonal rhythms as well as by the intrinsic unpredictable ebb and flow that characterizes all biological functioning. Physiological functions are perhaps the most obviously susceptible to these intrinsic influences, but psychological, and even social, functions are subject to such variations as well. The possibility of variance created by these internal factors must, of course, be taken into account.

Extrinsic factors, however, may exert even greater influence. Thus, the subject's freshness or fatigue at the time of study may affect every aspect under investigation for, like rhythm, these factors have an impact on the total state of the organism. This problem was considered to some extent in the discussion of rest—both rest preceding the experiment and rest periods interspersed throughout the experiment. In addition, passing indispositions, both physical and psychological, may alter attitudes and, indirectly, results.

Related to the temporal issue is the question of the stage of the development of the psychosis to be chosen for study. A discussion of the persons to be studied—the "Whom?" of our chain of queries—will deal with the problems here involved.

WHERE?

Previously, the importance of the specific setting of the experiment was noted. The *where* question concerns a broader aspect of the same problem, the *general* environment surrounding a study.

Because the range of settings available for study of the patient includes such places as the hospital ward, halfway house, home, school, and place of employment, the investigator must be ingenious in adapting his research techniques to the limitations encountered in nonexperimental and uncontrolled environments. He must also be aware of, and constantly monitor, the potential sources of error each setting introduces. Compensatory gains may derive, however, from having the freedom to deal with the subject in field situations that avert involvement in the thorny hierarchical problem.

As the scope of the study of schizophrenia broadens, from the earliest manifestations of the disorder through its most chronic phases, and the number of studies conducted outside the actual hospital ward increases, the development of techniques that deal adequately with phenomena occurring in environments not formally organized for research becomes particularly important.

SUBJECTS (WHOM)

We now turn to the final link in our chain-question—"*Whom*" are we to study? The problem, which requires more detailed discussion than some of the others, appears to be of two kinds, actually representing two aspects of one diagnostic problem—a primary and a secondary one. The former necessitates defining the characteristics of the core group to assure that *whom* is being distinguished from *not-whom*. In the secondary aspect one tries to make this distinction doubly secure by designating and comparing relevant control groups whose patterns of performance are to be differentiated from the experimental group's.

The question, *Who is schizophrenic?* is part of the broad, crucial problem of classification. (In an earlier paper (8) I dealt in greater detail with some of these issues.)

Despite the cogent arguments advanced about the pitfalls of classification, it is difficult to imagine how any researcher can adopt a professional orientation which does not acknowledge some form of classification as fundamental to dealing with the multiplicity of phenomena involved in the study of mental disorder. Classification is essential whether for purposes of therapy or research, but it is especially important for the latter. The objections to a particular classification system ordinarily arise because the method used differs from the one favored by the critic. No matter how vehemently a student may oppose existing systems of classification, he inevitably categorizes patients to some degree.

Some persons in the field object to what they call the "premature" classification of psychiatric phenomena, i.e., classification which, in their view, is adopted before sufficient information has been accumulated to justify such an attempt. The decision as to what is premature, especially in a field so subjective as the evaluation of mental status, is based primarily on the personal opinion of the individual involved. I think it would be a mistake to neglect *any* attempts at psychiatric classification, as long as they are based on a background of knowledge of the phenomena involved. The systematic study and thought exerted in past and present attempts at categorization (so completely outlined in Menninger et al. (17)) have advanced the understanding of mental disorders. It is necessary, however, for the proponent of a new method of classification to make a lucid presentation of his system to the relevant professional community and let its comment and reaction help determine the new method's validity and usefulness. Such disputation is characteristic of scientists' reaction to new methods and theories and, in the long run, helps to clear out the chaff.

Science is not possible without classification; it is essential to objective investigation, the core of the scientific method. The major difficulties in the classification of mental disorders, cited by many authors, are problems that beleaguer almost any attempt at categorization. Peculiar to schizophrenia are: reification—dealing with the abstract conception of a disorder rather than the actual behavior or symptoms manifested by the individual patient; elision—eliminating significant idiosyncratic characteristics of patients; partialization—extracting only a part and assuming it represents the total situation; privacy—using personal, rather than public, categories; and oversimplification—substituting an inadequate, simplistic, readily comprehensible explanation for the multitudinous phenomena so difficult to grasp in their complexity.

It is legitimate to point out these objections, even if they are the inevitable strictures that accompany attempts at categorization in any field. All categorizers must be on guard against them. Specifically, reification can be countered by constant anchoring in facts; elision of individuality, by following nomothetic with ideographic studies; partialization and privacy, by the use of multidisciplined approaches; and simplification, by constant awareness and continuing emphasis on the complexity of the problems. The classification problem in psychopathology compels one to consider how to develop a system which circumvents the pitfalls mentioned while making research work possible. (Mayr's chapter on "Behavior and Systematics" (18) has an interesting discussion of the problem of classification of behavior as related to systematics. Compare also Huxley (19) and Simpson (20, 21).) The growing sophistication and critical self-evaluation of workers in the field should gradually overcome such obstacles.

However, a source of difficulty more central to actual attempts to classify in psychopathology must be considered. The variety, looseness, and even lack of definitions of symptoms and characteristics, and the disagreements surrounding syndromes for diagnosis have resulted in discrepancies in successive descriptions of the same patient by the same expert, and discrepancies among different experts' descriptions of the same patient. Differences in diagnosis among experts and discrepancies and variations in diagnoses even in geographically proximate areas are further fruits of this confusion. The situation has fostered in many persons a pessimism about nosological activity and a readiness to throw over the whole system with the statement that classification in mental disorder, at least for the present, is too difficult, if not impossible.

But the reaction of others has been the opposite. Recognizing the vital importance of proper classification, particularly for research, such persons have insisted that the present difficulties stem from the means currently used rather than from the goal aspired to. They have therefore concentrated their energies on the systematic improvement of the successive steps of the classification process, with a persistent emphasis on high standards. The goal has been to achieve not only a careful definition and description of the characteristics represented in behavior, but a clear delineation of the characteristics comprising syndromes, and scrupulousness in the final classification and interpretation process.

Since the diagnostic aspect of the classification problem is so frequently emphasized and discussed, let me remind you that diagnosis *per se* is only one stage in the establishment of criteria for both index and control groups. Actually three different stages of the process of classification in psychopathology must be considered: (1) accurate description of the variety of phenomena the patient exhibits, (2) syndromization of these individual descriptions, and (3) the actual process of assigning patients to different categories. The concrete suggestions I advance here are those which in my experience have proven useful. I am sure that others will have equally practical, if different, recommendations to make.

Exclusion of those patients who would obviously contaminate the group will facilitate dealing clearly and directly with those in whom we are centrally interested—*schizophrenics*. Of course, as we inspect this population we find, among other variations, aged schizophrenics and young schizophrenics, schizophrenics with all kinds of associated physical diseases, such as tuberculosis and diabetes, and with all kinds of concomitant mental disorders, such as mental retardation, alcoholism, and manic-depressive and various organic psychoses. To obtain a *good* sample of this population, one would have to determine the incidence of these associated problems in the total population of schizophrenics and sample accordingly. This is a reasonable goal for some purposes, but it is *not* our interest here. Our goal is to try to determine the *nature* of schizophrenia—the essential quality of schizophrenosis. Consequently, our sample of schizophrenics should comprise those having the disorder in sufficiently uncomplicated form to obviate contaminations.

To achieve such a sample, we must impose some limitations. Excluded, for example, must be patients past a given chronological age, those with intercurrent physical disease, and those with associated mental disorders. It is hoped that such a procedure would provide for study a group of patients who, as nearly as can be assured, are "pure" cases of the disorder schizophrenia—a group meeting specified criteria with a fair degree of reliability.

Familiarity with the current mental-status-evaluation techniques routinely used by psychiatrists, or even those employed in elaborately prepared case studies, leaves one dissatisfied. An analysis of diagnostic methods uncovers several reasons for this. First, the methods lack quantifying means. Thus, it is difficult to correlate an individual's clinically derived psychological characteristics and symptoms with quantitatively expressed variables coming from research on psychological and physiological functioning.

An inexact definition also affects the terms used for the qualitative description of patient behavior. From a strict psychological viewpoint, the definitions used are often inadequate and lead to unreliability. Individual psychiatrists frequently characterize the same behavior differently in different patients or in the same patients at different times, or different psychiatrists may describe divergent types of behavior with identical or similar terms.

A careful review of the definitions, together with an adequate rating method, should provide the most satisfactory quantitative technique for certain aspects of psychiatric work. Despite the dangers lurking in oversimplification and excessive reliance on quantitative rating, it is difficult for anyone involved with psychiatric classification not to agree with Gordon Allport's opinion that, "Notwithstanding the dangers and difficulties encountered in devising and employing rating scales, we are forced to recognize this method as the only available objective criterion of personality. The sources of error must be gradually overcome by the improvement of the technic of rating" (22).

Specific advantages of a workable mental status rating scale are:

1. The roughly quantitative material on psychiatric characteristics obtained from such a scale would be suitable for correlation with

data from quantitative studies made on the same patient in other areas. For a single patient, one could use the ratings of one psychiatrist or the composite or modal (average) ratings of a group of psychiatrists. (The latter have been found to be more reliable from a technical standpoint.)

2. Reasonable, dependable, quantitative material for following up the same cases would be made available.

3. The personal factor which interferes with the objectivity of the conventional evaluative system would be partially eliminated. Although this factor is undoubtedly important in therapy, it often proves to be a marked handicap in investigation.

4. A mental-status scale offers increased dependability in the material needed for the determination of syndromes and even the determination of diagnostic types.

5. The mental-status scale keeps the psychiatrist alert to particular items of information he should try to obtain during the course of a mental-status examination. Eventually, the scale might even serve as the basis for a "standard interview," one that preserves the flexibility and open-endedness of administration any proper use of the interview technique calls for.

If we agree on the need for a rating scale, the next question is which characteristics or symptoms to rate. The sensible procedure, presumably, is to collect the salient characteristics used for diagnostic purposes by authorities in the field and supplement them with any additions the experience of the investigators participating may suggest. With these characteristics defined as clearly as possible, by means of reasonable guides, such as textbooks and dictionaries, and with a suitable rating scale worked out of, say, five or more points, the task is then to rate patients with this instrument, on the basis of both interview and observation. After several corrective steps in the refinement of the definitions and the selection of the traits, one may in the process eventually develop a suitable rating system.

We have thus far been discussing only the first of the three aspects of the problem of classification—how data derived from observation of the characteristics comprising syndromes may be gathered with some reasonable degree of dependability. For the next step in the diagnostic process —the determination of the syndromes to serve as the basis for diagnosing schizophrenia and placing the patient, whenever possible, in one of the subcategories of the disorder—one again has to rely on the standard texts and other literature, supplemented by the experience of the current staff. A list of the symptoms regarded as characteristic of schizophrenia and additional lists for the various standard subtypes of schizophrenia— simple, catatonic, paranoid, and hebephrenic—should be circulated among the psychiatrists and other staff members to involve them actively in this process. A final compilation, acceptable to all, and which all participants will agree to use as the criteria for diagnosis, can then be drawn up. The diagnostic criteria finally adopted at the Worcester State Hospital for our research on schizophrenia are shown in the accompanying Table and may serve as an example.

In presenting our Worcester criteria for diagnosis here, I emphasize that they are almost three decades old. Although at the time of their development we did not think it desirable to go into factor analysis—which we considered seriously—recent developments in this general area have apparently been found useful and productive. Our basic objection—the quality of the data going into the hopper for transformation into factors, clusters, facets, or what have you—of course, still stands. Given quality in this respect as an absolute imperative, these reductive techniques appear useful in this complex area.

I must also call your attention to two other points. The first is the fact that our criteria are largely descriptive, rather than inferential. In association with our descriptive criteria, we also carried out a fairly intensive rating scale analysis of the gamut of personality characteristics. This aspect of our research, however, never reached the stage where we could actually get into the more objective handling of dynamic hypotheses such as those represented in schemes like that of Beres on ego-function (23)—a scheme used so effectively by Grinker and his group in several studies (24). The second point worth emphasizing is that, in essence, we dealt with schizophrenia as an operational concept rather than as a disease. Through various paths we arrived at a set of criteria and then said openly, "This is the basis on which we have called our patients schizophrenic." The assumption was that other investigators would do likewise and make public their own processes of classification.

The major merit I would claim for our scheme is that it was developend with considerable care and emphasized factual data. But it is still only a beginning.

Now, having both the raw traits for characterization and the clinical grounds for combining these into syndromes, we arrive at the third aspect of the diagnostic process—the actual procedure for the final classification of the patient. This step should ordinarily be carried out at a diagnostic staff conference in which all those considered expert in diagnosis would have the opportunity to participate. After the person in charge of the particular patient presents the pertinent information, the participants discuss the clinical material on the patient, together with the data from his social history, and any other available data, such as that provided by psychological tests. The patient is then interviewed before the group—unless such a procedure is contraindicated by his condition—and an interpretative discussion usually follows.

On the basis of the material presented at the session, decisions must be made regarding diagnosis, prognosis, and suitability for the research program, decisions preferably arrived at by anonymous votes of the participants. The desirability of anonymity is, I am sure, clear to those familiar with the amount of contamination that opinions undergo in conventional staff conferences and the errors this almost inevitably introduces. In his personal evaluation each member of the staff indicates his opinion of the patient on the three above-mentioned dimensions. The chairman summarizes these views. If there is unanimous (or practically unanimous) agreement on the diagnosis of schizophrenia and the suitability of the patient for the research, he is accepted for the project. The prognostic designation is entered in the record to place staff members on their mettle and to introduce to the field a wider use of the important device of recorded prediction. (This is one of the many lessons I learned from my association with Alan Gregg, who deplored the rarity of the use of recorded predictive statements in psychiatry, and "predicted" that the profession would not grow up until it adopted such a procedure.)

With regard to types, the standard categories may be used if there is substantial agreement on the patient's subtype classification. If not, the categories of "mixed" and "unclassified" should be used liberally, for it is almost as important to keep the subtype classification "clean" as it is with primary diagnosis. In dealing with chronic patients at Worcester, we found it useful to create an additional category called "late indeterminate." It included chronic patients who had, at one time, clearly belonged in one of the standard subtype classifications, but who were currently considered "washed-out," or no longer manifesting the classic symptoms of any subtype. (The classification of "residual schizophrenia" suggested in the proposed 1967 Revision of the *ICD Classification of Diseases* (25) and the 1968 *Diagnostic and Statistical Manual of Mental Disorders* (26), comes close to, but appears not to be identical with, our "late indeterminate" category.)

After a patient is accepted for the study, he is interviewed by the psychiatrist in charge at frequent intervals throughout the period of active investigation, the interviewer making notations of the patient's mental state and behavior, preferably using the original rating-scale system in addition to the conventional narrative account. When necessary, changes in the original diagnosis and subtype category of any patient may be made at diagnostic conferences assembled for that purpose. In my expe-

Diagnostic Chart—Schizophrenia

	Common	Simple	Hebephrenic	Catatonic	Paranoid
1. Outstanding Characteristics	Abnormal development, instincts & feelings Defects of interest Blunting of emotions Ambivalence Disturbances of association & thought Autistic thinking Incoherence, disconnection General "disintegration"—in sense of queer & odd behavior	Gradual loss of interest	Thought—marked incoherence Bizarre ideas—changeable Mannerisms & grimaces Silliness	Phases of stupor and/or excitement Negativism	Delusional development Hallucinatory development
2.	Anamnestic Waning of interest Seclusiveness Dreaminess Oddness Overpiety Overconscientiousness Overdefensiveness Emotional instability Suspiciousness				
3. Onset	Usually in adolescence, (with change of disposition), few after 40 Slow & insidious (except some cases, partic. catatonic)	Early adolescence Insidious	Earlier than catatonic or paranoid Usually insidious, with change of disposition, depression, or irritability shown early	Acute, usually with change of disposition Initiated by depression, or excitement followed by stupor	Usually later than other types May begin as such or follow manic or acute catatonic state

DIAGNOSTIC CHART—SCHIZOPHRENIA (Cont'd)

	Common	Simple	Hebephrenic	Catatonic	Paranoid
4. Course	Usually chronic (except catatonic)	Chronic	Chronic	Frequently recover or go on to other type	Usually chronic
5. Personality	Sensitiveness Exaggerated self-consciousness	Good-natured Lackadaisical	Generally dis-integrated	Marked regression Acute	Suspicious Evasive
6. General Behavior	Odd, impulsive. apparently purpose-less acts	Lazy, neglectful conduct Tractable Rare, fleeting, commonly unexpressed	Manneristic Slovenly Silly	Stupor: (2 groups of symptoms) Negativism: Muscular tension Mutism Active opposition Diminution of activity Retention Hypersuggestibility: Cerea flexibilitas Automatic obedience Automatism Echopraxia Echolalia Excitement: Increased psycho-motor activity Markedly impulsive & compulsive acts Assaultive, destruc-tive, suicidal, homicidal, or auto-mutilative acts Mannerisms Stereotypy	Secondary in-tractability Meticulousness Homicidal (sometimes)

DIAGNOSTIC CHART—SCHIZOPHRENIA (Cont'd)

	Simple	Hebephrenic	Catatonic	Paranoid
7. Illusions & Hallucinations Common Frequent in most forms In most fields—especially auditory		Gen. present Numerous kinds—visual and auditory esp. Bizarre—dominant in early stages	Common	Common Particularly auditory & somatic
8. Stream of Mental Activity Tendency to disconn. Tendency to irrelevan. Intelligence ambivalence		Incoherence marked Neologisms common	Incoherence marked Stereotypy Perseveration	Peculiar phraseology (eg. stiltedness) Neologisms
9. Mental Content Autistic thinking (dereism)	Poverty of significant content	Poverty of significant content	Ideas of cosmic catastrophe	Grandiose ideas Persecutory ideas
10. Delusions Common	Rare, mild never grandiose	Fantastic, silly, changeable Often religious, sexual, somatic	Death and rebirth Ego expansion and contraction	Always present and dominant (but may be concealed) Toward coherent and systematized Often bizarre Commonly persecution and vengeance Commonly grandiose
11. Affective/Emotional Reactions Pathologic: Apathy, instability, ambivalence	Apathy relatively marked	Inappropriateness in quality & degree Pathological anger	Marked extremes	Relatively normal, but some inappropriateness of degree

DIAGNOSTIC CHART—SCHIZOPHRENIA (Cont'd)

Common	Simple	Hebephrenic	Catatonic	Paranoid
12. Orientation Commonly undisturbed for person & place May be disoriented for time Sometimes double orientation	Undisturbed	May be disturbed	May be disturbed, especially in excited states	Commonly undisturbed
13. Attention Active attention generally poor Passive attention generally good	Undisturbed	Active: poor Passive: moderate	Active: poor Passive: good	Active attention may be relatively the best
14. Memory Usually good	Usually good	Usually good	Usually good	Good—hypermnesia or paramnesia sometimes
15. Consciousness Generally clear	Clear	Clear	Apparently clouded in stuporous states	Clear
16. Judgment & Insight Serious defects common	Not prominent	May have insight in early stages	May have insight in certain stages	Markedly absent
17. General Deterioration Some degree present	Slow or arrested	Rapid or arrested	Variable: from none to marked	Commonly not marked

rience, I found that this constant review provided an additional device for maintaining the "cleanliness" of data.

In addition to the psychiatrist's observations, a log should be kept by the nursing staff and by special ward observers trained to report selected aspects of a patient's behavior. Notations of patient behavior and attitudes should also be made, even if less frequently, during "rest" periods —when the patient is not being actively studied.

Having selected the individual patients, one must next turn to the constitution of the *group*. At the very least, the group should be described as adequately as possible on a variety of relevant characteristics. These fall into two general categories: civil—such as age, sex, marital status, race, nationality, education; and psychiatric—such as age at first admission and duration of hospitalization.

In both categories, one is dealing with superficial indicators of class membership—*faute-de-mieux* indicators that are often far from satisfactory. Unless we examine this almost automatically accepted procedure most searchingly, we have no inkling of the compromises we make when, to simplify our task, we substitute class membership rubrics for the concrete, specific referents which they represent. For instance, when using the category "chronological age" we are essentially not really interested in the actual number of years a person has lived. We would much rather know his physiological, functional, vital age. When we accept as a label for "education" the number of grades a subject has completed, we are really interested in knowing how well he did in school and how much knowledge he has acquired. When we accept an "IQ" label, we really want to know how well a person can reason and use his knowledge. At the very least, we want to know how the IQ was determined: the nature of the test used and the conditions under which it was given. When we accept a figure for period of hospitalization (with its implications for "institutionalization"), we do so while recognizing the vast differences among institutions. We would really like to know the nature of the particular institution, not only its regime, but also the specific patient's reaction to it, and how he was affected by it. We frequently substitute these shorthand devices for the true referents because the necessary information is not available or is too difficult to seek out. In any event, we must recognize the limitations of these symbols and, whenever possible, try to obtain data on at least some of the referents.

But for a time to come we shall have to depend to a considerable extent on such class criteria. Despite the errors introduced in matching by such superficial class-membership criteria, they are still far outnumbered by the problems created by no matching or only casual matching. The errors introduced by the use of class criteria may not be cumulative; they may balance each other out, affecting similarly the control and index groups, although sometimes this is questionable. The complexities of trying to get at the referents make the task so difficult we have little choice but to compromise as we do. It is, therefore, doubly incumbent on us to remain aware of, and try to make adjustments for, possible errors and to retain some caution in the interpretations of our findings.

You will note that I have talked about the nature of schizophrenics only in the most general terms. I have deliberately avoided defining them in relation to premorbidity, reactivity, chronicity, and the other qualities relevant to the selection of a sample. The problem of choosing schizophrenics to work with is, to a considerable extent, determined by what might be thought of as *"the p complex"*—the influence of factors like predilection, propinquity, and pressure—on the choice of a sample. Since these factors are so much matters of individual opportunity and experience, it is particularly important that we describe the samples we use adequately.

The growing trend for *dichotomization* in schizophrenia is an aspect of the nosological problem. Because of a natural tendency to want to make material both more understandable and easier to handle in analysis, workers in the field have increasingly tended to divide schizophrenics into one or another dichotomy. Aside from the major distinction between dementia praecox and schizophrenia which a few persons still persist in using, such dichotomies as the process/reactive, typical/atypical, developmental/reactive, chronic/acute, and premorbid poor/premorbid good, have come into wide use.

Although these dichotomies are helpful when used conservatively, analyses based on them too often run the danger of oversimplification. Absolute constancy and consistency, whether within an individual or within a group of schizophrenics, are, of course, wills-o'-the-wisp. When we place patients in one or another of such dichotomous categories, we must keep in mind the truism that a biological process is almost invariably distributed along a continuum. Thus, when we choose to dichotomize, we choose to set up a criterion level along this continuum at which we separate the two classes. Even when the dichotomies are well-established, it is too much to expect reactions to remain constant within the designated level and range. Schizophrenia involves a natural process of action and reaction, of regression, or perhaps, better the Werner-Hartmann term, "dedifferentiation," and restitution—processes which go on most of the time, sometimes at an overt, easily discernible level, but frequently at a more cryptic level. Should the patient come for study during a reaction phase, one may be led to place him in the part of the dichotomy opposite that to which he characteristically belongs. For this reason, several readings on a patient should be taken. As I have already hinted, in work with schizophrenics one has to define clearly not only *about whom* one is saying what, but even more, about *which stage* in "whom's" progress one is saying what.

The class distinctions commonly used have created considerable discrepancy in the literature. Nonetheless, all of these dichotomies and characterizations have a distinct contribution to make. When they are based on careful description, one is surprised by the amount of corroborative overlap across the various dichotomies. The distinctions made among them appear to contain a common core of fact. Still needed, however, are more rigorous criteria for class membership and more dependable methods for defining the criteria, improvements which should eventually lead to a reduction in the number of dichotomies.

Yet another type of dichotomy warrants attention, one that represents not the two ends of a continuum, but rather disparate, bimodal distributions. It derives from the classic subtypes of schizophrenia already considered in this essay. As an illustration, my own data have suggested that the paranoid and the hebephrenic subtypes represent two different kinds of reactions to the basic schizophrenic disturbance. This dichotomy is also reflected in the rather prevalent tendency to compare paranoids with all other types of schizophrenia lumped together. Some justification can be offered for this procedure, as the early study by Hall on Worcester data in 1933 (27) demonstrated. And, to some extent, more recent data (28, 29) have supported this contrast. My own experience, however, raises some doubt about this procedure. I feel that something is being lost in lumping the group. Many of my studies certainly distinguished among the types now included under the "nonparanoid" rubric. I expect to consider this problem at some length in the context of presenting actual subtype findings.

CONTROLS

Many problems in schizophrenia call for controls that are peculiarly fitted to the needs of a particular study. For example, controls needed in genetic studies may call for the use of twins, monozygotic and dizygotic, or those reared by schizophrenic parents or by adopted parents. A different aspect of the control problem relates to heavily tested groups of schizophrenics, where one must be sure that the testing program itself does not modify the patients. It might therefore sometimes be necessary to do isolated tests on well-matched schizophrenics. Ultimately, it remains a problem for the investigator to define his controls in relation to his own particular study.

My own emphasis on schizophrenosis necessarily makes more difficult the problem of sampling. We have obviously not selected representative samples of schizophrenics as they occur in nature. Careful matching with control groups thus becomes one means available for correcting some errors introduced by our procedure. Let us first consider the kinds of groups needed and then the characteristics according to which they should be sampled.

It seems clear that we need groups representing disorders other than schizophrenia to determine whether our findings derive specifically from this disorder or from a wider psychopathology. We are interested, as well, in knowing how schizophrenics are differentiated from normal subjects. Since we encounter one kind of problem in selecting our disordered groups, and another in selecting the normal, each calls for separate examination.

In our consideration of sampling in schizophrenia, we came to appreciate the choice we had to make between getting a "good" sample—the subjects as they are distributed in nature, or a "pure" sample—one possessing the essential qualities of schizophrenosis uncontaminated by extraneous factors. We decided that, for our purposes, we needed the latter. For the selection of the comparison groups we must not only eliminate the same kinds of factors we judged as contaminating pure schizophrenia, but also must take the additional step of matching the group with the schizophrenics on certain descriptive criteria.

This task of descriptive matching is more complex than it appears at first glance. It affects even so simple a variable as age distribution. Suppose we select manic-depressive psychosis for one control group. That this psychosis naturally occurs later in life than does schizophrenia and distributes itself differently confronts us with a dilemma: do we take the modal age distribution of each of these psychoses for comparison, that is, match the psychoses by their respective natural distributions, or do we match the two groups by absolute mean age, equating them for the mean of the actual number of years the members of the respective groups have lived? The hospitalization periods of the two groups, which are also different in nature, raise a similar issue: do we match on the basis of the modal distributions of time spent in the hospital by persons with the respective psychoses or by absolute criteria? Such dilemmas become even more sharply defined if we choose to compare schizophrenia with general paresis or with senile psychosis, where we may end up with little or no age overlap between the two groups involved.

The answer to such questions would seem to lie in the goals of the investigator—the hypotheses that underlie his study. In some circumstances, he may decide that actual age and similar absolute matching best meet his needs; in other circumstances, he may turn instead to the natural, modal criteria. For instance, if he wishes to examine the hypothesis that the deteriorating effect of chronic schizophrenia is similar to that found in senility, he might accept *good* samples of each group and disregard the age matching. Or he may have an hypothesis about the "feminization" of response in male schizophrenics. In such a case he may match his male schizophrenics by absolute age to females with another psychosis or to normal females.

I have said nothing about the problem of nosology—the criteria for diagnosis—as it relates to the disordered group controls. The task is, of course, much like that I have described earlier for schizophrenia. The assumption is that similar care will be taken in classification and selection here, as it is for schizophrenia.

Let us now consider the *normal* subject controls. The problems of control here, though different in kind, are of equal importance. In general, great care would presumably be taken to match for "civil" characteristics such as age, sex, birth order, education, occupation. However, a major characteristic differentiating normal persons from schizophrenic and other disordered groups is the hospitalization (with its implication for "institutionalization") of one group but not the other. It is not easy to find controls for this variable. The investigator has to be ingenious in locating suitable groups. One possibility is to seek out long-institutionalized nonpsychotic groups, such as patients in chronic hospitals for the physically ill, patients in convalescent hospitals and homes, and inmates of prisons, and accept them for control, but only after cautious examination of the comparability of the conditions of such institutions with those of mental hospitals, as well as the "normality" of their residents. Having found such potential controls, the investigator has to establish favorable attitudes both with the institution personnel and among the inmates for participation in his studies. On occasion, though considerably more difficult to accomplish, it may even be neccessary to recruit normal persons for limited periods of actual residence in the same mental hospital to provide a level of living conditions more closely approximating those of the schizophrenics being studied. Such a program is particularly advisable for studies of certain physiological functions, such as those involving nutritional factors, which do not require markedly long periods of institutionalization.

Whatever the investigator does to achieve control, it is essential that he carefully describe in his report not only his procedures but also the nature of the samples he used. In this way, others may be able to evaluate the satisfactoriness of his matching, compare his samples with their own, and make the proper allowances for a complementary use of the material.

THE STATE OF THE FIELD

As I review the schizophrenia studies of the last several decades in the context of the research principles I have elaborated at such length, I believe that definite progress can be observed. My impression is that there has been increasing recognition of many of the factors I have mentioned, with a concomitant refinement in experimentation that has, to a considerable extent, taken them into account. We are far from Canopus, however, if that is our destination. Getting there is unavoidably slow, and we make progress haltingly. There are so many factors to deal with at once. And each investigator, and in some respects each discipline, tends to emphasize different ones. The complexity leads individual investigators and disciplines to make those compromises which we like to think of as the "few unavoidable and essentially unimportant" ones!

I do not believe, however, that equal progress has been made in acquiring sophisticated knowledge of patients—of knowing well with whom we are dealing. We may even have regressed in this respect. This neglect is reflected in the frequency of "single-shot" studies. Long-continued, deep involvement with patients is a luxury that few seem able to afford these days. I consider this most unfortunate, for I find it difficult to see how cross-sectional work with schizophrenics can, in any way, be as fundamentally productive as long-time studies.

I have always been somewhat resentful of investigators—particularly those in biochemistry and physiology—who do research on schizophrenics using blood and urine samples, feeling no need whatever to familiarize themselves with the sources of these samples. It is possible that this knowledge is not essential for what they are doing—but I wonder. The system seems to be highly unfair to the poor psychiatrists and psychologists who have to "waste" so much time in becoming acquainted with their patients.

SUMMARY AND CONCLUSIONS

I have considered the problem of doing research in schizophrenia in the context of a chain of queries: *Why* should *who* do *what* (*how, when, where*) to *whom*? In relation to each of these links I have tried to deal with some of the relevant issues involved.

Under *why,* I considered the motivations for doing research in this area: understanding schizophrenia, the better to cure the individual patient; prevention of schizophrenia; better understanding of the pathological process, particularly for its possible contribution to the understanding of normal process.

Under *who* I considered the range of disciplines relevant for research in schizophrenia, the types of interdisciplinary research and the concomitant problems each faces, and some of the special qualities needed by the individual investigator.

My discussion of *what* was brief, since I considered this a problem fundamentally determined by the background and perspicacity of the investigator.

The *how* question required the lengthiest discussion, since it encompasses so many of the difficulties of schizophrenia research. These conditions included: *method of approach* (the naturalistic, seminaturalistic, free-laboratory, and controlled-laboratory); general *time scale* (cross-sectional or longitudinal); *modes* of approach within specific methods (choice of emphasis on the descriptive or theoretical, multisimple or single recondite, direct or inferential, emphasis on technique or subject, method, or problem, qualitative or quantitative, molecular or molar, isolated or systematic, phenotypic or genotypic, nomothetic or ideographic, and contrived or spontaneous); *background status* of the subject—his psychosis, and the less permanent modifiers, from drugs to psychosocial influences; *conditions of stimulation* seen against a background of the general conditions of stimulation (from impersonal stimulation to personal affective stimulation under stress) with varying preparatory "rest" states (from sensory deprivation through nonresting conditions); *contexts of presentation of stimuli* (rest intervals, knowledge about the experiment, warnings of approaching stimulation, concurrent stimulation, frequency of stimulation, and the setting in which it occurs); intrinsic *nature of the stimuli*: their quality (focal or peripheral, brief or expanded, simple or complex, discrete or continuous, novel or old, repetitive or varied, ambiguous or defined), their intensity, and their frequency; and the *instructions of the experimenter.* Besides the stimulus situation, I considered the problems inherent in the subject's *response* part of the paradigm, both the portion involving his reaction to the experimenter's instructions and that deriving from his cooperation.

In relation to the *when* of the query chain I pointed to the problems created by internal rhythms, and to the need for keeping in mind, as well, such extrinsic factors as temporary fatigue and indisposition.

In relation to *where,* I considered the wide range of general environments in which the patient could be studied—not only the hospital ward, but the many extra-hospital situations, such as the home, school, and job. Such a widening of the range called for developing techniques to provide rigor of investigative conditions in these less-controlled environments.

The question of *whom*—last link in the chain—necessitated a consideration of the problems of classification as they relate to schizophrenia—the distinction between the *whom* and *not-whom,* and the various kinds of whoms involved, such as the chronic-acute and the premorbid good-premorbid bad. It also called for a discussion of the problem of relevant control groups. I presented several reasonable criticisms of classification schemes but concluded, nevertheless, that classification in scientific activity was inevitable. However, I advocated active efforts to deal with these criticisms and suggested some steps that might be taken. I then examined the three phases of the diagnostic problem: accurate, initial description of patient behavior and feelings, syndromization, and assignment of patients to categories. I made some suggestions for dealing with each of these phases as objectively as possible, including the use of rating scales, clear-cut criteria for syndromes, and anonymity in the process of assignment.

I then considered the problems raised by possible sources of contamination in the sampling, and suggested that we were not interested in obtaining *good* samples of the distribution of schizophrenics, but, rather, *pure* samples.

As to the nature of the control groups, I dealt with the constitution of the schizophrenic group as a whole and the details of matching with other groups, both pathological and normal. I considered particularly the problems created by the use of class membership criteria—the differences between the superficial symbols and the referents involved. I then touched, to some extent, on the problems raised by the use of dichotomies and subtypes. In closing my essay, I made a few remarks about the state of the field of research in schizophrenia as I see it.

Despite the length of the list I have presented, I am sure I have omitted some factors. But those presented should suffice! When the investigator has worked through such a roster of problems with at least some degree of definition and clarity, he comes to realize that schizophrenia presents such an immense task that only the beginnings of a unified picture are likely to be attained in the near future. Tolerance for any critical and honest efforts, even when they are not ideally controlled, is vitally needed. Such efforts are especially valuable when carried out by investigators who have an understanding of the patients, have treated them as human beings, are sensitive to the richness of their explicit and implicit clinical characteristics, and have approached the task in their own ways as carefully and diligently as they know how. When this kind of investigator provides us with what are bound to be only partial results, we can combine his results with the equally partial (and, one would hope, overlapping) results of others like him, to construct a composite picture which contains promise of sometime approximating the veridical one.

So here we are, finally, confronted by this formidable inventory of the complexities and difficulties of doing research in schizophrenia. Where do we go from here? For *me* it immediately brings to mind an admonition which has stuck with me from adolescence and which now seems peculiarly apt. It occurs in that delicious story "The Burglars" from *The Golden Age*. I don't know how many of you are old enough to remember Kenneth Grahame's nostalgic stories of childhood as related by one of the adults originally involved as a child in the events. For those of you who are, let me bring back to memory that appeal of Olympian Aunt Maria's—she was all of a venerable 26!—to the young curate on the occasion when she was out enjoying the night air with him on the garden bench. The curate had just nabbed the youngest nephew who was snooping around. The youngster was accounting for his presence outdoors, several hours beyond his usual bedtime, with a lurid story of being awakened by burglars he had seen approaching the house. (His story was classic, taken almost verbatim from the last penny-dreadful the brothers had been reading—you know, full of such phrases as "nefarious comrades," "armed to the teeth," and "vanished silently with horrid implications.") In the midst of spinning his yarn, they were startled by a sudden noise from the bushes. The curate made as if to head in that direction. It was then that Aunt Maria emitted her immortal plea: "Oh, Mr. Hodgitts! You are brave! For my sake do not be rash!" Aunt Maria's sensitive distinction seems a notably appropriate guide for us researchers in schizophrenia.

REFERENCES

1. SHAKOW, D.: "Contributions from Schizophrenia to the Understanding of Normal Psychological Function," in Simmel, M. (ed.): *The Reach of Mind: Essays in Memory of Kurt Goldstein*, New York: Springer Publishing Co., 1968.
2. WEISS, P.: Deformities as Cues to Understanding Development of Form, *Perspectives in Biology* 4:133-151 (Winter) 1961.
3. LUSZKI, M. B.: *Interdisciplinary Team Research Methods and Problems*, New York: New York University Press, 1958.
4. ROSENTHAL, R.: *Experimenter Effects in Behavioral Research*, New York: Appleton-Century-Crofts, 1966.
5. ARGYRIS, C.: Some Unintended Consequences of Rigorous Research, *Psychol Bull* 70:185-197 (Sept.) 1968.
6. FLEXNER, S.: Medical Research and Its Organization, *Science* 66:69-73 (July) 1927.
7. CHAMBERLIN, T. C.: The Method of Multi-Working Hypotheses, *Science* 148:754-759 (May) 1965.
8. SHAKOW, D.: "The Role of Classification in the Development of the Science of Psychopathology With Particular Reference to Research," in *Proceedings of the Conference on the Role and Methodology of Classification in Psychiatry and Psychopathology*, Washington, D.C.: American Psychiatric Association, 1966.
9. PLATT, J. R.: *The Step to Man*, New York: John Wiley & Sons, Inc., 1966.
10. CROZIER, W. J.: "The Study of Living Organisms," in Murchison, C. (ed.): *The Foundations of Experimental Psychology*, Worcester, Mass.: Clark University Press, 1929.
11. JAMES, W.: *Principles of Psychology*, vol. 2, New York: Henry Holt & Co., 1890, pp. 704.
12. JAMES, W.: *Principles of Psychology*, vol. 1, New York: Henry Holt & Co., 1890, p. 528.
13. SHAKOW, D.: Segmental Set: A Theory of the Formal Psychological Deficit in Schizophrenia, *Arch Gen Psychiat* 6:1-17 (Jan.) 1962.
14. SHAKOW, D.: Psychological Deficit in Schizophrenia, *Behav Sci* 8:275-305 (Oct.) 1963.
15. DUNBAR, H. F.: *Emotions and Bodily Changes*, ed. 4, New York: Columbia University Press, 1954.
16. LAING, R. D.: "The Study of Family and Social Contexts in Relation to the Origin of Schizophrenia," in Romano, J. (ed.): *The Origins of Schizophrenia*, Amsterdam: Excerpta Medica Press, 1967, pp. 139-146.
17. MENNINGER, K.; MAYMAN, M.; and PRUYSER, P.: *The Vital Balance*, New York: Viking Press, 1963.
18. MAYR, E.: "Behavior and Systematics," in Roe, A., and Simpson, G. G. (eds.): *Behavior and Evolution*, New Haven: Yale University Press, 1958.
19. HUXLEY, J. S.: "Introductory: Towards the New Systematics," in Huxley, J. S. (ed.): *The New Systematics*, Oxford, England: Clarendon Press, 1940.
20. SIMPSON, G. G.: *Principles of Animal Taxonomy*, New York: Columbia University Press, 1961.
21. SIMPSON, G. G.: Current Issues in Taxonomic Theory, *Science* 148:1078 (May) 1965.
22. ALLPORT, G. W.: Personality and Character, *Psychol Bull* 18:441-455 (Sept.) 1921.
23. BERES, D.: "Ego Deviation and the Concept of Schizophrenia," in Eissler, R., et al (eds.): *The Psychoanalytic Study of the Child*, vol. 11, New York: International Universities Press, Inc., 1956, pp. 164-235.
24. GRINKER, R. R., SR.; WERBLE, B.; and DRYE, R.: *The Borderline Syndrome*, New York: Basic Books, Inc., 1968.
25. *International Classification of Diseases for Use in the United States*, 8th rev., Washington, D.C.: US Government Printing Office, 1967.

26. *Diagnostic and Statistical Manual of Mental Disorders,* ed. 2, Washington, D.C.: American Psychiatric Association, 1968.

27. HALL, C. E.: The Position of the Paranoids in the Schizophrenic Group, Unpublished Dissertation, Clark University, Worcester, Mass., 1933.

28. SILVERMAN, J.: Scanning-Control Mechanism and "Cognitive Filtering" in Paranoid and Non-Paranoid Schizophrenia, *J Consult Psychol* 28:385-393 (Oct.) 1964.

29. RALPH, D. E., and McCARTHY, J. F.: Who Are Paranoid Schizophrenics: A Brief Comment, *Psycho Rep* 22:193-194 (Feb.) 1968.

Section II

DYNAMIC CONSIDERATIONS INCLUDING FAMILY INTERACTION

11

THE FAMILIES OF SCHIZOPHRENIC PATIENTS

Yrjö O. Alanen

My first study dealing with families of schizophrenic patients was confined to the mothers and to the mother-child relationship in schizophrenia. Employing the psychiatric interview, I investigated the mothers of 100 schizophrenic patients under 30 years of age, and the mothers of 20 neurotic patients and of 20 normal controls. The Rorschach test was administered to 92 of the mothers of schizophrenics and to all mothers in the control series. In a monograph (Alanen 1958) I classified the mothers I had studied into clinical categories on a unidimensional scale. The distribution that resulted is illustrated in Table 1.

TABLE 1

DISTRIBUTION OF MOTHERS OF SCHIZOPHRENICS, NEUROTICS AND
NORMAL PERSONS BY CLINICAL CATEGORY (ALANEN 1958)

Series	Clinical category of mothers A	B	C	D	A+B+C+D	E
Typical schizophrenics	7	5	27	9	48	6
Schizophreniform psychotics	5	4	12	12	33	8
Schizophrenia plus organic disorder	—	2	1	—	3	2
Total schizophrenics	12	11	40	21	84	16
Neurotics	—	1	1	7	9	11
Normals	—	—	1	5	6	14

For definition of clinical categories A-E *see* text.

I found that 12 of the mothers of schizophrenics had been manifestly psychotic and that a further 11 displayed unrealistic thought and behavior patterns bordering on the psychotic. These mothers were assigned to

---

Reprinted, by permission of author and editor, from: *Proceedings of the Royal Society of Medicine,* 63: 227-230, 1970.

the diagnostic categories A and B respectively. The most impressive finding, in my opinion, was the high frequency of mothers who were not included either in the psychotic or in the borderline group but were typified by a very accentuated constriction of affective life, poor self-control and an inability to feel themselves into the inner life of other people. Some of them were schizoid personalities; others were, above all, very aggressive and embittered; and, finally, some were very anxious and insecure, often with obsessional features. I separated these mothers from those whom I considered to be afflicted by "ordinary-level" psychoneurotic symptomatology. In Table 1 the schizoid and other nonpsychotic but emotionally very disordered mothers are included in category C and the ordinarily psychoneurotic mothers in category D. The last category, E, includes the mothers who manifested only slight neurotic traits or were completely healthy.

A larger proportion of the mothers of typically ("process") schizophrenic patients than of the mothers in the more benign schizophreniform psychosis group (diagnoses made according to Langfeldt 1953) fell within category C, which comprises the schizoid, aggressive and emotionally constricted mothers. I made a comparable observation when I tried to form a picture of the psychodynamic mother-child relationship in this study. Emotionally cold personalities with firmly dominating attitudes toward the child were definitely more frequent among mothers of typically schizophrenic patients than among those in the schizophreniform psychosis group, where warmer, more softly overprotective mother-child relationships were more common.

The psychoanalytic view of schizophrenia places a great emphasis on the disturbed early mother-child relationship. Although in my material this was often the case, it also seemed that the disturbing influence had not been uniformly concentrated in the patients' infancy or their mother relationships. More relevant appeared to be the frequent occurrence of continued disturbances, associated with a disordered mother-child relationship and liable to suppress the child's activity, and in some cases the father appeared to be more pathogenic than the mother.

The second study, conducted together with a number of my colleagues, was planned to investigate, through psychiatric interviews and a psychological test battery, members of the families of 30 schizophrenic and 30 neurotic patients (Alanen et al. 1966). Fifteen male and 15 female patients were included in both groups, and only typical schizophrenics with 'primary' symptoms and typical cases of neuroses treated in psychiatric hospitals were admitted. The descriptive findings regarding the parents and siblings of our index subjects are illustrated in Table 2.

TABLE 2

DISTRIBUTION OF PARENTS AND SIBLINGS OF TYPICAL SCHIZOPHRENIC AND
NEUROTIC PATIENTS BY CLINICAL CATEGORY (ALANEN *et al.* 1966)

| Series | Degree of disturbance category | | | | | | |
	VI	V	IV	III	II	I	?
Parents of schizophrenics	4	12	26	12	1	—	5
Fathers	1	6	14	5	—	—	4
Mothers	3	6	12	7	1	—	1
Parents of neurotics	—	1	10	25	16	2	6
Fathers	—	—	6	10	8	2	4
Mothers	—	1	4	15	8	—	2
Siblings of schizophrenics	4	6	10	11	18	—	—
Siblings of neurotics	—	—	4	17	24	4	—

Degree of disturbance categories: VI=schizophrenia; V=other functional psychoses, borderline psychotic features; IV=schizoid, paranoid and cyclic character disorders, alcoholism, psychopathy, sexual perversions, very severe character neuroses; III=milder psychoneurotic symptoms or personalities; II=normal with mild disorder traits; I=normal without disorder traits.

The earlier findings concerning the mothers of schizophrenics were confirmed. Table 2 also reveals, however, that disorders in the fathers were not less marked. Among the 55 parents of schizophrenics we had four who were schizophrenics themselves (category VI)—a proportion very compatible with the findings of most genetic studies. Of the 12 parents included in the next column (category V), five had psychotic-level paranoid symptoms, four displayed features suggestive of borderline schizophrenia, and three exhibited or had exhibited psychotic traits of an affective type. The most conspicuous feature about the distribution of the fathers and mothers of schizophrenics was their high frequency in category IV. Schizoid, paranoid and obsessional disorders formed a distinct majority in this group, and this was especially so for the mothers; about half the fathers in this group were alcoholics. Milder neurotic disturbances corresponding to category III were less frequent; but, as also appears from Table 2, they predominated in the group of parents of neurotic patients.

Among the siblings of schizophrenics the disturbances displayed greater variability than among their parents. There were four manifestly schizophrenic siblings and six who had borderline psychotic traits. Among the remainder, however, a wide variety of psychopathic and neurotic disorder patterns were found, though a considerable proportion of the siblings were regarded as normal. Neurotic disorders were comparatively common in the siblings of neurotics, but more than half of them were free from such disorders.

Findings of this kind suggest that, rather than being a specific and precisely circumscribed disease entity, schizophrenia should be regarded as the extreme degree of a more general tendency in these families toward developing psychic disorders of a particular kind. Genetic studies of illnesses that, in clinical practice, fall within the borderland between schizophrenia and other psychic disorders, as it were, point in the same direction (see, e.g. Shields 1968). Disorders other than schizophrenia were also of frequent occurrence in the families of schizophrenics according to the investigation conducted by Atkinson et al. (1968) in Newcastle; in this study no psychiatric diagnosis was recorded unless there was evidence that the relative had required psychiatric treatment or had experienced a major disruption of his social or working life as a result of illness or personality difficulties.

Such a view of schizophrenia does not, of course, imply anything concerning the nature of the causes of this disorder: these may be genetic, as well as associated with environmental factors. It is quite possible, indeed, that the disturbed relatives whose illness has not reached the stage of schizophrenia are suffering from the milder formes frustes of the same disorder, and that these also rest on a genetic basis. I would be inclined to think, however, that even if such a conception were accepted, our findings speak for polygenic rather than for specifically monogenic heredity. At this point I also wish to refer to the twin studies carried out by Tienari (1963, 1968) and Kringlen (1967) in the Scandinavian countries on the basis of population registers. Both found the strict concordance of monozygotic twins with respect to schizophrenia to be much lower than the figures reported in well-known previous studies (Kallmann 1946, Slater 1953).

I shall now try to give a brief account of some observations we made concerning the psychodynamics of the families of our schizophrenic patients.

Of 30 such families, 14 were regarded by us as schismatic and 7 as skewed in Lidz' sense (Lidz et al. 1957). Six of the families had broken before the patients reached the age of 12; thus only two or three families could be considered normal or well integrated as we characterized them. We also classified our families into two groups, chaotic and rigid, according to the nature of general atmosphere typical of them. Ten of the families were chaotic and 11 were rigid; six families had both chaotic and rigid features, and 3 were atypical. General incoherence was characteristic of the chaotic families, and in the worst cases the family atmosphere was colored with psychotic thought patterns and attitudes, which also typified the parents' relationships with their children. On the other hand, the atmosphere in rigid families was emotionally impoverished, schematized and unbending, and the parents (or one parent) usually related to their children in a very possessive or restrictive way, tinged with strict expectations. Although the children in both types of families undoubtedly had experienced severe emotional frustrations, the parents in these families could not be characterized as rejective towards their children; quite to the contrary, in many cases the children were quite important to the parents, providing them with compensation for disappointments encountered in their own childhood and in their marriages. The situation in such cases can be described by stating that children had remained the only object into which the parent could still direct his or her wishes for emotional satisfaction. Distinct differences were met between the roles of various siblings in many families, depending on both genetically based and psychological factors.

How could such disorders of the family environment be related to the pathogenesis of schizophrenia? The personality development of every individual is influenced by two sets of factors: his hereditary endowment and the experiences associated with his environment during growth. Neither set can eliminate the influence of the other: both are invariably present and contribute to the genesis of disorders in personality development, and I think that the genesis of schizophrenia is not an exception to this rules.

The family, and a child's parents in particular, occupy a key position in the process transmitting people's earliest and most fundamental experiences from one generation to the next. Parents influence their children's development both genetically and extragenetically. The nature of the extragenetic influences may be illuminated by dividing them into two broad groups as follows: parents have a part to play as their children's earliest emotional objects on the one hand, and as the persons with whom the children identify and from whom they learn on the other.

The family environments from which schizophrenics come are usually disturbed in both respects. In particular, they have lacked healthy models of identification from whom to learn inward adjustments and adjustments to external environments. Instead, many schizophrenics have learned in their childhood homes attitudes that markedly differ from those of other people in their environment, and even psychotic attitudes and modes of behavior, which they may employ in critical developmental phases as models conducive to illness. Another fact clearly in evidence is the pathogenic impact of ties of dependence. Where the parent has been accustomed to regard the child as a complement of his or her own personality, through which to satisfy unfulfilled wishes and onto which to direct projected fears and prohibitions, it will be difficult for the child to find a way to well-integrated independence. (In this connection, *see* also the concept of "double-bind" described by Bateson *et al.* 1956.)

I agree with Manfred Bleuler (1968) who stated that "if you know the life history of a schizophrenic in intimate detail, you always find close temporal connections between environmental circumstances and the psychotic evolution." Nevertheless, although factors precipitating the onset of psychosis can be discovered, the dynamically most important part is not played by such factors but, instead, by the personality that has remained weak and prone to regression. I think that in schizophrenics the process of neutralization, necessary for the development of the defensive functions of the ego, has remained defective and the underlying infantile instinctive drivings chaotically uncontrolled. The factors responsible for this state of affairs may include a lack of stable and socially useful identification patterns, as well as difficulty in reconciling needs and emotions associated with the early object relationships.

The practical result of our studies has been family psychotherapy of schizophrenic patients. As I see it, family therapy in its various forms should play an important role in the treatment of schizophrenics. The most effective form of therapy is usually that in which the patient and his parents—and sometimes some of the siblings—attend the therapeutic sessions conjointly. We have found that such a therapeutic situation in itself provides the schizophrenic patient with a powerful stimulus to leave his autistic inner world. After an initial contact, families of schizophrenics frequently show a willingness to come for therapy, either because one or both of the parents are afflicted by severe anxiety, or because of the symbiotic relationship they may have with the patient. This often makes it possible to help not only the patient but also the other family members. From the point of view of primary prevention, there would be reason to enlarge the scope of family therapy so as to include married schizophrenic patients' own families and by developing the after-care of patients along lines compatible with the family-therapeutic concept. This is all the more important in view of the constantly increasing number of cases in which schizophrenic patients are now able, by using the growing psychiatric outpatient services, to live at home with their families.

In conclusion, I would like to emphasize again that psychodynamically oriented family researchers—or at least a majority of them—do not deny the importance of genetic factors in the development of schizophrenia.

Rather, we are inclined to consider the genetic and environmental factors as a complementary chain of etiological causes. Neither do I believe that psychological and physiological approaches to the study of schizophrenia are mutually exclusive or irreconcilable. I expect that an approach to the problems of schizophrenia which seeks to combine and integrate results of studies representing different orientations and methods will prove most fruitful, and that psychodynamic study of the family and of family therapy will have an increasing part to play in the future.

REFERENCES

ALANEN, Y. O. (1958) The Mothers of Schizophrenic Patients. *Acta psychiat. scand.* 33, Suppl. 124.

ALANEN, Y. O., REKOLA, J. K., STEWEN, A., TAKALA, K., and TUOVINEN, M. (1966) *Acta psychiat. scand.* 42, Suppl. 189.

ATKINSON, M. W., GARSIDE, R. F., KAY, D. W. K., ROMNEY, D., and ROTH, M. (1968) *IV Wld Congr. Psychiat.* 3, 1777.

BATESON, G., JACKSON, D. D., HALE, J., and WEAKLAND, J. H. (1956) *Behav. Sci.* 1, 251.

BLEULER, M. (1968) In: The Transmission of Schizophrenia. Ed. D. Rosenthal and S. S. Kety, Oxford: p. 3.

KALLMANN, F. J. (1946) *Amer. J. Psychiat.* 103, 309.

KRINGLEN, E. (1967) Heredity and Environment in the Functional Psychoses. Oslo.

LANGFELDT, G. (1953) *Acta psychiat. scand.* 28, Suppl. 80, p. 7.

LIDZ, T., CORNELISON, A., TERRY, D., and FLECK, S. (1957) *Amer. J. Psychiat.* 114, 241.

SHIELDS, J. (1968) In: The Transmission of Schizophrenia. Ed. D. Rosenthal and S. S. Kety. Oxford; p. 95.

SLATER, E. (1953) *Spec. Rep. Ser. med. Res. Coun. (Lond.)* 278.

TIENARI, P. (1963) *Acta psychiat. scand.* 39, Suppl. 171; (1968) In The Transmission of Schizophrenia. Ed. D. Rosenthal and S. S. Kety. Oxford; p. 27.

11a.   DISCUSSION*

DR. ELIOT SLATER

(Institute of Psychiatry, London)

When Professor Alanen's famous book "The Mothers of Schizophrenic Patients" appeared in 1958, it caused something that can only be called a world sensation. It remains today one of the great clinical studies of the family background of schizophrenics, by a subtle and sensitive observer and a stimulating and original thinker. Professor Alanen has re-

---

* Reprinted, by permission of author and editor, from: *Proceedings of the Royal Society of Medicine,* 63: 230-231, 1970.

minded us of some of the main findings of the report of 1958, and he has given us a fascinating account of how his work and that of his colleagues has progressed since.

From a different standpoint, I hope to consider whether the genetic factors which Professor Alanen concedes, and the environmental factors which the geneticist concedes, can be brought into a meaningful synthesis.

Professor Alanen particularly studied the mothers of schizophrenics, but their fathers also have not escaped his attention; he thinks that in many cases they are just as pathogenic as the mothers, or even more so. This view is confirmed by the observations of Kallmann in Germany and of Bleuler in Switzerland, both of whom found that it was just as dangerous for the child to have a schizophrenic father as a schizophrenic mother. The point is an important one, since the child socially and emotionally is so much closer to the mother than the father, though on the genetic dimension at an equal distance from both.

Professor Alanen has found much more psychopathology in the mothers of schizophrenics than in the mothers of neurotic and of normal control groups: 63 out of the 100 mothers of schizophrenics showed gross psychopathology of grades A, B and C, as against 10% of the mothers of neurotics and 5% of the mothers of normals. Penetrating more deeply, he finds the relationship of parent to child more deviant and potentially dangerous in the schizophrenic group than the others.

Potentially dangerous, yes. But has the relationship been shown to be actually pathogenic? And pathogenic in a specifically schizophrenogenic way? We must remember that the genetic hypothesis leads one to expect constitutional deviations, schizoid personalities and the like, in the parents of schizophrenics; and abnormal personalities can be expected to behave in an abnormal way. But is this abnormal behavior the direct cause of the child's illness?

Professor Alanen has pointed out that parents may be very upset indeed when they see one of their children go mad. One may think that, under such a terrible blow, they might become aggressive and embittered, or anxious and insecure. They might perhaps, when put on the spot, give a resentful or defensive or slanted picture of the precursors of that catastrophe. I cannot feel that Professor Alanen's observations will bring much comfort and cheer to that person whom, if he exists, I would call the panpsycho-etiologist.

Let the geneticist offer a model for your consideration. We envisage a group of disorders, much akin clinically, of which some of the rarer syndromes are exogenously caused. A typical member of the group is determined by a single major autosomal gene, manifesting with reduced penetrance in the heterozygote. The condition shows itself very rarely under the age of 15, but after that is liable to cause a remitting and relapsing illness in which mental symptoms are prominent in 80% of cases—the symptoms we call schizophrenic, paranoia, depression, irritability, restlessness, hallucinations, confusion. The attacks may be precipitated by menstruation, pregnancy, infections and various drugs. Repeated attacks are likely to leave the patient with some degree of permanent damage. The disorder to which I refer is porphyria, particularly acute intermittent porphyria. But I could just as well have been referring to schizophrenia. Would it be fair to take the one as a working model to help us understand the other?

What, then, are the lessons we should draw from our contrasting views? Where should we devote our main efforts, along genetic-biochemical or along social-psychological lines? Practical consequences of immense importance hang upon our choice.

If we suppose a major gene to be the specific cause of some serious illness, we are tempted to think of the predisposed individual as being predestined. So he is, as long as we fail to recognize that this is the case. Once we confirm the genetic determination, we can discover the nature of the metabolic disorder; and then, inserting our chemical instrument into the "inevitable" chain of cause and effect, we break it off short. So it has been with phenylketonuria. Now that we know this condition is caused by a recessive gene, causing defective hydroxylation of phenylalanine, we can diagnose the abnormality in early infancy; we can put the child on an appropriate diet; and we can rear him to normality.

But what happens if we discover that the main cause of a serious condition lies in our psychological make-up and our social life? Recent history gives the answer. We have discovered that the smoking of cigarettes is currently the main cause of lung cancer, but society finds it impossible to make any effective use of this knowledge. Every year some 20,000 men and 4,000 women are dying of cancer of the trachea, bronchus and lung; and more cigarettes are being smoked every year. Rushing around the country in motor cars at high speeds costs us some 6-7,000 deaths a year, and many times more that number of disabled and maimed. There is hardly a soul who wishes to take any step to stop it. Our addiction to alcohol causes us large-scale problems in accidents and chronic disease. Prophylaxis remains impotent.

I pray that we shall find a specific genetic cause for schizophrenia, for then we may hope that something effective will be done in its prevention. If we find the causes lie in the bemused attitudes of only too human parents towards their children, we can be sure that the problem of prevention will be insoluble as long as the human family persists.

12

A CLINICAL EVALUATION OF CHILDREN WITH PSYCHOTIC PARENTS

E. James Anthony

In a metropolitan sample the author found three groups of disturbances among children of psychotic parents: precursive disturbances—forerunners of later adult psychoses; symbiotic—directly attributable to the type of relationship between child and sick parent; and induced or parapsychotic —attributable to the environment. The later two groups are susceptible to the effects of separation from the psychotic influence; this is less true in the first group, although there is some suggestion that specific therapeutic interventions may help avoid the development of an adult psychosis.

In a study of children with a psychotic parent, it has been found that a large number of quite disturbed subjects never get to see a psychiatrist for many different reasons: because they live in a relatively encapsulated microculture that manifests a high degree of tolerance for unusual or eccentric attitudes and behavior; because the children have learned to adapt themselves to a double standard of reality, conforming to realistic expectations at school and elsewhere while maintaining an irrational orientation within the home; because these families are often hypersensitive and suspicious of outsiders and regard their helpful intentions and interventions as intrusive and threatening; and because the children are often assiduously coached by the nonpsychotic parent in the concealment of bizarre happenings and conspire in the preservation of secrecy.

Read at the 124th annual meeting of the American Psychiatric Association, Boston, Mass., May 13-17, 1968.

Dr. Anthony is professor of child psychiatry, Washington University School of Medicine, 369 North Taylor Ave., St. Louis, Mo. 63108.

This work was supported by Public Health Service grants MH-12043 and MH-14052 from the National Institute of Mental Health.

Reprinted, by permission of author and editor, from: *The American Journal of Psychiatry*, 126: 177-184, 1969. Copyright 1969, the American Psychiatric Association.

For these reasons, and in the absence of a careful and thorough clinical appraisal, it is possible for the children, because of the subtle and surreptitious nature of their disturbances, to get by undetected into adolescence and adult life. Routine investigations and research based on school or agency assessments once removed from the children themselves will frequently come up with innocuous or negative findings. The further the research distance between investigator and child, the more likely is the latter to be rated high on adjustment.

The problem of adaptation has become further intensified by the introduction of new therapeutic measures and policies into mental hospitals that have had as a consequence the exposure of children, more often and for longer periods, to an impacting psychosis in varying conditions of remission and exacerbation. Most psychiatrists are in general agreement about the advantages of this new approach for the individual psychotic patient, especially in the mitigation of institutional influences on the personality, but the potential detriment to the younger family members resulting from the presence of an actively or inactively psychotic person in their midst has not received the meticulous scrutiny it deserves. As the traffic of patients between home and hospital increases, a point may well be reached when the mental health needs of the family as a whole come into sharp conflict with those of the individual patient.

THE RESEARCH SAMPLE

The research sample is drawn from several psychiatric, general, and special hospitals in the metropolitan area of St. Louis. It is made up of three groups. The first or experimental group comprises those families in which one parent is psychotic. The psychosis has been predominantly schizophrenia, but about ten percent of this group will be ultimately manic-depressive. The families are referred by the hospitals to which the sick parents have been admitted when certain criteria for selection have been met. These include intactness of the family—that is, both parents are alive and living together; the presence of children under the age of 17 and at least one child between the ages of six and 12; and an unequivocal diagnosis of psychosis without any contaminating factors of serious physical disability or disease or organic brain syndrome.

The second group is a comparison group involving families in which the parent has been admitted to the hospital with subacute or chronic physical illness, which has thus far been predominantly tuberculosis. The criteria for selection are the same except that the excluding factor is any form of mental illness requiring psychiatric treatment or hospitalization.

The third or control group comprises families in which neither parent gives any history of significant mental or physical illness requiring prolonged treatment or hospitalization.

With respect to the comparison groups, certain of the stresses of illness are the same for both—the concern over a sick parent, the separation as a result of hospitalization, and the disruption of regular home life with the experience of substitute care. It is difficult, however, to control for some of the factors such as the more disruptive impact of the remitting-relapsing type of illness as opposed to the more chronic condition, although the total duration of hospitalization, which is being controlled,

TABLE 1

DEMOGRAPHIC FEATURES OF THE RESEARCH SAMPLES (TOTAL N = 43)

Variables	Physically Ill Parents (Mean and Range)	Mentally Ill Parents (Mean and Range)
Mother's age	33.5 (23-48)	34.1 (23-47)
Father's age	43.5 (23-64)	37.4 (30-48)
Number of hospitalizations	2.3 (1-5)	3.3 (1-10)
Age at onset of illness	40.6 (23-64)	34.6 (23-48)
Socioeconomic class score*	59.63	52.4
Education level		
Mother	10.08	10.90
Father	8.67	11.52
Race White/Negro	3/10	12/9
Working mother	54%	24%
Children per family	4.31 (1-11)	3.76 (1-7)
Sex of children		
Female	2.17	2.41
Male	2.50	2.24

* From Social Class and Mental Illness(2), social class IV.

may be the same for both. There is also matching of socioeconomic, educational, and racial factors, the Negro component being ultimately restricted to between ten to 15 percent of the total sample.

The demographic features of the two comparison groups are shown in table 1.

CLINICAL APPRAISAL OF THE FAMILY MEMBERS

Each family member is interviewed and tested in a variety of ways by the research team of psychiatrists, psychologists, and social workers.

1. *The parent.* The diagnosis of the sick parent is initially made by the admitting hospital; then, by the research psychiatrist analyzing the

various components of psychotic attitude and behavior; and in addition, by a child psychiatrist recording his impression of how the predominant response of the parent might be perceived by the child in terms of avoidance, suspicion, sexual manipulation, or attack. An independent psychiatric judge finally places the patient in an official diagnostic category; gives him a score on the process-reactive (P-R) continuum, based on the premorbid adjustment; and empathizing with the child's view of the parent, also makes an assessment on an attacking-avoiding continuum.

It has been shown (4) that a high frequency of mental illness in the spouses of mental patients does exist and that although cumulative and detrimental interaction might be responsible for some of this, assortative mating also appears to be a factor. A psychiatric diagnosis, therefore, is also made on the nonpsychotic parent; in addition, he is rated on scales for helpfulness and harmfulness.

2. *The child*. After a careful clinical evaluation of the child dealing with both specific and general factors, a global rating of his adjustment is made ranging from normal and better than normal adjustments to varying degrees of maladjustment requiring counseling, outpatient treatment, or hospitalization (the rating is from 1 to 5, with 5 as severe maladjustment). In figures 1, 2, and 3 this global rating is placed in relation to the P-R scores of the parents, the child's view of the parents' behavior, and the helpfulness and harmfulness of the nonpsychotic parent.

In general, hebephrenic and catatonic schizophrenics tend to produce low P-R scores; paranoid and simple schizophrenics, intermediate ones; and subjects with schizo-affective, pseudoneurotic, schizophreniform, and manic-depressive psychoses, relatively high scores. It would seem, therefore, that, unexpectedly, the lower the P-R score, the less intense is the child's disturbance and vice versa; stated paradoxically, the more severely disturbed the parent is by usual clinical standards, the less disturbed the child seems to be.

The correlation found between the degree of the child's disturbance and the parental score on the avoiding-attacking continuum is also puzzling and would lend support to the view that a threatening posture is perceived as more alarming and therefore more disturbing by the child than a complete lack of attention or interest; it could be, however, that attacking behavior generates more immediate and overt disturbances and that remoteness has a delayed effect that builds up gradually and insidiously into a later character abnormality. There is some evidence to suggest that whereas the more reactive psychoses tend to create immediate disturbances in childhood, the process psychoses postpone their deleterious effects until adult life. The former, because of the large amount of affect

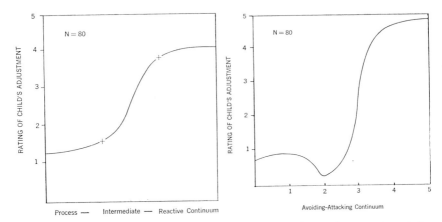

FIG. 1. The child's adjustment in relation to the process-reactive score of the parent.

FIG. 2. The child's adjustment in relation to his view of the parent's behavior.

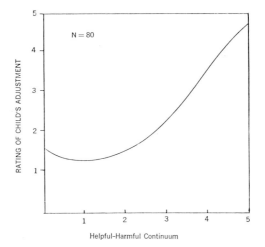

FIG. 3. The influence of the nonpsychotic spouse on the adjustment of the child.

available, are more likely to involve the child in chaotic interpersonal events and relationships, while the latter, because of withdrawal, are far less involving.

A closer clinical look at the child in an open-ended, semistandardized interview attempts to get at: 1) his basic tendency to internalize or externalize his conflicts; 2) his degree of self-awareness and body-awareness as manifested through a low threshold for subjective experiences; 3) his proclivity to withdrawal, regression, suspicion, diversion, negativism, or hostility with stressful questioning; 4) his compliance to suggestibility or authority; and 5) his over-identification and involvement with the sick parent and his sickness. The last item is assessed by the child's knowledge of the development of the psychosis, his concerns with causation, diagnosis, prognosis, and treatment, and his reactions, in terms of his own inner convictions, to the delusions and hallucinations to which he is exposed.

The cumulative impression is further reinforced by a series of miniature test inquiries. Given three houses—one in which he would live, a house next door, and a faraway house—how would he locate the various members of his family? Given three wishes, to what extent would he spontaneously include a wish for the cure and homecoming of the sick parent? Given a "day residue" of injury and indisposition, to what extent would he "make" a dream suggesting specific overconcern with the sick parent? Finally, in a doctors game, using miniature figures, what sort of patient would he like to diagnose and treat, and what would be the outcome? All these projective maneuvers are brought in as naturally as possible at different times during the interview so that the child does not receive the impression that the interviewer is unnaturally preoccupied with the subject of illness in general or with his parent's illness in particular.

SOME SPECIFIC AND NONSPECIFIC CLINICAL SYNDROMES

Three groups of clinical disturbances have thus far been isolated, two related specifically and one nonspecifically to the psychotic illness in the parent. There is a group of children whose disturbances appear to represent precursors of the later psychosis in the adult; a group whose disturbances are apparently directly attributable to a symbiotic type of relationship between child and sick parent; and a group that is disturbed by the vagaries of the peculiar environment engendered by the presence of psychosis.

There is a rough parallelism between the morbidity manifested by the child and the type of psychosis shown by the parent, as indicated in table 2.

When the psychotic illness in the parent is viewed simply as a stressful experience for the child, the intensity of the child's reaction is a function of the intensity and type of psychosis in the parent and of the constitutional and environmental vulnerability of the child. All the usual factors that are significant in the etiology of stressful disorders are operative here: the age at the time of onset, the duration of exposure, the intermittency of exposure, the disruption of normal routines, the presence of

TABLE 2

Parallel Morbidity in Child and Schizophrenic Parent

Severe	Child's Clinical Status		Mild
Extreme primitivization	Prepsychotic reactions	Externalized psychopathic reactions	Normal response
Parapsychotic reactions	Internalized neurotic reactions	Transient situational maladjustment	
Benign	Parent's Clinical Status		Malignant
Reactive schizophrenias (schizo-affective, schizophreniform, pseudoneurotic)	Intermediate group (paranoid schizophrenia, simple schizophrenia)	Process schizophrenias (hebephrenia, catatonia)	

adequate, helpful, and reality-oriented surrogation, and the pretraumatic experiences of the child.

Our data would support the view that the toddler phase is especially sensitive to the disturbing experiences of psychotic management, especially on the part of a chaotically reactive mother. This can result in an acute primitivization with a massive loss of developing ego skills. In the case of the older child, it may lead to transient situational disorders, acting out behavior, or to the development of such neurotic disturbances as nightmares, obsessions, and phobias. For reasons that are still inexplicable, certain children respond with a brittle normality (ten to 20 percent) or even with a "supernormality" (five to ten percent) that makes them into highly interesting, creative, and colorful individuals.

The two specific groups of disturbances—the "precursive" and the "symbiotic"—need further elaboration.

Antecedent Disturbances of Later Adult Psychosis

On the basis of the type of psychosis in the psychotic parent and the clinical status of the nonpsychotic spouse, an approximate estimate of genetic risk in this research sample would run between 15 and 20 percent, which is one in every five or six children. The summation of birth weight, birth size, body build, and body strength data is already suggestive of constitutional differences between the prepsychotic child and his siblings.

On a rating scale ranging from "most likely" to "least likely" to develop adult psychosis, about 16 percent of the subjects are currently falling into the "most likely" category. The characteristics of this class include a physical status score in the lowest quartile, an ectomorphic body build, a high score on the check list of precursive symptoms and behavior, a personality pattern classifiable as schizoid, paranoid, or cycloid in the older children, a tendency toward a thought disorder of an amorphous or analytic form, and the occurrence of characteristic episodes of withdrawal, mistrustfulness, or extreme regression.

Such micropsychotic episodes usually can be vividly remembered and clearly described by informants, since they represent a striking departure from the child's habitual behavior. The episodes last from three days to three months and then dissipate even without treatment. Separation from the sick parent seems to have little value in the prevention of further episodes. The microschizoid episode can be confused with sulkiness, except for the absence of antagonistic affect and the presence of a large number of strange subjective experiences. The child may appear unusually abstracted and unresponsive to his interests.

The microparanoidal episode is associated with an upsurge of suspiciousness and a sense of persecution that may develop loose systematization, especially in the older children. (Piaget's description of the child's developing thought makes it clear why the younger child in the preoperational stage can at best achieve only fleeting associations between malevolent ideas, while the older child, during the middle years, may achieve miniature systems based on simple dichotomous categorizations. With the development of abstract, propositional types of thinking, a coherent, internally consistent group of paranoid ideas becomes possible and firm enough to withstand confrontation.)

The hebephrenic episode is altogether less strikingly differentiated from the usual mode of behavior. The children appear "odd and peculiar" and, as Kraepelin first pointed out, already exhibit a considerable degree of "psychic weakness" in early childhood. He considered this childhood behavior as a manifestation of "existing disease" (3). In a few cases in our sample, vaguely demarcated episodes of silly, inappropriate, and clownish behavior have occurred from time to time, usually under the stimulus of some minor stress.

The childhood of later reactive psychotics does not seem to be characterized by these episodic developments; the children in this category tend to be persistently overexcitable, wild, undisciplined, nervous, and restless.

In round figures, current findings would suggest that of the prepsychotic disturbed group, 20 percent show hebephrenic episodes or characteristics; five percent, microschizoid or "shut-in" episodes or characteristics; five percent, microparanoidal episodes; and the remainder, varying degrees of hyperexcitability, normality, or what has been referred to as "superphrenia."

Induced or Parapsychotic Disturbances

In this condition delusions, hallucinations, and other psychotic symptoms are imposed by the psychotic parent on one or other of the children. These parapsychotic developments may take the form of folie à deux, Ganser syndrome, or a succession of twilight states. The conditions favoring such developments include a symbiotic relationship between mother and child, a lower than average intelligence in the child, a close identification with the sick parent, a high degree of suggestibility, especially in relation to bodily feelings, an almost abject passivity and submissiveness, and a marked involvement in the psychotic manifestations of the parent. The parapsychosis seems most prone to develop in the case of a mother and a daughter who is over the age of five. The sick parent may overtly make the acceptance of her delusional beliefs a precondition for object relations, so that it becomes a case of "love me, love my delusion."

In general the parapsychotic reactions mirror the parent's illness fairly closely, but unlike the prepsychotic reactions, they tend to disappear altogether when the child is permanently separated from the parent. The impact of a delusional system on a family of children can be roughly predicted from our measures of identification, involvement, suggestibility, and submissiveness. Conviction regarding the delusion may vary from child to child and in any particular child, depending on the presence or absence of the deluded parent and the presence or absence of other reality-oriented figures.

Case 1. The five-year-old daughter of a severely schizo-affective woman was admitted to the hospital in a state of acute panic. Her speech resembled that of a two year old; she was doubly incontinent and seemed unable to feed herself. From time to time she would emit shrill screams. From the account given, she had been grossly abused aggressively and sexually by the mother over a period of months. When the acute disturbance subsided, the child behaved like a robot and appeared to need direction before she could act at all. In interviews she would reiterate such questions as, "Why do you laugh?" "Do you feel happy when you smile?" "Why don't you look happy when you feel happy?" "If I pinch you, will you feel sad?" "Do you cry when you feel sad?" It almost seemed that the child was unable to connect in a logical, experiential way the sequence of stimulus, feeling, emotional expression, and affective label and that a lack of basic learning was involved. It seemed pertinent that the mother's affective responses were as incongruous and inconsistent as the rest of her behavior. *Diagnosis*: acute primitivization response.

Case 2. An eight-year-old girl of superior intelligence was doing quite well at school until one day when she misbehaved in a very minor way: She threw a rock on the playground so that a boy could bat it with a stick. She was immediately overcome with guilt and remorse, and everything that happened thereafter seemed directed toward trapping her into some terrible situation. She refused to return to school and became extremely suspicious of everyone. She would either say nothing in response to questions or ask why the question was asked. The reaction subsided completely after three months, and she resumed her normal behavior and was even able to laugh at the silly ideas she had had. A year and a half later another episode occurred that subsided in a few weeks without admission. The girl's mother had been hospitalized twice with the diagnosis of paranoid schizophrenia. *Diagnosis*: prepsychotic disturbance; microparanoidal episode.

Case 3. A 12-year-old girl believed completely with her mother that someone was poisoning the food at home, and like her mother, she refused to eat except in a restaurant. Her sister, two years younger, also refused to take food at home except when the mother ate with the family. When a seven-year-old brother was asked about the problem and why he was able to eat, he shrugged his shoulders and answered casually: "Well, I'm not dead yet!" *Diagnosis*: parapsychotic reaction, induced type.

Case 4. A boy, aged eight, the only son and youngest child of poor parents living under very dilapidated circumstances, came into the interview shaking his head from side to side and rolling his eyes upward. He lurched about the room and eventually sat on the floor in the corner, constantly contorting his features and gyrating his limbs. When asked what was the matter, he said in a silly, simpering way: "You think my brain has bust, but I am just nutty and fruity!" When asked his name, he would give his telephone number and eventually offered his sister's name. He said that he could not count from one to ten because he was stupid and that he could only count backward from ten to one.

His concocted psychosis reflected his stage of development and his cognitive and conceptual capacity. It also reflected popular misconceptions of school children about mental illness. His history and test responses indicated a strong involvement with his very psychotic father, to whom he had been devoted until the latter's hospitalization with paranoid schizophrenia a year previously. In one of his "saner" responses the boy said that when he grew up, he wanted to become like his dad so that he could fight all of his dad's enemies. The mechanism in this case was not an "identification with the crazy one," as with the folie à deux, but rather, when investigated more closely, a pathetic attempt to magically relieve the psychotic illness of the parent. *Diagnosis*: parapsychotic reaction, Ganser type.

EVALUATION OF THE HOME ENVIRONMENT

There are three main types of disorganization in the home environment or subculture of psychosis; in their fully developed forms they tend to reflect the type of psychotic disintegration of the parent as they do, to some extent, the type of disequilibrium in the child.

1. In the *process* environment, where the parent is hebephrenic or catatonic, the household suffers from neglect as a result of extreme degrees of laissez-faire. This is especially true when the sick parent is the mother. The children begin to lead separate lives of their own, unsupervised and undisciplined, and there is a high incidence of behavior problems and delinquency.

2. In the *paranoid* environment or "pseudo-community," there is "organized disorganization" in the sense that family life is incorporated into the workings of the delusional system, to the great bewilderment of the children.

3. The *reactive* environment is characterized by its inconsistency, chaotic management, contradictory communications, highly ambivalent but powerful affects, incoherent intentions and motives, and its disturbing degree of intrusiveness into the lives of the children. This "environment of irrationality" (5) envelops the family and makes for unpredictable storms and crises that hover over the lives of the children. At one moment they are pulled into intimate closeness, and at the next, they are thrust far away with bitter and unjustified accusations. The pulls of reality and unreality can set up peculiar conflicts of loyalty.

The following clinical vignettes attempt to illustrate the "climate" of these three environments, unmitigated by helpful spouses and surrogates.

Case 5. The family lived in a derelict building badly in need of repair. Two of the children, a boy aged nine and a girl aged seven, were squatting comfortably on a wall sharing a cigarette. The girl had no pants on and made no postural adjustments to disguise the fact. When asked the whereabouts of their mother, the boy said that "Old Annie" was where she always was, in the back room. "Take care you don't hurt her when you go in" he added; "she lies on the floor by the door." (There was a curious warmth in his voice, and he might have been speaking of a favorite pet.) A typical process type of environment.

Case 6. A paranoid schizophrenic man turned his home into a beleaguered fortress in which the family mounted watches against "the enemy" and weapon training was rigorously enforced. A great deal of secrecy prevailed, and no one was allowed to come and go without an examination of credentials. A child who went out shopping was closely interrogated on his return. One of the children complained bitterly that he even had to report before going to the bathroom! A typical paranoidal "pseudo-community."

Case 7. A five-year-old girl was believed by her father to be a love child of the mother by another man. At times he would become furious and, without reason, suddenly seize the little girl and start beating her and dragging her across the room by her hair. At other times he would observe that she was wearing clothes that he had brought her and a bracelet that he had given her, and he would then be overcome by the conviction that she was his daughter and completely like him in every way. He would then proceed to caress her passionately, frightening the child by his vehemence. A fairly typical chaotically reactive environment.

DISCUSSION

It would seem that careful clinical evaluation can bring to light a spectrum of disturbances manifested by children associated with high-risk psychotic heredities and high-risk psychotic environments. In 50 per cent of the cases, the subtle and unusual types of disturbance may be overlooked because they tend to be camouflaged by the family or made overt only in the family setting. It is possible that much of the precursive behavior is consolidated during the middle period of childhood and that later interventions become almost too late. It is also possible that certain therapeutic interventions might help to abort some of the gradual accumulation of disturbance that continues progressively throughout the child's development.

The full-scale investigation from which this clinical evaluation has been abstracted also comprises a naturalization section entailing a living-in experience with the family and an experimental section in which aspects of psychosis, such as incongruities of affect, thought, and communication, tendencies to magical thinking, and opportunities for persecutory interpretations of benign stimuli, are simulated in the laboratory. In addition, perceptual and psychological instabilities of response have been investigated and reported elsewhere (1).

SUMMARY

The goal of this study was to learn something about the hazards of having a psychotic parent. The existence of three groups of disturbances affecting the children of such parents during the period of childhood development has been demonstrated. There are disturbances that stem *from* the parental psychosis and represent antecedents of the adult psychosis; disturbances that are associated *with* the parental psychosis and result from its impact on over-influenceable children; and disturbances that are reactions *to* the parental psychosis and may take the form of transient situational maladjustments, anti-social behavior, or neurotic reactions. The latter two groups are susceptible to the effects of separation from the psychotic influence, while the former continues to manifest itself episodically despite separation; however, there is some suggestion that specific therapeutic interventions may lessen the frequency and intensity of the episodes and, in so doing, may mitigate or militate against the development of an adult psychosis.

REFERENCES

1. ANTHONY, E. J.: "The Developmental Precursors of Adult Schizophrenia," in Rosenthal, D., and Kety, S., eds.: The Transmission of Schizophrenia. Long Island City, N. Y.: Pergamon Press, 1969, pp. 293-316.
2. HOLLINGSHEAD, A. B., and REDLICH, F. C.: Social Class and Mental Illness. New York: John Wiley & Sons, 1958.
3. KRAEPELIN, E.: Zur diagnose und prognose der dementia praecox, Allgemeine Zeitschrift für Psychiatrie und psychischgerichtliche Medicin 56:254-264, 1899.
4. KREITMAN, N.: The Patient's Spouse, Brit. J. Psychiat. 110:159-173, 1964.
5. LIDZ, T., FLECK, S., and CORNELISON, A. R.: Schizophrenia and the Family. New York: International Universities Press, 1966.

13

COMMUNICATION IN FAMILIES OF SCHIZOPHRENIC PATIENTS

Describing Common Objects as a Test of Communication Between Family Members

David Feinsilver

There has been increasing focus on the study of distorted communication in families of schizophrenic patients during the past ten years, beginning with the work of Bateson et al. (1), Lidz et al. (2), and Wynne et al. (3). Most recently Singer and Wynne have shown that verbal communication in families of schizophrenic patients can be differentiated from communication in other families by the degree to which it demonstrates impaired focal attention, that is, by the degree to which it demonstrates stylistic qualities which impair the listener's ability to focus his attention on the meaning of what is being communicated. Singer and Wynne have examined the communication of parents in various settings and groupings: as they related, both individually and as a couple, to a tester during psychological tests (4-8), in a family by Rorschach (9), and in family therapy (10). Wild et al. (11) applied criteria developed by Singer and Wynne to the communication of individual parents with a tester during administration of the object sorting test. There have been, however, no attempts to study impaired focal attention in communication within total families of schizophrenic patients using the pairing of family members as the unit of investigation.

Submitted for publication July 22, 1969.

From the Yale University School of Medicine, Department of Psychiatry, New Haven, Conn. Dr. Feinsilver is currently with the Center for Studies of Schizophrenia, National Institute of Mental Health, Chevy Chase, Md.

Reprint requests to Center for Studies of Schizophrenia, NIMH, 5454 Wisconsin Ave., Chevy Chase, Md. 20015.

Reprinted, by permission of author and editor, from: *Archives of General Psychiatry*, 22:143-148, 1970.

It was observed in reviewing the protocols of the Wild study of the object sorting test that members of families of schizophrenic patients seemed to have a striking difficulty in identifying and talking about common objects. It was decided therefore to initiate an exploratory investigation designed to examine the ability of one family member to describe a common object to another family member and to compare this with the performance of families of normal controls. It was decided to pair off the various family members and, in addition to determining effectiveness of the pairings of the family as a whole, to compare the relative effectiveness of various pairings within the family, particularly comparing the communication of a parent to the schizophrenic patient with the communication of a parent to a nonschizophrenic sibling.

The process of describing common objects also involves the task of conceptualizing these objects properly and it was therefore decided to examine the descriptions for inappropriate conceptualization. This dimension of schizophrenic thinking was described first by Goldstein as a tendency to be overly concrete and similar to that of patients with organic deficits (12). Cameron, however, noted that the conceptual deficit of schizophrenic patients tended rather to reflect an inability to exclude irrelevant stimuli and to include too much and become over-generalized (13). He developed the concept of overinclusion, which in studies by other investigators (14, 15) seemed to differentiate schizophrenics from normals better than the category of overconcreteness (overexclusiveness). In this study therefore, inappropriate conceptualization is considered as thinking which is either overly concrete (overexclusive) or overly generalized (overinclusive).

It was also decided to examine the verbal interaction for the Singer-Wynne criteria for impaired focal attention and to observe whether these criteria, already amply demonstrated as a significant feature of the communication within families of schizophrenics in other settings, could also be quantified for this setting.

The basic hypotheses to be tested are:

Families of schizophrenic patients misidentify objects more frequently than families of normal controls.

Families of schizophrenic patients demonstrate descriptions which show inappropriate conceptualizations more frequently than families of normal controls.

Families of schizophrenic patients demonstrate communication which impairs focal attention more frequently than families of normal controls.

The communication from the parents to the schizophrenic patient is more impaired than to a nonschizophrenic sibling.

METHODS

Six families each consisting of a schizophrenic patient, sibling, mother, and father were selected from the various Yale Clinical Services. It was required that the patient be unequivocally diagnosed clinically as having had an acute schizophrenic episode with obvious evidence of schizophrenic thought disorder (confirmed by psychological testing if possible). It was required that at the time of participation in the study the patient should have been hospitalized from three to nine months, with his doctor judging him to be relatively reintegrated and capable of interacting with people in a nondisturbed manner. It was also required that the patient be a member of an intact family with a nonschizophrenic sibling (never symptomatic), and that all the family members participate voluntarily. Six normal control families in whom no member had ever been in psychiatric treatment were solicited as volunteers from among the Yale Hospital Staff, drawing from nursing, administrative, and custodial personnel, attempting to obtain a sample comparable to the families of the schizophrenics with respect to social class and intelligence. The ages of the children in the families were between 15 and 25 in both groups.

Because of the small size of the groups it was impossible to obtain adequate samples matched identically with respect to social class and intelligence. Each family member, however, was given the R. L. Thorndike Vocabulary Test of General Intelligence (16) and the social class of the family was determined by the Hollingshead-Redlich classification (17). The groups were found not to differ significantly with respect to social class and intelligence score and could therefore be considered equivalent. Furthermore, it was found in this study that social class and intelligence score showed low correlation with the variables being studied (Table 1).

A standard set of instructions was read to each family at the beginning of each testing session.

"The aim of this study is to see how well people in families can describe common objects to each other. You will be called into this room in pairs and will sit back-to-back. We will be recording this session and that is the reason for the microphones hanging from the ceiling."

"In turn, each member of the family will be given a series of common objects which he will describe to another member of the family who will not be able to see the objects and will have to identify them after the description is completed."

"The only requirements are:

"When you are describing you must give five separate characteristics

TABLE 1

SOCIAL CLASS AND INTELLIGENCE

Difference Between Families of Schizophrenics and Normals

	Schizophrenics	Normal	T	P
Social class*	3.0	2.0	1.67	<0.20
Intelligence score†	52.2	58.9	1.57	<0.20

Correlation With Grand Totals

	Correlation Coefficients
Social class	0.40
Intelligence score	0.41

* Hollingshead-Redlich Classification of the Family (17).
† Family sum of individual intelligence scores on R. L. Thorndike Test of General Intelligence (16).

TABLE 2

LIST OF OBJECTS

1. Battery	11. Diaper pin	21. Pliers
2. Bell	12. Doll	22. Plug, electric
3. Block	13. Knife	23. Pussywillow
4. Bra	14. Magnifying glass	24. Ribbon
5. Button	15. Match book	25. Rubber band
6. Candles	16. Nail	26. Scissors
7. Chewing gum	17. Nipple	27. Sock
8. Clay	18. Paper clip	28. Steel wool
9. Clothespin	19. Pipe cleaner	29. String
10. Cork stopper	20. Penny	30. Whistle

TABLE 3

SCORING RELIABILITY

	Correlation Coefficients
Object misidentification	0.99
Inappropriate conceptualization	0.89
Focal attention measures	
Closure	0.81
Disruptive	0.83
Peculiar	0.46
Drive	0.53
Loss of task	0.88
Totals	
Focal attention totals	0.82
Grand totals	0.84

of the object and when you are identifying you must wait until the five characteristics have been given before identifying the object."

"You may not use the name of the object in your description."

For each pairing, first one family member described a series of common objects and then the other member described a new series in return (Table 2). The sessions were taped, typescripts were made of each session, and the transactions scored by independent scorers according to criteria set forth in the scoring manual.

The following measures were scored.

MISIDENTIFICATION.—Scored if the first response given by the listener was not exactly correct.

INAPPROPRIATE CONCEPTUALIZATION.—Represents the degree of overly concrete or overly generalized thinking manifested. It was determined by categorizing each descriptive statement on a scale of one through four, with one being given for statements which are judged to represent an appropriate level of conceptualization, two for overly concrete (overexclusive) statements, three for overly generalized (overinclusive) statements, and four for statements which are judged as irrelevant or only loosely associated.

FOCAL ATTENTION MEASURES.—These measures, closure, disruptive, and peculiar are the categories developed by Singer and Wynne measuring impaired focal attention and the criteria for these categories have been adapted for this experimental design from their manual (8). Drive and loss of task are two additional categories which have been defined because they also represent ways in which focal attention is impaired in this setting.

Closure.—Scored when statements tended to detract from the clarity and finality of what was being focused upon, such as in fragmented speech, "It's used for . . . uh . . . well, it's made out of metal," or in following statements with disqualifying phrases, such as "I guess," "maybe."

Disruptive.—Scored when statements disrupted the trend of thought of the person describing such as by interruptions by the person waiting to identify or by extraneous remarks by either the person describing or the person identifying.

Peculiar.—Somewhat loosely defined and scored for statements manifesting peculiar wording or logic which diffuse the listener's attention by distorting meaning, such as quaint terms, "cuddly cloth," "hook-loop," or rhyming, "it's white and tight," and in non sequitur reasoning, "it's circular to make a noise."

Drive.—Scored when drive-laden material seemed to intrude inappropriately, such as in describing a pair of pliers as having a "mouth or gripper."

Loss of Task.—Represents the ways in which one's attention is diffused by blurring the task set. It was scored when instructions were ignored or when inappropriate questions were raised.

TOTALS.—*Focal Attention Totals.*—Represents the sum of the focal attention measures.

Grand Totals.—Represents the sum of all the measures being scored.

The scoring was done by the experimenter and the reliability was verified by training a second scorer according to a scoring manual and then having him score blindly 25% of the material chosen in a predetermined unbiased fashion. Using the correlation of the two scorers on all the measures taken together (Grand Totals) as a measure of overall reliability there is a high degree of interscorer reliability (correlation coefficient 0.84, Table 3). Taken separately, the scoring on each measure also correlates highly (correlation coefficient > 0.80), except for the two categories, peculiar and drive. These two categories seemed relevant, however, and require further refinement and verification.

RESULTS

The families of schizophrenic patients differed significantly from the families of normal controls by demonstrating a greater number of object misidentifications, a greater degree of inappropriate conceptualizations, and a greater degree of qualities which impair focal attention (Table 4). Grand Totals, representing all the measures taken together, differentiated the two groups at a level of significance $(P < 0.001)$, and Focal Attention Totals was particularly noteworthy, showing absolutely no overlapping between the two groups $(P < 0.001)$. Furthermore, the high level of significance between the two groups on either the Focal Attention Totals or Grand Totals does not change if the focal attention measures that did not show high reliability, Peculiar and Drive, are excluded $(P < 0.001)$. Considering the measures separately, Misidentification and the focal attention measures were each significant $(P < 0.05$ or $P < 0.01)$, but Inappropriate Conceptualization was only marginally significant $(P < 0.07)$.

Considering the pairings within the families of schizophrenics, using Focal Attention Totals as the measure of impaired communication, there were no significant differences between the communication from the parents to the schizophrenic patient and the communication from the parents to the non-schizophrenic sibling. It was also noted that there were no

TABLE 4

FAMILIES OF SCHIZOPHRENICS AND NORMALS

	Normal	Schizophrenic	T	P
Object				
misidentification	21.0	10.7	2.62	<0.05
Inappropriate				
conceptualization	40.0	27.8	1.90	<0.07
Focal attention measures				
Closure	26.3	14.7	2.75	<0.05
Disruptive	12.0	4.5	3.36	<0.01
Peculiar	46.0	24.8	2.80	<0.05
Drive	4.5	1.3	3.48	<0.01
Loss of task	43.2	17.2	2.84	<0.05
Totals				
Focal attention totals	132.0	62.5	5.31	<0.001
Grand totals	193.0	101.0	4.60	<0.001

TABLE 5

FAMILY PAIRINGS*

Normal

Child-child	3.8	
Parent-parent	4.6	
Mother-child	5.1	No significant differences
Child-father	5.4	
Child-mother	5.6	
Father-child	8.0	

Schizophrenic

Sibling-mother	7.0	
Patient-mother	7.7	
Mother-father	9.7	
Patient-father	9.8	
Father-mother	10.3	
Sibling-father	11.3	No significant differences
Mother-patient	11.4	
Father-sibling	11.4	
Sibling-patient	11.5	
Father-patient	11.7	
Patient-sibling	13.6	
Mother-sibling	14.0	

Differences Between Family Pairings of Normal vs Schizophrenics

	Normal	Schizophrenic	T	P
Child-child	3.8	12.7	5.01	<0.001
Parent-parent	4.6	10.0	3.33	<0.01
Mother-child	5.1	12.7	3.62	<0.01
Child-father	5.4	10.6	2.74	<0.05
Child-mother	5.6	7.4	1.42	ns
Father-child	8.0	11.6	1.26	ns

* Figures are for mean Focal Attention Totals for each pairing.

significant differences between any of the various pairings within the families of schizophrenics or within the families of normal controls. It was observed, however, in comparing the pairings within the normal family group with the pairings within the schizophrenic family group, that the greatest difference was between the normal child-child pairing and the schizophrenic child-child pairing $(P < 0.001$, Table 5).

TABLE 6

PARENTS TO SAME SEX VS. OPPOSITE SEX*

Mother to Daughter vs Son

	Daughter	Son	T	P
Schizophrenic	14.7	8.5	1.35	<0.20
Normal	4.4	5.6	1.04	ns
Combined	10.7	6.4	1.52	<0.20

Father to Son vs Daughter

	Son	Daughter	T	P
Schizophrenic	13.3	10.9	0.36	ns
Normal	11.7	4.1	1.58	<0.20
Combined	12.2	8.2	1.24	<0.20

Parent to Same Sex vs Opposite Sex

	Same	Opposite	T	P
Schizophrenic	13.9	10.3	1.36	<0.20
Normal	7.8	4.7	1.34	<0.20
Combined	11.2	6.9	1.95	<0.05

* Figures are for mean Focal Attention Totals for each pairing.

Although this study was not designed to investigate the effects of sex role on the communication within families and the samples were unevenly divided according to sex, it was decided to make an exploratory comparison between the parental communication to the children of the same sex and the parental communication to the opposite sex. Using Focal Attention Totals as the measure of impaired communication, grouping together the pairings within the schizophrenic family group and the normal family group, it was found that the parents communicated significantly better to children of the opposite sex than to children of the same sex $(P < 0.05$, Table 6). The differences when grouping either mothers or fathers alone, schizophrenic or normal, were not significant although tending in the same direction.

COMMENT

Although this study provides many significant findings, it should be emphasized that it is only a preliminary investigation of a technique which might prove useful in differentiating families of schizophrenics from other families. The study has been therefore carried out with only a few families and with limited controls and must be expanded before any definitive conclusions can be made. In addition to repeating this study with larger samples, it remains to be shown particularly that the impaired communication demonstrated in the families of schizophrenics is unique to these families and that they can be differentiated from families of other psychiatric populations such as sociopaths, depressives, and neurotics. Although the two groups in the study did not differ significantly with respect to social class and intelligence and the groups were therefore considered equivalent, future studies might provide a more adequate control for these important variables by matching the families.

The finding that families of schizophrenic patients can be differentiated from families of normal controls by showing a greater degree of object misidentifications, with the high reliability of this measure (correlation coefficient 0.99), suggests that Object Misidentification may provide a relatively simple objective indicator of impaired communication in families of schizophrenics.

The absolute differentiation of the two groups by the composite measure Focal Attention Totals suggests that this dimension seems to be a particularly valid indicator of families of schizophrenics, and these findings also further corroborate the work of Singer and Wynne. Although Inappropriate Conceptualization was only marginally significant ($P < 0.07$), the difference between the two groups may well be falsely lowered in this instance by the tendencies of schizophrenic families to interrupt their descriptions when having difficulty describing objects, resulting in fewer scorable descriptions at times when they were likely to produce inappropriate conceptualizations. This could be corrected in the future by insisting upon the requirement that the five descriptive statements be completed.

The failure to find any significant differences between the communication to the schizophrenic patient and his nonschizophrenic sibling nor between any of the pairings within the families, suggests that impaired communication as measured in this study, is probably a function of the total family and not of the patient, and it cannot alone account for the patient, rather than his sibling, becoming schizophrenic.

The highly significant difference between normal child-child pairing and the schizophrenic child-child pairing, compared with the lesser differences between the other pairings in the two groups, may be a reflection that a good-working coalition is part of normal sibling relationships and that this may be deficient in the relationship between schizophrenic patients and their siblings.

Finding that the parents of both groups when taken together communicate significantly better to children of the opposite sex than to children of the same sex suggests that, in general, the oedipal coalition may enhance communication whereas the competitive oedipal situation impedes it. Because these findings were not borne out when considering separately the smaller unevenly divided groups of mothers and fathers, both schizophrenic and normal, these findings must be considered particularly tentative.

SUMMARY

The task of communicating the essential attributes of common household objects from one person to another was explored as a test of communication between members of families of schizophrenic patients. A group of six families, each consisting of a mother, father, schizophrenic patient, and nonschizophrenic sibling, was compared with a control group of six normal families. The verbal interaction of all the various pairings within each family was scored according to the following categories: misidentification of the object, inappropriate conceptualization, and impaired focal attention. In every category the families of the schizophrenic patients performed significantly more poorly than the families of normal controls. A comparison of the various pairings within the families revealed that there were no significant differences between the communication from the parents to the schizophrenic patient and to his nonschizophrenic sibling. It is tentatively suggested that object misidentification in this setting may provide a relatively simple indicator of impaired communication within schizophrenic families.

Dr. Theodore Lidz, Chairman, Department of Psychiatry and Dr. Cynthia Wild, Assistant Professor of Psychology in the Department of Psychiatry, assisted in this study.

A detailed manual of the scoring criteria is available upon request.

REFERENCES

1. BATESON, G., et al: Toward a Theory of Schizophrenia, *Behav Sci* 1:251-264 (Oct.) 1956.
2. LIDZ, T., et al: The Transmission of Irrationality, *Arch Neurol Psychiat* 79:305-316 (March) 1958.

3. WYNNE, L., et al: Pseudo-Mutuality in the Family Relations of Schizophrenics, *Psychiatry* 21:205-220 (May) 1958.
4. WYNNE, L., and SINGER, M.: Thought Disorder and Family Relations of Schizophrenics, *Arch Gen Psychiat* 9:191-206 (Sept.) 1963.
5. SINGER, M., and WYNNE, L.: Thought Disorder and Family Relations of Schizophrenics: Methodology, *Arch Gen Psychiat* 12:187-200 (Feb.) 1965.
6. SINGER, M., and WYNNE, L.: Thought Disorder and Family Relations of Schizophrenics, Results and Implications, *Arch Gen Psychiat* 12:201-211 (Feb.) 1965.
7. SINGER, M., and WYNNE, L.: Communication Styles in Parents of Normals, Neurotics and Schizophrenics, *Psychiat Res Rep Amer Psychiat Assoc* 20:25-38 (Jan.) 1966.
8. SINGER, M., and WYNNE, L.: Principles for Scoring Communication Defects and Deviances in Parents of Schizophrenics: Rorschach and TAT Scoring Manual, *Psychiatry* 29:260-288 (Aug.) 1966.
9. LOVELAND, N.; WYNNE, L.; and SINGER, M.: The Family Rorschach: A New Method for Studying Family Interaction, *Family Process* 2:187 (March) 1963.
10. MORRIS, G., and WYNNE, L.: Schizophrenic Offspring and Parental Styles of Communication, *Psychiatry* 28:19 (Feb.) 1965.
11. WILD, C., et al: Measuring Disordered Styles of Thinking: Using the Object Sorting Test on Parents of Schizophrenic Patients, *Arch Gen Psychiat* 13:471-476 (Nov.) 1965.
12. GOLDSTEIN, K.: "Methodological Approach to the Study of Schizophrenic Thought Disorder," in Kosanin, J. S. (ed.): *Language and Thought in Schizophrenia*, Berkeley, Calif.: University of California Press, 1944, pp. 10-39.
13. CAMERON, N.: "Experimental Analysis of Schizophrenic Thinking," in Kosanin, J. S. (ed.): *Language and Thought in Schizophrenia*, Berkeley, Calif.: University of California Press, 1944, pp. 50-63.
14. EPSTEIN, S.: Overinclusive Thinking in a Schizophrenic and a Control Group, *J Consult Psychol* 17:384-388 (Nov.-Dec.) 1953.
15. CHAPMAN, L., and TAYLOR, J. A.: Breadth of Deviate Concepts Used by Schizophrenics, *J Abnorm Social Psychol* 54:118-123 (Feb.) 1957.
16. THORNDIKE, R. L.: Two Screening Tests of Verbal Intelligence, *J Appl Psychol* 26:128-135 (April) 1942.
17. HOLLINGSHEAD, A., and REDLICH, F.: *Social Class and Mental Illness*, New York: John Wiley & Sons, Inc., 1958.

14

SIBLING RELATIONS IN THE
SCHIZOPHRENIC FAMILY

W. W. Meissner

The literature on studies of family dynamics has been dominated by an interest in the role of family interactions as they influence the course and development of one or other member of the family. While the literature in this area has been abundant, only passing attention seems to have been paid to relations between siblings and to the place of the pathologically affected child in the family constellation. It is our purpose in the present study to review studies on sibling involvement in schizogenic families and to present clinical findings from a family in which the pattern of sibling involvement had striking impact on the development of schizophrenic illness within the family.

REVIEW OF THE LITERATURE

The number of studies on sibling relations in schizophrenia has not been very impressive. In very early studies of the schizophrenic process, the question was raised as to why certain of the offspring of a schizogenic family develop the clinical manifestations of the illness while others do not. The view was evolved that the development of the schizophrenic illness served a dynamic function in the family interaction, but the factors which were operating to select this child rather than that, as bearer of the illness, were not clear.

As more attention was paid to the "well" sibling, it became increasingly apparent that the siblings themselves carried a considerable degree of psychopathology (6). As studied in artistic productions, they showed well integrated functioning in relatively structured contexts; when the situa-

Massachusetts Mental Health Center, Boston, Mass.
I am grateful to Drs. H. Grunebaum and L. Hasenbush for their clarifying comments.
Reprinted, by permission of author and editor, from: *Family Process,* 9:1-25, 1970.

tion was relatively unstructured their performance became considerably more confused and fragmentary—in fact, approaching a schizophrenic level. This was in direct contradiction to the family's perception of the well-sibling as healthy, strong and successful. Their personalities showed a considerable degree of constraint and constriction. They seemed to be less involved in family difficulties and more detached from the family distress than the sick sibling (5). The constriction was seen as protecting the well-sibling from a subjective sense of conflict, thus permitting some emotional withdrawal from the family. The purchasing price was a certain shallowness in object-relations.

The Lidz group at Yale also focused on sibling involvement (8). They found that of twenty-four siblings of schizophrenic patients, three were clinically schizophrenic, seven were classifiable as borderline, and eight suffered from a variety of clinical neuroses. They too found marked constriction and flight from the family as characteristic of siblings with reasonably good adjustment. Flight from the disturbing family environment as well as a maintained aloofness had definite protective advantages. It provided the adaptive function of allowing the well-sibling to separate emotionally from the pathological processes within the family and thus avoid the threat of overwhelming involvement (10, 14, 15).

In the extensive study of family processes in the pathogenesis of schizophrenia and neurotic disorders, Alanen and his coworkers (1) brought to light a considerable amount of information about sibling relations in schizophrenia. The level of sibling psychopathology was, as in the Lidz study, significant and was found to be higher than the comparable group of siblings of neurotics. This reflects the generally greater degree of disturbance in the schizophrenic families. The parents of schizophrenic families were generally gravely disturbed and narcissistic persons with marked tendencies to projection. They showed greater variety in both type and severity of disturbance. Another interesting finding is that same-sex siblings, i.e., brothers of male schizophrenics and sisters of female schizophrenics, tended to be more disturbed than opposite-sex siblings. This was a significant finding in the Lidz studies as well. It seems that certain family environments are more pathogenic for males and others for females (8).

Although the categories cannot always be applied neatly, the Lidz group has distinguished marital schism from marital skew in schizophrenic families (9). In schismatic families, the parents were in conflict with each other, each trying to coerce the other and meeting either defiance or a temporary and resentful submission. Each undercut the value and self-esteem of the other, each tried to get the children on their side, each fostered distrust and devaluation of the other in the children. The threat of family dissolution hangs like a cloud over the heads of the children. Without affection and support from each other, these parents turn to the children to fill their emotional needs. The schizophrenic child is caught in the schism more so than his siblings. He may become the "scapegoat"; or he may try to widen the split to gain one parent for himself; or he may try to bridge the gap, dividing his loyalties and trying to fill the emotional needs of both parents; or he may be caught in the bind in which loyalty to one parent means rejection by the other (1).

In other families of the skewed type, the influence of the dominant parent is not countered by the other parent. The patient becomes the object of a vigorous intrusiveness of the dominant parent which develops a symbiotic bond. The pattern is most typical in the relation between schizophrenic boys and their mothers. The father is usually quite passive and distant so that identification with him is impaired. The mother's involvement with the son allows the other siblings a degree of independence and differentiation.

Parents of schizophrenics were significantly disturbed people, as we have noted, but they also revealed ambivalent and frustrating relations with their own parents. The influence of the extended family on the development of pathology in the nuclear family has been recognized as important (2). Many of the mothers were caught up in hostile relations with their own parents, particularly their mothers. By contrast, the fathers showed conspicuous dependent tendencies. It was noted that the conflicts between parents and their parents were quite similar to the conflicts which obtained in their relations with their children (1).

In schizophrenic families, parents can reach decisions about nonschizophrenic siblings relatively easily, but not about the schizophrenic child (7, 13). The mother is inclined to leave the nonschizophrenic child to herself but cannot leave her schizophrenic child alone without anxiety— even though the relationship is often stressful and hostile (11). In consequence, the schizophrenic child is often compliant and dependent while the nonschizophrenic sibling is more independent and ignores parental demands (10).

One of the basic questions involved in the family study of schizophrenia is why the patient becomes ill rather than other children. This is undoubtedly a complex issue with many facets. The schizophrenic child is markedly dependent, more so than less disturbed neurotic children and more so than his siblings. Such dependency seems to be a primary factor in pathogenesis. The development of autistic withdrawal is regarded as a secondary regression in response to the frustration of dependency needs (1). The patient is caught up in intense symbiotic ties which the siblings were able to avoid. The patients were the more involved and more disturbed children in the family from their earliest years. The influences, therefore, which determine the schizophrenic process are operative very early. Such data, retrospective and based on parental re-collections, are suspect but they suggested that events surrounding the patient's birth and influencing the subsequent mother-child relationship are of great significance (1, 8). The period around the patient's birth was often exceptionally difficult and stressful, but more important seems to be the effect of this external disequilibrium on the mother's inner psychic state. The data suggest that the vicissitudes of nursing may indicate the beginning of a more chronically faulty mother-child relationship (8).

The future schizophrenic child's involvement with its parents seems to be central to the pathogenic process. The parents were marked by trends to narcissism and projection. They showed strong inclinations to provoke excessive dependency needs in the patients and to create symbiotic ties with them. Such ties resulted from the transferral of unfulfilled parental needs to the children. Such unsatisfied needs arise from the emotional divorce and schism between the parents as well as from emotional frustrations and conflicts derived from relations with their own parents (4).

The families of female schizophrenics show some specific characteristics which have important bearing on the family discussed below. The most prominent pattern observed in families of female schizophrenics consists in a mother who is hostile or rejecting and a father who stimulates ambivalent and anxious feelings of closeness in the child. Most of the patients are described as "father's girls," especially in schismatic families. They are closer to and more dependent on the father than the sisters. The fathers in turn show a possessive closeness to the schizophrenic daughter. They are conspicuously narcissistic and paranoid. In the Alanen study (1) they were also found to have a vulnerable self-esteem that had been violated by marital frustrations. This resulted in the father's seeking emotional compensation and affective support from the daughter. They were also sexually inadequate men and displayed seductive features in their relationships with the patient daughters. As Lidz has suggested (9) it is the daughter who sides with the father and seeks his love who becomes psychotic.

The schizophrenic girl also has difficulties in relation to her mother. In families with more than one daughter, the mother's relation to the schizophrenic daughter is considerably more hostile than to the patient's sister.

In fact, the mother's relation to the sibling was often narcissistically possessive so that the mother tended to identify this daughter with herself. The patients found it virtually impossible to identify with the mother and usually allied themselves with the father. The patient was invariably the child most exposed to the mother's rejecting or hostile attitudes, and the difference in the mother's attitude to the siblings was marked.

It is possible, then, to outline some of the important psychodynamic elements which underly the pathogenesis of schizophrenia in females. In the mother we find an inadequate sense of feminine identity and her inability to give the child genuine warmth and affection. The readiness to reject the patient is reinforced by frustrations and lack of satisfaction in the marital relation. This provokes in the child intense, unsatisfied cravings for affection and strong dependency tendencies. It also provokes aggressive feelings toward the mother and associated guilt feelings. Aggression, in addition, is dangerous since it makes the prospect of affectionate closeness to the mother even more remote. Feminine identification is impaired and the child turns to the father as a source of affection and an object for identification. The father's narcissistically paranoid and seductive response seeking affection and alliance in the daughter, evokes a strong oedipal configuration. Since the closeness is not counterbalanced, it provokes anxiety and guilt. In the schismatic family, closeness to the father further alienates the patient from her mother (1).

It is not always clear what factors are involved in getting the schizophrenic child caught up in this interaction. Differences between the children may play a primary role. The child may be born at a particularly difficult time for the mother with related disturbances in the pattern of mutual communication. The birth of the child itself may also be responsible for the mother's crisis in adjustment. The even minimal degrees of passivity and proneness to dependency in the child may feed into the parent's need for symbiotic closeness. Other factors may indeed be at work. A major factor is that pathogenic parental attitudes are in large measure rejective as seen from the patient's point of view. They feel rejected and unloved, but at the same time the expression of aggression by the patient is strongly prohibited and produces guilt. This may develop into a scapegoating pattern in which parental hostility is drawn to the patient and away from the other siblings (17).

Family environments associated with schizophrenia show a variety of patterns. The family structure may be governed by a symbiotic union between parent and child which keeps the child dependent and helpless. The environment may be simply chaotic, such that the basic needs of the child are neglected. Or it may be depressive and dominated by a sense of emptiness and loss. The parents may respond to the child by withdrawal and indifference to the child's needs, or there may be a vacillation between depressive indifference, hostile attack and guilt-ridden concern. These families frequently contain a mother who is chronically depressed or is undergoing periods of depression during the patient's childhood. Another important variant is that at some point in his development the schizophrenic child comes to be considered an outsider and is rejected, distrusted, or even forced to leave the home (16).

The interlocking of parental pathologies, innate characteristics of the children, environmental stresses, family patterns, extended family influences as well as other as yet unspecified determinants form a convergence of factors which focus the pathogenic process in the family on the child or children who will become schizophrenic. There seems to be a certain economy in the operation of these factors in so far as the focus on one child allows the others to escape the schizophrenogenic influence. It may be that the presence of one schizophrenic child in the family diminishes the probability of schizophrenic illness in other children, but it does not eliminate it. Where more than one child is involved in the schizophrenic process, different factors may be operating to produce the schizophrenic illness in each case.

CASE PRESENTATION

We would like to turn at this point to a consideration of a family in which there were three daughters, two of them schizophrenic. This family has been treated in conjoint family therapy with a psychiatrist and social worker acting as co-therapists.* The oldest daughter, Amy, has been treated concurrently in intensive individual psychotherapy as has the youngest daughter, Alice. They are being treated by different therapists. The parents are also being seen in casework relationship with the social worker. Extensive psychodiagnostic testing has been done on all family members and on the family as a group, but this data will be reported elsewhere. Our primary focus is directed to the problem of how two of the daughters in this family were caught up in the family interaction in such a way as to produce a schizophrenic result, while the third daughter has achieved a relatively normal and healthy adjustment. It is our feeling that only by careful attention to clinical detail can further light be shed on this problem.

---

* Therapy was conducted by the author and Miss Dorothy Stewart, M.S.W.

The DiMaggio Family

The DiMaggio family to all outward appearances is an average middle class suburban dwelling family with three daughters. The distinguishing feature of this family is that two of the three daughters have been hospitalized with a diagnosis of paranoid schizophrenia. To understand the factors contributing to this state of affairs, we will begin the story in the grandparental generation.

The paternal grandfather (PGF) was born and raised in Italy. He was one of three sons raised by the mother since his father had deserted the family. His older and younger brothers received some education, but PGF received little or none. The older brother emigrated to the United States and the rest of the family followed shortly after the turn of the century. PGF was 27 years old at the time. His adaptation to the new world was hampered by his inability to learn English along with his tendency to reticent withdrawal and dependence.

Paternal grandmother (PGM) came from Italy when she was only fifteen years old. She came with five older brothers, leaving their parents in Italy. She became a substitute mother for the family, doing the cooking and housekeeping and working as a seamstress. PGF and PGM met and were married in 1911. Because of the strength of the PGM's family ties, they were much closer to her family than to his. PGF was very unsure of himself, never really learned to speak English, and was generally quite dependent on PGM. He was described as rather rigid and puritanical. PGM was by far the stronger figure. She could read and write, and is described as genteel and cultured. She ran the house, disciplined the children, and was a "guiding light" to the rest of the family.

They had three sons, born in 1914, 1916, and 1920. The second oldest was the father (F) of our nuclear family. He was quiet, reserved, and very shy as a child. There was a constant struggle with his older brother. The family operated on the principle of the right of primogeniture. Consequently the oldest son received all privileges and was given first rights in everything. F got clothing, toys, etc., only after his older brother had used them. The oldest brother got a car at 17; F had to wait until he was 27. F resented this bitterly and swore that in his own family his children would be treated equally without any privileges for the first-born.

Despite these difficulties, F was clearly his mother's favorite and became very close to her and dependent on her. Toward his father, conversely, he felt distant and cold. As a boy Mr. DiMaggio stuttered badly and was in general shy and unsure of himself. In school he did poorly but finally graduated from high school in 1934. Jobs were difficult to find and he was unable to find employment for over two years. He had strong feelings of worthlessness, felt he was a terrible burden to his parents, and recalls thinking seriously of running away from home. He finally got a menial job with a large local department store where he has worked ever since. He finally was able to become a salesman and has been quite successful at this part of his work. Becoming a salesman was apparently a great triumph of will-power and resolve for him. His speech is larded with aphorisms of self-improvement—"You're as good as you think you are!"; "You can do anything if you want to bad enough!" He presents himself constantly to his family and to others as a man who started life with unbelievable handicaps but who has managed to overcome them all —stuttering, poor aptitude for study, poor family background, feelings of inadequacy, etc.—by sheer determination and strength of will.

To turn now to Mrs. DiMaggio's family, the father (MGF) was born in Norway, where he had worked as a sailor and fisherman. He came to the USA a little after 1900. He worked here as a house painter and finally started his own painting business which he maintained for many years. He met his wife after being in this country for some time and they were married in 1914. She was from an English Yankee family that had lived in this country for several generations. While MGF was quiet and passive and kept more to himself, MGM was more talkative, demanding and determined to have her way. It is not clear whether either was more dominant, but it seems clear that there was a schism between them which was accompanied by a considerable degree of argument and conflict. Mrs. DiMaggio had a sister, two years older than herself, and there was a good deal of rivalry between the two girls for their parents' affection. Mrs. DiMaggio was her father's girl while her sister was much closer to MGM. Mrs. DiMaggio and her father did many things together and she became quite a tomboy. Her closeness to MGF was matched by the conflictual and bickering relationship with MGM.

When the depression hit in the early 1930's, MGF's business began to fail. As the business failed, he became more and more depressed and started to drink. Mrs. DiMaggio recalls one day when she came home from school she found her father weeping bitterly; the experience left a profound impression on her. MGF continued to drink and began to consume heavy amounts of alcohol. This pattern persisted for years and when he had a lot to drink he would become very antagonistic and argumentative. This would produce terrible arguments between him and MGM which nearly tore the house apart.

In recent years MGF's health has been precarious. His alcoholism resulted in cirrhosis with esophageal varices which finally bled. In 1958 he developed a laryngeal carcinoma which was treated over the succeeding years but with continual deterioration. During this period of MGF's illness, the MGM, always an energetic and determined woman, went to work in a library and continued this means of support until she was 80 years old. She remains a vigorous and fairly active person with many hobbies and interests.

Mr. and Mrs. DiMaggio met in the early 1940's and were married in 1943. At the time, she was very unhappy at home, and was getting along very poorly with her parents. She saw marriage as a way of escaping that situation. She was very poorly prepared for marriage. She knew nothing about housekeeping or cooking. She had an overwhelming insecurity and doubt about her own capacities to function as wife and mother. In the early part of the marriage, Mr. DiMaggio had to do almost everything. He did the cooking and the cleaning and tried to teach her. This was a very stressful period for both of them. She felt terribly inadequate and he felt resentment that he had to shoulder his wife's burdens as well. He more or less supported her through this period but it seems clear that the experience served to reinforce his deeply fixed and almost unconscious perception of her as weak and defective and her feelings about herself as an inadequate and defective woman.

Sexual relations between the couple were quite frequent, but Mrs. DiMaggio usually found relations difficult and never got much enjoyment out of them. The first two pregnancies were planned. Amy was born in 1947. The pregnancy was difficult. Mrs. DiMaggio felt increasingly tense and anxious and depressed as it progressed. The delivery, however, was normal and she breast-fed the baby for about eight months. Taking care of the baby was difficult for her. She was extremely anxious about all aspects of baby-care and would become quite depressed and upset by the demands of mothering. The second daughter, Anny, was born in 1949. The pregnancy was again difficult and accompanied by considerable anxiety and depression. After the delivery, Mrs. DiMaggio continued to be quite depressed and seemed disinterested in the child. She nursed her for about three months but unlike Amy she fed very well from the beginning. The couple decided that they would not have any more children at that point. Mrs. DiMaggio, however, became pregnant again in 1951 but this time miscarried. There was another unplanned pregnancy which produced the last daughter, Alice, in 1954.*

Although Alice's conception was unplanned and Mrs. DiMaggio admits that it was a great disappointment to her, she feels that she and her husband were able to accept the child. Alice's pregnancy was fraught with problems. Mrs. DiMaggio became quite depressed during the course of it and after the baby was delivered suffered a complete breakdown. The postpartum psychosis was marked by anxiety and intense depression, required hospitalization and was treated with ECT and psychotherapy. The total course of hospitalization was over a year, and the attendant disruption of the family was considerable. The children were sent to live with their grandparents and little Alice was put in a foster home where she was to remain for 14 months. It is interesting to note that during this same period Mr. DiMaggio's mother became quite ill. He describes himself making almost daily the painful round of visits to his wife and then to his mother. If we recall his deep devotion to her and his dependence

---

* The three names, Amy, Anny, and Alice, are confusingly alike. They mirror the actual similarity of the daughters' names. Even family members would often misname each other, suggesting the diffusion and merging of identities in the family.

on her, we can imagine the inner stress that he must have undergone at this time. PGM finally died in 1958. It becomes obvious as he talks about these events that his mother's death was one of the most painful losses Mr. DiMaggio has suffered. His father died in 1950 but that event is hardly referred to at all.

Three years after Alice's birth, Mrs. DiMaggio became pregnant again. This time the pregnancy was interrupted. A hysterectomy was performed for psychiatric reasons. Since that time their sexual relationship has deteriorated badly. Mrs. DiMaggio has been somewhat frigid all along but since her operation has been quite resistant to her husband's advances. This remains a major source of schism between them and is something that Mr. DiMaggio holds against her. The implicit message is that she is defective as a woman because she cannot and will not give him the satisfaction he expects as a man. There is a footnote to this message. It is that she is also defective because she never gave him a male child. Mr. DiMaggio feels cheated on this account.

The Children

The effect of these events on Amy, the oldest of the three daughters, was profound. She was about seven years old when these events surrounding M's breakdown took place. She had always been a very shy, timid and well behaved child. Of all the sisters, she was the most feminine, preferring to spend long hours playing with dolls rather than joining in the rougher play of the neighborhood children. She was always quite attached to her mother and apparently made more emotional demands than Mrs. DiMaggio felt able to fill. In consequence Amy grew up with the feeling that she was unloved and rejected. The intense need for love and affection from her parents, especially her mother, was complicated by two factors. The first was Mrs. DiMaggio's inability to give herself warmly and lovingly to her children both because of her inner inhibition and because of her continuing depression. The second was the presence of a sister two years younger. The former had a very strong impact since it meant that M's self-doubt, insecurity, and poor self-esteem must have come across to Amy as a rejection which dominated the climate of her early years. The latter was also of crucial importance, because it meant that the already rejecting and unavailable mother had also to be shared with a sibling.

One of the consequences of the unavailability of M to Amy was a turning to her father for affection and emotional support. On his part, Mr. DiMaggio whose strong sexual needs were being frustrated, tended to turn to his daughters for emotional rewards. The emotional involvement between himself and his oldest daughter became very strong. The stage was set for a very powerful oedipal involvement. Mr. DiMaggio takes a warm, almost mothering and protecting position in relation to her which is quite seductive in quality. It is as though he were trying to be mother and father both, but that the role of mothering one comes easier to him.

When M broke down, Amy felt the loss as catastrophic and moreover felt responsible for what had happened to M. She felt terribly guilty about it. These feelings undoubtedly reflect her underlying rage at M for the more or less chronic feeling of rejection as well as the more acute abandonment. These events and their attendant feelings drove Amy closer to her F and made her even more dependent on him. Despite the forces drawing father and daughter together and despite the seductive closeness and possessiveness of their relationship, F was really less available to Amy during his wife's illness than at any other time. He was taken up with concerns about his wife's illness and his own guilt feelings in regard to it, about the necessity for his youngest child being put in a foster home, and perhaps more significantly, about his own mother's serious illness which carried its own burden of grief, guilt, recrimination, and loss.

Another important factor which underlined and reinforced many of these dynamic influences was Mr. DiMaggio's attitude toward the right of primogeniture and its impact on his children. His own position as second-born had fixed him intensely on the determination that in his family there would be no distinction between first and second born children. Consequently, the relative treatment of the two older girls, Amy and Anny, was administered with absolute equality. They were treated equally in all matters. They got the same kind of presents, enjoyed the same privileges, went to bed at the same time, and shared the same responsibilities. Since Amy was two years older, this treatment was seen unequivocally by her as preferential treatment of her sister. As she put it, "I had all of the responsibilities of being two years older, but none of the privileges." The impact of this rigid equality was very marked. It provided a continuing mechanism for undercutting her and played into her feelings of rejection and lack of love from her parents. In her attempts to gain compensatory affection and consideration from F, she was continually frustrated by what she perceived as preferential treatment of her sister. The application of this principle acted to intensify and frustrate her longings for closeness to her F and made her dependent clinging to him all the more crucial. At the same time it continually fed her feelings of rejection and abandonment and fanned the underlying rage and resentment she felt toward both her parents.

Something else that proved important started about the time mother got sick. F dealt with M's illness by trying to protect her from irritations and one can speculate that Amy's demands for attention and affection were difficult for M to deal with. F would often tell Amy not to bother M and not to cause trouble. The implicit message was that Amy was responsible for M's troubles. Later on, when M returned from the hospital, F would tell Amy frequently not to cause any trouble because M *might get sick again*. This phrase deserves emphasis because it is one that has become a leitmotif for this family. The threat of M's fragility and the gloomy possibility of her becoming sick again hang over this family like a dark cloud. Its effect is to prohibit the expression of anger or aggression within the family. Mr. DiMaggio does not allow himself to express his obvious rage at his wife. Rather he shifts it into much more subtle forms of hostility by which he undercuts her authority in the family and undermines her relationships with the children. For Amy it made any expression of anger terribly threatening because not only would it produce that cataclysmic loss of her mother that she dreaded, but it meant that Amy herself would be responsible for what would happen. The only recourse for her was to cling more closely and desperately to her parents, to believe what they wanted her to believe, to do what they wanted her to do. At the same time, while the expression of angry feelings was so threatening and devastating, the climate of the family was thoroughly permeated with angry feelings which were expressed in implicit and indirect ways.

It is not difficult to guess that Amy grew up a timid, quite withdrawn, isolated, phobia-ridden and terribly depressed and guilty child. She had one or two not-too-close girl friends and remained very much in the circle of close family. She did well in school but always with the complaint of teachers that she was isolated from other children and did not work up to her potential. She always felt socially awkward, worried about her appearance, afraid of saying or doing the wrong thing. This masked the underlying fear of the dreadful consequences of revealing the hateful and destructive feelings which lay close beneath the surface. Contact with nonfamily became difficult, so much so that riding on a bus nearly paralyzed her with fear. Paranoid ideation, ideas of reference, and anxiety became overwhelming. She had developed a tenuous relation with her only boy friend toward the end of high school, and when he precipitiously dropped her and married she plunged into a rapidly deteriorating course which led to her hospitalization. She became increasingly withdrawn, spending most of the time in bed. Relations within the family became progressively more deteriorated. Struggles with her parents and demands for attention particularly directed to her mother grew in intensity. She finally developed the delusion that her family was trying to get rid of her and kill her. This was combined with a paralyzing dread that members of her family were going to die, particularly her father. The parents sought psychiatric help but the situation at home continued to deteriorate and Amy was finally hospitalized. It is interesting to note that Mr. DiMaggio resisted this move for over a year.

The second daughter is Anny. She is two years younger than Amy and is the healthy member of the family. At the time of writing she is 19 years of age. She is the tallest member of the family and while she is really no more attractive than Amy she presents herself with considerable self-possession and poise. Her manner is charming and seductively feminine. Her opinions are well formed, confidently asserted, and often differ considerably from her parents, particularly her father. Her manner often suggests that she is almost an independent observer and commentator on what is going on in the family: a veritable one person Greek chorus. But her involvement emotionally in the troubles of her family is very deep.

One of the most striking features of Anny's story is that she was completely unaware of her mother's illness. This seems incredible in view of the fact that M's illness was an overwhelming feature of family life for both her F and Amy. But Anny had apparently bypassed the event—she was five years old when it occurred—and consequently had sidestepped the pathogenic influences that related to it. Her development has been strikingly successful. She has always had many friends, was successful in school and was always extremely popular. In high school she was a leader, was elected class president several years, and led an active social life. She had many boy friends and an abundance of dates. Her relationship with Amy was close when they were young and it is clear that the older Amy leaned on and depended on her younger sister. As Anny's outside interest grew, however, she spent less and less time at home and was able to spend less time sympathizing with Amy's problems. As they grew older Anny grew less dependent on and involved with her parents, while Amy grew more so. Anny's extrafamiliar involvement was experienced by Amy as rejection and abandonment and the loss of another prop on which she had depended.

Anny was the beneficiary of the abrogation of primogeniture that ruled the family. Her experience in the family was thus one of continual privilege rather than one of continual undermining. While she was still quite young she came to be regarded by both parents as the stable member of the family. They both confided in her in a way which never obtained with Amy. Amy again saw this development as preferment of her sister and exclusion and rejection of herself. At many points along the line, Anny was able to demonstrate initiative and engaged in activities from which Amy felt excluded. The exclusion was due, of course, to her own inhibitions and conflicts, not to any prohibitions from her parents. An example was driving the car. Anny learned to drive and obtained a license at the earliest possible opportunity. Amy was so caught up in fears and doubts that she never learned to drive. Anny's use of the car, however, became another instance of preferment and privilege.

One of the most significant aspects of Anny's role in the family is her relationship with her parents. She demonstrates considerable independence of judgement and action from her parents. She recalls that, when she was younger, F or M would tell her not to do something and if she still wanted to do it, she would generally do it without letting them know about it. Rather than argue endlessly with her father, she chose to listen to what he had to say then make up her own mind. The contrast here with Amy is striking. Amy could not deviate from the parents' wishes, particularly her father's. It was essential to adhere faithfully to whatever he thought or believed or directed—presumably the threat of independence and self-assertion were too overwhelming for Amy.

The consequence of these influences was that Anny grew up with a certain amount of distance from her parents and a certain amount of independence and autonomy. She was able to remain unentangled in the pathological influences in the family and could become "her own person." As conditions at home deteriorated and the situation became intolerably conflictual, Anny moved out of the house and started living in an apartment. This was done without recrimination and with parental acknowledgement of her autonomous decision.

The third daughter is Alice. Alice is now fourteen years old, and is very precocious, and in many ways is the most attractive of the 'daughters, physically. There is little doubt that the circumstances of her birth are of the utmost importance to her pathology. She has always been a petulant child and difficult to control, sometimes quite defiant. She has done quite well in school until the last year or two. She began to have difficulties, particularly with reading. Teachers complained that she was often inattentive and seemed to be looking off into space. On occasions she would burst out into tears in the classroom and they became increasingly concerned about her behavior. It came to light during the course of the family interviews that she was having terrifying nightmares, that she suffered from some severe phobic anxieties, that she dreaded some catastrophe that was going to befall her family because of her, that she was hearing voices that told her how evil she was, that she did not deserve to live and that she should kill herself. She also saw evil faces on occasions, faces of dead people and death's-heads. She also cherished a secret delusion that she was different from the rest of her family, that she was from a different race from another world. These delusions were quite frightening to her and it became necessary to hospitalize her after only a few months of family treatment.

The combination of facts, that her conception was unwanted, that her mother suffered a postpartum psychosis after her pregnancy, that she lived in a foster home for 14 months and then was taken care of by a mother who suffered from continuing depression and an inadequate sense of her own mothering capacity, and that her birth occasioned such devastating disruption in the family—set the stage for Alice's pathological involvement in the family. Her interaction with the family is dominated by the feeling that she is not wanted by her parents and that she is not really a member of the family. While the circumstances of birth prepared the situation, there are also factors at work which prolong the impression. Mrs. DiMaggio has a similar problem with Alice as with Amy—she cannot meet the demands that Alice generates for affection and attention. It is as though Alice were constantly testing to see whether her mother really loves and wants her but her need cannot be satisfied. When M tries to set limits, usually in exasperation, this becomes another reflection which confirms her basic premise. Alice is capable of petulant outbursts but rage is difficult and threatening for her because it destroys the closeness with her parents that she so desperately seeks.

Alice's relationship with her father is interesting as well. Alice is uniquely capable among the three daughters of eliciting anger in her father. His demeanor to her is generally in his usual style of affectionate and seductive mothering. But when Alice becomes willful and defiant, F becomes very upset and has great difficulty in controlling his anger. The fact that he becomes so enraged is proof to her that he doesn't want her as his daughter.

The family romance is plainly between Mr. DiMaggio and Anny. Anny is the tallest, strongest, and best endowed sexually of the three daughters. Mr. DiMaggio relates to her as a fellow adult, almost as to a spouse—even more so than his wife. She is, of course, the second oldest child, as he was. In the intense sibling rivalry for father's affections, Anny is clearly the winner. This further undercuts the two sick daughters. It intensifies Amy's need to cling dependently to her father and to seek the elusive and threatening emotional closeness to him. Alice is intensely jealous of her older sister. Anny is bigger, older, has well developed breasts and has "made it" sexually. Alice is smaller, has no breasts to speak of and has strongly emerging desires for sexual expression but is terribly frightened by her own emergent sexuality. In the competition for father she feels that she has lost out. She cannot gain father's love and affection as a female. She carries the delusion that the child that miscarried in 1951 was a boy and she identifies with that dead fetus. If she could become like that dead fetus, she could gain father's love—not as a girl but as the boy he always wanted so badly.

Alice's involvement with Amy is one of intense sibling rivalry and hatred. There is an intense competition for F's affection particularly. The feeling between the two pathologically affected girls has broken out in physical fights on several occasions. These have strengthened Amy's conviction that Alice is trying to kill her. Alice does indeed express the murderous wish to kill her sister. Amy has in fact become the target for Alice's pent-up rage and resentment against the rest of the family for what she feels is rejection and not being wanted. Alice's relationship to Anny is more positive but is strongly colored by the feeling that Anny doesn't care about her and isn't interested in her. Quite recently Anny announced in one of the family sessions her engagement and intentions of marriage. The two sisters reacted very characteristically. Amy broke down in tears of self-pity, reflecting how badly she felt because her younger sister was getting married and she was still so sick and had to be in a hospital and would probably never be able to get married. Alice reacted in an outburst of tearful rage, accusing Anny of leaving her, of never caring about her, and of abandoning the family.

Family Interaction

I would like to focus on the style of family interaction since it has important implications for understanding the pathology in this family. The style of the family is set largely by the interactions between the parents and their interlocking personalities and pathologies. There is no clear-cut pattern of dominance-and-dependence. Rather both parents seem dependent in their own way and their relation is schismatic if anything. Mr. DiMaggio is the most verbal member of the family and takes up an undue proportion of the talking time in the family sessions. His anxiety is apparent and his depression is more subtle. He characteristically takes a position and then clings doggedly to it in the face of whatever confrontation the family or the therapist is capable of presenting to him. He responds often as though what has been said to him has made no impression whatsoever on him. He states a position and does not change it. If one of the family refutes his view of things, he inevitably distorts facts with a dogged insistence that he is right. He is incapable of letting anyone else in the family have the last word. If an argument ends, it ends because the other person gives up. When the argument ends, it ends with his re-enunciation of his original position. The family calls this phenomenon a "no-win" situation. It is interesting that Mischler and Waxler (13) in their extensive study of family patterns of interaction, have pointed to this kind of circularity and rigidity as characteristic of schizophrenic families.

The reaction of the two older daughters to this phenomenon is quite distinct. Anny will engage her father but only for a limited time. After two or three exchanges she seems to sense that the same old thing is going on and simply drops the argument with a "what's-the-use" attitude. Amy, on the other hand, engages in the argument with an intense degree of involvement. She matches her father point for point and as the argument progresses the intensity of feeling and volume of expression grow so that they end up shouting at each other. The involvement on both sides is such that neither gives any sign of giving in or wanting to end the argument. Amy shows an almost fiendish pleasure in this kind of debate, but while the contestants seem to relish it the other members of the family are quite upset by it. For Amy there is a curious satisfaction in this kind of exchange because in it she seems more engaged with her father than at any other time. The family has analogized the father's style in this matter to his salesmanship. He is like the salesman who will not let his customer escape without buying. Mr. DiMaggio is constantly selling to his family and he does not give up until they buy what he has to sell. The only one who buys is Amy.

Something that is insidious, but nonetheless striking, is Mr. DiMaggio's paranoid thinking. This is expressed in many subtle ways but sometimes becomes quite explicit. He is terribly self-conscious. He is constantly afraid of what people think of him, what they say about him. He feels that other men at work are jealous of him, that they try to keep sales away from him and that they are trying to get him fired. At times he has expressed thoughts that his family is against him, that they don't want him around, and even that they are trying to drive him crazy. The parallelism between this more hidden aspect of his character and the more apparent pathology of both sick daughters, particularly Amy, is quite striking.

The role of parental authority is extremely important for Mr. DiMaggio. Undoubtedly influenced by his Italian roots, he feels strongly that the father is to be the strong person in the family and that his word should be law. He feels that the father should make all the decisions in the family—and that no one else should make decisions. The difficulty is that he is quite unable to compromise or change his decisions—much in

the style of his taking any position—and he has great difficulty in enforc-
ing them. This is particularly a problem with Alice who openly defies and
struggles against parental restrictions. The challenge to his authority and
rigidity enrages him and threatens him. He has great difficulty managing
these feelings and when he does take some disciplinary measure he inevitably turns around almost immediately and undoes it by making some
palliating concession. Particularly threatening to him is any assertion of
authority on the part of his wife. He repeatedly undercuts her authority
in many subtle ways. She feels that she has no real say about what is done
in the family and feels devalued in her role as mother. Frequently he
has reopened decisions she has made vis-à-vis the children and then has
not supported her decision. When she objects to this, they become engaged in a typical no-win argument which only frustrates and enrages her
the more. Expression of anger is a problem for her as well.

There is chronic competition for the affection of the children which
comes up around both the sick girls and curiously not around Anny. The
quality of this aspect of the family interaction and its impact can be
gathered from the following episode. Mrs. DiMaggio and Alice got into
an argument just prior to Mr. DiMaggio's coming home one evening. He
came in to find his wife quite angry in the kitchen and Alice weeping
bitterly in her room. He went to comfort his daughter saying that she
shouldn't cry because he loved her. M also loved her but couldn't show
it so well because she had been sick. He then called to M to come upstairs
and show Alice how much she loved her. It was quite apparent that at
that point, M, who was very angry at Alice, was not about to come up and
show Alice how much she loved her. The impact of this kind of maneuver
is to reinforce the children's pathological feelings of rejection, to undercut
his wife's position, to reinforce the impression that M is somehow defective, and to reinforce his own position as the parent who really cares and
is solicitous.

Family studies have made it clear that such maneuvers which prolong
and enforce the family pathology are not present without some collusion
from the spouse. In the present case, the collusion is quite apparent. Mrs.
DiMaggio's pathology interlocks quite nicely with her husband's. His
sadism feeds into her masochism. His insistence on the exercise of parental authority feeds into her impoverished self-esteem. His undercutting
of her mothering position and his continual competition with her over
mothering tasks feeds into her self-depreciation and feelings of feminine
inadequacy. She holds in her anger and avoids any direct confrontation
with her husband, but the anger is expressed in more diffuse and indirect
ways. The whole family atmosphere is permeated with angry feelings

which by and large remain unexpressed and beneath the surface. The feelings are picked up with great sensitivity by the two pathologically affected daughters and expressed by them in psychotic ways.

DISCUSSION

The basic question to which we are addressing ourselves in this study has to do with the factors that determine which child or children in the family become schizophrenic. I have discussed elsewhere (12) reasons why double-bind theories, communication theories and theories of role relations do not satisfy this basic question. They provide, in general, *ex post factum* explanations which make the patterns of disturbed interactions intelligible given the fact of illness, but they do not allow us to discriminate why this child rather than that became schizophrenic. We must look to more fundamental and primary levels of the family process.

In our family, the oldest and the youngest daughters became schizophrenic while the middle daughter escaped. The sick daughters became schizophrenic in entirely different contexts and for entirely different reasons. We can argue, then, that the pathogenic factors impinge upon the involved child in a variety of ways which need to be explored and understood. Our family seems to fit the characteristics of families which have a maximally pathogenic effect on the involved female children. The family is dominated by the hostile insecurity and depression of the mother and the father's narcissistic paranoia and seductive seeking of affective response from the children. The mother's feminine inadequacy and incapacity to give warmth and affection create feelings of rejection, intense longing for affection, resentful anger and guilt in the daughters. Feminine identity is impaired and the child is forced into strong emotional ties with the father. The closeness to the father is further alienating from the mother and provokes intense oedipal conflicts.

The question as to why the oldest and youngest daughters became involved in the family pathology must acknowledge that there was already a family pathology erected on the parental pathologies. The parents shared and blended their own inadequate personalities in such a way as to provide the matrix within which the children could be pathologically affected. The mother's sense of inadequacy, masochism, depression and inability to express positive warmth locked into the father's sense of masculine inadequacy, conflicts over dependency, sadism, and excessive needs for affection. Between the two there evolved a complex system of emotional interaction which provided a mutually provocative framework for their antagonism and hostility. She was continually undercut and devalued. She had to struggle at all times with a destructive rage which she could not directly express but which was expressed in many indirect ways both intrapsychically and intrafamiliarly. Her husband was, on his side of it, continually deprived and frustrated, his needs for dependent clinging and affection unfulfilled and his resentment continually stirred.

The important point, it seems to me, is that the parental interaction provided an ongoing system of emotional influences into which the future schizophrenic children are drawn. But what determines that they should be drawn into it?

The oldest daughter, the first born child, was introduced to this emotional system without any buffers. Her involvement was initially a function of her mother's mothering difficulties. Her early history is dominated by a longing for closeness and affection from the mother which was never satisfied. The added impediment of a sibling with whom the limited supply of affection had to be shared added to the basic problem. The rest of the family interaction, particularly as influenced by the father's influence in the denial of primogeniture and the reinforcement of her guilt, acted to continually undercut her position in the family. The other side of it was her deep sense of narcissistic entitlement which demanded attention, love and affection from her parents. The frustration of that demand brought forth her rage which was then channeled into depressive and phobic symptoms and finally into paranoid concerns. The family style contributes to the shape the sick member's pathology takes, but the essential fact is that the sick member gets caught up in the emotional system and its elaborate interplay.

The second daughter, who remains relatively healthy, is first of all protected from the involvement in the family system because the older sister has been taken up in the emotional entanglements of the system and provides sufficient satisfaction to the neurotic needs of mother and father around which the system is organized. She escapes the emotional involvement and thereby escapes the harmful emotional influences that are exchanged within the system. Consequently she is much freer to interact with the parents in a more positive and healthy way. Rather than assimilating from them their more pathological aspects she can identify with the healthier dimensions of both parents. In addition the family interaction acts continually to put her in a more favored position so that instead of the continually undercutting influences to which her older sister is subjected she has the opportunity of internalizing good parental images rather than bad and can undergo a more normal development of self-differentiation and self-esteem. She is the second of the siblings, and thus occupies the position which her father occupied in his nuclear family.

This reinforces the ties of identification between them. She is also the biggest, strongest, most uninhibited and independent of the three girls. She thus became F's "boy." She can form her own identity, hold her own opinions, be "her own person," without guilt and the threat of loss of love. The whole complex of guilt, hostility, recrimination and heartache which surrounds her mother's illness seems to have passed her by so as to have no place in her conscious memory. And all of the pathogenic influences which swirled around that event, which came to bear on her older sister so intensely, left her untouched.

The youngest daughter in this family was also quite sick and becomes involved in the family emotional system but in entirely different ways and for entirely different reasons than her older sister. Instead of the pattern of hostile dependence of her sister, the youngest daughter falls into a pattern of hostile rejection. This has been described as scapegoating (3, 17). She begins as an unwanted child, spends the first fourteen months of her life living outside the family, and her birth is surrounded by all the intense feelings and unexpressed attitudes that accompanied mother's illness. At an unconscious level, she is blamed by the family and particularly by the father for what happened to mother. She is the "bad seed" that did so much damage to mother, and the family mechanisms are subtly at work to reinforce this impression. She senses this implicit rejection and acts in such a way as to set it up and elicit it in the rest of the family. Once again the complex interplay of projection and introjection makes her into the blighted and defective ovum who deserves only to be cast out and killed. The family struggles ineffectually at a conscious level to refute this perception, but the sick child picks up and expresses what remains unconscious in the family system—just as her older schizophrenic sister picks up and reflects the unconscious paranoid elements in the family system.

It is impressive that both sick daughters are intensely involved in and responsive to the pathological affect in the family while the healthy daughter more or less prescinds from it. It is the emotional ties that accompany involvement which impede differentiation of self, progressive identification and structuralization which underly the emergence of a more mature and autonomous personality.

Our focus in the present study has been on the conjunction of factors which relate to the degree of involvement of respective siblings in the family pathology. Given the pathological matrix based on the emotional interaction of the parents, each child is drawn into that interaction in different ways and for different reasons. There is an economy in involvement which affects the first child most deeply and thereby leaves the

second child immune. The third child comes at a time of maximal instability and in tragic circumstances which permit her intense involvement
as well. There is in this descriptive material a clinical theory of pathogenesis in the family. It is hoped that further clinical studies may add
further plausibility to the view expressed here.

SUMMARY

The present clinical study is directed at the question of why one or the
other child is subjected to the pathogenic influences in the family and
the others are not. A clinical study is presented of a family in which there
are two schizophrenic daughters and one presumably healthy daughter.
The material supports the view that schizophrenia is a function of involvement in the emotional system generated by the interaction of parental pathologies. The involvement of a given child depends upon the
relative stability and equilibrium in the family system. In this family,
involvement of the first child stabilized the system sufficiently to allow
the second child to escape. The equilibrium can be further disturbed by
intrafamilial or extrafamilial influences, allowing further involvement
of other siblings. Specific mechanisms in the family dynamics preserve
and intensify pathogenic influences on the involved children, as well as
confirm and preserve the uninvolvement of healthy siblings.

REFERENCES

1. ALANEN, Y. O., et al., "The Family in the Pathogenesis of Schizophrenic and
   Neurotic Disorders," *Acta Psychiat. Scand.*, 42 (Suppl. 189), 1-654, 1966.
2. BELL, N. W., "Extended Family Relations of Disturbed and Well Families," *Fam.
   Proc.*, 1, 175-193, 1962.
3. BOSZORMENYI-NAGY, I., and FRAMO, J. L. (Eds.), *Intensive Family Therapy*,
   Hoeber Medical Div., Harper and Row, New York, 1965.
4. BOWEN, M., "A Family Concept of Schizophrenia," in D. Jackson (Ed.), *The Etiology of Schizophrenia*, Basic Books, New York, 1960, 346-372.
5. DAY, J., and DURATKOWSKA, H. Y., "The Psychiatric Patient and His 'Well' Sibling. A Comparison Through Their Art Productions," *Bull. Art Therapy*,
   Winter, 1, 51-56, 1962.
6. DELAY, J., DENIKER, P., and GREEN, A., "Le Milieu Familial des Schizophrènes. III
   Résultats et Hypothèses," *Encephale*, 51, 5-73, 1962.
7. DYSINGER, R. H., "The Family as the Unit of Study and Treatment, Workshop,
   1959. 2. A Family Perspective on the Diagnosis of Individual Members," *Am.
   J. Orthopsychiat.*, 31, 61-68, 1961.
8. LIDZ, T., FLECK, S., ALANEN, Y. O., and CORNELISON, A., "Schizophrenic Patients and
   Their Siblings," *Psychiatry*, 26, 1-18, 1963.
9. LIDZ, T., FLECK, S., and CORNELISON, A., *Schizophrenia and the Family*, Int. Univ.
   Press, New York, 1966.
10. LU, Y., "Contradictory Parental Expectations in Schizophrenia: Dependence and
   Responsibility," *Arch. Gen. Psychiat.*, 6, 219-234, 1962.

11. LU, Y., "Mother-Child Role Relations in Schizophrenia: A Comparison of Schizophrenic Patients with Nonschizophrenic Siblings," *Psychiatry*, 24, 133-142, 1961.
12. MEISSNER, S. J., W. W., "Thinking about the Family—Psychiatric Aspects," *Fam. Proc.*, 3, 1-40, 1964.
13. MISCHLER, E. G., and WAXLER, N. E., *Interaction in Families: An Experimental Study of Family Processes and Schizophrenia*, Wiley, New York, 1968.
14. SERRANO, A. C., McDANALD, E. C., GOOLISHIAN, H. A., MacGREGOR, R., and RITCHIE, A. M., "Adolescent Maladjustment and Family Dynamics," *Am. J. Psychiat.*, 118, 897-901, 1962.
15. SPIEGEL, J. P., "The Resolution of Role Conflict within the Family," *Psychiatry*, 20, 1-16, 1957.
16. WARING, M., and RICKE, D., "Family Patterns of Children Who Become Adult Schizophrenics," *J. Nerv. Ment. Dis.*, 140, 351-364, 1965.
17. VOGEL, E. F., and BELL, N. W., "The Emotionally Disturbed Child as the Family Scapegoat," in N. W. Bell and E. F. Vogel (Eds.), *A Modern Introduction to the Family*, The Free Press, Glencoe, Illinois, 1960, 382-397.

Section III

SOCIAL, DEVELOPMENTAL, AND EXISTENTIAL FACTORS

15

CRISES AND LIFE CHANGES PRECEDING THE ONSET OR RELAPSE OF ACUTE SCHIZOPHRENIA: CLINICAL ASPECTS

J. L. T. Birley and G. W. Brown

In a previous publication (Brown and Birley, 1968) we have presented some findings which suggest that life changes and crises frequently precipitate the acute onset, relapse or exacerbation of schizophrenic states. To summarize: consecutively admitted patients diagnosed as suffering from schizophrenia were seen at mental hospitals serving a known catchment area. The first fifty whose onsets occurred within three months of admission and could be accurately dated within a week were included. Both the patient and at least one other informant were interviewed about the occurrence of certain previously defined and datable events occurring to the patient or to close relatives. These included such events as moving house, starting or leaving a job, admission to hospital, birth, marriage or death during the twelve weeks prior to onset. These were classified, according to their apparent independence of the patient's control, as "independent" or "possibly independent." The former were those which could be regarded as outside his control, e.g. discovering a burglary or hearing of a brother's serious illness. "Possibly independent" events were those which were considered to have been within the patient's control but which had not been brought about by any unusual behavior on the patient's part. They were chiefly changes of job, or of opposite sex friends. (Loss of job would, under certain circumstances, be rated as "independent," e.g., when a whole firm closed down.)

In the three weeks immediately prior to onset, 23 (46 percent) of the patients had experienced at least one "independent" event, as compared

Reprinted, by permission of author and editor, from: *The British Journal of Psychiatry,* 116:327-333, 1970.

to an average of 12 per cent of patients experiencing such an event in each of the three earlier three-week periods. If both types of event are considered, the corresponding figures are 60 percent and 23 percent. The same interview, covering the same type of events, was given to a comparison group of 325 persons at their places of work. The percentage of these persons experiencing an event remained the same *for all four three-week periods* (independent events: 14 percent; all events: 19 percent)—a proportion very similar to that found for the patients during *their earlier three three-week periods.* For the comparison group, unlike the patients, there was *no* increase in the percentage of persons experiencing an event during the three-week period immediately prior to interview.

We interpret these results as indicating that, prior to onset, there had been a real increase in the rate of events which could not have been brought about by abnormal behavior on the patient's part, nor could it be an effect of biased reporting, nor of any tendency to forget events which had occurred more than three weeks prior to interview.

This paper is concerned with some of the clinical issues involved in this study. In particular are these patients a "special group" as judged by age, sex, length of illness or symptomatology; do these findings apply equally to those experiencing first onsets, relapses, or exacerbations; and how are the results affected when another possible precipitant —stopping or reducing phenothiazines—is taken into account.

METHODS

The patients were seen as part of a larger study of admissions to hospitals serving a defined catchment area (approx. 1,000,000) in South-East London. The case notes of every patient were screened soon after admission. If certain diagnostic symptoms were mentioned (see under "Diagnosis") or if the diagnosis of schizophrenia or "schizo-affective" or "paranoid state" had been considered as a possibility, then the patient was interviewed, first to establish a diagnosis and secondly to get details of onset and the incidence of events prior to onset. This generally involved at least two interviews. For the great majority of the patients it was possible to get an account from relatives or other informants.

The interview concerning events is described in our previous article. Our approach was to ask about the occurrence of various types of events affecting the patient or close relative, which could be dated to a definite point in time and which usually involved either danger, significant changes in health, status or way of life: the promise of these, or fulfillment, or disappointments. We included events which on commonsense grounds might be regarded as "disturbing" but could be either pleasant (e.g. marriage, moving to a better home), unpleasant (e.g. bereavement, severe illness or injury), or neutral (e.g. brother announces engagement). In practice, of course, the emotions actually experienced may be very different: marriage may be an unpleasant ordeal, and an injury a pleasant escape.

In addition, careful enquiry was made as to whether the patient was taking phenothiazines or other drugs, or whether these had been reduced or omitted either by the patient's initiative, or on medical advice, during the past year.

Diagnosis

Diagnosis was based largely on symptoms expressed at a comprehensive and standardized clinical interview (Wing *et al.*, 1967), which was concerned with the recent mental state of the patient. For a diagnosis of schizophrenia to be made, the patient must have shown at least one of the following groups of symptoms, in the presence of clear consciousness:

1. Subjective experience of disordered thought or body control.

2. Delusions of persecution or reference which were thought to be undeserved and not occurring in the context of severe depression.

3. Grandiose, religious, somatic, or bizarre delusions but not in a setting of severe depression or mania.

4. Consistent hallucinations, not depressive in content and not symptomatic of alcohol addiction.

Persistent incoherence of speech and catatonic motor disorders were also taken into account, but in practice all the admitted patients with either or both of these symptoms also showed evidence of schizophrenic delusions or hallucinations.

On the basis of these symptoms the patients were categorized into two groups: "definite schizophrenia" and "probable schizophrenia." We found this necessary because there were many patients, usually of a younger age, for whom schizophrenia seemed the most likely diagnosis, but owing to an admixture of other symptoms, such as depression, excitement, depersonalization, and of episodes of comparatively brief duration, we could not come to a firm conclusion. Such conditions would roughly correspond to the "schizophreniform states" described by Langfeldt (1939). We felt it important to include these patients, since it is known that, whilst their outcome is generally more favourable, a considerable proportion relapse, and some may develop a more definite schizophrenic illness later. (Holmboe and Astrup, 1957; Welmer and Strömgren, 1958.)

Onset

We distinguished three different types of onset according to the mental state of the patient prior to the development of a state of acute schizophrenia.

1. From "normal" to schizophrenia (29 patients).

2. From "non-schizophrenic" symptoms, e.g. depression, irritability, or withdrawal, to schizophrenia (8 patients).

3. Exacerbation of "mild" to "severe" schizophrenia (15 patients).

RESULTS

(1) *Selection of patients*

The first 50 patients whose onsets had occurred within three months of admission and could be dated within a week were selected from a total of 123 consecutive admissions diagnosed by us as suffering from schizophrenia. The 73 other patients were excluded on the following grounds:

1. No change or only gradual deterioration during the three months prior to admission: 53 patients.

2. Some definite change during the three months prior to admission, but this could not be dated to within a week: 16 patients.

3. Inadequate information: 4 patients.

There were no statistically significant differences by age, sex and diagnosis between the excluded and the included patients. The excluded group tended to be rather older and contained a somewhat higher proportion of patients diagnosed as "definitely schizophrenic." By definition, the included group contained more patients with a short previous history. There were also more patients experiencing their first admission in the included group (24/50—48 percent) than in the excluded group (25/73—34 percent), but the difference is not statistically significant.

The admitting hospitals' diagnoses of the 50 included patients were as follows:

(a) "Schizophrenia" (45 patients).

(b) "Schizo-affective psychosis" (4 patients).

(c) "Mixed affective state with paranoid ideas" (1 patient).

(2) *Age and sex*

There were 24 men and 26 women in the series. Diagnosis was not related to sex, but those diagnosed as "probably schizophrenic" were younger (range 15-52, mean 29.3) than those diagnosed as "definitely schizophrenic" (range 17-71, mean 38.2 years). Diagnosis was also related to type of onset (Table 1). There were more onsets from "normal to schizophrenia" among patients diagnosed as "probably schizophrenic" than amongst those diagnosed as "definitely schizophrenic" (18/24 (75 percent) v. 11/26 (42 percent) $\chi^2 = 4.5$, p < .05).

(3) *Relationship of events to type of diagnosis and symptomatology* (Table 1)

Between the "definitely" and the "probably" schizophrenic patients there was no difference in the proportion experiencing an independent event in the three weeks prior to onset (46 percent). Rather more of the "probably schizophrenic" than of the "definitely schizophrenic" patients experienced an event of some description in the final three weeks, but the difference is not statistically significant (17/24 (71 per cent) v. 13/26 (50 percent)).

As our clinical interview covered a considerable range of symptoms, a more detailed analysis of symptomatology was possible. The frequencies of 21 different types of symptoms were compared between 30 patients who had experienced any event in the final three weeks and the 20 who had not. All differences were small and insignificant except in two instances. Depressive delusions were more frequently expressed by those patients who had experienced any event in the final three weeks (6/30 v. 1/20) and so were preoccupations with death (9/30 v. 2/20). For only 2 of these 9 patients was the "event" a death of a relative. On the other hand, depressive mood changes and feelings of guilt were found equally in both groups of patients.

(4) *Relationship of events to type of onset* (Table 1)

The proportion of patients experiencing any event in the final three weeks was the same for those with a "normal to schizophrenic" onset as for those with exacerbations of "mild to severe schizophrenia" (20/29 (65 percent) v. 9/13 (69 percent)). For those patients with an onset from "non-schizophrenic" symptoms to "schizophrenia" the proportion experiencing any event in the final three weeks was considerably less (1/8 (13 percent)). This difference, we believe, can be attributed to the design of the study which excluded our considering changes from normal to non-schizophrenic symptoms, as we expected these to be too indistinct to be dated accurately. For 3 of these 8 patients (all diagnosed as "definitely schizophrenic") a clear-cut disturbing event occurred shortly before a change in their mental state from "normal" to "non-schizophrenic" symptoms. These events were:

1. (Spinster aged 22) mother committed suicide, 11 weeks prior to onset.

2. (Bachelor aged 71) moved by Council to live on his own in a strange neighborhood, 11 weeks prior to onset.

3. (Spinster aged 47) sister arrived suddenly asking to stay after being attacked by her mentally disturbed son, 4 weeks prior to onset.

TABLE 1

EXPERIENCE OF EVENTS DURING 3 WEEKS PRIOR TO ONSET AND TYPE
OF ONSET, DIAGNOSIS, AND FIRST OR READMISSION

Type of onset	Diagnosis	Experience of at least one event during 3 weeks prior to onset			
		Independent event	Possibly independent event only	No event	Total patients
Normal to	Definite schizophrenia	5	1	5	11
schizophrenia	Probable schizophrenia	9	5	4	18
Non-schizophrenic	Definite schizophrenia	1	—	5	6
symptoms to	Probable schizophrenia	—	—	2	2
schizophrenia	Definite schizophrenia	6	—	3	9
Exacerbation of mild to	Probable schizophrenia	2	1	1	4
severe schizophrenia..	Definite schizophrenia	12	1	13	26
All onsets	Probable schizophrenia	11	6	7	24
	First admissions	12	4	8	24
	Readmissions	11	3	12	26
	All patients	23	7	20	50

After a varying interval, these patients' "non-schizophrenic" symptoms changed quite abruptly to "schizophrenic" ones. If the development of "non-schizophrenic" symptoms had been taken as "onset" in these cases, the proportion with independent events in the three weeks prior to onset would have been the same as for patients with the other two types of onset (4/8 (50 percent)). Clearly, this would be altering our design, but it indicates that further studies should consider such changes if possible.

(5) *"First admission" and "Readmission"* (Table 1)

Rather more of the "probably schizophrenic" than the "definitely schizophrenic" patients were experiencing their first admission, but the difference is not statistically significant (14/24 (58 percent) *v.* 10/26 (38 percent)). There was little difference in the proportion of patients experiencing any event in the final three weeks between the first admitted and the readmitted patients (16/24 (67 percent) *v.* 14/26 (54 percent)).

(6) *"First episodes" v. "Relapses"*

Eight of the 13 patients experiencing an exacerbation of "mild" to "severe" symptoms were in their first episodes of schizophrenia, but for most of these 8 the episodes had been of several years' duration, usually with previous admissions. Of the remaining 37 patients, 15 were experiencing their first-ever episode, and 22 a relapse. The proportion of patients experiencing any event in the final three weeks was very similar in the two groups (10/15 (67 percent) *v.* 12/22 (55 percent)).

TABLE 2

RELATIONSHIP BETWEEN PHENOTHIAZINE MEDICATION
AND THE EXPERIENCE OF ANY EVENT IN
THE 3 WEEKS PRIOR TO ONSET

Phenothiazine medication	Experience of at least one event during 3 weeks prior to onset		
	Yes	No	Total
Stopped or reduced phenothiazines	4	9	13
On no phenothiazines in past year	23	9	32
Taking phenothiazines at onset	3	2	5

(7) *Phenothiazine Medication* (Table 2)

Eleven patients had stopped their phenothiazines, and two others had reduced theirs by at least a half, during a period between 6 weeks and 11 months (average 4.5 months) prior to onset. This had been done for apparently quite "healthy" reasons—they were feeling well, and were often acting on medical advice or approval. Of these 13 patients only 4 (31 per cent) had experienced any event in the three weeks prior to onset, compared to 23 (72 per cent) of the 32 patients who had not taken any phenothiazines in the past year ($\chi^2 = 4.8$, p<.05). Putting it another way, 9 (45 per cent) of the 20 patients who had not experienced any event in the past three weeks gave a history of stopping or reducing their drugs, compared to only 4 (13 per cent) of the 30 patients who had experienced any event.

There were five patients who had been taking phenothiazines regularly at the time of onset. Three of these had experienced an event in the preceding three weeks. Both the other two had experienced a disturbing event, but earlier on. One, already mentioned, had lost her mother through suicide in week 11. The other, a boy of 19, whose father had left home some years previously, was present at the death of his grandfather in week 5.

DISCUSSION

Opinions about the role of precipitating events in schizophrenia have been confused by the tendency to make assumptions about etiology on the basis of symptomatology. Thus K. Schneider (1959) makes the distinction between "true psychoses," which have a "somatic etiology" and can be "precipitated" by external events, and "psychic reactions" which can be "caused" by external events. These two are "polar opposites" which, he claims, can be distinguished from each other by their symptomatology. Schneider would therefore not agree with the diagnosis "psychogenic" or "reactive psychosis"—a contradiction in his terms. It is a popular one, nevertheless, in Scandinavia, although most Scandinavian studies indicate that the symptoms of "reactive" and "true" psychoses overlap each other to a considerable extent, and the diagnosis seems to depend more on outcome than on symptomatology or apparent "psychogenesis" (Faergeman, 1946, 1963; Strömgren, 1965).

In his pioneer studies of the contributions of "stress" and "genetic predisposition" in the precipitation of schizophrenia and manic depressive states, Strecker (1922) took the precaution of stating that he was making no claim about etiology. He had in mind the concept of a single etiological factor. We believe, as do many others (see review by Rosenbaum, 1968), that several possible factors may have to combine to produce a "schizophrenic state"—for instance, some biological change in the brain, an acquired "style" of coping behavior, and some difficulty or change in the environment. Outcome presumably depends upon how much one or more of these can be rectified: a poor outcome need not necessarily be due to a "somatic etiology." It may reflect a persistently unsuitable environment (Wing and Brown, 1961; Brown and Wing, 1962; Brown et al., 1962). At the onset of the illness the contribution of any particular factor may vary considerably. At times "inherent" factors, at others "exogenous" ones will be over-riding. Significantly, Schneider remarks that "at the battle-front it is often hard to make a differential diagnosis between twilight states and schizophrenia. In the isolated cases it can be impossible for the most practised eye not to be deceived."

In designing our study, our aim was *not* to consider every possible psychological precipitant but to establish whether or not certain types of potentially disturbing events, which could be dated, and ascertained in a nonpsychiatric population, occurred more frequently in a period prior to the acute onset, relapse, or exacerbation of a schizophrenic state. We have established that the rate of such events was increased in the three weeks prior to onset, and that these were events which could not have been directly brought about by the patient's illness.

In considering the clinical aspects of the patients, we have found no evidence that our findings apply only to patients of a certain age, sex or symptomatology. The finding that "probably schizophrenic" were rather younger than the "definitely schizophrenic" patients, and were more likely to experience an onset from "normal to schizophrenia," agrees with the general impression that acute schizophrenia is often accompanied by affective disturbance. Of those patients diagnosed as "definitely schizophrenic," only eleven experienced an onset of normal to schizophrenia" but the proportion of these experiencing any event in the previous three weeks (6/11—(54 per cent)) was the same as that of the whole series (60 per cent). The finding that patients experiencing a recent event were more likely to be preoccupied with thoughts of death and depressive delusions agrees with the observations of Vaillant (1964) that "concern with death" and "depression" were positively correlated with precipitating events in his series of schizophrenic patients.

There have been many reports to indicate that stopping or reducing phenothiazines may bring about a relapse or exacerbation of schizophrenia (Good et al., 1958; Wold, 1960; Caffey et al., 1964). We were interested to find that of the patients who had stopped their drugs, the proportion experiencing any event in the final three weeks (31 per cent) was little different from the average rate for all the patients in the earlier three-week periods (23 per cent). For these patients, therefore, the most important factor seems to have been stopping phenothiazines. In contrast, we found that all of the patients who relapsed while taking phenothiazines had experienced a disturbing event. In two cases this had occurred more than three weeks prior to onset. It is possible that taking phenothiazines may delay reactions to disturbing events.

Recently, Steinberg and Durell (1968) have reported that, shortly after enlistment, there is an increased incidence of schizophrenic illness. This agrees with a study by Wallis (1965), who found that, between the ages of 15 and 20, but not at other ages, the incidence of schizophrenia in the British navy is very much higher than the national average. It is thus rather curious that there is now better evidence for the importance of precipitating events in schizophrenia than there is for affective states where, apart from childbirth (Pugh *et al.*, 1963) the findings are inconclusive (Forrest *et al.*, 1965; Hudgens *et al.*, 1967). This may be due to the methodological difficulties involved in assessing onset in affective illness—a problem upon which we are engaged at present.

In addition to any theoretical interest, our findings have important implications for the after-care of schizophrenic patients who are now exposed rightly to a more "eventful" existence than the harmful monotony of an old-style mental hospital. Their relapse rate remains high, and we need to know why this is the case. If certain types of crisis or life change can precipitate relapse, it is important to know what these are, and how they can be dealt with or avoided. It may be that taking phenothiazines helps some patients cope better; it may be that psychological preparation may help others. Certainly such events need to be taken into consideration when assessing the effects of any drug in maintaining schizophrenic patients in the community.

SUMMARY

From a consecutive series of 123 patients diagnosed as suffering from schizophrenia, the first 50 were selected who had experienced an acute onset or relapse within three months of admission. They and their relatives were interviewed concerning the occurrence, during the 12 weeks prior to onset, of certain previously defined events which might, on commonsense grounds, be considered as potentially disturbing. Sixty per cent of the patients had experienced at least one such an event during the three weeks prior to onset compared to an average of 23 per cent during the three earlier three-week periods.

Diagnostically, the patients were divided into two groups—"definite" and "probable" schizophrenia. In addition, the frequency of 21 different symptoms was looked at. Onsets were classified into (1) "normal to schizophrenic," (2) "non-specific to schizophrenic" and (3) "exacerbation from mild to severe schizophrenia."

There were no significant differences by age, sex and diagnostic category between the 50 included and the 73 excluded patients. Within the acute onset group, there were no differences by age, sex and diagnostic category or symptomatology between those who had and those who had not experienced any event in the final three weeks, except that certain depressive preoccupations were commoner in the former. Thirteen patients gave a history of stopping or considerably reducing their phenothiazines medication. The proportion of these experiencing any event in the final three weeks (31 per cent) was significantly lower than for the rest of the patients (72 per cent) and not different from the "average rate" (23 per cent) for all patients in the earlier three weeks periods.

We conclude firstly that both life events and reducing or stopping phenothiazines contribute as precipitants of acute schizophrenia, and secondly that the symptomatology of acute schizophrenia is largely unrelated to its precipitants.

ACKNOWLEDGMENTS

The authors are grateful to the staff of the Bethlem Royal, Bexley, Cane Hill, Maudsley, St. Francis, St. Olave's, and St. Thomas's Hospitals for their permission to carry out this research and for their generous co-operation during the work.

REFERENCES

BROWN, G. W., BIRLEY, J. L. T., (1968). 'Crises and life changes and the onset of schizophrenia.' *J. Hlth. soc. Behav.*, 9, 203-14.

—— WING, J. K. (1962). 'A comparative clinical and social survey of three mental hospitals.' The Sociological Review Monogr. 5. *Sociology and Medicine: Studies within the Framework of the British National Health Service.* Ed. P. Halmos.

BROWN, G. W., MONCK, E. M., CARSTAIRS, G. M., WING, J. K. (1962). 'Influence of family life on the course of schizophrenic illness.' *Brit. J. prev. soc. Med.* 16, 55-68.

CAFFEY, E. M., DIAMOND, L. S., FRANK, T. V., GRASBERGER, J. C., HERMAN, L., KLETT, C. J., ROTHSTEIN, C. (1964). 'Discontinuation or reduction of chemotherapy in chronic schizophrenia.' *J. chron. Dis.*, 17, 347-58.

FAERGEMAN, P. (1946). 'Early differential diagnosis between psychogenic psychosis and schizophrenia.' *Acta psychiat. neurol. Scand.*, 21, 275-9.

—— (1963). *Psychogenic Psychosis.* London: Butterworths.

FORREST, A. D., FRASER, R. H., PRIEST, R. G. (1965). Environmental factors in depressive illness. *Brit. J. Psychiat.*, 111, 243-53.

GOOD, W. W., STERLING, M., HOLTZMAN, W. H. (1958). 'Termination of chlorpromazine with schizophrenic patients.' *Amer. J. Psychiat.*, 115, 443-8.

HOLMBOE, R., ASTRUP, C. (1957). 'A follow-up study of 255 patients with acute schizophrenia and schizophreniform psychoses.' *Acta psychiat. neurol. Scand.*, Suppl. 115.

HUDGENS, R. W.. MORRISON, J. R., BARCHHA, R. G. (1967). 'Life events and the onset of primary affective symptoms.' *Arch. gen. Psychiat.*, 16, 134-45.

LANGFELDT, G. (1939). *The Schizophreniform States.* Copenhagen.

PUGH, T. F., JERATH, B. K., SCHMIDT, T. W. M., REED, R. B. (1963). 'Rates of mental disease related to child-bearing.' *New Eng. J. Med.*, 1224-8.

ROSENBAUM, C. P. (1968). 'Metabolic, physiological, anatomic and genetic studies in the schizophrenias: a review and analysis.' *J. nerv. ment. Dis.*, 146, 103-26.

SCHNEIDER, K. (1959). *Clinical Psychopathology.* (5th edn.) Grune and Stratton.

STEINBERG, H. R., DURELL, J. (1968). 'A stressful situation as a precipitant of schizophrenic symptoms.' *Brit. J. Psychiat.*, 114, 1097-105.

STRECKER, E. A. (1922). 'A preliminary study of the precipitating situation in two hundred cases of mental disease.' *Amer. J. Psychiat.*, 1, 503-36.

STRÖMGREN, E. (1965). 'Schizophreniform psychoses.' *Acta psychiat. Scand.* 41, 483-9.

VAILLANT, G. E. (1964). 'Prospective prediction of schizophrenic remission.' *Arch. gen. Psychiat.*, 11. 509-18.

WALLIS, G. G. (1965). 'An epidemiological and follow-up study of schizophrenia in the Royal Navy.' M.D. Thesis. University of London.

WELMER, J., STRÖMGREN. E. (1958). 'Clinical and genetic studies on benign schizophreniform psychoses based on follow-up.' *Acta psychiat. neurol. Scand.*, 33, 377-99.

WING, J. K., BROWN, G. W. (1961). 'Social treatment of chronic schizophrenia: a comparative study of three mental hospitals.' *J. ment. Sci.*, 107, 847-861.

—— BIRLEY, J. L. T., COOPER, J. E., GRAHAM, P., ISAACS, A. (1967). 'Reliability of procedure for measuring and classifying "present psychiatric state." ' *Brit. J. Psychiat.*, 113, 499-515.

WOLD, P. E. (1960). 'A long term evaluation of chlorpromazine in six chronic schizophrenic patients.' *J. nerv. ment. Dis.*, 130, 151-4.

16

PREMORBID ASOCIAL ADJUSTMENT AND PROGNOSIS IN SCHIZOPHRENIA

Rachel Gittelman-Klein and Donald F. Klein

In the extensive literature concerning the personality characteristics of schizophrenics, major emphasis has been placed on the role premorbid asocial adjustment plays in the development of schizophrenia (1-11).

Kraepelin was one of the first to discuss the early childhood personality characteristics of dementia praecox patients. He emphasized a pattern, most frequently reported in men who as children "exhibited a quiet, shy retiring disposition, made no friends, lived only for themselves" (7).

Hoch (4, 12) labeled such patients as having a "shut-in" personality. Bleuler also described an early disturbance reflecting the child's lack of interest in the environment (13).

The concept that the childhood of the adult schizophrenic was often characterized by inadequate social interaction gained wide acceptance (11). A variety of labels were used to refer to the shut-in premorbid personalities of schizophrenic patients, such as "schizophrenic constitutions" (10), "schizoid personalities" (2, 3, 6), "constitutional schizophrenia" (1), "introverted personalities" (14), and "process symptoms" (15). The qualitative referents of these terms unanimously reflected Hoch's description.

There was disagreement, however, as to what the shut-in, schizoid personality signified. Some clinicians, among them Kraepelin, Bleuler, and Kretschmer, felt that these early disturbances were the first signs of the disease. Meyer, on the other hand, felt that these early traits did not represent disease onset but were dynamic factors predisposing to schizophrenia (16, 17).

Although much was written in the early 1900's regarding the childhood

Reprint requests to Research Department, Hillside Hospital, Box 38, Glen Oaks, New York 11004.

Reprinted, by permission of author and editor, from: *The Journal of Psychiatric Research,* 7:35-53, 1969.

social inadequacies of adult schizophrenics, Hoch only was explicit about their prognostically negative role (12). In view of Hoch's explicit statement regarding the relationship of premorbid adjustment to outcome, it is surprising that relatively little attention was given to this issue. Rather, the length of time during which the psychosis developed (i.e. insidious vs. acute onset) was considered by clinicians the major factor influencing the course of schizophrenia (18, 19).

Kant (14, 15, 20) and Langfeldt (21-23) emphasized the prognostic value of the psychotic symptomatology. Kant also stressed the role of "introversion" in the prognosis of schizophrenia. He did not, however, clarify what he meant by the discrimination between extrovert versus introvert, or at what point in the patient's life it should be made. He stated that the malignant or process symptoms consisted of disorganization, dulling and autism. These changes, which he did not specify or describe further, developed gradually, preceded the outbreak of the psychosis and later gave specific coloring to the clinical picture (14, 15).

EMPIRICAL FINDINGS

Wittman (24) compared the outcome of electroshock therapy in two groups of 66 adult schizophrenics each. One group had received psychiatric treatment and psychological tests between the ages of 10 to 16 (early treatment group); the other had not. Half the referrals of the early treatment group were for school retardation. The author reported that in the original psychological reports of the early treatment group 48 patients had been said to be "slow, listless, inattentive, and indifferent." Wittman therefore felt that the early treatment group represented the shut-in type of personality. Since fewer of the early treatment group showed improvement following shock therapy, she concluded that the shut-in personality had prognostic value.

Wittman's study has several shortcomings. The two samples were not matched or studied with regard to other variables which may influence outcome. Thus, the IQ's of the early treatment group range from defective to above average. Those of the non-treated group are not given and may have differed. More important, the patients in childhood had deviant, but not necessarily shut-in personality patterns. A less inferential conclusion is that a history of psychiatric treatment in childhood is prognostic of a poor response to shock therapy in adult schizophrenia. This study did not test the prognostic value of the shut-in personality.

Phillips (25) related the scores obtained by 31 patients on a case history form to their level of functioning 6-12 months after receiving some form of shock therapy. He found that the better the patient's adjustment on the case history variables, the better his treatment outcome. However, the only two premorbid ratings which did not relate to outcome were those dealing with the adequacy of early social functioning. The results of this study are therefore in contradiction to Wittman's (24).

Several investigators have used the absence of a premorbid schizoid personality as a positive sign in scales of prognosis (26-29). They all report a significant positive association between the absence of a premorbid schizoid personality and good outcome for schizophrenic, as well as nonschizophrenic patients. These studies are remarkable in providing follow-up information for extended periods of time. Vaillant (29) studied 172 schizophrenics. Of 44 who remitted fully, 34 per cent had had a schizoid personality; of 128 who did not fully remit, 76 per cent had been schizoid. For a subgroup of 100 patients followed 12-24 months after hospital admission, Vaillant reports a tetrachoric correlation of 0.69 between non-schizoid adjustment and remission.

From a cohort of 350 patients, Stephens, Astrup and Mangrum (28) selected a group of 50 patients each; one group had the best outcomes, whereas the other had the worst. They found that the "not schizoid" item had a tetrachoric correlation of 0.51 with recovery.

However, perhaps because the above authors' interests were not specifically in the role of early asociality in outcome, the terms schizoid and nonschizoid are not defined. Astrup and Noreik (27), who are unique in giving reliability data, report 62 per cent agreement on ratings of schizoid personality, a relatively low agreement. Further, no information is given as to when during the patients' lives a schizoid personality was identified (26-30).

The use of a dichotomy, schizoid vs. nonschizoid, in predicting post-hospital course, has yielded positive results. However, though empirically valid in studies of prognosis, it is not clear that such a dichotomy does exist, and that it corresponds to clinical phenomena.

In another study (31) two groups were selected by specific stringent criteria of differential outcome; recovery was defined as having spent no more than six months in the hospital and avoiding rehospitalization for at least five years; nonrecovery consisted of having been in the hospital for more than six months. The total Phillips scale scores of 83 schizophrenic women were predictive of recovery. However, the relative predictive value of each item is not given. Therefore, it is not possible to evaluate the contribution of the item indicative of early asociality to the significant correlation between total score and outcome.

Other studies have also related scores on various prognostic scales to outcome (30, 32-35). Besides the limitations of the recovery criterion of three of these studies (27, 29, 31), i.e. length of hospitalization, they also all give results for total scale scores only. Therefore, it is not possible to determine the specific relationship of premorbid socialization to outcome.

Another study gives the relationship of asociality to outcome for a mixed group of psychotic patients, but not for the schizophrenic subgroup (27).

In view of the abundant clinical references to the malignant implications of early asocial behavior for adult schizophrenia and the lack of specific empirical data, a study was undertaken to assess the specific relationship of premorbid socialization patterns to posthospital adjustment in schizophrenia.

HYPOTHESES

The general hypothesis is that premorbid schizoid or asocial functioning is positively related to poor posthospital adjustment in adult schizophrenics. Specifically, it is hypothesized that premorbid asocial traits are associated with poor outcome as defined by:

1. poor overall outcome with regard to symptomatology and maintenance of role appropriate behavior,
2. poor psychiatric outcome; i.e. number of rehospitalizations and time spent in psychiatric hospitals,
3. poor occupational outcome, and
4. poor interpersonal functioning in posthospital adjustment.

METHOD

The study was undertaken at Hillside Hospital, a 196-bed, voluntary psychiatric hospital. Patients are admitted who, upon psychiatric screening, are felt to be good candidates for psychotherapy and milieu therapy.

Sample

A total of 177 patients were followed 2 years after discharge from the hospital. The sample and follow-up procedures have been reported elsewhere (36). Of the 177 Ss, 127 (68 women and 59 men) had been diagnosed as schizophrenic at their discharge conference by a joint decision of the clinical staff. The patients ranged in age from 17 to 59. In this study, all patients 41 years and older ($N = 12$) were eliminated from the sample since economic, social, or psychological characterists of patients differ as a function of age (37).

Of the 115 patients 40 years of age and under, 7 were deceased before follow-up, 13 refused to participate in the study, and 2 were not located. Of the remaining 93 schizophrenic patients, 86 were personally interviewed by a social worker who did not know the patient's history. These constitute the study sample.

Table 1 sumarizes some patient characteristics. Social class was rated according to Hollingshead and Redlich's schema (38).

TABLE 1

Patient Characteristics ($N = 86$)

	N	N Married	Age in years		Years of education		Social class		I.Q.		Months of index hospitalization	
			Mean	S.D.	Mean	S.D.	Mean	S.D.	Mean	S.D.	Mean	S.D.
Men	39	4	22.82	5.30	13.41	2.34	3.23	1.21	112.46	17.08	9.40	3.93
Women	47	12	23.89	5.75	13.21	2.07	3.13	1.00	108.02	14.49	9.83	4.03
Total	86	16	23.41	5.58	13.31	2.20	3.17	1.10	110.16	15.94	9.64	3.99

Ratings of Premorbid Asocial Adjustment

The data used for rating premorbid history came from three sources: first, the patients' case histories, an extensive report written by the treating psychiatrist on the basis of information obtained from patient and relatives; second, social histories gathered from the patient's family by the hospital Social Service Department; third, reports from previous treatment sources.

Prior to rating the life history of the patients, no material pertaining to the patient's hospital course was read. This precaution was easily observed since current hospital data were clearly separated from other data.

A scale was devised limited to aspects of a shut-in, schizoid, withdrawn, asocial premorbid personality during preadolescence and adolescence (Table 2). A high score always indicates an asocial type of functioning.*

The undefined scale points are for interpolation. The extremes indicating marked difficulty in social activities are still less severe than the disturbed interpersonal relationships of autistic children. The deviant

---

* Since completion of the study, the scale has been revised. The new version is available from the authors.

TABLE 2

Case History Ratings for Premorbid Schizoid Adjustment

Sixth year to adolescence

Withdrawal
0   Normal social interaction
1   Somewhat timid and quiet
2   Timid and quiet, reluctant to approach people
3
4   Withdrawn, unrelated—no interest in approaching others; not attracted to other children

Peer relationships
0   Many friends with a few close relationships
1   Few but close friends
2   Casual friends only
3   A few occasional casual friends only
4
5   Social isolate, no friends

*Interests**
Active   x   Normal   x   Introverted interests   x   No interests
0   1   2   3   4   5   6
Active: Interested in a variety of school and social activities and hobbies.
Introverted interests: One or a few hobbies which require no contact with others (i.e. stamp collection, reading, movie going, school work)

Adolescence

Withdrawal   As above
Peer relationships   As above
*Interests**   As above.

Socio-sexual adjustment†
0   Healthy interest in girls/boys, steady *close* relationships with sexual intercourse or sexual play
1.5   Went out with girls/boys regularly, steady *close* relationships with little or no sexual play
3   Went out with girls/boys regularly, steady *casual* relationships with sexual intercourse
4.5   Went out with girls/boys regularly, passing *casual* relationships with sexual intercourse
6   Casual occasional contact with girls/boys with sexual intercourse or sexual play
7.5   Casual occasional contact with girls/boys without sexual play
9   Interested in girls/boys, but never went out on dates
10.5   Homosexual involvement only
12   No desire to be with girls/boys, never went out on dates

* Modification of item 3 of Elgin Prognostic Scale (41).
† Modification of item B of Premorbid History of Phillips Scale (25).

peer relationships observed in autistic children are not included in this scale since it was designed to rate children living at home and functioning within normal settings (i.e. schools, churches, etc.). Therefore, high scale ratings for premorbid asocial behavior should not be construed as indicating that the patients, as children, were already schizophrenic. Further, ratings are to be made only for behavior anteceding the first manifestations of the psychotic onset.

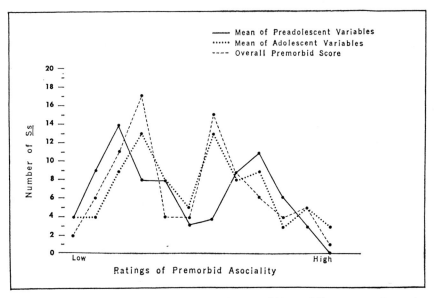

Fig. 1.—Frequency distributions of ratings of premorbid asociality: mean of preadolescent variables ($N = 79$), mean of adolescent variables ($N = 83$), and overall premorbid score ($N = 84$).

Overall scores were computed by averaging all scored items if at least three of the seven premorbid variables had been rated.

Items were scored only if explicit statements concerning the patient's functioning were present. Inferential judgments were strictly avoided, even though "impressions" were often obtainable from case histories. Further, the items as stated represent only one aspect of deviant adjustment, namely, asocial vs. social interactions with the environment in general, and peers specifically. There were other patterns of malfunctioning observed, such as exploitative, unstable, or aggressive social relationships, etc. These deviant patterns were not included in the shut-in, asocial type of adjustment. As a result, the low schizoid ratings for some patients cannot be construed to indicate normal premorbid adjustment.

Thirty cases were rated independently by two psychologists who had previously scored 10 cases jointly for training purposes. The Pearson r for Overall Premorbid Score was 0.87. Rater reliability was 0.85 and 0.77 for the means of the preadolescent and adolescent variables respectively. Thus, the inter-rater reliability of the scale and the data-extraction procedures are established.

TABLE 3

MEANS AND STANDARD DEVIATIONS OF SCORES ON PREMORBID RATINGS*

	Total			Men			Women			P of F	P of t
	$\bar{x}$	S.D.	N	$\bar{x}$	S.D.	N	$\bar{x}$	S.D.	N		
Preadolescent withdrawal	4.71	4.47	70	5.71	4.72	31	3.92	4.08	39	ns	ns
Preadolescent peer relationships	5.29	3.15	78	6.49	3.32	34	4.36	2.67	44	ns	0.01
Preadolescent interests	5.56	2.52	68	6.71	2.61	31	4.70	2.41	37	ns	0.01
Mean of preadolescent variables	5.20	3.01	79	6.28	3.10	35	4.36	2.66	44	ns	0.01
Adolescent withdrawal	4.36	4.44	73	4.80	4.92	35	3.95	3.90	38	ns	ns
Adolescent peer relationships	5.64	2.99	83	5.94	2.95	38	5.39	3.00	45	ns	ns
Adolescent interests	5.72	2.86	78	6.06	3.03	36	5.42	2.66	42	ns	ns
Adolescent sexual adjustment	7.10	2.99	78	7.86	3.10	37	6.40	2.73	41	ns	ns
Mean of adolescent variables	5.70	2.80	83	6.14	2.99	38	5.29	2.57	45	ns	ns
Overall premorbid score	5.47	2.74	84	6.08	2.39	39	4.93	2.94	45	ns	ns

* The F and t tests were performed to test differences between the variance and means respectively for the men and women Ss.

RESULTS

Only 2 of the 86 patients had fewer than three scoreable childhood characteristics and therefore could not be assigned an Overall Premorbid Score but were included in all other analyses.

The frequency distribution of the Overall Premorbid Score as well as that of the means of preadolescent variables and adolescent variables are given in Fig. 1. Their bimodality is evident.

The means and standard deviations of the scale items are given by sex for the total group in Table 3.

The greater degree of asocial functioning in the men, as reflected in a higher Overall Premorbid Score, is due to the greater degree of schizoid characteristics during preadolescence, but not during adolescence. This finding corroborates Kraepelin's report that these characteristics are more often observed in men.

The 21 intercorrelations of the seven premorbid variables range from 0.51 to 0.76 (for 80 d.f., $p = 0.01$, $r = 0.28$). The high degree of homogeneity underlying the premorbid variables is felt to be desirable, since the aim in devising this scale was to obtain an unequivocal score for shut-in personalities.

TABLE 4

MEANS AND STANDARD DEVIATIONS OF OUTCOME VARIABLES*

	Total			Men			Women			P of F	P of t
	x̄	S.D.	N	x̄	S.D.	N	x̄	S.D.	N		
Overall outcome	3.88	1.77	86	3.97	1.82	39	3.81	1.73	47	ns	ns
Number of rehospitalizations	0.74	0.94	86	0.80	0.92	39	0.69	0.95	47	ns	ns
Time spent in hospital (months)	4.71	3.48	86	5.26	3.94	39	4.25	2.99	47	0.05	ns
Occupational adjustment	17.89	5.95	84	17.56	6.26	39	18.18	5.66	45	ns	ns
Parasitic adjustment	2.28	1.85	81	2.37	2.03	38	2.21	1.66	43	ns	ns
Social isolation	3.25	2.15	84	3.53	2.14	39	3.02	2.13	45	ns	ns

* The F and t tests are for the variances and means respectively of the men's and women's scores.

Ratings of Posthospital Adjustment

The items used to evaluate outcome are included in the Appendix. Except for one variable, item 1, Overall Outcome, all follow-up data were obtained by the social worker during the interview with the patient.

The Overall Outcome scale was devised by a research psychiatrist (DFK), who was familiar with every patient in the study. Outcome categories were based on all the posthospital data available (i.e. doctors' reports, hospital records, patient and relative reports). The cases were then independently rated by a social worker and a psychologist, neither of whom had seen the patients. Rater reliability was beyond the 0.0001 level of significance on the Binomial Test of Agreement. Disagreements were resolved by consensus.

The means and standard deviations of the outcome variables are given in Table 4, the intercorrelations of the outcome variables in Table 5.

Because of the relatively large number of correlations performed, the critical level of confidence of $p < 0.01$ (one-tailed tests) was selected for all correlational analyses.

TABLE 5

INTERCORRELATION MATRIX OF OUTCOME VARIABLES

	1	2	3	4	5	6
1. Overall outcome	—	0.56	0.66	0.87	0.64	0.24
2. Number of rehospitalizations			0.70	0.41	0.46	0.07
3. Time spent in hospital				0.57	0.48	0.09
4. Occupational adjustment					0.53	0.20
5. Parasitic adjustment						0.07
6. Social isolation						—

for d.f. $= 80$, and $p = 0.01$ (one-tailed), $r = 0.26$.

TABLE 6

THE RELATIONSHIP OF OVERALL PREMORBID SCORES AND OUTCOME FOR THE TOTAL GROUP (OUTCOME VARIABLES)

	Overall outcome	Number of re-hospitalizations	Time spent in hospital	Occupational adjustment	Parasitic adjustment	Social isolation
Overall Premorbid Score	0.58†	0.41†	0.43†	0.41†	0.49†	0.34†
Number of subjects	84	84	84	82	81	82

For d.f. $= 80$ and $p = 0.01$ (one-tailed), $r = 0.26$.
† $p < 0.0005$, one-tailed.

Overall Outcome is most highly associated with the other follow-up variables since the global outcome rating subsumes the other variables.

That outcome ratings of Social Isolation are not significantly associated ($p > 0.01$) with other outcome characteristics is unexpected. This issue is discussed below.

To test the hypotheses regarding the relationship of premorbid asocial type functioning to outcome, a correlational analysis was performed. Subjects with missing data were excluded from the relevant analyses. Therefore, correlations vary in the number of subjects from 66 to 86 Ss.

Relationships between Overall Premorbid Score and Posthospital Adjustment

The Overall Premorbid score is significantly associated with all outcome variables, indicating that the greater the degree of premorbid asocial, withdrawn personality characteristics, the worse the likelihood of recovery from a schizophrenic episode and maintaining oneself adequately in the community (Table 6).

Overall Outcome. Thirty-six of the 84 *Ss* rated fell within the first three outcome categories, the remaining 48 patients had very poor outcomes, as defined by the ability to maintain appropriate social roles on a fairly consistent basis.

Overall Outcome had a correlation of 0.58 with Overall Premorbid Score. This correlation supports the hypothesis that premorbid asocial character is associated with poor functioning following hospitalization for schizophrenia.

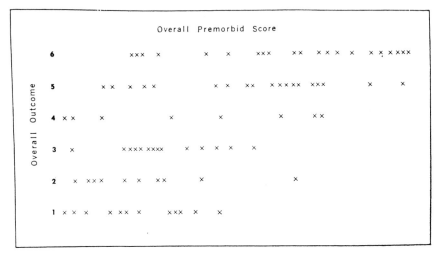

FIG. 2.—Scattergram of relationship between Overall Premorbid Score and posthospital Overall Outcome (*N* = 84).

A scattergram of the association of Overall Premorbid Scores to Overall Outcome shows a curvilinear relationship (see Fig. 2). That is, the Overall Outcome of patients with low Overall Premorbid Scores (i.e. nonasocial patients) is distributed over the whole range of the Outcome Scores; about two-thirds of them having good Overall Outcome, another third having poor outcome. However, all the asocial patients (i.e. with high Overall Premorbid Scores), with only one exception, had poor Overall Outcome. Thus, high premorbid schizoid characteristics invariably predict a narrow range of posthospital adjustments whereas patients with relatively few premorbid asocial traits have a wide range of outcomes.

Psychiatric Status. Psychiatric status was defined by the number of rehospitalizations during the two year follow-up and by the amount of time spent in a psychiatric hospital during the two year follow-up period (Appendix, items 2 and 3 respectively). The two items were recorded for each twelve-month period of the two-year follow-up. The scores were therefore added to yield a single rating, ranging from 2 to 14. The mean number of rehospitalizations was 0.74. Half of the patients were rehospitalized during the 2-year follow-up period; among the rehospitalized patients most (65 per cent) were rehospitalized once, while the rest had from two to five rehospitalizations. Rehospitalized patients spent an average of 5-6 months in the hospital.

The Overall Premorbid Score correlated significantly with the Number of Rehospitalization ($r = 0.41$) and with Time Spent in Psychiatric Hospitals ($r = 0.43$).

Occupational Adjustment. The four items (Appendix, items 4, 5, 6, 7) pertaining to patients' work functioning were all highly intercorrelated (r's $= 0.62$ to 0.74) and therefore were added together to derive a single score as an index of Occupational Adjustment. Thus, the range of scores possible was from 4 to 28, the higher the score, the better the level of occupational adjustment.

As hypothesized, the Overall Premorbid Score correlated significantly with Occupational Adjustment ($r = 0.41$). Altogether, 19 patients' scores were in the opposite direction from that hypothesized. Specifically, 12 patients with low Overall Premorbid Scores were rated as having poor posthospital Occupational Adjustment, whereas seven patients with high Overall Premordial Scores had at least average occupational functioning.

Interpersonal Functioning. This category of adjustment included the degree of the patient's dependence on his environment and lack of self-support (Appendix, item 8, Parasitic Adjustment), and the patient's friendship patterns or the extent to which he had been socially active (Appendix, item 9, Social Isolation). Of the 81 patients rated on the extent to which they were parasitic, 51 were rated as being totally nonparasitic. As predicted, the Overall Premorbid Score was significantly correlated with the follow-up rating of Parasitic Adjustment ($r = 0.49$) supporting the contention that discharged schizophrenics with poor early social interaction are more likely to be socio-economically dependent than other patients.

The rating of Social Isolation would appear *a priori* most closely related to the premorbid variables. Yet, even though the correlation between the Overall Premorbid Score and Social Isolation is significant ($r = 0.34$), it is relatively low.

The correlations between the individual premorbid scale items and outcome are given in Table 7. The preadolescent and adolescent variables are equally predictive of posthospital adjustment.

COMMENT

This study affirms that early withdrawn, asocial behavior, and a lack of interest in activities involving one's peers are uniformly associated

TABLE 7

RELATIONSHIPS OF PREMORBID VARIABLES AND OUTCOME FOR THE TOTAL GROUP

	Overall outcome	Number of rehospital- izations	Time spent in hospital	Occupational adjustment	Parasitic adjustment	Social isolation
1. Preadolescent withdrawal	0.51	0.48	0.40	0.36	0.43	0.31
2. Preadolescent peer relationships	0.46	0.31	0.34	0.36	0.39	0.20
3. Preadolescent interest	0.52	0.30	0.35	0.38	0.36	0.12
4. Mean of preadolescent variables	0.54	0.42	0.42	0.41	0.44	0.26
5. Adolescent withdrawal	0.52	0.44	0.42	0.28	0.39	0.38
6. Adolescent peer relationships	0.40	0.27	0.28	0.30	0.34	0.25
7. Adolescent interests	0.56	0.31	0.39	0.39	0.38	0.30
8. Adolescent sexual adjustment	0.44	0.27	0.28	0.30	0.25	0.39
9. Mean of adolescent variables	0.55	0.36	0.39	0.37	0.38	0.39

For d.f. $= 80$, and $p = 0.01$ (one-tailed), $r = 0.26$.

with a decreased frequency of successful, lasting recovery in schizophrenic patients, as measured by follow-up variables. This consistent negative outcome associated with the bimodal score distribution argues strongly for the presence of a qualitatively distinct schizoid type.

As a result, the procedure of using a dichotomy between schizoid and nonschizoid premorbid personalities (26-30) appears justified.

However, the nonschizoid group does not constitute an entity if overall global outcome is used for differentiating and identifying clinical subgroups. Within the nonschizoid schizophrenics about one-third do very poorly while the rest do relatively well. Therefore there seems to be at least two outcome groups subsumed among nonschizoid patients. This finding is consistent with those of Rioch and Lubin (39) who correlated psychological test results with outcome. They noted that "a prognosis of non-improvement could be made with virtual certainty on the basis of poor test performance, but good test performance was not prognostic." However, other investigators (26, 28, 29) report remissions among schizophrenics classified as schizoid. Vaillant points out that, in his sample, remission among most schizoid patients consisted of a resumption of a chronically schizoid functioning. Therefore, differences in definitions of outcome may lead to varying results. Similarly, differences in the definitions of what qualifies as schizoid functioning may also cause discrepancies. Thus, it is not uncommon for nonschizoid individuals to withdraw gradually for relatively extended periods of time, such as one year, prior to manifesting florid psychotic symptoms. In our schema, these patients are not considered schizoid, in others', they might be. Further, reliability may also be a factor. Poor reliability of categorization of the predictive variable introduces error. As noted, no reliability data are given by Vaillant (29), and in one instance (27) the percentage of agreement is relatively low.

Diagnostic accuracy is crucial to the study of prognosis to insure that the observed heterogeneity of outcome is not due to diagnostic error. The diagnosis of schizophrenia is probably more reliable for the schizoid patients. Misdiagnoses are more likely to occur among patients without histories of chronic social maladaptation. This possible source of error may account for part of the outcome variance within the nonschizoid group. We are currently undertaking an investigation of the role of differing diagnostic criteria in the prediction of posthospital outcome.

The issue of developmental sequence has never been dealt with systematically in prognostic studies since patients have been labeled as schizoid without consideration of the period in which this type of adjustment occurred.

It might be worthwhile to investigate the relative role that schizoid characteristics play in the course of schizophrenia with reference to when they occur, and to investigate whether an increase in socialization in adolescence mitigates the effect of autistic trends in early childhood. It may be that individuals who do not remain chronically withdrawn throughout their life represent a subgroup of the shut-in personality.

Differing outcomes may reflect contrasting treatment courses rather than premorbid patient differences. It is possible, for a variety of reasons, that the non-asocial patients received more effective treatments than the asocial patients and therefore functioned better after hospital discharge.

Phenothiazines have been found to affect positively the long-term adjustment of schizophrenics. If the non-asocial patients in this study received significantly more phenothiazines than the asocial patients after discharge from the hospital, the above interpretations relating premorbid differences *per se* to outcome might be unjustified. To investigate this possibility, the patients were divided into premorbid asocial vs. non-asocial groups. A median cut-off score of the Overall Premorbid Scores was used (a score of 5.8 represented the median of the scale which ranges from 0 to 12). Outcome measures of length of posthospital phenothiazine treatment were dichotomized between "less than three months of treatment" and "at least three months," during each outcome year.

There was a significant difference in length of phenothiazine treatment between the two premorbid groups. The asocial patients received phenothiazine for longer periods of time than the non-asocial patients during the first and second outcome year following the index hospitalization (χ^2 with Yates' correction for the first and second year are, respectively, 3.87, $p < 0.05$; 7.00, $p < 0.01$).

It is not possible to give an unequivocal explanation for the difference in length of phenothiazine administration between the two patient groups since we had no control over the treatment and no data are available from the treating physicians as to their reasons for prescribing phenothiazines. However, the most plausible explanation seems to be that patients who were chronically malfunctioning and adjusting poorly were more likely to receive phenothiazines. In any case, the relatively good outcome of the non-asocial patients cannot be interpreted as being due to their having received more extensive phenothiazine treatment.

Relevance of the Study to the Process-Reactive Literature

The patient descriptions used in this study are reminiscent of those found in the literature on process-reactive schizophrenia. However, we did not use the so-called process-reactive scales (25, 40, 41) because of several considerations.

Three scales referred to above neither specify a single patient-relevant dimension nor isolate a patient type. It has been repeatedly argued that such scales tap a single continuous dimension, or ordering construct, along which patients can be ranked. To posit that a single dimension has been identified requires that all instruments or scale items assumed to reflect that dimension yield highly intercorrelated results. Since factor analysis of the Elgin and Phillips scale items has shown that they represent several orthogonal factors (42, 43) the notion of unidimensionality is unjustified.

It is sometimes not realized that a "dimension" can be generated by discrete types. If one had a bimodal sample composed of midgets and giants, and applied several different criteria of height, then intercorrelated them, one would isolate an underlying height dimension. It would not be an artifact since giants are taller than midgets, and specifying this ordinal relationship requires a dimensional construct. However, the existence of such a dimension tells us nothing about the frequency distribution or continuity along this dimension. Our bimodally distributed data imply that the schizophrenics with early childhood asociality are a distinctive homogeneous type and not a tail of a normal distribution (Fig. 1).

As stated above, process-reactive scales not only fail to define a single dimension, but also fail to identify homogeneous patient groups. The scales were empirically devised by selecting many items of prognostic value from the literature. As a result, they are a mixture of items hopefully related to prognosis but not necessarily to each other. Since a patient's score on these scales is the arithmetic mean of all items, patients with identical scores may have markedly differing scale profiles. Therefore, the scales do not isolate clinically homogeneous patient subgroupings, although they may be "homogeneous" with respect to outcome. It is therefore erroneous to equate, as is done, these scale scores with a patient-descriptive label, such as process or reactive schizophrenia. A more accurate patient description on the basis of scores on process-reactive scales as they exist would be, for instance, poor prognosis or good prognosis patients. To sum up, these scales are best considered simply empirical compound prognostic measures that identify neither a dimension nor patient types.

Our interest was not to devise an empirically optimal scale for prognosis in schizophrenia. Rather, the goal was to investigate whether a specific type of developmental pattern that occurs prior to manifest clinical schizophrenia is related to clinical course. The scales of process-reactive schizophrenia, as well as other prognostic scales, are all inappropriate for such a purpose since, in addition to the above considerations, they are not restricted to premorbid functioning but include confounding aspects of current patient status or behavior. However, it is of interest to note that the prognostic value of the scale used in this study is equivalent to that of the compound process-reactive and prognostic scales (25-27, 29-31, 33, 41, 44). It may be that these scales' empirical value lies solely in their relationship to premorbid asociality and that little, if anything, is gained from the other scale items.

To determine this fact requires detailed multivariate analyses. Astrup and Noreik (27) have presented linear multiple regression equations indicating that schizoid personality is only one of several "independent" predictors of outcome. However, we have shown that such analyses can be misleading unless curvilinear relationships are considered (45). The relationship between the prognostic scales and outcome is markedly curvilinear in Vaillant's study (29), indicating that curvilinearity is not an academic consideration.

Correspondence of the Findings to Clinical Theories of Prognosis

The large number of schizophrenic patients found to have been asocial and withdrawn in their early years corroborates the clinical observations of Kraepelin, Bleuler, and especially Hoch. The finding that these schizophrenic patients have a distinctly poor outcome is also consonant with the observations of many clinicians.

Both Sullivan (19) and Langfeldt (21, 22, 46, 47) retained the early Kraepelinian view of dementia praecox followed by an inevitable malignant course and made a clear distinction between this syndrome and schizophrenia. However, they conceptualized the two syndromes differently. Langfeldt separated the groups exclusively on the basis of psychotic symptomatology. He considered schizoid personality prognostically malignant only in the presence of malignant symptoms. Therefore, since schizoid traits have no prognostic value in themselves, Langfeldt is implicitly negative about their role in the course of schizophrenia. Sullivan maintained that the two discrete pathological entities differed in origin and types of onset. He felt that dementia praecox inevitably had an insidious onset and followed a malignant course. But he was, on the whole, optimistic about the course of "schizophrenia" since he viewed it as a disturbance of mental function, or regression, in individuals often capable of reintegration and adequate adjustment. Sullivan (48) even noted cases who were able to achieve a relatively superior level following a schizophrenic episode. This observation has not been confirmed by other clinicians.

Our results do not support Langfeldt's formulations regarding the inconsistent role of premorbid shut-in personalities. In contrast, these traits were consistently predictive of poor overall outcome.

If the premorbid asocial group is equated with the clinical syndrome of dementia praecox and the other group with schizophrenia, using Sullivanian terminology, our results suport Sullivan's observations concerning the lack of uniformity of outcome in schizophrenia.

Our results support the theory that the global diagnosis of schizophrenia subsumes separate clinical subgroups. Several investigators have criticized the concept of discrete pathological entities within schizophrenia as implying separate etiological factors for each subgroup. This viewpoint is simplistic since the identification of such groups does not cast light upon etiology in any way. No study of the clinical course of schizophrenia or its associated developmental, psychological, or biological characteristics can definitively resolve the issue of etiological antecedents in schizophrenia. Only the discovery of specific causal factors will get to the bottom of this problem. However, the isolation of subgroups with similar developmental history, symptomatology, outcome and response to treatment may facilitate the identification of etiological factors.

A case can be made for psychogenic causality in all types of schizophrenia hypothesizing different psychological antecedents for each subgroup (49, 50). As good a case can be made for a theory of CNS dysfunction in all the various groups of schizophrenia by maintaining that the nature of the organic pathology differs among the clinical entities (51). As Zigler and Phillips (52) have aptly pointed out, whether schizophrenia is made up of one, two or more syndromes should not affect the nature of the hypotheses regarding its genesis.

SUMMARY

This study tested the hypothesis that a premorbid schizoid personality predicted poor outcome among hospitalized schizophrenics. A scale was devised limited to items specifically reflecting premorbid asocial, schizoid adjustment in preadolescence and adolescence.

The patients' scores were clearly bimodally distributed, suggesting that a premorbid schizoid adjustment does not manifest itself in a graduated, normally distributed fashion. Rather, it appears to be an either-or phenomenon.

The posthospital adjustment of 86 schizophrenics was evaluated by interviews with patients two years after discharge. Posthospital outcome measures consisted of: an overall outcome rating, the number of hospitalizations and time spent in psychiatric hospitals, occupational adjustment, and interpersonal functioning, for two years following the index hospitalization.

The theory that premorbid asocial schizophrenics had a poorer chance for a favorable outcome was confirmed. Outcome could be predicted with relative certainty for the premorbid asocial group who all functioned very inadequately after hospitalization. The posthospital adjustment of non-asocial patients varied from very good to very poor.

The relationships of the findings to the concept of process-reactive schizophrenia and clinical theories of prognosis are discussed.

ACKNOWLEDGMENTS

This paper is based, in part, on a Ph.D. dissertation submitted by R. K. Gittelman, Teachers College, Columbia University. Gratitude is expressed to Professors Rosalea A. Schonbar, Joel R. Davitz and Laurence F. Shaffer for their interest and valuable assistance.

This paper was supported in part by the NIMH, USPHS Grants MH05090, MH-08004 and MH10191.

REFERENCES

1. BOWMAN, K. M. and KASANIN, J. Constitutional schizophrenia. *Am. J. Psychiat.* 13, 645-658, 1933.

2. CALDWELL, J. M., JR. Schizophrenic psychoses: Report of 100 cases in U.S. Army. *Am. J. Psychiat.* 97, 1061-1072, 1941.

3. CLAUDE, H., BOREL, A., and ROBIN, G. Schizoid vs. cycloid constitution. *Encéphale* 19, 209-216, 1924.

4. HOCH, A. A study of the mental make-up in the functional psychoses. *J. nerv. ment. Dis.* 230-236, 1909.

5. KASANIN, J. S. Developmental roots of schizophrenia. *Am. J. Psychiat.* 101, 770-776, 1945.

6. KASANIN, J. and ROSEN, Z. A. Clinical variables in schizoid personalities. *Archs. Neurol. Psychiat.* 30, 538-566, 1933.

7. KRAEPELIN, E. *Dementia Praecox and Paraphrenia,* E. & S. Livingstone, Edinburgh, 1919.

8. KRETSCHMER, E. *Physique and Character,* Harcourt & Brace, New York, 1926.

9. KRETSCHMER, E. *Der sensitive Beziehungswahn,* Berlin, 1918. Cited by K. Jaspers. *General Psychopathology,* University of Chicago Press, Chicago, 1963.

10. SADLER, W. S. *Theory and Practice of Psychiatry,* C. V. Mosby, St. Louis, 1936.

11. STECKLER, E. A. and WILEY, G. F. Prognosis in schizophrenia. *Proc. Ass. Res. nerv. ment. Dis.* 5, 403-431, 1928.

12. HOCH, A. Constitutional factors in the dementia praecox group. *Rev. Neurol. Psychiat.* 8, 463-474, 1910.

13. BLEULER, E. P. *Dementia Praecox or the Group of Schizophrenias,* International University Press, New York, 1950.

14. KANT, O. A comparative study of recovered and deteriorated schizophrenic patients. *J. nerv. ment. Dis.* 93, 616-624, 1941.

15. KANT, O. The evaluation of prognostic criteria in schizophrenia. *J. nerv. ment. Dis.* 100, 598-605, 1944.

16. MEYER, A. An attempt at analysis of the neurotic constitution. *Am. J. Psychol.* 14, 90-143, 1903.

17. MEYER, A. The dynamic interpretation of dementia praecox. *Am. J. Psychol.* 21, 385-403, 1910.

18. SULLIVAN, H. S. The relation of onset to outcome in schizophrenia. *Proc. Ass. Res. nerv. ment. Dis.* 10, 111-118, 1931.

19. SULLIVAN, H. S. *Conceptions of Modern Psychiatry,* The William Alanson White Psychiatric Foundation, Washington, D.C., 1947.

20. KANT, O. Types and analyses of the clinical pictures of recovered schizophrenics. *Psychiat. Quart.* 14, 676-700, 1940.

21. LANGFELDT, G. The prognosis in schizophrenia and the factors influencing the course of the disease. *Acta psychiat. neurol. scand.* Suppl. 13, 1-228, 1937.

22. LANGFELDT, G. The diagnosis of schizophrenia. *Am. J. Psychiat.* 108, 123-125, 1951.

23. LANGFELDT, G. Some points regarding the symptomatology and diagnosis of schizophrenia. *Acta psychiat. neurol. scand.* Suppl. 80, 7-26, 1952.

24. WITTMAN, PHYLLIS. Diagnostic and prognostic significance of the shut-in personality as a prodromal factor in schizophrenia. *J. clin. Psychol.* 4, 211-214, 1948.

25. PHILLIPS, L. Case history data and prognosis in schizophrenia. *J. nerv. ment. Dis.* 117, 515-525, 1953.

26. ASTRUP, C., FOSSUM, A. and HOLMBOE, R. *Prognosis in Functional Psychoses,* C. C. Thomas, Springfield, Illinois, 1962.

27. ASTRUP, C. and NOREIK, K. *Functional Psychoses—Diagnostic and Prognostic Models,* C. C. Thomas, Springfield, Illinois, 1966.

28. STEPHENS, J. H., ASTRUP, C. and MANGRUM, J. C. Prognostic factors in recovered and deteriorated schizophrenics. *Am. J. Psychiat.* 122, 1116-1121, 1966.

29. VAILLANT, G. E. Prospective prediction of schizophrenic remission. *Archs. gen. Psychiat.* 11, 509-518, 1964.

30. STEPHENS, J. H., ASTRUP, C. and MANGRUM, J. C. Prognosis in schizophrenia: Prognostic scales cross-validated in American and Norwegian patients. *Archs. gen. Psychiat.* 16, 693-698, 1967.

31. FARINA, A., GARMEZY, N., ZALUSKY, M. and BECKER, J. Premorbid behavior and prognosis in female schizophrenic patients. *J. consult. Psychol.* 26, 56-60, 1962.

32. CHAPMAN, L. J., DAY, DOROTHY and BURSTEIN, A. The process-reactive distinction and prognosis in schizophrenia. *J. nerv. ment. Dis.* 133, 383-391, 1961.

33. FARINA, A. and WEBB, W. Premorbid adjustment and subsequent discharge. *J. nerv. ment. Dis.* 124, 612-613, 1956.

34. GARFIELD, S. L. and SUNDLAND, D. M. Prognostic scales in schizophrenia. *J. consult. Psychol.* 30, 18-24, 1966.

35. SUGERMAN, A. A. Prognostic factors in schizophrenia: A developmental approach. Unpublished dissertation. Downstate Medical Center, New York, 1962.

36. LEVENSTEIN, S., KLEIN, D. F. and POLLACK, M. Follow-up study of formerly hospitalized voluntary psychiatric patients: the first two years. *Am. J. Psychiat.* 122, 1102-1109, 1966.

37. POLLACK, M. Comparison of childhood, adolescent, and adult schizophrenias. *Archs. gen. Psychiat.* 2, 652-660, 1960.

38. HOLLINGSHEAD, A. B. and REDLICH, F. C. *Social Class and Mental Illness,* John Wiley, New York, 1958.

39. RIOCH, MARGARET J. and LUBIN, A. Prognosis of social adjustment for mental hospital patients under psychotherapy. *J. consult. Psychol.* 4, 313-318, 1959.

40. KANTOR, R. E., WALLNER, J. M. and WINDER, C. L. Process and reactive schizophrenia. *J. consult. Psychol.* 17, 157-162, 1953.

41. WITTMAN, PHYLLIS. A scale for measuring prognosis in schizophrenia patients. *Elgin State Hospital Papers* 4, 20-33, 1941.

42. BECKER, W. C. The process-reactive distinction: A key to the problem of schizophrenia? *J. nerv. ment. Dis.* 129, 442-449, 1959.

43. NUTTALL, R. L. and SOLOMON, L. T. Factorial structure and prognostic significance of premorbid adjustment in schizophrenia. *J. consult. Psychol.* 29, 362-372, 1965.

44. WITTMAN, PHYLLIS and STEINBERG, L. Follow-up of an objective evaluation of prognosis in dementia praecox and manic-depressive psychosis. *Elgin State Hospital Papers* 5, 216-227, 1944.

45. GITTELMAN-KLEIN, R. and KLEIN, D. F. Marital status as a prognostic indicator in schizophrenia. *J. nerv. ment. Dis.* 147, 289-296, 1968.

46. LANGFELDT, G. The prognosis in schizophrenia. *Acta psychiat. neurol. scand.* Suppl. 110, 1-66, 1956.

47. LANGFELDT, G. Diagnosis and prognosis of schizophrenia. *Proc. R. Soc. Med.* 53, 1047-1052, 1960.

48. SULLIVAN, H. S. Schizophrenia; its conservative and malignant features. *Am. J. Psychiat.* 4, 77-91, 1924.

49. GARMEZY, N. and RODNICK, E. H. Premorbid adjustment and performance in

schizophrenia—Implications for interpreting heterogeneity in schizophrenia. *J. nerv. ment. Dis.* 129, 450-466, 1959.

50. GARMEZY. N. Process and reactive schizophrenia: Some conceptions and issues. In *The Role and Methodology of Classification in Psychiatry and Psychopathology* (Edited by Katz, M. M., Cole, J. O. and Barton, W. E.), National Institute of Mental Health, Chevy Chase, Md., 1965.

51. KLEIN, D. F. Behavioral effects of imipramine and phenothiazines: Implications for a psychiatric pathogenetic theory and theories of drug action. In *Recent Advances in Biological Psychiatry* (Edited by Wortis, J.), pp. 273-283, Plenum Press, New York, 1964.

52. ZIGLER, E. and PHILLIPS, L. Social competence and the process-reactive distinction. *J. Abnorm. Soc. Psychol.* 65, 215-222, 1962.

Appendix

ITEM 1

Overall outcome categories

1. Continuous adequate functioning with none or only slight symptomatology. Patient may or may not be receiving psychotherapy.
2. Adequate functioning for extended periods of time but patient may have had one-to-two recurrences of symptomatology which were accompanied by impaired functioning. Each relapse lasted less than three months, with or without hospitalization.
3. Moderately adequate functioning in appropriate social role but patient remained continuously symptomatic possibly with fluctuations of severity. The patient's social role was maintained under moderately protective circumstances. Patient was receiving continuous psychiatric care. Brief (less than 1 month) or no hospitalization.
4. Continuous life disruptive mood fluctuations with or without delusional or psychotic episodes. Patient was unable to maintain an overall good level of functioning but may have had intervals of adequate adjustment. May or may not have been hospitalized.
5. Continuous marked symptomatology. Patient's adjustment ranged from very low level of self-support to completely parasitic.
6. Continuous marked symptomatology. Adjustment from very low level of self-support to completely parasitic and hospitalized more than 3 months.

ITEM 2

Number of rehospitalizations

Number of new admissions to psychiatric hospitals in each 12 month period. Count admissions followed by transfer, e.g., Kings County and sent to Creedmoor, as *One*. However, direct transfer from Hillside Hospital to another psychiatric facility counts as one new admission.

1. No new admission.
2. 1 new admission.
3. 2 new admissions.
4. 3 new admissions.
5. 4 new admissions.
6. 5 new admissions.
7. More than 5 new admissions.
9. No information.

ITEM 3

Time spent in psychiatric hospitals

Amount of time spent in psychiatric hospitalizations during each 12 month period.

1. No time in hospital.
2. Up to 1 month.
3. 2 months.
4. 3 months.

5. 4-6 months.
6. 7-9 months.
7. 10-12 months.
9. No information.

ITEM 4

Occupational adjustment

Complete on all patients, including housewives, students and retired persons in terms of ordinary daily activities which would be expected for the person's occupational status.

1. Unable to work or function due to mental illness.

2. Unable to work or function part of the time, which might include long periods of continuous inability to work or frequent long absence from work.
3.
4. Able to work or function most of the time, with only short periods of inability to work, such as occasional days or weeks off.

5. Able to work or function steadily, but because of patient's problems there is definitely impaired efficiency or functioning below capacity.
6.

7. Able to work or function steadily and efficiently at capacity.
8. Not applicable.

9. No information.

ITEM 5

Industriousness

Work here includes keeping house or going to school.

1. Never works.

2. No period of sustained work (over 3 months).
3. Usually unreliable as a worker, unusually slow or takes time off for insufficient reasons, may have been fired or not able to take care of house.
4.

5. Average worker: works well but does not over work. Adequate.
6. Hard worker: Conscientious. Does a good job.
7. Very industrious and exceptionally hard working.

8. Not applicable—Hospitalized during entire 12-month period.
9. No information.

ITEM 6

Per cent time working

Percentage period gainfully employed or working appropriately as student or house-wife—include vacation time as employment.

1. No gainful employment.
2. Less than ½ time.
3. About ¼ time.
4. About ½ time.
5.
6. About ¾ time.
7. 90 to 100 per cent—i.e., worked continuously.
9. No information.

ITEM 7

Responsibility

Ability to assume responsibility.

1. Unable to plan own work without supervision.
2.
3. Only limited responsibility or self-direction can be handled by patient.
4. Average and ordinary in regard to taking responsibility.
5.
6. Handles responsibility well or organizes own work well without supervision.
7. Exceptionally able in assuming responsibility.
9. No information.

ITEM 8

Parasitic adjustment

Patient has maintained a very low level of self care. With family and/or community support he was able to remain in the community in a largely parasitic and dependent role. When such support was withdrawn, psychiatric hospitalization was necessary.

1. No resemblance.
2. A little resemblance.
3. Mild resemblance.
4. Moderate resemblance.
5. Quite a bit.
6. Marked resemblance.
7. Perfect description.
9. No information.

ITEM 9

Social isolation

1. Has good friends and enjoys spending time with them.
2. Has friends and spends time with them but does not always enjoy doing so.
3.
4. Has a few friends, but has trouble getting along with them or spends little time with them.
5. Has no close friends, but does spend a little time in social activities.
6. Has almost no friends but would like to have more social contact.
7. Has almost no friends and usually prefers to be by himself.
9. No information.

17

FREQUENCY OF SEPARATION AND DIVORCE AMONG WOMEN AGED 16-49 SUFFERING FROM SCHIZOPHRENIA AND AFFECTIVE DISORDERS

Barbara C. Stevens

INTRODUCTION

Previous studies on marital breakdown among schizophrenics and manic-depressives have either failed to study the periods of marriage after first admission (Dayton (1940); Ödegard (1953)) or they have analyzed the periods before and after admission together with inadequate control over the relevant demographic variables (Blacker (1958); Brown, Bone, Dalison & Wing (1966)). However, these studies suggest that the frequency of marital breakdown is comparatively high among schizophrenics, whereas it appears that patients with affective disorders do not part from their spouses so often.

The aim of the present inquiry was to analyze marital status changes before and after first admission by the relevant clinical and sociological variables, and to compare frequency of separation and divorce among these patients with that expected in the corresponding general population.

MATERIAL

Selection of Sample

This inquiry was part of a large investigation into the marriage and fertility of psychotics which has been published elsewhere (Stevens (1969a)). The sample was composed of 1,295 women aged 16-49 who were admitted to a London mental hospital during the years 1955-63 and

Reprinted, by permission of author and editor, from: *Acta Psychiatrica Scandanavica*, 46:136-150, 1970.

who were finally diagnosed as suffering from schizophrenia, or an affective disorder. Owing to the difficulty in distinguishing between reactive and endogenous depression from case records (Lewis (1934); Lewis (1944)) it was not possible to obtain a sample of manic-depressives, and the affective sample included any woman whose diagnosis was primarily a disorder of mood, involving either a depression or a hypomanic or manic condition.

It should be emphasized that this sample is essentially composed of women whose first admission was during their childbearing period, at the time when the marital relationship and fertility would be most affected by the illness. Because of this selection by age, the two main clinical groups are similar in duration of marriage, thus allowing comparisons between them concerning separation and divorce. A sample which included older women with affective disorders would have been very difficult to compare with the schizophrenics because of earlier age on first admission of the latter group.

METHOD

Collection of Data

1. *From clinical and legal records*

A schedule was designed for coding on to I.B.M. cards, and details were obtained from each patient's records on the following variables: marital status on first admission and changes in marital status before admission; any marital status changes after first admission, and marital status on last discharge; age on first admission; pre-morbid personality (as described in a questionnaire sent to relatives and doctors by the hospital); total length of hospital stay; consultant's final diagnosis; and religion of patient. For ever-married patients data was collected on age at first marriage, first husband's occupation, duration of marriage on first admission, and at last discharge, and number of live born children before and after admission.

2. *The postal follow-up study*

This was undertaken along the lines suggested by Laurence (1959); details were obtained from patients, relatives, general practitioners and other hospitals on marital status changes; fertility, husband's occupation and clinical condition since discharge. This part of the study was completed by August 31st, 1966.

3. General population data

This was derived from Rowntree (1964) who published data collected from a large random sample of the British population during 1959-60 as part of a study of marriage and family growth carried out by the Population Investigation Committee in collaboration with Social Surveys (Gallup Poll) Ltd.

TABLE 1

CLINICAL STRUCTURE OF THE SAMPLE BY AGE ON FIRST PSYCHIATRIC
ADMISSION COMPARED WITH THAT FOR ALL ADMISSIONS IN ENGLAND
AND WALES* FOR THE SAME TYPES OF MENTAL ILLNESS

Age on first admission 1955-1963	Total schizo- phrenic women	Per cent distri- bution of sample	Per cent distri- bution of all adms. 1959	Total women suf- fering from affective disorders	Per cent distri- bution of sample	Per cent distri- bution of all adms. 1959	Total** No. of patients
16-19	77	9.7	8.6	20	4.2	3.0	97
20-9	316	39.7	31.2	147	30.9	19.0	463
30-9	262	32.9	37.6	170	35.7	38.6	432
40-9	141	17.7	22.7	139	29.2	39.5	280
Total	796	100.0	100.0	476	100.0	100.0	1,272

* *Source*: The Registrar General's Statistical Review of England and Wales for the year 1959, Supplement on Mental Health, Appendix Table M 24(i)F for the childbearing ages, p. 78.
** This table excludes 23 patients whose age on first admission was not known.

Data Processing

Data from each patient was coded on to two Hollerith cards and the analysis was by Mr. P. Wakeford's Social Survey Programme on the I.B.M. 1440 Computer at the London School of Economics.

RESULTS

Representative Nature of the Sample

Table 1 gives the age structure of the sample on first ever admission in comparison with the Registrar General's data for all admissions in England and Wales: the sample appears to be representative of the main clinical groups, and the slight bias incurred towards the younger age groups was considered an advantage in such a study of marriage and fertility.

General Results: Before Admission

Table 2 gives the clinical structure of the sample, and the marital status changes during the period before first admission. It demonstrates that fewer of the schizophrenics have married compared with the women suffering from affective disorders: this means that more of the latter clinical group are exposed to the risk of separation or divorce before admission. The proportion who marries cannot be reliably compared owing to the lack of control over the relevant variables of age on admission and age at marriage, and a demographic analysis of probability of marriage has been published elsewhere (Stevens (1969b)). Table 2 demonstrates that in most diagnoses the type of schizophrenia was not specified, and although it was possible to tabulate separately some of the paranoid, catatonic and schizo-affective sub-groups, it was felt that the size of these would be increased if some of the undifferentiated group could have been allocated to them at the time of the original clinical diagnosis. For the purpose of this analysis all the schizophrenics were considered as one group, including the schizo-affectives.

If the proportion of ever married patients who became separated or divorced is calculated from Table 2, it is found that 17.7 percent of 407 schizophrenic women and 15.7 percent of 388 women with affective disorders parted from their first husbands during the period before first admission; the difference between these proportions was quite insignificant at the 5 percent level. However, it should be emphasized that the schizophrenics are a younger group on first admission (see Table 1), and that some of them have not been exposed to the chance of separation or divorce for as long as the women suffering from affective disorders so that these similar proportions found in both clinical groups may mask a greater liability to marital breakdown among the schizophrenics. The important factor of duration of marriage is considered below in comparisons with data from the general population.

General Results: After Admission

The period after admission was analyzed in two stages, firstly from first admission until last discharge from Springfield Hospital, and secondly from last discharge until the end of the follow-up period. Tables 3 and 4 give the marital status changes during these periods for both single and married patients on first admission. If the total numbers of ever married patients in each main clinical group are derived from these tables and considered separately, analysis showed that marital breakdown was much more frequent after admission among the schizophrenics:

TABLE 2

MARITAL STATUS CHANGES BEFORE FIRST ADMISSION: SCHIZOPHRENIC WOMEN COMPARED WITH WOMEN SUFFERING FROM AFFECTIVE DISORDERS; FOR FIRST MARRIAGES ONLY

Number of patients in each clinical group experiencing various types of change in marital status

Diagnosis	None*	Married for 1st time	Separated	Separated and Reconciled	Divorced	Marriage declared null	Wid.	Reconciled Widowed	N.K.	N
Schizophrenia—type unspecified	295	190	20	1	17	2	6	—	2	533
Paranoid schizophrenia	60	75	16	—	13	—	7	—	1	172
Catatonic schizophrenia	21	14	1	—	1	—	2	—	—	39
Schizo-affectives	30	34	1	—	2	—	2	—	—	69
All affective disorders	94	311	32	1	29	—	14	1	1	482
Total—all diagnoses	500	624	70	1	62	2	31	1	4	1,295

* Never married.

TABLE 3

MARITAL STATUS CHANGES BETWEEN FIRST EVER ADMISSION AND LAST DISCHARGE BY DIAGNOSIS

Diagnosis	N.A.*	None**	Number of patients experiencing various types of change in marital status								N
			Married	Separated	Separated and Reconciled	Divorced	Marriage declared null	Div. on grounds of insanity	Wid.	N.K.	
Schizophrenia—type unspecified	138	315	31	22	5	11	2	1	4	4	533
Paranoid schizophrenia	69	85	4	4	2	3	—	—	2	3	172
Catatonic schizophrenia	13	23	1	—	1	—	—	—	—	1	39
Schizo-affectives	20	41	4	3	—	—	—	—	1	—	69
Affective disorders	234	205	10	10	2	12	—	—	7	2	482
Total—All diagnoses	474	669	50	39	10	26	2	1	14	10	1,295

* N.A. = Not applicable, i.e. first admissions involving no observation of marriage after admission.
** None = No change from marital status on first admission.

TABLE 4

MARITAL STATUS CHANGES DURING THE FOLLOW-UP BY DIAGNOSIS

Diagnosis	N.A.*	None**	Married	Separated	Separated and Reconciled	Divorced	Marriage declared null	Div. on grounds of insanity	Wid.	Reconciled and Wid.	N.K.	N
						Marital status changes during the follow-up						
Schizophrenia	81	294	17	10	4	11	2	1	2	—	111	533
Paranoid schizophrenia	18	100	2	6	1	7	—	—	2	—	36	172
Catatonic schizophrenia	6	23	—	1	—	1	—	—	—	—	8	39
Schizo-affectives	7	44	4	1	1	—	1	—	—	—	12	69
All affectives	17	306	15	6	—	13	1	—	8	1	115	482
Totals	129	767	38	24	6	32	3	1	12	1	282	1,295

* N.A. = Not applicable, i.e. no period of observation after admission.
** No change in marital status since last discharge.

18.3 percent of 470 ever married schizophrenics became separated or divorced after admission compared with only 10.2 percent of 413 women suffering from affective disorders. The difference between these proportions was statistically significant at the 1 percent level. There are probably more separations and divorces among the fifth of the sample which could not be traced (see Table 4), and these proportions may be considered as minimum estimates. The non-response rate did not vary much between clinical groups so that there is no reason to question the validity of the significant difference discovered in frequency of marital breakdown.

Comparisons with Data from the General Population Taking into Consideration Duration of Marriage

Rowntree (1964) gives the proportion of marriages of 10-20 years duration ending in divorce or separation as 6.5-10.2 percent. Table 5 is based on the periods both before and after admission, and allows comparisons between the two main clinical groups controlled for duration of marriage: at least 15 percent of the patients in each main clinical group has been married for under 10 years and at least 40 percent in each group had been married for over 20 years. It appears that the increased frequency of broken marriages in our sample is partly due to some of the patients' marriages being of longer duration than those in Rowntree's sample. However, this would not explain the high frequency of separation and divorce before first admission, especially among the schizophrenics who are a comparatively younger group on first admission.

Table 5 shows that when the periods before and after admission are combined, the two clinical groups were not very different in duration of marriage: 151 of 374 schizophrenics, or 40.4 percent, had been married for 22 years or longer in 1966, compared with 169 of 360 affectives, or 46.9 percent; the difference between these proportions was not significant at the five percent level. This is due to the age criterion, 16-49, adopted for selecting the series. When *date and duration of marriage are controlled*, comparisons between the schizophrenics and the women suffering from affective disorders indicated that the schizophrenics were always a little more liable to become separated or divorced than the affectives. Considering the marriages of over 22 years duration, 32.5 percent of the schizophrenics had become separated, divorced or widowed compared with 25.4 percent of the affectives. This difference was quite insignificant at the 5 percent level. Among patients married since 1945, 23.3 percent of the schizophrenics had become separated, divorced or widowed compared with 19.9 percent of the affectives; again a slight, but insignificant, difference

TABLE 5

DURATION OF ENDED MARRIAGES BY DATE OF MARRIAGE IN RELATION TO ALL MARRIAGES: SCHIZOPHRENICS COMPARED WITH AFFECTIVES*

Quin-quennial date of marriage	Schizophrenics					Affectives				
	Duration of ended marriages**			No. of marriages not ended	Percent of marriages ended**	Duration of ended marriages**			No. of marriages not ended	Percent of marriages ended**
	Under 10 yrs	10-19 years	Over 20 yrs			Under 10 yrs	10-19 years	Over 20 yrs		
1925-9	2	1	—	2	60.0	—	—	—	1	—
1930-4	3	2	4	17	34.6	2	3	1	28	17.6
1935-9	5	8	4	41	29.3	6	8	6	60	25.0
1940-4	11	9	—	42	32.2	9	8	—	37	31.5
1945-9	18	13	—	69	31.0	12	6	—	60	23.1
1950-4	11	—	—	52	17.5	11	—	—	42	20.8
1955-9	9	—	—	34	20.9	6	—	—	41	12.8
1960s	1	—	—	16	5.9	3	—	—	10	23.1
N.K.	—	—	—	26	—	1	—	—	23	4.2
Total	60	33	8	299	25.3	50	25	7	302	21.3

* 1955-1963 admission sample follow-up until August 1966.
** Ended marriages in this table includes patients who are separated or divorced, and small number of widowed patients.

is found, and since there are fewer widows among the schizophrenics the tendency to marital breakdown always appears slightly higher in this clinical group.

Analysis by Social and Psychological Variables: Age and Marriage

In both clinical groups marital breakdown was more frequent among those patients who married before they were twenty than among those marrying at a later age. Still considering first marriages only, among the 400 ever married schizophrenics there were 53 who married before they were 20: 5.7 percent of these were separated before their first admission and 18.9 percent were divorced during this period. The proportion divorced before admission was lower at 7.2 percent for those 279 schizophrenics who married at 20-29, and 7.9 percent for 38 patients who married at 30-39. Among the women suffering from affective disorders 72 were married before the age of 20, and of these 13.9 percent became separated and 15.3 percent divorced before their first admission. Among 264 such patients who married in their twenties, the proportion who separated from their husbands dropped to 7.2 percent, and 6.4 percent were divorced. Only 24 women in this clinical group were married at

30-39 and of these only 4.2 percent separated and none were divorced. These findings agree with Rowntree's (1964), and appear to demonstrate the importance of immaturity in the brides as a factor in marital breakdown.

Analysis of marital status changes during the period after admission indicated no clear difference in frequency of separation and divorce by age at marriage of the patient.

Religion

Among the schizophrenic women there were no differences in frequency of separation and divorce when analyzed by religion of patient: 15.9 percent of the Protestants and 15.7 percent of the Roman Catholics parted from their husbands during the period before admission. Among the women suffering from affective disorders, 12.9 percent of the Protestants and 21 percent of the Roman Catholics had become separated or divorced; this agrees with Rowntree's finding that slightly more Roman Catholics separate than Protestants. No analysis was attempted of the period after admission owing to lack of data on religion of husbands.

Occupation of Husband

Husband's occupation was graded by the 1960 Registrar General's Classification of Occupations into non-manual and manual categories. There appeared a tendency for separation and divorce to be more frequent in the non-manual group, especially among the schizophrenics before admission. Rowntree had found no very great difference in her sample of the general population: 9.2 percent of 392 women married to non-manual workers experienced broken marriages, compared with 7.3 percent of 466 normal women married to skilled manual workers. It was decided that further analysis of the clinical sample would be unprofitable, in view of the fact that most separations had occurred in the group of patients giving no reliable data on former husband's occupation.

Number of Live Born Children

Separation and divorce appeared more frequently among patients in both clinical groups having fewer than two children: 21.3 percent of 103 schizophrenics who were infertile became separated or divorced from their husbands before admission, compared with 16.6 percent of 96 having two children. Among the women suffering from affective disorder 21.6 percent of 74 infertile couples had parted, compared with only 4.6 percent of 104 such patients who had two children. In this sample the children of women in both clinical groups were generally young and dependent, and they appeared to be a factor in prevented complete marital breakdown. If an older sample of affectives had been selected, their children would probably be grown up and their welfare would be a less important consideration in the prevention of separation, or divorce. After admission there were not enough patients having two or more children to permit analysis of separation and divorce. These findings again tend to agree with Rowntree's; she found that 13.9 percent of 228 infertile couples had parted compared with only 6.8 percent of 601 women having two or three children. Exact comparisons are impossible owing to variations in duration of marriage between her sample and the present one.

Pre-Morbid Personality

The importance of pre-morbid personality had been demonstrated in the analysis of probability of marriage (Stevens (1969b)) and it was decided to analyze proportions becoming separated or divorced from their husbands by this variable. Twenty percent of 185 schizophrenic patients exhibiting markedly abnormal personalities had become separated or divorced before admission compared with 11.8 percent of 85 schizophrenics who had always appeared normal to their relatives; the difference between these proportions did not quite reach the 5 percent significance level, and neither did the differentials in the group of women who were suffering from affective disorders, although they were in the same direction.

Age on First Admission

Marital breakdown was more frequent among schizophrenic women who were aged 30 and over on their first admission: 12.5 percent of the 128 schizophrenics who were admitted in their twenties had experienced a broken first marriage, compared with 25 percent who were not admitted until the age of 40 or over. No such differential was detected among the women with affective disorders. There are probably other factors involved in the schizophrenic group: those admitted later during the childbearing period may be those of a paranoid type of insidious onset whose marital relations would be more disturbed than those suffering from other forms of schizophrenia of sudden onset.

Total Length of Hospital Stay

Table 6 indicates that the proportion of patients who became separated or divorced after admission increased as length of hospital stay increased in both clinical groups. The difference in proportion parting between the very short and long stay schizophrenics is significant at the 1 percent level, and the difference between the short and medium stay schizophrenics was significant at the 5 percent level. The differentials among the women with affective disorders did not reach significance, mainly owing to the small size of the long stay group and resultant large standard errors.

TABLE 6

Proportion of Patients Parting from Their Husbands After First Admission by Diagnosis and Length of Hospital Stay*

Total length of stay	Schizophrenics		Affectives	
	N	Percentage separated or divorced	N	Percentage separated or divorced
Under 6 months......	82	6.1	79	5.1
6 months — 2 years...	107	16.8	67	9.0
Over 2 years..........	64	25.0	16	18.8

* This table is based on a sub-sample of married patients who were not first admissions on selection, and whose clinical notes gave exact information on total length of stay in hospital, and marital status changes.

Note on Assortative Mating

Among 440 ever married schizophrenic women, 2.5 percent had husbands who were definitely mentally ill, compared with 4.9 percent of 386 ever married women suffering from affective disorders. These husbands had all had out-patient or in-patient treatment, and the groups did not include husbands whose personalities were abnormal but who had never been seen by a psychiatrist. Even in this sample of women aged 16-49, the women suffering from affective disorders are a slightly older group than the schizophrenics, so that their husbands are generally a little older and would therefore have had a slightly greater chance of seeing a psychiatrist than the husbands of the schizophrenics. This may partially explain the slightly higher proportion of mentally ill husbands among the affective group. Data from case records suggested that more patients seemed to become ill as a result of their husband's mental disorder than husbands who become ill as a reaction to the patient's illness, but further investigation is necessary in view of the complexity of the marital relationship.

Reliability of Data
Checks on the Reliability of Clinical Diagnoses

For the purpose of the analysis the consultant's last diagnosis was accepted. However, a five percent random sub-sample was selected, and Dr. J. K. Wing read the clinical notes of 63 patients thus selected, and made his own diagnosis. In 41 cases Dr. Wing's diagnosis was the same as that accepted, and in a further 14 cases his diagnosis did not involve changes from the main clinical groups used in the analysis: it therefore appears that about 87 percent of the random sub-sample were considered to be reliably diagnosed.

A further check on diagnosis was made by writing to all other hospitals each patient had been in for their clinical opinion: 80 percent of each clinical group involved no change in diagnosis.

Reliability of Data in Case Records

Two-thirds of the case histories came from a source other than the patient such as husband, mother, doctors or social workers. There was an important difference by diagnosis: in 6 to 8 percent of the schizophrenics the patient herself was the only source of information, compared with 29 percent of women with affective disorders giving their own histories, and this difference was significant at the 1 percent level. This is probably due to the fact that more of the depressed women were not deluded and were able to give their own histories.

Non-response Bias

Method of tracing patients during the follow-up were cross tabulated with the variables of marital status, personality, social class by husband's occupation, religion and race, in order to determine sources of bias. Although 80 percent of the total simple were successfully traced, married patients were easier to trace than single and separated patients, especially among women with affective disorders: 30 percent of 84 single women in the latter group could not be traced, compared with 27 percent of 33 who had separated, 30 percent of 23 who had been divorced, and 18.5 percent of 313 patients who were married and living with their husbands. In the schizophrenic sample, 19 percent of the 360 single women were not traced, compared with 29 percent of the 56 who were separated, 17 percent of the divorced group and only 15.4 percent of the 324 married patients. It is therefore possible that during the follow-up a bias has been incurred towards the married, and that some patients who have separated or become divorced or have married again have been under-represented.

Analysis of the other relevant variables indicated no significant sources of bias except that patients whose hospital stay was short were slightly more difficult to trace than long stay patients in both clinical groups. It was considered that these differentials in non-response should not seriously bias the results on frequency of separation and divorce, except that there may be some slight underestimation of marital breakdown which should be compensated for in the general results by the slight bias towards chronic patients, who appeared more likely to become separated or divorced than patients whose hospital stay was short.

DISCUSSION

The frequency of separation and divorce before admission among both schizophrenic women aged 16-49 and women of this age suffering from affective illnesses was considerably in excess of that expected on the basis of controlled comparisons with Rowntree's general population data. This finding supports earlier results based on first admissions, such as for the paranoid schizophrenic group in an American sample (Dayton (1940)), and Ödegard's (1953) findings on Norwegian schizophrenics. Ödegard considered that schizophrenics are selectively excluded in marriage, and that paranoid traits especially are conducive to high frequency of marital breakdown. Blacker's (1958) results on admission to the Bethlem-Maudsley Hospital during 1952-54 also indicated a high frequency of marital breakdown among schizophrenics; 13 percent had become separated or divorced from their husbands, and 22 percent of patients with paranoid states.

The results of the present inquiry on the women aged 16-49 with affective disorders indicated that they appear to be as prone to marital breakdown before illness as the schizophrenics, which disagrees with Ödegard and Blacker's results on patients of all ages indicating that manic-depressives have a low rate of separation and divorce. Ödegard (1953) found no evidence for manic-depressives being excluded from marriage and Blacker (1958) found that only 6 percent of 781 ever married manic-depressives had parted from their husbands, this percentage being similar to that expected in a sample of normal women such as Rowntree's; the difference in age structure between Blacker's sample and the present one may partly account for the lower proportion of broken marriages in his sample of manic-depressives; he had included patients whose illness was essentially involutional in nature, whose marriages had had a longer period in which to become stable before the illness than the marriage of the younger women in this study. Blacker's estimate included some marital status changes after admission and did not clearly distinguish between these and changes before admission. The present study really emphasizes the significant role of personality in marital disruption in both schizophrenics and women suffering mainly from severe depression, rather than the illness itself. This is in accordance with similar findings on the importance of pre-morbid personality in probability of marriage before admission, Stevens (1969b)). However, it is probable that schizophrenics are slightly more liable to marital breakdown before admission than women with affective disorders when the important factor of duration of marriage is controlled; the schizophrenics are younger and have been exposed to the chance of separation for a shorter period than the women with affective disorders, but *in spite of this* they experience as many separations as the women suffering from depression or mania.

The results on marital breakdown after admission were more expected on the basis of previous studies: the frequency of separation and divorce was significantly higher among the schizophrenics during this period than among the affectives which accords very much with Brown, Bone, Dalison & Wing's (1966) results on schizophrenics and Blacker's results on manic-depressives. Blacker found that 13 percent of 994 ever married neurotic depressives had parted from their husbands, which was as high a proportion as among his non-paranoid schizophrenics. The present sample of affectives included some neurotic depressives, but presumably Blacker's estimate was predominantly of the period before admission and it included patients over the age of 50 and cannot be strictly compared with our estimates based solely on separation after admission.

The analysis by age at marriage, fertility and religion indicated that patients exhibited the same basic trends as the general population, as demonstrated by Rowntree's results: patients who married before the age of 20 were more likely to experience a separation or divorce than those who married later, and patients who were Roman Catholics or had less than two children appeared a little more likely to separate than those who were more fertile, or were of Protestant faith.

With regard to factors more intrinsic to the clinical condition of the patients, there appeared to be a relationship between pre-morbid abnormalities of personality and high frequency of separation; this agrees with the results of Slater & Woodside (1951) on marriages of neurotic and normal soldiers, in that they also demonstrated the role of abnormal personality traits in marital unhappiness. Among the schizophrenics, those experiencing a chronic psychosis involving long periods in hospital were significantly more likely to part from their husbands after admission than those whose hospital stay was shorter, and whose course of illness was less severe.

There appeared to be some assortative mating in the sample, but the extent of this was lower among the schizophrenics than found by Macsorley (1964). Only 2.5 percent of the husbands of our patients had seen a psychiatrist compared with 5.1 percent of her sample. Our estimate for women with affective disorders of 4.9 percent is nearer hers. There was more evidence for concordance of clinical condition between patients and husbands in the affective sample, as was found by Nielsen (1964). However, such data could be interpreted as much by concepts of psychopathological marital interaction as by an assortative mating hypothesis. Kreitman (1968) undertook a detailed study of married couples who were both patients and favors a neurotic interaction hypothesis for findings on patients with neurosis and personality disorders, but considered that assortative mating may occur in psychotics.

Further investigation is necessary requiring intensive interviews before the high frequency of separation and divorce among patients may be reliably interpreted in psychopathological and other terms.

SUMMARY

1. A large representative sample of 1,295 women aged 16-49 suffering from schizophrenia and affective disorders was selected from admissions to a London mental Hospital between 1955 and 1963, and followed up until 1966 by a postal inquiry. Data on separation and divorce was analyzed for the 407 ever married schizophrenics and the 388 ever married women with affective disorders, by the relevant social and clinical variables.

2. During the period before first admission, 17.7 percent of the married schizophrenics and 15.7 percent of the married women with affective disorders had become separated or divorced. This frequency is higher than that of 6-10 percent expected from Rowntree's national sample of British women, some of whom had been married for similar periods to the patients, and these results indicate the significance of pre-morbid personality in marital breakdown, rather than factors associated with the illness itself.

3. After admission, 18.3 percent of the schizophrenics became separated or divorced from their husbands compared with only 10.2 percent of women with affective disorders, this difference was significant at the 1 percent level.

4. Analysis of frequency of separation and divorce by the sociological variables of age at marriage, religion, occupation of husband and number of live born children indicated that patients followed the same basic trends as normal women, as given by Rowntree (1964).

5. Patients who had abnormal pre-morbid personality traits were more likely to become separated or divorced than those who appeared to their relatives to have been normal.

6. Patients who required long periods in hospital became separated and divorced more often than those whose illness was less chronic.

7. Further inquiry is necessary before any explanation may be made of the high frequency of separation and divorce in psychopathological or other terms.

ACKNOWLEDGMENTS

I should like to thank the Medical Research Council for financial support in the form of the Mapother Fellowship, and Mr. *N. H. Carrier*, Professor Sir *Aubrey Lewis*, Professor *D. V. Glass* and Dr. *J. K. Wing* for excellent advice; Dr. *H. C. Beccle* and Dr. *M. Markowe* for facilities provided at Springfield Hospital, Tooting; and Mr. *P. Wakeford* for use of his computer programme. These results were part of the author's Ph.D. Thesis in Sociology awarded by London University in 1967.

REFERENCES

BLACKER, C. P. (1958): Disruption of marriage. Some possibilities of prevention. *Lancet* 1, 578-581.

BROWN, G. W., B. DALISON & J. K. WING (1966): Schizophrenia and Social Care. Maudsley Monograph No. 17, Oxford University Press, London.

DAYTON, N. (1940): New Facts on Mental Disorder. Thomas, Baltimore.

KREITMAN, N. (1968): Married couples admitted to mental hospital. Part 1: Diagnostic similarity and relation of illness to marriage. Part 2: Family history, age and duration of marriage. *Brit. J. Psychiat.* 114, 699-718.

LAURENCE, K. M. (1959): Tracing patients. *Lancet* 2, 208-212.

LEWIS, A. J. (1934): Melancholia. A clinical survey of depressive states. *J. ment. Sci.* 80, 277-378.

LEWIS, A. J. (1944): Depression. *J. ment. Sci.* 90, 256-265.

MACSORLEY, K. (1964): An investigation into the fertility rates on mentally ill patients. *Ann. hum. Genet.* 27, 247-256.

NIELSEN, J. (1964): Mental disorders in married couples. *Brit. J. Psychiat.* 110, 683-697.

ÖDEGÅRD, Ö. (1953): New data on marriage and mental disease. *J. ment. Sci.* 99, 778-785.

ROWNTREE, G. (1964): Some aspects of marriage breakdown in Britain during the last thirty years. *Pop. Studies* 18, 147-163.

SLATER, E., & M. WOODSIDE (1951): Patterns of Marriage. Cassell. (London).

STEVENS, B. C. (1969a): Marriage and Fertility of Women Suffering from Schizophrenia and Affective Disorders. Maudsley Monograph No. 19, Oxford University Press, London.

STEVENS, B. C. (1969b): Probability of marriage and fertility of women suffering from schizophrenia and affective disorders. *Pop. Studies* 23, 435-454.

Section IV

BIOCHEMICAL STUDIES

18

INVESTIGATION OF p-METHOXYAM-
PHETAMINE EXCRETION IN AMPHET-
AMINE INDUCED PSYCHOSIS

B. M. Angrist, J. W. Schweitzer, A. J. Friedhoff,
and S. Gershon

Many differences exist between the symptoms of schizophrenia and those of drug-induced states caused by agents like LSD or mescaline (1). Amphetamine psychosis, by contrast, can in some cases replicate virtually all of the manifestations of natural schizophrenic illness (2-5). Such a correspondence justifies a study of the biochemical basis of this condition.

A provocative hypothesis about the genesis of amphetamine psychosis has been proposed (6). Smythies et al. suggest that p-methoxyamphetamine (PMA) may be formed from amphetamine in patients who develop psychotic symptoms. In an animal test system utilizing a conditioned avoidance response and analysis of reaction time which is designed to correlate with human psychotogenicity (6, 7), Smythies has found PMA to be highly potent as a disruptor of behavior—second only, in this respect, to LSD of all the compounds tested (6). Shulgin et al. have established that PMA is psychotogenic in humans and also that it has an order of potency of approximately five times that of mescaline (8). The doses of amphetamine required to induce a psychosis in humans are such that pharmacologically active amounts of this metabolite could be produced. We therefore examined the urine of subjects who were receiving amphetamine in psychotogenic doses to ascertain the presence or absence of PMA.

The subjects were four physically healthy non-schizophrenic volunteers to whom amphetamine was administered orally in doses of 5-50 mg/h for as long as was tolerated. A mean total cumulative dose of 629

Reprinted, by permission of author and editor, from: *Nature,* 225:651-652, 1970.

mg was admiinstered over an average period of 51 hours. The method of administration and behavioral effects have been reported (5).

Urine was collected continuously in 6-12 hours pooled specimens throughout amphetamine administration. The specimens representing hours before and immediately after amphetamine was last administered were examined. Urinary amphetamine was assayed by a method in which an internal standard, phenethylamine, is added to a 5 ml. aliquot of each urine sample, in duplicate. The amines, extracted with chloroform at pH 10, are acetylated directly with acetic anhydride. The residue on evaporation is dissolved in dioxane and a portion is injected into an F

TABLE 1

Schedule of Testing for PMA Excretion

Subject and trial		Cumu-lative dose (mg)	Duration of adminis-tration (h)	Urine volume (ml.)	Amphetamine excreted (mg)	Psychotic symptoms
1	A	325	28.75	95	10.0	Present
	B	745	64.25	36.5	14.2	Present
	C (+R)	950	54	735	123	Absent
2	A	390	45.75	485	18.3	Minimal
	B	590	74.75	325	23.4	Minimal
3	A	955	71.5	245	21.4	Absent
	B (+R)	465	26	405	9.20	Absent
4	A	595	46	79	9.05	Present
	B (+R)	645	47	490	14.9	Absent

PMA was not detected in any of the trials. R indicates pretreatment with reserpine, which seemed to prevent the occurrence of psychotic symptoms (5).

and M "Biomedical 400" gas chromatograph fitted with a six-foot U tube packed with 8 percent ethylene glycol adipate on "Chromosorb W." For 8 inches at the two ends the packing was 3 percent "SE-30" on "Diatoport S." The column temperature was 215°.

The amount of amphetamine present can be calculated by comparing the height of its chromatographic peak with that of the internal standard (9). PMA was assayed with the same method. Retention times for N-acetylamphetamine and N-acetyl-PMA were, respectively, 4 and 15 minutes. From peak height measurements of standard amounts (0.1—1.0 μg) of N-acetyl-PMA and, independently, from recovery studies of PMA added to urine, it is estimated that the limit of detectability of PMA in these urines is about 70-80 μg/l. of urine. In none of the nine studies was PMA detected even though large amounts of amphetamine were present in these urine samples (Table 1).

Our study does not support the suggested formation of PMA from ingested amphetamine as a mechanism for the genesis of amphetamine psychosis, but the distinct possibility remains that amphetamine could undergo such transformation within the central nervous system and not peripherally, and then subsequently be further transformed before being excreted in the urine. Even the transient production of such a substance, should it occur at critical sites in the central nervous system, could cause significant behavioral effects. In partial support of this alternative, we have found that N-^{3}H-acetyl-PMA is almost entirely O-demethylated in rats *in vivo*.

We thank Dr. Alexander Shulgin for the *p*-methoxyamphetamine used as a chromatographic standard for preliminary studies. The standards were synthesized in our laboratory.

REFERENCES

1. HOLLISTER, L., *Chemical Psychosis, LSD and Related Drugs,* 117 (Thomas, Springfield, 1968).
2. CONNELL, P. H., *Amphetamine Psychosis,* Maudsley Monographs, No. 5, 75 (Oxford University Press, London, 1958).
3. GRIFFITH, J. J., OATES, J., & CAVANAUGH, J., *Amer. Med. Assoc.,* 205, 39, 1968).
4. ANGRIST, B. M., & GERSHON, S., *Schizophrenia. Current Concepts and Research* (edit. by Siva Sankar, D. V.), 508 (P. J. D. Publications Ltd., 1969).
5. ANGRIST, B. M., & GERSHON, S., *Proc. Soc. Biol. Psychiat.,* 1970 (in the press).
6. SMYTHIES, J. R., JOHNSTON, U. S., BRADLEY, R. J., BENNINGTON, F., MORIN, R. D., & CLARK, JUN., L. C., *Nature,* 216, 128 (1967).
7. SMYTHIES, J. R., COPPER, A., & KREITMAN, N., *Biological Psychiatry, A Review of Recent Advances,* 70 (Springer-Verlag, New York, 1968).
8. SHULGIN, A. T., SARGENT, T., & NARANJO, C., *Nature,* 221, 537 (1969).
9. ANGRIST, B. M., SCHWEITZER, J. W., FRIEDHOFF, A. J., GERSHON, S., HEKIMIAN, L. J., & FLOYD, A., *Internat. Pharmacopsychiat.* 2, 125 (1969).

19

HETEROGENEITY OF N- AND O-METHYLTRANSFERASES

Julius Axelrod and Elliot S. Vesell

Laboratory of Clinical Science, National Institute of Mental Health
Laboratory of Chemical Pharmacology, National Heart Institute
National Institutes of Health, Bethesda, Maryland

SUMMARY

The methyltransferases phenylethanolamine N-methyltransferase, histamine N-methyltransferase (EC 2.1.1.8), catechol O-methyltransferase (EC 2.1.1.6), and hydroxyindole O-methyltransferase, from tissues of several species, were subjected to starch block electrophoresis. Adrenal phenylethanolamine N-methyltransferase and pineal hydroxyindole O-methyltransferase were heterogeneous among different species with respect to electrophoretic mobility on starch block, heat stability, and substrate specificity, but they were homogeneous within a given species. Multiple forms of histamine N-methyltransferase and catechol O-methyltransferase occurred in tissues within a given species as well as among different species. They had different electrophoretic mobilities, heat stabilities, and kinetic properties.

INTRODUCTION

Several methyltransferases are involved in the activation and inactivation of the biogenic amines norepinephrine, histamine, and serotonin. These enzymes catalyze the N-methylation of norepinephrine and other β-hydroxylphenylamines (phenylethanolamine N-methyltransferase) (1, 2), the O-methylation of catecholamines (catechol O-methyltransferase, EC 2.1.1.6) (3), the N-methylation of histamine (histamine N-methyltransferase, EC 2.1.1.8) (4), and the O-methylation of N-acetylserotonin (hydroxyindole O-methyltransferase) (5).

In view of the marked species differences in the total activity and

Reprinted, by permission of author and editor, from: *Molecular Pharmacology,* 6: 78-84, 1970.

tissue distribution of these enzymes, a study was undertaken to ascertain whether biochemically distinguishable forms of the enzyme possessing different catalytic properties could be identified. This report describes certain physico-chemical properties of such distinct forms. Phenylethanolamine N-methyltransferase, catechol O-methyltransferase, histamine N-methyltransferase, and hydroxyindole O-methyltransferase exhibited multiple molecular forms in different species and, in certain cases, within the tissues of the same animal.

MATERIALS AND METHODS

Adult male animals were used unless otherwise stated. Tissues from rats (Sprague-Dawley), mice (NIH stock), mongrel dogs and cats, and guinea pigs (Hartley strain) were removed, placed on cracked ice, and homogenized within 1 hour after the animals had been killed. Pineal glands from quails (*Corturnix corturnix japonica*) were kindly supplied by Dr. Jean Lauber, University of Alberta, shipped in Dry Ice, and examined 1 week later. Bovine tissues were removed within 1 hour after the cattle had been killed in a local slaughterhouse and were stored for 1 week at —10°. Human tissues, obtained within 8 hours from two normal young men who had been killed in an accident, were stored at —10° for 1 day. Tissues were homogenized, and the supernatant fractions were subjected to starch block electrophoresis within 8 hours. All experiments were repeated two to five times with different tissue preparations from each species.

Tissues were homogenized in 3-10 volumes of ice-cold water, depending on the tissue, and centrifuged at 100,000 $\times$ g for 30 minutes in a refrigerated Spinco centrifuge. The fatty layer was removed by aspiration, and the clear supernatant fraction was subjected to starch block electrophoresis. A starch block was prepared in 0.05 M sodium barbital buffer, pH 8.6, as described previously (6). A 1-2-ml aliquot of the supernatant fraction, containing 2-10 units of enzyme activity (1 unit is equivalent to 1 mμmole of N- or O-methylated product formed per hour), was applied at the origin. Electrophoresis was carried out at 4° for 18 hours at 360 V. and 80 mamp. The starch block was cut into 0.5-inch segments, and the enzyme was eluted from each segment with 2 ml of 0.05 M sodium phosphate buffer, pH 7.9.

To examine the efficacy and reproducibility of the electrophoretic technique, supernatant fractions from dog and rat adrenals, containing equal amounts of phenylethanolamine N-methyltransferase activity, were mixed and inserted into a starch block. After electrophoresis there were two distinct peaks of enzyme activity, which were the same as those obtained when the extracts from each animal were subjected separately to electrophoresis (Fig. 1A). After electrophoretic separation, the peak tube of phenylethanolamine N-methyltransferase activity from rat adrenals was eluted and again subjected to starch block electrophoresis. There was no change in mobility of the enzyme purified by electrophoresis. Duplicate determinations gave the same electrophoretic pattern.

An aliquot from each eluate was transferred to a 15-ml centrifuge tube and assayed for various methyltransferases by a modification of procedures described previously.

Phenylethanolamine N-methyltransferase (2), histamine N-methyltransferase (4), catechol O-methyltransferase (7), and hydroxyindole O-methyltransferase (5) were measured as follows.

Phenylethanolamine N-methyltransferase. DL-Phenylethanolamine (25 µg), ^{14}C-methyl-S-adenosylmethionine (New England Nuclear Corporation) (1.0 mµmole; 50µCi/µmole), sodium phosphate buffer (0.5 M, pH 7.9), and enzyme preparation to make a final volume of 250 µl were incubated for 1 hour at 37°. The reaction was stopped by addition of 0.5 ml of sodium borate buffer, pH 10, and the ^{14}C-methylphenylethanolamine formed enzymatically was extracted with 6 ml of toluene containing 3% by volume of isoamyl alcohol. A 4-ml aliquot of the extract was transferred to a counting vial containing 1 ml of ethanol and 10 ml of phosphor, and the radioactivity was measured.

Histamine N-methyltransferase, hydroxyindole O-methyltransferase, and catechol O-methltransferase. The procedure was similar to that used for phenylethanolamine N-methyltransferase, except that the following substrates were used: histamine dihydrochloride (25 µg) for histamine N-methyltransferase, N-acetylserotonin (50 µg) (Regis Chemical Company, Chicago) for hydroxyindole O-methyltransferase, and l-norepinephrine bitartrate (25 µg) for catechol O-methyltransferase. $MgCl_2$ (2 µmoles) was added to the incubation mixture for the catechol O-methltransferase assay. The enzymatic products ^{14}C-methylhistamine, ^{14}C-melatonin, and ^{14}C-metanephrine formed in the respective reactions were extracted into a 6-ml mixture of toluene and isoamyl alcohol (3:2 by volume).

K_m values were determined by Wilkinson's method (8), using a digital computer and the FORTRAN program written by Cleland (9). Statistical differences were obtained by the procedure of Steele and Torrie (10).

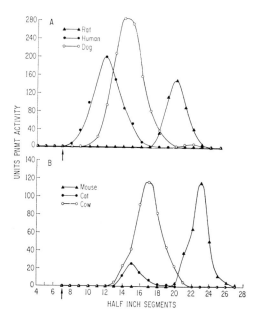

Fig. 1. *Electrophoretic mobility on starch block of adrenal phenylethanolamine N-methyltransferase (PNMT) from several mammalian species* Electrophoresis was performed on supernatant fractions in 0.05 M sodium barbital buffer, pH 8.6, at 4° for 18 hr. Arrows indicate origin.

RESULTS

Separation of different forms of phenylethanolamine N-methyltransferase from mammalian adrenal glands. The adrenal gland was used as a source of phenylethanolamine N-methyltransferase because the enzyme is highly localized in this organ (2). The electrophoretic separations of phenylethanolamine N-methyltransferase obtained from human, dog, mouse, rat, cat, and cow adrenal glands are shown in Fig. 1A and B. These illustrate electrophoretic patterns obtained for adrenal glands from six species, as revealed by separations on two starch blocks. Human, dog, and rat adrenals contain a distinct form of phenylethanolamine N-methyltransferase as shown by their differing electrophoretic mobilities (Fig. 1A). The electrophoretic mobilities of phenylethanolamine N-methyltransferases obtained from cow and cat adrenals were similar (Fig. 1B), but the phenylethanolamine N-methyltransferases from these species differed in electrophoretic mobility from that of the mouse (Fig. 1B). The cat and cow phenylethanolamine N-methyltransferases exhibited electrophoretic mobilities resembling that of the dog. In many experiments, mouse phenylethanolamine N-methyltransferase was similar in electrophoretic mobility to that of the rat. To distinguish further among the phenylethanolamine N-methyltransferase activities from various species, peak tubes were diluted to contain similar enzyme activities, and stability to heat was examined (Table 1). Although the cat phenyletha-

TABLE 1

HEAT STABILITY OF PHENYLETHANOLAMINE N-METHYLTRANSFERASE FROM VARIOUS SPECIES

Peak tubes in Fig. 1A and B were diluted to contain approximately similar concentrations of phenylethanolamine N-methyltransferase. Aliquots were heated for 2 and 5 min. at 48° in 0.05 M sodium phosphate buffer, pH 7.9. Results are expressed as percentage of phenylethanolamine N-methyltransferase activity remaining.

Species	Heat stability	
	2 min.	5 min.
	% enzyme remaining	
Rat	90	65
Mouse	50	20
Cat	55	20
Human	40	20
Dog	88	70
Cow	90	68

nolamine N-methyltransferase had an electrophoretic mobility similar to those of dog and cow, the cat enzyme was considerably less stable to heat. The rat phenylethanolamine N-methyltransferase was also more heat-stable than that of the mouse. These results suggest the existence of at least five distinguishable forms of phenylethanolamine N-methyltransferase among the six mammalian species examined.

Phenylethanolamine N-methyltransferase methylates β-hydroxyphenylamine derivatives, but not phenylethylamines (2). The relative activities of phenylethanolamine N-methyltransferases separated electrophoretically from various species were examined with respect to their ability to N-methylate several phenylamine derivatives. The phenylethanolamine N-methyltransferases obtained from rat, human, and cow methylated phenylethanolamine derivatives, but not phenylethylamines (Table 2). However, dog phenylethanolamine N-methyltransferase showed small but definite activity toward some phenylethylamine derivatives. Dog and human phenylethanolamine N-methyltransferases methylated norephedrine to greater extents than did rat phenylethanolamine N-methyltransferase (Table 2).

Histamine N-methyltransferase. The electrophoretic mobility of histamine N-methyltransferase was examined in several guinea pig tissues, and

TABLE 2

SUBSTRATE SPECIFICITY OF PHENYLETHANOLAMINE
N-METHYLTRANSFERASE

Phenylethanolamine N-methyltransferases obtained from peak tubes (Fig. 1A and B) were incubated with 0.1 μmole of substrates and cofactors as described in *Materials and Methods. The* ^{14}C-methylated products were extracted as described previously (2). Results are expressed as percentage of relative activity.

Substrate	Rat	Human	Dog	Cow
	%	%	%	%
DL-Phenylethanolamine	100	100	100	100
Phenylethylamine	<1	<1	4	0
DL-Normetanephrine	70	70	71	80
3-Methoxy-4-hydroxyphenyl-ethylamine	<1	0	3	0
DL-Norephedrine	2	10	18	
D-Amphetamine	0	0	0	0

in human, cow, cat, dog, and guinea pig liver. The electrophoretic mobility of this enzyme was first studied in guinea pig stomach, liver, lung, and brain (Fig. 2A and B). All these tissues showed a single peak of activity with similar electrophoretic mobility. The livers of human, dog, and cat were then subjected to starch block electrophoresis and examined for histamine N-methyltransferase activity. The results, shown in Fig. 2B, reveal at least three distinct forms of histamine N-methyltransferase. Dog and guinea pig liver histamine N-methyltransferases had similar electrophoretic mobilities but differed from those of human and cat liver. The human and dog also had a smaller peak of histamine N-methyltransferase activity, which, to achieve adequate definition, required larger amounts of histamine N-methyltransferase activity to be applied to the starch block (Fig. 2C). The dog and human each showed two peaks of

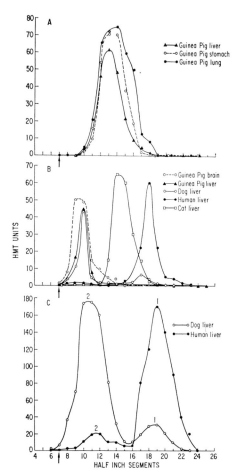

FIG. 2. *Electrophoretic mobility on starch block of histamine N-methyltransferase (HMT) from several mammalian species and tissues*

Conditions were the same as described in Fig. 1 and MATERIALS AND METHODS.

histamine N-methyltransferase activity: a major, slow-moving peak in the dog, and a larger, faster-moving peak in the human (Fig. 2C).

Heat stability and K_m values with respect to histamine were determined for the histamine N-methyltransferases electrophoretically separated from various species (Table 3). Cat histamine N-methyltransferase was most heat-stable, and the human peak 2 enzyme was least stable. There was also a wide range of K_m values for histamine. The two human enzymes

TABLE 3

Some Properties of Histamine N-methyltransferase from Various Species Separated by Starch Block Electrophoresis

Peak tubes (Fig. 2A-C) were diluted to contain similar concentrations of histamine N-methyltransferase. Aliquots were heated at 51° in 0.05 M sodium phosphate buffer, pH 7.9, for 3 min. Results are expressed as the percentage of histamine N-methyltransferase activity remaining. K_m values were obtained before heating, using varied amounts of histamine and a constant amount of S-adenosylmethionine (2.5×10^{-6} M). Peak 2 (human) K_m was significantly different from peak 1 ($p < 0.001$). K_m for cat was significantly different from that of all other species ($p < 0.05$). Dog peaks 1 and 2 were not statistically different.

Species	Heat stability % enzyme remaining	K_m μM ± SEM
Cat	63	81 ± 22
Dog, peak 2	49	10 ± 2.3
Dog, peak 1	55	24 ± 7.3
Guinea pig	49	
Human, peak 1	46	950 ± 97
Human, peak 2	33	20 ± 0.4

showed a 40-fold difference in K_m values, whereas two dog enzymes showed a smaller difference, which was not statistically different.

Catechol O-methyltransferase. The electrophoretic mobilities of cathechol O-methyltransferases from rat heart, kidney, brain, and liver and from cat, human, and dog liver were examined. The rat tissues exhibited two isozymes of catechol O-methyltransferase after starch block electrophoresis (Fig. 3A and B). In the rat, isozymes from one tissue had the same electrophoretic mobility as the corresponding isozymes from the other tissue. The heat stability and K_m values of the two catechol O-methyltransferase isozymes from rat liver were found to differ (Table 4).

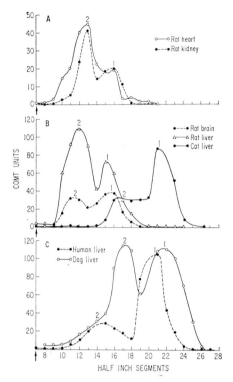

FIG. 3. *Electrophoretic mobility on starch block of catechol O-methyltransferase (COMT) from several mammalian species and tissues*

Conditions were the same as described in Fig. 1 and MATERIALS AND METHODS.

Two electrophoretically distinguishable forms of catechol O-methyltransferase were also separated from human, dog, and cat livers (Fig. 3B and C). These isozymes appeared to have different electrophoretic mobilities, heat stabilities, and K_m values from those of the rat (Table 4). In the dog and cat the fast-moving peak was the major isozyme, whereas in the rat and human the slower-moving peak had most enzyme activity. Because of the extreme instability of human catechol O-methyltransferase after starch block electrophoresis, K_m values could not be determined.

Hydroxyindole O-methyltransferase. The melatonin-forming enzyme hydroxyindole O-methyltransferase is uniquely localized in the pineal gland (5). The electrophoretic behavior of this enzyme obtained from a mammal (cow) and a bird (quail) was studied. Each had a single peak

TABLE 4

PROPERTIES OF CATECHOL O-METHYLTRANSFERASES FROM VARIOUS SPECIES

Peak tubes (Fig. 3A-C) were diluted to contain similar concentrations of catechol O-methyltransferase. An aliquot was heated at 51° in 0.05 M sodium phosphate buffer, pH 7.9, for 3 min. Results are expressed as percentage of catechol O-methyltransferase activity remaining. K_m values were obtained before heating, using varied amounts of norepinephrine and a constant amount of S-adenosylmethionine (2.5×10^{-6} M). Cat peak 1 K_m differs from all other species ($p < 0.05$). The K_m value for catechol O-methyltransferase rat peak 1 differs from that of peak 2 ($p < 0.05$).

Species	Heat stability	K_m
	% enzyme remaining	μM $\pm$ SEM
Human, peak 2	50	
Human, peak 1	48	
Dog, peak 2	54	39 $\pm$ 2.7
Dog, peak 1	15	39 $\pm$ 4.9
Cat, peak 1	7	57 $\pm$ 15
Rat, peak 2	33	43 $\pm$ 12
Rat, peak 1	45	194 $\pm$ 58

TABLE 5

PROPERTIES OF HYDROXYINDOLE O-METHYLTRANSFERASE FROM COW AND QUAIL

Peak tubes (Fig. 4) were diluted to contain similar concentrations of hydroxyindole O-methyltransferase. An aliquot was heated at 51° in 0.1 M sodium phosphate buffer, pH 7.9, for 3 min. Results are expressed as percentage of hydroxyindole O-methyltransferase activity remaining. K_m values were obtained before heating, using varied amounts of N-acetylserotonin and a constant amount of S-adenosylmethionine (2.5×10^{-6} M). Hydroxyindole O-methyltransferases from quail and cow were statistically different ($p < 0.001$).

Species	Heat stability	K_m
	% enzyme remaining	μM $\pm$ SEM
Cow	35	51 $\pm$ 5.8
Quail	2	4.8 $\pm$ 0.65

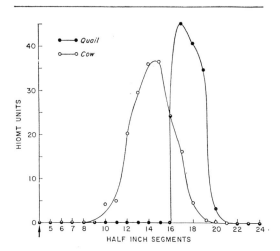

FIG. 4. *Electrophoretic mobility on starch block of cow and quail hydroxyindole O-methyltransferase (HIOMT)*
Conditions were the same as described in Fig. 1 and MATERIALS AND METHODS.

of hydroxyindole O-methyltransferase activity. The electrophoretic mobility of the quail hydroxyindole O-methyltransferase was faster than that of the cow (Fig. 4). The hydroxyindole O-methyltransferases from these species differed markedly in heat stability and K_m values (Table 5). Previous work has shown that cow and quail hydroxyindole O-methyltransferases also differ in substrate specificity (11). Quail hydroxyindole O-methyltransferase O-methylates both serotonin and N-acetylserotonin, whereas cow hydroxyindole O-methyltrasferase is highly specific for N-acetylserotonin.

DISCUSSION

These results show that species differences exist in the physicochemical properties of the methyltransferase enzymes involved in biogenic amine synthesis and metabolism. Under the conditions of these experiments, phenylethanolamine N-methyltransferase and hydroxyindole O-methyltransferase appeared to be electrophoretically homogeneous within a given species, but species differences in adrenal phenylethanolamine N-methyltransferase and pineal hydrozyindole O-methyltransferase were identified by starch block electrophoresis and heat stability. Although these enzymes were homogeneous by starch block electrophoresis with sodium barbital buffer at pH 8.6, other conditions of electrophoresis or physicochemical techniques might uncover heterogeneity. Previous work has revealed different forms of phenylethanolamine N-methyltransferase in frog and rat (12). Rat phenylethanolamine N-methyltransferase was induced by corticoids, whereas the frog phenylethanolamine N-methyl-transferase was not. Histamine N-methyltransferase and catechol O-me-thyltransferase were heterogeneous electrophoretically within a given species. These multiple forms of histamine N-methyltransferase and cate-chol O-methyltransferase were further distinguished by differences in heat stability and kinetic properties. Previously, rat liver catechol O-methyltransferase was shown to exhibit at least two forms of activity by acrylamide electrophoresis (13).

Isozymes have become a commonly encountered biological phenom-enon (14). Availability of multiple forms of isozymes has been shown to permit selective and flexible regulation of physiologically important reactions. A variety of mechanisms whereby isozymes act to allow finer metabolic control have been documented (14). For example, Stadtman has described differential feedback inhibition of several isozymes at branched metabolic pathways (14). Fritz has reported allosteric control of lactate dehydrogenase-5 by oxalacetate (15). With respect to the multiplicity of enzymes involved in the synthesis and degradation of biogenic amines, the distinct physiological roles performed by each iso-zyme remain to be elucidated. Possibly some forms are subject to induc-tion by steroids or drugs, whereas others are not (16). Certain isozymes may represent synthetic or degradative by-products without additional physiological significance. Some of these isozymes may even be artifacts, arising during the processes of tissue homogenization and electrophoresis, although their markedly different physicochemical properties suggest that they do exist within the cell.

ACKNOWLEDGMENTS

We thank Dorothy M. Rutherford and Wallace W. Holland for their excellent technical assistance.

REFERENCES

1. KIRSHNER, N., & GOODALL, M.: Biochim. Biophys. Acta 24:658 (1957).
2. AXELROD, J.: J. Biol. Chem. 237:1657 (1962).
3. AXELROD, J.: Science 126:400 (1957).
4. BROWN, D. D., TOMCHICK, R., & AXELROD, J.: J. Biol. Chem. 234:2948 (1959).
5. AXELROD, J., & WEISSBACH, H.: J. Biol. Chem. 236:211 (1961).

6. Kunkel, H. G. *in* "Methods of Biochemical Analysis" (D. Glick, ed.), Vol. 1, p. 141. Interscience, New York, 1954.
7. Axelrod, J., & Tomchick, R.: *J. Biol. Chem.* 233:702 (1958).
8. Wilkinson, G. N.: *Biochem. J.* 80:324 (1961).
9. Cleland, W. W.: *Nature* 198:463 (1964).
10. Steele, R. C. D., & Torrie, J. H.: "Principles and Procedures of Statistics." McGraw-Hill, New York, 1960.
11. Axelrod, J., & Lauber, J. K.: *Biochem. Pharmacol.* 17:828 (1968).
12. Wurtman, R. J., Axelrod, J., Vesell, E. S., & Ross, G. T.: *Endocrinology* 82:584 (1968).
13. Anderson, P. J., & D'Iorio, A.: *Biochem. Pharmacol.* 17:1943 (1968).
14. Conference on Multiple Molecular Forms of Enzymes (E. S. Vesell, ed.), *Ann. N. Y. Acad. Sci.*, 151:1-681 (1968).
15. Fritz, P. J.: *Science* 156:82 (1967).
16. Kovacs, E. M., & Heisler, S.: *Fed. Proc.* 28:353 (1969).

20

HISTOCHEMICAL ABNORMALITIES OF SKELETAL MUSCLE IN PATIENTS WITH ACUTE PSYCHOSES

W. King Engel and Herbert Meltzer

Abstract. *In 29 acutely psychotic patients (mostly schizophrenic), histochemical abnormalities of a myopathic type were demonstrated in skeletal muscle biopsies from 13 and were generally correlated with elevation of the "muscle" type isoenzymes of creatine phosphokinase in the patients' serum. The incidence was much higher than found in normal controls, hospitalized neurotic psychiatric patients, or parents of acutely psychotic patients. A diazo-coupling type of "alkaline phosphatase" reaction was particularly useful in identifying abnormal muscle fibers.*

A rise in the blood of the "muscle" type isozymes of creatine phosphokinase (CPK) associated with acute exacerbation of psychoses of various kinds has been reported (1). Histochemical abnormalities of a myopathic type have now been demonstrated in skeletal muscle biopsies from such patients.

Muscle biopsies were obtained from 29 patients with acute exacerbations of psychoses, 22 of whom were schizophrenic, the others having affective, paranoid, or involutional psychoses. They were compared with biopsies from two chronic schizophrenic patients, 11 hospitalized nonpsychotic psychiatric patients, four parents (one also an acute psychotic) of acutely psychotic patients, 45 nonpsychiatric normal control subjects, and 142 nonpsychiatric patients with various neuro-muscular diseases. Biopsies averaging 8 by 8 by 12 mm were obtained from the gastrocnemius or vastus lateralis. No patient had any significant trauma, including that caused by needles, to the muscle prior to its being biopsied. The specimens were rapidly frozen within 5 minutes of removal (2), and

Reprinted, by permission of author and editor, from: *Science*, 168:273-276, 10 April 1970. Copyright 1970 by the American Association for the Advancement of Science.

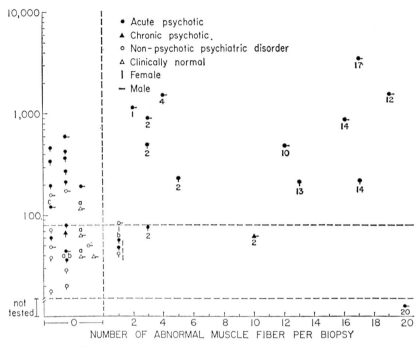

FIG. 1.—Muscle biopsy abnormalities correlated with serum CPK values and clinical psychiatric diagnosis. A serum CPK value of more than 80 I.U./liter is abnormal for ambulatory patients. (a) Parent of acute psychotic; (b) patient seen in remission from acute psychosis, could have had elevated CPK during exacerbation; (c) patient had none of the four counted changes, but 25 percent of fibers contained rods. Subscripts: number of alkaline phosphatase-positive fibers within the total abnormal fibers per patient.

kept well frozen until sections were cut from each specimen. Sections stained with the methods for modified trichrome (3) reduced nicotinamide adenine dinucleotide-tetrazolium reductase (NADH-TR) (4), myofibrillar adenosine triphosphatase at pH 9.4 (5), basophilia (thionine), and "alkaline phosphatase" (AP) by the α-naphthol phosphate and fast blue RR method at pH 8.8 (6, 7). Biopsies from 41 of the 42 psychotic and neurotic patients, from four relatives of the acutely psychotic patients, and from one normal control were processed and read by one of us in Bethesda (W.K.E.) without any knowledge of the clinical state or CPK levels which were evaluated by the other (H.M.) in Chicago. At the end of the study the data were collated for possible correlations. The other 187 nonpsychiatric normal and disease controls were

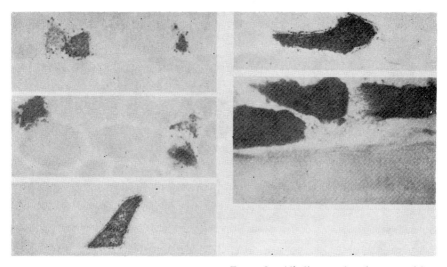

Fig. 2.—Alkaline phosphatase-positive muscle fibers are dark; normal fibers are unstained. Examples from five acutely psychotic patients.

part of a larger histochemical evaluation of the "alkaline phosphatase" reaction in neuromuscular disease (7).

The number of abnormal muscle fibers per biopsy was recorded (Fig. 1). Abnormalities were of four types: (i) alkaline phosphatase—positive fibers (Fig. 2); (ii) necrotic fibers undergoing phagocytosis demonstrated with the modified trichrome method (Fig. 3); (iii) fibers with a typical moderate architectural and staining abnormality (broadening and ir-regularity of the intermyofibrillar network seen with the modified tri-chrome and NADH-TR reactions), with slight to moderate reduction in size and internal nuclei but without phagocytosis (Fig. 4); and (iv) end-stage atrophic necrosis (Fig. 5).

On the basis of our histochemical experience with more than 1500 abnormal and normal muscle biopsies from various types of patients, we do not consider the following to be of definite pathologic signifi-cance (8) and have discounted them in the present study: slight type 2 fiber atrophy, less than 15 striated annulet fibers, cytoplasmic bodies in less than five fibers, rods in less than five fibers, or fewer than five small angular fibers excessively dark with NADPH-TR reaction. (All biopsies contained more than 1500 fibers.)

The muscle biopsy findings (Fig. 1) show (i) 13 of 29 acutely psychotic patients had abnormal biopsies with two or more abnormal fibers (as defined for this study) per biopsy, while another two were borderline (one abnormal fiber). As a corollary, about half (11 out of 21) with CPK levels greater than 80 I.U./liter had abnormal biopsies (an additional acute schizophrenic patient hospitalized at NIH had 20 abnormal fibers, but CPK activity was not studied). (ii) Of the two chronically psychotic patients, one had a normal biopsy and the other, a definitely abnormal one; in both patients CPK activity was essentially normal. (iii) Among the 11 patients with nonpsychotic psychiatric disorders,

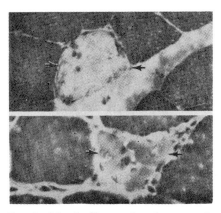

Fig. 3.—Muscle fiber undergoing necrosis and phagocytosis. Examples from two acutely psychotic patients; modified trichrome stain.

nine had normal biopsies and two had borderline biopsies (one abnormal fiber); one of the latter two had a slightly elevated CPK. (iv) Three parents of acutely psychotic patients had normal biopsies and CPK's even though one was acutely psychotic herself; one parent of an acutely psychotic manic-depressive patient had mild elevation of CPK and minor morphologic changes consisting of about 5 percent of the fibers with internal nuclei and 40 type 2 fibers with striated annulets. (v) No abnormal fibers were found in the 44 normal control subjects (7).

In one acutely psychotic patient (acute paranoia) with slight elevation of CPK (peak of 122 units), more than 25 percent of the muscle fibers contained rod-shaped particles characteristic histochemically (Fig. 6) and electron microscopically (9) of rod (nemaline) myopathy (10).

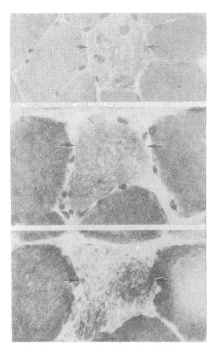

Fig. 4.—Moderate architectural abnormality of muscle fiber. Bottom two figures are serial sections. Top two are modified trichrome stain, bottom one is NADPH-TR reductase. Examples from two acutely psychotic patients.

Because none of the previous patients with rod myopathy was psychotic and because this patient's muscle biopsy had none of the four types of muscle fiber abnormalities mentioned above, the association was tentatively considered fortuitous (since strength was normal, he was considered a subclinical case of rod myopathy). Three other acute psychotics had one fiber each containing several rodlike particles, but this is not necessarily pathologic (10).

A positive AP reaction is a striking indicator of abnormal muscle fibers in the acutely psychotic patients. Since normal human skeletal muscle fibers are not stained with this reaction (7), all AP-positive fibers are considered abnormal. The AP-positive fiber is not undergoing total necrosis with phagocytosis. It is probably undergoing either a milder form of degeneration or a certain stage of regeneration, or both, simultaneously (7). Alkaline phosphatase—positive fibers are numerous in active myopathies and sometimes in severe denervation (11). Since the biopsies from psychotic patients which contained AP-positive abnormal fibers did not show moderate or severe denervation (and the one with very slight denervation had 14 AP-positive fibers, 13 fibers more than any of the 20 nonpsychotic disease controls with slight denervation) nor severe type 2 fiber atrophy, the abnormal fibers are interpreted as indicative of a mild myopathic process. They are of the same type and distribution as in carriers of Duchenne muscular dystrophy (7) but are more prevalent in the acutely psychotic patients in whom they occur.

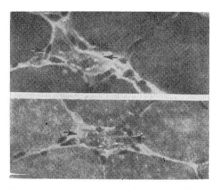

FIG. 5.—End-stage atrophic necrosis of muscle fiber. Examples from two acutely psychotic patients; modified trichrome stain.

The other three types of muscle fiber abnormalities recorded are the changes characteristic of the myopathies, including the muscular dystrophies and the various forms of polymyositis. When any or all are the predominant feature of a biopsy they are considered diagnostic of a myopathy (8).

There seem to be general correlations between the presence of histochemically abnormal muscle fibers, acute psychosis, and elevated blood CPK (Fig. 1). If these correlations reflect a unified biological phenomenon, two facts could be invoked to explain those acutely psychotic patients who had normal CPK activity or muscle biopsy, or both: (i) muscle biopsy is a small sampling procedure that can miss involved fibers (2); and (ii) elevations of blood CPK which occur with acute exacerbations of psychoses are transient (1). Furthermore, it is likely that not all acutely psychotic patients have a myopathy; and conceivably the diagnosis of acute psychosis was not always infallible. It may be postulated that the nonpsychotic psychiatric patients with borderline abnormal biopsies may represent intermediate forms of the myopathy and mental disturbance present in the acutely psychotic patients.

There did not appear to be extraneous causes for the muscle fiber histochemical abnormalities in these patients, such as antecedent muscle trauma, other neuromuscular disease or type of drug treatment. Three of the six acutely psychotic patients with ten or more AP-positive fibers had not received phenothiazines prior to the biopsy. More patients must be studied to completely exclude such factors.

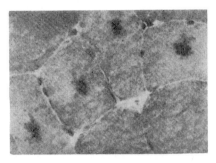

Fig. 6.—Clusters of darkly stained rods in the centers of four otherwise normal type 2 muscle fibers. Acutely psychotic patient; modified trichrome stain.

If extraneous factors are not responsible for the histochemical abnormalities in the acutely psychotic patients, the AP-positive fibers represent morphologic evidence of an extracerebral organic disease process in some acutely psychotic patients. It remains to be determined what relationship, if any, these muscle abnormalities have to the mental disturbance in such patients; but their high degree of correlation with acute psychosis supports the possibility of a significant relationship.

REFERENCES

1. MELTZER, H. *Science* 159, 1368 (1968); *Arch. Gen. Psychiat.* 21, 102 (1969); ——, L. Elkin, R. Moline, *ibid.*, in press.
2. ENGEL, W. K. & BROOKE, M. H. In *Neurological Diagnostic Techniques*, W. S. Fields, Ed. (Thomas, Springfield, Ill., 1966), pp. 90-146.
3. ENGEL, W. K. & CUNNINGHAM, G. G. *Neurology* 13, 919 (1963).
4. HESS, R., SCARPELLI, D. G. & PEARSE, A. G. E. *J. Biophys. Biochem. Cytol.* 4, 735 (1958).
5. PADYKULA, H. A. & HERMAN, E. *J. Histochem. Cytochem.* 3, 170 (1955).

6. ASHMORE, C. R.. DOERR, L., SOMES, R. G. JR. *Science* 160, 319 (1968).
7. ENGEL, W. K. & CUNNINGHAM, G. G. *J. Histochem. Cytochem.* 18, 55 (1970).
8. ENGEL, W. K. *Clin. Orthop.* 39, 80 (1965).
9. FISCHMAN, D. Personal communication.
10. ENGEL, W. K. In *Exploratory Concepts in Muscular Dystrophy and Related Disorders*, A. T. Milhorat, Ed. (Excerpta Medica Foundation, New York, 1967), pp. 27-40.
11. It has been shown in human muscle biopsies (7) (i) that no AP-positive fibers were present in 43 biopsies from normal subjects or in 37 with various benign neuromuscular disorders (including slight and moderate type 2 muscle fiber atrophy); (ii) that many AP-positive fibers are found in active muscular dystrophies, polymyositis, and moderate and severe denervation atrophy (a small number are found in clinically normal carriers of Duchenne pseudohypertrophic X-linked muscular dystrophy, in which they are a typical lesion); (iii) that rare (two or less) AP-positive fibers occur in certain myopathies with moderate clinical neuromuscular symptoms (of 20 patients with mild denervation four had two AP-positive fibers and others none); five patients with severe type 2 muscle fiber atrophy had up to three AP-positive fibers.
12. We thank Dr. M. Matz and Miss Sarah Burnett for assistance in obtaining the muscle biopsies and G. G. Cunningham for performing the histochemical reactions. Supported in part (H.M.) by grant 17-340 from the State of Illinois and PHS grant 1-RO1-MH-16127 to H.M.

21

AMINO ACID TRANSPORT AND THE PLASMA FACTOR IN SCHIZOPHRENIA

Charles E. Frohman, Kenneth A. Warner, Clifford T. Barry, and Robert E. Arthur

The properties of the alpha-2-globulin isolated from plasma of schizo-phrenic patients have been investigated. This protein causes an increase of the uptake of amino acid by cells. Particularly striking is the increase in uptake of glutamic acid, tryptophan, and 5-hydroxytryptophan. Further experiments indicate that an active transport system is being affected rather than the rate of diffusion.

INTRODUCTION

The alpha-2-globulin which is being studied by various laboratories has also been under intensive study at the Lafayette Clinic. The following report deals with a number of studies and in particularly focused on the effect of this factor on amino acid transport.

In the past few years, considerable evidence has accumulated supporting the existence of an active plasma factor in many schizophrenic patients. This evidence has been reviewed fully elsewhere (Frohman, 1968) and will only be summarized briefly here. Frohman and coworkers (1960) have isolated a protein factor which is an alpha-2-globulin and which affects cellular oxidation as evidenced by the increased ratio of lactic acid to pyruvic acid in chicken erythrocytes following incubation with the factor. Vartanyan has isolated a protein which is identical to this substance (Krasnov, 1965). Bergen and Pennell (1960) have also isolated a protein which when administered to rats caused the rats to

Supported in part by a Grant-in-aid from the National Institute of Mental Health No. MH-04816-08. The Lafayette Clinic, Detroit, Michigan, and Wayne State University School of Medicine, Detroit, Michigan.

Reprinted, by permission of author and editor, from: *Biological Psychiatry,* 1:201-207, 1969, published by Plenum Publishing Corporation, New York.

take longer to solve a simple rope climbing test to receive a food reward. A double blind study involving exchange of the isolated substances from Bergen's laboratory and from Frohman's gave good evidence that these two groups are also working with an identical protein (Bergen *et al.,* 1968).

Three other groups have also isolated a protein from the plasma of schizophrenic patients (Ehrensvard *et al.,* 1960; Haavaldsen *et al.,* 1958; Heath and Krupp, 1967), but the opportunity has not presented itself for determining if these three proteins are identical to the alpha-2-globulin reported by Frohman, Bergen, and Vartanyan. There is a strong possibility because of their characteristics that two of these factors, those of Walaas and Ehrensvard, are identical to the alpha-2-globulin. The protein reported by Heath appears to be a different substance since it is a gamma globulin.

Ryan and coworkers (1966) claim that the alpha-2-globulin is an immune lysin and that all of its other properties are merely secondary to its hemolytic property. However, it has been demonstrated that the pure factor has no hemolytic properties and that these properties are the result of a beta globulin which often occurs along with the alpha-2-globulin (Frohman, 1968).

METHOD

The subjects used for the following experiments were chronic schizophrenic patients who had been living on a research ward for several years. They had been drug-free for a minimum of 2 years and eating a diet supplemented with animal protein. The control subjects were laboratory personnel. None of them had ever received either tranquilizers or energizers at any time in their life. They were compltely drug-free for 1 week before the blood was drawn.

Effect of the Protein Factor on Transport of Various Amino Acids

Blood was removed from chickens carefully protected from excitement, by heart puncture and was prevented from clotting by the addition of 50 units of heparin for each 10 ml of whole blood. Forty-five ml of blood was removed from each chicken. The cells were removed, washed with a minimum of four volumes of 0.9% saline and then added to a modified Krebs-Ringer solution in a ratio of two parts cells to three parts solution. To 20 ml of this mixture was added 4 ml of plasma from either a control or a schizophrenic subject or 4 ml of a solution containing an amount of the alpha-2-globulin equivalent to 20 ml of plasma. Next,

1 ml of amino acid carrier solution of appropriate concentration was added. In the following experiments, carrier was added to bring the level in the mixture to one-fifth of, equal to, and five times the normal amino acid level of the plasma. The object here was to test the effect that the concentration of each amino acid in question had on transport. Just prior to incubation, 1 ml of a solution containing 8 μc of labeled amino acid per ml was added. The mixture was incubated at 37 C. Three-ml aliquots were removed at zero time and at 5, 10, 20, 30, 45, 60, 75, and 90 minutes of incubation. Each aliquot was immediately centrifuged, in the cold, to separate the cells from the medium. A Folin-Wu filtrate was made from the medium, and an aliquot of filtrate was counted in a Beckman Scintillation Counter. In the tryptophan study a second aliquot of filtrate was placed on an amino acid analyzer to measure the amount of the amino acid and obtain a pure sample of the amino acid so that its specific activity and counts could be measured. The cells which were removed from the incubation were washed twice with 0.9% saline, and a Folin-Wu filtrate was prepared from them and analyzed in the same manner as the filtrate from the medium. The results are shown in Table 1.

RESULTS OF THE FIRST EXPERIMENT

Plasma from schizophrenic patients caused a significant increase in the uptake of glutamic acid ($p<0.001$), tryptophan ($p<0.001$), 5-hydroxytryptophan ($p<0.001$), and alinine ($p<0.001$). Its effect on tyrosine barely reached significance ($p<0.05$). There was no significant effect on the uptake of phenylalanine, serine, methionine, histidine, lysine, alpha-aminoisobutyric acid or aspartic acid. Similar results were obtained using the isolated alpha-2-globulin. One should note that three of the four amino acids affected by plasma from the patients or by the alpha-2-globulin are precursors of neurohumoral substances (i.e., tryptophan and 5-hydroxytryptophan are precursors of serotonin and glutamic acid is the precursor of GABA).

The level and specific activity of tryptophan in the cells after 60 minutes incubation is shown in Table 2. There were 53.5 nanomoles of tryptophan per ml of cells incubated in plasma from control subjects. These values differ significantly at the 1% level of confidence (t test). Tryptophan isolated from cells incubated in plasma from schizophrenic patients has a significantly higher specific activity than from cells incubated in plasma from control subjects ($p<0.05$, t test). This may indicate that the tryptophan in the incubate containing plasma from schizo-

TABLE 1

Uptake of Amino Acid by Chicken Erythrocytes in the Presence of Plasma from Control Subjects and Schizophrenic Patients

Amino acid	Controls N = 12 cpma ×10⁻³	SD	Range	Schizophrenics N = 13 cpma ×10⁻³	SD	Range	b
Glutamic acid	5	± 1	3-8	12	± 3	7-16	0.001
Tryptophan	93	±20	68-138	142	±35	113-199	0.001
Hydroxytryptophan	7	± 2	5-10	12	± 3	8-16	0.001
Phenylalanine	292	±33	246-375	317	±32	263-387	N.S.
Tyrosine	87	±17	59-113	116	±33	77-163	0.05
Alanine	116	±11	90-137	165	±15	128-231	0.001
Serine	184	±42	148-219	197	±43	151-226	N.S.
Methionine	47	±12	20-65	49	±12	23-65	N.S.
Histidine	53	±19	45-80	64	±13	55-94	N.S.
Lysine	30	± 8	21-41	39	±14	23-55	N.S.
Alpha-aminoisobutyric	20	± 4	16-24	24	± 5	17-29	N.S.
Aspartic	6	± 2	3-13	7	± 3	5-16	N.S.

a Values are cpm/g cell at 60 min.
b Significance of difference between schizophrenics and controls.

TABLE 2

Tryptophan in Cells After 60-min Incubation in Modified Krebbs-Ringer Solution with 55 μg Tryptophan/ml and 0.44 μc of Tryptophan/ml

	Concentration of tryptophan, nanomoles/ml	Specific activity of tryptophan in the cell, dpm/nanomole	% dpm as tryptophan
Schizophrenics	53.5	2357	85.9
Controls	42.9	1891	83.4

phrenic patients is closer to equilibrium than that in the control incubate.

Effect of Temperature on Tryptophan Uptake

The above experiment using labeled tryptophan was repeated but with incubations at 1 C, 6 C, 13 C, 25 C, and 37 C. The results are shown in Fig. 1. The slope of the curve for effect of temperature on tryptophan uptake is quite different at lower temperatures than at higher temperatures. At temperatures from 0 C to 13 C the slope of the

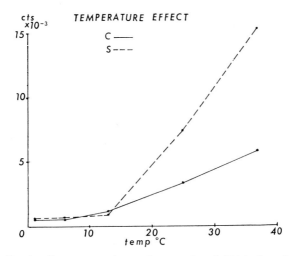

FIG. 1.—Counts per minute of tryptophan-3-C14 in 1 g of cells incubated with 0.44 μc labeled tryptophan and plasma from control or schizophrenic subjects for 60 min at various temperatures.

curve was 27 dpm/degree for both groups of subjects while at higher temperatures the slope was 348 dpm/degree for the cells incubated in plasma from schizophrenic subjects and 682 dpm/degree for the cells incubated in control plasma. That is, the uptake by cells did not differentiate between plasma from schizophrenic patients and plasma from control subjects at the lower temperatures but did so increasingly as the temperature approached 37 C.

Effect of Ouabain on the Plasma Factor

Sufficient ouabain to make the concentration 10^{-3} M was added to the incubation mixture containing labeled tryptophan. Failure of ouabain to affect the uptake of tryptophan in the presence of the factor is shown in Fig. 2.

Effect of the Factor on Tryptophan Efflux

Forty-eight ml of washed chicken erythrocytes were added to a mixture of 72 ml of modified Krebs-Ringer solution, 24 ml of plasma from a control subject, and 12 ml of a solution containing 30 μc of labeled tryptophan per ml. The mixture was incubated at 37 C for 100 minutes.

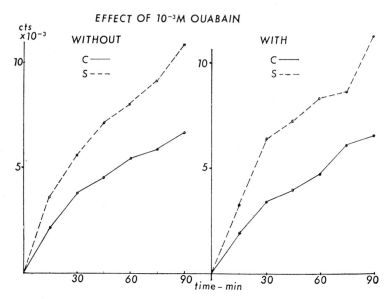

F𝚒𝚐. 2.—Effect of 10-3 M ouabain on uptake of labeled tryptophan in the presence of plasma from control of schizophrenic subjects. The ordinate represents counts per minute × 10-3 tryptophan in 1 g of cells at the times indicated on the abscissa.

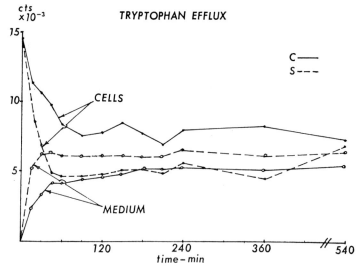

F𝚒𝚐. 3.—Decrease of tryptophan-3-C14 in cells previously loaded with tryptophan-3-C14 and increase of the compound in medium containing plasma from control or schizophrenic subjects. Results are in counts per minute per gram cells.

At the end of the incubation, the tryptophan-loaded cells were removed by centrifugation at 4 C. They were then washed three times with cold saline. Twenty ml of cells loaded in this manner were added to a mixture of 30 ml of modified Krebs-Ringer solution and 10 ml of plasma from schizophrenic patients, or plasma from control subjects, or an equivalent solution of purified alpha-2-globulin. This mixture was incubated at 37 C. Aliquots were taken at 0, 15, 30, 45, 60, 90, 120, 150, and 180 minutes. The cells and medium were separated and amino acid measured as in previous experiments. The results are shown in Fig. 3. Plasma from schizophrenic patients caused more tryptophan to leave the cells than plasma from the controls; however, the difference between the effect of plasma from schizophrenic patients and control subjects on tryptophan efflux was not as great as in the influx experiments.

DISCUSSION

It is quite clear that the alpha-2-globulin, or plasma rich in alpha-2-globulin, increases the rate of accumulation of tryptophan, 5-hydroxy-tryptophan, glumatic acid, and alanine in the cell. It remains to be determined what mechanism of transport of the four amino acids is affected by this substance. Since amino acids probably can enter and leave the cell by means of simple diffusion, it might be hypothesized that a change in the nature of the cell membrane may permit material to diffuse in and out more rapidly. Under these circumstances one would not expect a significant change in the rate of diffusion in only a few amino acids but rather to have all of them affected (i.e., the rate of accumulation of tryptophan and 5-hydroxytryptophan is increased but phenylalanine is unaffected). One would also expect that the temperature coefficient would be considerably less in diffusion than in active transport. Note in Fig. 1 that the change in rate of accumulation of tryptophan in the cell has two different slopes. The slope at the lower temperature probably represents diffusion while that at the higher temperature probably represents active transport. The difference between the effect of plasma from control subjects and that of plasma from schizophrenic subjects is apparent only at the higher temperatures. Therefore, it is very unlikely that diffusion is the process affected by the plasma factor.

Since both the influx and the efflux of amino acids are affected by this substance, one might suspect that exchange is the process that is affected. This process as described by Christensen involves moving amino acids in and out of the cells at equal rates (Eavenson and Christensen,

1967). Final levels of the acids in the cells are not affected and the process is closely tied to the transport of sodium and therefore should be inhibited by ouabain, a sodium transport inhibitor. Failure of ouabain to inhibit the activity of the plasma factor demonstrates that this activity is not dependent on sodium transport. There is a significant difference in the increase in levels of tryptophan in cells incubated in plasma from schizophrenic subjects as compared with cells incubated in plasma from control subjects; in addition, influx of tryptophan was affected more profoundly by the alpha-2-globulin than was efflux. Because of these three observations (the failure of ouabain to inhibit, the increased accumulation of tryptophan, and the differential effect on influx and efflux), it can be definitely stated that exchange is not affected by the plasma factor. Consequently, the exact mechanism of the active transport system that appears to be affected remains to be determined.

Regardless of the mechanism, it remains a fact that three very important precursors of neurohumoral substances enter the cells more rapidly in the presence of plasma from schizophrenic patients than in the presence of plasma from control subjects. Glutamic acid is a precursor of gamma-aminobutyric acid, a substance which is quite important in neurohumoral transmission; tryptophan and 5-hydroxytryptophan are precursors of serotonin, another important neurohumoral transmitter. Recently serotonin has been shown to be involved in the production of sleep: administration of p-chlorophenylalanine (an inhibitor of serotonin production) in sufficient amounts prevents sleep in animals (Snyder, in press). Caldwell and Domino (1967) have reported that in patients with a high level of the alpha-2-globulin, stage 4 sleep either is decreased or is completely absent. The level of alpha-2-globulin correlates with the amount of stage 4 sleep with a coefficient of—0.550 ($p<0.05$). It is possible that the lack of stage 4 sleep in the high factor patients is in some way related to the factor-induced disturbance in the uptake of tryptophan (the precursor of serotonin) and that the high level of the factor and the lack of stage 4 sleep are both related to a neural mechanism involved in the production of schizophrenia. The *in vitro* studies upon which this hypothesis is based are currently being tested in neural tissue *in vivo*.

REFERENCES

BERGEN, J. R., PENNELL, R. B., FREEMAN, H., & HOAGLAND, H. (1960). Rat behavior in response to a blood factor from normal and psychotic persons. *Arch. Neurol.* 2: 146.
BERGEN, J. R., FROHMAN, C. E., MITTAG, T. W., ARTHUR, R. E., GRINSPOON, L., & FREE-

MAN, H. (1968). Plasma factors in schizophrenia: A collaborative study. *Arch. Gen. Psychiat.* 18: 471.

CALDWELL, D., & DOMINO, E. (1967). Electroencephalographic and eye movement patterns during sleep in chronic schizophrenic patients. *Electroencephalog. Clin. Neurophysiol.* 22: 414.

EAVENSON, E., & CHRISTENSEN, N. (1967. Transport systems for neutral amino acids in the pigeon erythrocyte. *J. Biol. Chem.* 242: 5386.

EHRENSVARD, G., LILJEKVIST, J., & HEATH, R. G. (1960). Oxidation of 3-hydroxyanthranilic acid by human serum. *Acta Chem. Scand.* 14: 2081.

FROHMAN, C. E. (1968). Studies on the plasma factors in schizophrenia, in *Mind as a Tissue*, Rupp, C. (ed.), Hoeber of Harper and Row, New York, p. 181.

FROHMAN, C. E., LUBY, E. D., TOURNEY, G., BECKETT, P. G. S., & GOTTLIEB, J. S. (1960). Steps toward the isolation of a serum factor in schizophrenia. *Am. J. Psychiat.* 117: 401.

HAAVALDSEN, R., LINGJAERDE, O., & WALAAS, O. (1958). Disturbances of carbohydrate metabolism in schizophrenics. *Confinia Neurol.* 18: 270.

HEATH, R. G., & KRUPP, I. M. (1967). Schizophrenia as an immunologic disorder. *Arch. Gen. Psychiat.* 16: 1.

KRASNOV, A. I. (1965). Influence of blood serum from schizophrenic patients on the carbohydrate metabolism in chicken erythrocytes. *Neuropathol. Psychiat. (Korsakov)* 65: 1206.

RYAN, J. W., BROWN, J. D., & DURELL, J. (1966). Antibodies affecting metabolism of chicken erythrocytes: Examination of schizophrenic and other subjects. *Science* 151: 1408.

SNYDER, S. H. (in press). Catecholamines, brain functions, and how psychotropic drugs act, in *Principles of Psychopharmacology*, Clark, W. G. (ed.), Academic Press, New York.

22

THE PLASMA FACTOR AND TRANS-
PORT OF INDOLEAMINO ACIDS

Charles E. Frohman, Kenneth A. Warner, Hak S. Yoon,
Robert E. Arthur, and Jacques S. Gottlieb

More properties of the α-2-globulin isolated from plasma of schizophrenic patients have been investigated. This protein causes an increase in the uptake of tryptophan, 5-hydroxytryptophan, and pyrrolidone carboxylic acid by cells. The mechanism affected is an active transport mechanism which follows the first order reaction equation. The factor appears to affect the final equilibrium concentration rather than the rate constant. An antifactor present in cells has been partially isolated. It appears to destroy the activity of the α-2-globulin.

INTRODUCTION

Previous reports have described the isolation and properties of a protein which is elevated in the plasma of many schizophrenic patients (Frohman *et al.*, 1960). This protein is an α-2-globulin with a molecular weight of about 400,000. It contains approximately 80% lipid, and is quite labile. This protein has a pronounced effect on the transport of amino acids into the cell, most markedly on transport of indoleamino acids (Frohman *et al.*, 1969). Its activity can be protected with the addition of small amounts of mercaptoethanol, ascorbic acid, or glutathione which would suggest that the biological activity of the protein is dependent on the ratio of sulfhydryl groups to disulfide groups in the molecule (Bergen, 1967).

Evidence has accumulated that two other research groups, Bergen and Pennell at the Worcester Foundation for Experimental Biology, and

Research supported in part by a Grant-in-aid from the National Institute of Mental Health No. MH-04816-08. The Lafayette Clinic, Detroit, Michigan, and Wayne State University School of Medicine, Detroit, Michigan.

Reprinted, by permission of author and editor, from: *Biological Psychiatry,* I: 377-385, 1969, published by Plenum Publishing Corporation, New York.

Vartanyan at the First Institute of Psychiatry at the National Academy of Science, Moscow, are working on the same protein. Bergen and Pennell have shown that when injected, this protein both increases the time it takes a rat to climb a rope to receive a food reward, and affects the evoked potentials in unanesthetized rabbits. They claim that this activity depends on an unidentified small molecule (Bergen *et al.*, 1962). Vartanyan and coworkers have demonstrated that the integrity of the cell membrane is affected by the protein (Krasnova, 1965). The following report deals with further inquiries into the effect of this substance on amino acid transport.

The subjects used for the following experiments were male, chronic schizophrenic patients, aged 18-40, who had been living in a research ward for several years. They had been drug-free for a minimum of 2 years and had been eating a diet supplemented with vitamins and animal protein and were exercised daily. The control subjects were male laboratory personnel in the same age range as the patients.

EFFECT OF THE PROTEIN FACTOR ON TRANSPORT
OF VARIOUS AMINO ACIDS

Blood was removed by heart puncture from chickens carefully protected from excitement, and was prevented from clotting by the addition of 50 units of heparin for each ml of whole blood. The cells were removed, washed with a minimum of 4 vol of 0.85% saline and then added to a modified Krebs-Ringer solution in a ratio of two parts cells to three parts solution. To 20 ml of this mixture was added 4 ml of plasma from either a control or a schizophrenic subject, or 4 ml of a solution containing an amount of the α-2-globulin equivalent to 4 ml of plasma. Next, 1 ml of amino acid carrier solution of appropriate concentration was added. This carrier, in the first set of experiments, was added to bring the level in the mixture to one-fifth of, equal to, and five times the normal amino acid level of the plasma. The object was to test the effect that the concentration of each amino acid in question had on transport. Just prior to incubation, 1 ml of a solution containing 8 μc of labeled amino acid per ml was added. The mixture was incubated at 37 C. Three-ml aliquots were removed at zero time and at 5, 10, 20, 30, 45, 60, 75 and 90 minutes of incubation. Each aliquot was immediately centrifuged, in the cold, to separate cells from the medium. Folin-Wu filtrates were made from the washed cells, and aliquots of the filtrates were counted in a Beckman scintillation counter. The results are shown in Table 1.

Plasma from schizophrenic patients caused a significant increase in the apparent uptake of glutamic acid $(p<0.001)$, tryptophan $(p<0.001$, and 5-hydroxytryptophan $(p<0.001)$. Its effect on proline, tyrosine, aspartic acid, arginine, histidine, and alanine barely reach significance $(p<0.05)$. There was no significant effect on the uptake of phenylalanine, serine, methionine, lysine, or α-aminoisobutyric acid even though all amino acids tended to go into the cell more rapidly in the presence

TABLE 1

UPTAKE OF AMINO ACID BY CHICKEN ERYTHROCYTES IN THE
PRESENCE OF PLASMA FROM CONTROL SUBJECTS
AND SCHIZOPHRENIC PATIENTS[a]

Amino acid	Controls $N = 12$		Schizophrenics $N = 13$		
	dpm $\times 10^{-3}$	SD	dpm $\times 10^{-3}$	SD	b
Glutamic acid	5	± 1	12	± 3	0.001
Tryptophan	93	± 20	142	± 35	0.001
5-Hydroxytryptophan	7	± 2	12	± 3	0.001
Phenylalanine	292	± 33	317	± 32	n.s.
Tyrosine	87	± 17	116	± 33	0.05
Alanine	116	± 11	165	± 15	0.05
Serine	184	± 42	197	± 43	n.s.
Methionine	47	± 12	49	± 12	n.s.
Histidine	51	± 19	66	± 13	0.05
Lysine	30	± 8	39	± 14	n.s.
α-Aminoisobutyric	20	± 4	24	± 5	n.s.
Aspartic acid	6	± 2	10	± 3	0.05
Proline	118	± 45	91	± 40	0.05
Agrinine	71	± 16	86	± 20	0.05

a Samples were taken after 1-hr incubation.
b Significance of difference between schizophrenics and controls.

of plasma from schizophrenic patients. The level of carrier had no effect on the rate of uptake of amino acids within the limits set for the experiment. Similar results were obtained when using the isolated α-2-globulin instead of plasma.

Investigations were undertaken to determine if the carboxyl group and the amine group of the amino acid were necessary for the activity of the α-2-globulin. To determine if the carboxyl group was necessary, the effect of the protein on several biologically active amines closely related to the most strongly affected amino acids was used. In the same procedure as described previously, serotonin, dopamine, and tryptamine were substituted for the amino acids. None of these compounds contain a carboxyl group. The protein did not increase the rate of uptake of any of these amines by chicken erythrocytes (Table 2). Therefore it was concluded that a carboxyl group on the substrate is necessary for the activity of the factor.

TABLE 2

EFFECT OF PLASMA FROM SCHIZOPHRENIC
SUBJECTS ON UPTAKE OF SOME AMINES[a]

	Controls N = 13		Schizophrenics N = 13	
	Mean	SD	Mean	SD
Serotonin	19	± 5	16	± 3
Tryptamine	74	±24	66	±21
Dopamine	20	± 5	19	± 5

a Values are dpm × 10⁻³ per ml cells after 60 min incubation.

TABLE 3

EFFECT OF PLASMA FROM SCHIZOPHRENIC
SUBJECTS ON UPTAKE OF
SOME ORGANIC ACIDS

	Controls N = 13		Schizophrenics N = 13	
	Mean	SD	Mean	SD
Acetate	90,057	±45,427	92,000	±48,391
Succinate	1947	±440	2582[a]	±625
Citrate	763	±200	1432[b]	±400

a Differs at 5% level of confidence.
b Differs at 0.1% level of confidence.

To test the effect of the amino group on the substrate, the experiment was repeated substituting acetate, succinate, and citrate for the amino acids. None of these compounds contain an amino group. The α-2-globulin significantly increased the uptake of both succinate and citrate (Table 3). Therefore the amine group is apparently not necessary for the activity of the protein.

Previously reported temperature studies, and studies of the effect of ouabain on the increase in tryptophan uptake with the substance, indi-

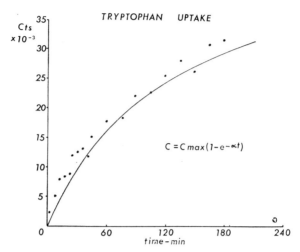

FIG. 1.—Fit of tryptophan uptake data to first order reaction curve ($r = 0.9975$). Dots represent data from one experiment using plasma from schizophrenic subjects. The line represents the theoretical curve.

cated that an active transport mechanism was affected (Frohman *et al.*, 1969). The results of the tryptophan experiment were analyzed more closely to determine if the nature of the affected reaction could be discovered. The results fit very closely a standard first-order reaction equation ($r = 0.9975$): $C = C_{max} (1 - e_{\alpha t})$ where α is the combination of the influx and efflux constants, t represents time, and C_{max} represents the maximum steady state equilibrium concentration (Fig. 1). Substituting the date into this equation and solving for α indicated that there was no significant difference in α for plasma from control subjects and plasma from schizophrenic patients (Table 4). However, C_{max} differed at the 1% level of confidence between the two groups. Theoretically, then, the rate of passage of certain amino acids into and out of cells should not be affected by plasma from schizophrenic patients any more than by plasma from control subjects. However, the final equilibrium concentration should be significantly higher in those cells incubated with plasma from schizophrenic patients, as contrasted with those incubated with plasma from control subjects.

To test these predictions, the original study was modified using glutamic acid, tryptophan, and 5-hydroxytryptophan (the three acids previously showing the greatest significant difference in uptake) and in addition the acids were isolated from the filtrate in the following manner. Aliquots of the cell filtrates at 60 min incubation were placed on an amino acid analyzer and the amount of amino acid present in the cells was measured. The amino acid analyzer was equipped with a stream splitter so that pure amino acid samples could be collected and their radioactivity determined. The results of this experiment are shown in Table 5.

It can be seen that the concentration of tryptophan and 5-hydroxytryptophan in the cells incubated with plasma from schizophrenic patients is

TABLE 4

VALUES FOR THE RATE CONSTANT (α) AND THE EQUILIBRIUM CONCENTRATION (C_{max}) FOR TRYPTOPHAN

	α	C_{max}, nanomole/ml
Controls	0.010214	45.2
Schizophrenics	0.010153	58.9[a]

a Differs significantly at the 0.01 level of confidence.

TABLE 5

AMINO ACID IN CELLS AFTER 60 MIN INCUBATION

	Controls			Schizophrenics		
	Nanomoles amino acid	dpm $\times 10^{-3}$	Count/min per nmole[b]	Nanomoles amino acid	dpm $\times 10^{-3}$	Count/min per nmole
Tryptophan	42.9	96	2,240	53.5[a]	142[a]	2,654
SD	± 3.5	± 20		± 6.4	± 35	
5-Hydroxytryptophan	14.3	7	482	21.6[a]	12[a]	551
SD	± 1.4	± 2		± 3.3	± 3	
Glutamic acid	1.3	3	230	1.4	3	215
SD	± 0.4	± 1		± 0.4	± 1	

a Differed significantly at 0.1% level of confidence.
b Specific activity.

significantly higher, and that the disintegrations per minute (dpm) from intracellular tryptophan and 5-hydroxytryptophan are also increased. Specific activity of cellular tryptophan and 5-hydroxytryptophan do not differ significantly. Therefore, in the case of these two acids, the equilibrium concentration (C_{max}) is indeed greater in the presence of plasma from schizophrenic patients than in the presence of plasma from control subjects. The glutamic acid data, however, present a different situation. No difference exists in the final glutamic acid content of the cells in plasma from control subjects or schizophrenic patients. To make it even more perplexing, the dpm present in glutamic acid in the cells are the same with plasma from both control and schizophrenic subjects. Thus, the apparent difference in glutamic acid uptake in the first study, and the lack of difference in glutamic acid levels in the second study, cannot be related to more rapid equilibration in plasma from schizophrenic patients. Instead, the difference in counts in cells must be the result of entry into the cell of some labeled material other than glutamic acid. Since a very small percentage of the glutamic acid incubated with the cell enters it (the ratio of extracellular glutamic acid to intracellular glutamic acid in the incubation mixture is 99:1), the possibility that an impurity in the labeled glutamic acid was giving the false results was investigated. When glutamic acid is placed in a weakly acid solution, about 2% of the glutamic acid is converted to pyrrolidone carboxylic acid; there would be more than enough of this impurity present to cause the observed effect. When the uptake of pure pyrrolidone carboxylic acid was measured, plasma from schizophrenic patients caused a 200% increase in the uptake of this compound. With this finding, it is evident that glutamic acid in the first experiment was not affected by plasma from schizophrenic patients. The second glutamic acid experiments and the experiments with pyrrolidone carboxylic acid showed that the apparent difference in glutamic acid uptake was in reality due to a derivative of glutamic acid present as an impurity in the incubation mixtures.

EFFECT OF ANTIFACTOR ON TRYPTOPHAN UPTAKE

We have reported previously the presence in chicken erythrocytes of an antifactor which destroyed the activity of the α-2-globulin. Norepinephrine given in physiological amounts to chickens *in vivo* 15 min before the cells were drawn greatly increased the activity of this antifactor (Frohman *et al.*, 1964). Norepinephrine had no effect on the factor or antifactor *in vitro*. However, since this earlier work was concerned with the use of the lactate/pyruvate ratio as a bioassay, we attempted to determine if the antifactor also could prevent the factor-induced increase in tryptophan uptake by chicken erythrocytes. Partially purified antifactor, equivalent to 5 ml of cells, was added to the standard incubation mixture described previously and the rate of uptake of tryptophan was measured. Results are shown in Table 6. The antifactor caused a significant decrease in uptake of tryptophan in the presence of the α-2-globulin ($p < 0.001$). However, the antifactor had no effect on the uptake of tryptophan if the α-2-globulin was not present in the mixture.

In an attempt to isolate the antifactor, chicken erythrocytes containing

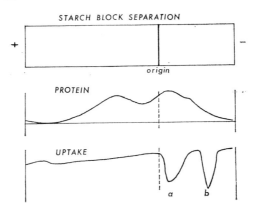

Fig. 2.—Separation of the antifactor using a preparative starch block. The top diagram shows the polarity and the point of application of the sample on the starch block. The middle diagram shows the protein concentration of each fraction. The bottom diagram represents the uptake of tryptophan by chicken erythrocytes incubated with plasma from schizophrenic patients and fractions from the starch block.

high levels of the antifactor were hemolyzed. The resulting protein solution was placed on a preparative starch block for electrophoresis. The sample was run for 8 hr in a Veronal buffer, pH 8.65, at 275 v and 75 ma. The results of the separation are shown in Fig. 2. Note that the antifactor moved towards the negative pole and appeared in two different positions in the protein pattern. When the material in peak "b" was again separated on the starch block, it again was resolved into two peaks. It was concluded that the protein containing antifactor activity exists in two equilibrium forms, a dimer (peak a) and a monomer (peak b). Most of the hemoglobin came out along with peak "a" so that purification of the dimer form of antifactor by this method was virtually impossible.

It was of interest to determine if the antifactor was present in brain tissue as well as in chicken erythrocytes. Chickens were injected with 800 μg of norepinephrine and were sacrificed 15 min later and their brains removed and homogenized in 2 vol of 0.85% sodium chloride. The soluble protein was then separated by starch block electrophoresis in the same manner as the protein from the erythrocytes. The brain tissue possessed almost four times as much antifactor activity as the chicken erythrocytes (Table 7). However, the separation of the antifactor on starch block was even poorer with brain proteins than with chicken erythrocyte proteins. In order to obtain a better product, the scheme shown in Fig. 3 was used. The brain was extracted with cold chloroform-methanol solution (2:1 v/v), then the extract was fractionated by ammonium sulfate precipitation. The fractions were dissolved in 0.5 M phosphate buffer, pH 7.4, and dialyzed against the same buffer until all traces of ammonium ion were removed. They were then tested in a system consisting of chicken erythrocytes in plasma from schizophrenic patients. The plasma was

TABLE 6

EFFECT OF ANTIFACTOR ON UPTAKE OF TRYPTOPHAN BY CHICKEN ERYTHROCYTES IN THE PRESENCE OF THE α-2-GLOBULIN

Plasma equivalents in incubation mixture		Tryptophan uptake
α-2-Globulin	Antifactor	dpm/ml cells
0	0	8057
2	0	14,696
2	1	10,342
2	2	8621
2	4	7942
0	2	8104

TABLE 7

COMPARISON OF ACTIVITY OF ANTIFACTOR IN CHICKEN BRAIN AND CHICKEN ERYTHROCYTES

Tissue equivalent[a] mg	Tryptophan uptake dpm/ml cells	
	Brain	Erythrocytes
0	21,654	21,654
200	19,403	21,550
400	17,516	20,654
800	15,994	19,235
1200	15,961	16,540
1600		15,868

[a] Amount of antifactor added to incubation mixture was derived from this weight of tissue.

added to supply the α-2-globulin. The active antifactor was not precipitated by 20% ammonium sulfate but was completely precipitated by 40% ammonium sulfate (Fig. 3). The resulting material was further purified on DEAE cellulose using a gradient elution system consisting of 0.05 M phosphate buffer, pH 7.4, in flask 1, and 0.04M NaH_2PO_4 in 0.14M NaCl in flask 2. The results of this separation are shown in Fig. 4.

With this system of separation, the antifactor from brain is now closer

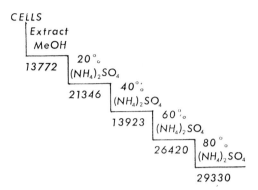

FIG. 3.—Scheme for ammonium sulfate fractionation of the antifactor. The values below the horizontal lines represent the uptake of tryptophan by chicken erythrocytes in dpm per ml of cells. The erythrocytes were incubated with plasma from schizophrenic patients and fraction from the isolation. Without the antifactor fraction the uptake was 29,500. Fractions containing antifactor lowered the dpm of tryptophan taken up by the cell.

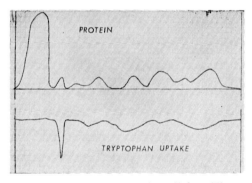

FIG. 4.—Separation of antifactor on DEAE cellulose. The top line represents protein content in the fractions. The bottom line represents tryptophan uptake in incubation mixtures consisting of chicken erythrocytes, tryptophan. Krebs-Ringer solution, α-2-globulin, and a fraction from the column.

to being isolated. Once it is isolated, our next step will be to manufacture antibodies to this substance to determine if it is missing in cells from schizophrenic patients. If the antifactor is low or missing in the tissue of schizophrenic patients, it would explain the elevation of the activity of the α-2-globulin in these subjects; a lower level of antifactor would result in less destruction of the α-2-globulin activity.

Certainly more studies of the effect of the α-2-globulin on tryptophan uptake and on the production of metabolites of tryptophan by brain tissue in its presence are warranted. Also, the discovery that pyrrolidone carboxylic acid, instead of glutamic acid, is a compound affected by the α-2-globulin suggests further study.

Since pyrrolidone carboxylic acid is present in most biological systems (it is an intermediate in the conversion of glutamic acid to proline), this compound might prove interesting for further investigation concerning the effect of the α-2-globulin on it, and whether there is any subsequent effect on behavior. Studies on the influence of the α-2-globulin on the uptake and metabolism of tryptophan, 5-hydroxytryptophan, and pyrrolidone carboxylic acid are continuing in our laboratories.

REFERENCES

BERGEN, J. R. (1967). Possible relationships of plasma factors to schizophrenia, in *Molecular Basis of Some Aspects of Mental Activity,* Vol. 2, Walaas, O. (ed.), Academic Press, New York, p. 257.

BERGEN, J. R., KOELLA, W. P., FREEMAN, H., & HOAGLAND, H. (1962).A human plasma factor inducing behavior and electrophysiological changes in animals. II. Changes in animals. *Ann. N.Y. Acad. Sci.* 96: 469.

FROHMAN, C. E., LUBY, E. D., TOURNEY, G., BECKETT, P. G. S., & GOTTLIEB, J. S. (1960). Steps toward the isolation of a serum factor in schizophrenia. *Am. J. Psychiat.* 117: 401.

FROHMAN, C. E., BECKETT, P. G. S., & GOTTLIEB, J. S. (1964). Control of the plasma factor in schizophrenia, in *Recent Advances in Biological Psychiatry,* Vol. 7, Wortis, J. (ed.), Plenum Press, New York, p. 45.

FROHMAN, C. E., WARNER, K. A., BARRY, C. T., & ARTHUR, R. E. (1969). Amino acid transport and the plasma factor in schizophrenia. *Biol. Psychiat.* 1: 201.

KRASNOV, A. I. (1965). Influence of blood serum from schizophrenic patients on the carbohydrate metabolism in chicken erythrocytes. *Zh. Nevropat. Psikhiat. Korsakov.* 65: 1206.

23

A THEORY OF NEURONAL MALFUNCTION IN SCHIZOPHRENIA

Jacques S. Gottlieb, Charles E. Frohman,
and Peter G. S. Beckett

A considerable amount of biological research into schizophrenia, mainly upon blood fluids, is performed throughout the world. The authors report their latest findings on a plasma protein factor and relate these findings to other domestic research and to recent research in other nations, particularly the Soviet Union. They hypothesize that a malcontrolled blood protein contributes to the genesis of schizophrenia by selectively altering neuronal permeability to precursors of important neurotransmitters; if this occurs, it would disrupt information processing in the brain.

Investigations into the various aspects of the syndromes called schizophrenia have been expanding rapidly on a world-wide basis. In 1966 there were 863 publications, of which 663 were in the English language—498 published in the United States (17). Although a large number of the publications were concerned with pharmacologic and psychotherapeutic evaluations, there remained a significant number of studies from the biological and psychosocial sciences. The language barrier complicates the problem of keeping abreast with all the findings.

This presentation is concerned with only one aspect of the investigative effort directed toward understanding schizophrenia. It is limited to cer-

Based on a paper read at the 124th annual meeting of the American Psychiatric Association, Boston, Mass., May 13-17, 1968.

The authors are associated with the Lafayette Clinic, 951 E. Lafayette, Detroit, Mich. 48207, where Dr. Gottlieb is director, Dr. Frohman is head, biochemistry laboratories, and Dr. Beckett is associate director; and with Wayne State University, where Dr. Gottlieb is professor and chairman, department of psychiatry, Dr. Frohman is assistant professor, department of biochemistry, and Dr. Beckett is professor, department of psychiatry.

tain aspects of the biochemistry of schizophrenia. Because of a lack of an animal model, essentially all the studies in this area have been restricted to the study of body fluids, particularly blood and urine. In this report attempts will be made to incorporate into American thinking some of the findings in the world literature, particularly some recent ones from the Soviet Union.

A number of laboratories have reported either normal substances in excess or abnormal substances in the blood of patients with schizophrenia. The literature is considerable; while some of the reports are conflicting and controversial, there is now evidence that several factors are present in the plasma of patients with schizophrenia. These factors may play a role in the pathogenesis of the disorder.

THE PLASMA ALPHA-2-GLOBULIN

Most of the evidence, as summarized in Table 1, is concerned with the isolation and identification of a protein that moves electrophoretically as an alpha-2-globulin. At least three of these laboratories (Lafayette Clinic, Worcester Foundation for Experimental Biology, and the Institute of Psychiatry, Academy of Sciences of the USSR) have been studying the same factor. Dr. Bergen of the Worcester group (6) uses a rat rope climbing technique for bio-assay and a zinc precipitation technique for the isolation of the factor. Dr. Frohman of the Lafayette Clinic group (6) uses the lactate to pyruvate ratio (L/P ratio) in an incubation mixture as a bio-assay and a physical separation procedure for the isolation of the protein. Nevertheless, in crossover studies between these two groups, the plasma substance isolated by each research group has been demonstrated to be active in the other's bio-assay system (6). It is quite certain that the factor isolated by the Russian investigator is the same, as they have used Frohman's techniques throughout (22,25).

This alpha-2-globulin is very labile, has a high molecular weight of about 400,000, and occurs in a concentration of about 50 μg. per 100 ml. of blood. About 80 percent of this molecule is composed of lipid. It constitutes about 1:150,000 of the proteins of the plasma. It appears to be consistently elevated in about 60 percent of patients.

One aspect of the study of this substance has been the attempt to determine whether it is a carrier of a small molecule that is responsible for its activity or whether the activity depends upon the intact protein itself. Bergen and Pennell and their associates (2) have presented some evidence that a small molecule ordinarily attached to this protein may pass through an artificial membrane and attach itself to a comparable protein on the other side. Pennell (26) has obtained further evidence that upon oxidation the small molecule forms a chromogenic derivative that has an absorption spectrum that would indicate a quinoid structure. This quinoid could arise from either the oxidation of catecholamines or the oxidation of indoles. These observations have not, however, as yet been confirmed.

Another characteristic of the alpha-2-globulin is that its level increases

TABLE 1

SUMMARY OF REPORTS OF SUBSTANCES IN PLASMA OF
PATIENTS WITH SCHIZOPHRENIA

Investigator	Identifying property	Protein Type
Bergen (2)	Delays climbing time in rats	α^2
Frohman (13)	Raises the L/P ratio	α^2
	Amino acid increase	α^2
Ehrensvard (7)	Amine oxidase activity	α or β
Krasnova (22) & Lozovsky (25)	Raises the L/P ratio	α or β
Ryan (29)	Hemolysis	?
Turner (37)	Hemolysis	?
Lideman (24)	Hemolysis	?
Lozovsky (25)	Hemolysis	?
Frohman (11)	Hemolysis	?
Tikhonov (36)	Increases membrane permeability	β^2
Uzunov (39)	Increases membrane permeability	?
Lideman (24)	Increases membrane permeability	?
Romasenko (28)	Increases membrane permeability	?
Frohman (10)	Increases membrane permeability	α^2
Semenov (30)	Brain antigens	?
	Brain auto-antibodies	?
Kuznetsova (23)	Brain auto-antibodies	?
Kolyaskina (21)	Brain auto-antibodies	?
Heath (19)	Brain auto-antibodies	γ

when the organism is stressed by either physical exercise, a cold pressor test, or a psychological test (12). The inconsistency of response within patients from test to test suggests, however, that the physiologic mechanism responsible for the increase has not been identified. Lozovsky and associates (25) have reported that ACTH given to patients increases the L/P ratio of serum in the incubation mixture, suggesting that this may be closer to the physiologic mechanism controlling plasma levels of the alpha-2-globulin. From these studies, it would appear plausible to propose that the alpha-2-globulin is a substance normally important in the organism's response to stress that is out of control in the *schizophrenic* patient.

There appears to be a close association between the effects of the alpha-2-globulin on the L/P ratio and the production of hemolysis in the incubation mixture. This phenomenon has been observed by Frohman (11), Ryan and associates (29), Lideman of the USSR (24), and others (25, 37). Ryan and co-workers (29) have suggested that the increase in the L/P ratio when chicken erythrocytes are incubated with serum from schizophrenic patients is a result of an immune lysin. It seemed quite important therefore to determine whether the alpha-2-globulin was indeed an immune lysin and whether the elevation of the L/P ratio was due to the hemolysis. Consequently, the following study was undertaken.

Thirty-two fractions from plasma of ten individual schizophrenic patients characterized by a high L/P ratio and ten individual control subjects were studied for their effect on both the L/P ratio and on hemolysis. The patients were all typically schizophrenic; they were male, chronically ill, had been drug free for years, were in good nutritional status, and exercised daily.

The techniques of fractionation of the plasma proteins used in this study are outlined briefly as follows: The euglobulin fraction of each subject's plasma was precipitated by dialysis against distilled water. The euglobulins were then taken up in 0.02M Tris buffer, pH 3.4, and separated into 32 tubes by curtain electrophoresis on a Spinco C.P. apparatus, using 700 v. and 35 m.a. current. The resulting fractions in tubes 1 and 2 contained no protein, the gamma-globulins appeared in tubes 3 to 10, the beta-2-globulins in tubes 11 to 14, the beta-1-globulins in tubes 15 to 17, the alpha-2-globulins in tubes 18 and 19, the alpha-1-globulins in tubes 20 to 23, and the albumins in tubes 24 to 31; tube 32 was free of protein. From schizophrenic plasma, the fraction in tube 18 was an alpha-2-globulin which, when incubated with chicken erythrocytes, caused a higher equilibrium ratio of lactate to pyruvate in the incubation mixture than did the equivalent fraction from the control subjects' plasma.

Only fraction 18 from the schizophrenic patients' plasma increased the L/P ratio significantly, and only fractions 11, 12, and 13 increased hemolysis. Table 2 shows the mean of L/P ratios from chicken erythrocytes incubated with pooled fractions 11, 12, and 13, and with fraction 18. Table 2 also shows the mean percentage of hemolysis caused by these fractions both in the presence and in the absence of guinea pig complement.

Protein in fraction 18 from the schizophrenic patients caused an increase in the L/P ratio as compared to control subjects (F test, p < .01), but had little effect on hemolysis. In contrast, the proteins isolated in pooled fractions 11, 12, and 13 from schizophrenic patients had no different effect on the L/P ratio than the equivalent fractions from control subjects. However, these latter proteins (beta-2-globulins from the plasma of schizophrenic patients) produced considerable hemolysis of the cell

TABLE 2

Means of L/P Ratios and Hemolysis Determinations in the
Presence of Protein Fractions Obtained from the Plasma
of 10 Schizophrenic and 10 Control Subjects

Subject	Fraction Number	Type Protein	L/P Ratio Without Complement	L/P Ratio With Complement	Percent Hemolysis Without Complement	Percent Hemolysis With Complement
Schizophrenic	18	α-2-globulin	14.95 ±7.4	15.20 ±7.9	0.5 ±0.6	1.3 ±1.4
Control	18	α-2-globulin	6.47 ±2.3	6.56 ±2.3	0.2 ±0.2	1.0 ±0.8
Schizophrenic	11, 12, 13	β-2-globulin	7.21 ±3.1	7.32 ±3.2	2.0 ±1.8	44.8 ±13.7
Control	11, 12, 13	β-2-globulin	7.40 ±3.4	7.31 ±3.4	0.5 ±0.4	12.2 ±7.4

when complement was added: pooled fractions 11, 12, and 13 from all subjects hemolyzed cells more than fraction 18 from all subjects (Lindquist type 1 analysis of variance, p < .001); pooled fractions 11, 12, and 13 from schizophrenic patients hemolyzed cells more than pooled fractions 11, 12, and 13 from control subjects (F test, p < .01). Fraction 18 is an alpha-2-globulin, whereas fractions 11, 12, and 13 consist of beta-2-globulins. Therefore, in plasma from patients who have schizophrenia, the protein responsible for an increase in the L/P ratio is different from the protein responsible for hemolysis.

Lozovsky (25) of the USSR has also demonstrated different properties for these two proteins. He has found that the substance responsible for the increase in the L/P ratio is much more labile than the substance responsible for the hemolysis. Lozovsky's findings therefore support the study reported above.

THE BLOOD FACTORS AND THE CELL MEMBRANE

The concurrence of a hemolysin and a factor that increases the L/P ratio could be explained by postulating a substance or substances in the serum of schizophrenic patients that affect cell membrane permeability. The only direct evidence of the effect of serum of patients upon membrane permeability has been obtained by a number of USSR scientists. Tikhonov and associates (36) reported that under the electron microscope the membrane of the mitochondria of the cells of the rat's cerebral cortex showed swelling and fragmentation when these subcellular particles were incubated with serum from patients with schizophrenia. Uzunov and associates (39) reported that more P^{32} was incorporated into the erythrocytes of patients with schizophrenia due to an increase in the permeability of the cell membrane.

Lideman and associates (24) reported morphological changes in the membrane of chicken red cells when the cells were incubated with serum from patients with schizophrenia. They also reported extensive lesions in the ultrastructure of the myelin of the surviving femoral nerve of the frog when it was incubated in the same way. Romasenko (28) reported a study in which rats were injected with serum from patients; by electron microscopy he observed a deterioration in the membranes of both cells and mitochondria of the fifth layer of the cerebral cortex. The direct evidence presented by these investigators therefore suggests the presence of a membranolytic substance in the serum of patients with schizophrenia.

Indirect evidence by Frohman and his associates (10) through in vitro studies of the effect of the alpha-2-globulin on the chicken red cell implicates the alpha-2-globulin as having membranolytic activity. One may hypothesize that if this increase in the permeability of cell membranes is a fact, then certain substances may cross the membrane from within the cell and act as antigens to which subsequent auto-antibodies may be formed. The beta-2-globulin, a hemolysin, may be such an auto-antibody.

If there is an increase in cell membrane permeability, it may well explain the number of reports of brain antigens and antibrain antibodies in the serum of patients with schizophrenia. Semenov and associates (30), using an antibody and complement fixation test, reported antigens from brain in the serum of patients. They also reported brain antigens and their corresponding antibodies in the cerebral spinal fluid of patients. Kuznetsova (23) reported auto-antibodies in the serum active against mitochondria of neurons. Kolyaskina and associates (21) reported that the auto-antibodies to neural tissue occurred in the serum of about 25 percent of patients.

However, she made the point that when nonschizophrenic subjects were stressed, 30 percent had positive reactions. This is similar to the report of Goodman and associates (15), who showed that antibodies to thyroglobulin increased in medical students under stress to a level similar to that obtained in a schizophrenic population. The most detailed report of an auto-antibody in the serum of patients with schizophrenia is by Heath and associates (19). They describe a specific gamma globulin with unique antibody activity to an antigen in a specific part of the septum of the brain.

From these various studies it would appear probable that substances might pass through the membranes of neural tissue with greater facility in patients with schizophrenia than in control subjects. The evidence also suggests that some of the substances that might escape from within the cell could act as antigens to which auto-antibodies could be formed. If further studies support these hypotheses, an immunochemical mechanism would appear to be involved as part of the pathophysiology of this disorder.

METABOLIC EFFECTS OF THE ALPHA-2-GLOBULIN

For several years it has been known that the alpha-2-globulin disturbs the process of phosphorylation (16). This substance prevents the adaptive shift under stress of glucose metabolism from the hexosemonophosphate shunt to the Embden-Myerhof scheme (14). In vitro studies, first by Haavaldsen and associates (18) of Norway, using a rat diaphragm as a substrate, and later by Frohman (13), using both rat diaphragms and chicken red cells as substrate, showed that glucose uptake by cells was diminished by serum from patients. (Utena of Japan (38) has reported that cerebral tissues obtained from patients at neurosurgery took up glucose at lower rates than corresponding tissue from controls.)

Pursuing these metabolic disturbances further, Frohman and associates (10) found that a greater percentage of noncarbohydrate material was passing through the cell membrane in the presence of the alpha-2-globulin from schizophrenic patients. A series of in vitro studies was initiated of the rate of accumulation of certain amino acids in chicken red cells when incubated with plasma from patients who have high levels of alpha-2-globulin in comparison with the effect of plasma from control subjects.

Table 3 presents the data on 11 amino acids: phenylalanine, glutamic acid, tryptophan, 5-hydroxytryptophan, alanine, methionine, alpha-amino isobutyric acid, serine, tyrosine, histidine, and lysine. Of these, only glutamic acid, tryptophan, 5-hydroxytryptophan, and alanine accumulated in cells in excessive amounts when incubated in the plasma from patients. It is of particular interest that three of those amino acids that accumulated in excess in the chicken cells are precursors of neural transmitters. Glutamic acid is metabolized to gamma amino butyric acid (GABA), a potent dendritic inhibitor, while tryptophan and 5-hydroxytryptophan are metabolized to tryptamine and serotonin.

TABLE 3

Uptake of Amino Acid by Chicken Erythrocytes in the Presence of Plasma from Control Subjects and Schizophrenic Patients

Amino Acid	Controls (N = 12)		High-Factor Schizophrenics (N = 13)		
	Counts	S.D.	Counts	S.D.	*
Glutamic acid	5,384	± 1,487	12,211	± 3,293	0.001
Tryptophan	93,629	±20,743	142,062	±35,285	0.001
5-Hydroxytryptophan	69,480	±17,462	119,220	±30,425	0.001
Phenylalanine	292,613	±33,315	317,231	±32,112	n.s.
Tyrosine	87,711	±17,499	116,685	±33,073	0.05
Alanine	116,800	±11,952	165,740	±15,490	0.001
Serine	184,028	±42,284	197,596	±43,612	n.s.
Methionine	47,060	±12,358	49,420	±12,358	n.s.
Histidine	53,620	±19,660	64,940	±13,880	n.s.
Lysine	30,920	± 8,740	39,320	±14,700	n.s.
α-amino isobutyric	20,600	± 4,632	24,860	± 5,465	n.s.

* Significance of difference between high-factor schizophrenics and controls.

SUBSTANCES IN URINE

Numerous studies of the constituents of the urine of patients with schizophrenia have sought metabolites, either abnormal or in excess amounts, that would characterize and give some clue to the pathophysiology of the disorder. A great deal of the literature has been summarized in the book *Amines and Schizophrenia* (20). There is considerable evidence that the urine of schizophrenic patients contains either O-methylated catecholamines or N-methylated indoleamines or both; these may derive from central neurotransmitters. The substances include: 3, 4-dimethoxyphenylethylamine (DMPEA, a substance possibly formed from dopamine, which in turn is derived from phenylalanine) and bufotenin (1, 3, 8, 9, 31, 34, 35) (N, N-dimethyl serotonin, possibly formed from serotonin, which in turn is derived from tryptophan or 5-hydroxytryptophan). Moreover, a number of studies (4, 27, 32, 33) suggest that when patients, in conjunction with an MAO inhibitor, are loaded with tryptophan or with methyl donors as methionine or betaine or with a thiol activator as cysteine, worsening of symptoms occurs. There is also an increase in N-dimethylated indoleamines as N-dimethyl trypta-mine and N, N-dimethyl serotonin (bufotenin) in the urine. Some of these substances may produce psychotogenic effects.

DISCUSSION

It is of considerable interest, therefore, that on the one hand there is an active substance—alpha-2-globulin—in the blood of certain patients with schizophrenia that is responsible for an accumulation of glutamic acid and tryptophan within the cell, while on the other hand certain methylated metabolites of phenylalanine and tryptophan have been noted in the urine.

The three amino acids implicated by these studies—glutamic acid, phenylalanine, and tryptophan—are all considered important precursors of neurotransmitter substances. Glutamic acid goes to gamma aminobu-tyric acid (GABA), phenylalanine metabolizes to dopamine and nor-epinephrine, and tryptophan to tryptamine and serotonin. Information processing most probably depends upon the control or regulation of these biogenic amines; an excess of any one may distort their relationships. Moreover, emergency pathways of metabolism as that of N-methylation in addition to O-methylation may be required to handle any excess of phe-nylalanine or tryptophan. Metabolites may thus be formed as N-dime-thylated indoleamines that may also affect synaptic transmission and, in so doing, affect information processing.

The studies of the effect of the alpha-2-globulin of the serum on the metabolism of chicken red cells in vitro certainly raise the question as to whether the same effects are produced in neural tissue in vivo. It was noted that the alpha-2-globulin affected the accumulation within cells of several amino acids that are important as "mother substances" of sub-stances that affect synaptic transmission. It is important to attempt to confirm this finding with in vivo studies; such studies are currently under way.

Glutamic acid and its metabolite (GABA) present a unique problem that can only be resolved by study of the effects of the serum alpha-2-globulin on neural tissue itself. Not only is glutamic acid formed in neurons and GABA present only in nervous tissue, but there are no known metabolites to be sought in the urine.

The reports of DMPEA in excess in the urine of patients and the accumulation of phenylalanine in cells as normal under the influence of the alpha-2-globulin would seem to be incompatible. DMPEA is present in patients' urine primarily during the acute phases of their illness; in chronic patients it is practically absent or nearly so. All studies of the effect of the alpha-2-globulin on the accumulation of phenylalanine were done on chronic patients; hence, in chronic patients, if DMPEA is being formed, the amount may be so small as to be undetectable in urine by current techniques.

Reports of the presence of metabolites (N-dimethylated indoleamines) of tryptophan in the urine of patients on the one hand, and the alpha-2-globulin of the blood responsible for an increased accumulation of tryptophan and 5-hydroxytryptophan in cells on the other, would appear to be more than coincidental. This certainly suggests a metabolic disturbance that may be an important part of the pathophysiology of the disorder. Supportive evidence comes from the same patients characterized by the alpha-2-globulin, for they are also characterized by a significant reduction of slow wave sleep, a function most likely mediated by serotonin (5).

One may therefore propose a general hypothesis that in patients with schizophrenia there is a blood protein that promotes the malfunction of noradrenergic and/or serotonergic neuronal systems within the brain. If this hypothesis proves to be true, then one would expect malfunction in the hypothalamus and limbic areas, parts of the brain concerned with emotional functioning, and mid-brain and reticular areas having to do with activation and sleep.

SUMMARY

A hypothesis has been presented concerning a possible disturbance of neural function in certain patients with schizophrenia. The evidence suggests that a specific alpha-2-globulin is present in the serum of all individuals and that it has an important adaptive role, but that in some patients with schizophrenia the level of this protein is out of control. This macro lipo-protein may affect metabolism by selectively increasing cell permeability. As a consequence, certain substances could possibly escape from cells in excess while other substances could enter cells in excess. This would explain the presence of a hemolysin in the serum of patients with schizophrenia as well as the presence of brain antigens and auto-antibodies.

More important, the selective alteration in membrane permeability would also explain the excess accumulation of glutamic acid, tryptophan, and 5-hydroxytryptophan in chicken erythrocytes in in vitro experiments. If a similar excess of tryptophan were to accumulate in vivo in neural cells, an excess of its metabolites would probably be present. The likely increase of such metabolites as serotonin and N-dimethylated indole-amines might then result in a disturbance in synaptic transmission and consequently in information processing.

There is much work to be done before this hypothesis can be verified, modified, or discarded. Our own research is finding answers for some of the numerous questions that it raises.

REFERENCES

1. ACEBAL, E. M.: The Influence of the Treatment With "Triperidol" on the Elimination of Bufotenin in Schizophrenic Patients, presented at the 42nd anniversary congress of the Pan American Medical Association, Buenos Aires, Argentina, November, 1967.

2. BERGEN, J. R., PENNELL, R. B., SARAVIS, C. A., & HOAGLAND, H.: "Further Experiments with Plasma Proteins in Schizophrenics," in Heath, R. G., ed.: Serological Fractions in Schizophrenia. New York: Harper & Row, 1963, pp. 67-76.

3. BONHOUR, A.: The Reaction of Bufotenin and the Clinical State of Mentally Disturbed Patients, presented at the 42nd anniversary congress of the Pan American Medical Association, Buenos Aires, Argentina, November, 1967.

4. BRUNE, G. G., & HIMWICH, H. E.: "Biogenic Amines and Behavior in Schizophrenic Patients," in Wortis, J., ed.: Recent Advances in Biological Psychiatry. New York: Plenum Press, 1963, pp. 144-160.

5. CALDWELL, D. F., & DOMINO, E. F.: Electroencephalographic and Eye Movement Patterns During Sleep in Chronic Schizophrenic Patients, Electroenceph. Clin. Neurophysiol. 12:414-420, 1967.

6. Cooperative Study: Plasma Factors in Schizophrenia, Arch. Gen. Psychiat. 18: 471-476, 1968.

7. EHRENSVARD, G.: "Discussion," in Walass, O., ed.: Molecular Basis of Some Aspects of Mental Activity, vol. 2. London: Academic Press, 1967, p. 311.

8. FISCHER, E.: Recent Studies on the Possible Dismetabolic-Endotoxic Origin of Schizophrenia, presented at the 42nd anniversary congress of the Pan American Medical Association, Buenos Aires, Argentina, November, 1967.

9. FISCHER, E., FERNANDEZ LAGRAVERE, T. A., VAZQUEZ, A. J., & DI STEPHANO, A. O.: A Bufotenine-like Substance in the Urine of Schizophrenics, J. Nerv. Ment. Dis. 133:441-444, 1961.

10. FROHMAN, C. E.: "Studies on the Plasma Factor in Schizophrenia," in Rupp, C., ed.: Mind as a Tissue. New York: Harper & Row, 1968, pp. 181-195.

11. FROHMAN, C. E.: unpublished data.

12. FROHMAN, C. E., BECKETT, P. G. S., GRISELL, J. L., LATHAM, L. K., & GOTTLIEB, J. S.: Biologic Responsiveness to Environmental Stimuli in Schizophrenia, Compr. Psychiat. 7:494-500, 1966.

13. FROHMAN, C. E., CZAJKOWSKI, N. P., LUBY, E. D., GOTTLIEB, J. S., & SENF, R.: Further Evidence of a Plasma Factor in Schizophrenia, Arch. Gen. Psychiat. 2:263-267, 1960.

14. FROHMAN, C. E., LATHAM, L. K., BECKETT, P. G. S., & GOTTLIEB, J. S.: Evidence of a Plasma Factor in Schizophrenia, Arch. Gen. Psychiat. 2:255-262, 1960.

15. GOODMAN, M., ROSENBLATT, M., GOTTLIEB, J. S., MILLER, J., & CHEN, C. H.: Effect of Age, Sex, and Schizophrenia on Thyroid Autoantibody Production, *Arch. Gen. Psychiat.* 8:518-526, 1963.

16. GOTTLIEB, J. S., FROHMAN, C. E., BECKETT, P. G. S., TOURNEY, G., & SENF, R.: Production of High-Energy Phosphate Bonds in Schizophrenia, *Arch. Gen. Psychiat.* 1:243-249, 1959.

17. GRISELL, J.: "Current Research Trends in Schizophrenia and Information Retrieval Analysis," in Gottlieb, J. S., and Tourney, G., eds.: Lafayette Clinic Studies in Schizophrenia. Detroit: Wayne State University Press, 1971.

18. HAAVALDSEN, R., LINGJAERDE, O., & WALAAS, O.: Disturbance of Carbohydrate Metabolism in Schizophrenics, *Confin. Neurol.* 18:270, 1958.

19. HEATH, R. G., KRUPP, I. M., BYERS, L. W., & LILJEKVIST, J. I.: Schizophrenia as an Immunologic Disorder, *Arch. Gen. Psychiat.* 16:1-33, 1967.

20. HIMWICH, H. E., KETY, S. S., & SMYTHIES, J. R., eds.: Amines and Schizophrenia. New York: Pergamon Press, 1967.

21. KOLYASKINA, G., KUSHNER, S., & GASKIN, L.: "Certain Immunological Changes in Schizophrenic Patients," in Vartanyan, M., ed.: Transactions of the Symposium on Biological Research in Schizophrenia. Moscow: Lenin Printing Co. (Pravda), 1967, pp. 238-239.

22. KRASNOVA, A. I.: The Influence of the Blood Serum of Patients Having Schizophrenia on Carbohydrate Metabolism in Chicken Erythrocytes, *Zh. Nevropat. Psikhiat. Korsakov* 68:1206-1211, 1965.

23. KUZNETSOVA, N.: "Some Data Concerning the Immunological Properties of Brain Mitochondria," in Vartanyan, M., ed.: Transactions of the Symposium on Biological Research in Schizophrenia. Moscow: Lenin Printing Co. (Pravda), 1967, pp. 221-224.

24. LIDEMAN, R., & BOKOVA, J.: "The Possible Nature and Mechanism of Action of the Active Factor of the Blood Serum of Schizophrenic Patients," in Vartanyan, M., ed.: Transactions of the Symposium on Biological Research in Schizophrenia. Moscow: Lenin Printing Co. (Pravda), 1967, pp. 169-172.

25. LOZOVSKY, D., KRASNOVA, A., FACTOR, M., POLYANSKAYA, N., & POPOVA, N.: "The Effect of the Serum of Schizophrenic Patients Upon Certain Glucose Transformations," in Vartanyan, M., ed.: Transactions of the Symposium on Biological Research in Schizophrenia. Moscow: Lenin Printing Co. (Pravda), 1967, pp. 151-156.

26. PENNELL, R.: "Biological Properties of the Blood Serum of Schizophrenic Patients," in Vartanyan, M., ed.: Transactions of the Symposium on Biological Research in Schizophrenia. Moscow: Lenin Printing Co. (Pravda), 1967, pp. 161-163.

27. POLLIN, W., CARDON, V., & KETY, S. S.: Effects of Amino Acid Feedings in Schizophrenic Patients. *Science* 133:104-105, 1961.

28. ROMASENKO, V.: "Certain Morphological and Histochemical Changes in Animals Induced by Schizophrenia Patients' Blood Serum," in Vartanyan, M., ed.: Transactions of the Symposium on Biological Research in Schizophrenia. Moscow: Lenin Printing Co. (Pravda), 1967, pp. 176-182.

29. RYAN, J. S., BROWN, J. D., & DURELL, J.: Antibodies Affecting Metabolism of Chicken Erythrocytes: Examination of Schizophrenic and Other Subjects, *Science* 151:1408-1410, 1966.

30. SEMENOV, S., GLEBOV, V., & CHUPRIKOV, A.: "Autoimmune Organ Specific Reactions as One of the Factors of Pathobiology of Schizophrenia," in Vartanyan, M., ed.: Transactions of the Symposium on Biological Research in Schizophrenia. Moscow: Lenin Printing Co. (Pravda), 1967, pp. 230-233.

31. SIREIX, D. W., & MARINI, F. A.: A Study About the Elimination of Bufotenin of Urine, presented at the 42nd anniversary congress of the Pan American Medical Association, Buenos Aires, Argentina, November, 1967.

32. SMYTHIES, J. R., & OSMOND, H.: Schizophrenia: A New Approach, *J. Ment. Sci.* 98:309-315, 1952.

33. SPAIDE, J., TANIMUKAI, H., BUENO, J. R., & HIMWICH, H. E.: Behavioral and Biochemical Alterations in Schizophrenic Patients, *Arch. Gen. Psychiat.* 18:658-665, 1968.

34. SPATZ, H.: Determination of Bufotenin in Urine of Schizophrenics, presented at the 42nd anniversary congress of the Pan American Medical Association, Buenos Aires, Argentina, November, 1967.

35. TANIMUKAI, H., GINTHER, R., SPAIDE, J., BUENO, J. R., & HIMWICH, H. E.: Psychotogenic N-Dimethylated Indoleamines and Behavior in Schizophrenic Patients, presented at the 42nd annual meeting of the Society of Biological Psychiatry, Detroit, Michigan, May 5, 1967.

36. TIKHONOV, V., LOZOVSKY, D., & GLEZER, I.: "Effects of Blood Serum from Patients upon Potassium Ion Stimulated Respiration of Rat Brain Slices," in Vartanyan, M., ed.: Transactions of the Symposium on Biological Research in Schizophrenia. Moscow: Lenin Printing Co. (Pravda), 1967, pp. 156-158.

37. TURNER, W. J., & CHIPPS, H. I.: A Heterophil Hemolysin in Human Blood: I. Distribution in Schizophrenics and Nonschizophrenics, *Arch. Gen. Psychiat.* 15: 373-377, 1966.

38. UTENA, H.: "Neurochemical Studies of Chronic Methamphetamine Intoxication as a Model of Schizophrenia," in Vartanyan, M., ed.: Transactions of the Symposium on Biological Research in Schizophrenia. Moscow: Lenin Printing Co. (Pravda), 1967, pp. 188-191.

39. UZUNOV, G., IORDANOV, B., & DOSEVA, I.: "Cellular Membrane Permeability in Schizophrenia," in Vartanyan, M., ed.: Transactions of the Symposium on Biological Research in Schizophrenia. Moscow: Lenin Printing Co. (Pravda), 1967, pp. 163-169.

24

PERSPECTIVES FOR BIOLOGICAL PSYCHIATRY

Robert G. Heath

In the early 1940's, American psychiatry was so preoccupied with the psychoanalytic approach to the understanding of human behavior that contributions of the basic neurosciences seemed negligible. It was this climate that inspired the formation of the Society of Biological Psychiatry in 1947. The principal aim of the founders was to bring into focus the obvious—that human behavior is a consequence of activity of the nervous system. And this was somewhat of a challenge since many of us who trained during the war years were seduced by the attractive promises forecast for psychoanalysis. General psychiatry, seemingly in a state of arrested development, focused on static classification of disordered behavior and offered little hope for its effective remedy. On the other hand, psychoanalysis provided the inexperienced trainee with glib explanations for all types of behavior, and promised specific, effective preventions and treatments.

Vulnerable trainees were not the only ones influenced by these promises; so were many civic leaders and philanthropists. One reflection of the intensity of the psychoanalytic fervor was the development of the child guidance centers. Advocates rationalized that behavioral disorders could be prevented, and that the population of mental hospitals could eventually be reduced significantly if children could be seen early enough by persons trained in Freudian dynamics. It has taken many years to demonstrate conclusively the shortcomings of this one-sided approach. So tempting was the lure that it eclipsed the fact that the only real advances toward specific diagnosis, treatment and, in many instances, eradication

Presented at the Annual Meeting of the Society of Biological Psychiatry, Miami Beach, Florida, May 4, 1969.

Reprinted, by permission of author and editor, from: *Biological Psychiatry*, 2: 81-88, 1970, published by Plenum Publishing Corporation, New York.

of disordered behavior, had issued from intense, patient, and often un-dramatic biologic research. The history of these advances has been the subject of previous Presidential addresses, of which the review by Dr. Paul Hoch in 1960 was perhaps the most complete (Hoch, 1961).

The treatment of paresis and pellagra probably most dramatically illus-trates the substantial results of intense biologic research in psychiatry. Until a few years ago, general paresis accounted for about 10% of mental hospital admissions; today it is almost non-existent. Similarly, patients with pellagra represented about 19% of admissions to mental hospitals in some southern states; today pellagra causes psychosis only rarely. The problem of alcoholic psychosis has been mitigated considerably through treatment with vitamins. As Dr. Hoch emphasized ten years ago, signifi-cant progress has been made in treatment of chronic psychotic disorders associated with arteriosclerosis and senility through effective use of tran-quilizing drugs. Further progress toward solving these major behavioral disorders will parallel progress in basic research on arteriosclerosis. Al-ready, recognition that certain metabolic disorders, such as diabetes, may hasten and intensify arteriosclerotic changes has given considerable im-petus to the search for treatment of such disorders.

Dr. Hoch also emphasized our lack of understanding of the basic mechanisms underlying chronic alcoholism and drug dependency, and the futility of treatments then being used. The subsequent introduction of methadone in the treatment of drug addicts had led to their social rehabilitation in many instances. Methadone is itself a narcotic which apparently occupies receptor sites for heroin and other potent narcotic analgesics. When the addict is pretreated with methadone, ingestion of more harmful narcotics has no significant effect. Because methadone is cheap and its behavioral effects do not disturb effective social functioning, the heroin addict, freed of his $65 to $75 a day habit becomes employ-able and no longer needs to commit crimes to finance his drug habit. Thus, although not a cure for drug addiction, methadone is proving to be an effective treatment.

For some time, mood-elevating drugs have been used successfully in treatment of some depressed patients, but until recently the manic pa-tient has represented a difficult therapeutic problem because drugs avail-able were only minimally effective. Recently, results obtained with use of lithium for this disorder have proved gratifying, albeit the need for caution and collection of careful statistics has been expressed ("Lithium," 1969). In light of the dramatic, predictable behavioral responses these patients achieve when blood-lithium reaches the proper level, the concept seems shallow and wanting that manic or elated behavior is implicitly the result of the fulfillment fantasy of recapturing the ever-flowing breast. The often impressive response of the depressive patient to mood-elevating drugs, as well as his instantaneous response to electrical stimulation of the septal region, similarly casts doubt on the psychodynamic explanation for the condition which focuses on retroflect rage from loss of an imagined love object. But it would be shortsighted to consider that one observation completely nullifies the other, that because biologic treatment produces such dramatic response, there is no validity to the concept that psychologic factors are causative. Considering data from the two approaches together provides the best opportunity for understanding how psychologic factors and brain activity are interrelated. Learned behavioral patterns and their associated affects are determinants in brain function. And chemical or physiologic manipulation of brain function obviously alters behavior. Existing treatments do this principally by altering affect. In each of the incidents cited, however, biologic treatment exerts a greater effect than the psychologic approach.

Research interest and activity in recent years have probably been most intense in biologic exploration of schizophrenia, the primary theme of this meeting. At least this is the most exciting to me; investigations of schizophrenia have been the primary focus of research efforts in the Tulane Department of Psychiatry and Neurology for 20 years. Although developments thus far have not been definitive, there is reason for optimism. In his survey 10 years ago, Dr. Hoch noted the diffuseness of our knowledge of the functional psychoses, particularly schizophrenia, at both the clinical-descriptive and biologic levels. Now at last, the biologic etiology at least has more general acceptance, and basic investigations at several research centers are beginning to converge to some degree. I am convinced that schizophrenia is a distinct single disease entity—an opinion that seemingly deviates from concepts presented by some other investigators at this meeting, as well as in some published reports. But I think the difference is more apparent than real. It is essentially semantic, arising from a tendency to use the terms, psychosis and schizophrenia, reciprocally. Psychosis denotes a syndrome, a group of signs and symptoms, characteristic of many disease processes affecting the brain. In this context psychosis is somewhat analogous to the syndrome of epilepsy which is a group of symptoms that can derive from a variety of brain pathologies. Neither psychosis nor epilepsy is a disease process, and they should not be presented as such. One paper delivered at this meeting is entitled "A Study of Drug-Induced Schizophrenia," but it actually was a study of drug-induced psychosis. Another presentation included a slide diagram depicting various components of schizophrenia being stripped away, basic pathologic parts that have been demonstrated to induce psychotic behavior in disease processes such as neurosyphilis, pellagra and, more recently, temporal lobe epilepsy. It was implied that a few more peelings would dispose of schizophrenia. I profoundly oppose this concept. The well-trained psychiatrist can separate, on clinical grounds alone, these other disorders from schizophrenia. Schizophrenia is but one of many brain pathologies characterized by psychosis. While there are many psychotic features that the schizophrenic patient may share in common with patients with other brain pathologies, schizophrenia has unique clinical features. And the Tulane research group postulates that a unique brain pathology will be demonstrated for schizophrenia, that it will be identified as a single disease entity with the principal clinical feature being production of psychotic signs and symptoms which tend to remit and relapse.

"Functional psychosis" implies absence of brain disease, but it was coined in the days when available technics failed to disclose disease. With the introduction of newer methods, clear-cut brain disease is now being demonstrated with these disorders. Depth electrode technics introduced at Tulane in 1950 permitted long-term study of patients with a variety of psychiatric and neurologic disorders and showed a clear-cut physiologic abnormality in the form of spike or slow-wave activity, or both, in the rostral septal region concomitant with psychotic behavior (Heath, 1967). Occasionally, there were associated abnormalities in other parts of the limbic system, particularly the hippocampus and amygdala, but if the patient was not psychotic, the septal recordings were not affected. These same findings have recently been reported from other research centers. The correlation of psychotic behavior and the septal aberration prevails, regardless of the cause of the psychosis.

The major focus of the Tulane investigations since 1954 has been to determine the nature of the basic disease process in schizophrenia which affects the brain at a focal site, the septal region, and induces the well-known, usually intermittent, behavioral aberrations. Our recent findings suggest that schizophrenia may represent an immunologic disorder, that the schizophrenic patient produces an antibody which affects specific cells of the septal region, thereby inducing abnormal brain activity and the consequent psychotic signs and symptoms. Our data indicate that the antibody is a subfraction of gamma G immunoglobulin (IgG) (Heath and Krupp, 1967). The antibody concept is substantiated by the finding that the antibody binding fragment, obtained by papain digestion of the IgG, evokes psychosis-inducing activity in assay monkeys.

We know, however, that this is not the whole story of schizophrenia.

We are probably still some distance from establishing the specific nature of this disease. And the frustrations that have plagued all of us who are whittling away at this problem seem also destined to remain for some time. With methods now available, we have demonstrated the passive transfer phenomenon in rhesus monkeys (induction of EEG and behavioral changes) with taraxein (IgG) fractioned from serum of about half of our acutely symptomatic patient-donors. Even with serum of these donors, however, we have not been able to demonstrate the psychosis-inducing IgG consistently. We do not now know all the reasons for these inconsistencies, although several explanations seem plausible. An unidentified cofactor or factors, for example, may be involved. Indeed, the findings in several laboratories, including the Worcester Foundation for Experimental Biology and the Lafayette Clinic, suggest this possibility.

But the most important trend in recent years has been the more definitive focus on the role of protein fractions in schizophrenia, suggesting an immunologic cause, that is, a protein (antibody?) -inducing alteration in membrane permeability and neural transmission. Despite the seemingly overwhelming vicissitudes we are encountering in our current research endeavors, I believe that in the foreseeable future schizophrenia will be established as still another disease process that fits the neurologic model. In other words, the basic disease process affects brain cells with resultant psychotic signs and symptoms, and by virtue of this mechanism there is an analogy to the processes at work in other well delineated psychotic disorders: nutritional diseases such as pellagra; infectious diseases such as general paresis; vascular diseases such as cerebral arteriosclerosis; and other basic pathologic states that affect the brain to produce psychosis. Once the basic disease process of schizophrenia is elucidated, successful treatment will not be long in following.

In our studies of schizophrenia at Tulane, we have become intrigued with certain patients whose symptoms resemble those of schizophrenic psychosis. Conventional scalp electroencephalograms (EEG) for these patients, however, show abnormalities that are usually focal over the temporal region. Although most symptoms of patients with this disorder are indistinguishable from those of the psychotic schizophrenic, there are some distinguishing characteristics. Episodes of psychotic behavior of these patients are usually shorter than the psychotic episodes of the schizophrenic patient and characteristically feature more overt and impulsive expressions of the emergency emotions of fear and rage. In periods of remission, they do not exhibit the primary symptoms of schizophrenia described by Bleuler, 1950; instead, behavior is more like that of a healthy person.

The temporal lobe EEG abnormality is pronounced during psychotic episodes and becomes minimal or even disappears during interpsychotic periods. This syndrome was originally described a number of years ago by Dr. Fred Gibbs, but insufficient attention has since been devoted to its delineation. Patients with this temporal lobe abnormality who were included in our depth electrode series showed continuous epileptogenic EEG abnormalities in deep temporal lobe structures, even when there was no manifestation on the surface. But when the patients became psychotic, the epileptogenic discharge was always propagated into the rostral septal region as well. Many patients with this disorder have had operations for ablation of portions of the temporal lobe, and histologic study of the ablated tissues rather consistently shows sclerotic cells. On postmortem study of brains of other patients with this syndrome, similar histologic changes have been detected in various temporal lobe structures. The cause of the sclerosis no doubt varies from one subject to the next, ranging from anoxia at birth to head trauma, infection, and other less clearly defined disease processes.

I have emphasized this group of patients because they are often included with the schizophrenics on the basis of behavioral similarities. But since the underlying disease affecting the brain is different, these patients clearly represent a separate, distinct, disorder. A common characteristic of the schizophrenic patient and the patient with temporal lobe disorder and, in fact, of all psychotic patients regardless of cause, is the physiologic aberration in the rostral septal region during episodes of psychotic behavior. It is in the septal region of the brain that stimulation has been shown to induce feelings of pleasure and alerting, whereas impaired function of this brain site is associated with reduced awareness and anhedonia.

Therapeutic results with various combinations of anticonvulsant medications are sometimes gratifying in patients with temporal lobe disorder. This is an interesting group of patients worthy of further study. This disorder too, like schizophrenia, fits the neurologic disease model, with demonstrable structural brain disease responsible for signs and symptoms.

Present knowledge indicates that there are also many patients who have behavioral disorders *not* based on the classical neurologic model. In such disorders, brain structure is intact, and the aberrant behavior is the result of faulty learning experiences. To use computer analogy, the structurally intact machine has been poorly programmed. This is in contrast to the classical neurologic model, in which the behavioral abnormality is the result of a loose wire or a blown tube. There is a spectrum of behavior from the normal on the one extreme to the severely neurotic and disturbed at the other.

It cannot be questioned that the significant advances in the treatment of mental illness have come from the sphere of basic biology. And it seems undeniable that there is a one-to-one relation between brain activity and mental activity, although such a relation may be impossible to establish, since mental activity is largely subjective. Despite the difficulties in relating mind and brain, the one being dependent on introspective data and the other on physical or inspective data, we should do our best to bridge the gap by making whatever cross-correlations we can. The most significant future advances will come from just such a bilateral approach. To discard the subjective or introspective data simply because it is hard to evaluate would deprive us of valuable information—in fact, essential information for studying the mind as a reflection of brain activity. Much information that is sound and has withstood the test of time has been derived from use of the technics of reported introspection, that is, intensive investigation of mental activity of individuals. The fact, too, that there has been much unsubstantiated theoretic dogma and that effective treatment by this method has fallen short of expectations does not mean that we should discard all findings based on subjective patient reporting.

In the past a few psychoanalysts attempted to base psychodynamic formulations on sound physiologic data. One such pioneer, who has been insufficiently recognized, is Dr. Sandor Rado (1956), whose adaptational psychodynamic framework is based on physiology, a subject in which he is well versed. Increasingly, young psychiatrists trained in psychoanalysis are becoming aware that psychoanalytic theory must be related to brain physiology. The so-called psychodynamic data, and theory based on these data, constitute the best signpost available to point the way for productive biological research of behavior. In fact, this information could well be the most important result of the 70 years of psychoanalytic studies, if coupled with the intuitive investigations of the sensitive, humane psychiatrist, who can separate out data which are useful. The basic scientist, in attempting to investigate behavior, would be helpless without such data and would not know what experiment to do with his technics.

If behavior is approached holistically, introspective and inspective data being related wherever possible, two spheres of investigation become apparent, offering preventive and therapeutic potentials exceeding even those gains that would be achieved by elimination of schizophrenia or, in fact, of all unsolved organic psychotic disorders. One is concerned with the controlled manipulation of the pleasure response and the other, with manipulation of memory by biologic methods.

By electrical stimulation of the brain of a large number of patients, as well as chemical stimulation to precise brain regions of a smaller number of patients, feelings of pleasure can be induced. Reports of patients so stimulated illustrate that an inverse relation exists between pleasure and pain. Induction of pleasure is a specific immediate antidote for both painful emotional feelings and physical pain. This central neurophysiologic mechanism for pleasure has been studied in animals as well, and extensively through application of self-stimulation technics first introduced by Dr. James Olds (1962). The ability to manipulate this mechanism, that is, to induce pleasure, not only offers possibilities for testing existing psychodynamic theories of behavior, but provides a potentially more influential approach than heretofore available for modifying behavioral patterns. Certainly, most psychodynamic theorists would agree that inappropriate anxiety is the nuclear factor in neurotic behavior. Signs and symptoms represent the inadequate reparative attempts to alleviate the inappropriate anxiety. If these theories are correct, then instantaneous replacement of irrelevant anxiety with positive pleasant feelings might provide the key to replacing undesirable behavior with more adaptive patterns. Our limited experience in patients indicates that this is a possibility. Repugnance for the sexual act, for example, can be transformed to sexual satisfaction by physical induction of pleasure by electrical means. The neurotic avoidance patterns of the phobic patient can be rapidly eliminated and depressive symptoms can be promptly dispelled with brain stimulation. On the basis of preliminary studies, these therapeutic potentials deserve extensive exploration.

Attitude, that is, motivation, is recognized to have a significant role in learning. The ability to induce desirable motivational states could aid considerably in establishing healthy patterns of behavior, specifically by influencing the affect associated with learned patterns. If acts for the benefit of society or for ourselves could be made consistently pleasurable, and those detrimental could be made painful by appropriately programmed technics, then our automatic self-operating behavioral patterns, or conscience, would be much healthier.

True, electrical stimulation of the brain has been confined to a very small number of very sick patients. But the data obtained from such limited studies may lead to a practical means of stimulating specific brain structures—perhaps through use of chemical compounds. As with nearly all potentially useful agents, however, there is danger, since unscrupulous use could motivate recipients toward undesirable, maladaptive acts of behavior. Already there is widespread use of narcotics which activate this system, but with undesirable side-effects that far outweigh the potential benefits derived from activating the pleasure response. The need for an effective pleasure-inducing compound is vividly illustrated, however, by the large numbers of people so impoverished in their capacity to experience enjoyment that they undergo the tortures of addiction for the fleeting pleasure offered by narcotics. An interesting side-note is that a large number of the addicts studied in our program have shown, even with the insensitive conventional scalp EEG, suggestible evidence of malfunction of the central physiologic pathways for pleasure. This finding suggests that addiction is a complication of desperate attempts at self-treatment.

Learning obviously contributes to the determination of one's affective response to environmental stimuli. The demonstration that stimulation of specific brain sites alters affect, and therefore affective response to environmental stimuli, provides us with at least some rough initial data about the way in which the brain acts as a substrate for the physiologic phenomena of thinking and feeling.

The second significant field in which integration of the inspective-introspective approach should prove fruitful concerns the physiologic basis of memory and its relation to behavior. In recent years this has been one of the most active and exciting fields of research in biologic psychiatry. It is unnecessary to go into detail about this work, since it was the theme of our Society meeting two years ago. The significance of these investigations was comprehensively presented by Dr. Ralph Gerard. Studies of the process of memory are being conducted in all the basic neurosciences, and have become a subject of preoccupation for many bio-mathematicians as well.

Man's behavior, although principally biologically motivated, is also determined by learned experiences, that is, memory. Incoming stimuli are perceived and behaviorally responded to in accordance with previous experiences. Considerable psychodynamic research has been devoted to the establishment of relationships between previous experiences and present behavioral patterns. The data suggest that certain periods in life are critical in establishing basic patterns, a concept that has recently come under the intense investigation of animal behaviorists. The psychoanalytic concept of transference is based on the reappearance of these early behavioral patterns in the doctor-patient relationship; psychotherapy with the transference technic is essentially an attempt to give insight into and correctively manipulate the interpersonal relationship.

Although this approach has yielded considerable data, it has not proved very effective therapeutically. The doctor and patient both gain insight as fixed behavioral patterns become evident, but faulty patterns based on early memory are not readily changed. It would seem, however, that if it became possible to obliterate memories, or through chemical means to facilitate the imprinting of new memories, or to do both, then behavior could be redirected (effective repatterning) to provide beneficial psychotherapy. Even with better use of existing technology, however, improvement in the learning mechanism is feasible and is now, in fact, being tried in some experimental schools. In his address two years ago, Dr. Gerard advocated extensive computerized programming of the learning process.

Judging from the progress of basic biological research, before long appropriate relearning of behavior will probably be possible through use of biologic methods combined with programmed learning. These methods, if combined with the proper use of pleasure, would constitute a specific and logical, effective approach to the treatment of behavioral disorders derived from faulty learning experiences. Methods may be developed for widespread application of one or both of these approaches to the modification of behavior derived from poor programming. If so, it could help to eliminate the prejudices, biases, and negative emotions that pervade various cultures of our world, which have created the dangerous unrest and turmoil so provocatively described last year by Dr. Hudson Hoagland in his Presidential Address.

If we look into each of these major aspects of behavior and psychiatric illness, it is evident that the basis of all psychiatry is biologic. Although all behavior is a result of nervous system activity, our biologic approach will be advanced if we simultaneously look at mental activity, a product of the biologic process. It becomes obvious that the terms "psychiatry" and "biologic psychiatry" are synonymous. But for sentimental and historical significance, "biologic psychiatry" will probably continue to specify those studies conducted by a group of neuroscientists devoted to the intensive investigation of the relation between brain function and disordered behavior.

REFERENCES

BLUELER, E. (1950). *Dementia Praecox or The Group of Schizophrenias,* International Universities Press, New York.

HEATH, R. G. (1967). Schizophrenia: Studies of pathogenesis, *in Biological and Clinical Aspects of the Central Nervous System,* Symposium of Sandoz Ltd., Basle.

HEATH, R. G. & KRUPP, I. M. (1967). Schizophrenia as an immunologic disorder. *Arch. Gen. Psychiat.* 16:1.

HOCH, P. H. (1961). Introduction: The achievements of biological psychiatry, in *Recent Advances in Biological Psychiatry, Vol. III,* Wortis, J. (ed.), Grune and Stratton, New York, pp. 1-10.

"Lithium" (leading article) (1969). *Lancet* 1:709.

OLDS, J. (1962). Hypothalmic substraits of reward. *Physiol.* Rev. 42:554.

RADO, S. (1956). Emergency behavior—with an introduction to the dynamics of conscience, *in Psychoanalysis of Behavior—the Collected Papers of Sandor Rado, Vol. I:* 1922-1956, Grune and Stratton, New York, pp. 214-234.

25

RELATION OF TARAXEIN TO SCHIZOPHRENIA

Robert G. Heath, Andrew F. Guschwan,

and John W. Coffey

Since 1956, numerous reports have been published describing taraxein, a protein fraction obtained from serum of schizophrenic patients which has now been characterized as a specific subfraction of schizophrenic gamma G. immunoglobulin (IgG) (1-3). When administered to normal monkeys, taraxein induces focal electroencephalographic (EEG) changes in the septal region, and occasionally in the hippocampus and amygdaloid nucleus, concomitant with catatonic signs. Its intravenous administration to volunteer-subjects induces a range of behavioral signs and symptoms characteristic of the psychotic schizophrenic patient.

In this study, conducted in an attempt to delineate more clearly the relation of taraxein to the clinical disorder of schizophrenia, clinical data were collected for the last 56 subjects (since December 1966) from whom serum was obtained for fractionating and subsequent assaying in the rhesus monkey.

MATERIALS AND METHODS

The 38 schizophrenic patient-donors for this study were selected from routine admissions to the Tulane Psychiatry Service of Charity Hospital of Louisiana at New Orleans. The two principal criteria for selection were (1) establishment, after initial examination, of a tentative diagnosis

From Tulane University School of Medicine, 1430 Tulane Avenue, New Orleans, La., 70112.

Supported by a grant-in-aid from the Ittleson Family Foundation, New York, N. Y.

Presented at the Annual Meeting of the American Psychiatric Association, May, 1969, Miami Beach, Florida.

Reprinted, by permission of author and editor, from: *Diseases of the Nervous System*, 31:391-395, 1970.

of schizophrenia and (2) conspicuous manifestation of severe psychosis. In some subjects, initially selected as schizophrenic, more complete study resulted in a change in diagnosis; such patients then served as control donors.

About half the schizophrenic patient-donors were on medication at the time of hospital admission. For the others, we tried to withhold medication for one or more blood drawings, but the patient's welfare was always a principal consideration. History of medication was always made a part of the donor's file.

Of the 18 control subjects participating in the study, 6 were healthy medical students or staff members well known to the research staff. The other 12 control subjects were patients with other diseases: 2 with systemic lupus erythematosus, 4 with myasthenia gravis, one with rheumatoid arthritis, one with multiple sclerosis, one with psychosis with brain trauma, 2 with toxic psychosis, and one with Marfan's disease. While participating in the study, all patient-donors were maintained on an adequate hospital diet with vitamin supplement.

For most of the schizophrenic patients (and some of the control subjects), serial blood drawings were done with use of the plasmapheresis ion exchange double blood-pack, which permitted about 500 ml of serum to be obtained as often as every two or three days. In this way, we could determine if psychosis-inducing (taraxein) activity in the monkey assay fluctuated with the clinical state of the donor. Plasma was withdrawn from some schizophrenic donors as few as two times and from one as many as 25 times. The plasma was thrombinized and stored as serum at minus 20°C until it was fractionated. In most instances a donor's serum was fractionated two to four times, but serum of one patient was fractionated on 64 occasions. (Sometimes blood was withdrawn only once from a subject because diagnosis was not clear-cut or, in the case of a schizophrenic patient, there was prompt remission of psychotic signs and symptoms. Such patient-subjects are not included in this survey.)

Routinely, the fractionation procedure involved diluting 70 ml serum 1:1 with phosphate buffered saline, pH 7.5. The diluted serum was then brought to 50% saturation of ammonium sulfate by addition of an equal volume of saturated ammonium sulfate solution. The precipitant formed was removed by centrifugation and dissolved in a small amount of 0.05 M TRIS HCl buffer, pH 7.5. The dissolved precipitate was dialyzed overnight against the same buffer and then applied to a 2.5 x 100 cm DEAE Sephadex A-50 column, which had been equilibrated with 0.05 M TRIS HCl buffer, pH 7.5. The column was eluted with this same buffer. Two of these columns were usually processed simultaneously (Fig. 1).

The relative protein concentration of the eluate from the columns was registered by an ultraviolet absorption detector. About the first half of the protein eluted from each column was pooled and concentrated by ultrafiltration to 20 ml.

The pooled globulin was then rechromatographed on a column similar to the first, except that it was 45 cm long. The rechromatograph procedure is the same as that used with 100 cm columns. The protein eluted

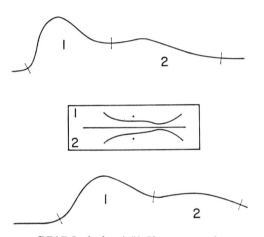

DEAE Sephadex A-50 Chromatographs
70 ml Serum TRIS pH 7.5
Fig. 1.—See title on figure. Immunoelectrophoretic analyses of each fraction show presence of IgG only.

from the 45 cm column was in a much smaller volume of buffer and was a subfraction of the IgG eluted from the 100 cm column. The elution pattern registered on the ultraviolet absorption meter consisted of one high, sharp peak, a portion of which usually contained the active protein, and one low, flattened peak consisting of inactive protein. The eluate so obtained was divided into four fractions containing about equal amounts of protein (Fig. 2). Each fraction was concentrated to 15 ml by ultrafiltration and aliquoted for injection into the assay monkey. Total protein content of these fractions ranged from 0.3 mg/ml to 3.0 mg/ml. All procedures were carried out at 4°C.

The assay rhesus monkeys were prepared with depth and cortical electrodes and a cannula was placed in the anterior horn of the left lateral ventricle of each by methods of Heath and associates (4, 5). Electrodes

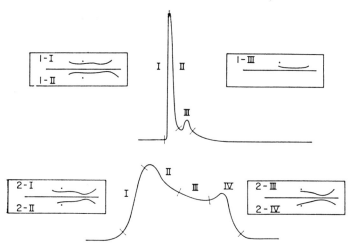

DEAE Sephadex A-50 Rechromatographs
of Fractions 1 and 2 TRIS pH 7.5

Fig. 2.—See title on figure. Immunoelectrophoretic analyses of each
fraction reveals that the sample tested in the monkey assay contained
a subfraction of pure IgG.

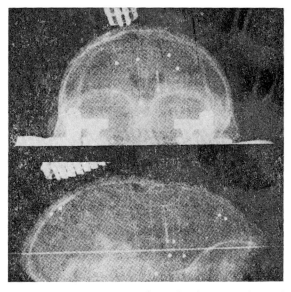

Fig. 3.—X-ray of monkey skull showing cannulas and
electrodes fixed into position.

were routinely implanted into the septal region, caudate nucleus, hypothalamus, hippocampus (bilaterally) , and over the cortex in several frontal and occipital regions (Fig. 3) .

When given intraventricularly, the serum globulin was introduced into
the monkey in increments of 0.3 ml at three hourly intervals while EEGs

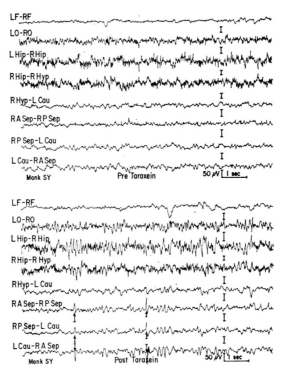

Fig. 4.—Surface and depth EEGs of a monkey that
received taraxein.

were being obtained. To determine if we were observing the same psychosis-inducing activity with intraventricular injections as we have observed since 1955 with intravenous use of serum fractions in rhesus
monkeys, we sometimes tested the serum globulins by both routes. The
fraction was injected intravenously as rapidly as possible while EEGs
were being made.

Psychosis-inducing (taraxein) activity was graded on the basis of aberrations induced in the EEG, predominantly in the septal region and
sometimes reflected in other deep limbic structures (Fig. 4) . To make the

evaluation more objective, we have recently used electronic indicators which measure changes in frequency and detect spike or slow-wave activity, or both, in the EEG (6).

RESULTS

Taraxein activity was demonstrated in serum fractions of 30 of the 38 schizophrenic patient-donors in the series at least once, and usually repeatedly. We failed to demonstrate psychosis-inducing activity in at least one sample of serum of 29 of these 30 patients. The one schizophrenic patient whose serum fractions were always psychosis-inducing in the monkey was an acutely catatonic subject with waxy flexibility. His serum was withdrawn and fractionated on four different occasions. Serum fractions of the schizophrenic donor who was used most (64 fractionations for testing from 25 blood drawings) yielded taraxein activity in the monkey test on 49 occasions.

Fractions of all control sera were inert when tested in the monkey with one exception—the serum fractions of one of the 4 patients with myasthenia gravis. On two of the four occasions when his serum was fractionated and tested in the monkey, it was psychosis-inducing. This patient-donor showed no evidence of schizophrenia on psychiatric examination or psychologic testing.

DISCUSSION

The most consistent observation from our studies is that taraxein activity is demonstrable in serum fractions of a high percentage of schizophrenic patients if plasma is withdrawn when the donors are showing full-blown secondary signs and symptoms of schizophrenia, including undeniable gross delusions and hallucinations. We have failed to demonstrate taraxein activity in serum fractions of the same patients when they were showing significant remission in signs and symptoms. And we have failed to show taraxein activity in serum fractions of chronic schizophrenic patients unless signs and symptoms of the disease are in an acute stage of exacerbation.

Medication that donors are taking does not seem to play a significant role in this phenomenon. Taraxein activity has been demonstrated in serum fractions of patients receiving medications as well as those who are receiving none. Psychosis-inducing activity has been demonstrated in plasma of patients of all diagnostic subtypes of schizophrenia (paranoid, catatonic, hebephrenic, undifferentiated). In the present study, the greatest number of schizophrenic patient-donors from whom we obtained taraxein activity were paranoid (47%), but this was proportional to the percentage of paranoid patients in the total sample (18 of 38). Of the group whose serum fractions were consistently inactive, distribution was similar; five of the donors were paranoid and 3 were undifferentiated. There was no correlation that was apparent between taraxein activity and sex or race of the plasma-donor; of the 38 schizophrenic donors, 22 were males and 16 were females, and 55% of this group were Negroes. Nor does diet seem to play a role.

Beyond these general observations, it becomes too complex at present to correlate more specifically the clinical disease, schizophrenia, and taraxein. A few of the more obvious problems that are difficult to evaluate can be cited.

Although fractionation of sera by DEAE Sephadex A-50 ion exchange chromatography has proved by far the most effective method for obtaining taraxein, the columns are by no means identical from one run to the next. When the same serum has been fractionated more than once, we have often observed differences in activity, as well as physical qualities, of the fractions. When ammonium sulfate precipitation has been the first step, we have applied half of the resuspended precipitate to each of two 2.5 x 100 cm columns that were packed together seemingly under identical conditions, and there have been significant differences between the fractions yielded by the two columns. Variations have included rate of flow, concentration of proteins eluting from the columns in equivalent time periods, and positions where taraxein activity appears on the uvicord graph.

Column fractionation is still an imprecise technic, particularly with the ion exchange medium. But our minor modifications of the column fractionation method are increasing our effectiveness in obtaining taraxein. Fractions obtained by this method contain only IgG, but since taraxein is such a minute portion of the schizophrenic IgG fraction, there are major problems in technic. For the monkey assay it is necessary to obtain the IgG subfraction. Assay of the entire IgG fraction of schizophrenic serum does not yield taraxein activity, and we postulate that it has been too overdiluted by inactive IgG molecules.

Adequate data have been accumulated to suggest that serum taraxein levels of schizophrenic patients are highest with onset of acute signs and symptoms. Only on a few occasions have we demonstrated taraxein in serum fractions of chronic schizophrenic and in remitting acutely schizophrenic patients. But other variables compound the problem. Just as responses of the assay monkeys to administration of taraxein vary, so have the responses of human volunteer recipients of taraxein. These observations, coupled with findings indicating that taraxein levels fluctuate in schizophrenic patients at different stages in the course of the disease, lead us to surmise that one or more co-factors may be involved. Support for this speculation are the reports from other research centers, including the Worcester Foundation for Experimental Biology, the Lafayette Clinic at Detroit, and the Soviet Academy of Medical Sciences, that other globulin fractions of schizophrenic sera are often implicated in the disease.

In appraising the data, one must remember that ours is an imprecise system. A successful passive transfer, even if it works only rarely, has considerable significance because so many variables are involved. The passive transfer of taraxein is dependent on the state of the patient-donor of serum, on the efficiency of the fractionation procedure used to purify the schizophrenic IgG (taraxein), and on the condition of the recipient assay monkey or human volunteer. The fact that we have occassionally refractionated IgG that has been inactive in the monkey test and have later obtained psychosis-inducing taraxein suggests that the taraxein titer is sometimes below threshold for our assay system.

Passive transfer demonstration can never be an accurate diagnostic test. But we believe it gives direction for eventual development of a diagnostic test, and we are pursuing this in our laboratories.

Although our data suggest that taraxein is present in all subtypes of acutely ill schizophrenic patients and that it induces aberrations in brain activity and consequent behavioral signs and symptoms of the disease, the many variables involved prevent us, at this stage of our investigations, to substantiate our contention that schizophrenia is probably a single disease entity.

REFERENCES

1. HEATH, R. G., MARTENS, S., LEACH, B. E., COHEN, M., & ANGEL, C.: Effect on behavior in humans with the administration of taraxein. *Amer. J. Psychiat.* 114:14, 1957.
2. HEATH, R. G., KRUPP, I. M., BYERS, L. W., & LILJEKVIST, J.: Schizophrenia as an immunologic disorder. *Arch. Gen. Psychiat.* 16:1, 1967.
3. HEATH, R. G., & KRUPP, I. M.: Schizophrenia as a specific biologic disease. *Amer. J. Psychiat.* 124:37, 1968.
4. BECKER, H. C., FOUNDS, W. L., PEACOCK, S. M., HEATH, R. G., LLEWELLYN, R. C., & MICKLE, W. A.: A roentgenographic stereotaxic technique for implanting and maintaining electrodes in the brain of man. *Electroenceph. Clin. Neurophysiol.* 9:533, 1957.
5. HEATH, R. G., & FOUNDS, W. L.: A perfusion cannula for intracerebral microinjections. *Electroenceph. Clin. Neurophysiol.* 12:930, 1960.
6. SALTZBERG, B., LUSTICK, L., & HEATH, R. G.: Correlates of depth spiking in scalp-recorded electroencephalograms in monkeys. Presented at the meeting of the Society of Biological Psychiatry, Miami, May, 1969.

26

COMPARATIVE BEHAVIORAL AND BIOCHEMICAL EFFECTS OF TRANYL-CYPROMINE AND CYSTEINE ON NORMAL CONTROLS AND SCHIZOPHRENIC PATIENTS

H. E. Himwich, N. Narasimhachari, B. Heller, J. Spaide,
L. Haskovec, M. Fujimori, and K. Tabushi

Beginning with the investigations of Pollin et al. in 1961, twelve papers (1-12) have been written on schizophrenic patients regarding the behavioral effects evoked whether by feeding DL-methionine or L-cysteine simultaneously with the administration of an MAO inhibitor, either iproniazid (Marsilid), isocarboxazid (Marplan) or tranylcypromine (Parnate). Behavioral worsenings, though not necessarily of the same kinds, were reported in all of these instances associated with the administration of the combined treatments. In seven of these twelve studies (5, 6, 7, 8, 10, 11, 12) increases of tryptophan metabolites, especially tryptamine, were found in the urine before and during the worsening of behavioral symptoms. Chromatographic studies have been made in only two series of patients for N-dimethyltryptaminic compounds: N-dimethyltryptamine (DMT), 5-hydroxy-N-dimethyltryptamine (bufotenin) and 5-methoxy-N-dimethyltryptamine (5-MeODMT). The formation of these potentially psychotomimetic derivatives from the naturally occurring amines is facilitated by the enzyme discovered by Axelrod (13) chiefly in the rabbit lung (Fig. 1) and more recently by Morgan and Mandell in human brain (14). In one of these, Tanimukai et al. (12), using thin-layer chromatography chiefly, reported three potentially psychotomimetic N-dimethyltryp-

Reprinted, by permission of author and editor, from: *Life Sciences*, 9:1021-1032, 1970.

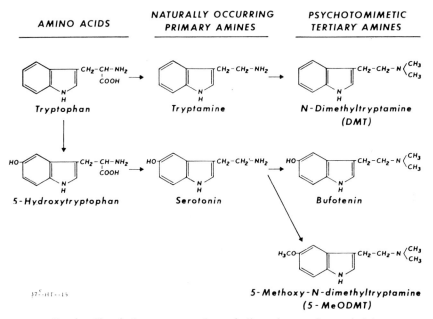

FIG. 1.—Chemical structures and metabolic pathways of some indole compounds.

taminic compounds in the urine of four chronic schizophrenic patients while experiencing exacerbations of their schizophrenic symptoms and in the other, Kakimoto et al. (9) had negative findings. However, the latter employed paper chromatography which is less sensitive than the thin-layer method. Despite the long continued interest in the behavioral alterations and biochemical changes evoked by the combined treatments, there have been no results on normal controls, and the purpose of the present experiments is to make up for this lack.

METHODS

In previous work from our laboratory, Tanimukai et al. (12, 15) have made behavioral and biochemical observations on four chronic schizophrenic patients before, during and after a chemical stress evoked by tranylcypromine and L-cysteine. In the present observations, the methods of the previous experiments were largely repeated. These investigations started on July 1, 1969, simultaneously for six normal controls, college boys between 19 and 22 years of age, and two schizophrenic patients, 57 and 60 years of age. The two groups were not only studied under similar environmental conditions but also by the same biochemical methods. The study was begun with a control period of 21 days, during which behavioral and biochemical baselines were established. For the experimental period, 10 mg of tranylcypromine were given to all the subjects three times a day for seven days. On day eight, L-cysteine was added and the combined medication was administered for 20 days. The L-cysteine was administered in 5 gram increments up to a maximum of 20 g per day. Each dose level was given for a five-day period. The experimental period was followed by one of after-loading, two weeks for the normals and three weeks for the schizophrenic patients, and during this time they received neither tranylcypromine nor cysteine. Thus, the study was completed on September 1 for the normals and on September 8 for the two schizophrenics.

The subjects were placed on a rigorously controlled, weighed diet and the actual individual food intakes were recorded. All foods known to contain preformed indoleamines were eliminated. The calculated tryptophan, methionine and cysteine contents of the diet offered were 1.27, 2.64, and 1.62 g per day respectively. The entire study was done on a double-blind basis.

The six normal controls were selected from a group of thirty-five volunteers. They were the sole occupants of the same ward which had been used in all previous observations on schizophrenic patients. Two chronic schizophrenic patients with active symptoms were chosen and they occupied a ward across the hall but had their meals in the same ward though in a different room than the normal controls. All psychoactive drugs were withheld from the schizophrenics prior to the study, 17 days for No. 1 and 62 days for No. 2, as well as throughout its duration.

Rounds were made daily on all eight subjects. Once each week the psychiatrists specifically assessed the behavior of the controls as well as that of the two schizophrenic patients. The evaluations of the subjects were done on a tripartite basis. Rockland and Pollin's (16) total rating score is the sum of three major components, general appearance and manner, affect and mood, and thought content and thought process. In addition, a second, ad hoc, more "loose" type of psychiatric evaluation was constructed. It consisted of the classic categories of psychiatric evaluation such as thinking process, mood, clarity of consciousness and perception of the surroundings, level of energy, drive and psychomotor activity, sleep, dreams and physical side effects. The weekly physical checkups included the measurement of blood pressure, heart rate, respiratory rate, weight, temperature, and a standardized neurological examination.

Twenty-four hour collections of urine were made throughout the study. These were acidified to pH 2 with 6 N HCl and stored frozen at —20°C before use. Ten percent of the 24-hour urine collection was used for the analyses of tryptamine (17), total 3-indoleacetic acid (3-IAA) (18), and creatinine (19).

For the separation of amines from the urine samples, at least 75% of 24-hour collection (concentrated to 10% of volume) was used either for ion exchange chromatography on Dowex 50 (H+ form) or solvent extraction by ethyl acetate at pH 10-10.4. The basic fractions were then again fractionated to separate the primary and secondary amines (20) and final purified concentrates used for thin-layer (TLC) and gas-liquid (GLC) chromatographic identification. Recovery experiments were carried out by adding known quantities of DMT, bufotenin and 5-MeODMT (10 μg each) to urine samples which were negative for these compounds and subjecting them to the same methods of separation. Recoveries of 75-80% were obtained in both ion exchange and solvent extraction methods. Two spray reagents, p-dimethylaminocinnamaldehyde and diazotized o-tolidine, were used for identification in TLC method. For gas-liquid chromatography, the free amines and their trimethylsilyl (TMS) derivatives were used. The trimethylsilyl derivatives were prepared by a method recently developed by Narasimhachari et al. (21), using "Regisil" [Bis (trimethylsilyl) trifluoroacetamide plus 1% trimethylchlorosilane] where the trimethylsilyl group was shown to be on the indolic nitrogen by mass spectrometry. The trimethylsilyl derivatives of amine fractions from the urine samples were run on a 6 ft. 3% SE 30 column on a programmed temperature 140° with a rate of rise of 5° per minute and with a standard hydrocarbon mixture (C_{12}-C_{24}). The methylene unit values (MU) of the distinct peaks in the samples were compared with the values obtained for standards. In some cases heptafluorobutyryl (HFB) derivatives were used (22) for GLC. In a few cases, where TLC and GLC results were positive for DMT or 5-MeODMT or bufotenin, the samples were run on preparative TLC or preparative GLC methods and the fractions corresponding to these three amines were collected and read on Aminco Bowman Spectrofluorometer and fluorescence spectra recorded at activation 295 mμ. In this study the results were reported as positive for any of these three dimethylated indoleamines only when they were positive by at least two of the methods used for their identification.

RESULTS

Fig. 2 is a diagrammatic representation of the behavioral and chromatographic results. The symptoms of Patient No. 1 were more florid than those of Patient No. 2 and, correspondingly, the highest total scores were 56 and 44 respectively.

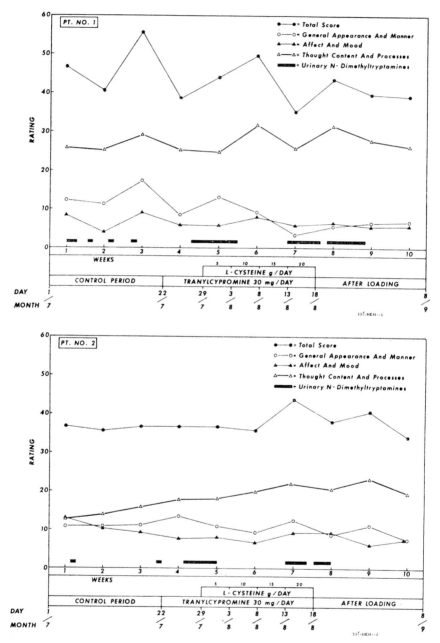

FIG. 2.—Patients' behavioral ratings according to Rockland and Pollin (16) and detection of urinary N-dimethyltryptamines.

During the control period, Patient No. 1 proved to be a clear-cut para-noid, chronic schizophrenic with florid and continuous auditory hallucin-ations and paranoid delusions. His delusional ideas were systematized and centered around the army and its officers. An analysis of the total scores reveals that the second and third peaks are obviously related to increases in thought content and processes because the other two para-meters decreased in intensity at these times in comparison with the controls. The disturbances of the thought processes included some ap-parently new delusions in which all of his five brothers occupied import-ant positions.

Chromatographic examinations revealed that the 24-hour urinary sam-ples were sporadically positive for DMT or DMT and bufotenin on July 4, 5, 8, 12, and 16 and negative for the other 16 days of the control period. From July 22 to July 28 on tranylcypromine alone and July 29 to August 2 when the patient received tranylcypromine plus 5 g of L-cysteine, he showed DMT and bufotenin or DMT, bufotenin and 5-MeODMT and in greated concentrations than during the control period. These appeared in the urine preceding significant behavioral worsenings. The highest concentrations were observed from August 13 to August 26 with the single exception of August 19. These values were higher than any observed in Patient No. 2.

During the control period, Patient No. 2 was found to be a hebephrenic type of chronic schizophrenic, socially withdrawn and intellectually re-gressed. His thinking was fragmented with obsessional traits and thought content was poor. He exhibited only moderate variations in general ap-pearance and manner as well as in mood and affect (see Fig. 2, Patient No. 2). The increased total scores during and following the administra-tion of tranylcypromine and L-cysteine were largely due to worsening of thought content and processes, especially of his obsessional thinking as well as the formation of new delusions.

Chromatographic evaluations revealed that during the control period he showed mere traces of DMT and only for two days, July 5 and 21, of the 21-day control period. From July 26 through July 31, DMT and bufotenin or DMT, bufotenin and 5-MeODMT were detected in his urine and in larger concentrations than during the control period. Finally, from August 13 through August 20, with the single exception of August 17, DMT and bufotenin were observed in the highest concentrations for this patient.

Both patients continued to excrete these urinary compounds during the first part of the after-loading period, Patient No. 1 for nine days and Patient No. 2 for three days. It may be said in general that the three

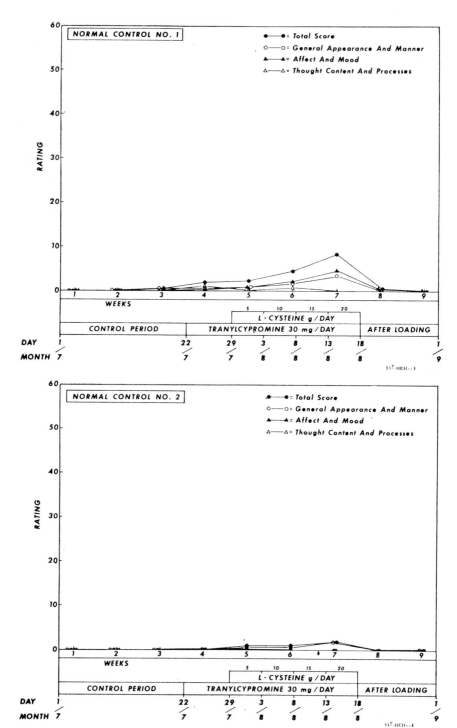

Fig. 3.—Behavioral ratings of normal controls according to Rockland and Pollin (16) and detection of urinary N-dimethyltryptamines.

N-dimethyltryptaminic compounds were detected in the urine before and during behavioral worsening. It is essential to interpose a remark in regard to the concentrations of the urinary N-dimethyltryptamines. The differences between them were semiquantitative and comparative, depending upon the relative heights of the peaks of the gas-liquid chromatograms.

In Fig. 3 are presented the results of two normal controls. Control No. 1 yielded the highest total score according to the rating scale of Rockland and Pollin (16) and Control No. 2 the lowest, 8.2 and 2.0 respectively. No psychopathological symptoms such as hallucinations, illusions, delusions, obsessions or psychotic behavior, were observed in any of the controls. During the experimental load they reacted with rather nonspecific physical side effects such as fatigue, dizziness, nausea and insomnia. These were mild during the initial phases of experimental loading, but gradually became more severe towards the end. At the peak of the combined treatment, occasional severe gastric cramps and diarrhea as well as severe insomnia occurred in most of the controls. These side effects were much more prominent in the controls than in the patients. The mild depressions which occurred in two normals appeared to be psychological reactions to the physical side effects of the combined treatment rather than results of the biochemical load *per se* and ceased soon after the treatments were stopped. Dreams, however, were more numerous, vivid and frequently in technicolor, especially during the first part of the after-loading period. Neither in the schizophrenics nor in the normals were disturbances of consciousness observed in terms of impairment of the sensorium or in awareness of their identity and environment.

In regard to chromatographic results, in no instance were any of the three N-dimethylated compounds detected in the urine specimens using our criterion of identification by two different methods. It is true, however, that occasionally a bufotenin-like spot was detected by TLC using p-dimethylaminocinnamaldehyde but not with diazotized o-tolidine and in accordance with our criterion of a minimum detection by two methods those urines are reported negative. The question of bufotenin in the urine is complicated and has been reviewed by Himwich (23).

Neither 3-indoleacetic acid (3-IAA) nor creatinine exhibited significant changes throughout the study. The starting and peak loading values of urinary tryptamine, $\mu g/day$, were for the first normal 200 and the second normal 100 and rose to 3040 and 1750 respectively. Patient No. 1 started at 40 and Patient No. 2 at 130 and increased to 1220 and 2850 respectively. The average tryptamine levels during the period of tranylcypromine and cysteine loading for the two normals were 2333 $\mu g \pm 455$ (SD) and 1443 $\mu g \pm 328$ (SD) and for the two patients, 834 $\mu g \pm 205$ (SD) and 1966

μg $\pm$ 537 respectively. It is, therefore, evident that in the production of N-dimethyltryptamines the actual amounts of tryptamine in urine and presumably in the blood are not the limiting factor but rather the ability to methylate tryptamine.

It is true that our normals and patients did not belong to the same age group. But there is evidence in the literature that N-methylation is not an age dependent phenomenon. Morgan and Mandell (14) have shown the presence of an enzyme which N-methylates various indole ethylamine substrates both in infant parietal cortex and in adult frontal cortex. Furthermore, studies similar to ours made on chronic patients (24) from 21-52 years of age have also disclosed N-dimethylated trypta-mines in the urine. In our studies with acute schizophrenics, Heller et al. (25) demonstrated the presence of N-dimethylated indoleamines in blood and urine samples in nonmedicated acute schizophrenics 22-55 years of age. Thus, the age differences between our normals and patients could not have contributed to the differences in the behavioral alterations and biochemical changes observed in our two groups of patients.

SUMMARY

In view of the previous and present positive results on schizophrenic patients, it is important to note that in no instance did any of the six normal controls exhibit any signs of schizophrenic-like symptoms. Though the normals, like the schizophrenics revealed increases of urinary trypta-mine, unlike the schizophrenics, their chromatograms were negative even for bufotenin, indicating a biological difference between the two groups of subjects, namely, that the normals may not be able to dimethylate tryptamines. The close association between the worsening of the schizo-phrenic symptoms and the increased concentrations and frequency of occurrence in the urine of the three N-dimethyltryptaminic compounds is noted. Furthermore, an etiological significance of a biochemical factor is indicated by the detection of the urinary N-dimethyltryptamines before behavioral worsening became apparent.

ACKNOWLEDGMENTS

We gratefully acknowledge the financial aid extended for this study by Geigy Pharmaceuticals, Division of Geigy Chemical Corporation and Roche Laboratories, Division of Hoffmann-La Roche Inc.; the gift of tranylcypromine from Smith, Kline and French Laboratories; Mrs. Rowena Ginther for helping with the management of diets; Mr. LeRoy Elam, Clinical Psychologist, for helping in the selection of the normal controls by evaluating the MMPI results; and various members of our nurs-ing department for their essential assistance with the patients.

REFERENCES

1. POLLIN, W., CARDON, P. V. & KETY, S. S. *Science* 133, 104 (1961).
2. PARK, L. C., BALDESSARINI, R. J., & KETY, S. S. *Arch. Gen. Psychiat.* 12, 346 (1965).
3. BRUNE, G. G., & HIMWICH, H. E. *Neuro-Psychopharmacology*, p. 465. Elsevier, Amsterdam (1961).
4. BRUNE, G. G., & HIMWICH, H. E. *J. nerv. ment. Dis.* 134, 447 (1962).
5. BRUNE, G. G., & HIMWICH, H. E. *Recent Advances in Biological Psychiatry*, p. 144. Plenum Press, New York (1963).
6. BERLET, H. H., MATSUMOTO, K., PSCHEIDT, G. R., SPAIDE, J., BULL, C., & HIMWICH, H. E. *Arch. Gen. Psychiat.* 13, 521 (1965).
7. ALEXANDER, F., CURTIS, G. C., III, SPRINGE, H., & CROSLEY, A. P. JR. *J. nerv. ment. Dis.* 137, 135 (1963).
8. SPRINGE, H., PARKER, C. M., JAMESON, D., & ALEXANDER, F. *J. nerv. ment. Dis.* 137, 246 (1963).
9. KAKIMOTO, Y., SANO, I., KANAZAWA, A., TSUJIO, T., & KANEKO, Z. *Nature* 216, 1110 (1967).
10. SPAIDE, J., TANIMUKAI, H., BUENO, J., & HIMWICH, H. E. *Arch. Gen. Psychiat.* 18, 658 (1968).
11. SPAIDE, J., NEVELN, L., TOLENTINO, J., & HIMWICH, H. E. *Biol. Psychiat.* 1, 227 (1969).
12. TANIMUKAI, H., GINTHER, R., SPAIDE, J., BUENO, J. R., & HIMWICH, H. E. *Brit J. Psychiat.* (in press).
13. AXELROD, J. *Science,* 134, 343 (1961).
14. MORGAN, M., & MANDELL, A. J. *Science,* 165, 492 (1969).
15. TANIMUKAI, H., GINTHER, R., SPAIDE, J., BUENO, J. R., & HIMWICH, H. E. *Recent Advances in Biological Psychiatry*, p. 6. Plenum Press, New York (1968).
16. ROCKLAND, L. H., & POLLIN, W. *Arch. Gen. Psychiat.* 12, 23 (1965).
17. SJOERDSMA, A., OATES, J. A., ZALTZMAN, P., & UDENFRIEND, S. *J. Pharmac. exp. Ther.* 126, 217 (1959).
18. WEISSBACH, H., KING, W., SJOERDSMA, A., & UDENFRIEND, S. *J. biol. Chem.* 234, 81 (1959).
19. HAWK, P. B., OSER, B. L., & SUMMERSON, W. H. *Practical Physiological Chemistry*, p. 839. Blakiston Co., Philadelphia (1951).
20. GROSS, H., & FRANZEN, FR. *Biochem. Z.* 340, 403 (1964).
21. NARASIMHACHARI, N., SPAIDE, J., & HELLER, B. (in preparation).
22. VESSMAN, J., MOSS, A. M., HORNING, M. G., & HORNING, E. C. *Analyt. Letters* 2, 81, (1969).
23. HIMWICH, H. E. *Biochemistry, Schizophrenias and the Affective Illnesses*, p. 79. Williams & Wilkins, Baltimore (1970).
24. ROSENGARTEN, H., SZEMIS, A., PIOTROWSKI, A., ROMASZEWSKA, K., MATSUMOTO, H., STENCKA, K., & JUS, A. (in preparation).
25. HELLER, B., NARASIMHACHARI, N., SPAIDE, J., HASKOVEC, L., & HIMWICH, H. E. *Experientia* 26, 503 (1970).

27

SERUM-ENZYME CHANGES IN NEWLY ADMITTED PSYCHIATRIC PATIENTS

Herbert Meltzer, Leonard Elkun, and Ronald A. Moline

Increased activity of the enzymes creatine phosphokinase (CPK) (E.C.2.7.3.2) and aldolase (E.C.4.1.2.7) has been reported in the serum of acutely psychotic patients of all diagnostic types: acute schizophrenic patients, manic-depressive patients, and patients with psychotic depression (1-5). Chronically psychotic patients, schizophrenic or depressed, did not have any increase in the activity of these enzymes even when they were experiencing an exacerbation of their psychosis which necessitated rehospitalization (3-5). Nonpsychotic severely anxious or depressed hospitalized psychiatric patients also had no increase in the activity of these enzymes (3, 4).

The increased activity of CPK or aldolase, or both, was generally present at the onset of a psychotic episode in the acute patients and lasted for five to ten days after hospitalization, but could be as brief as 1 day or, in one instance, as long as 51 days (3, 4). The increased enzyme activities ranged from 5-fold to 50-fold above the limits of controls (3, 4). Other enzymes were surveyed in the serum of the acutely psychotic patients: lactic dehydrogenase (LDH), acid phosphatase, alkaline phosphatase, serum glutamic oxalacetic transaminase (SGOT), and serum glutamic pyruvic transaminase (SGPT) (3, 4). No increase in the activity of these enzymes was found in the specimens with increased CPK or aldolase activity (3, 4). Isozyme studies established that the increased CPK and aldolase activity was of the muscle type, rather than brain or

Submitted for publication April 17, 1969.

From the Department of Psychiatry, University of Chicago Pritzker School of Medicine (Drs. Meltzer, Elkun, and Moline), and the Illinois State Psychiatric Institute, Chicago (Dr. Moline).

Reprint requests to Department of Psychiatry, 950 E. 59th St., Chicago 60637 (Dr. Meltzer).

Reprinted, by permission of author and editor, from: *Archives of General Psychiatry*, 21:731-738, 1969.

liver (3, 4). The possible influence of physical activity, nonspecific stress, oral medication, corticosteroid excretion, and tissue catabolism on the serum activity of these enzymes was considered and these factors did not appear to account for the increased enzyme activity (3, 4). Intramuscular injections of chlorpromazine (Thorazine) can produce increased activity of CPK or aldolase in some patients (6-8).

Since the increased CPK activity appeared to be confined to the acutely psychotic patients, did not appear to be due to the nonspecific factors mentioned above, and, moreover, increased activity of the muscle-type CPK has been found to occur in patients with known acute brain diseases such as brain trauma and cerebrovascular accidents (9, 10), it was proposed that the determination of serum-CPK activity might be a useful test for confirming the diagnosis of acute psychosis and could be the basis for distinguishing a subgroup of acute psychosis with a common pathophysiologic basis. The present study was organized to confirm and extend some of these findings and hypotheses.

METHODS

Patients.—Blood samples were obtained at the time of admission from 251 patients admitted to the Illinois State Psychiatric Institute and the Psychiatry, Neurology, Medical, and Neurosurgical Services of Billings Hospital of the University of Chicago. Diagnosis was established by the clinical staff of these institutions according to the classification of the *Diagnostic and Statistical Manual of Mental Disorders-II,* of the American Psychiatric Association. Discharge diagnoses were used wherever possible, rather than admission diagnoses. The patients were grouped into acutely psychotic patients experiencing their first hospitalization for a psychotic episode, acutely psychotic patients undergoing more than their first hospitalization for a psychotic episode, chronically psychotic patients, nonpsychotic psychiatric patients (neuroses and character disorders), patients with organic brain syndromes, acute or chronic, including cases of toxic psychoses, and neurologic and neurosurgical patients. Careful note was made as to whether any of the patients had received intramuscular medications of any kind prior to obtaining the blood sample.

Serum, or occasionally plasma, was collected as soon as possible after admission to the hospital. This was usually within 16 hours and never more than 48 hours. Twenty-three patients were hospitalized on a research ward at the Illinois State Psychiatric Institute and had blood taken on an almost daily basis, generally at 8:00 A.M. but at other times as well. After clotting for one hour at room temperature, the serum was removed and frozen for assay at a later time, generally within 48 hours. Enzyme activity has been found to be stable for at least one month's time at 0°C (11).

CPK, aldolase, SGOT, and LDH were determined by spectrophotometric methods in which series of coupled enzyme reactions result in the reduction of nicotinamide nucleotides (12-15). As a check on our standard assay for CPK, the CPK activity in serum was occasionally determined by another method which does not involve a series of coupled enzyme reactions, but measures the phosphate released from the hydrolysis of creatine phosphate synthesized by CPK action (16).

The isoenzymes of CPK were determined by two methods: cellulose acetate electrophoresis (17) and a batch-separation method (employing DEAE-Sephadex) (9, 18).

Controls.—Normal limits of serum-CPK activity with the method used in our laboratory were obtained by determining the activity in 125 subjects who were accepted as blood donors at Billings Hospital or who had no disease at the time of preemployment physical exams. Serum samples were also obtained from 20 laboratory workers and hospital employees.

RESULTS

Serum-CPK Activity in Normals.—The mean serum-CPK activity of the 145 controls is presented in Table 1, along with separate data for male and female controls. The frequency distribution of the enzyme activity for men and women is presented as part of Table 2. The data in Table 2 suggest that the serum-CPK activity of normal controls is not normally distributed, particularly for women, being slightly skewed towards lower values. Mean, "trimmed" mean, and median values are not, however, appreciably different. The serum-CPK activity for men and for women is significantly different at the 0.05 level of confidence, using the Mann-Whitney U test. The upper limit of normal of CPK in our laboratory, for admission blood samples, is 82 international units (IU) per liter (mean $+$ three standard deviations). For hospitalized subjects, the upper limit of normal for serum-CPK activity is 50 IU-liter.

Acute Psychotic Reaction, First Hospitalization.—Of the 26 acutely psychotic patients of this type, 13 had significantly increased activity of serum-CPK activity in their admission serum sample. Of these 13, ten were diagnosed as schizophrenic, two as psychotic depression, and one as manic-depressive, manic phase. Of the schizophrenic patients, five had predominantly paranoid symptoms, two were the acute undifferentiated type, two were the schizo-affective type, depressed, and one was the catatonic type, excited. The mean serum-CPK activity was 412.7 IU/liter ± SE 120 IU/liter (range 121 to 1,530 IU/liter). The frequency-distribution data for this group of patients are presented in Table 2. The increased activity was present for approximately 10 to 30 days from the estimated onset of the psychosis, declining progressively towards normal limits. The median number of days of elevation was ten. The median number of days in the hospital in which the elevation was detected was six.

Of the 13 acutely psychotic patients with normal serum-CPK activity at admission, on their first hospitalization, 12 were diagnosed as schizo-

TABLE 1

SERUM-CPK (IU/LITER) ACTIVITY OF NORMAL CONTROLS

Patients	Mean	Standard Deviation	Standard Error of the Mean	Minimum	Maximum
Total Group (No. = 145)	33.147	16.56	1.37	7	165
Men (No. = 78)	39.84	19.92	2.56	12	138
Women (No. = 67)	29.22	22.46	2.80	7	165

phrenic: of these five were the paranoid type, five were the acute un-differentiated type, and two were catatonic type, excited. One patient was diagnosed as a postpartum psychosis. The mean serum-CPK activity of these patients at the time of admission was 25.5 IU/liter ± SE 5.0 IU/liter (range 7 to 68 IU/liter). The frequency-distribution data for this group of patients are presented in Table 2. Three of these patients were hospitalized on a research unit and daily serum-CPK activity was obtained. During the first two weeks of their hospitalization two of these patients had minor increases in the serum activity of CPK: 73 IU/liter and 80 IU/liter as peak values, with additional serum specimens with lesser increases preceding and following these peak values. Periods of minor increases in serum-CPK activity were generally not seen in the chronically psychotic and nonpsychotic patients studied longitudinally.

Since the increase in serum-CPK activity was short-lived even in those patients in whom it was found, a possible explanation for the failure to find the increase in one half of the acutely psychotic patients was that the first blood sample was obtained much longer after the onset of their psychoses than was the case for the first group. This was investigated by carefully reading the charts of the patients and sometimes questioning their physicians to establish the number of days between the onset of their psychoses and the time the blood sample for CPK determination was obtained (Table 3). The median number of such days for the group with high CPK was five, for the other group, six, although three of the patients in the latter group had such long intervals between onset of illness and blood sampling that had an increase been present at the onset of psychosis it would have been missed.

Psychotic Reactions with More than One Previous Admission.—Of the 94 patients in this group, 18 had increased activity of serum CPK. For these 18 patients, the mean serum-CPK activity was 370.7 IU/liter ± SE 100 IU/liter (range 105 to 1,530 IU/liter). The frequency-distribution data for this group of patients are presented in Table 2. Eleven of these 18 patients were diagnosed as acutely psychotic rather than chronically psychotic. These 11 patients had had only one or two previous admissions, the longest of which was for seven months, while many lasted only several weeks. There is some evidence that the patients with more than one admission, diagnosed as acutely psychotic, come from a different population than those diagnosed as chronic psychotic. Mean serum-CPK activity was 537.6 IU/liter ± SE 144.5 IU/liter. The frequency-distribution data of this group of acutely psychotic patients are presented in Table 2. The other seven patients were diagnosed as chronic schizophrenic reactions because of very poor recovery from their initial psychotic episodes. One had been hospitalized six times over a six-year period. The serum-CPK activity of these six chronically psychotic patients was 128.4 IU/liter ± SE 8.7 IU/liter. These two groups were significantly different from each other at greater than the 0.001 level of confidence, using the Mann-Whitney U test.

These six chronic schizophrenic patients with relatively small increases in the activity of their serum-CPK activity are to be compared with 73 other patients diagnosed as chronic schizophrenic reaction, chronic psychotic reaction, or chronic psychotic depression who had no increase in the activity of their serum-CPK activity. For these 73 patients, the mean serum-CPK activity was 27.2 IU/liter ± SE 2.2 IU/liter (range 6 to 89 IU/liter). The frequency-distribution data for this group of patients are presented in Table 2. Seven of these patients hospitalized on a research unit had daily determinations of serum-CPK activity and at no time was an increase in serum-CPK activity detected. Interestingly, no patient diagnosed as acutely psychotic who had had more than one psychiatric admission had normal serum-CPK activity.

Nonpsychotic Psychiatric Patients.—Admission blood samples were ob-

TABLE 2

FREQUENCY DISTRIBUTION OF PEAK SERUM-CPK ACTIVITY IN NORMAL CONTROLS, PSYCHIATRIC PATIENTS, AND NEUROLOGIC PATIENTS

Diagnostic Groups	Total	0-10	11-20	21-30	31-40	41-50	51-80	81-100	101-150	151-200	201-500	501-1,000	1,001-2,000
Normal men	78	—	11	13	25	11	16	1	1	—	—	—	—
Normal women	67	1	28	20	8	2	7	—	1	—	—	—	—
Acute psychotics, 1st hospitalization	26	2	4	3	3	—	1	—	3	2	5	1	2
Acute psychotics, multiple hospitalizations	11	—	—	—	—	—	—	—	1	2	4	2	2
Chronic psychotics	80	11	21	18	11	4	6	2	6	1	—	2	—
Nonpsychotics	94	18	25	21	15	6	8	1	—	—	—	—	—
Chronic brain syndromes	7	1	2	2	1	1	—	—	—	—	—	—	—
Acute brain syndromes	6	—	—	—	—	—	—	—	2	—	3	—	1
Neurologic patients	20	1	2	1	4	2	6	—	—	2	2	—	—

tained from 94 nonpsychotic hospitalized psychiatric patients: anxiety reaction (No. = 9); depressive reaction (No. = 37); character disorder (No. = 26); adolescent reaction (No. = 8); and chronic alcoholism (No. = 14). None of these patients had an increase of serum-CPK activity. For this group, the mean serum-CPK activity was 25.4 IU/liter ± SE 1.8 IU/liter (range 3 to 81 IU/liter) (Table 2). Two such patients were studied intensively, and had no increase in serum-CPK activity at any time during their hospitalization.

Chronic Brain Syndromes.—Eight such cases were studied. One had increased activity of serum CPK (127 IU/liter) while the others were all within normal limits (range 6 to 44 IU/liter) (Table 2).

TABLE 3

Estimated Duration of Psychotic Symptoms Prior to First Determination of Serum-CPK Activity

Patients	Duration (Days)								
	3	4	5	6	7	8-10	11-12	15	20-25
Acutely psychotic patients with normal CPK activity	—	3	1	2	—	—	1	1	2
Acutely psychotic patients with increased CPK activity	5	4	2	4	2	2	2	—	—

Acute Brain Syndromes.—Six such patients were studied, all of whom had increases in serum-CPK activity: mean 343.3 IU/liter ± SE 166.3 IU/liter (range 106 to 1,167 IU/liter) (Table 2). Three patients, including the patient with CPK activity of 1,167 IU/liter, had a febrile illness as the origin of their acute deleria; one had taken an overdosage of barbiturates; one was withdrawing from barbiturates; and one said he had taken marijuana, lysergic acid diethylamide, and amphetamines.

Neurologic Patients.—Serum-CPK activity was determined for 19 patients admitted to the neurological and neurosurgical services of Billings Hospital. Four had elevated activity of serum CPK, ranging from 111 IU/liter to 216 IU/liter. This included one case of cerebrovascular occlusion, two cases of brain trauma, and one case of a ruptured aneurysm. Normal CPK activity was found in the other cases of cerebrovascular accidents, brain trauma, meningitis, and brain tumor.

Alternative Assay of CPK.—Serum-CPK activity was also increased by this method—colorimetric determination of phosphate from hydrolysis of creatine phosphate—in many of the specimens with increased activity according to the spectrophotometric method. Because the colorimetric method is less sensitive, a few of the specimens with the lowest increases by the spectrophotometric method appeared normal by the colorimetric method.

Isoenzyme Studies.—The CPK activity in all the sera tested, which included all sera with activity of CPK greater than 100 IU/liter, in psychiatric and neurological patients was exclusively of the muscle type. By electrophoresis, only the muscle-type CPK was noted. By the batch-separation method, a small amount of brain-type CPK appeared to be present but, when this was electrophoresed, it too proved to be of the muscle-type.

Other Serum Enzymes.—Increased activity of aldolase was found in many of the sera with the largest increases in the activity of CPK. The increases were generally much smaller in magnitude relative to normal limits than the CPK increases, e.g., threefold to sixfold above normal limits. No increases in the activity of SGOT and LDH were noted.

COMMENT

This survey study was undertaken to disprove or confirm some of our previous conceptions that an increase in the activity of CPK is present in a variety of acutely psychotic states and certain neurological disorders and that CPK activity is not increased in other types of psychiatric patients. The results just reported have confirmed these hypotheses although some patients whose illness was of the recurrent type and who were felt to be chronically psychotic had slight but significant increases in CPK activity.

One of the strengths and weaknesses of this study is that the diagnoses of the psychiatric patients were made by over 30 resident and staff physicians of two hospitals, independently of any knowledge of enzyme activity, of course. This allowed a greater opportunity for misclassification than if one or two physicians had seen all of the patients. But because of this, it is perhaps more significant that not one of 94 nonpsychotic patients had an increase in CPK activity. While a few of the patients seen as chronically psychotic had modest increases in the activity of serum CPK (7 of 80), 24 of 37 acutely psychotic patients had increases in CPK activity ranging to 50 times the mean of the controls in this study. The diagnosis of acute psychosis would appear to be much more highly correlated with increased CPK activity than any other psychiatric diagnosis, while neurotic and psychotic patients fall into two mutually exclusive populations by this biochemical parameter. Thus, psychiatrists can sort out psychiatric patients into two populations, such that many of the

members of one of these populations have a readily estimatable biochemical characteristic.

As we have shown, this biochemical characteristic is an increased activity of muscle-type CPK in serum. We have described elsewhere our
efforts to assure that we were, in fact, assaying CPK (3). The alternative
assay for CPK used here also demonstrated marked increases in CPK activity. We have assayed the serum-CPK activity of muscular dystrophy
patients and found large increases in those patients. Serum aldolase activity, but not LDH, SGOT, alkaline phosphatase, and acid phosphatase,
was also increased in acutely psychotic patients but not as frequently as
CPK activity. The increase in CPK activity may be as high as that in
some cases of muscular dystrophy but generally it is much lower. It
tends to be present only in the first two to four weeks of an acute psychosis and then declines to normal levels. We have found several patients
where the increase in CPK activity was much more prolonged, either continuously or discontinuously. We have noted in a few patients that the
increases in CPK activity may begin just prior to a major exacerbation of
the psychotic process (3, 4).

Is the biochemical characteristic of some acute psychotics a nonspecific
phenomenon or does it reflect some basic pathophysiologic process common to the acute psychoses? Elsewhere we have presented considerable
data as to why it does not appear that the enzyme increases are due to
psychotropic medications, increased corticosteroid secretion, weight loss,
and activity (3, 4). More information is now available to us with regard
to psychotropic medications, weight loss, and activity.

Orally administered phenothiazines have neither produced nor diminished the activity of CPK in the patients we have studied intensively.
The length of the period of increased enzyme activity in patients receiving
phenothiazines on our research ward tends to be somewhat greater in
those subjects receiving phenothiazines but only by a few days. We have
found intramuscularly administered chlorpromazine produces a substantial increase of serum-CPK activity in 20% of acute psychotics. Other
types of medication given intramuscularly produce no increase in CPK
activity at all or, at most, in just a few patients. For this reason, we
have not included in this report the results from any blood samples taken
from a patient given an intramuscular injection prior to venipuncture.
The possibility of false positives due to intramuscular injections of chlorpromazine should be carefully considered in future studies of this area of
research.

A recent study of the serum-CPK activity of children suffering from
kwashiorkor or marasmus in Africa found *lowered* activity of these en-

zymes in the serum of these patients (19). It is hardly likely that the few weeks of poor food intake which sometimes accompany acute psychotic episodes could produce substantial increases in CPK activity.

We have studied the effects of an exhausting, standardized exercise test on acutely psychotic patients and found it to have a slight effect on serum enzyme activity (20). The increase in CPK activity from the exercise was much less than that which occurred during the acute psychotic episodes. It seems highly unlikely that the increased physical activity manifested by some of our patients during the acute phase of their psychoses could produce the massive increases in CPK activity lasting for many days.

Thirteen of the acutely psychotic patients had no increase in CPK activity at the time of their admission to the hospital. It does not appear that prolonged delay before hospitalization is the explanation for the failure to find the enzyme increases. We are currently exploring the possibility that they may represent a separate group of schizophrenic patients. It has long been suspected that several distinct syndromes are included in schizophrenia. It may be that increases in CPK activity as part of the psychotic process may reflect two or more distinct subgroups of schizophrenia, with unique pathophysiologic bases. It could be that, however, with careful longitudinal study, many of these patients would have increased activity of CPK at a later phase of their illness. This was noted in two patients in this study and in one-third of a group of acute schizophrenic patients studied longitudinally on a blind basis (21).

If it is possible to trace the changes in serum-CPK or aldolase activity to some fundamental pathophysiologic process common to the acute psychoses, this would establish that the "functional" psychoses are really organic diseases. We have speculated elsewhere how toxic agents could be responsible for the hypothetical changes in brain activity which mediate the behavioral manifestations of the acute psychoses and the hypothetical muscle disturbance which leads to increased activity of CPK and aldolase in serum (3, 4).

The increase in enzyme activity in serum is much more likely to be due to increased release of the enzymes from muscle than a decrease in the rate of removal of the enzymes from serum. It could also be due to changes in the activity of the enzyme without any changes in the concentration of the enzyme, by the presence of increased amounts of an enzyme activator or decreased amounts of an enzyme inhibitor. The transient increase in release of CPK from muscle, if that is the reason for the increase in enzyme activity, does not, itself, lead to serious consequences for the psychotic patient. The amounts present in serum are only a small fraction of the enzyme activity in muscle which is constantly being resynthesized. There is also little possibility that the CPK or aldolase in serum "causes" the psychosis in any way. Much greater activity of CPK and aldolase is present in the serum of patients with some primary muscle disorders who have little or no mental disturbance. It is of interest that psychosis has been linked to myotonica dystrophia, a primary muscle disease in which there are no changes in serum-CPK and aldolase activity (22). It is quite likely nevertheless, that additional enzymes, proteins, and other substances are increased in the serum along with CPK and aldolase and one of these substances might be contributing to cerebral dysfunction. There is no evidence that CPK or aldolase is also being released from brain where it plays a critical role in energy metabolism. The negative evidence is the barely detectable activity of CPK in the cerebrospinal fluid of several psychotic patients with high serum CPK (3, 4).

We have found increased activity of serum CPK, or aldolase, or both in three separate groups of acutely psychotic patients (4, 21). Three other investigators have reported comparable results (1, 2, 5). Similar changes do not appear to occur in other types of psychiatric patients. Thus, a determination of CPK activity of greater than 80 IU/liter by the method utilized in this study in an acutely disturbed psychiatric patient should strongly support a diagnosis of acute psychosis. The increases in aldolase activity tend to be of smaller magnitude but increases are present in a few patients who have no increase in CPK activity (5, 21). Clearly, the finding of normal serum-CPK or aldolase activity does not rule out the diagnosis of acute psychosis since a number of unequivocally acutely psychotic patients do not have increased activity of the enzyme. Even where the enzyme activity is increased, other possible causes of the increase should be carefully considered: intramuscular injections of chlorpromazine, prolonged intense physical activity, myocardial infarction, muscle trauma, brain trauma, hypothyroidism, primary myopathies, etc.

Although we have demonstrated that the most likely nonspecific causes of the increase in CPK or aldolase activity do not account for the enzyme changes in the acutely psychotic patients, it would seem that even if causal nonspecific factors are discovered these increases in enzyme activity would still be useful in differentiating psychiatric patients into distinct subgroups. The determination of CPK or aldolase activity, or both, could provide a standardized way for distinguishing a group of severely disturbed psychiatric patients with the recent or impending acute onset of a thought disorder, or affective disorder, or both. This would mean that an investigator could type his patients as to serum-CPK or aldolase activity and expect that other investigators could assemble similar groups of subjects.

In addition, the serum-CPK activity may identify the optimal time to look for whatever other physiological abnormalities may be present in acutely psychotic patients. For example, we have recently demonstrated a very high correlation between decreases in the amount of nondreaming sleep in acutely psychotic patients and their serum-CPK activity (23). Such sleep disturbances are generally not present when CPK activity has returned to normal even if the patients are still manifestly psychotic.

SUMMARY

The activity of creatine phosphokinase (CPK), aldolase, serum glutamic oxalacetic transaminase (SGOT), and lactic dehydrogenase (LDH) was studied in newly admitted psychiatric patients and normal controls. Serum-CPK activity was increased in 24 of 37 acutely psychotic patients, some of whom had had repeated admissions. The CPK activity was 20 times the upper limits of normal in some specimens. The CPK was the muscle-type, not the brain-type. There were some increases in aldolase activity but not in SGOT or LDH activity in the acutely psychotic patients. There were no increases in serum-CPK activity in nonpsychotic psychiatric patients, but patients with toxic psychoses and with some acute brain diseases, such as brain trauma, had increased CPK activity. The implications of these findings for diagnosis and further research are discussed.

Supported in part by grant No. MH-16127-01 from the U.S. Public Health Service and grant No. 17-340 from the state of Illinois.

The professional staff of ward 10-west assisted in caring for some of the patients in this study. Mrs. Suzanne Mrovack and Mrs. Lana Moore provided technical assistance and Mrs. Joseph Piscopo and Mr. Gaspare Scaturro assisted in collecting the specimens in this study.

GENERIC AND TRADE NAMES OF DRUG

Chlorpromazine—*Thorazine.*

REFERENCES

1. SCHIAVONE, D. J., & KALDOR, J.: Creatine Phosphokinase Levels and Cerebral Disease, *Med. J. Aust.* 2:790-792 (Nov. 6) 1965.
2. BENGZON, A.; HIPPIUS, H.; & KANIG, K.: Some Changes in the Serum During Treatment With Psychotropic Drugs, *J. Nerv. Ment. Dis.* 143:369-376 (Oct.) 1966.

3. MELTZER, H.: Creatine Kinase and Aldolase in Serum: Abnormality Common to Acute Psychoses, *Science* 159:1368-1370 (March 22) 1968.

4. MELTZER, H.: Muscle Enzyme Release in the Acute Psychoses, *Arch. Gen. Psych.* 21:102-112 (July) 1969.

5. COFFEY, J. W.: Serum Phosphokinase, Aldolase, and Copper in Acute and Chronic Schizophrenics, read before the Society of Biological Psychiatry, Miami Beach, Fla. May 3, 1969.

6. WARNOCK, D. G., & ELLMAN, G. L. Intramuscular Chlorpromazine and Creatine Kinase: Acute Psychoses or Local Muscle Trauma? *Science* 164:726 (May 9) 1969.

7. MELTZER, H.: Effect of Intramuscular Injections on Serum CPK Activity, *Science* 164:726-727 (May 9) 1969.

8. MELTZER, H.: Effect of Intramuscular Injections on Serum CPK Activity, to be published.

9. DUBO, H., et al: Serum Creatine-Kinase in Case of Stroke, Head Injury, and Meningitis, *Lancet* 2:743-748 (Oct. 7) 1967.

10. CAO, A., et al: Creatine Kinase Isoenzymes in Serum of Children With Neurological Disorders, *Clin. Chim. Acta.* 23:475-478 (March) 1969.

11. KAR, N. C., & PEARSON, C. M.: Activation of Creatine Phosphokinase by Sulfhydryl Compounds in Normal and Muscular Dystrophy Sera, *Proc. Soc. Exp. Biol. Med.* 118:662-664 (March) 1965.

12. ROSALKI, S. B.: An Improved Procedure for Serum Creatine Phosphokinase Determination, *J. Lab. Clin. Med.* 69:696-705 (April) 1967.

13. BRUNS, F. H., & BERGMEYER, H. U.: "Fructose-1, 6-diphosphate Adolase," in Bergmeyer, H. U. (ed.): *Methods of Enzymatic Analysis,* New York: Academic Press, Inc., 1965, pp. 728-731.

14. KARMAN, A.; WROBLEWSKI, F.; & LaDUE, J. S.: Transaminase Activity in Human Blood, *J. Clin. Lab. Invest.* 34:126-131 (Jan) 1955.

15. WACKER, W. E. C.; ULMER, D. D.; & VALLEE, B. L.: Metalboenzymes and Myocarcardial Infarction: II. Malic and Lactic Dehydrogenase Activities and Zinc Concentrations in Serum, *New Eng. J. Med.* 255:449-456 (Sept) 1956.

16. KUBY, S. A.; NODA, L.; & LARDY, H. A.: Adenosinetriphosphate-Creatine Transphosphorylase: I. Isolation of the Crystalline Enzyme From Rabbit Muscle, *J. Biol. Chem.* 209:191-201 (July) 1954.

17. TRAINER, T. D., & GRUENIG, D.: A Rapid Method for the Analysis of Creatine Phosphokinase Isoenzymes, *Clin. Chim. Acta.* 21:151-154 (July) 1968.

18. RICHTERICH, R.; SCHAFROTH, P.; & AEBI, H.: A Study of Lactic Dehydrogenase Isoenzyme Patterns of Human Tissues by Adsorption-Elution on Sephadex-DEAE, *Clin. Chim. Acta.* 8:178-192 (March) 1963.

19. BALMER, S. E., & RUTISHAUER, I. H. E.: Serum Creatine Kinase in Malnutrition, *J. Pediat.* 73:783-787 (Nov.) 1968.

20. MELTZER, H., & MOLINE, R.: Effect of Exercise on Serum CPK Activity in Psychiatric Patients, to be published.

21. MELTZER, H.; SHADER, R.; & GRINSPOON, L.: Serum CPK and Aldolase Activity in Acute Schizophrenia, read before the American Psychiatric Association, Miami Beach, Fla., May 7, 1969.

22. JOHNSON, J.: Myotonia Congenita (Thompsen's Disease) and Hereditary Psychosis, *Brit. J. Psychiat.* 113:1025-1030 (Sept.) 1967.

23. MELTZER, H., et al.: The Relationship Between Sleep Disturbance and Serum CPK activity in Acutely Psychotic Patients, to be published.

28

PSYCHOENDOCRINOLOGY OF EGO DISINTEGRATION

Edward J. Sachar, Stanley S. Kanter, Daniel Buie,

Ralph Engle, and Robert Mehlman

The authors describe the clinical and endocrine characteristics of the state of acute ego disorganization that initiated the schizophrenic episodes of four young men. Corticosteroid excretion during this phase reached levels 250 percent of subsequent recovery values, far exceeding the elevation seen in normals under stress. The patients subsequently recovered along two separate clinical pathways, which were associated with distinctive changes in adrenal cortical activity. The findings suggest neuroendocrine differences between psychotic and neurotic anxiety.

This paper will report endocrine and psychological observations on a group of acutely schizophrenic men who were followed longitudinally through clinical phases in their illnesses. The paper will focus, in particular, on fluctuations in the adrenal-cortical stress response during stages of "ego disintegration" and "ego reintegration."

This work is an extension of previous research by the senior author and associates in 1963 (25), which reported endocrine changes in associa-

Based on a paper read at the 124th annual meeting of the American Psychiatric Association, Boston, Mass., May 13-17, 1968.

Dr. Sachar is associate professor of psychiatry, Albert Einstein College of Medicine at Montefiore Hospital, 111 E. 210th St., Bronx, N. Y. 10467. Drs. Kanter, Engle, and Mehlman are with Harvard Medical School, Boston, Mass., where Dr. Kanter is clinical associate in psychiatry, Dr. Engle is instructor in psychiatry, and Dr. Mehlman is assistant in psychiatry. Dr. Buie is assistant professor of psychiatry, Tufts University School of Medicine, Boston, Mass.

This work was supported by Public Health Service grants MH-06745 and MH-05077 from the National Institute of Mental Health and Career Development Award 5K 3-MH-22613, also from NIMH.

The assistance of the medical and nursing staffs of the clinical research center, Massachusetts Mental Health Center, is acknowledged.

tion with shifts in clinical states in acutely schizophrenic men. This earlier paper described a sequence of clinical phases occurring in the patients as their illness evolved and emphasized stages of "acute psychotic turmoil," "psychotic equilibrium," "anaclitic depression," and "recovery" (Figure 1).

The period of acute psychotic turmoil (or panic, or ego disintegration), which initiated the psychotic episodes in those patients, was shown to be associated with very great elevations in corticosteroid and epinephrine excretion. One of the characteristics of this stage of psychotic turmoil is a massive breakdown of ego defenses that formerly kept stressful conflicts

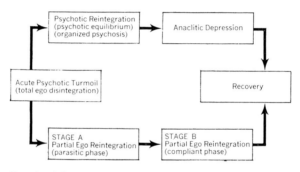

FIG. 1.—Scheme describing two clinical sequences of recovery from the state of acute psychotic turmoil (ego disintegration).

out of mind, and associated with this breakdown is a flood of disintegrative annihilation anxiety. It was, therefore, predicted that this hormonal upheaval would occur as part of the stress response.

However, as the patients went on to enter the phase of psychotic equilibrium—that is, the phase of psychotic restitution, or of the organized psychotic system—emotional distress decreased and corticosteroid and epinephrine excretion diminished toward normal levels. These endocrine changes, which were also predicted, were felt to be consistent with the formulation that the organized psychotic delusional system serves, in part, defensive functions, protecting the patient from unbearable internal stress at the expense of breaking with reality. Indeed, in therapy, as these patients began to give up their psychotic delusions and to grapple once more with painful reality issues, they moved through a transient phase termed "anaclitic depression" in which the affects of depression and anxiety were again prominent, and in which corticosteroid excretion once more increased, presumably as part of the stress response. "Recovery" periods, when the patients returned to their premorbid ego-defensive organization, were associated with a fall in corticosteroid and epinephrine excretion to normal levels. Corticosteroid excretion during periods of organized psychosis and recovery were similar.

The present research was planned with two major goals. The first was to determine whether the findings of the earlier study could be replicated in another setting, again with special emphasis on the psychological and endocrine differences between the states of "acute psychotic turmoil," "organized psychosis," and "anaclitic depression." Our hypothesis was that these different states of ego disequilibrium and ego equilibrium would be associated with shifting degrees of adrenal-cortical activation, as in the earlier study.

The second goal was to study in more detail a different sort of clinical transition seen in many acutely schizophrenic patients—that is, through two stages of partial ego reintegration that occur as patients move from acute psychotic turmoil on into recovery without forming an organized delusional system. In this clinical sequence (Figure 1) the patient emerges from the period of acute psychotic ego disintegration into stage A, an early phase of tenuous ego reintegration, termed the "parasitic" phase, then into stage B, a second, somewhat better integrated phase, termed the "compliant" phase, and then into final reintegration or recovery. The hypothesis here was that adrenal-cortical activity, as an index of psychic distress, would decrease as ego reintegration increased, particularly as the ego defenses previously shattered gradually became effective again in protecting the patient from anxiety.

Table 1 summarizes the hypotheses about fluctuation in corticosteroid excretion during the two sequences of clinical phases. The unifying assumption is that the greater the degree of ego decompensation, the greater the degree of adrenal-cortical activity.

METHODS

Patient selection criteria called for male patients who were physically healthy and between 18 and 35, who had previously been functioning adequately, and who were now experiencing their first psychotic episodes, sharp in onset, characterized by severe panic and ego disintegration, and diagnosable as acute schizophrenic reactions, confusional type (29). With regard to treatment arrangements, the patients were all hospitalized within 24 hours of the onset of psychosis and without medication in the clinical research center of the Massachusetts Mental Health Center. This 11-bed psychiatric research ward was set up for intensive study and treatment of schizophrenic men. A high staff-to-patient ratio permitted patients in this psychoendocrine study to be managed with interpersonal rather than drug therapy. In addition to special nursing care, each patient was seen in intensive psychotherapy throughout hospitalization, by one of us. (A complicating feature of the therapeutic milieu, however, was the fact that only one bed was available for the acute schizophrenics, the other ten beds being occupied by chronic schizophrenics.)

TABLE 1

HYPOTHESIZED PSYCHOENDOCRINE CORRELATIONS

Expected Rank 17-OHCS Output	Clinical Phase	Clinical Phase	Rank of Decompensation of Ego Defenses
1 (highest)	Acute psychotic turmoil	Acute psychotic turmoil	1 (highest)
2	Partial reintegration Stage "A" "Parasitic" phase	Anaclitic depression	2
3	Partial reintegration Stage "B" "Compliant" phase	Psychotic equilibrium (Psychotic reorganization)	3
4 (lowest)	Recovery		4 (lowest)

Endocrine assessments included daily measurements of 24-hour urinary 17-hydroxycorticosteroid (17-OHCS) excretion (Glenn-Nelson method) (11) and determinations of 8 a.m. plasma 17-OHCS levels several times each week (method of Murphy and associates) (18). Completeness of urine collections was assured by close supervision of patients and monitoring of creatinine values. In some instances urine losses of less than 15 percent were "corrected," using the creatinine values as a guide.

Clinical observations, recorded without knowledge of endocrine data, included: 1) detailed shift-by-shift nurses' notes; 2) a nurse's Behavioral Disturbance Index rating scale (BDI) (9); and 3) summaries of psychotherapy interviews. These clinical materials were reviewed initially by one of us (S.S.K.), who classified and demarcated the clinical stages in each patient's course according to criteria that will be described. The group of us then met in a workshop for further review, with the final judgments arrived at by consensus. As in the previous study, all of these evaluations were carried out without knowledge of endocrine data.

Descriptive clinical criteria were used for classifying each patient's course into the specified stages. The acute psychotic turmoil, or severe ego disintegration, was defined by the cardinal features of: 1) a breakthrough of painful psychological conflicts into consciousness, by which one infers that there has been 2) a massive breakdown of defenses (especially repression) previously relied on for keeping unbearable conflicts out of mind. 3) There is, at the same time, an upsurge of severe annihilation anxiety, with fears of imminent death and sometimes with fantasies of world destruction. 4) Fluid, unstable delusions and ideas of reference are rapidly formed and discarded. 5) Concurrently, the patient is flooded with bizarre body sensations and primitive sexual and aggressive impulses. 6) The (ego-maintained) thresholds to outer stimulation fall, so that the patient becomes hypersensitive to stimulation of all types. 7) Cognitive confusion is also a major feature, as in 8) primary process thinking, which is used almost exclusively. 9) Typical also is a loss of a sense of identity. For example, the patient may feel that he is falling apart, dissolving, merging with others, changing in size, and so forth. 10) There is a loss of the ability to relate to other people in a consistent way; and 11) there is typically a severe sleep disturbance.

The phase of psychotic ego reintegration or psychotic equilibrium, seen in certain patients as an outcome of the phase of acute psychotic turmoil, was defined by cardinal criteria of: 1) the development of a fixed, stable, organized psychotic defense system, which replaces the shattered reality-oriented defenses 2) with a corollary projection or denial of conflict; 3) the denial or projection of primitive impulses and sensations (e.g., "rays from outer space") ; 4) marked reduction of anxiety; 5) the replacement of cognitive confusion by psychotic restructuring of the environment; 6) the development of a new psychotic omnipotent sense of identity; and 7) the placing of real people at an emotional distance while the delusional system becomes of primary interest.

The stage of anaclitic depression is seen in some patients as they emerge from the phase of psychotic equilibrium. It was defined according to the following clinical criteria: 1) a breakdown of the psychotic defense system, with replacement by tenuously held, ineffective dependent and neurasthenic defense patterns; 2) a reexperience of internal conflict; 3) a prominent sense of loneliness and fears of abandonment, with 4) depression and anxiety as concomitant affects; 5) reexperience of unusual body sensations, in hypochondriacal fashion; 6) a replacement of the omnipotent self-image with a defective and devalued self-image; and 7) perception of real people as urgently needed and powerful, invested with some of the omnipotency previously attributed to the self.

"Recovery," or ego reintegration, is associated with a return to premorbid characterological patterns of defenses and object relations that are reality-oriented, effective in keeping painful conflict from consciousness, capable of minimizing anxiety and depression, and permissive of a return to social functioning.

As indicated previously, some patients move from the phase of acute psychotic turmoil or ego disintegration without developing a psychotic ego organization. Instead, they move through transient stages of partial ego reintegration as they progress toward recovery. Stage A, or the "parasitic" stage of partial ego reintegration, was defined by the following clinical criteria: 1) a "parasitic" dependency on staff with 2) reliance on "borrowed" coping mechanisms and defenses. (Patients at this point can cope with their internal and external environments only by using therapeutic personnel as auxiliary egos, relying on staff members to explain, interpret, and clarify in concrete terms all details of their experiences. For example, "I am a nurse, you are John, these sensations are coming from inside you, I will help you control them, etc.") With this type of relationship, the patient experiences 3) a return of tenuous ability to distinguish self from others; 4) more circumscribed episodes of anxiety, confusion, and disturbing body sensations; 5) reduced stimulability; 6) reduced impulsiveness; 7) the beginning of a return to secondary process thinking; and 8) less awareness of conflict.

In Stage B, or the "compliant" stage of partial ego reintegration, one sees 1) a compliant dependence upon others; 2) a return to fragile premorbid defense mechanisms. (In dynamic terms, it appears that the patient at this point can rely in general on his own ego-coping mechanisms but cannot tolerate any tension or disagreement arising between himself and the therapist upon whom he depends. When this occurs, there is usually a regression to stage A of partial ego reintegration or a return to the psychotic turmoil.) 3) Episodes of anxiety and confusion are rare, and the anxiety is much less global and intense in character; 4) reality testing and secondary process thinking are present, although tenuous; and 5) disturbing body sensations and impulses are largely absent.

Following this stage, final reintegration can then occur.

RESULTS

All four of the patients in the study showed striking corticosteroid elevations (reaching levels of two and one-half times their recovery values) during the period of acute psychotic turmoil, and subsequent changes in corticosteroid excretion closely paralleled changes in clinical state, as predicted in table 1 ($p < .001$). A summary of the results follows, and more detailed psychological and endocrine data are presented in two illustrative case reports and in figures 2 to 5. Mean corticosteroid excretion for each patient during each clinical phase is presented in table 2.

Clinical Observations

Four patients fitting the clinical criteria for selection were admitted to the ward for psychoendocrine study. All of them were in states of severe psychotic turmoil on admission, and all were discharged in remission. In terms of diagnosis, all could be classified as acute schizo-affective reactions or acute schizophrenic reactions, confusional type.

TABLE 2

MEAN CORTICOSTEROID EXCRETION DURING CLINICAL PHASES
(MG. PER DAY)

Case	Clinical Phases			
	Turmoil		Organized Psychosis	Anaclitic Depression
1	9.5		4.1	6.3
	Turmoil	Stage A	Stage B	Recovery
2	12.3	9.1	6.7	5.5
3	10.8	—	7.7	6.1
4	9.8	7.1	5.5	4.5
		6.4		

All four patients manifested a striking consistency in clinical features during the period of acute psychotic turmoil, closely corresponding to the criteria outlined in the methods section. All experienced panic with annihilation fears. Thus patient 4 begged, "Don't let me die!" and patient 3 not only anticipated his own death but pictured the sky opening up and his family members dropping as corpses to the ground. All experienced a sense of loss of identity. Patient 3 feared that he was becoming fused with a male attendant, and patient 4 believed he was, in turn, becoming a baby, an animal, a killer, a sex maniac, and so forth. All formed unstable delusions that could be rapidly given up. To quote patient 3, "Doctor, that attendant threw a shock into me! No, [shaking his head] he said something that shocked me! No [sweating profusely], I was shocked by something he said."

All were extremely sensitive to stimuli of all types: Patient 3 developed erections in the presence of both male and female staff, and patient 4

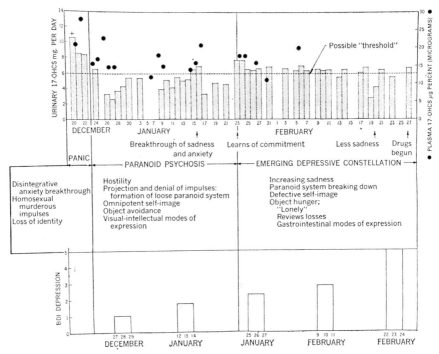

Fig. 2.—Illustration of clinical and endocrinological data for Case 1. (Bars represent daily urinary corticosteroid excretion, and dots represent 8 a.m. plasma cortisol levels.)

feared ejaculating if he got too close to the nurses. Bizarre body sensations were a problem to all four: Patient 4 found that the body tinglings and tensions disrupted his sense of balance and coordination. Some of the other clinical features are described further in the two illustrative case reports.

The patients were then treated with intensive interpersonal therapy without the use of phenothiazines, offering an unusual opportunity to study the clinical evolution of the psychoses unmodified by medication. Of these four patients, one (case 1) then followed the first clinical sequence: that is, from acute psychotic turmoil to organized psychosis to anaclitic depression. This patient was the only one of the group who was unable to achieve a recovery without an eventual course of phenothiazines.

The other three cases followed the second clinical sequence: that is, from acute psychotic turmoil to stage A, the "parasitic" phase of partial ego reintegration to stage B, the "compliant" phase of partial ego reintegration to recovery. Two of these three patients moved in a progressive manner through each stage toward recovery, while the other (case 4) followed a stormy course, moving back and forth throughout his hospitalization between different stages of ego disintegration and reintegration.

Two additional cases—one of an acute amphetamine psychosis (case 6) and another of a paranoid psychotic reaction without ego disintegration (case 5)—provided interesting contrast data in both psychological and endocrine areas.

Endocrine Changes

Mean urinary 17-OHCS excretion during periods of acute psychotic turmoil averaged 215 percent of subsequent recovery levels in the same patients, with the peak values during turmoil phases reaching levels of approximately 250 percent of recovery values (see table 2). (In the instance of case 1, 17-OHCS levels during the period of organized paranoid psychosis were used as a baseline for comparison, since recovery data were not available.)

Mean absolute urinary 17-OHCS levels during the turmoil periods ranged from 9.5 to 12.3 mg. per day, with peak values ranging from 11 to 15 mg. per day. It should be noted that, because of urine losses on the most disturbed days, it is likely that the true peak values are somewhat higher. Although these absolute corticosteroid values are generally high, some of them fall in the upper range of "normal" as observed in studies of hospitalized healthy male subjects in the same age range (24). However, as those studies have emphasized, because of the great constitutional differences in 17-OHCS excretion between subjects, partly weight-related, the absolute 17-OHCS excretion level gains significance primarily when compared with subsequent values in the same subjects, using each subject as his own control. In this respect, in both intensity and duration, the elevations in 17-OHCS excretion seen in these acutely psychotic patients exceed by far the fluctuations seen in normal subjects even under conditions of severe stress.

As predicted, 17-OHCS excretion diminished in association with subsequent stages of ego reintegration. Stage A ("parasitic" phase) values averaged 160 percent of recovery values, and stage B (compliant phase) averaged 125 percent of recovery levels. In the case that moved via the first clinical sequence through organized psychosis and then anaclitic depression, levels during the phase of anaclitic depression averaged 150 percent of the levels during the phase of organized psychosis. In terms of corticosteroid excretion, then, as well as in certain of the clinical features,

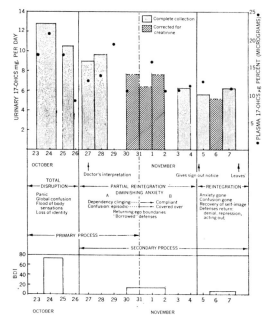

FIG. 3.—Illustration of clinical and endocrinological data for Case 2. (Bars represent daily
urinary corticosteroid excretion, and dots
represent 8 a.m. plasma cortisol levels.)

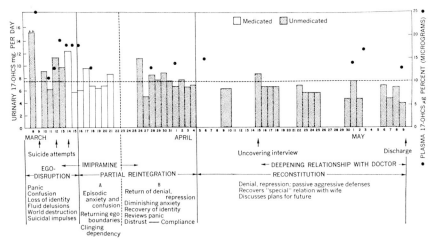

FIG. 4.—Illustration of clinical and endocrinological data for Case 3. (Bars represent
daily urinary corticosteroid excretion, and dots represent 8 a.m. plasma cortisol levels.)

the phase of anaclitic depression seems most comparable to stage A, the "parasitic" phase of partial ego reintegration.

Psychoendocrine Correlations

In line with the hypothesis of the study, as outlined in table 1, the clinical phases of each patient were rank ordered in terms of expected rank of corticosteroid excretion and then correlated with actual ranks of mean hormone excretion. Correlations were consistent throughout.

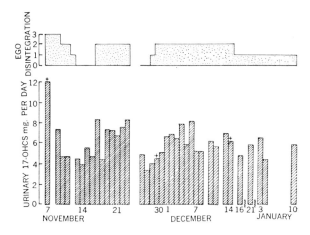

Fig. 5.—Illustration, in Case 4, of daily urinary corticosteroid excretion and stages of ego disintegration (3 = total disintegration, 2 = stage A, 1 = stage B, 0 = recovery).

In order to test the statistical significance of the consistency, a rank order correlation matrix for the group of four cases was constructed. Three stages only were available for analysis from two of the cases since patient 1 did not achieve a full recovery during the period of endocrine study, and since patient 3 required chlorpromazine briefly during stage A of partial reintegration. Accordingly, three phases only were selected from the other two cases as well, the period of acute turmoil and stages A and B of partial reintegration. Using the binomial test for the probability of these correlations occurring by chance, it is found that p = 1/1,296, or less than .001.

Contrasting Patients

Two patients with different psychotic pictures were also studied in the same setting, providing useful contrast data. Case 5 was a 32-year-old man who developed an acute paranoid psychosis of a circumscribed type, without the cardinal features of ego disintegration. As predicted, there was virtually no endocrine disturbance on either of his two admissions.

Case 6 was that of a 19-year-old man with an acute amphetamine psychosis, who demonstrated some features mimicking an acute turmoil state (fear of being killed, hypersensitivity to stimuli), but without such cardinal features as loss of identity, significant confusion, or appearance of primitive conflicts and impulses. Corticosteroid excretion was only mildly elevated (20 percent) in this case.

Plasma Cortisol Results

The 8 a.m. plasma cortisol values did not appear to correlate as strikingly with clinical state as did the 24-hour urinary 17-OHCS levels. While the highest individual and highest mean plasma cortisol values occurred in each case during the phase of acute psychotic turmoil, the absolute levels were not unusually high, nor was there a clear differentiation in each stage of reintegration.

This discrepancy between the urinary and plasma values can probably be accounted for by the fact that the plasma levels represent a single point in time, whereas the urinary values are a better index of overall adrenal activity over time. In patients with a normal sleep pattern, 8 a.m. plasma cortisol levels usually indicate the peak of the daily circadian curve, but sleep was so disrupted in these patients that it is likely that their circadian rhythms were also disrupted. More frequent blood sampling through the day is necessary to get a more accurate estimate of this dimension and, in our patients, it would probably have indicated elevated evening levels.

CASE REPORTS

Case 1. This case is an illustration of the first clinical sequence (see figure 2).

Acute psychotic turmoil (December 20-23). The patient, a 20-year-old Harvard sophomore, had become disorganized and excited in association with impending failure in his courses and in the wake of an unsuccessful love affair with his first girl friend.

On admission to the ward he was frightened and angry, afraid to go to sleep, and fearful that his brain was being taken over by some extraterrestrial force. He was confused about his identity, sorting out all his identity cards and consulting them frequently. He was torn between feelings of helplessness and feelings that he might become uncontrollable. On one occasion he bolted from the ward. He experienced murderous impulses and feared that he might destroy the attendants and that he might pass right through the walls of his room. He was unable to make decisions and was easily confused. He expressed concerns about passivity, homosexuality, and his lost girl friend.

Organized paranoid psychosis (December 24-January 23). Within a few days, the patient had organized a paranoid system, involving electrical circuits and complex astronomical delusions (in which Venus figured prominently). In his new psychotic identity, he was a member of a powerful military fighting unit. He declared staff members "theoretically dead," so that he did not have to kill them. He spent much of his time at the blackboard working at his system and avoided meaningful interpersonal contacts. He remained belligerent, but no longer frightened.

The patient's therapist persisted in trying to penetrate the patient's delusions to help him talk in a more direct fashion about his concerns. The patient touched on these issues briefly January 14, 15, and 16, but then backed away, maintaining he was going to leave the hospital.

Anaclitic depression (January 23-February 27). On January 23 the patient learned he was about to be committed. Subsequently he appeared more sad and more willing to face issues in his therapy, although he frequently retreated to paranoid thinking. He reviewed, with tears, the loss of his girl friend, whom he acknowledged he drove away because of his fears of closeness. He hinted at the fear of mutual destruction involved in intimacy, and his imagery shifted from the visual intellectual forms used in the previous phase to oral metaphors. He described with sadness and anger the death of his father when he was 16, just as they were getting close, and he touched on his yearnings for his mother, who had died when he was two. He complained increasingly of loneliness, talked of himself as a failure, and finally declared with pain that he had been "frozen" all his life. Shortly after this acknowledgment, the patient became severely disturbed and had to be started on medication.

Case 2. This case is an illustration of the second clinical sequence (see figure 3).

Total ego disintegration (October 27-31). The patient was a 24-year-old man who had become confused and frightened following his decision to break with his previous way of life and to enroll in electricians school, as part of preparation for marriage to his fiancee of long standing.

After admission he was very frightened and extremely confused and distractible. He experienced vivid perceptual distortions and intense body sensations, particularly sexual ones; his body shuddered almost convulsively as he was periodically flooded with feelings. His impulsive behavior became increasingly bizarre, and at times several attendants were required to hold him down. His speech deteriorated to a babble; when intelligible, he seemed to be expressing concerns about dying and confusion about his identity—was he a man or a woman, an adult or a baby, a big shot or a nothing, a good person or an evil one, and so forth.

Stage A, partial reintegration (October 31-November 5). On October 31, his therapist made an emphatic clarification to the patient, relating his current turmoil to the life decision he had attempted to make. The patient responded with a cry. "You're right!" and then in a burst of tears, said "I have been so frightened." Reintegration proceeded from that point. His verbal expressions coalesced into coherent sentences, his associations became less loose, and confusional episodes became more circumscribed and less frequent. Anxiety diminished, as long as the patient could remain dependent in a clinging way on staff members. With his therapist, he began to piece together the concerns that had overwhelmed him. Among other factors, his decision to marry meant separation from his mother, a domineering, nearly psychotic religious fanatic; his attempt to get training as an electrician involved separation from his father with whom he had worked in the same bakery for several years. He feared that unless he changed his life he would become a "hood" like many of his friends, and his inability to comprehend school work signified doom to all of his life hopes for maturation.

Stage B, partial reintegration (November 1-5). By November 1, the patient was judged to have reintegrated further. His behavior was calm and quite appropriate and his speech coherent. He reestablished contact with friends and family, and with his doctor he continued to review his recent turmoil. He seemed unusually compliant, however, and at moments of stress loosening of his associations and concreteness of thinking were evident, although the patient was quite skillful in covering these over.

Reconstitution (November 5 to discharge). By November 5, the patient had reconstituted to his premorbid Runyonesque character, and he promptly announced his decision to sign out. "I'm a guy who likes to move, doc, and I can't see sittin' around on a ward with a bunch of nuts!" He dealt with his psychotic concerns primarily by denial and repression: "I guess I tried to do too much at once; I'll take things easier from now on." Efforts to persuade him to stay were unsuccessful, and he left on the ninth of November.

DISCUSSION

The Acute Psychotic Turmoil

We have described in some detail the psychological phenomena and adrenal-cortical responses occurring during the clinical phase we have termed "acute psychotic turmoil," or "ego disintegration," as it occurs during schizophrenic episodes. This state has been described under various names by numerous authors who have emphasized one or another aspect of the clinical phenomena. For example, Weiner reviewed the extensive literature describing it in schizophrenic reactions under the term "acute confusional type," emphasizing the features of suddenness of onset, psychological precipitant, confusion, and panic (29). Bowers has emphasized the experience of identity dissolution and the heightened reactivity to sensory stimuli (4). Mann and Semrad used the term "acute psychotic turmoil," and they speculated, in 1960, that endocrine disturbance probably accompanied the psychological upheaval (15).

The results of this investigation bear out the speculation of Mann and Semrad and confirm and extend the findings of the earlier study by the senior author and associates (25). The state of acute psychotic turmoil as seen in schizophrenics is associated with very marked hypersecretion of the adrenal cortex, presumably on the basis of hypothalamic pituitary activation. The relative magnitude of the elevations (to two and one-half times "basal" levels) far exceeds those observed in numerous studies of normal subjects under stress. Indeed, the data presented in this and the previous paper suggest that the disintegrative anxiety connected with psychotic ego disruption is associated with a kind of neuroendocrine "storm."

The results gain further significance when compared with observations of psychoendocrine responses in normals. One of the major findings of psychoendocrine research in the 1960s has been the consistent demonstration that normal subjects show relatively *mild* urinary adrenal-cortical responses to stress. For example, normal men coping with the stress of hospital admission also showed a urinary adrenal-cortical response during the first two to three days of hospitalization, but the average increase was only about 20 percent above basal levels (8, 17, 24). In numerous studies of normals under severe life stress—the parents of dying children (30), women awaiting surgery for possible cancer of the breast (14), soldiers coping with basic training (19), and under attack in Vietnam (3)—the maximal 24-hour urinary corticosteroid responses have been in the range of 25-30 percent elevations above normal, with most of the subjects showing slighter responses. Those few showing larger increases have rarely sustained them for more than a day.

In all of the studies, those subjects judged "well defended" have shown little adrenal response, and those judged "poorly defended" the greater responses. But the upper limits of the response range have been far lower than those seen in the schizophrenic patients in this study and the preceding one. It appears that it is only when the "buffer" system of ego defenses is shattered, with the arousal of disintegrative anxiety, that massive two- to threefold increases in urinary adrenal-cortical responses occur (22). Thus, within the group of patients in this study, it is interesting to note that the two patients (cases 5 and 6) with psychotic reactions who did *not* manifest the features of massive ego disintegration also did not show substantial elevations of corticosteroid output after hospitalization.

This view is further supported by a review of the literature on adrenal-cortical responses in depressive illnesses. As the senior author has pointed out elsewhere, adrenal-cortical elevations in the vast majority of depressions fall in the "mild" range similar to that seen in normals under stress (20, 21). Only a small group of depressed patients do show very large adrenal-cortical responses, and these are nearly always patients undergoing psychotic decompensation with beginning delusion formation (6, 21).

Psychotic ego disintegration in the depressive is similar in many respects to the type we have described in acute schizophrenic reactions, but there are some differences. For example, the depressive undergoing ego disintegration rarely experiences the loss of a sense of identity, the hypersensitivity to stimuli, or the murderous impulses of the schizophrenic. However, he does typically experience the fluid ideas of reference, the feeling of going crazy, the disintegrative annihilation anxiety, the sense of bodily disintegration, and sometimes a sense of world destruction and imminent doom (6, 21). It has been reported that depressed patients, prior to successful suicide, also run very high corticosteroid levels (5), suggesting that impending suicide and impending psychosis may be comparable ego states (22).

Although we assume, on the basis of many animal studies (16), that the primary mechanism of the increased adrenal-cortical activity in the acute psychotic turmoil is mediated by the influence of limbic system structures involved in emotional states on the hypothalamic neuroendocrine centers, the possibility remains that there may be secondary effects of the high hormone levels on the brain of the psychotic. For example, the patient's hyperreactivity to stimuli might conceivably be influenced in part by the corticosteroid effects on sensory thresholds (although *decreased* sensitivity is suggested by one study) (12).

Phase of Organized Psychosis

One outcome of the state of acute ego disintegration is a reintegration at the psychotic level. This stage of psychosis has also been described in various terms by various authors: the stage of organized psychosis, psychotic restitution, psychotic insight, psychotic solution, psychotic equilibrium, chronic established psychosis, etc. For the purposes of this paper we wish to emphasize the distinction, *psychologically and endocrinologically,* between this phase and the stages of ego disintegration. Freud

(10), Arieti (1), and Boisin (2) are among the numerous writers who have made this psychological distinction and have viewed the fixed delusional system as a psychotic "solution" to the terrifying conflicts and confusion of the state of turmoil. They argue, in other words, that there is a psychodynamic connection between the elaboration of a psychotic system and the panic's subsidence.

In terms of endocrine function, there is a striking drop to normal in the adrenal-cortical stress response as the patient enters this stage of his illness, as seen in case 1 of this paper and in the four cases of the preceding paper by the senior author and associates (25). This return of endocrine function to normal is associated with the diminution in the emotional turmoil. If the psychodynamic frame of reference is kept, however, then one might add that the organization of a delusional system functions in the service of both psychological and physiological homeostasis, protecting the patient from intense anxiety and concomitant endocrine disturbance.

Phase of Anaclitic Depression

The depression that often occurs as schizophrenics give up their psychotic system has not been widely described in the clinical literature. Semrad and Zaslow have summarized the clinical features of this transition (26), and Jacobson has pointed out some of the significant clinical differences between schizophrenic depressions and the typical nonschizophrenic depressive illnesses (13). We have used the term "anaclitic" because the prominent features include feelings of loneliness, yearnings for nurturing care and separation anxiety.

In the previous paper, the senior author and associates described this phase as it occurred in four acute schizophrenics, associated in each instance with a significant urinary corticosteroid elevation (25). Steinberg and associates subsequently confirmed these clinical observations but were not able to detect a concomitant corticosteroid elevation (28). The reason, almost certainly, is that their patients were receiving chlorpromazine, which has been shown to block the adrenal cortical stress response (27). In the case described in this paper (case 1), both the clinical and adrenal-cortical findings further confirm the observations made by the senior author and associates in 1963 (25).

It should also be noted that this is the fifth case we have reported in which endocrine measures have been made during the transition between a paranoid phase and a depressive phase (23, 25). In each instance the depressive phase has been associated with elevated corticosteroid excretion as compared with the paranoid stage. The shift could be interpreted in terms of the difference in the affects—the depressive state being associated with sadness and anxiety, the paranoid state with hostile belligerency, and the suggestion being that the former affects evoke more of a response in the adrenal than the latter. Another way of restating the matter would be to note that apparently in these patients it was more stressful for them to see their problems as coming from within themselves rather than from outside themselves.

The Stages of Partial Ego Reintegration

A second pathway of recovery from the acute psychotic turmoil, which was followed in three of our cases, involves gradual ego reintegration. We have described in some detail two stages of partial ego reintegration—a "parasitic" and a "compliant" phase—that occur as part of this transition in the unmedicated patient. To our knowledge, only Carlson has referred to these progressive stages of repair in terms of ego psychology (7). Utilizing a somewhat different scheme from ours she described her observations on the "acute confusional" state in college students.

The theoretical implications of these ego states in terms of developmental ego stages and the practical implications for interpersonal therapeutic techniques at different points in the patient's course will be dealt with in subsequent papers. Here we would emphasize the subsiding endocrine disturbance and point out that it is consistant with the stages of recompensation of ego defensive functions, along the lines predicted.

Corticosteroid Response, Ego Function, and the Two-Type Theory of Anxiety

As our data indicate, it is only when the patient emerging from turmoil enters phase B, the "compliant" stage of partial reintegration, that the urinary corticosteroid levels become comparable to those seen in anxious normals (about 25 percent elevation over "basal" or "recovery" values). Phase B is also the stage when the patient's own reality-oriented premorbid defenses become tenuously operative again. The nature of the patient's anxiety also changes at this point. As we have indicated, it is less global, no longer disintegrative, more episodic—in other words, much more like "signal" anxiety as opposed to the primary, "annihilation" anxiety experienced earlier. The differences in the magnitude of the corticosteroid response at the peak of the patient's acute turmoil and at phase B of ego reintegration might be attributed to differences in the degree or *intensity* of his anxiety. On the other hand, it may be that the *quality* of his anxiety also has changed, to the "signal" type, along with a return of his premorbid ego defenses (especially repression). The striking differences in the upper range of corticosteroid response reached by the stressed anxious normal and the schizophrenic in turmoil might, therefore, be construed as endocrine evidence for the two-type theory of anxiety: i.e., "signal" versus "primary," or "neurotic" versus "psychotic."

SUMMARY

Psychological and endocrine observations are reported on four first-episode acutely schizophrenic men who were hospitalized in the state of acute psychotic turmoil or ego disintegration, and then followed, unmedicated, through stages of illness to recovery. On the basis of hypotheses of a previous paper by the senior author and associates (25), predictions were made as to the direction and relative magnitude of changes in urinary corticosteroid excretion as the patients moved through clinical stages of illness.

We have described in detail the clinical features of the state of acute psychotic turmoil. During this phase, there were marked elevations of urinary corticosteroid excretion to 250 percent of each patient's basal levels, presumably as a function of the stress response. These extreme, sustained elevations in corticosteroid excretion were far in excess of what is observed in normals under stress and suggest that the psychotic turmoil is associated with a neuroendocrine as well as an emotional "storm."

Two pathways of recovery from the stage of turmoil are also described. The first pathway involves the formation of an organized psychotic system, which is then followed by a phase of "anaclitic depression" as the patient gives up his delusional system. In one case this sequence involved the development of a paranoid system, and corticosteroids promptly fell to normal levels, about 40 percent of the levels seen during the preceding turmoil. As the patient subsequently moved through the period of "anaclitic depression," corticosteroid levels again rose to about 150 percent of his "normal" levels.

A second pathway of recovery from the acute psychotic turmoil occurred in three cases. In this clinical sequence, the patient does not form an organized psychosis but moves through two intermediate stages of partial ego reintegration, a "parasitic" and a "compliant" phase, before recovery. Urinary corticosteroid levels during these two phases also diminished progressively.

The psychiatrists, working without knowledge of endocrine data, correctly predicted the direction and relative magnitude of changes in corticosteroid excretion in all four cases $(p < .001)$.

Two additional cases of acute psychotic reactions *without* massive ego disruption were also studied. As predicted, the changes in corticosteroid excretion were slight.

The results of this study confirm and extend the findings of the previous study by the senior author and associates (25) of endocrine changes during the course of acute schizophrenic reactions.

REFERENCES

1. ARIETI, S.: Interpretation of Schizophrenia. New York: Robert Brunner, 1955.
2. BOISIN, A. T., JENKINS, R. L. & LORR, M.: Schizophrenic Ideation as Striving Toward the Solution of Conflict. *J. Clin. Psychol.* 10:389-391, 1954.
3. BOURNE, P., ROSE, R. M., & MASON, J. W.: Urinary 17-OHCS Levels: Data on Seven Helicopter Ambulance Medics in Combat. *Arch. Gen. Psychiat.* 17:104-110, 1967.
4. BOWERS, M. B.: Pathogenesis of Acute Schizophrenic Psychosis, *Arch. Gen. Psychiat.* 19:348-355, 1968.
5. BUNNEY, W. E. JR. & FAWCETT, J. A.: Possibility of a Biochemical Test for Suicide Potential, *Arch. Gen. Psychiat,* 13:232-239, 1965.
6. BUNNEY, W. E. JR., MASON, J. W., ROATCH, J. F., & HAMBURG, D. A.: A Psychoendocrine Study of Severe Psychotic Depressive Crises. *Amer. J. Psychiat.* 122:72-80, 1965.
7. CARLSON, H.: Relation of the Acute Confusional State to Ego Development, *Int. J. Psychoanal.* 42:517-536, 1961.
8. FISHMAN, J., HAMBURG, D., HANDLON, J., MASON, J., & SACHAR, E.: Emotional and Adrenal Cortical Responses to a New Experience, *Arch. Gen. Psychiat.* 6:271-278, 1962.
9. FRAMO, J. T., & ALDERSTEIN, A. M.: A Behavioral Disturbance Index, *J. Clin. Psychol.* 17:260-264, 1961.
10. FREUD, S.: "Psychoanalytic Notes Upon an Autobiographical Account of a Case of Paranoia" (1911), in Collected Papers, vol. 3. London: Hogarth Press, 1949, pp. 387-470.
11. GLENN, E., & NELSON, D.: Chemical Method for the Determination of 17-Hydroxycorticosteroids and 17-Ketosteroids in Urine Following Hydrolysis with B-Glucuronidase, *J. Clin. Endocr.* 13:911-921, 1953.
12. HENKEN, R., McGLONE, R., DALY, R., & BUTLER, F.: Studies on Auditory Thresholds in Normal Man and in Patients with Adrenal Cortical Insufficiency: The Role of Adrenal Steroids, *J. Clin. Invest.* 46:429-435, 1967.
13. JACOBSON, E.: "Problems in the Differentiation Between Schizophrenic and Melancholic States of Depression," in Loewenstein, R., Newman, L., Schur, M., and Solnit, A., eds.: Psychoanalysis—A General Psychology. New York: International Universities Press, 1966.
14. KATZ, J., GALLAGHER, T., HELLMAN, L., ACKMAN, P., ROTHWAX, Y., SACHAR, E., & WEINER, H.: Psychoendocrine Aspects of Cancer of the Breast, *Psychosom. Med.* in press.
15. MANN, J., & SEMRAD, E.: "Conversion as Process and Conversion as Symptom in Psychosis," in Deutsch, F., ed.: On the Mysterious Leap from the Mind to the Body. New York: International Universities Press, 1959.
16. MASON, J.: The Organization of Psychoendocrine Mechanisms. *Psychosom. Med.* 30:563-808, 1968.

17. MASON, J., SACHAR, E., HAMBURG, D., FISHMAN, J., & HANDLON, J.: Corticosteroid Responses to Hospital Admission, *Arch. Gen. Psychiat.* 13:1-8, 1965.
18. MURPHY, B., ENGLEBERG, W., & PATEE, C.: Simple Method for the Determination of Plasma Corticoids, *J. Clin. Endocr.* 23:293-300, 1963.
19. ROSE, R., POE, R., & MASON, J.: Psychological State and Body Size as Determinants of 17-OHCS Excretion, *Arch. Intern. Med.* 121:406-413, 1968.
20. SACHAR, E.: Corticosteroids in Depressive Illness. I: A Review of Control Issues and the Literature, *Arch. Gen. Psychiat.* 17:544-553, 1967.
21. SACHAR, E.: Corticosteroids in Depressive Illness. II: A Longitudinal Psychoendocrine Study, *Arch. Gen. Psychiat.* 17:554-567, 1967.
22. SACHAR, E.: "Psychological Homeostasis and Endocrine Function," in Mandell, A., and Mandell, M., eds.: Psychochemical Research in Man: Methods, Strategy and Theory. New York: Academic Press, 1969, pp. 219-233.
23. SACHAR, E., HARMATZ, J., BERGEN, H., & COHLER, J.: Corticosteroid Responses to Milieu Therapy of Chronic Schizophrenics, *Arch. Gen. Psychiat.* 15:310-319, 1966.
24. SACHAR, E., MASON, J., FISHMAN, J., HAMBURG, D., & HANDLON, J.: Corticosteroid Excretion in Normal Young Adults Living Under "Basal" Conditions, *Psychosom. Med.* 27:435-445, 1965.
25. SACHAR, E., MASON, J., KOLMER, H., & ARTISS, K.: Psychoendocrine Aspects of Acute Schizophrenic Reactions, *Psychosom. Med.* 25:510-537, 1963.
26. SEMRAD, E. & ZASLOW, S.: Assisting Psychotic Patients to Recompensate, *Ment. Hosp.* 15:361-366, 1964.
27. SHADER, R., GILLER, D., & DiMASCIO, A.: Endocrine and Metabolic Effects of Psychotropic Drugs. IV: Hypothalamic-Pituitary-Adrenal Axis. *Conn. Med.* 32: 539-543, 1968.
28. STEINBERG, H., GREEN, R., & DURELL, J.: Depression Occurring During the Course of Recovery from Schizophrenic Symptoms, *Amer. J. Psychiat.* 124:699-705, 1967.
29. WEINER, H.: "Diagnosis and Symptomatology," in Bellak, L., ed.: Schizophrenia: A Review of the Syndrome. New York: Logos Books, 1958, pp. 151-153.
30. WOLFF, C., FRIEDMAN, S., HOFER, M., & MASON, J.: Relationship Between Psychological Defenses and Mean Urinary 17-OHCS Excretion Rates, I-II, *Psychosom. Med.* 26:576-609, 1964.

29

THE "PINK SPOT" IN SCHIZOPHRENICS AND ITS ABSENCE IN HOMOCYSTINURICS

J. Philip Welch, Courtney G. Clower, and R. Neil Schimke

In 1952 Osmond and Smythies, with Harley-Mason, suggested that schizophrenia might be due to an abnormality in the metabolism of epinephrine, by which a mescaline-like substance such as dimethoxy-phenylethylamine (DMPE) might be produced by O-methylation at the third and fourth positions. It was felt then that DMPE might have "psychotomimetic properties" similar to mescaline.

In 1962 Friedhoff and Van Winkle (1962a) using a single dimension method of paper chromatography reported the occurrence of a "pink spot," which they believed to be DMPE, in the urine of 15/19 schizophrenic patients and 0/14 controls. The amounts present were later reported to be in the range of 20-150 micrograms (Friedhoff and Van Winkle, 1962b). This study aroused considerable interest, resulting in several attempts to reproduce these findings.

Some studies (Takesada et al., 1963; Kuehl et al., 1964; Sen and McGeer, 1964; Bourdillon et al., 1965) have produced evidence apparently confirming the presence of DMPE in the urine of some schizophrenics, though with varying prevalence. Some workers, however, have failed to find DMPE in such individuals (Perry, 1963; Perry et al., 1964, 1966; Faurbye and Pind, 1964, 1966; Williams et al., 1966). The identity of the substance found by Friedhoff and Van Winkle has also been questioned by some investigators (Boulton and Felton, 1966b; Bell and Somerville, 1966; Pind and Faurbye, 1966; Boulton et al., 1967; Perry et al., 1967), though Friedhoff and his collaborators have amassed a consider-

Reprinted, by permission of author and editor, from: *The British Journal of Psychiatry*, 115:163-167, 1969.

able body of evidence in favor of its being DMPE (Friedhoff, 1966). Evidence to identify DMPE in the urine from schizophrenics has also been presented by Creveling and Daly (1967), using mass spectrometry following extraction and chromatographic separations. The difficulties and uncertainties of this field of endeavor are exemplified by the report of Kuehl and co-workers (1966) who have failed to replicate their own earlier results in which DMPE had been found in the urine of some schizophrenics. Sen and McGeer (1964) also claimed to have found 4-methoxyphenylethylamine (4MPE) in the urine of 11 of 22 schizophrenics examined. This finding has not been confirmed and others (Perry *et al.*, 1966) have been unable to replicate it.

If an abnormal pathway of transmethylation is involved in the pathogenesis of some schizophrenic disorders, an investigation of individuals or families known to carry genes for inborn errors of metabolism involving such processes might be profitable. A disorder particularly worthy of investigation is homocystinuria since in this the error consists of a block to the production of crystathionine, with the creation of a large "methyl pool" and increased levels of plasma methionine in some homozygotes. Carson and her colleagues (1963) reported two homocystinuric siblings whose mother (heterozygous for homocystinuria) was schizophrenic, while five other members of the maternal side showed clear evidence of schizophrenia. Perry (1967) has made mention of three other families showing homocystinuria and psychosis. Two families had a number of psychotic individuals extending over three generations on one side of the family, while the third showed a first cousin of the proband with a severe behavior disorder. In addition some of the present authors reported a case study of a woman homozygous for homocystinuria and also diagnosed as schizophrenic (Spiro *et al.*, 1965), as was her mother.

We report here the results of a search for urinary DMPE and 4MPE in two selected groups, one composed of schizophrenics and the other of homozygotes and heterozygotes for homocystinuria.

METHOD OF URINARY ANALYSIS FOR DMPE AND 4MPE

(a) *Collection and Extraction* (modified from Takesada *et al.*, 1963) —Urine was collected over 24 hours, usually with 10 ml. 11.6*N* HCl as preservative. Urines were kept cold during collection and adjusted to pH2 with HCl immediately following collection. Following filtration (Whatman #42 paper) they were passed through a 1×8 cm. column of Dowex 50×2 (100-200 mesh).* The column was washed with 25 ml.

---

* Bio Rad Laboratories, 32nd and Griffin, Richmond, California.

distilled water and amines were eluted with 50 ml. 1N NH$_4$OH in 65 percent. (v/v) ethanol. The eluate, with 20 microlitres of acetic acid, was evaporated to dryness in a rotary evaporator at 50° C. and the residue resuspended in a small volume (2-3 ml.) of 0.2 N NaOH. The pH was adjusted to 10 and the residue extracted with chloroform† (1 ml. ×3). The chloroform extracts were pooled and extracted first with 0.02 N NaOH (1 ml. X 3) (discarded), and then with 0.05 N HCl (1 ml. × 3).

(b) *Electrophoresis and Chromatography.*—The HCl extract was evaporated to dryness under vacuum at room temperature, the residue being applied to paper (Whatman 3MM. 45 cm. × 145 cm.) for high voltage electrophoresis at pH 4.7 (5,000 volts for 4$\frac{1}{4}$ hours under Varsol.). This procedure produced good resolution in most cases, but a minority of control subjects showed other faint spots at the DMPE region. (These were shown to be not DMPE by the staining reaction described by Friedhoff and Van Winkle, 1962b.) For further resolution a chromatographic run was added, the solvent being made by thoroughly shaking equal volumes of tertiary amyl alcohol and a mixture consisting of 10 percent. (v/v) Pyridine, 0.4 percent. (v/v) acetic acid and water to 100 and using the top layer only. A strip containing the DMPE and 4MPE regions (shown by guide strips) was cut from the electrophoresis run and sewn into paper according to the method of Naughton and Hagopian (1962) for descending chromatography at right angles to the electrophoresis run. This two-dimensional procedure resulted in clear separation of the DMPE and 4MPE spots from normetanephrine, tyramine, dopamine, 3-hydroxy 4-methoxyphenylethylamine, and 3-methoxy 4-hydroxyphenylethylamine. DMPE and 4MPE were ascertained by the staining reaction described by Friedhoff and Van Winkle (1963b).

Recovery rates using control urine adulterated with DMPE and 4MPE varied somewhat but was approximately 50 percent. Five micrograms of DMPE or 4MPE could be readily detected on the final chromatogram. Of ten samples containing 8 μgm. DMPE and 10 μgm. 4MPE all but one were read as positive for both DMPE and 4MPE, and samples containing $\geqq$ 16 μgm (DMPE or 4MPE) were in our experience invariably positive. Very small amounts of DMPE and 4MPE, i.e. less than 5 μgm/L are probably not detected by this procedure; however, the levels of DMPE reported by Friedhoff and Van Winkle were in the 20-150 microgram range.

---

† Spectroquality, Matheson Coleman and Bell, East Rutherford, New Jersey.

RESULTS

We have looked for DMPE and/or 4MPE in the urines from a group of seventeen hospitalized schizophrenic patients. At least two psychiatrists agreed upon the diagnosis, and most of the patients had been presented in psychiatric staff conferences, with unanimous agreement on diagnosis. All were maintained on the standard hospital diet (see table).

TABLE I

SCHIZOPHRENICS EXAMINED FOR URINARY DMPE AND/OR 4MPE

Patient	Sex	Age	Length of illness	Diagnosis	Medication
P.D.	M	15	6 months	A.U.T.	None
A.H.	F	15	3 months	A.U.T.	None
J.McG.	M	19	5 years	C.U.T.	None
M.B.	F	18	3 years	A.U.T.	Chloropromazine
F.W.	M	16	7 years	C.U.T.	None
C.P.	M	24	11 years	C.U.T.	None
M.B.	F	25	8 years	C.T.	Chloropromazine
G.H.	F	22	6 months	A.U.T.	Thioridazine
M.W.	F	30	2 years	P.T.	Thioridazine
H.C.	M	24	4 years	C.U.T.	None
G.D.	F	35	3 years	S.A.T.	Chloropromazine
R.P.	M	40	2 years	P.T. (chronic)	Thioridazine
N.A.	F	21	3 years	C.U.T.	None
H.M.	F	22	3 years	A.U.T.	Trifluoderazine
R.M.	F	21	6 years	S.A.T.	Trifluoderazine
I.L.	F	31	1 year	P.T.	Fluphenazine
V.N.*	F	26	7 years	P.T.	Fluphenazine

A.U.T. = Schizophrenic Reaction, acute, undifferentiated type.
C.U.T. = Schizophrenic Reaction, chronic, undifferentiated type.
C.T. = Schizophrenic Reaction catatonic type.
P.T. = Schizophrenic Reaction, paranoid type.
S.A.T. = Schizophrenic Reaction, schizo-affective type.
* Positive for "pink spot."

In only one case was a spot found on chromatography in the place expected for DMPE and exhibiting the staining reaction described by Friedhoff and Van Winkle (1963b) for DMPE. Its intensity by visual inspection was such that it could have been produced by about 10-15 micrograms of DMPE in the original 24-hour collection (corrected for losses). There was no suggestion of the presence of 4MPE in this patient. Although this patient was on fluphenazine hydrochloride 2 mgm. b.i.d. at the time of collection, urine from another acute paranoid schizophrenic on comparable doses of this drug did not yield the "pink spot." Our records indicate no evidence of hyperexcitability at the time of collection. It has not been possible to obtain a further specimen from this patient to confirm the result or to characterize further the substance responsible.

No ninhydrin-positive spots corresponding to 4MPE were seen in 14 cases, while a technical error prevented any conclusion about the other four. Eleven of the eighteen patients studied were on phenothiazine drugs at the time of urine collection. While the possibility of an inter-action between DMPE and one or more drugs or drug products cannot be excluded, in no instance were there other ninhydrin-positive areas on the final chromatogram which obscured the DMPE or 4MPE areas.

A second study was carried out on persons carrying the gene for homo-cystinuria. Three separate 24-hour urine specimens were obtained from a 25-year-old homocystinuric and schizophrenic female (the patient re-ported by Spiro *et al.,* 1965) and two such specimens from her mother, who has also shown signs of schizophrenia. No evidence of DMPE or 4MPE was found in any sample. As a test of the procedure the third urine sample from the proband was divided into two equal portions, one of which was adulterated with 8 μgm. DMPE and 10 μgm. 4MPE. Readily detectable amounts of 4MPE and DMPE were found in the chromato-gram of the adulterated half-sample while the other half-sample was blank at the corresponding areas. In addition, 24-hour urine specimens were examined from four other patients homozygous for homocystinuria and three other individuals heterozygous for homocystinuria, but not schizophrenics. Urine from the heterozygotes was collected following a load of 200 mgm./kg. methionine given orally in each case, in an attempt to increase the chance of discovering a "pink spot" substance related to methionine metabolism. Neither DMPE nor 4MPE were found in any sample. There was no evidence of schizophrenia in any of these persons who carried the gene for homocystinuria, other than in the mother and daughter mentioned above.

DISCUSSION AND CONCLUSIONS

There is evidence that DMPE may cause behavioral changes in ani-mals (Bergen, 1965; Smythies and Sykes, 1966), though the administra-tion of DMPE to man has been without effect (Shulgin *et al.,* 1966). There is experimental evidence in man, however, to support a more general hypothesis involving a disorder of transmethylation in at least some forms of schizophrenia (Pollin *et al.,* 1961; Park *et al.,* 1965; Kety, 1967). The finding of mentally disturbed subjects among the relatives of homocystinurics intriguingly suggest some link with the transmethylation hypothesis. However, our results show that if there is some relationship between homocystinuria and some form of schizophrenia it is not associated with the urinary excretion of DMPE or 4MPE.

The frequency with which "pink spot" positive individuals have been reported among groups of schizophrenics has varied enormously. Our finding of one such positive among urine samples from eighteen schizophrenics is consistent with other recent studies (Boulton and Felton, 1966b; Bell and Somerville, 1966). It is not clear yet whether this low frequency differs from that in the general population, and the data of Bourdillon *et al.* (1965) on control subjects must be treated with reserve, particularly since the twice-reported occurrence of a "pink spot" in a high percentage of patients with Parkinson's disease (Barbeau *et al.,* 1963; Boulton and Felton, 1966a). A detailed review of the literature to date (Welch and Clower, 1968) indicates that the "DMPE story" contains many conflicting and confusing findings. Currently, it seems uncertain that DMPE is involved in the pathogenesis of any form of schizophrenia, though the involvement of a compound of this general type remains worthy of investigation.

SUMMARY

Dimethoxyphenylethylamine (the "pink spot") and 4-methoxyphenylethylamine can be identified by high voltage electrophoresis followed by paper chromatography at right angles.

Urine extracts from 18 schizophrenics yielded a "pink spot," in only one case. Patients suffering from homocystinuria, and related heterozygous carriers, whether schizophrenic or not, failed to show either substance in their urine.

ACKNOWLEDGMENTS

We are most grateful to Drs. S. H. Boyer, H. M. Dintzis and M. A. Naughton for much help and advice during the course of this study. We also wish to thank K. and K. Laboratories for supplies of 3,4-dimethoxyphenylethylamine and Hoffmann-La Roche for supplies of 4-methoxyphenylethylamine.

REFERENCES

BARBEAU, A., DeGROOT, J-A., JOLY, J. G., RAYMOND-TREMBLAY, D., & DONALDSON, J. (1963). "Urinary excretion of a 3,4-dimethoxyphenylethylamine-like substance in Parkinson's disease." *Rev. Can. Biol.,* 22, 469-472.

BELL, C. E., & SOMERVILLE, A. R. (1966). "Identity of the 'pink spot'." *Nature,* 211, 1405-1406.

BERGEN, J. R. (1965). "Possible relationship of a plasma factor to schizophrenia." *Trans. N. York Acad. Sci.,* 28, 40-46.

BOULTON, A. A., & FELTON, C. A. (1966a). "The pink spot: a red herring?" *Lancet,* 2, 964-965.

———— (1966b). "The 'pink spot' and schizophrenia." *Nature,* 211, 1404-1405.

———— POLLITT, R. J., & MAJER, J. R. (1967). "Identity of a urinary 'pink spot' in schizophrenia and Parkinson's disease." *Nature,* 215, 132-134.

BOURDILLON, R. E., CLARKE, C. A., RIDGES, A. P., SHEPPARD, P. M., HARPER, P., & LESLIE, S. A. (1965). " 'Pink Spot' in the urine of schizophrenics." *Nature,* 208, 453-455.

CARSON, N. A. J., CUSWORTH, D. C., DENT, C. E., FIELD, C. M. B., NEILL, D. W. & WESTALL, R. G. (1963). "Homocystinuria: a new inborn error of metabolism associated with mental deficiency." *Arch. Dis. Childh.,* 38, 425-436.

CREVELING, C. R., & DALY, J. W. (1967). "Identification of 3,4-dimethoxyphenylethylamine from schizophrenic urine by mass spectrometry," *Nature,* 216, 190-191.

FAURBYE, A., & PIND, K. (1964). "Investigation of the occurrence of the dopamine metabolite 3,4-dimethoxyphenylethylamine in the urine of schizophrenics. *Acta psychiat. Scand.,* 40, 240-243.

———— ———— (1966). "Failure to detect 3,4-dimethoxyphenylethylamine in the urine of psychotic children. *Acta psychiat. Scand. Suppl.,* 191, 136-148.

FRIEDHOFF, A. J. (1966). "The Pink spot: a red herring?" *Lancet,* 2, 1188.

———— & VAN WINKLE, E. (1962a). "Isolation and characterization of a compound from the urine of schizophrenics." *Nature,* 194, 897-898.

FRIEDHOFF, A. J., & VAN WINKLE, E. (1962b). "The characteristics of an amine found in the urine of schizophrenic patients." *J. nerv. ment. Dis.,* 135, 550-555.

———— ———— (1963). "A method for the detection of β-phenylethylamines and β-phenylethylamino-acids." *J. Chromatog.,* 11, 272-274.

KETY, S. S. (1967). Discussion comment in *Amines and Schizophrenia* (Ed. H. E. Himwich, S. S. Kety and J. R. Smythies), 129, 131. Pergamon Press, New York.

KUEHL, F. A., JR., HICHENS, M., ORMOND, R. E., MEISINGER, M. A. P., GALE, P. H., CIRILLO, V. J., & BRINK, N. G. (1964). "*Para-o* methylation of dopamine in schizophrenic and normal individuals." *Nature,* 203, 154-155.

———— ORMAND, R. E., & VAN DEN LEUVEL, W. J. A. (1966). "Occurrence of 3,4-dimethoxyphenylacetic acid in urines of normal and schizophrenic individuals." *Nature,* 211, 606-608.

NAUGHTON, M. A., & HAGOPIAN, H. (1962). "Some applications of two-dimensional ionophoresis." *Analyt. Biochem.,* 3, 276-284.

OSMOND, H., & SMYTHIES, J. R. (1952). "Schizophrenia: a new approach." *J. Ment. Sci.,* 98, 309-315.

PARK, L. C., BALDESSARINI, R. J., & KETY, S. S. (1965). "Methionine effects on chronic schizophrenics." *Arch. gen. Psychiat.,* 12, 346-351.

PERRY, T. L. (1963). "*N*-Methylmetanephrine excretion by juvenile psychotics." *Science,* 139, 587-589.

———— (1967). Discussion comment in *Amines and Schizophrenia.* (Eds. H. E. Himwich, S. S. Kety and J. R. Smythies), 265, Pergamon Press, New York.

PERRY, T. L., HANSEN, S., & MacDOUGALL, L. (1967). "Identity and significance of some pink spots in schizophrenia and other conditions." *Nature,* 214, 484-485.

———— ———— & MacINTYRE, L. (1964). "Failure to detect 3,4-dimethoxyphenylethylamine in the urine of schizophrenics." *Nature,* 202, 519-520.

PERRY, T. L., HANSEN, S., MacDOUGALL, L., & SCHWARTZ, C. J. (1966). "Urinary amines in chronic schizophrenia." *Nature,* 212, 146-148.

PIND, K., & FAURBYE, A. (1966). "Does 3,4-dimethoxyphenylethylamine occur in the urine from schizophrenics and normal persons?" *Acta psychiat. Scand.,* 42, 246-251.

POLLIN, W., CARDON, P. V. JR., & KETY, S. S. (1961). "Effects of amino acid feedings in schizophrenic patients treated with iproniazid." *Science,* 133, 104-105.

SEN, N. P. & McGEER, P. L. (1964). "4-methoxyphenylethylamine and 3,4-dimethoxyphenylethylamine in human urine." *Biochem. and biophys. Research Commun.,* 14, 227-232.

SHULGIN, A. T., SARGENT, T., & NARANJO, C. (1966). "Role of 3,4-dimethoxyphenylethylamine in schizophrenia." *Nature,* 212, 1606-1607.

SMYTHIES, J. R., & SYKES, E. A. (1966). "Structure-activity relationship studies on mescaline: the effect of dimethoxyphenylethylamine and N:N-dimethyl-mescaline on the conditioned avoidance response in the rat." *Psychopharmacologia (Berl.),* 8, 324-330.

SPIRO, H. R., SCHIMKE, R. N., & WELCH, J. P. (1965). "Schizophrenia in a patient with a defect in methionine metabolism." *J. nerv. ment. Dis.,* 141, 285-290.

TAKESADA, M., KAKIMOTO, Y., SANO, I., KANEKO, Z. (1963). "3,4-dimethoxyphenylethylamine and other amines in the urine of schizophrenic patients." *Nature,* 199, 203-204.

WELCH, J. P., & CLOWER, C. G. (1968). "3,4-dimethoxyphenylethylamine and schizophrenia." To be published.

WILLIAMS, C. H., GIBSON, J. G., McCORMICK, W. O. (1966). "3,4-dimethoxyphenylethylamine in schizophrenia." *Nature,* 211, 1195.

Section V

GENETIC STUDIES

30

THE MORBIDITY RATE AND ENVIRONMENTAL INFLUENCE IN MONOZYGOTIC CO-TWINS OF SCHIZOPHRENICS

K. Abe

INTRODUCTION

The purpose of this paper is to present some of the findings concerning the morbidity rate of monozygotic co-twins of schizophrenics and the possible influence on it of environmental factors. The work is based on a statistical study of the clinical records available at the MRC Psychiatric Genetics Research Unit.

In the classical twin method, the so-called "concordance rate" was employed to estimate the relative importance of hereditary and environmental factors, that is, the proportion of pairs where both partners show the same trait. In a disease like schizophrenia, where there is a wide variability in the age at first manifestation of the disease, the concordance rate depends greatly on the length of observation; that is, the longer the co-twins are observed, the higher the proportion of them to have the opportunity of falling ill, and the higher the concordance rate. It would be more reasonable to obtain the rate, not as a constant but rather as a function of the length of the follow-up period. The present paper deals with this problem and also discusses how this function is modified by environmental factors.

MATERIALS AND METHODS

Schizophrenic twins and their monozygotic partners were derived from two sources:

Reprinted, by permission of author and editor, from: *The British Journal of Psychiatry*, 115:519-531, 1969.

(1) Slater's series (1953) : twins obtained from the standing population of 20,640 patients from ten London County Council mental hospitals in 1936-1939 and consecutive admissions to the Maudsley Hospital from 1936-1939. This series includes 37 pairs of monozygotic twins, of which one or both were diagnosed schizophrenic. Of the total of 37, 4 pairs in which one of the twins died before the onset of schizophrenia in the other were excluded as they provided no information for this study.

(2) Twins seen between 1948 and 1964 at the Bethlem Royal and Maudsley Hospitals (Gottesman and Shields, 1966) . On admission, every patient is routinely asked whether he was born a twin. From this series 24 monozygotic pairs were taken in whom the co-twin was alive at the time of onset of schizophrenia in the first twin.

Throughout this paper "the first twin" refers to the one who became schizophrenic first and "the second twin" refers to the other, whether or not he became schizophrenic during the observation period. This was without regard to status as index case or otherwise.

Altogether there were 57 pairs of monozygotic twins available for this study. At the time of onset in the first twin all of their co-twins were alive and well, hence we had originally 57 well co-twins. However, the morbidity risk is not merely a proportion of cases who became ill among those who were well at the beginning of the observation, because the latter figure decreases during the observation period because of mortality and so forth. For an exact estimation of the morbidity risk, Weinberg's exact method by morbidity table (Rüdin, 1916) was used (Table 1) .

Whenever possible, the author went back to the hospital record, and the time of onset was determined in the following way: the description under the item "previous illness" and "present illness" by the doctor in charge was given the first preference, and the time of first manifestation of psychopathological symptoms, usually delusion or hallucination, was taken as described.

Usually some indication was given by the doctor in charge as to how long ago the illness started before the patient came to the hospital, and this was taken as the time of onset. Where the original record was not available, the author relied upon the histories obtained later by the staff of the Psychiatric Genetics Research Unit.

RESULTS

Figure 1 shows the percentage of well co-twins in relation to the time after the first twin's onset. The loss of cases by disappearance from

TABLE 1

No. of years after the onset in first twin	(1) Disappeared from observation without becoming schizophrenic	(2) Became schizophrenic during the period	(3) No. well at the end of the period	(4) No. remained well in the middle of the period	(5) Ri (2) divided by (4)	(6) 1—Ri	(7) Successive multiplication II (1—R₁)
0—1	0	10	47	52	0.192	0.808	0.808
2	0	8	39	43	0.186	0.814	0.658
3	1	1	37	38	0.026	0.974	0.641
4	2	3	32	34.5	0.087	0.913	0.585
5	3	1	28	30	0.033	0.967	0.571
6	1	2	25	26.5	0.075	0.925	0.529
7	2	1	22	23.5	0.043	0.957	0.506
8	0	1	21	21.5	0.047	0.953	0.482
9	0	0	21	21	0	1	—
10	2	1	18	19.5	0.051	0.949	0.457
11	1	0	17	17.5	0	1	—
12	1	0	16	16.5	0	1	—
13	2	1	13	14.5	0.069	0.931	0.426
14	1	1	11	12	0.083	0.917	0.390
15	1	0	10	10.5	0	1	—
16	0	0	10	10	0	1	—
17	1	0	9	9.5	0	1	—
18	0	1	8	8.5	0.118	0.882	0.344
19	0	0	8	8	0	1	—
20	1	1	6	7	0.143	0.857	0.295
21	1	0	5	5.5	0	1	—
22	1	1	3	4	0.250	0.750	0.221
28	1	0	2	—	—	—	—
30	1	0	1	—	—	—	—
31	0	1	0	—	—	—	—
Total	23	34					

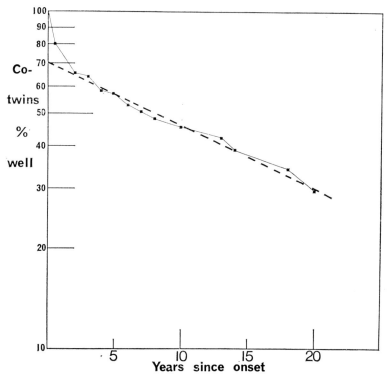

FIG. 1.—Proportion (%) of co-twins still well, in relation to the time elapsed after the first twin's onset.

observation, e.g. due to mortality, has been accounted for by the method already explained. The ordinate is in logarithmic scale.

The morbidity rate in the initial two years is disproportionately high, and afterwards becomes relatively low and steady, that is the co-twins as a whole have a high risk of falling ill within two years following the first twin's onset, and if they pass this period their risk of falling ill for a unit time thereafter is low and does not fluctuate very much from year to year.

(1) Living Together and Closeness of Onset

In order to examine this initial high morbidity and the nature of factors operating, co-twins were divided into two sub-groups:

(A) The "together" group; the co-twins in this group were living together at the time of the first onset in their twin. The co-twins were

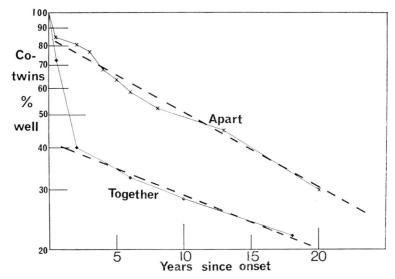

F‌ig. 2.—Proportion of well co-twins in relation to the time elapsed after the first twin's onset in "apart" and "together" group respectively.

thus living together with the psychotic twin in a period ranging from several days to several months, i.e. during the whole onset-admission intervals of the first twin in most of the cases.

(B) The "apart" group, i.e. those co-twins who were already living separately before the onset in the first twin, and thus were in general less exposed to the influence of the psychotic twins, although in a few cases the co-twin regularly visited the patient in the hospital and was showing concern for the patient.

Out of the total of 57 co-twins 25 fell into Group A and 27 into Group B. The remaining five pairs were excluded from consideration because it was difficult to know from the record whether the twins were living together at the onset in the first twin. The morbidity rates in these two groups are shown in Fig. 2. The initial disproportionately high morbidity is much more marked in the "together" group, suggesting that environmental influences played an important role here. The tendency is clearly demonstrated in Table 2, the difference being significant at 0.02 level. However, since the younger the twins the more of them were living together (Table 3), it can be suspected that the high initial morbidity in the "together" group might be due to their, on average, younger age.

To examine this point, we may exclude the co-twins younger than

TABLE 2

CO-TWINS CLASSIFIED ACCORDING TO WHETHER OR NOT THEY WERE
LIVING TOGETHER AT THE TIME OF ONSET OF SCHIZOPHRENIA IN
THE FIRST TWIN, AND WHETHER OR NOT THEIR ONSET FOLLOWED
WITHIN TWO YEARS AFTER THAT OF THE FIRST

| | Second twin's onset | | |
	Within 2 years	Later or never	Total
Twins living together	13	12	25
Twins living apart	5	22	27
Total	18	34	52

$\chi^2 = 6.43$
$0.01 < p < 0.02$

TABLE 3

PAIRS OF TWINS CLASSIFIED ACCORDING TO THE FIRST TWIN'S AGE
OF ONSET AND WHETHER OR NOT THEY WERE LIVING TOGETHER.
(THE DISTRIBUTION HAPPENED TO BE THE SAME AS IN TABLE 2)

| | First twin's age of onset | | |
	Before 20	After 20	Total
Twins living together	13	12	25
Twins living apart	5	22	27
Total	18	34	52

20 years of age at the time of onset in the first twin, and discordant cases. We are then left with ten pairs in the "together group," average age at onset 27.7 years, and ten pairs in the "apart" group, average age 27.4 years; and these groups will be comparable with regard to the question: in which group do second twins who fall ill do so the sooner after the onset in the first twin? The answer is shown in Table 4, and once again the same trend is clearly shown. Therefore the closeness in the age of onset cannot be explained by the younger age of the "together" group, but is to be regarded as a result of their living together and therefore as due to environmental factors.

The closeness in the age of onset in the "together" group can theoretically be caused by circumstances of the following types:

Type 1. The pairs living together were exposed to the same relatively *recent* environmental change acting as a precipitant of the onset in both of the twins.

Type 2. Onset in one of the twins acted as one of the important precipitating factors in the onset of the other.

Since most of the "apart" group had been living together until 18-20 years of age, early long-standing environmental factors, for example childhood environment, should have influenced both "apart" and "together" groups in the same way, and are therefore unlikely to be con-

TABLE 4

INTRA-PAIR DIFFERENCE IN THE TIME OF ONSET IN "CONCORDANT" TWIN PAIRS, ACCORDING TO WHETHER THEY WERE LIVING TOGETHER OR APART AT THE TIME OF ONSET IN THE FIRST TWIN. OUT OF THE TOTAL OF 32 CONCORDANT TWIN PAIRS, 12 PAIRS WITH AGE OF ONSET EARLIER THAN 20 IN ONE OR BOTH OF THE TWINS WERE EXCLUDED

		Second twin's onset		Mean age at onset in first twin (in years)	Mean difference in age of onset (in years)	S.D. of the difference (in years)
Group	Within 2 years	Later	Total			
"Together"	7	3	10	27.7	2.06	1.66
"Apart"	2	8	10	27.4	8.25	7.27
	—	—	—			
Total	9	11	20			

For the first three columns:
By Fisher's exact test $p = 0.035$.

tributing to the difference of initial morbidity between these two groups. For evidence of influences of Type 1 we should therefore look for environmental factors which started to act on both of the twins relatively recently.

(2) *Living Together with a Psychotic Twin as a Precipitating Situation*

Let us first consider the hypothesis that the closeness of onset in the "together" group is due to Type 2 influences and due to either a direct influence by the psychotic twin or an indirect influence through the modified environment, e.g. the family environment, which continues to be influenced by the ill twin, that is, direct or indirect influence by the presence of the psychotic twin in the family. Since the length of time in which the twin and co-twin were living together can be expressed

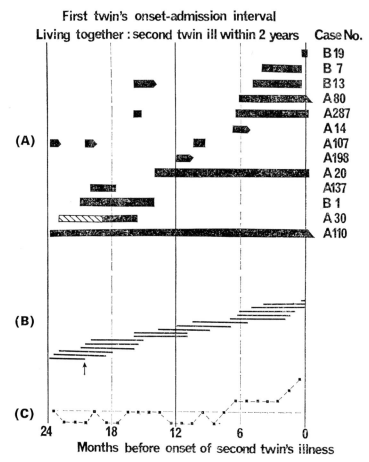

Fig. 3.— (A) The actual timing and duration of exposure of the second twins to the illnesses of the first twins over the 24 months preceding the onset in the second twin. (B) The expected timing of the exposure of the second twins, taking the average onset-admission interval of the first twins, extending in horizontal lines of equal length from the observed time of onset in each individual first twin. Each month is taken as a single point in time, at which there must be an integral number of second twins exposed or not exposed.

An adjustment was made for case A107: the first and the fifth bar from the left originate from the two successive onsets (3 months apart) of a single case. The portion of the first horizontal bar superimposed by the fifth was taken away as a single case cannot be counted twice at the same time. The adjustment is partially responsible for the total of the difference (C in Table VI) being 1 instead of 0. (C) The difference A-B.

in terms of the first twin's onset-admission interval in the "together" group, the interval was calculated for each of the first twins from the records. In cases treated on an out-patient basis, where there was no admission, the onset-remission interval was taken. These two intervals were taken as the best estimates of the duration of the stress imposed on the second twin by the first. In all of these cases, the second twin appears to have been living together not only at the time of onset but also at the time of admission of the first twin, therefore the second twin may be considered to be exposed to the former's influence during the whole interval.

Figure 3a is for those pairs where the second twin was living together with the first and fell ill within two years, and we proceed to examine whether the mean onset-admission interval in first twins in this group is longer than in other groups of cases. Out of the total 52 cases of Table 3, three cases with the first onset dating before 1910 were excluded because of relatively scanty information and disproportionately long onset-admission interval; thus Case A110 of Fig. 3 was excluded in the following analysis. Further, five cases had to be excluded because of the difficulty of obtaining an exact date of admission or onset.

The remaining 44 cases were divided into four groups according to whether or not the twins were living together and the intra-pair difference of onsets. The average length of the interval is shown in Table 5. If Group (1) is compared with all the other cases combined, there are significantly more long-interval cases in Group (1) (by Fisher's exact test, $p = 0.0022$).

However, if (1) is compared with (2), although the mean interval in the former is more than twice as long as in the latter the difference falls short of the conventional 5 percent level of significance ($t = 1.91$, $0.05 < p < 0.1$). Although the finding is suggestive, it is not a statistically sufficient proof of the hypothesis. The hypothesis is further examined from a different angle in the next paragraph.

(3) The Time of Exposure in Relation to the Second Twin's Onset

Next to be examined was how the period of exposure was distributed relative to the second twin's onset in the group where the second twin's onset followed within two years. If the length of exposure to the first twin's influence does not affect the time of onset of the second twin at all, the length of the onset-admission interval would be independent of the subsequent onset in the second twin. The expected distribution of exposure in such a condition was estimated as follows. The mean

TABLE 5

THE FIRST TWIN'S ONSET-ADMISSION INTERVAL IN PAIRS IN WHICH BOTH OF THE TWINS WERE LIVING TOGETHER AND THE SECOND TWIN'S ONSET FOLLOWED WITHIN TWO YEARS, AND IN OTHER GROUPS

	Group	First twin's onset-admission interval			Mean (in months)
		< 2 months	≧ 2 months	Total	
Living together—2nd twin's onset:					
Within 2 years	(1)	3	9	12	5.25
After 2 years	(2)	5	3	8	2.50
Living apart—2nd twin's onset:					
Within two years	(3)	4	1	5	1.10
After 2 years	(4)	14	5	19	1.95
Total		26	18	44	

The difference of the means between Group (1) and (2)—$t = 1.91$: $0.05 < p < 0.1$.

onset-admission interval was calculated from the sum of all the observed onset-admission intervals in this group, and for each month prior to the second twin's onset the number of cases were calculated in which the second twin should theoretically be under exposure to the first twin's influence. Fig. 3 shows under A the actual timing and duration of exposure of the second twins to the illnesses of the first twin over the 24 months preceding the onset in the second twin. Under B is shown the expected timing of the exposure of the second twins, taking the average onset-admission interval of the first twins, extending in horizontal lines of equal length from the observed time of onset in each individual first twin. Each month is taken as a single point in time, at which there must be an integral number of second twins exposed or not exposed. The expected value was subtracted from the observed number of cases under exposure, for each month, to see if there were any tendency for the exposure to occur excessively in a certain particular time relative to the second twin's onset. The result is shown in Fig. 3C, demonstrating an excessive number of cases with exposure occurring near the second twin's onset. There is a significant tendency for exposure to occur in fewer cases in months remote from the second twin's onset.

The significance of the trend is, by "the turning point method" (Yule and Kendall, 1958, p. 638),

$$\frac{p'-p''}{\sqrt{\text{var } p}} = \frac{14.66-7}{\sqrt{3.95}} = 3.85$$

where p' and var p are the theoretical mean and variance of the number of turning points and p'' the actual number of the points, and by "serial correlation method,"

$$\frac{r_1}{\sqrt{\text{var } r_1}} = \frac{0.654}{0.209} = 3.13$$

Where r_1 is the serial correlation of order 1 obtained from the series C of Table 6 (also Fig. 3C).

Both ratios are larger than 3 (i.e. three times the standard deviation) and therefore significant.

(4) *A Common Environmental Factor as a Precipitant of the Onset in Both of the Twins Living together*

Now we have to consider the possibility of a Type 1 factor being the only responsible cause of the closeness of onset. Since intra-pair differ-

TABLE 6

No. of months prior to 2nd twin's onset	A No. of 2nd twins exposed to 1st twin's illness	B Expected No. of 2nd twins exposed	C Difference (A-B)
24	2	2	0
23	2	3	—1
22	2	3	—1
21	4	5	—1
20	5	5	0
19	4	5	—1
18	3	4	—1
17	3	3	0
16	4	4	0
15	3	3	0
14	3	3	0
13	2	3	—1
12	3	4	—1
11	3	4	—1
10	3	3	0
9	2	3	—1
8	2	2	0
7	4	3	1
6	5	4	1
5	5	4	1
4	6	5	1
3	6	5	1
2	6	4	2
1	7	4	3
		Total	1

ences of physical or psychological measures of monozygotic twins show approximately a distribution of the right half of the normal curve—with the maximum at *o* differences and tapering off towards the right—one can expect intra-pair differences of resistance to a hypothetical exogenous factor, measured by the number of days exposed to this factor before falling ill, to be distributed somewhat similarly, although it may not be an exact normal curve.

If we allow the efficacy of the exogenous factor to vary from case to case (but not within the pair), but assume that both of the twins started to be exposed to the factor at about the same time and to the same intensity, the distribution of the intra-pair difference of the onset would be a curve with decreasing frequency with increase along the abscissa (the difference), since it can be considered theoretically as a sum of normal curves of varying shape with a maximum at *o* difference.

The observed distribution (Table 7), however, shows the opposite tendency—a significant increase towards the right with a regression co-

TABLE 7

INTRA-PAIR DIFFERENCE OF FIRST ONSET IN TWINS SHOWN IN FIG. 3A

	Intra-pair difference between onsets (in months)				
	0-5.9	6-11.9	12-17.9	18-23.9	Total
No. of pairs	2	3	3	5	13

Regression coefficient $b = 0.15$ $t(b) = 5.66$ $0.02 < p < 0.05$.

efficient $b = 0.15$, $t_{(b)} = 5.66$ and $0.02 < p < 0.05$; and the hypothesis that the closeness of the age of onset in the "together" group is only due to the fact that they happened to be living together when a certain exogenous factor operated, influential enough to precipitate the onset in both, is not likely to be supported at least in its pure form as described above.

(5) Later Steady "Decay" and Analogy to the Radioactive Isotope

Let us now come back to the curve in Fig. 1 and consider the steady decrease of percentage of well co-twins after the initial dip for two years.
The equation of the straight line was found to be

$$N = 70 \, e^{-0.0424 \, t} \qquad \ldots \ldots \ldots \quad (1)$$

where N is the percentage of cases (co-twins) remaining well t-years after the onset in the first twin, in the absence of mortality and provided that all co-twins have been followed up at least for t years. The equation is of the form $N = Ae^{-kt}$ which applies to the decay of radioactive isotopes; the half life in this case would be 16.3 years.

Taking the logarithm of both sides and differentiating we have

$$\log N = \log A - kt$$

$$\frac{d \log N}{dt} = -k$$

$$\frac{1}{N}\frac{dN}{dt} = -k \qquad \ldots \ldots \ldots \quad (2)$$

That is, of co-twins still remaining well, a fraction k falls ill in unit time over the total period of observation just as it is a constant fraction of radioactive isotope that decays in unit time.

In Fig. 2 we see that the slope of decrease is smaller in the "together" group, which is reasonably to be expected after two years of rapid removal of easily decayable elements from the group by environmental factors.

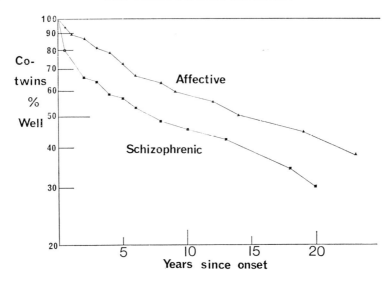

F<small>IG</small>. 4.—Proportion of well co-twins in relation to the time elapsed after the first twin's onset, in schizophrenic and affective groups.

However, this difference is not found to be statistically significant. In Fig. 4 the morbidity rate of affective disorder calculated in the same way was compared with that of the schizophrenics. The first onset of affective disorder was taken as the time of onset, as in the schizophrenic series, with any individual who falls ill leaving observation at that moment of time. It is interesting that these two groups show almost the same later decay rate. The value of k in the formula therefore may be fairly constant among different types of functional psychoses.

(6) *Concordance Rate or Morbidity Risk*

Another use of the regression line of Fig. 1 is to estimate what proportion of the co-twins would be spared from illness if they could be followed up 25 years after the onset in the first schizophrenic twin. Twenty-five years' follow up may be considered long enough, since even where one twin were to fall ill as early as 20 years of age, the surviving co-twin would, after 25 years, have reached the age of 45. The risk of becoming schizophrenic for the first time after this age is low, even in the general population. Since also there is a positive correlation in the age of onset between the twins, one may expect a very low probability of one twin falling ill 25 years after the onset in the other.

As the number of twins followed up more than 15 years is rather small, we cannot extend the curve itself from the tail end: we simply extend the regression line up to $t = 25$, which gives the value of $N = 24.3$, and assume the percentage of twins remaining untouched by schizophrenia to be around this level. Hence about 75.7 per cent of the co-twins can be expected to become schizophrenic given 25 years in which to do so.

This might be regarded as an assessment of the morbidity risk of the monozygotic twins of schizophrenics and can be compared with Kallmann's (1946) 85.8 per cent and Slater's (1953) 76.3 percent age-corrected estimate.

DISCUSSION

The morbidity of the co-twins of schizophrenics was found to be an exponential function of the time elapsed after the first twin's onset except in the initial two years. The initial high morbidity is due to the cases with small intra-pair difference in onsets. Provided the other conditions are the same, the larger the proportion of such cases, the higher is the correlation coefficient. The environmental factors found to influence this initial high morbidity may also be regarded as influencing the correlation coefficient. This initial high morbidity was much more marked in those second twins who were living together with the first twin at the time of the first twin's onset, suggesting an environmental factor.

It is also important to consider here whether or not any bias in selection of the material can produce such a finding. If the twins of the "apart" group are in general followed up for a shorter period, which may be due to some difficulty in locating the twin and so forth—in fact they are followed up at an average of 14.78 years and this is shorter by about four years compared with 18.52 years of the "together" group—there may be an underestimation of cases with larger intra-pair difference, which would however, result in an opposite tendency to the finding obtained. Therefore the above finding cannot be explained by a selection bias. Although the onset-admission interval was not significantly longer in twins who were living together and where the second twin became ill within two years, the exposure in them was found to have occurred more frequently just before or during the onset of the second twin, a finding in favor of the "interaction hypothesis."

There was no support for the hypothesis that the closeness of the age of onset in this "living together" group is entirely due to the fact that they happened to be living together when an exogenous factor influential enough to precipitate the onset in both came into operation. This does not, however, rule out the presence of such a mechanism: it may be responsible in some cases. For this mechanism to be in conformity with the findings, we should have to assume that in general the responsible exogenous factor is of a long-lasting nature and that the twins are in general exposed to this factor very differently, i.e. different intensity and/or length of time, otherwise it would be difficult to account for the predominance of cases with intra-pair difference of onset larger than a year.

It would be of much interest to examine whether the exponential function (Equation 1) can be demonstrated in the data obtained by other investigators. Luxemburger's (1936) and Kallmann's data would have been suitable for this purpose if they had given the data on the length of follow-up of the discordant twins which are indispensable for the calculation of R_i in Table 1. Mitsuda's (1964) report on 16 pairs of monozygotic twins includes the length of follow-up of each discordant twin. The data were analysed using the method described above (Weinberg's non-abridged method), and the value of N is shown in Fig. 5. The curve shows no initial dip. The main difference in composition between his and the present material is that his material contains six pairs who were reared apart from infancy (and in none of these pairs is the difference in the age of onset less than three years), while the present material contains only one pair reared apart. There has been a tendency in Japan to separate twins in childhood. Whether or not the absence of the initial dip in Mitsuda's material can be adequately accounted for by these differences is still open to question, though it is a reasonable speculation. An interesting finding here is that his data, like those in Figs. 1 and 2, show no large deviation from a straight line.

To examine the meaning of the straight line to which the data in Figs. 1, 2 and 5 have been approximated, let us take the following situation and see what kind of function is expected for N. Suppose there is no intra-pair correlation in the time of onset, and the onset occurs randomly among the subjects so predisposed, whose number in the initial state is N_0. Then each of N_0 co-twins has theoretically an equal chance of having an onset at any moment, just as every atom of radium has an equal chance of decaying. Consequently,

$$-dN = cN\, dt$$

and hence

$$N = N_0 e^{-ct} \quad . \quad . \quad . \quad . \quad . \quad . \quad . \quad . \quad (3)$$

where N is the expected number of cases remaining well at time t in the

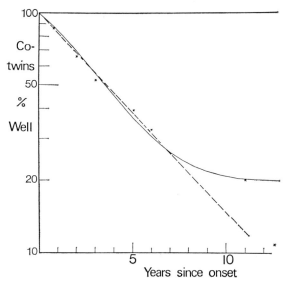

FIG. 5.—Mitsuda's schizophrenic twin data analysed by the method shown in Table 1, with expected values from Equation 3 (- - - - -) and 4 (———).

absence of mortality and other loss of cases during the observation period, and c a constant. Here the genetic predisposition influences which of the subjects in the population is capable of becoming ill (that is to define the size of N_0) but not *when* the onset occurs.

If there is an intra-pair correlation in the age of onset, and if we assume an originally normal distribution of the intra-pair differences in age of onset, it can be shown that, in place of Equation 3, we shall have

$$N = 1 - B \int_0^t e^{-\frac{t^2}{2\sigma^2}} dt \quad .. \quad (4)$$

where B is a constant to be adjusted.

To see how these equations 3 and 4 fit the observed data, the expected values from these equations are shown in Fig. 5 along with Mitsuda's data; the type 4 equation of best fit was found to be

$$N = 1 - \frac{0 \cdot 3}{3 \cdot 76 \sqrt{\pi}} \sqrt{2} \int_0^t e^{-\frac{1}{2}\left(\frac{t}{3 \cdot 76}\right)^2} dt$$

As N approaches 0.2 as t increases, 0.2 of the co-twins ultimately can be expected to remain well. The standard deviation (σ) of the difference in the age of onset would be 3.76 years. However, owing to the small size of the sample, it is difficult to decide which type of equation fits the observed data better; this is also the case with the present material.

It is apparent that the initial dip, which is very marked in the "together" group and was found to be mainly due to environmental influence, contributes much to the correlation coefficient, although it does not follow that there is no genetic influence on the age of onset. There is some evidence in the literature for such a genetic influence; for example Luxemburger (1936) and Abe (1966).

Since a linear approximation in Figs. 1, 2 and 5 does not seem to be very unsatisfactory, we may say that genetic influence on the age of onset is presumably not so strong as to make linear approximation totally inadequate; and at least if we take a short period, the onset can be regarded as occurring fairly randomly *after the initial two years*.

SUMMARY

From the data on 57 co-twins of schizophrenics available at the MRC Psychiatric Genetics Research Unit, the morbidity rate of the monozygotic co-twins was obtained, using a modified Weinberg method, as a function of time elapsed after the onset in the twin who first became ill (referred to as "the first twin") and examined in relationship to modifying exogenous factors.

(1) The morbidity was found to be an exponential curve $N = 70e^{0.0424\,t}$, where N is the percentage of co-twins still remaining well t-years after the first twin's onset, except in the initial two years where the morbidity is significantly higher and deviates from this formula. A similar exponential curve also fitted Mitsuda's schizophrenic twin data.

(2) This "initial high morbidity" was much more marked in the second twins who were living together with the first twin at the time of the first twin's onset, suggesting an environmental factor as being responsible for this deviation.

(3) There was no support for the hypothesis that the closeness of the age of onset in this "living together" group is entirely due to the fact that they happened to be living together when an exogenous factor influential enough to precipitate the onset in both, occurred.

(4) The onset-admission interval was longer in twins who were living together and where the second twin became ill within two years, but the difference was not statistically significant. However, the exposure was found to have occurred more frequently just before or during the onset

of the second twin, a statistically significant finding suggesting the significance of exposure to the first twin's influence.

(5) An estimation of morbidity risk was obtained and was found to be 75.7 per cent.

ACKNOWLEDGMENTS

The author is very grateful to Dr. Eliot Slater and Mr. James Shields for giving him access to their original case records and for valuable assistance, and to Dr. John S. Price for useful criticism during the present study.

REFERENCES

ABE, K. (1966). "Susceptibility to psychoses and precipitating factors; a study of families with two or more psychotic members." *Psychiat. Neurol.*, 151, 276-290.

GOTTESMAN, I. I., & SHIELDS, J. (1966). "Schizophrenia in twins: 16 years' consecutive admissions to a psychiatric clinic." *Brit. J. Psychiat.*, 112, 809-818.

KALLMANN, F. J. (1946). "The genetic theory of schizophrenia. An analysis of 691 schizophrenic twin index families." *Amer. J. Psychiat.*, 103, 309-322.

LUXENBURGER, H. (1936). "Untersuchungen an schizophrenen Zwillingen und ihren Geschwistern zur Prüfung der Realität von Manifestationsschwankungen." *Z. ges. Neurol. Psychiat.*, 154, 351-394.

MITSUDA, H. (1964). "Clinical genetics in psychiatry." *Jap. J. hum. Genet.*, 9, 61-81.

RÜDIN, E. (1916). "Studien über Vererbung und Entstehung geistiger Störungen." *I. Zur Vererbung und Neuentstehung der Dementia Praecox.* Berlin: Springer.

SLATER, E. (1953). *Psychotic and Neurotic Illnesses in Twins.* Med. Res. Coun. Spec. Rept. Ser., No. 278. London: H.M.S.O.

YULE, G. U., & KENDALL, M. G. (1958). *An Introduction to the Theory of Statistics* (14th edition). London: Griffin.

31

COMPARISON OF HOSPITALIZATION MEASURES IN SCHIZOPHRENIC PATIENTS WITH AND WITHOUT A FAMILY HISTORY OF SCHIZOPHRENIA

L. Erlenmeyer-Kimling and Susan Nicol

It is well known that an individual with a family history of schizophrenia carries an increased risk of manifesting the disorder in comparison with members of the population at large. Also, within the population of schizophrenic patients, individuals may or may not have other members of the family affected. Obviously also, schizophrenic patients may be distinguished by gradations of severity of the illness. Whether familial incidence of schizophrenia and severity co-vary, however, remains an open question.

Although it is a question of some theoretical interest, this problem has received attention chiefly in investigations centered on the search for prognostic indicators. Early findings suggested that the presence of mental illness in the relatives of psychotic patients might be correlated with favorable outcome. Later analysis by specific types of disorders in the family members showed that only the more benign affective disorders occurred with greater frequency among the relatives of remitted or improved schizophrenics than in the families of chronic cases (Kant, 1942; Langfeldt, 1939; Vaillant, 1962). Indeed, data from several studies indicated that schizophrenic patients whose disease processes followed a deteriorating course were more likely to have family histories positive for schizophrenia than were "recovered" patients (Kant, 1942; Nameche et al., 1964; Vaillant, 1962). Astrup's data (1966), though not strictly comparable to those of other investigators due to the inclusion in his patient group of cases with other functional psychoses, similarly pointed

Reprinted, by permission of author and editor, from: *The British Journal of Psychiatry*, 115:321-334, 1969.

to an association between chronicity and a family history of schizophrenia.

Other data, however, yield no evidence of co-variation between family history of schizophrenia and severity. Malamud and Render (1939), for example, found no difference in the proportions of recovered and chronic schizophrenic patients with schizophrenic relatives. It is to be noted, moreover, that, while studies of relatives concordant for schizophrenia show a moderate degree of within-family similarity in course and outcome of the illness (cf. Tsuang, 1967), considerable variability in severity across multiple-affected families can also be demonstrated.

New data relevant to the problem became available in the course of a survey of schizophrenic patients admitted to hospitals in 1934-1936 and 1954-1956 (Erlenmeyer-Kimling et al., 1966). Although the survey was concerned primarily with marriage and fertility trends, the longitudinal follow-up of the patients provided hospitalization histories and family mental health data that lend themselves to other types of analyses as well. Since patients in each of the two admission samples were found to vary widely on measures of severity it was considered that any association between severity and familial incidence of schizophrenia should be reflected in comparisons of quantitative aspects of hospitalization of patients with and without schizophrenic relatives.

SUBJECTS AND METHODS

Schizophrenic patients (index cases) for the main survey of marriage and fertility trends were drawn from samples of consecutive admissions, during the years 1934-1936 and 1954-1956, to eleven State mental hospitals in New York. From the 3,337 index cases studied subsamples of the white cases were drawn for follow-up beyond the admission period. Detailed descriptions of the sampling, diagnostic verification, random selection of cases for follow-up, and the follow-up procedures are reported elsewhere (Erlenmeyer-Kimling et al., in press). In the follow-up phase complete hospitalization histories were obtained on 1,899 cases up to the date of death or to the time that the investigation was in progress (i.e. 1961-1965). Completion of the family histories, including ascertainment of mental illnesses, was also undertaken. A diagnosis of schizophrenia was entered for a relative only when there had been at least one admission to a mental hospital and when the clinical records could be submitted to one or more staff psychiatrists for independent evaluations of mental status.

Out of the pool of (white) index cases with completed hospitalization and family data, and with at least one sibling, patients could be separated into those with and those without schizophrenia among their first-degree relatives. In total 263 patients were identified as having at least one family member (parent, sibling or both) who had been hospitalized for schizophrenia. The proportion of such patients was about the same among the followed cases from each of the two admission periods (19.0 per cent in the 1934-1936 group and 16.6 per cent in the 1954-1956 group).

For the present set of analyses it was planned to match each of the cases with positive family history with one of the negative family history cases from the pool for the following variables: sex, admission period, year of birth, sibship size, and area of residence in New York State. I.B.M. punch cards from the main survey were used to sort the cases on the several variables. Adequate matching could not be achieved for four of the cases with schizophrenic relatives and they were accordingly discarded from the further analyses. Six patients of twin birth were also discarded, since they could not be matched for twinship as well as for all the other matching criteria. The number of cases entering into the analyses therefore was 253 patients with positive family history and 253 matchmates with negative family history. The 506 index cases had a total of 3,355 first-degree relatives (1,012 parents and 2,343 siblings). The two types of cases are hereafter distinguished as the "family history" cases and the "matchmates."

The family history cases were divided into three principal groups: *Group I*—158 cases with schizophrenia in siblings only (187 affected siblings); *Group II*—71 cases with schizophrenia in parents only (27 affected fathers and 45 affected mothers—one case having two affected parents); *Group III*—24 cases with schizophrenia in parents and siblings (32 affected siblings, 10 affected fathers and 15 affected mothers—one case again having two affected parents). These groups were further divisible into four subgroups each, by sex of the index case and by admission period (1934-1936 or 1954-1956). The twelve subgroups (Table 1) have been separately analyzed to allow for identification of possible differential effects according to the relationship of the affected family member to the index case or according to the sex of the index case, and to allow the groups from the two admission periods to serve as replicates of each other.

Each matchmate of course belonged to the same sex and admission period as the family history case. Precise matching within a pair could not be achieved on all of the other variables. When this was not possible the matching was equalized within the subgroup to which the pair belonged. Thus, for example, it was possible to match the members of

TABLE 1

NUMBER OF MATCHED PAIRS (FAMILY HISTORY CASE AND MATCHMATE) AND MEAN YEAR OF BIRTH* FOR EACH SUBGROUP

Sex and admission period	Group I (cases with schizophrenia in siblings only) and their matchmates		Group II (cases with schizophrenia in parents only) and their matchmates		Group III (cases with schizophrenia in parents and siblings) and their matchmates	
	Number of pairs	Mean year of birth	Number of pairs	Mean year of birth	Number of pairs	Mean year of birth
1934-36 Male	57	1903	21	1909	4	1906
Female	44	1902	19	1908	7	1905
1954-56 Male	25	1919	11	1923	5	1925
Female	32	1922	20	1917	8	1921
Total	158		71		24	

* Mean year of birth is the same for family history cases and for matchmates within each subgroup.

only 84 pairs for exact year of birth. The intrapair difference, however, never exceeded five years, and the mean birthyears within each subgroup were the same for the family history cases and the matchmates (Table 1). Area of residence (based on admitting hospital) was precisely matched in 221 pairs; although the remaining 32 pairs could not be matched precisely on this variable the ratio of metropolitan to non-metropolitan cases was the same for family history cases as for the match-mates within subgroups. Sibship size was exactly matched in 230 pairs; the 23 discrepant pairs all came from sibship sizes greater than five, and in all but two of these pairs the matchmate had more siblings than did the family history case.

In a few instances a family history case was found to have more than one potential matchmate after all of the above variables had been taken into account. The alternatives were then screened on still another variable, viz. year of last information, and the one most closely coinciding with the family history case on this variable was chosen as the matchmate.

Data analyses reported in the following section are of two kinds: (a) comparisons of other variables that might be associated with prognosis but that could not be included in the matching procedure; (b) comparisons of hospitalization measures as indices of severity.

RESULTS

A. *Comparisons of Other Prognostic Variables*

The purpose of the matching was to equate the cases with and without schizophrenic relatives as closely as possible on other variables before proceeding to the evaluation of severity. Matching obviously could not be extended to include all of the factors that have been considered by various investigators to be indicators of prognosis. In order to assess residual differences between the family history cases and their matchmates other than the presence or absence of schizophrenic relatives comparisons were made with respect to the following variables: (1) history of other psychiatric disorders in first-degree relatives; (2) educational level; (3) marital status at admission; (4) ages at onset and at first admission; and (5) duration of illness prior to admission.

(1) *Frequency of other psychiatric disorders in first-degree relatives.* Other psychiatric disorders here include: epilepsy, general paresis, involutional psychosis, manic-depressive psychosis, mental deficiency with and without psychosis, personality disorders, psychoses of aging, and psychosis with encephalitis. Of 1,244 nonschizophrenic parents and siblings belonging to the family history cases, 43 (20 parents, 23 sib-

lings belonging to 36 index cases) were hospitalized for one of these other psychiatric disorders. By contrast only 25 (12 parents, 13 siblings belonging to 22 index cases) of the 1,695 relatives of the matchmates required hospitalization for these disorders. The difference between the two frequencies is highly significant ($\chi^2 = 9.97$, p $<.005$). It is important to note that the families of the two types of cases did not differ with respect to either manic-depressive psychosis or neurotic depressions, the ten relatives with these diagnoses being evenly divided between the family history cases and the matchmates. It is not clear how other investigators of the association between family history and severity have classified the affective disorders; if involutional psychosis is to be included the family history cases would be considered to have a proportionately higher number of relatives with affective disorders (11 for them and 7 for the matchmates).

In addition another ten relatives who had never been hospitalized were known to have committed suicide, and 57 relatives were recorded as showing psychiatric conditions which did not lead to hospitalization. Some of the latter had clear-cut diagnoses, such as epilepsy or cerebral arteriosclerosis, but were capable of being managed at home. In other cases, however, the condition was not clearly referable to a specific diagnostic entity and some of these relatives may have represented marginal conditions on the schizophrenia spectrum. It is not claimed that the procedures used in this investigation were capable of providing a good estimate of marginal and sub-clinical deviations in relatives. Nevertheless, it was found that the family history cases once again had a disproportionately higher frequency of parents and siblings with the various conditions for which information was available: 32 of the 57 relatives with non-hospitalized disorders and 6 of the 10 suicides belonged to the family history cases.

(2) *Education.* No differences in educational level were found between the family history cases and their matchmates within the subgroups, and it was of particular interest that the Group II patients achieved the same educational standing as subjects from potentially less disruptive backgrounds. Cases from the 1954-1956 admission period had an average of ten years of schooling compared to nine years for cases from the 1934-1936 admission period in line with the rise in educational level in the population as a whole over this time. No differences were found between males and females within the same admission period.

(3) *Marital status.* In general the marriage rates at first admission for the 506 subjects studied here were comparable to those found in the main survey of marriage and fertility for the larger samples of index

TABLE 2
Age at First Admission for Family History Cases and Matchmates, by Subgroup

Sex and admission period			Group I	Matches	Group II	Matches	Group III	Matches
1934-36	Male	X±SE	27.3±1.0	27.5±1.1	24.0±1.2	25.4±1.8	23.2±3.5	25.0±2.7
		Median	25.0	25.0	22.0	24.0	24.5	27.0
	Female	X±SE	27.9±1.3	29.4±1.5	24.5±1.2	23.8±1.3	26.3±3.3	29.7±3.4
		Median	25.0	28.0	23.0	23.0	22.0	26.0
1954-56	Male	X±SE	29.0±1.9	30.6±2.0	25.3±3.6	29.6±2.7	24.6±2.8	25.2±2.1
		Median	29.0	30.0	25.0	27.0	24.0	24.0
	Female	X±SE	27.6±1.5	30.2±1.3	31.6±2.0	34.8±1.9	30.9±3.8	29.9±3.6
		Median	26.5	30.5	33.0	36.5	31.5	29.0

t values (2 tail) not significant within subgroups.

cases (Erlenmeyer-Kimling *et al.,* in press). As in the main survey the subjects from the 1954-1956 admission period had higher marriage rates than those from the 1934-1936 period and proportionately more females of each period were married than males. The number of family history cases married by first admission was approximately the same as for the matchmates within all subgroups with the single exception of the Group I females, 1954-1956, where the family history cases had a significantly lower marriage rate.

(4) *Age at onset, age at first admission, and duration of illness prior to admission.* The admission to hospital in 1934-1936 or 1954-1956 did not necessarily represent the first admission for a given index case. Thus, even though the family history cases and their matchmates were equated for year of birth and for admission in 1934-1936 or 1954-1956, they could be compared for possible differences in age at first admission.

The mean age at first admission did not differ significantly for the family history cases and their matchmates within any of the subgroups (Table 2). On the intrapair comparisons the family history cases were found to have been admitted at younger ages than their matchmates in 50 percent of the pairs and at the same age in 10 percent. The intrapair difference moreover tended to be quite small (e.g. 5 years or less in 69 percent of the pairs) whereas data from studies relating differential prognosis to age at admission (cf. Israel and Johnson, 1956) have been based on substantially larger disparities (e.g. 15 years or more).

Data on age at onset (not presented here) were similar in all respects to the data on age at first admission. The average interval elapsing between onset and first admission was 3.0 years for the family history cases and 3.2 years for the matchmates. In so far as the estimation of onset may be regarded as reliable, then, it appears that the duration of illness prior to admission was about the same for both types of cases.

To summarize the comparisons of prognostic factors on which the family history cases and their matchmates were free to vary there were no important differences found with the exception of family history of other psychiatric disorders.

B. *Comparisons of Hospitalization Histories*

Indices of severity were based on: the total number of months hospitalized, number of months in hospital per admission, and final outcome. Analyses of these measures were performed for two different follow-up intervals. In the first both members of a pair were followed to the same age, i.e. for the same amount of time in the life-span. In the second set of analyses all cases were followed for a standard interval beyond admission. In the comparisons of the family history cases and their matchmates attention was given to variability of the distributions as well as to central tendencies. Finally two sets of analyses were performed in an attempt to evaluate patterns of hospitalization.

Data from the analyses based on equal follow-up in the life-span are summarized in Table 3. The cases with schizophrenic siblings (Group I) did not differ significantly from their matchmates in either mean length of hospitalization or variability. Nor was there a consistent directional trend across subgroups, although either admission period taken alone might have given the impression that the Group I cases tended to spend less time (1934-1936) or more time (1954-1956) in hospital than their matchmates. The final outcome measure (percent of cases hospitalized at the end of follow-up) also failed to differentiate between the two types of cases; although one of the subgroups (females, 1954-1956) showed a higher proportion of hospitalized family history cases than matchmates the difference was not significant and the other three subgroups revealed identical, or nearly identical, final outcome status for both types of cases. It will be noted from Table 3 that the two measures, length of hospitalization (correspondingly, percentage of time spent in hospital) and final outcome status, are not necessarily correlated within subgroups. Of the two, final outcome status is more subject to chance fluctuations and an attempt to place the two measures in perspective will be presented subsequently with the analysis of hospitalization patterns.

Comparisons involving the cases with schizophrenic parents (Group II) showed a distinct trend with respect to mean length of hospitalization but not with respect to variability or final outcome. Although the mean difference in length of hospitalization reached a significant level on the t-test for only one of the subgroups (females, 1954-1956), the direction of the difference was the same in all four subgroups, with the family history cases tending to spend more time in hospital than their matchmates. Moreover, intrapair comparisons on the sign test (Siegel, 1956) were significant at the .03 level for all subgroups combined. The data in Table 3 also demonstrate that the Group II cases on the whole were hospitalized for a greater percentage of their lives than were the Group I cases (with the single exception of the males, 1954-1956) or than the Group I matchmates. The apparently consistent trend toward increased severity for the Group II cases that seems to emerge from the measures relating to length of hospitalization does not hold for the data on final outcome. The proportion of patients hospitalized at the end of follow-up was greater for the family history cases in only two of the subgroups

TABLE 3

NUMBER OF YEARS FOLLOWED IN LIFE-SPAN, NUMBER OF YEARS HOSPITALIZED, PERCENT OF TIME HOSPITALIZED, AND PERCENT OF CASES HOSPITALIZED AT FINAL EVALUATION, BY SUBGROUP

Sex and admission period	Group I	Matches	Group II	Matches	Group III	Matches
1934-36 Males						
Mean years followed	53.6	53.6	49.0	49.0	56.8	56.8
Mean years hospitalized	15.4±1.6	16.7±1.6	16.7±2.7	12.9±2.6	27.2±4.3	21.3±7.0
% of time hospitalized	28.7	31.2	34.1	26.3	47.9	37.5
% of cases hospitalized at final evaluation	70.1	68.4	76.2	57.1	75.0	75.0
1934-36 Females						
Mean years followed	55.0	55.0	48.6	48.6	56.6	56.6
Mean years hospitalized	14.6±1.8	15.4±1.7	15.2±2.5	13.0±2.4	16.6±4.3	14.8±3.6
% of time hospitalized	26.5	28.0	31.3	26.7	29.3	26.1
% of cases hospitalized at final evaluation	61.4	61.4	63.1	68.4	71.4	42.9
1954-56 Males						
Mean years followed	42.5	42.5	38.6	38.6	35.8	35.8
Mean years hospitalized	6.2±1.5	4.0±0.9	4.5±1.4	2.8±0.9	4.7±2.7	10.1±4.5
% of time hospitalized	14.6	9.4	11.6	7.2	13.1	28.2
% of cases hospitalized at final evaluation	36.0	36.0	27.3	27.3	20.0	80.0
1954-56 Females						
Mean years followed	39.6	39.6	44.5	44.5	40.8	40.8
Mean years hospitalized	4.5±0.8	3.2±1.0	6.9±1.7*	2.5±0.5*	3.6±1.1	6.1±0.9
% of time hospitalized	11.4	8.1	15.5	5.6	8.8	15.0
% of cases hospitalized at final evaluation	28.1	18.7	35.0	25.0	50.0	37.5

*$t = 2.46$, $p < .02$ (2 tail).

(males, 1934-1936 and females, 1954-1956), neither of them differing significantly from the matchmates.

The Group III cases (with schizophrenia in parents and siblings) showed no distinct trend in relation to their matchmates either on the measures in Table 3 or on the other measures of hospitalization to be presented. Because of the small size of the subgroups and the extreme variability within subgroups, however, the comparisons were considered to be of doubtful reliability, and data on these cases will be omitted from most of the analyses that follow.

In the second set of analyses the follow-up intervals were standardized across pairs by evaluating all cases from the 1934-1936 period as of 15 years after first admission and all cases from the 1954-1956 period as of 5 years after admission. The standard intervals permit more meaningful comparisons across analysis groups. Twenty-three of the 229 pairs from Groups I and II had to be excluded from these analyses because one or both members had not been followed for the required time. In all of these pairs one or both members died before the end of the standard interval (in 16 pairs the family history case died, in 5 the matchmate died, and in 2 pairs both members died). (It should not be assumed from these figures that patients with a positive family history of schizophrenia have a higher death rate than patients with a negative family history since in the matching procedure an attempt was made to exclude potential matchmates whose follow-up histories were fore-shortened by death.)

In Table 4 it may be seen that the Group I cases continued to be indistinguishable from their matchmates in terms of the percentage distribution of months hospitalized and the mean length of hospitalization during the standard interval. The data for the Group II cases are here less clear. The directional trend, observed in the previous analysis in the comparisons of mean values for the Group II cases with those of their matchmates, continues to be seen in Table 4 but perhaps merits less emphasis here since in this analysis the sign test of the intrapair differences failed to yield significant results. It may be noted also that the mean length of hospitalization was not necessarily greater for the Group II cases than for Group I or their matchmates. Additional indications of increased chronicity for the Group II patients were seen, however, in that these cases were more likely to remain continuously hospitalized throughout the interval than were any of the other patient groups.

The measures examined thus far have been the straightforward ones concerned with overall length of hospitalization and with final outcome status. In order to assess more fully any possible differences in patterning of hospitalization of the cases with positive and negative family histories

TABLE 4

PERCENT DISTRIBUTION OF CASES BY MONTHS HOSPITALIZED AND MEAN LENGTH OF HOSPITALIZATION IN STANDARD (15- OR 5-YEAR) INTERVAL FOLLOWING FIRST ADMISSION BY SUBGROUP

1934-1936 Cases

Number of months hospitalized	Male Group I (N = 49 prs.)	Matches	Male Group II (N = 18 prs.)	Matches	Female Group I (N = 39 prs.)	Matches	Female Group II (N = 17 prs.)	Matches
0- 24	26.5	18.4	27.7	38.9	30.8	15.4	23.5	17.6
25- 60	18.4	10.2	5.6	5.6	15.4	20.5	11.8	29.5
61-120	12.2	14.3	5.6	16.6	12.8	15.4	23.5	17.6
121-179	20.5	26.5	22.2	16.7	20.5	20.5	5.9	5.9
180 (continuously hospitalized)	22.4	30.6	38.9	22.2	20.5	28.2	35.3	29.4
Total	100.0%	100.0%	100.0%	100.0%	100.0%	100.0%	100.0%	100.0%
$\bar{X}\pm SE$	93.6±9.6	115.2±9.6	118.8±18.0	85.2±18.0	90.0±12.0	105.6±10.8	96.0±16.8	91.2±16.8

1954-1956 Cases

Number of months hospitalized	Male Group I (N = 23 prs.)	Matches	Male Group II (N = 11 prs.)	Matches	Female Group I (N = 31 prs.)	Matches	Female Group II (N = 18 prs.)	Matches
0-12	34.8	47.8	72.7	54.5	35.5	51.6	33.3	66.6
13-24	26.1	21.8	—	36.4	19.4	16.1	11.1	11.1
25-36	13.0	13.0	9.1	—	22.6	9.7	5.6	5.6
37-48	8.7	8.7	—	9.1	6.4	9.7	5.6	—
49-59	4.4	4.4	—	—	3.2	6.5	11.1	—
60 (continuously hospitalized)	13.0	4.3	18.2	—	12.9	6.4	33.3	16.7
Total	100.0%	100.0%	100.0%	100.0%	100.0%	100.0%	100.0%	100.0%
$\bar{X}\pm SE$	25.6±4.0	19.1±3.8	18.4±6.8	14.7±3.4	23.8±3.5	20.3±3.5	33.0±5.9*	17.2±5.0*

* t = 2.04, p < .05 (2 tail).

two further sets of analyses were used. In the first attempt toward pattern analysis comparisons were made between the family history cases and their matchmates with respect to number of admissions and mean number of years hospitalized per admission during equal time in life-span. No differences in mean number of admissions were found within any of the subgroups. For the mean number of years hospitalized per admission (Table 5), the Group I cases were again similar to their matchmates, while the Group II cases gave evidence of greater chronicity, with the means for each of these subgroups exceeding those for their own matchmates or for the Group I cases and their matches.

TABLE 5

NUMBER OF YEARS HOSPITALIZED PER ADMISSION (BOTH MEMBERS OF A PAIR FOLLOWED EQUAL NUMBER OF YEARS IN LIFE-SPAN), BY SUBGROUP

Sex and admission period		Group I	Matches	Group II	Matches
1934-36 Male	X+SE	9.6+1.4	10.9+1.3	12.2+2.6	8.8+2.1
Female	X+SE	8.7+1.5	9.6+1.3	11.4+2.6	8.1+2.2
1954-56 Male	X+SE	2.9+0.8	1.7+0.4	2.9+1.1	1.2+0.3
Female	X+SE	2.1+0.4	2.2+0.9	4.2+1.1	2.0+0.5

t values (2 tail) not significant within subgroups.

It has been noticed that final outcome and length of hospitalization are not necessarily correlated measures, in that the group with the highest proportion of hospitalized cases at final evaluation need not be the group with the greatest mean length of hospitalization. A more refined analysis of hospitalization patterns may help to clarify this. At least six patterns of hospitalization may be distinguished among individuals, three resulting in hospitalized status at final evaluation and three in discharged status. These are: (1) continuous hospitalization from first admission; (2) continuous hospitalization following second admission; (3) multiple admissions, in hospital at final evaluation; (4) multiple admissions, discharged at final evaluation; (5) discharged after second admission, never readmitted; and (6) discharged after first admission, never readmitted. Of these only patterns (1) and (6) are expected to be highly correlated (in opposite directions) with length of hospitalization, although even for pattern (6) the correlation might not be high. Patterns (2) and (5) should show greater individual variations reflecting differences in the length of first admission and the lag between first hospitalization and readmission. Patterns (3) and (4) presumably will show the greatest variation, and indeed final outcome may be largely a matter of chance with these patterns, contingent upon the particular point in time at which final evaluation is made.

When the index cases were classified according to the six patterns no differences were found in the overall distributions (χ^2 tests not significant) of the family history cases and their matchmates within the subgroups. Thus the cases with positive family history for schizophrenia were as likely to show both the extreme and the more variable intermediate patterns of hospitalization as were the cases with negative family history. The pattern distributions differed across subgroups, however, with some subgroups containing relatively high proportions of cases in the pattern classes (3) and (4) and others containing relatively few such cases. The low degree of correlation between final outcome and length of hospitalization observed in some of the previous comparisons is therefore not surprising.

Although allocation of the cases to the six patterns is desirable in a full analysis of the hospitalization histories because it makes maximum use of all information about each individual case, the smaller subgroups are distributed too thinly across the patterns to allow meaningful comparisons of length of hospitalization by pattern class. In Table 6, therefore, mean length of time in hospital is given for all hospitalized as well as for all discharged cases rather than for the separate patterns. (It should be mentioned that while the calculations in Table 6 are based on equal follow-up in the life-span for both members of a pair the 23 pairs in which one or both members died have been excluded, so that the figures are not identical to those presented in Table 3.) It is clear here that for each type of outcome, hospitalized or discharged, the mean length of time spent in hospital can vary widely. As usual, comparisons of Group I cases with the matchmates even out with three of the means among the hospitalized cases being greater for the matchmates and three of the means among the discharged cases being less for the matchmates. As usual also, the means for the Group II cases exceed those of the matchmates in the majority of the comparisons—three comparisons among the hospitalized cases and all four among the discharged (sign test, $p < .035$). The same is true when Group III cases (schizophrenia in parent and sibling) are added to Group II. Finally, while Group II gives no trend with respect to final outcome status in comparison with the matchmates the combination of Groups II and III shows that in three out of the four subgroups the proportion of cases hospitalized at final evaluation is higher for the family history cases than for the combined matchmates.

TABLE 6

Final Outcome Status (Percent Hospitalized or Discharged) and Mean Length of Time in Hospital (in Months) by Final Outcome Status, by Subgroup. (Both Members of a Pair Followed Equal Number of Years in Life-Span, Omitting 23 Pairs in Which One or Both Members Died Before End of Standard Interval.)

Sex and admission period	Number of cases	At final evaluation H = % hospitalized	At final evaluation D = % discharged	Mean months hospitalized in life span For H	Mean months hospitalized in life span For D
Group I, 1934-36 Males	49	65.3	34.7	306	49
Matches	49	67.4	32.6	339	46
Group I, 1934-36 Females	39	61.5	38.5	267	36
Matches	39	61.5	38.5	288	64
Group I, 1954-56 Males	23	39.1	60.9	150	36
Matches	23	39.1	60.9	107	15
Group I, 1954-56 Females	31	25.8	74.2	104	36
Matches	31	16.1	83.9	121	22
Group II, 1934-36 Males	18	77.8	22.2	273	15
Matches	18	55.6	44.4	292	14
Group II, 1934-36 Females	17	58.8	41.2	285	74
Matches	17	64.7	35.3	238	35
Group II, 1954-56 Males	11	27.3	72.7	123	29
Matches	11	27.3	72.7	66	21
Group II, 1954-56 Females	18	38.9	61.1	161	34
Matches	18	16.7	83.3	57	20
Groups II and III, 1934-36 Males	22	77.3	22.7	290	47
Combined Matches	22	59.1	40.9	303	13
Groups II and III, 1934-36 Females	24	62.5	37.5	272	76
Combined Matches	24	58.3	41.7	247	61
Groups II and III, 1954-56 Males	15	20.0	80.0	123	35
Combined Matches	15	46.7	53.3	63	21
Groups II and III, 1954-56 Females	26	42.3	57.7	137	30
Combined Matches	26	23.1	76.9	78	29

DISCUSSION

In evaluating the quantitative aspects of the hospitalization histories it was reasoned that a strong association between family history of schizophrenia and severity would be supported if patients with schizophrenic relatives were found to show reduced variability and displacements of mean values on the several measures compared to patients with negative family histories. No such trend was observed for patients with schizophrenic siblings.

The picture was less sharply defined for patients with schizophrenia in the parental generation. The range of variability was as great for these patients on all measures as for the other types of cases, the distributions of hospitalization patterns were not distorted, and only by the rather doubtful procedure of including the small group of cases with schizophrenia in both parents and siblings could the final outcome status of the family history cases be seen to diverge from that of the cases with negative histories. Few of the differences in mean values in comparison with their own matchmates reached significant levels. On the other hand a trend, which fluctuated in strength but not in direction, was demonstrated in all such comparisons in the four sets of analyses (i.e. means during equal time in life-span, means during standard interval, mean length per admission, and means by final outcome status) as well as in some of the comparisons with the Group I cases and their matchmates. In aggregate, the data suggest that the patients with schizophrenic parents are likely to have somewhat poorer histories of hospitalization than patients whose siblings are schizophrenic or than patients with negative family histories, if the criterion of severity is amount of time or proportion of life-span spent in hospital. Other criteria give no indication of increased severity and the only firm conclusion that may be drawn is that there is no *strong* association between a history of schizophrenia in the parents and the degree of severity shown by the schizophrenic index case.

The approaches used in the present study differed on several counts from those followed in the majority of studies that have considered family history as a prognostic variable. Rather than preclassifying patients according to severity ratings and then assessing family history along with other variables of potential prognostic importance, the procedure in this study was reversed in order to focus directly on familial occurrence of the disorder and to minimize, through the matching, the influence of other variables upon the hospitalization patterns of the index cases. The cases studied here thus could be (and were) distributed over the entire spectrum of severity that is representative of schizophrenic persons with at least one hospital admission, while patients in the earlier research tended to fall into either extreme of the spectrum.

At issue in all of these studies is the problem of formulating satisfactory ratings of severity. Clinical evaluations may actually give the best estimates in the individual patients even though they are the least objective of the possible measures. The clinical method is unfortunately extremely difficult in large follow-up studies where the material must be revalidated at a later date through personal contact with each subject. For this reason few of the previous studies have employed clinical evaluations and all of them have used some measure of hospitalization as an index of severity.

In the present analyses several measures of hospitalization and final outcome at the end of defined periods of follow-up have been used as the indices. As has been seen, the different measures do not always give uniform results in the comparisons of the cases with positive and negative family history. Final outcome has been considered as a weaker and less reliable measure than length of time spent in hospital. Knowledge of the pattern of hospitalization prior to the date of final follow-up is helpful in determining the reliability of the final outcome status assigned to the individual patient. For example, if the patient has been in hospital for a number of years at the time of follow-up it is reasonable to assume that hospitalized status reliably presents not only the current condition but the future expectations for that patient; similarly, if the patient has been out of hospital for a long period discharged status may be considered a reliable classification.

The classification of final outcome for a patient who has been in and out of hospital many times during the follow-up interval yields, however, only a time-limited statement about his current status, a statement that is not necessarily representative of his status one year before or one year after the evaluation date. The amount of time spent in hospital during a follow-up period provides a somewhat more reliable index, although even this measure is not a completely safe guide to the state of functioning of the individual, since some fairly well integrated patients remain in hospital for long periods merely because they have no place to go, while others, though less well integrated, are maintained at home for varying lengths of time. Theoretically errors of classification of this type should balance out across individuals. Practically, when the comparisons are between cases whose relatives are also affected and possibly unable to provide support and cases whose relatives are unaffected, length of hospitalization may not give a true picture of state of functioning in the two groups. It is conceivable, therefore, that the trend observed for the patients with schizophrenic parents with respect to length of hospitalization would prove to be an artefact if other assessments of behavioral functioning could be applied. The development of more refined methods for the evaluation of severity is badly needed for comparative studies. In the meantime studies of the present type have recourse only to the less than satisfactory objective measures that are available and the observations reported must be understood to be limited to the given set of criteria used.

The use of subgroups in the present study made it possible to establish that there were no differential effects by sex of the index case, as well as to validate trends across the two admission periods which could be considered as independent replicates. Most important, separate evaluations were made according to the relationship of the affected family member to the index case, although only first-degree relatives were considered here in contrast to the previous work. The study therefore lost some of the generality of the data that grouped together first-degree and collateral relatives but gained in the ability to specify the kinds of differential patterns that existed among the patients from the various family types. It would be of interest to know, for example, whether the finding of an association between a deteriorating course and positive family history in some of the other studies (Kant, 1942; Nameche et al., 1964; Vaillant, 1962) could be attributed largely to cases with schizophrenic parents. If so, additional weight would be given to the trend indicated in the current study. Other than the trend noted for the patients with schizophrenic parents the data here are in line with those of Malamud and Render (1939), showing no influence of family history on severity.

In addition to the question of the prognostic implications of schizophrenic family history the present type of study may be considered in relation to several theoretical issues that have been raised in connection with schizophrenia. For example, it may be noted that etiologic hypotheses that disregard genetic factors altogether cannot account for the lack of differences in severity between patients with schizophrenic siblings and patients from equal-sized sibships that contain no other affected members. Logically, when environmental stress is posed as the sole factor of importance it should follow that situations which are sufficiently stressful to induce schizophrenic psychoses in two or more members of a sibship should also be sufficient to increase the probability of severe expressions in the members of such sibships.

It has been suggested also that severity is influenced primarily by environmental factors (cf. Rosenthal, 1966). Such a view could have been upheld if a marked differential in the probability of severity had been found for patients with schizophrenic parents; of all persons that manifest schizophrenia they are most likely as a group to have been exposed to highly stressful backgrounds during development. But the severity indices of these patients were not found to be as sharply distinguished from those of the other patient groups as the hypothesis would indicate.

It may be thought that data on the severity of cases with and without a family history of schizophrenia could provide a test for the view that schizophrenia is divisible into genetic and nongenetic cases. Unfortunately this is not so. While phenocopies can be expected to occur only among the matchmates, it cannot be assumed that all, or even a large proportion, of the matchmates are phenocopies merely on the basis of absence of affected first-degree relatives. On that basis over 80 percent of the index cases in the main samples from which the present material is drawn would be considered to be phenocopies. A reasonable assumption under any genetic theory, however, would be that nongenetic cases account for a relatively small proportion of the total patient population, and indeed when adequate genealogical information is available it is usually possible to establish a family history of schizophrenia in collateral relatives for a large proportion of the patients. Information about collateral relatives of the matchmates is too scanty to afford the means of separating the cases into those with and without a history of schizophrenia in second- or third-degree relatives. Except for the distinction between matchmates with other psychiatric conditions in first-degree relatives and those without, it is not possible to identify the most probable cases of phenocopying among the matchmates. All that may be said is that if phenocopies are expected to be less severely affected than genetic cases there cannot be a large proportion of nongenetic phenocopies among the matchmates.

It should be pointed out that the lack of association between severity and family history of schizophrenia found here for the cases with affected siblings in no way conflicts with observations on monozygotic twins, where within-pair concordances for schizophrenia and severity in the index twin have been found to be associated (cf. Gottesman and Shields, 1966). The two members of a monozygotic twin pair represent replicates of the same genotype (disregarding possible differences arising through somatic point mutations or through errors at cell division) and it is not surprising that the heredity-environment interaction pattern follows an approximately similar course in both twins. The findings applicable to monozygotic twins cannot necessarily be generalized to other categories of relationship. For siblings specifically shared genes are placed against differing genotypic backgrounds that *in toto* interact differently with incoming environmental stimuli. It is less likely, therefore, that manifestation within the sibship and severity in the individual members of the sibship will be correlated. A similar absence of association between severity and concordance for schizophrenia should be found in dizygotic twins.

Indeed unless interaction effects and departures from additivity are taken into account it can be shown that the data as a whole are not consistent with expectations from any of the genetic hypotheses. Thus, to the extent that the data may be taken as showing a slightly increased probability of severity in patients with schizophrenic parents, they are not in line with straightforward monogenic theories or with recessive and multiple allelic heterogeneity theories, which would predict no differences among the three types of cases studied. Nor are they in line with heterogeneity theories that assume dominant and recessive forms, since the dominant forms presumably would be found most frequently in cases with schizophrenic parents and presumably also would display milder expression than recessive forms. Under a polygenic-threshold model it would be expected that both types of family history cases would be more severely affected than the matchmates, which has not been found in the comparisons involving the cases with schizophrenic siblings.

The foregoing are expectations from several of the major genetic theories when little or no allowance is made for gene-environment interaction. In fact, however, all of the theories do take into account nonadditive interaction effects, and it is possible within each genetic framework to view severity as a product of environmental stress and genotypic predisposition, just as for the basic manifestation of the disorder. Both the modest trend toward increased severity that was observed for the cases with schizophrenic parents, in whom environmental stresses would be most likely to be elevated, and the failure to demonstrate differences between the cases with schizophrenic siblings and the negative family history cases are in good agreement with this interaction point of view. The difficulty of using the present data on severity as a means of differentiating among genetic theories is precisely this: if interaction is not accorded a prominent role the data fit none of the theories, while the postulate of a strong interaction effect means that almost any set of findings on family history and severity can be consistent with each of the theories. The point to be made here, therefore, is that the analyses of severity in relation to familial incidence of schizophrenia are not likely to be effective in evaluating genetic hypotheses unless different types of severity indices, less contaminated by interaction effects, become available.

SUMMARY

To minimize the influence of variables other than family history in the comparisons of the hospitalization patterns, 253 family history cases were matched to patients with negative family history (matchmates) on a number of variables and were further contrasted with respect to several other variables of possible prognostic significance. The two types of cases were found to be similar on all such variables with the exception of the frequency of psychiatric disorders in relatives. Results of the hospitalization analyses showed the patients with schizophrenic siblings not to be different from their matchmates on any of the measures used as indices of severity. Although no strong association between history of schizophrenia in the parents and degree of severity was established, the data in aggregate suggested that patients with schizophrenic parents are likely to have somewhat poorer histories of hospitalization than any of the other patient groups. Data were discussed in relation to previous studies that have considered family history as a prognostic indicator and in relation to several theoretical issues regarding schizophrenia. The results of the analyses were considered to be in line with the interaction model of schizophrenia, in which severity, like the basic manifestation of the disorder, is viewed as a product of interaction between environmental stress and genotypic predisposition. It was concluded that the analysis of familial incidence of schizophrenia and severity on currently existing measures is not a useful means of differentiating among genetic hypotheses.

ACKNOWLEDGMENTS

The authors gratefully acknowledge the assistance of Miss Elyse Van den Bosch and Miss Rita Cyens who helped with the majority of the computations in this study. Research reported in this paper was supported by grant MH-03532 from the National Institute of Mental Health, United States Public Health Service.

REFERENCES

ASTRUP, C. (1966). "The prognostic importance of genetic factors in functional psychoses." *Brit. J. Psychiat.*, 112, 1293-1297.
ERLENMEYER-KIMLING, L., NICOL, S., RAINER, J. D., & DEMING, W. E. (in press). "Comparison of fertility rates of schizophrenic patients in New York State." *Amer. J. Psychiat.*
—— RAINER, J. D., & KALLMANN, F. J. (1966). "Current reproductive trends in schizophrenia." In: (eds. P. H. Hoch and J. Zubin) *Psychopathology of Schizophrenia.* New York: Grune & Stratton.
GOTTESMAN, I. I., & SHIELDS, J. (1966). "Schizophrenia in twins: 16 years' consecutive admissions to a psychiatric clinic." *Brit. J. Psychiat.*, 112, 809-818.

ISRAEL, R. H., & JOHNSON, N. A. (1956). "Discharge and readmission rates in 4,254 consecutive first admissions of schizophrenia." *Amer. J. Psychiat.*, 112, 903-909.

KANT, O. (1942). "The incidence of psychoses and other mental abnormalities in the families of recovered and deteriorated schizophrenic patients." *Psychiat. Quart.*, 16, 176-186.

LANGFELDT, G. (1939). *The Schizophreniform States.* Copenhagen: E. Munksgaard.

MALAMUD, W., & RENDER, N. (1939) "Course and prognosis in schizophrenia." *Amer. J. Psychiat.*, 95, 1039-1055.

NAMECHE, G., WARING, M., & RICKS, D. (1964). "Early indicators of outcome in schizophrenia." *J. nerv. ment. Dis.*, 139, 232-240.

ROSENTHAL, D. (1966). "The offspring of schizophrenic couples." *J. psychiat. Res.*, 4, 169-188.

SIEGEL, S. (1956). *Nonparametric Statistics.* New York: McGraw-Hill.

TSUANG, MING-TSO (1967)."A study of pairs of sibs both hospitalized for mental disorder." *Brit. J. Psychiat.*, 113, 283-300.

VAILLANT, G. E. (1962). "The prediction of recovery in schizophrenia." *J. nerv. ment. Dis.*, 135, 534-543.

32

A DANISH TWIN STUDY OF SCHIZOPHRENIA

Margit Fischer, B. Harvald, and M. Hauge

Previous studies on schizophrenia in twins have quite recently been reviewed in detail by Gottesman and Shields (1966a) and Shields (1968). The indications of concordance in different series are highly diverging, in monozygotic pairs ranging from near unity to zero. The high concordance rates found by Luxenburger (1928), Kallmann (1946) and Slater (1953) stress the importance of genetic factors in the etiology of schizophrenia, whereas the low concordance rate in two recent Scandinavian twin series (Tienari, 1963; Kringlen, 1966) has given rise to the question whether special genetic or environmental factors prevail in some populations. It has, therefore, been found of interest to study schizophrenia in a Danish twin population.

MATERIAL AND METHOD

The existence in Denmark of two nationwide registers, the Danish Twin Register and a Danish Psychiatric Register, has opened the possibility of ascertaining twin index cases from among the members of a fairly complete twin population.

The Danish Twin Register, comprising all twins born in Denmark within the period 1870-1910 and all same-sexed twins born 1911-20, was started in 1954 by two of the present authors (B.H. and M.H.) as a follow-up study of all twins born in Denmark in the periods mentioned. Pairs broken prior to their sixth birthday were, however, excluded from the more intensive studies as has been described in detail in a recent account of the Twin Register (Hauge et al., 1968); this report also gives complete information about the methods of collecting the material and

Reprinted, by permission of author and editor, from: *The British Journal of Psychiatry,* 115:981-990, 1969.

of establishing the zygosity diagnosis as well as a survey of the present composition of the material and the representativeness of the sample.

The study material, which excludes the early broken pairs, can be divided into two main parts: (*i*) *Part T* which comprises pairs known to have attained the age of 6 years as unbroken pairs and about whom the medical history is available; (*ii*) *Part U* which includes those pairs so far untraced. It is expected that a considerable proportion of these pairs will ultimately be found to have been broken before their sixth birthday, which would imply that they should be excluded from the study material. As only same-sexed pairs have been taken into consideration in the present study the size of the basic material is further reduced. The actual composition of this material is as follows:

Pairs born 1870-1910: *Part T:* 5,112   *Part U:* 3,233
Pairs born 1911-20: *Part T:* 1,611   *Part U:* 1,332

making a total of 11,288 same-sexed pairs.

The Psychiatric Register was established in the Institute of Human Genetics, Copenhagen, around 1940 as a central registration of all admissions to psychiatric departments and mental hospitals. Out-patients have not been registered.

The ascertainment of probands took place by two approaches: the medical data collected in the twin register were scrutinized, and all twins found to have signs or symptoms of psychic disorder or deviation were selected; next the twin register and the psychiatric register were cross-matched, which led to the selection of all individuals appearing in both. By these procedures a file of probands was constructed, which may be termed the Psychiatric Twin Register. The actual composition of this register appears from Table 1.

The index cases for the present study were ascertained in the Psychiatric Twin Register. All available case material of twins with schizophrenia, schizophreniform psychosis, paranoid psychosis and atypical psychosis was carefully reviewed, and supplemented by personal interviews (by Margit Fischer) in doubtful cases. All twins complying with the following criteria were accepted as probands: presence of a psychiatric disorder with disintegration of personality and affect, associated with impaired relation to reality, disturbance of thought, hallucinations or delusions; the disorder considered to be chronic, often progressive, sometimes with remissions, but never with complete cure. This type of schizophrenia is often called process schizophrenia.

TABLE 1

PRESENT COMPOSITION OF THE PSYCHIATRIC TWIN REGISTER

Diagnosis	Number of pairs
1. Schizophrenia	70
2. Manic-depressive psychosis	68
3. Paranoid psychosis	16
4. Psychotic or neurotic depression	67
5. Neuroses other than depressive	21
6. Personality disorder	50
7. Suicide without psychiatric classification.. (Suicide in pairs included under diagnoses 1-6: 22; total suicides therefore 77)	55
8. Other diagnoses	48
Total	395

A total of seventy-eight probands was ascertained, belonging to seventy twin pairs. All probands had at some time been hospitalized under the diagnosis of schizophrenia. Table 2 shows the distribution as to sex, period of birth and zygosity type. Furthermore, the size of the basic study material from which the probands have been drawn is shown in this table.

RESULTS

All relevant details of the findings in the probands and their co-twins are given in the Appendix. This survey gives the basis of the zygosity diagnosis, the age of onset if known, the age at the first admission to a psychiatric ward of the schizophrenic cases, an evaluation of the outcome of the disease as well as the age at which the twins disappeared from observation. Eight pairs with uncertain zygosity have been discarded from the following analyses.

Twenty-five schizophrenic probands belong to a total of twenty-one MZ (monozygotic) pairs. Among the co-twins of these probands nine were found to have schizophrenia with a clinical picture fulfilling the requirements used in the selection of probands. Calculated on the basis of these strict criteria the probandwise concordance rate in MZ twins is:

$9/25 = 0.36 =$ MZ grade 1 concordance rate. Among the probands of forty-five probands from a total of forty-one DZ (dizygotic) same-sexed pairs eight were found who fulfilled the same diagnostic criteria. Thus,

$8/45 = 0.18 =$ DZ same sex grade 1 concordance rate.

In the evaluation of the concordance in the present material it would

TABLE 2

DISTRIBUTION OF PROBANDS WITH SCHIZOPHRENIA

Year of birth	Same-sexed male pairs					Same-sexed female pairs				
	No. of pairs in basic material*	No. of probands				No. of pairs in basic material*	No. of probands			
		MZ	DZ	UZ	Total		MZ	DZ	UZ	Total
1870	73	0	0	0	0	92	0	0	0	0
1871-80	834	1	1	1	3	914	1	0	0	1
1881-90	911	2	1	0	3	1,017	3	5	0	8
1891-1900	964	3	4	1	8	1,063	2	6	2	10
1901-10	1,204	2	7	2	11	1,273	6	7	0	13
1911-20	1,359	3	8	2	13	1,584	2	6	0	8
Total	5,345	11	21	6	38	5,943	14	24	2	40

MZ = monozygotic; DZ = dizygotic; UZ = zygosity type uncertain.
* Parts T+U of the Danish Twin Register (see text).

be reasonable to include co-twins who suffered from schizophreniform, paranoid or atypical psychoses. The resulting rates will be as follows:

MZ grade 2 concordance rate $= 14/25 = 0.56$
DZ $_{\text{same sex}}$ grade 2 concordance rate $= 12/45 = 0.26$

The difference between these two rates is significant at the 5 percent level.

If finally concordance is extended to include also cases where the co-twin has manifested psychic deviations of different types without having been psychotic, the grade 3 concordance rates will be 0.64 and 0.41 for MZ and DZ twins, respectively.

The rather special age composition of the present material has opened an unusual opportunity for prolonged observation. This is of the utmost importance in the discordant pairs where the unaffected partners in this series have been under observation for an average period of twenty-five years after the first admission of the proband to a psychiatric ward (24.6 years in MZ pairs, 24.5 in DZ pairs). Thus, age correction should not be expected to cause significant changes in the concordance figures. The exclusion of two MZ and two DZ pairs all discordant, in which the co-twins died before a diagnosis of schizophrenia was established in the proband, leads to only insignificant changes of the concordance rates: Grade 1: MZ 0.39, DZ 0.19; Grade 2: MZ 0.61, DZ 0.28.

COMMENTS

It is quite clear that the original goal of collecting all twins with schizophrenia, born in the period mentioned, has not been fully accomplished in the present study. As may be seen from Table 2, the proportion of probands is not the same in all five decades included, being much lower in the oldest part of the twin population. It seems improbable that this variation should be due to changes in population incidence. It is much more likely that some probands from the earlier part of the period have been lost, primarily on account of insufficient diagnostic intensity in a period with undeveloped medical care. On the other hand, the loss of probands from the later periods seems to be rather limited.

The intensive study of Fremming (1947) provides good schizophrenia risk figures for the Danish population, based on a sample of about 5,000 persons born in the years 1883-7 in a geographically delimited area and followed-up to an average age of about 60. Fremming found thirty-four schizophrenics in this population out of which five cases, however, are considered as not surely to be in the group of process-schizophrenia (Fremming's cases 11, 13, 15, 17 and 23). The twin material includes a total of about 5,300 pairs born in the period 1901-20, and in this part of the material forty-five probands have been ascertained. Irrespective of differences of mortality, which is furthermore known to be much higher in twins than in the general population, especially during the first years of life, it seems justifiable to assume that ascertainment has been fairly complete in the present study, at least as far as the later part of the material is concerned.

The loss of material from the earlier period may be suspected to comprise mainly milder non-institutionalized cases, but also some severely affected concordant pairs where both partners have died early. Thus it is impossible to evaluate the influence of this bias on the over-all concordance rates.

Whereas it is very well possible that incomplete ascertainment will influence the final result only to a limited extent it is quite clear that all diagnostic misclassifications will be of the greatest importance in a small material. This holds true both with regard to the clinical diagnosis in the co-twins and to the zygosity diagnosis.

The rather high age of the present sample means a certain advantage with respect to clinical diagnosis because of the long period of observation, which also implies that most or all cases of schizophrenia in the co-twins have appeared at the time of examination. On the other hand many of the pairs were broken before the initiation of the present study, which implies that the proband and the co-twin could only in part of the cases be examined in the same way and undergo the same psychological test-procedures. The broken pairs constitute a problem with respect to zygosity diagnosis, which explains the rather large group with an uncertain zygosity diagnosis in this series. As far as the classified pairs are concerned, the proportion of MZ probands is $25/78 = 32.2$ percent, a value which comes close to population expectancy. This gives support to the assumption that only a few pairs have been misclassified.

In the present material, where it has been intended to ascertain as probands all persons born within a given period and in a well defined area who fulfill the diagnostic criteria described above, it seems clear that the proband method of calculating the concordance rate is preferable (cf. Allen, Harvald and Shields, 1967). The proband concordance rate expresses the chance that the co-twin of a proband is likewise affected. In some pairs there will be two independently ascertained probands which will increase the numerical value of the concordance rate calculated in this way as compared with the value obtained when the pairwise con-

TABLE 3

TWIN STUDIES OF SCHIZOPHRENIA, CONCORDANCE ACCORDING TO "PAIR-METHOD"

Author	MZ "Strict" schizophrenia	MZ Including "borderline" cases	DZ same sex "Strict" schizophrenia	DZ same sex Including "borderline" cases
Luxenburger, 1928* (Germany)	7/14 50%	10/14 71%	0/13 0%	0/13 0%
Rosanoff et al., 1934 (U.S.A.)	18/41 44%	25/41 61%	5/53 9%	7/53 13%
Essen-Möller, 1941* (Sweden)	1/7 14%	5/7 71%	2/24 8%	4/24 17%
Kallmann, 1946* (U.S.A.)		120/174 69% 86%†		34/296 11%
Slater, 1953* (U.K.)		24/37 65% 76%†		8/58 14%
Inouye, 1963‡ § (Japan)		33/55 60%		2/11 18%
Tienari 1963 ‡§ || (Finland)	0/16 0%	0/16 0%		
Kringlen 1966 *§ (Norway)	14/50 28%	19/50 38%	6/94 6%	13/94 14%
Gottesman and Shields, 1966* (U.K.)	10/24 42%	13/24 54%	3/33 9%	6/33 18%
Fischer et al., 1968* (Denmark)	5/21 24%	10/21 48%	4/41 10%	8/41 19%

* Excluding "early broken" pairs.
† Age-corrected.
‡ Only including pairs where both partners were alive at the time of examination.
§ Including probands with "borderline" schizophrenia.
|| Male probands.

cordance rate is used in which all concordant pairs are counted only once.

In Table 3 all major schizophrenia twin series are presented. The table gives the raw concordance figures, based simply on the number of concordant pairs in each material. It should be stressed that these figures are in no way directly comparable, primarily because the necessity of clearly indicating whether one or both partners of concordant pairs have been ascertained independently has been disregarded in most previous studies. Age differences between the materials will also influence the comparability unless special corrections have been introduced. It is not always made clear if such corrections have been made, e.g. by excluding pairs in which the co-twin died at an early age.

The factors just mentioned may give part of the explanation of the rather impressive differences among the series included in Table 3. The diagnostic delimitation of schizophrenia, however, is not the same in all series; thus, there can be no doubt that the concept of schizophrenia is comparatively broad in Kallmann's study.

Irrespective of the differences between the various twin studies in schizophrenia they all indicate that genetic factors influence the population variability with respect to this disease. When, on the other hand, it is attempted to estimate the relative importance of genetic and environmental factors on the basis of these series, widely different values are obtained. The concordance rates of the present study seem to leave more than 50 percent of population variability to environmental factors; our figures come rather close to the results of previous Scandinavian investigations.

Thus it is conspicuous that the Scandinavian studies all seem to indicate a relatively low rate of concordance. This may be a consequence of stricter diagnostic criteria, but another characteristic of the three recent Scandinavian studies should also be taken into consideration: they can claim to represent all diagnosed cases from the whole population within a given period and as such their relatively low concordance rate may be a more correct estimate of a population parameter.

Should heterogeneity with respect to schizophrenia-provoking environmental factors exist in a population, one would expect to find lower concordance rates in material representing the total population than in series sampled from among the patients of a single hospital or city with a more homogenous environmental background. Furthermore the degree of heterogeneity with respect to relevant environmental factors may well vary from one population to another. This problem, however, cannot be discussed successfully until significant exogenous factors have been singled out.

In their discussion of the mode of inheritance of schizophrenia Gottesman and Shields (1966a, b) found considerable support for a polygenic theory. One of their arguments in favor of this hypothesis was a rather close correlation between severity and concordance. In the present material the average age at first admission was found to be 33.2 years in probands of concordant pairs and 33.3 years in probands of discordant pairs. The average outcome (cf. the Appendix) was slightly milder in probands of concordant pairs. These results seem to be at variance with the findings of Gottesman and Shields. This can of course be due to the limited size of the material but may on the other hand suggest that ascertainment in our material has been slightly influenced by concordance. The disagreement on this point could, however, also reflect the difference of sampling procedure between the British and the Danish material, the Danish representing the total population in which heterogeneity with respect to environmental influences may obscure genetic relationships, which appear more clearly in a material with a more uniform environmental background.

All genetic studies on schizophrenia clearly suffer from the lack of a clearcut biochemical or symptomatic delimination of a well defined disease entity. In the present study it was therefore decided to apply rather sharp diagnostic criteria in the selection of probands, knowing that this would limit the validity of all conclusions based on this series to this degree of morbidity. When, later on, all groups of twins included in the Psychiatric Twin Register have been examined it will be possible to define other groups of probands with less clear-cut schizophrenic traits, and eventually by the study of their co-twins to elucidate the interplay between different psychic abnormalities.

SUMMARY

From among a population of same-sexed Danish twins born 1870-1920 a total of seventy-eight probands with process-schizophrenia were selected. Among the co-twins of twenty-five MZ probands nine were found to have schizophrenia, and a further five co-twins had presented schizophrenic traits; the corresponding figures for the co-twins of forty-five DZ probands were eight and five respectively. In eight probands zygosity could not be determined with sufficient certainty. If partners with schizophreniform, paranoid or atypical psychoses are accepted as concordant, the probandwise MZ and DZ concordance rates will be 0.56 and 0.26.

This difference is significant, which in agreement with earlier twin studies indicates that genetic factors influence population variability with regard to schizophrenia. The actual value of the MZ concordance rate in the present study is, however, in the lower range of all previously obtained figures, in this respect corresponding with two recent Scandinavian studies. It is characteristic of these three studies as opposed to all others that the probands have been selected from a total population.

ACKNOWLEDGMENTS

This study was supported by research grants C-948 and GM 09418 from the National Institutes of Health, U.S. Public Health Service, Department of Health, Education and Welfare, Bethesda, Maryland, U.S.A.; from Statens Almindelige Videnskabsfond, Copenhagen, Fonden til Laegevidenskabens Fremme, Copenhagen, and F. L. Smidth & Co. A/S's Jubilaeumsfond, Copenhagen, Denmark.

REFERENCES

ALLEN, G., HARVALD, B., & SHIELDS, J. (1967). "Measures of twin concordance." *Acta genet. (Basel)*, 17, 475-81.

ESSEN-MÖLLER, E. (1941). *Psychiatrische Untersuchungen an einer Serie von Zwillingen.* Copenhagen: Munksgard.

FREMMING, K. (1947). *Morbid Risk of Mental Diseases and other Abnormal Psychic States among Average Danish Populations.* Copenhagen: Munksgard.

GOTTESMAN, I. I., & SHIELDS, J. (1966a). "Contributions of twin studies to perspectives in schizophrenia." In: B. A. Maher (ed.): *Progress in Experimental Personality Research.* Vol. 3, pp. 1-84. New York: Academic Press.

GOTTESMAN, I. I., & SHIELDS, J. (1966b). "Schizophrenia in twins: 16 years consecutive admissions to a psychiatric clinic." *Brit. J. Psychiat.*, 112, 809-18.

HAUGE, M., HARVALD, B., FISCHER, MARGIT, GOTLIEB JENSEN, K., JUEL-NIELSEN, N., RAEBILD, INGRID, SHAPIRO, R., & VIDEBECH, T. (1968). "The Danish twin register." *Acta genet. med. (Roma)*, 17, (in Press).

INOUYE, E. (1963). "Similarity and dissimilarity of schizophrenia in twins." *Proceedings of the Third World Congress on Psychiatry.* Vol. 1, pp. 524-30. Montreal: University of Toronto Press.

KALLMAN, F. J. (1946). "The genetic theory of schizophrenia. An analysis of 794 twin index families." *Amer. J. Psychiat.*, 103, 309-22.

KRINGLEN, E. (1966). "Schizophrenia in twins. An epidemiological-clinical study." *Psychiatry*, 29, 172-84.

LUXENBURGER, H. (1928). "Vorläufiger Bericht über psychiatrischen Serieuntersuchungen an Zwillingen." *Z. ges. Neurol. Psychiat.*, 176, 297-326.

ROSANOFF, A. J., HANDY, I. M., PLESSET, I. R., & BRUSH, S. (1934). "The etiology of so-called schizophrenic psychoses. With special reference to their occurrence in twins." *Amer. J. Psychiat.*, 91, 247-86.

SHIELDS, J. (1968). "Summary of the genetic evidence." *J. psychiat. Res.*, Vol. Suppl., 95-126.

SLATER, E. (1953). *Psychotic and Neurotic Illnesses in Twins.* Her Majesty's Stationery Office, London.

TIENARI, P. (1963). "Psychiatric illnesses in identical twins." *Acta psychiat. Scand.*, Suppl. 171, pp. 1-195.

APPENDIX I

KEY

Sex: f = female, m = male.

Method of zygosity determination:

   ant = diagnosis based on degree of similarity/dissimilarity of general appearance and selected anthropological traits; information about whether partners have repeatedly or never been mistaken for one another.

   ser = diagnosis based on extensive serological examinations (for details, cf. Hauge *et al.*, 1968).

   A, B = the partners of a pair; probands are marked by *.

Age at first admission refers only to admission to psychiatric wards.

Age at disappearance from observation: +indicates disappearance due to death.

Type of outcome:

   0 = complete cure.

   1 = good remission, socially adjusted.

   2 = incomplete remission, not institutionalized but a social burden.

   3 = incomplete remission, institutionalized.

   4 = still psychotic, not institutionalized.

   5 = no remission, institutionalized.

   6 = deterioration, institutionalized.

Concordance rating:

   C1 = grade 1 concordance: co-twin schizophrenia.

   C2 = grade 2 concordance: co-twin psychotic, but not schizophrenic as judged by the proband criteria.

   C3 = grade 3 concordance: co-twin not psychotic but "nervous," "odd" and/or neurotic.

   C4 = grade 4 = discordant, co-twin normal.

   * = proband.

APPENDIX II

SURVEY OF THE MATERIAL

Pair No./year of birth	Sex	Method of zygosity determination		Diagnosis	Approx. age at onset	Age at first admiss.	Age at disapp. from obs.	Type of outcome	Concordance rating
a. MONOZYGOTIC PAIRS									
006/1878	f	ant	A*:	schizophrenia	25-30	36	53+	5	C_4
			B:	normal			53+		
009/1894	f	ant	A*:	schizophrenia	33	35	65+	5-6	C_4
			B:	normal, death following surgical treatment of peptic ulcer			18+		
015/1901	f	ser	A*:	schizophrenia	28	28	66	4	C_1
			B*:	schizophrenia	29	29	66	2	
018/1887	f	ant	A*:	schizophrenia	35	41	50+	6	C_1
			B*:	schizophrenia	30-35	70	80	4	
025/1899	m	ant	A*:	schizophrenia	30	31	57+	5-6	C_3
			B:	lived alone, regarded as odd, "a crank"			64+	1(?)	
026/1901	f	ant	A*:	schizophrenia	40-45	54	64+	2	C_4
			B:	normal, died from bronchial asthma			37+		
031/1896	m	ser	A*:	schizophrenia	27	27	71	3	C_4
			B:	normal			71		
032/1906	f	ser	A*:	schizophrenia	40	51	61	5	C_1
			B*:	schizophrenia	43	49	61	4	
043/1888	m	ant	A*:	schizophrenia	23	33	79+	5	C_4
			B:	normal			46+		
044/1902	m	ser	A*:	schizophrenia	26	26	65	6	C_1
			B*:	schizophrenia	27	27	65	1-2	
045/1908	f	ant	A*:	schizophrenia	52	52	59	1	C_2
			B:	acute psychosis	23	23	23+	?	

Pair No./year of birth	Sex	Method of zygosity determination	Diagnosis	Approx. age at onset	Age at first admiss.	Age at disapp. from obs.	Type of outcome	Concordance rating
060/1883	m	ant	A*: schizophrenia	38	39	43+	5	C$_3$
			B: "nervous"			82+	?	
062/1898	f	ant	A*: schizophrenia	32	32	34+	5	C$_4$
			B: normal			69		
118/1911	m	ser	A*: schizophrenia	35	41	56	5	C$_2$
			B: periods of atypical psychosis	45		56	2	
119/1912	f	ser	A*: schizophrenia	20	24	55	6	C$_2$
			B: periods of atypical psychosis	17	21	55	2	
142/1913	m	ser	A*: schizophrenia	27	29	53	3(5)	C$_2$
			B: paranoid psychosis	44	47	53	1	
143/1913	m	ser	A*: schizophrenia	21	23	53	2	C$_2$
			B: periods of schizophreniform psychosis	28	48	53	0-1	
403/1882	f	ant	A*: schizophrenia	50?	52	80+	5	C$_4$
			B: normal			77+		
405/1879	m	ant	A*: schizophrenia	23	29	74+	5	C$_4$
			B: normal until senile dementia at age 80			88		
408/1899	m	ser	A*: schizophrenia	23	24	68	5	C$_4$
			B: normal			68		
417/1915	f	ser	A*: schizophrenia	20	30	52	5	C$_1$
			B: schizophrenia	17		52	1-2	
b. DIZYGOTIC PAIRS								
001/1901	f	ant	A*: schizophrenia	20	20	61+	6	C$_1$
			B*: schizophrenia	26	26	36+	5	
011/1909	m	ant	A*: schizophrenia	22	22	27+	5	C$_2$
			B: schizophreniform psychosis	35	35	58	1-2	
034/1899	f	ant	A*: schizophrenia	23	23	67	5	C$_4$
			B: normal, died after childbirth			27+		

Pair No./year of birth	Sex	Method of zygosity determination		Diagnosis	Approx. age at onset	Age at first admiss.	Age at disapp. from obs.	Type of outcome	Concordance rating
036/ 1908	f	ser	A*:	schizophrenia		22	61	6	C₃
			B:	ulcus duodeni refused cooperation G.P. says: very peculiar			61		
069/ 1911	m	ant	A*:	schizophrenia		34	55	3	C₃
			B:	"very nervous," died after traffic accident			52+		
083/ 1913	f	ant	A*:	schizophrenia		23	54	5	C₂
			B:	atypical psychosis with hysterical symptoms		22	27+	2	
085/ 1920	m	ser	A*:	schizophrenia		22	46	3	C₄
			B:	normal, diabetes insipidus			46		
087/ 1913	f	ser	A*:	schizophrenia		32	54	5	C₄
			B:	normal			54		
089/ 1917	f	ant	A*:	schizophrenia		42	49	2	C₄
			B:	normal			49		
094/ 1916	f	ant	A*:	schizophrenia		36	50	4	C₄
			B:	normal, refused cooperation			50		
097/ 1920	m	ser	A*:	schizophrenia		24	46	5	C₄
			B:	normal			46		
131/ 1912	m	ser	A*:	schizophrenia age 51 thyrotoxicosis		33	54	4	C₄
			B:	normal			54		
134/ 1914	m	ant	A*:	schizophrenia partly remission emigrated 1964		33	54	1	C₄
			B:	normal			50		
160/ 1912	m	ser	A*:	schizophrenia		23	52	5	C₄
			B:	normal			52		
183/ 1920	f	ser	A*:	schizophrenia		31	46	2	C₄
			B:	normal			46		

Pair No./year of birth	Sex	Method of zygosity determination		Diagnosis	Approx. age at onset	Age at first admiss.	Age at disapp. from obs.	Type of outcome	Concordance rating
199/ 1918	m		A*:	schizophrenia		22	48	3	C$_4$
		ser	B:	normal			48		
200/ 1916	m	ser	A*:	schizophrenia		40	50	1	C$_4$
			B:	normal			50		
201/ 1920	f	ant	A*:	schizophrenia		24	24+	?	C$_4$
			B:	normal			46		
251/ 1896	m	ant	A*:	schizophrenia		65	67+	3	C$_4$
			B:	normal, died after chance-shot (suicide?)			60+		
259/ 1903	m	ant	A*:	schizophrenia		19	58	3	C$_2$
			B:	atypical psychosis (depressive and paranoid symptoms) suicide		20	23+	?	
370/ 1900	f	ant	A*:	schizophrenia (?)		47	49+	?	C$_3$
			B:	1960: seemed paranoid at visit. Refused further co-operation. 1965: admitt. neurosis, depressive		65	65	0-1	
401/ 1898	f	ant	A*:	schizophrenia		25	55+	5	?
			B:	normal, died from epid. influenza			20+		
402/ 1881	f	ant	A*:	schizophrenia		23	55+	6	C$_4$
			B:	normal			86		
404/ 1888	f	ant	A*:	schizophrenia		30	34+	5	C$_3$
			B:	neurosis			78		
406/ 1886	f	ant	A*:	schizophrenia		27	80	6	C$_4$
			B:	normal			76+		
407/ 1885	f	ant	A*:	schizophrenia		24	47+	5	C$_1$
			B*:	schizophrenia		40 (?)	43+	3	
409/ 1891	m	ant	A*:	schizophrenia		68	69	4	C$_4$
			B:	normal			67+		

Pair No./year of birth	Sex	Method of zygosity determination	Diagnosis	Approx. age at onset	Age at first admiss.	Age at disapp. from obs.	Type of outcome	Concordance rating
410/1902	m	ser	A*: schizophrenia		31	65	4	C_1
			B*: schizophrenia		45	65	2	
411/1906	m	ser	A*: schizophrenia	40	33	61	4	C_4
			B: normal			61	4	
413/1895	f	ant	A*: schizophrenia, partly remission about age 40, died from brain tumor		26	50+	1-2	C_1
			B*: schizophrenia, many adm. in G.H. from age 31		41	73	3	
414/1907	f	ser	A*: schizophrenia		32	60	4	C_3
			B: neurosis depressiva		53	60	1-2	
415/1910	f	ant	A*: schizophrenia		24	56	4	C_4
			B: normal, died after childbirth			33		
420/1905	m	ant	A*: schizophrenia		43	61	2	C_4
			B: normal			61		
422/1874	m	ser	A*: schizophrenia		36	87+	5-6	C_3
			B: "nervous"		66	88	0-1	
423/1900	m	ser	A*: schizophrenia		24	67	5	C_4
			B: mental retardation, lives in institution		26	67		
437/1903	f	ant	A*: schizophrenia		43	64	2	C_4
			B: normal until age 59, later depressive and organic symptoms (?tumor frontalis), suicide age 60		59	60+	?	
438/1910	f	ant	A*: schizophrenia, mental retardation		31	56	3	C_4
			B: normal, refused co-operation			56		

Pair No./year of birth	Sex	Method of zygosity determination	Diagnosis	Approx. age at onset	Age at first admiss.	Age at disapp. from obs.	Type of outcome	Concordance rating
439/1898	f	ant	A*: schizophrenia		26	68	3	C_4
			B: normal, refused co-operation			56		
C. PAIRS OF UNCERTAIN ZYGOSITY								
013/1903	m		A*: schizophrenia		22	64	6	C_4
			B: normal			55+		
046/1877	m		A*: schizophrenia		27	40+	5	C_4
			B: normal			44+		
070/1914	m		A*: schizophrenia		25	52	5	C_2
			B: encephalitides seq., mental retardation, psychotic episodes		15	30+	5	
110/1911	m		A*: schizophrenia, refused co-operation		32	55	1-2	?
			B: died in childhood			8+		
356/1904	m		A*: schizophrenia		34	34+	?	C_3
			B: suicide no further information			18+		
400/1900	f		A*: schizophrenia		27	62	5	?
			B: died in childhood			15+		
412/1898	f		A*: schizophrenia, refused co-operation		53	68	2	?
			B: died in childhood					
419/1886	m		A*: schizophrenia		29	75+	5	C_3
			B: lived in social institution, no further information			57+	?	

33

THE GENETICS OF SCHIZOPHRENIC AND SCHIZOID DISEASE

Leonard L. Heston

The contribution of genetic factors to the etiology of schizophrenia has been confirmed decisively. Because the investigations that have led to this result have uncovered questions cutting across several fields of inquiry, a fresh look at some central aspects of the schizophrenia problem is warranted. These questions and the factual background underlying them are the main concerns of this article. Because emphasis is placed on formulating testable hypotheses, the evidence is organized in support of a particular genetic theory.

THE BASIC EVIDENCE

During the first half of this century, systematic family studies demonstrated that the distribution of schizophrenia is that of a genetic disease. Relatives of schizophrenics were found to be afflicted with the illness much more frequently than members of the general population. The child of a schizophrenic parent, for example, was found to have a risk of schizophrenia about 15 times that of a member of the population at large. It was found that, among all classes of relatives, the closer the genetic relationship to a schizophrenic proband (or index case) is, the greater is the likelihood of schizophrenia in the relative. Finally, and most telling of all, monozygotic twins were found to be concordant with respect to schizophrenia about four times as often as dizygotic twins. Several authorities have critically reviewed these basic data (1, 2). But, despite the supporting evidence, a genetic etiology for schizophrenia was not widely accepted, especially in this country. It was pointed out that the investigators did not pay enough attention to important pro-

Reprinted, by permission of author and editor, from: *Science,* 167:249-256, 16 January 1970.

cedural matters, such as providing sampling safeguards and insuring against bias on the part of the investigator. But the paramount objection to a genetic interpretation of the evidence was the objection that the whole research strategy was faulty. The results of these studies, it was held, were just as compatible with transmission of schizophrenia through the social environment as with transmission through genes. The closer the genetic relationship, the closer the social relationship. Were genes or was noxious social learning responsible for the familial clustering of schizophrenia?

Recently, several studies have been aimed at closing those methodological and conceptual gaps. In these newer studies diagnoses either were made by raters who did not know the genetic background of the subjects or were taken unchanged from medical records. Care was taken to remove sampling biases, and, most importantly, control groups were used. The strategy permitted separation of the effects of genes from the effects of social environment through the use, as subjects, of children reared in adoptive or foster homes.

The results of one such study are shown in Table 1 (3). The experimental subjects were individuals born to schizophrenic mothers, and the controls were individuals born to parents who had no record of psychiatric disturbance. The members of both groups had been permanently separated from their biological mothers in the first month of life and reared mainly in foster or adoptive homes. The subjects, as adults, were assessed through psychiatric interviews and review of every available record—for example, school, police, Veterans Administration, and medical —and then evaluated by a team of clinicians. The significant excess of schizophrenia found among those subjects whose biological mothers were schizophrenic seems impossible to explain except on a genetic basis. Moreover, among those same experimental subjects, and thus also linked to schizophrenia by the evidence, was an even greater excess of various apparently nonschizophrenic disorders. The latter finding, which is reflected in nearly every entry in Table 1, is a central concern throughout this article.

The preliminary results from a very similar study which stressed exemplary investigative safeguards were much the same. Rosenthal et al. (4) reported that biological children of schizophrenics reared in adoptive homes exhibited "schizophrenic spectrum" disorders in significant excess over similarly reared controls. The "schizophrenic spectrum"—an expression coined in a quite reasonable attempt to find a term that would encompass the various disorders seen among biological relatives of schizophrenics—included schizophrenia, possible schizophrenia, borderline states, certain paranoid disorders, schizoid disorders, and the condition known as inadequate personality.

Karlsson (5), as one result of his study of schizophrenia in Icelandic families, found that 6 of 29 persons, some of them siblings, born to a schizophrenic parent but reared in foster homes developed schizophrenia. None of their 28 foster sibs who were reared in the same homes developed schizophrenia. This difference, too, is significant. Karlsson did not ascertain any disorders other than typical schizophrenia, among his subjects.

In two ingeniously designed research projects, adopted individuals served as the starting point. Wender et al. (6) studied the biological and adoptive parents of ten adopted schizophrenics and the adoptive parents of ten normal persons. The biological parents of the schizophrenics were found to exhibit significantly more psychopathology than either group of adoptive parents. In a similar but wider-ranging study conducted by Kety et al. (7), psychopathology, again reported as "schizophrenic spectrum" disorders, was found to be concentrated in significant excess among the biological relatives of adopted schizophrenics. The adoptive families of schizophrenics were indistinguishable from the adoptive and biological families of adopted controls. Since the psychopathology found in these studies was significantly greater among the group of biological relatives of the schizophrenic probands than among the adoptive relatives who actually lived with them, this evidence too strongly favors genetic over social transmission of schizophrenia.

The results of the studies of adopted and foster children—results which are strikingly consistent from study to study, considering the vagaries of research in this area—present seemingly insurmountable difficulties for adherents of environmental theories of schizophrenia. The evidence must surely compel acknowledgment of a genetic contribution to schizophrenia, and probably to related disorders as well. To go further, however, requires information on other types of genetic relationships and larger numbers of subjects. Happily, the older family studies can now meet these needs. For perhaps the most important contribution of the recent studies of adopted and foster children is the fact that they have confirmed the results of the older studies in all material respects. The familial clustering of psychopathology that had been documented in such detail has been linked to one critical variable, a genetic relationship to schizophrenia.

THE SCHIZOID

The presence of so much psychopathology other than typical schizophrenia among relatives of schizophrenics was first noticed by physicians on visiting days in the earliest asylums. Isaac Ray, writing in 1863, gave a good description (8). Because the relatives' disabilities resembled schizophrenia, investigators associated with the Munich school called these disabilities "schizoid" (schizophrenic-like). Describing the schizoid individual, delimiting schizoid from psychiatric and general populations, and placing the schizoid in relation to the schizophrenic were central concerns of the psychiatry of that day. After perhaps the longest detour in the modern history of science, we have come full circle in returning to the same concerns. Meanwhile, problems of nomenclature have developed.

To me, "schizoid" and "schizophrenic spectrum" seem to denote precisely the same disabilities, except that the latter term also includes schizophrenia. One consideration that may have led Kety (7), Rosenthal (4), Wender (6), and their co-workers to coin the new term is the obvious danger of confusing "schizoid" with "schizoid personality." The latter term, a diagnosis in the American Psychiatric Association and World Health Organization nomenclature, although descended from descriptions of the abnormal relatives of schizophrenics, has evolved and changed in meaning so that it is no longer applicable to most of those relatives. For example, it was not often applied to relatives of schizophrenics by the rating clinicians in the studies of adopted and foster children. But other diagnoses currently considered applicable to such individuals also fit these relatives imperfectly, so no formal categorization is now available. Because of a central trait of the schizoid—his clinical resemblance to the schizophrenic—and because of the desirability of maintaining continuity with older studies, I use the term "schizoid" as a name for the schizophrenic-like disabilities seen in relatives of schizophrenics, or for the individual manifesting such disabilities.

Nearly all observers of the schizoid have noted his clinical resemblance to the schizophrenic, but clinical criteria adequate to reliably distinguish the schizoid from members of a general or a psychiatric population or even from other kinds of abnormal persons with a coincidental genealogical connection to a schizophrenic are most imperfect (9). Though unsatisfactory, the only means of identifying many—perhaps most—schizoids remains genealogical, and a clinical understanding of the schizoid can best be gained by reading descriptions of abnormal relatives of schizophrenics (see 10-13 for good examples). The circularity thus introduced is regrettable but inescapable. The schizoid exists, and he sometimes shows as much impairment psychiatrically as a typical schizophrenic.

Several problematical behaviors have been associated with the schizoid. Among males, antisocial behavior has been found commonly enough to warrant the older subdesignation "schizoid psychopath." Entries in the

TABLE 1

RESULTS OF A STUDY OF INDIVIDUALS BORN TO SCHIZOPHRENIC MOTHERS
AND REARED IN ADOPTIVE OR FOSTER HOMES, AND OF CONTROLS BORN
TO NORMAL PARENTS AND SIMILARLY REARED

Item	Control	Experimental	Exact probability (Fisher's test)
Number of subjects	50	47	
Number of males	33	30	
Age, mean (years)	36.3	35.8	
Number adopted	19	22	
MHSRS, means*	80.1	65.2	0.0006
Number with schizophrenia	0	5	.024
Number with mental deficiency (I.Q. <70)†	0	4	.052
Number with antisocial personalities	2	9	.017
Number with neurotic personality disorder‡	7	13	.052
Persons spending more than 1 year in penal or psychiatric institution			
Number	2	11	.006
Total years incarcerated	15	112	
Number of felons	2	7	.054
Number serving in armed forces	17	21	
Number discharged from armed forces on psychiatric or behavioral grounds	1	8	.021
Social group, first home, mean§	4.2	4.5	
Social group, present, mean§	4.7	5.4	
I.Q., mean	103.7	94.0	
Years in school, mean	12.4	11.6	
Number of children, total	84	71	
Number of divorces, total	7	6	
Number never married, >30 yrs of age	4	9	

* The MHSRS is a global rating of psychopathology moving from 0 to 100 with decreasing psychopathology. Total group mean, 72.8; S.D., 18.4.
† One mental defective was also schizophrenic; another had antisocial personality.
‡ Considerable duplication occurs in the entries under "neurotic personality disorder"; this designation includes subjects diagnosed as having various types of personality disorder and neurosis whose psychiatric disability was judged to be a significant handicap.
§ Group 1, highest social class; group 7, lowest.

police records of the schizoid psychopaths in my study reflected impulsive, seemingly illogical crime such as arson, unreasoning assault, and poorly planned theft (3). Social isolation, heavy intake of alcohol, and sexual deviance have been noted frequently. Other schizoids, both male and female, have been described as eccentric, suspicion-ridden recluses. The main disability of still other schizoids, mostly females, has been found to be incapacitating attacks of panic or unreasoning fear in response to ordinary social challenges.

On a more technical level the resemblance to schizophrenia is more apparent. Rigidity of thinking, blunting of affect, anhedonia, exquisite sensitivity, suspiciousness, and a relative poverty of ideas—in variable combinations and intensities—characterize both the schizoid and the schizophrenic, though such characteristics are less prominent in the former. Though schizoids do not show a well-marked thought disorder, delusions, and hallucinations, descriptions of some of the behavioral lapses of schizoids, especially the schizoid psychopath, are bizarre enough to suggest micropsychotic episodes.

Slater took a different approach. He listed a series of explicatives, partially reproduced in Table 2, used by relatives of schizophrenics when

TABLE 2

EXPLICATIVES USED BY RELATIVES OF SCHIZOPHRENICS IN DESCRIBING THEIR SCHIZOID RELATIVES. [AFTER SLATER (13)]

Paranoid eccentricities: suspicious, sensitive, sullen, touchy, grouchy, morose, resentful, unforgiving, difficult, quarrelsome, self-conscious, jealous, litigious, critical, and others.

Eccentricities: giggly, opinionated, pedantic, narrow-minded, meticulous, obstinate, humorless, rigid, little-minded, spiritualists, and many others.

Lack of feeling: passive, cruel, calculating, placid, hard and stingy, unsympathetic, cold, withdrawn, little-feeling, and others.

Reserve: shy, serious, haughty, snobbish, studious, unforthcoming, taciturn, unsociable, seeks solitude, and so on.

Anergic: dependent, tired, slack, unreliable, subservient, and so on.

describing their abnormal but nonschizophrenic relatives (13). Slater went on to say (13, p. 83) that "the same or similar words or phrases occur in descriptions of abnormal personalities from other kinds of families, but much less frequently, not in such concentrated form, and they are usually submerged by descriptions of a very different tone."

Because Kallmann's investigations of the families of schizophrenics were by far the most extensive that have been made, his concept of the schizoid is of critical importance (11). From his description (11, p. 102) it is clear that he relied heavily on the schizoid's clinical resemblance to the schizophrenic. Kallmann regarded the distinguishing features of the schizoid to be the "fundamental symptoms of schizophrenia in the milder form of characterological abnormalities . . . dominating the personality of the individual in question." Kallmann also looked analytically at traits other than those obviously associated with schizophrenia or schizoidia that seemed to occur in excess among relatives of schizophrenics, with the aim of including or excluding them from the group of schizoid traits. On various grounds he excluded all the traits that he considered.

One of the traits which Kallmann considered and rejected, mental deficiency, perhaps deserves another look. About 6 to 10 percent of schizophrenics (see 14) and their first-degree relatives (see 3, 11) are mentally subnormal, as compared with 3 percent of the general population. The expected reciprocal relationship, an excess of schizophrenics among mental defectives or their relatives, was found by Penrose (15) and Böök (16) among mental defectives but not by Reed and Reed (17) in their monumental survey of the relatives of mental defectives. Also, Kallmann found a much higher rate of mental deficiency (10.8 percent) among relatives of simple schizophrenics, where there is a clinical commonality of sorts, than among relatives of other subtypes in the Kraepelinian classification. The evidence for or against an association between schizophrenia and mental deficiency is inconclusive, and more data are needed before the matter can be decided.

Obviously there is much yet to be learned before we can describe and delimit schizoidia. However, the same thing can be said of schizophrenia itself, and in this regard study of the schizoid may lighten some dark corners. Schizophrenia is defined operationally, not etiologically. It is the clinician who determines whether schizophrenia is present. But of course the limits of the clinical entity may not correspond to those of the etiological entity. In fact the linking of schizoidia to schizophrenia by genetic evidence raises serious questions about the etiological reality of the clinical definition of schizophrenia. There has always been a fuzzy border about schizophrenia along which several named entities, including abortive, ambulatory, borderline, latent, pseudoneurotic, pseudopsychopathic, and reactive schizophrenia and the "schizotype" of Meehl (18) have seemed to lie. These terms may best be viewed as attempts to cope with an operationally defined border between schizoidia and schizophrenia that is clinically imprecise because it is biologically unreal.

QUANTITATIVE ASPECTS

Given a schizophrenic who has a monozygotic twin, the empirical probability that his twin will also be schizophrenic has been found to be about 0.46 (Table 3). Most of the remaining 54 percent of monozygotic twins of schizophrenics have also been found to be abnormal. From clinical descriptions included in five studies (12, 13, 19-21) it appears that nearly all of the abnormal though nonschizophrenic co-twins were schizoid.

Overall, only about 13 percent of the monozygotic twins of schizophrenics have been regarded as normal or nearly normal, and, because most of the errors inherent in this sort of research tend to increase the proportion of apparent normals, this is surely an overestimate. But, while a critic could easily quibble about any of the proportions in Table 3, a crude but critical conclusion is inescapable: monozygotic twins of schizophrenics are about as likely to be schizoid as schizophrenic. What then is inherited? These considerations led Essen-Möller (19) to regard schizoidia as the basic inherited trait, and Kringlen, in a careful and sensitive analysis of

TABLE 3

DATA ON MONOZYGOTIC TWINS OF SCHIZOPHRENICS

Investigator	Pairs (No.)	Schizophrenia (No.)	Other significant abnormality (No.)	Normal, or mild abnormality*
Essen-Möller (19)	9	0	8	1
Slater (13)	37	18	11	8
Tienari (41)	16	1	12	3
Kringlen (12)	45	14	17	14
Inouye (42)	53	20	29	4
Gottesman and Shields (23)	24	10	8	6
Kallmann† (43)	174	103	62	9
Totals	358	166 (46.4%)	147 (41.1%)	45 (12.6%)

* Investigators' diagnoses: ? schizophrenia, schizophreniform, transient schizophrenia, reactive psychosis, borderline state, schizoid, suicide, psychopathic, neurosis, and variations of these diagnoses.
† From Shields, Gottesman, and Slater (44).

twin research, including his own major study, seems to have reached a similar conclusion, although he regarded the predisposition as less specific (12). At the very least a prima facie case has been made for considering the whole group of schizoid and schizophrenic disorders as alternative expressions of a single genotype. Moreover, because monozygotic twins are identical genetically, there is presumptive evidence that the range of variability within pairs can in principle be accounted for by environmental factors. The genes allow a range of outcomes.

A critical point to be established is the proportion of schizoids or schizophrenics among the first-degree relatives (parents, sibs, children) of schizophrenics. Table 4 gives Kallmann's results. No one else has investigated so many relatives of schizophrenics, and few others have conducted field studies intensive enough to identify schizoids. The more intensive modern studies have tended to show somewhat larger proportions of afflicted relatives (3, 10, 22). So did Slater among dizygotic twins of schizophrenics (13). The proportions found by Gottesman and Shields (23) and by Ödegard (24) were somewhat smaller. Kallmann's values may be taken as fair average estimates of the proportion of schizoids or schizophrenics among first-degree relatives of schizophrenics.

Table 4 also shows the results of four studies of the children of two schizophrenics. An estimated 66 percent of the children of these matings were schizoid or schizophrenic, again, this is surely an underestimate because the subjects were still quite young. The results of one such study, that of Lewis (25), was not included. Lewis did not give ages, and he stated that his follow-up was incomplete. Rosenthal has recently reviewed these studies (26).

An important unknown must now be considered. There is no adequate estimate of the proportion of schizoids in the general population. Then, is the clustering of schizoids among relatives of schizophrenics greater than might occur by chance? Although the proportion of schizoids found in families of schizophrenics is surely greater than that expected by even the most pessimistic observer of the general population, a better answer is that neither the relatives of other kinds of psychiatric patients nor the controls used in psychiatric studies have been found to be afflicted in significant numbers with disorders of a schizoid character or with any kind of behavioral disorder to the extent seen in relatives of schizophrenics. Further evidence—the small proportion of schizoids found among descendants of normal relatives of schizophrenics—is discussed below.

While the lack of data for the general population and the related lack of data for the families of schizoid probands preclude estimates of gene frequency, it should be noted that schizoid disorders surely afflict a large proportion of the population. With only isolated exceptions, schizophrenia afflicts about 1 percent of any population. If each schizophrenic has five living first-degree relatives (about the number in Kallmann's study), a simple extrapolation yields an estimate of 4 percent for the proportion of schizoids plus schizophrenics in the general population. This crude estimate can only make the point that any population, and especially any psychiatric population (persons identified because they came to psychiatric clinics or hospitals), is likely to contain large numbers of schizoids. One of the most neutral implications of this conclusion has an obvious application to the choosing of control groups for research in schizophrenia.

GENETIC HYPOTHESIS

The most parsimonious explanation of the data is given by the hypothesis that a defect in a single autosomal gene accounts for the genetic contribution to both schizoid and schizophrenic disease (the "dominance hypothesis"). By including schizoid disease (schizoidia), this hypothesis extends that of Slater (27). The view that schizoidia and schizophrenia are a single disease genetically is supported by their clinical similarity and is virtually required by the finding that the disorders occur with equal probability in monozygotic twins of schizophrenics. Further sup-

TABLE 4

PERCENTAGES OF FIRST-DEGREE RELATIVES FOUND TO BE
SCHIZOPHRENIC OR SCHIZOID

Relationship	Number of individuals	Schizophrenia* (%)	Schizoid (%)	Total: schizoid plus schizophrenic (%)
Children†	1000	16.4	32.6	49.0
Siblings‡	1191	14.3	31.5	45.8
Parents‡	2741	9.2	34.8	44.0
Children of two schizophrenics§	171	33.9	32.2	66.1

* Age-corrected rates.
† From (11).
‡ From (43).
§ From Kallmann (11), Kahn (45), Schulz (46), and Elsässer (47).

port for the hypothesis is presented in Fig. 1. The proportions of affected first-degree relatives fit reasonably well with the theoretical proportions expected under the dominance hypothesis.

Kallmann presented some data on second-degree relatives (11). Among 822 grandchildren of his schizophrenic probands he found 4.3 percent to be schizophrenic and 22.8 percent to be schizoid. The corresponding rates for nephews and nieces were considerably lower (3.9 and 6.2 percent). However, Kallmann pointed out that the normal sibs of his schizophrenic probands contributed many more nephews and nieces than the schizoid or schizophrenic sibs did. While the total of 27.1 percent for affected grandchildren is certainly close to the 25 percent expected under the dominance hypothesis, the proportions of affected nephews and nieces may or may not be compatible with that hypothesis.

The segregation of schizophrenia and schizoidia within families fits well with the dominance hypothesis. In Kallmann's study, which included

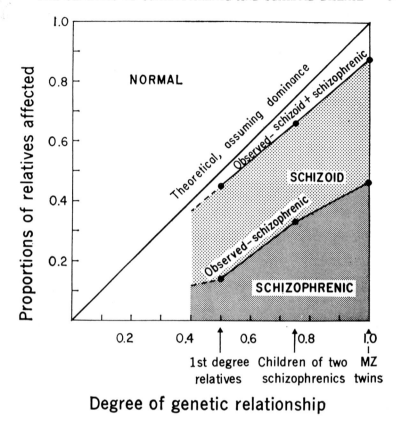

Fig. 1.—Observed and expected proportion of schizoids and schizophrenics.

three generations, the normal children of his schizophrenic probands produced few schizophrenic or schizoid children (1.8 and 2.6 percent, respectively), no more than might be expected in a general population. This is in contrast to the corresponding values of 13.7 and 33.4 percent for the children of the schizoid or schizophrenic children of Kallmann's schizophrenic probands (11).

The matter cannot be so simple, of course. The mechanisms involved in a disease like schizoidia-schizophrenia will surely be found to be extremely complex. Even phenylketonuria, which only a few years ago provided a prototype of rigorous simplicity for behavioral genetics, has turned out to be enormously complicated by secondary biochemical effects and by other, mostly unknown, factors (28). Heterogenity is also likely. Probably the most completely known genetic disease in humans, glucose-

6-phosphate dehydrogenase deficiency, occurs in at least 18 variants, each one presumably due to an amino acid substitution at a different place in the same enzyme (29). But research must proceed from hypotheses based on present understanding. From that viewpoint, and for practical purposes, it is not at all unreasonable to proceed on the working assumption that most schizoidia-schizophrenia is associated with defects in a single basic biochemical or physiological pathway, transmitted by a single mode of inheritance. It matters little that new research will no doubt turn up complexities that cannot even be imagined today.

Apart from insights gained from analogies to other genetic diseases, there are factual reasons for expecting that many elements in addition to a single main gene go into the mix that results in schizoidia-schizophrenia. First of all, there remain small deviations from the theoretical expectations under the dominance hypothesis, deviations which have been cited by Shields (2). These mainly take the form of a greater resemblance between relatives than can be explained by simple dominance. For example, the monozygotic twin of a severely afflicted individual is more likely to be schizophrenic than the twin of a mildly affected individual. If only a single gene were involved one would expect the risk of schizophrenia for a monozygotic twin of any schizophrenic to be equal to that of any other. Likewise, the larger the proportion of schizophrenic relatives is, the greater is the risk of schizophrenia for any given individual. Another sort of problem is that of accounting for the variability seen among schizophrenics; this becomes more difficult when schizoids are included. Although there are no grounds for expecting any particular degree of resemblance between affected persons, it has often been argued that, if only one gene were involved, the range of observable phenotypes should be smaller than is the case. And the persistence of schizophrenia presents a problem. Before the introduction of antipsychotic drugs, schizophrenics reproduced at a rate 30 percent lower (16), and schizoids at a rate 22 percent lower (11), than the rate for the general population. Such reproductive deficits should have lowered the rates of occurrence of a disorder due to a main gene of large effect far below the presently observed rates for schizophrenia.

Attempts to account for such findings have led to widespread espousal of polygenic theories of schizophrenia (12, 24, 30). As Gottesman and Shields have pointed out (31), the facts are explained adequately by polygenic theory. Most polygenic theorists have regarded schizophrenia as a threshold trait. But clinically schizoidia and schizophrenia seem to form a continuum of psychopathology, much as first described by Kretschmer (32). If there is a threshold it probably falls between the schizoid and the normal condition, but it seems that any such "threshold" is as likely to be a function of lack of diagnostic precision as a function of the disease. It is not necessary to consider other aspects of the polygenic argument here. Known modifiers of the phenotypic expression of the disease point toward plausible solutions of the problems encountered by the dominance hypothesis and toward resolution of the apparent differences between main-gene and polygenic theories.

MODIFYING FACTORS

One class of modifiers must be environmental events in the broadest sense—events occurring from conception onward that produce some change in the organism. The nature-nurture dilemma is unreal. It is change in the environment of the cell that induces change in the genetically mediated metabolic systems of the cell. The functional state of the cell is a result of the interplay of these determinants. But realization that phenotypic traits depend on interaction between gene and environment imposes conditions on research aimed at assessing the environment contribution. Genes function within cells. They interact with chemical, thermal, or other physical events and not with the abstractions ("stress," for example) that too often have passed for environmental data. The ultimate questions implicit in the concept of gene-environment interaction are, for example: How does a noxious learning experience alter the environment of the cell? What response is elicited from the genetic program of the cell? How is the later operation of the cell modified? Of course, such questions cannot be approached directly today. But unless the environmental contribution is too variable from case to case to allow generalization, it should be possible to build up a series of associations between environment and behavior that would point toward the environmental events that enter into the gene-environment interaction. The critical requirement is that such associations be potentially translatable into events that occur at the level of the gene. Despite all the research that has been done on the effects of environment on the development of schizophrenia, and despite the scope for environmental factors demonstrated by the differences between members of monozygotic twin pairs, practically no associations that meet this requirement have been established. Clinicians have learned to predict the effects of environmental features on their patients, but it is difficult to see any etiological clues in this body of experience. On general clinical grounds it makes sense to continue to study the effects of environmentally stimulated autonomic and endocrine responses. An association between lower birth weight and the development of schizophrenia in one member of a monozygotic twin pair has been reported (21), but it must be quite imperfect in view of the failure of other investigators to confirm it (12, 23). Perhaps differences in autonomic responses among children of schizophrenics that were described in a preliminary report from a wide-ranging prospective study (33) are the most promising associations so far defined. Almost everything remains to be done.

A second class of modifiers consists of complex traits that have been linked to schizophrenia by decades of empirical research. Somatotype has been found by several investigators to be associated with major modification of schizophrenia. Mesomorphs are underrepresented among schizophrenics, and especially underrepresented among schizophrenics younger than 25. Ectomorphs are correspondingly overrepresented. Schizophrenic mesomorphs are predominantly paranoid and have a shorter mean period of hospitalization that other schizophrenics. Parnell (34), who has reviewed the subject and contributed his own data, found all these associations to be statistically significant. A relation between intelligence and the prognosis in schizophrenia is well known: the higher the intelligence the better the prognosis. But higher intelligence may also affect the expression of schizophrenia. Lane and Albee (35) found that the I.Q. of children who later became schizophrenic was seven points lower than that of their siblings who remained nonschizophrenic. There are a host of other established associations between complex traits and schizophrenia— for example, patterns of autonomic nervous system reactivity, immunological phenomena, resistance to certain chronic diseases, and tolerance of wound shock. Some such traits appear to be only oddities, given our present knowledge; others are known to be linked to favorable or unfavorable prognosis in schizophrenia, and still others are known only to be more frequent or infrequent among schizophrenics. Several reviews of these findings are available (36).

The large number of such complex traits and the magnitude of the modification of schizophrenia associated with some of them must mean that they have a significant role in the ecology of the disease. For one thing, they suggest a plausible solution to the puzzle posed by the persistence of high rates of schizophrenia. Sir Julian Huxley et al. (37) postulated that the gene responsible for schizophrenia conferred sufficient physiological or reproductive advantages to maintain a balanced polymorphism. They listed several physiological traits found in schizophrenics that could be due to pleiotropism. Although the number of traits listed seems large, widespread pleiotropism might result from a mutation at a regulatory locus (38). But many modifying traits are clearly not due to pleiotropism, and some of those—particularly differences in somatotype and intelligence—which demonstrably affect the outcome in schizophrenia must have conferred general biological advantages through much of man's history as well. In either event, schizophrenics possessing advantageous traits would be expected to reproduce at relatively higher rates than those not possessing such traits. Over time, the evolutionary process would, theoretically, act to establish sets of favorable traits that, on the average, would tend to accompany schizophrenia. Theory aside, the popular association between genius and insanity, thought to be erroneous by Kallmann, was given some substance by Karlsson's finding that creative achievements and schizophrenia occurred in the same family lines (39). I reported a similar impression; however, the evidence was not gathered systematically (40). Although the problem posed by the persistence of schizophrenia remains theoretical and unsolved, further exploration of modifying traits provides as likely a path as any other now in view toward solution of the puzzle.

Modifying traits also suggest an approach to the problem of deviations from strict expectations under the dominance hypothesis. As pointed out above, polygenic theory can account for such deviations. But traits like somatotype and intelligence are themselves almost certainly polygenic. Polygenic modifiers of a single main gene explain the same facts, and indeed would yield the same mathematical results as simple additive polygenic theory per se. A multitude of genes summating to produce schizophrenia directly or a single main gene plus groups of genes summating to produce modifying traits account equally well for findings such as the tendency of monozygotic twins to be concordant with respect to severity of illness.

CONCLUSION

A main gene of large effect modified by multiple factors, including polygenic traits, suggests a number of testable hypotheses. Biochemical or other effects of a main gene should be present in schizoids as well as in schizophrenics. In family studies, the critical test of the place of the schizoid would be his reproductive performance in matings with normal individuals; 50 percent of the offspring of such matings should be schizoid or schizophrenic. However, polygenic modifiers should, on the average, maintain lesser degrees of disability in particular families. Thus, schizoid parents should have fewer schizophrenic but more schizoid children than schizophrenic parents. There is incomplete support for this contention in Kallmann's study (11) of the grandchildren of his schizophrenic subjects: the schizoid children of his schizophrenic probands had more schizoid and fewer schizophrenic children than their schizophrenic siblings, but members of the third generation, the grandchildren of the probands, were too young to yield decisive evidence. Along the same lines, it would be expected that nearly all schizophrenics should have at least one schizoid or schizophrenic parent. Although the work of Kallmann and the intensive family studies of Alanen (10) and Lidz (22) support this expectation, more rigorous evidence is needed. The traits that favorably modify schizophrenia should be more apparent among schizoid than among schizophrenic relatives of schizophrenics. One would hypothesize, for example, that the more mesomorphic or more intelligent among the children of schizophrenics would tend to have less severe illnesses and to have more children than the less mesomorphic or less intelligent. These hypotheses, and many more that are implicit in the preceding discussion, constitute a significant refinement of the genetic hypotheses so far explored in schizophrenia.

SUMMARY

The importance of genetic factors in the development of schizophrenia has by now been established beyond reasonable dispute, although it is clear that environment too plays its etiologic role. The results of recent research have refocused attention on schizoid disorders, a term applied to psychiatric disorders resembling schizophrenia which afflict relatives of schizophrenics. The many conceptual and research problems presented by the schizoid are considered.

Schizoids and schizophrenics occur with about the same frequency among monozygotic twins of schizophrenics. About 45 percent of the sibs, parents, and children of a schizophrenic are schizoid or schizophrenics, as are about 66 percent of the children of two schizophrenics. From the known risk of schizophrenia for the population as a whole, it is estimated that at least 4 percent of the general population will be afflicted with schizoid-schizophrenic disease.

Since monozygotic twins are identical genetically, it appears that the same genotype is compatible with either schizophrenic or schizoid disease. The proportions of affected first-degree relatives and the segregation of affected individuals within families closely approximate theoretical expectations based on the hypothesis of a defect in a single autosomal dominant gene. However, modifying traits play a significant role; this is discussed and integrated into the main genetic hypothesis. Emphasis is placed on hypotheses testable by future research.

REFERENCES

1. SLATER, E., in *The Transmission of Schizophrenia*, D. Rosenthal and S. Kety, Eds. (Pergamon, Oxford, 1968); D. Rosenthal, in *The Origins of Schizophrenia*, J. Romano, Ed. (Excerpta Medica Foundation, New York, 1967).
2. SHIELDS, J., in *The Transmission of Schizophrenia*, D. Rosenthal and S. Kety, Eds. (Pergamon, Oxford, 1968).
3. HESTON, L. L., *Brit. J. Psychiat.* 112, 819 (1966).
4. ROSENTHAL, D., WENDER, P., KETY, S., SCHULSINGER, F., ÖSTERGARD, L., WELNER, J., in *The Transmission of Schizophrenia*, D. Rosenthal and S. Kety, Eds. (Pergamon, Oxford, 1968).
5. KARLSSON, J., *The Biolgical Basis of Schizophrenia* (Thomas, Springfield, Ill., 1966).
6. WENDER, P., ROSENTHAL, D., KETY, S., in *The Transmission of Schizophrenia*, D. Rosenthal and S. Kety, Eds. (Pergamon, Oxford, 1968).
7. KETY, S., ROSENTHAL, D., SCHULSINGER, F., WENDER, P., *ibid.*
8. RAY, I., *Mental Hygiene* (Hafner, New York, new ed., 1968).
9. PLANANSKY, K. *J. Nerv. Ment. Dis.* 142, 318 (1966); E. Essen-Möller, *Mschr. Psychiat. Neurol.* 112, 258 (1946).
10. ALANEN, Y. O. *Acta Psychiat. Scand., Suppl. No. 189* (1966).
11. KALLMANN, F. J., *The Genetics of Schizophrenia* (Augustin, New York, 1938).
12. KRINGLEN, E., "Heredity and Environment in the Functional Psychoses," *Norwegian Monogr. Med. Sci. Univ. Oslo* (1967).
13. SLATER, E., with the assistance of J. Shields, "Psychotic and Neurotic Illness in Twins," *Med. Res. Counc. (Great Brit.) Spec. Rep. Ser. No. 278* (1953).
14. HALLGREN, B., & SJÓGREN, T., *Acta Psychiat. Neurol. Scand., Suppl. No. 140* (1959).
15. PENROSE, L. S., *A Clinical and Genetic Study of 1280 Cases of Mental Defect* (Her Majesty's Stationery Office, London (1938).
16. BÖÖK, J. A., *Acta Genet.* 4, 1 (1953).
17. REED, E. W., & REED, S. C., *Mental Retardation: A Family Study* (Saunders, Philadelphia, 1965).
18. MEEHL, P. E. *Amer. Psychol.* 17, 827 (1962).
19. ESSEN-MÖLLER, E. *Acta Psychiat., Suppl. No. 23* (1941).
20. TIENARI, P. *Acta Psychiat., Suppl. No. 171* (1963).
21. POLLIN, W., STABENAU, J. R., TUPIN, J., *Psychiatry* 28, 60, (1965).
22. LIDZ, T., FLECK, S., CORNELISON, A., *Schizophrenia and the Family* (International Universities Press, New York, 1966).
23. GOTTESMAN, I. I., & SHIELDS, J., *Brit. J. Psychiat.* 112, 809 (1966).
24. ÖDEGARD, Ö., *Acta Psychiat., Suppl. No. 169* (1963), p. 94.
25. LEWIS, A., *Acta Genet.* 7, 349 (1957).
26. ROSENTHAL, D., *J. Psychiat. Res.* 4, 169 (1966).
27. SLATER, E., *Acta Genet.* 8, 50 (1958).
28. JOHNSON, C., *J. Iowa Med. Soc.* 59, 27 (1968).
29. HARRIS, H., *Brit. Med. J.* 2, 135 (1968).
30. ROSENTHAL, D., *The Genain Quadruplets* (Basic Books, New York, 1963).
31. GOTTESMAN, I., & SHIELDS, J., *Proc. Nat. Acad. Sci. U.S.* 58, 199 (1967).
32. KRETSCHMER, E., *Physique and Character* (W. Sprott, Trans.) (Paul, Trench and Trubner, London, 1925).
33. MEDNICK, S., & SCHULSINGER, F., in *The Transmission of Schizophrenia*, D. Rosenthal and S. Kety, Eds. (Pergamon, Oxford, 1968).
34. PARNELL, R., *Behavior and Physique* (Arnold, London, 1958).
35. LANE, E. A., & ALBEE, G. W., *Amer. J. Orthopsychiat.* 35, 747 (1965).
36. GELLHORN, E., & LOOFBOURROW, G., *Emotions and Emotional Disorders: A Neurophysiological Study* (Harper & Row, New York, 1963); W. Ross, J. Hay, M.

McDowal, *Psychosom. Med.* 12, 170 (1950); P. Huston and M. Pepernik, in *Schizophrenia, A Review of the Syndrome*, L. Bellak, Ed. (Logos, New York, 1958); C. Rosenbaum, *J. Nerv. Ment. Dis,* 146, 103 (1968); H. Freeman, in *Schizophrenia, A Review of the Syndrome*, L. Bellak, Ed. (Logos, New York, 1958); L. Rees, in *Schizophrenia: Somatic Aspects,* D. Richter, Ed. (Macmillan, New York, 1957).

37. Huxley, J., Mayr, E., Osmond, H., Hoffer, A., *Nature* 204, 220 (1964).
38. Britten, R. J., & Davidson, E. H., *Science* 165, 349 (1969).
39. Karlsson, J., in *The Transmission of Schizophrenia*, D. Rosenthal and S. Kety, Eds. (Pergamon, Oxford, 1968).
40. Heston, L., & Denney, D., *ibid.*
41. Tienari, P., *ibid.*
42. Inouye, E., in *Proceedings, Third World Congress of Psychiatry* (Univ. of Toronto Press, Montreal, 1961), vol. 1, p. 524.
43. Kallmann, F. J., *Amer. J. Psychiat.* 103, 309 (1946).
44. Shields, J., Gottesman, I., Slater, E., *Acta Psychiat. Scand.* 43, 385 (1967).
45. Kahn, E., *Monogr. Gesamtgeb. Neurol. Psychiat.* 36, 1 (1923).
46. Schulz, B., *Z. Gesamte Neurol. Psychiat.* 168, 322 (1940).
47. Elsässer, G., *Die Nachkommen gelsteskranker Elternpaare* (Thieme, Stuttgart, 1952).
48. I thank James Shields, John Price, Irving Gottesman, and Russell Noyes, who commented on various phases of this manuscript.

34

THE ROLE OF GENETICS IN THE ETIOLOGY OF THE SCHIZOPHRENIAS

Paul H. Wender

Both experiential and genetic factors have been implicated in the etiology of schizophrenia but their relative roles have been impossible to assess. Recent studies using the technique of adoption to separate the effects of "nature" and "nurture" have shown that genetic factors play an important role in the etiology of schizophrenia and may also play a role in the development of other psychiatric illnesses.

In the past few years a body of impressive data has emerged demonstrating the role of genetics in the etiology of the schizophrenic syndromes. It is the purpose of this paper to summarize the findings of this research and discuss the relevance of these, as yet not widely known, studies.

Before proceeding, it might be useful to underscore the importance of such research. The schizophrenias are not uncommon disorders. The usual figure given for lifetime incidence is about 1%. This figure is based on hospitalized cases (5); if the number of people hospitalized is only one-half to one-third (7) of those who have the disorder, the prevalence figure must be doubled or even tripled. But the problem may be even more extensive, since the boundaries of the syndrome are so unclear. It is possible that conditions which bear a phenomenological resemblance to schizophrenia, such as schizoid disorders and borderline states, may share etiological factors as well. These latter disorders are extremely common; some clinics report (e.g. Gaw et al. (8)) that as many as one-

Presented at the 1968 annual meeting of the American Orthopsychiatric Association, Chicago, Illinois.

Reprinted, by permission of author and editor, from: *American Journal of Orthopsychiatry*, 39:447-458, 1969. Copyright, The American Orthopsychiatric Association, Inc.

half of their applicants have been so diagnosed. Clearly, then, what might be in question is the etiology of the disorder of a substantial proportion of the psychiatrically disturbed population.

What are the theories concerning the genesis of the schizophrenias? Primarily they are explications of an observation of considerable antiquity: that there is a familial clustering of psychiatric disease. A suitably early reference may be found in Thomas Willis who wrote in 1685 that: "It is a common observation, that men born of parents that are sometimes wont to be mad, will be obnoxious to the same disease. . . ." In the intervening 280 years, studies exploring the etiology of the schizophrenias have implicated both genetic and environmental factors but have not yet been able to assess the relative roles of each factor in the development of the syndrome. These studies have employed two major lines of investigation:

1. Consanguinity studies—assessment of the prevalence of mental disease in the relatives of schizophrenic patients. Such studies (13, 25) have demonstrated that there is a significantly higher prevalence of psychopathology among the relatives of schizophrenics as compared to the general population and that the closer the biological relationship the greater the prevalence of psychopathology in these relatives, culminating in the high concordance rate of schizophrenia in monozygotic twins. Results of such studies have been traditionally explained as due to the operation of genetic factors.

2. Psychodynamic and family studies—studies of the psychological environment to which schizophrenic patients have been exposed. These studies (1, 3, 17, 18) have revealed that schizophrenics have been reared in and exposed to a disturbed psychological environment. They have been interpreted to show that the disease is a learned reaction to, modeling after or identification with such familial pathology.

What makes interpretation of both types of studies difficult, if not impossible, is the confounding of biological and psychological relatedness: the deviant psychological experiences have usually been received at the hands of the patient's biological relatives. One cannot decide to what extent the disturbance of the schizophrenic offspring has been genetically or psychologically transmitted since the cognitive, affective, and child-rearing abnormalities of the parents might be the manifestation of a genetic disorder in the parents rather than the cause of the illness in the child. The data accumulated to date are compatible with both the biological and the social transmission of schizophrenia and do not permit the evaluation of the relative contributions of either.*

In the past few years a method of resolving this dilemma occurred independently to several people: Leonard Heston (11), Jon Karlsson (14), and each of our collaborative team at the NIH—Seymour Kety (15), David Rosenthal (23), and myself (29). This method involves the study of persons adopted in infancy. Since in such circumstances the biological parents are not the parents who rear the children, the transmitters of biological heredity and social experience are separated and their relative roles may be evaluated. Why this method had not been previously applied to the problem of the psychoses and why it suddenly occurred to several people at once is an interesting question; the technique had been used to evaluate the contributions of nature and nurture in intelligence 30 years ago (24) and to the problem of alcoholism (22) 20 years ago.

THE ADOPTION STUDIES

Studies utilizing the technique of adoption have employed three approaches attempting to answer three questions. The first question is: Does heredity play any role in the etiology of the schizophrenia and, if so, what is the manifestation of the genetic diathesis? The two relevant studies are that of Leonard Heston (11) and that of Rosenthal, Wender, Kety, Walner, Schulsinger, and Østergaard (23). Both studies have evaluated the personalities of adults born to schizophrenic parents but raised from infancy in foster homes (Heston) or adoptive homes (Rosenthal et al.) Both studies have employed the obvious control group of children born to normal biological parents and reared in foster or adoptive homes. Heston's evaluations of subjects were made primarily on the basis of clinical interviews while the Rosenthal study employed psychological tests as well. At this time results of the Heston study have been fully analyzed, those of the Rosenthal study have not. Without describing the methodology of these studies—for which the reader is referred to the

---

* The studies of monozygotic ("identical") twins do provide some definitive information regarding the role of genetics in the etiology of schizophrenia. This information is usually incorrectly interpreted. Since in no study conducted today has it been found that 100% of "identical" twin pairs are concordant with regard to schizophrenia, one can only conclude that the etiology of the disease cannot be 100% genetic. However this does not document—as some people would seem to believe—that psychological factors necessarily play an etiological role in the development of the disorder. All that is nongenetic is not necessarily psychological: biological but nongenetic factors have been implicated in several such studies (27). It is of some interest that the concordance rate of schizophrenia in monozygotic twins is approximately that of diabetes, a disease not generally regarded as primarily psychological in origin (10).

original articles—I would like to summarize the major results. In these studies the phrase "index group" refers to the offspring of schizophrenic parents reared in foster or adoptive homes while the phrase "control group" refers to the offspring of nonschizophrenic parents reared in foster or adoptive homes. Table 1 presents the findings of each study and summarizes the results of both studies taken together.

TABLE 1

Distribution of Schizophrenic Diagnoses Among Offspring of Schizophrenic Parents (Index Cases) and Nonschizophrenic Parents (Control Cases)

	Schizophrenic	Borderline or Schizoid Schizophrenic States		Other	Total
HESTON (1966)					
Index Cases	5	8		34	47
Control Cases	0	0		50	50

Schizophrenic+Borderline schizophrenics+Schizoid vs. "Others," p<.001 (exact probability test).

	Schizophrenic	Borderline or Schizoid Schizophrenic States		Other	Total
ROSENTHAL ET AL. (1967)					
Index Cases	3	6	4	26	39
Control Cases	0	1	5	41	47

Schizophrenic+Borderline schizophrenics+Schizoid vs. "Others," p<.02 (exact probability test).

	Schizophrenic	Borderline or Schizoid Schizophrenic States		Other	Total
COMBINED DATA					
Index Cases	8 (9%)[a]	18 (21%)[b]		60 (70%)[c]	86
Control Cases	0	6		91	97

The probability that the excess of:
[a] Schizophrenics in the index group is chance, p<.003 (exact probability test).
[b] Borderline schizophrenics or schizoids in the index group is chance, p<.001 (exact probability test).
[c] Schizophrenics+borderline schizophrenics or schizoids in the index group is chance, p<.001 (exact probability test).

In summary we find that about 9% of the offspring of schizophrenic parents become schizophrenic when reared in adoptive or foster homes as opposed to none of the offspring of nonschizophrenic mothers reared in adoptive or foster homes. The rate of 9% is well within the range of the percentage of offspring of schizophrenics who become schizophrenic when reared by their own parents. Likewise, more than 30% of the index group manifested psychiatric pathology in the schizophrenic or borderline spectrum as opposed to 6% in the control group. (These differences are highly significant statistically, p<.001, exact probability test.) In other words, about one-third of the offspring of one schizophrenic parent develop psychiatric disorders of a schizophrenic character even when they are reared away from their schizophrenic biological parents. This is comparable to the fraction who develop such pathology when reared by their schizophrenic parents (2). The results of these two studies are apparent: there is a markedly increased prevalence of schizophrenic psychopathology among the biological offspring of schizophrenic parents, a finding strongly implicating genetic factors in the development of *some* forms of schizophrenia. Note that I state "some forms"—logically such a research design can (and has) only shown that some schizophrenic parents genetically transmit this disorder to their offspring. The design cannot demonstrate the converse: that all schizophrenics have schizophrenic parents, or that all schizophrenics have a genetic component to their illness.

Two additional results—not cited in the tables—are of considerable interest. Both relate to what seem to be other manifestations of the genetic tendency. Heston's study revealed that in addition to the 5 schizophrenic subjects in the index group, 21 other index subjects manifested appreciable psychopathology, including 9 sociopaths* and 13 other personality disorders (emotionally unstable personalities and mixed psychoneurotic reactions). Among the control group there were, by comparison, 2 sociopaths and 7 personality disorders. The difference in frequency between the two groups is again significant (p<.02 for sociopathy, p<.05 for the personality disorders, exact probability test). The second unexpected result was that among those index subjects who demonstrated no psychiatric pathology Heston felt there were a large number of talented, creative, and colorful people—a provocative suggestion of the often cited relationship of madness and genius.

Let me reemphasize the first of these two findings, which if replicated in other studies suggests not only that genetic factors play a role in the etiology of schizophrenia but that such factors play a role in the development of a wide variety of psychiatric difficulties. As will be seen, the evidence from the second group of studies supports this finding.

Although there is a preponderance of psychopathology among the offspring of psychotic parents, there is some psychopathology among the offspring of the control parents. What is the implication of this fact? Does it demonstrate that such psychopathology can originate without a genetic basis? Not necessarily. In both studies it is not asserted that the parents of the control subjects were psychologically healthy but only that they had never received psychiatric attention. What fraction of persons

---

* Eight were noted as "schizoid psychopath" and have been included in the category of "borderline schizophrenic" or "schizoid" states in Table 1.

with the schizophrenic syndrome do receive psychiatric attention at some time during their lives? In the Rosenthal study it was found that of 20 persons who were schizoid, borderline, or schizophrenic, only one had ever received psychiatric care. Judging from the Rosenthal data—as well as population surveys, e.g., Mental Health in the Metropolis (26)—only a small fraction of seriously disturbed persons do receive psychiatric attention. Accordingly, there is a fair probability that the control population's parents contained ill but undiagnosed persons. (This assertion documents the obvious—in general it would seem that women giving up their children for adoption are more apt to be disturbed than those who do not). Preliminary analyses of the Rosenthal data suggests that severity of psychopathology in the parent is not closely correlated with the severity of pathology in the offspring; that is, borderline schizophrenic patients are as apt to have children in the schizophrenic spectrum as are chronically schizophrenic parents. If this is so, the psychiatric disturbance in the offspring of the control group may be due to genetic transmission from mildly disturbed and undiagnosed parents within this group.* Hence, there is no necessary reason for attributing disturbance to the offspring of the control group to psychological environmental factors. It is *possible* that the disturbances in both the experimental and control groups are entirely genetic. It is also logically possible that psychological factors do play a role in the development of psychiatric illness within both groups. One cannot make a decision between these two possibilities on the basis of these data. An obvious question relates to whether the experiences associated with adoption are psychologically noxious. One might then argue that some psychological experiences related to adoption interact with a biological predisposition to produce psychopathology in the index group. An admission that this is so is tantamount—because the control group did not in general become ill—to stating that the biological predisposition is so great that factors that do not make a genetically normal child ill will make a predisposed child severely disturbed; that is, genetically transmitted characteristics are *at least* necessary, if not sufficient. It is worth noting in passing that virtually no disease is entirely genetic. Even phenylketonuria, which is generally considered to be a "genetic disorder," has an environmental component. The child who has the disease will become ill only if he eats substances containing the amino acid, phenylalanine. If most edible substances did not contain phenylalanine, a child with phenylketonuria would become ill only if he

---

* A method which might permit clarification of the above problem would be to interview and screen the parents of the control group, including only the offspring of those parents who manifested no psychiatric disturbance.

ate special foods, those containing phenylalanine. Since, in fact, most proteins do contain phenylalanine an afflicted child becomes ill under any natural environmental circumstances. (When such a child is fed a diet deficient in phenylalanine the manifestation of the disease may, perhaps, be avoided). Similarly, the genetically predisposed child might not become schizophrenic if reared in an unusual way. All that may be said from this data is that given an apparently adequate psychological environment such a child does become ill.

The first experimental design answers one question: Can schizophrenia be genetically transmitted? The answer is affirmative. The design cannot

TABLE 2

DISTRIBUTION IN THE RELATIVES OF SCHIZOPHRENIC CASES AND THEIR CONTROLS

| | Relatives with Schizophrenia or Probable Schizophrenia | |
	Biological Relatives	Adoptive Relatives
Index Cases (n=33)	11 (150)[a]	1 (74)
Control Cases (n=33)	3 (156)	3 (83)

p<.05 (exact probability test, one-tailed).
[a] Figures in brackets indicate the total number of relatives at risk, e.g., for the upper left-hand cell, there were 150 biological relatives of adopted schizophrenics (index cases) and of these relatives 11 were schizophrenics or probable schizophrenics.

answer the question: What fraction of schizophrenics is genetically produced? To answer this question another design must be employed. In this second design one starts with adult schizophrenics, adopted in infancy, and determines which of them have psychiatric illness in their biological relatives. If schizophrenia is a genetically transmitted disorder, one should find an increased prevalence of schizophrenia among the biological relatives of the schizophrenics as compared to the biological relatives of normal adopted adults. Likewise, if schizophrenia is a psychologically transmitted disorder, one should expect to find an increased prevalence of psychopathology among the adopting relatives of the schizophrenic subjects.

Such a study has been conducted and is reported by Kety, Rosenthal, Wender and Schulsinger (15). These authors report the prevalence of psychopathology among the biological and adoptive relatives of 33 adopted schizophrenics (the index cases) and 33 matched adopted nonhospitalized subjects (the control cases). The prevalence of schizophrenia and other psychiatric disorders among these relatives was determined by finding the number of such relatives who had received such psychiatric diagnoses from hospitals and clinics. The results are presented in Table 2.

As may be seen, there is a significantly increased prevalence of schizophrenia among the biological relatives of the adopted schizophrenics but not among the adoptive parents of these subjects. This result is highly significant statistically (p<.05, exact probability test). This result, too, is compatible with the genetic but not the psychological transmission hypothesis. Since Heston's study had shown that schizophrenic parents produced offspring with a variety of psychopathology, it was logical to

TABLE 3

DISTRIBUTION IN THE RELATIVES OF SCHIZOPHRENIC INDEX CASES
AND THEIR CONTROLS

	Relatives with Schizophrenia, Probable Schizophrenia, Psychopathy, Character Disorder, Inadequate Personality	
	Biological Relatives	Adoptive Relatives
Index Cases (n=33)	20 (150)	4 (74)
Control Cases (n=33)	7 (156)	3 (83)

p<.01 (exact probability test, one-tailed).

reverse the process, that is, to ask how many of the biological relatives of schizophrenic subjects had received comparable diagnoses. Accordingly, the following diagnoses were grouped together under the neologism "schizophrenic spectrum disorder": schizophrenia; probable schizophrenia; psychopathy; neurotic character disorder; inadequate personality. The results are presented in Table 3.

As may be seen, the prevalence of all these illnesses is significantly greater among the biological relatives of the schizophrenics (p<.01 exact probability test), a result again compatible with Heston's finding of a general increase of psychopathology among the offspring of schizophrenic parents.

The above study has one methodological and one logical weakness. The methodological weakness is that the diagnoses were made on the basis of formally recognized mental illness. Consequently the rates of illness among the relatives are too low. Likewise the "control group" may have been far from psychologically healthy because a weak criterion of health was used: that of never having received psychiatric therapy for mental illness. A *logical* weakness is that such a method could only set a *lower* limit on the fraction of schizophrenics who have a genetic predisposition. The reason for this is as follows: For any genetic trait which is not transmitted by a simple dominant gene, not all of the family of a child with that trait will demonstrate it. For example, if both parents are carrying a heterozygous recessive trait, neither will show the trait and perhaps one or more of the children will show it. This is the usual state of affairs among the parents of children with phenylketonuria. In this study, at least one child, an adopted schizophrenic, showed the trait in question. If the trait were a simple recessive one, one would expect that about

TABLE 4

GLOBAL SEVERITY OF PSYCHOPATHOLOGY RATING SCALE

1 Normal—without any disorder traits.
2 Normal—with minor psychoneurotic traits.
3 Psychoneurosis or mild character neuroses.
4 Moderate to marked character neuroses.
5 Severe character neuroses, moderate to marked cyclothymic character, schizoid character, paranoid character.
6 Borderline schizophrenia, acute psychoses.
7 Schizophrenic psychosis.

40% of the sibships would not manifest that trait.* That is, even if the disease were *entirely* genetic, 40% of the cases would have a negative family history.

In neither of the groups of studies discussed was the psychological environment of the adopted schizophrenic evaluated. Proponents of the psychological mode of transmission (1, 3, 17, 18, 30, 31) have clearly described the aberrant interpersonal and cognitive environment to which the future schizophrenic is exposed during his formative years. Although such work is important, one cannot determine, as I have already explained, whether such an environment is a manifestation of illness in the parents rather than the cause of illness in the child.

To attempt to unravel this problem a third type of study has been conducted. In this study (29) the *adoptive* parents of schizophrenics were

---

* In the Kety et al. study, the average number of sibs per patient was three—that is the average number of offspring per biological parent was about four. In this study, the actual number of sibships who did not manifest a psychiatric illness was about 65%. For further explication of this point see any textbook of human genetics, e.g., Curt Stern's *Principles of Human Genetics* (28).

compared with a group of parents who had reared their own schizo-phrenic children. The parents of these two groups and those of a third comparison group, the adoptive parents of normal adults, were evaluated with psychiatric interviews and psychological tests. At present only the psychiatric interviews have been evaluated. On the basis of these inter-views each parent was evaluated and assigned a score on a global psycho-pathology scale which is shown in Table 4. The average severity of psy-

TABLE 5

FREQUENCY AND SEVERITY OF PSYCHOPATHOLOGY IN THE THREE
GROUPS OF PARENTS

Group		1-2	2.5-3	3.5-4	4.5-5	5.5-6	6.5-7	Mean
Biological Schizophrenic	Fathers	1	1	1	6	1	0	4.2
	Mothers	0	0	4	3	1	2	4.9
Adopted Schizophrenic	Fathers	1	4	3	2	0	0	3.3
	Mothers	1	3	4	1	1	0	3.5
Adopted Normals	Fathers	2	6	2	0	0	0	2.6
	Mothers	2	4	4	0	0	0	3.0

Significances, one-tailed t-test:
Adoptive Schizophrenic Parents vs. Biological Schizophrenic Parents, p<.005.
Adoptive Schizophrenic Parents vs. Adoptive Normal Parents, p<.05.
Adoptive Schizophrenic Mothers vs. Biological Schizophrenic Mothers, p<.05.
Adoptive Schizophrenic Mothers vs. Adopted Normal Mothers, NS.
Adoptive Schizophrenic Fathers vs. Biological Schizophrenic Fathers, p<.05.
Adoptive Schizophrenic Fathers vs. Adoptive Normal Fathers, NS.

chopathology among the three groups was calculated, and results are presented in Table 5.

The biological parents were considerably more disturbed than the adop-tive parents of schizophrenic patients. The difference is highly significant (p<.005, t-test). Likewise the adoptive parents of the schizophrenic adults were somewhat more disturbed than the adoptive parents of the normal subjects—this difference is significant but less so (p<.05, t-test). Some sampling problems and a methodological problem (the interviewers knew into which group the parents fell) dictate less than unqualified acceptance of these data; a replication is planned. Nonetheless, this ex-periment again suggests that the reported and here observed psycho-pathology in the parents of schizophrenic persons is a manifestation of a genetically transmitted disturbance in the parents rather than the cause of illness in the patient. This last assertion contravenes the mandate of one's psychological intuition. It is virtually impossible to see how the aberrant psychological environments that have been described can fail to leave their pathological toll. Perhaps the psychopathology among the offspring of schizophrenic parents reared in adoptive homes would be still greater if these homes provided the type of environments which have been deemed schizophrenogenic. Nonetheless, if these data are correct— and, as stated, the experiment needs replication—one cannot but conclude that the role of deviant psychological experiences in the etiology of schizophrenia has been overestimated.

DISCUSSION

I would like to turn now to some of the questions that have been raised but not answered by these studies.

1. *Schizophrenia Spectrum Disorders.* One of the most surprising findings of the Heston and Kety studies was the increased amount of nonschizophrenic pathology (i.e., psychopathy, character disorders, etc.) among the relatives of schizophrenic patients. Because of the designs of these studies such pathology could not have been the effect of psychological causes but rather must have been due to genetic inheritance. To repeat, not only do some schizophrenias have a genetic basis but apparently so do some phenomenologically nonschizophrenic psychiatric syndromes as well.

If a graduated continuum of psychiatric pathology, a spectrum, does exist, the nineteenth century concept* of a neuropathological trait with varying manifestations may have to be exhumed and resuscitated. The efforts of nosologists to break the continuum of psychological malfunction into discrete nonoverlapping psychiatric diagnostic categories may be not only difficult (which is obvious) but impossible. Because of the difficulty nosologists have had in describing discrete nonoverlapping psychiatric diagnostic categories, some psychiatrists (e.g., Menninger (20)) have argued that the reason for this continuum is that there really are no psychiatric diseases and that all apparently qualitatively different forms of mental illness differ only quantitatively; different forms of malfunc-

---

* The observation that mental disease—not particular forms of mental illness— cluster in families had been made considerably earlier. In his *Anatomy of Melancholy* published in 1651 Burton (6) observed: "and that which is to be more wondered at, it [melancholy] skips in some families and goes to the son, or takes every other, and sometimes every third in a lineal descent, *and does not always produce the same, but some like, and some symbolizing disease* [my italics].

tion are the result of the degree of regression along a continuous path of psychological development common to all people.

The demonstration of a continuum often leads to an incorrect conclusion: because a continuum exists, no diseases exist. Without quibbling about the meaning of the word "disease" it should be obvious that although intelligence is distributed along a continuum, certain biological pathological states ("diseases") exist which produce low intelligence. Likewise, height is distributed along a continuum, but no one would argue that achondroplastic dwarfs or persons with pituitary giantism did not have "diseases." In summary, the existence of a phenomenological continuum of psychopathology in no way militates against the view that biological "diseases" exist in this continuum. The data discussed suggest that there may be an underlying continuum of biological disposition which is manifested in the observed symptomatic continuum.

2. *What Is Transmitted?* Another question, related to the one already discussed, is the question of what is transmitted. To begin with, what are the primary psychological traits that are inherited? Are they any or all of the "fundamental" psychological characteristics posited by several authors to form the psychological anlage of schizophrenia? A partial list of such traits would include: dissociation (4); introversion (12); weakness of repression; overreaction to anxiety-producing stimuli (19); and anhedonia (21).

A second question is simply the mechanism of genetic transmission. What gene or genes are involved? What are the effects of their interaction? What is their degree of penetrance?

A third related question regards what is biologically transmitted. Using the computer as an analogy to the brain, at least three possible mechanisms suggest themselves. (1) Some of the components (neurons) may be aberrant. In this model some groups of cells have a metabolic abnormality which might be manifested in a variety of ways including a raised or lowered threshold of excitability, lack of modification through use ("effective learning"), etc. Such aberrant functioning might be detectable with present biochemical techniques. (2) The wiring may be aberrant. In this model the individual elements (neurons, vacuum tubes, transistors) function adequately but are interconnected incorrectly. Such an abnormality would probably be difficult, if not impossible, to ascertain with current biological techniques. (3) The inbuilt "programs" are aberrant. In this instance both the elements and their interconnections are adequate but the instinctive "programs" are aberrant. In a normal child certain complex patterns of behavior emerge on a fairly predictable timetable: stranger anxiety during the second half of the first year; separation anxiety during the second year; oppositional behavior during the second and third years. Such preprogrammed behavior seems to fulfill an important role in normal development. As Levy (16) suggests, without the period of preprogrammed rebellion a two-year-old might not begin to develop independence; one might easily see a child lacking this program as becoming an excessively dependent and "good" child closely bound to his mother—in fact a child with some characteristics often described in preschizophrenics. An aberration in which the mechanisms were intact but the neural instructions which govern were somehow malfunctioning would be an abnormality whose biological basis would probably be impossible to detect with current techniques of biological analysis.

3. *The Role of Experiential Factors*. To begin with, what have these experiments demonstrated with regard to the etiology of schizophrenia? They demonstrate that biological factors—almost certainly genetic—play a predominant role in the etiology of some fraction of the schizophrenic syndromes. The followup studies—studies of the offspring of schizophrenics reared in adoptive homes—can logically demonstrate only that schizophrenia can be genetic. Such studies cannot determine in what fraction of schizophrenias genetic factors are predominant. Studies of the relatives of adopted schizophrenics—the second class of studies discussed—should be able to help answer this question. As already discussed, even if the syndrome were entirely genetic, unless it were transmitted as a simple dominant trait (and it appears not to be), one would not expect to find a family history in all instances. (Certainly one would not expect all schizophrenics to be genetically produced. If some schizophrenic adults are, so to speak, "ex-schizophrenic children," then since a large fraction of schizophrenic children suffer from organic brain damage (9), one would expect that the predominant etiology of some adult schizophrenic syndrome would also be organic brain damage).

A most important question not answered by these studies is to what extent (and how) experiential factors play a role in the genesis of the schizophrenias. The adoptive parents study could only show that some schizophrenics have fairly normal parents. But what are the effects of disturbed parenting? Can experential factors alone produce schizophrenia? Some light may be shed on this question by a study, now in progress, of the psychological fate of offspring of normal biological parents reared by schizophrenic, presumably schizophrenogenic, adopting parents. Finally, how and to what extent do experiential factors interact with the documented biological factors? Neither the Heston nor the Rosenthal study employ a comparison group of adults reared by their own schizo-

phrenic parents. Such a comparison group is necessary to determine if—
and if, how much—deviant environmental factors contribute to the impaired psychological and social functioning seen in schizophrenic individuals. It is possible that although schizophrenics' offspring reared in
adoptive homes are as apt to develop schizophrenic symptoms as when
reared by their own parents (which the data seem to indicate), the severity and type of these symptoms may be affected by circumstances of
rearing.

Theories regarding the genesis of psychopathology are many. Facts are
less abundant. Most theorists acknowledge the importance of both constitutional (or hereditary) and experiential factors. Such assertions are not
very useful. What is essential is specifying *which* kinds of experience
interacting with *which* kinds of biological background *when* result in
what kinds of personality development. The strategy of adoption studies
may permit the construction of specific and useful theories, both for
deviant and normal human psychological development.

SUMMARY

Previous research into the etiology of schizophrenia had been unable
to assess the relative roles of experiential and genetic factors in the
production of this syndrome. Recent studies, using the technique of adoption to separate biological and experiential factors, have permitted a
partial answer to this question. Genetic factors have been demonstrated
to play an important role in the etiology of schizophrenia and, in addition, evidence has emerged suggesting that genetically transmitted characteristics play a role in the development of other psychiatric illnesses.
These data do not permit a full answer to the question of the extent of
influence of environmental factors on the severity and nature of schizophrenic manifestations, nor do they demonstrate that, in all instances,
schizophrenia is determined by genetic factors.

REFERENCES

1. ALANEN, Y. 1958. The mothers of schizophrenic patients. *Acta Psychiat. et Neurol. Scand. Suppl.* 124.
2. ALANEN, Y., et al. 1963. Mental disorders in the siblings of schizophrenic patients. *Acta Psychiat. Scand. Suppl.* 169.
3. ALANEN, Y., et al. 1966. The family in the pathogenesis of schizophrenic and neu-rotic disorders. *Acta Psychiat. Scand. Suppl.* 189.
4. BLEULER, E. 1950. Dementia Praecox or the Group of Schizophrenias. International Universities Press, New York.
5. BÖÖK, J. 1960. Genetical aspects of schizophrenic psychoses. *In* The Etiology of Schizophrenia, D. Jackson (ed.). Basic Books, New York.

6. BURTON, R. 1651. The Anatomy of Melancholy. Edited by F. Dell and P. Jordan-Smith. Farrar & Rinehart, New York. 1927 edition: 185.

7. ENGELHARDT, D. 1967. Drug treatment of chronic ambulatory patients. *Amer. J. Psychiat.* 123:1329-1337.

8. GAW, E., et al. 1953. How common is schizophrenia? *Bull. Menn. Clinic,* 17:20-28.

9. GITTLEMAN, M., & BIRCH, H. 1967. Childhood schizophrenia. *Arch. Gen. Psychiat.* 17:16-26.

10. HARVALD, B., & HAUGE, M. 1965. Hereditary factors elucidated by twin studies, *In* Genetics and the Epidemiology of Chronic Diseases, J. Neel et al. (eds.). No. 1163, U.S. Gov't. Printing Office, Wash., D.C.

11. HESTON, L. 1966. Psychiatric disorders in foster home reared children of schizophrenic mothers. *Brit. J. Psychiat.* 112:819-825.

12. JUNG, C. 1909. The Psychology of Dementia Praecox. Nervous and Mental Disease Pub. Co., New York and Washington.

13. KALLMAN, F. 1938. The Genetics of Schizophrenia. J. J. Augustin, New York.

14. KARLSON, J. 1966. The Biological Basis of Schizophrenia. Charles C Thomas, Springfield, Ill.

15. KETY, S., et al. (In press). The Types and Frequencies of Mental Illness in the Biological and Adopted Families of Adopted Schizophrenics: A Preliminary Report.

16. LEVY, D. 1955. Oppositional syndromes and oppositional behavior. *In* Psychopathology of Childhood, P. Hoch and J. Zubin (eds.). Grune & Stratton, New York.

17. LIDZ, T., et al. 1958. The intrafamilial environment of the schizophrenic patient: IV Parental personalities and family interaction. *Amer. J. Orthopsychiat.* 28: 764-776.

18. LIDZ, T., et al. 1958. The intrafamilial environment of the schizophrenic patient: VI Transmission of Irrationality. *Arch. Neurol. & Psychiat.* 79:305-316.

19. MEDNICK, S. 1958. A learning theory approach to research in schizophrenia. *Psych. Bull.* 55:316-327.

20. MENNINGER, K. 1963. The Vital Balance. The Viking Press, New York.

21. RADO, S. 1956. Psychoanalyses of Behavior. Grune & Stratton, New York.

22. ROE, A., & MITTLEMAN, B. 1945. Adult adjustment of foster children of alcoholic and psychotic parentage and the influence of the foster home. *Memoirs, Quart. J. of Study of Alcohol,* No. 3.

23. ROSENTHAL, D., et al. (In press). Schizophrenics' Offspring Reared in Adoptive Homes.

24. SKODAK, M., & SKEELS, H. 1949. A final follow-up study of one hundred adopted children. *J. Genet. Psychol.* 75:85-125.

25. SLATER, E., & SHIELDS, J. 1953. Psychotic and neurotic illness in twins. Medical Research Council Special Report, Series No. 278. Her Majesty's Stationery Office, London.

26. SROLE, L., et al. 1962. Mental Health in the Metropolis. McGraw-Hill, New York.

27. STABENAU, J., & POLLIN, W. 1967. Early characteristics of monozygotic twins discordant for schizophrenia. *Arch. Gen. Psychiat.* 17:723-734.

28. STERN, C. 1956. Principles of Human Genetics. W. H. Freeman & Co., San Francisco.

29. WENDER, P., et al. (In press). A Psychiatric Evaluation of the Adoptive Parents of Schizophrenics.

30. WYNNE, L., & SINGER, M. 1963. Thought disorder and family relations of schizophrenics: I—A research strategy. *Arch. Gen. Psychiat.* 9:191.

31. WYNNE, L., & SINGER, M. 1963. Thought disorder and family relations of schizophrenics: II—A classification of forms of thinking. *Arch. Gen. Psychiat.* 9:199.

Section VI

COGNITIVE AND PERCEPTUAL STUDIES

35

SCHIZOPHRENIA AND INTERFERENCE
An Analogy With a Malfunctioning Computer

Enoch Callaway III

The subject of schizophrenia is responsible for a fast growing but increasingly indigestible mass of clinical descriptions and experiments. Many of these data are valuable, but some conceptual scheme for ordering and organizing these observations would be helpful. The obvious parallels between human thought processes and computer programs have inspired some useful models; thus, I was led to explore a computer analogy for schizophrenic thought-process disorder.

Some years ago, before phenothiazines, a fire broke out on the back ward of a state hospital. Most of the patients were hallucinated, chronic, process schizophrenics. However, they quickly queued up and marched out as sane as you please. Mannerisms, responses to hallucinations, and other gross signs of disorder vanished until after they reached the safety of the yard; then things returned to normal, or, in this case, to abnormal.

With such a clear goal and with such a clear and practiced method of reaching it, the excitement of the fire did not disorganize their behavior. Ordinarily, of course, the behavior of such patients deteriorates with excitement. According to McGhie, such patients are even ". . . likely to be at a disadvantage in a large noisy ward where there is much irregular activity and where the senses are bombarded simultaneously by multiple stimuli" (1).

Submitted for publication Aug. 29, 1969.

From the Langley Porter Neuropsychiatric Institute, California Department of Mental Hygiene, and the University of California School of Medicine, Department of Psychiatry, San Francisco.

Reprint requests to Langley Porter Neuropsychiatric Institute, 401 Parnassus Ave., San Francisco 94122 (Dr. Callaway).

Reprinted, by permission of author and editor, from: *Archives of General Psychiatry*, 22:193-208, 1970.

With or without excitement, patients on that "back ward" usually showed signs of thought disorder. That is to say, they had shifting, unstable, "segmental" (2) sets, their associations showed "lawful disorganization" (3), their language reflected "disattention defect" (4), and their behavior suggested "perceptual inconstancy" (5). Looked on as computers, something seemed to be interfering with the running of their programs.

Some years later, I came to know a computer that had schizophrenic associations. Simple programs worked fine, but occasionally, during the running of a particularly large program, out would come an inappropriate message. The problem was finally traced to a defective ground in one section. This particular program used most of the hardware, including the defective section. Static discharge from the operator to the console occasionally produced interference, resulting in a wrong decision by the computer. This would set in operation a part of the program that was inappropriate at that particular occasion, thus resulting in the "schizophrenic association."

THE ANASTOMOTIC COMPUTER

This model of the human schizophrenic as a computer that suffers interference in running its programs is, of course, too simple. In the examples just given, both schizophrenic patients and the "schizophrenic" computer could run simple programs successfully. However, it is doubtful if simple programs run in patients by avoiding defective circuits, as in the case of the "schizophrenic" computer.

More likely, all human computers operate with defective circuits. Individual components are unreliable, and there may be errors in interconnections. Winograd and Cowan (6) have shown that for finite periods, arbitrarily small error frequencies can be achieved in spite of fallible elements and a certain randomness of connection. This reliability is achieved by redundant computation performed by complex modules. Computation is redundant since any one function is computed by more than one module; and modules are complex in that any one module must be able to compute a diverse mixture of many functions. The redundancy required for a given reliability is reduced by increasing the complexity of individual modules.

The resulting networks were labeled anastomotic because their structure resembled the neural nets of the cerebral cortex. Given a relation between structure and function, the anastomotic nets in our brains may be related to the relatively reliable functioning that we achieve despite our unreliable parts.

Our computer model thus must be somewhat more complex. However, it is important not to confuse complexity of modules in the computer to complexity of input to the computer. Module complexity enhances the efficiency of redundancy in reducing errors. Input complexity, on the other hand, increases the chance of error by reducing the redundancy that can be utilized. Finally, erroneous computations interfere with the function of a program.

THE INTERFERENCE THEORY OF SCHIZOPHRENIA

Buss and Lang (7, 8) reviewed the research literature on schizophrenia extensively and arrived at five theories which have been advanced to explain this disorder. These are: (1) social censure, (2) sensitivity to affective stimuli, (3) insufficient motivation, (4) regression, and (5) interference. They conclude that interference theory is the best of the lot.

According to Buss and Lang,

> . . . when a schizophrenic is faced with a task, he cannot attend properly or in a sustained fashion, maintain a set, or change the set quickly when necessary. His ongoing response tendencies suffer interference from irrelevant, external cues and from "internal" stimuli which consist of deviant thoughts and associations. These irrelevant, distracting, mediated stimuli prevent him from maintaining a clear focus on the task at hand, and the result is psychological deficit (7).

I know of nothing published since those two papers to invalidate that conclusion. For example, another inability "to change the set quickly" was subsequently demonstrated in experiments by Kristofferson (9) on time for shifting attention between sensory modalities.

Somewhat more complex issues are raised by recent studies on interference with "ongoing response tendencies." A well-studied sort of interference is seen in subjects deprived of sleep. In such subjects, sustained attention is interfered with by brief periods of drowsiness or lapses of attention. This suggests a possible analogy between schizophrenia and sleep loss.

Schizophrenics do poorly on a reaction time (experimenter-paced) task although tapping speed (subject-paced) may be normal (2). After sleep loss, persons experience lapses (blocks in attention), and also show more impairment on experimenter-paced tasks than on subject-paced tasks. If the sleep-deprived subject is allowed to pace his own performance, he can compensate for his lapses by working hard during lucid intervals. The schizophrenic's shifting sets might be analogous to the blocks of a sleep-loss subject, and these lapses due to shifting sets might be similarly compensated for in a subject-paced task.

Cromwell et al. (10), however, found that schizophrenics were relatively worse on a particular self-paced complex reaction time task than on a subject-paced task. This particular self-paced task required the subjects to set a warning interval, initiate a trial, and then perform it. The normals enjoyed the subject-paced portion of the experiment and did as well as or better than on the experimenter-paced task. The schizophrenics performed particularly poorly on the subject-paced task, and they complained of being disturbed by shifting back and forth between the various things they had to do. That is to say, they seemed to have trouble with the more complex program. Tapping is simple, and so complexity seems more critical than whether or not the subject or the experimenter paces the task.

The interference that bedevils the schizophrenic seems different from the interruptions that occur when a sleepy person drowses briefly. When a person lapses for a moment, whether from drowsiness or from petit mal epilepsy, he is like a computer that has executed a "halt." Although the program is interrupted, it can be restarted where it left off. Only time is lost. The schizophrenic's interference does not merely interrupt an ongoing program or set, occasionally it diverts it and then again it causes it to persist when it should have been diverted. The result is the characteristic variability of performance. For example, consider the study done by Foulds et al. (11) who evaluated measures of proverb interpretation, object classification, and grid-test performance that were expected to correlate with thought-process disorder. Only a measure of inconsistency from the Bannister-Fransella Grid Test (12) was significantly correlated with psychiatrists' ratings of thought disorder in schizophrenic patients.

PLANS AND PROGRAMS

Schizophrenic thought disorder is diagnosed when actions, associations, and transactions with the environment appear to be interfered. I find it useful to consider that these appearances result from interference with something in the schizophrenic analogous to the programs in a computer.

In what follows, one could usually get by with using words such as "set," "cognition," or "ego function" instead of "program" and avoid using the computer model. A model is to some extent a matter of taste, and although I feel that the computer model handles the data more gracefully and simply, and that it suggests new approaches more readily than do the available alternatives, you can decide that for yourself. The important point is that this model is presented as an aid to thought, and not as a set of verities.

With this caution, we can now usefully be more specific about programs in the human computer. Miller et al. (13) use the word "plan" for the human counterpart of a computer program. For them, a "plan" is a building block for a new psychology, much as the stimulus-response oversimplification of the reflex arc was the building block of classical behaviorism. The difference lies in the fact that even the smallest plan contains a feed-back loop. The stimulus-response model is like a light switch—press the button and the light results. A plan has a purpose, and it takes some action until its purpose is accomplished. A plan, then, is more like a thermostat, turning on the furnace until the desired level of room heat is achieved. In the Miller et al. analogy, a plan corresponds to a computer program.

The power of a programmable computer is closely related to its ability to carry out operations until some goal is reached. In this way, each step does not have to be spelled out, since the computer can be left to decide when the appropriate goal is attained. One example of goal-directed computer action is the DO loop which, in FORTRAN language, defines how many times a set of operations should be repeated. The power that comes with being able to specify even such a simple goal can only be truly appreciated after practical programming experience. One programmer put a sign over his desk that read, "God bless the DO loop." The next morning, he found a label pasted over the sign which proclaimed, "God *is* a DO loop."

Whether or not the reification of teleology is the manifestation of God in our time, it certainly is the hallmark of modern technology. Psychiatric clinicians have never been able to avoid taking goals and purposes into consideration. Computer programs serve as a concrete model for purposive human plans and so bring the clinician hope of a new intellectual respectability.

Miller et al. (13) diagram plans in what they call "TOTE" units (for *Test, Operate, Test, Exit*). TOTE units may be nested and one TOTE may contain other TOTEs, as diagrammed in the Figure. In this way, simple plans may be built up into higher level plans.

Primitive neuronal interaction can problably be diagrammed as plans. The reflex has its plan, as does the simplest motor act. Such elements are combined into simple tactical plans, and tactical plans may be made use of by high level strategic or executive plans.

The highest level executive plan may modify itself as events progress and may organize and call up subplans as needed. Miller et al. call such

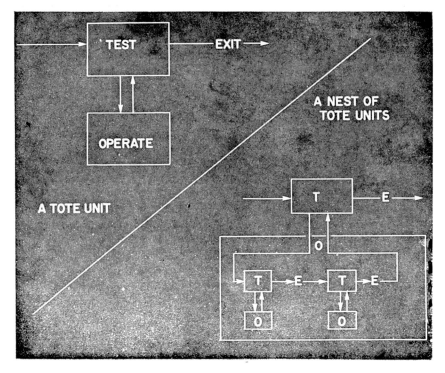

Diagrams of plans as conceived by Miller et al. (13).

plans "meta-plans." Neisser (14) refers to them as "executive programs." Since we are emphasizing the computer analogy, we will speak of programs even though we have in mind something quite like what Miller et al. refer to with their technical use of "plan."

The role of language in the regulation of behavior has been emphasized by Luria (15). Complex sequences of programs and language occur simultaneously both phylogenetically and developmentally. Thus, it comes as no surprise that complex human programs are often formulated and stored in verbal symbols.

INTERFERENCE AS A SOURCE OF AROUSAL

Consider now the human computer operating with its inevitable background of noise and its inherently unreliable components. Ordinarily, we can count on what McCulloch (16) refers to as the "agathe tyche" of neural nets. They usually have enough of that beneficent luck to operate reliably in spite of their chancy parts. Occasionally, though, even in the best of us a net looses its gamble and makes a wrong choice.

In other words, even the computers in you and me make occasional errors at various levels. For minor slips, superordinate programs together with various sorts of corrective feedback allow us to compensate smoothly enough. More rarely, the slips are bad enough to throw off an entire strategic program, thus producing a major interruption. In general, a program is disrupted most if interference occurs with the *Test* section of a TOTE; and in a nest of TOTEs, the closer we come to the executive or highest level, the more disruptive will be any defective *Test*.

Mandler (17) has discussed the interruption of behavior at length. He points out that the more the outcome of the interruption is consistent with the ongoing program, the less disruptive it is. The state produced by a faulty *Test* in more primitive or low level subroutines is unlikely to be completely inconsistent with the governing or executive program and so such errors do not disrupt behavior as much as higher level errors.

Mandler has also shown that the more organized a program is, the more visceral arousal accompanies its interruption. In our scheme of things, diffuse or poorly organized programs would be most vulnerable to interruptions. This, so it would be maladaptive if the organism set off, marked visceral arousal in response to the interruption of poorly organized programs. On the other hand, when using simpler, better or-ganized, and more practiced programs, long sequences can be run off without testing and checking. Thus, more redundant computations can be used to insure reliability. In this way, well-practiced programs become more resistant to interruption, both internal and external. When, how-ever, such a program was interrupted, either by neural noise or by an unplanned for environmental situation, then some visceral reorganization to prepare for a potential emergency would be adaptive.

This can be more specifically related to schizophrenia. Organization may protect programs from interruption, and certain paranoid individ-uals successfully ward off interference by developing highly organized programs. If, however, such organization fails to protect the individual's programs against interruption, we would expect autonomic signs of arousal such as Venables and Wing (18) found in disorganized and withdrawn schizophrenics.

Happiness is being able to carry out one's programs. By contrast, to have one's programs forever interrupted must be a particularly dreadful kind of hell. When schizophrenia is viewed as internal interference with programs, schizophrenic overarousal appears as a result of schizophrenia.

This is an interesting alternative to the theory that increased drive or arousal is a causal factor in schizophrenia.

AROUSAL AS A SOURCE OF INTERFERENCE

Interference as a source of arousal does not, of course, rule out arousal as a source of interference.

Kornetsky and Mirsky (19) believe that the schizophrenic is over-aroused and that performance is related to arousal by a " $\cap$ " function. In general, as arousal increases, performance at first improves, but then at high levels of arousal, performance gets worse. This follows the so-called Yerkes-Dodson law (20). Kornetsky and Mirsky believe that interference in schizophrenia results from overarousal (in contrast to the notion that arousal results from interference with programs). They rely on a quasi-neuro-physiological model and make good use of pharmacological evidence which will be referred to later.

While Kornetsky and Mirsky see arousal in terms of reticular activation, Storms and Broen (3, 21) assign a somewhat similar role to the concept of Hullian drive. Increased drive increases the likelihood of all responses. Normally, the dominant response is augmented. In schizophrenics, however, a response potential ceiling is postulated. With increased drive, the low ceiling prevents further potentiation of the dominant response. Weaker competing responses may then reach a level equal to the originally dominant response and so be expressed in behavior. Thus, the concept of response ceiling replaces the inverted "U" as the cause for the supposed interfering effects of drive-arousal in schizophrenia.

A particularly good feature of the Storms and Broen model is that it focuses on the relationship between drive and competing responses. Schizophrenics, in their variable behavior, do not act in an entirely unexpected way. Instead, they give competing but ordinarily subordinate responses. A normal person might, for example, do almost anything a schizophrenic would do, but for the normal it would be an unusual thing, and so have little effect on the general course of his life. A review of many observations supporting this concept led Storms and Broen to coin the very apt phrase "lawful disorganization" (3) for schizophrenic behavior.

Unfortunately, both the reticular activation model and Hullian drive model are somewhat at variance with such things as the adequate performance of the patients during the fire mentioned above.

Laboratory evidence can also be cited. Thus, Rosenbaum (22) found that on reaction-time tasks, schizophrenic subjects had slowed reaction times when they were told their speed after each trial and were urged to do better (social motivation) and fast reaction times when a 50-v shock was administered through the telegraph key along with the signal to release the key (shock motivation). Perhaps this particular form of social motivation introduced greater complexity and so made the subjects' plans more vulnerable to interference. For the arousal or drive theory, one would have to make the somewhat gratuitous assumption that shock did not increase arousal or drive in schizophrenics enough to counteract the attention-directing effect of shock (23).

The best evidence against the "arousal" or "drive" theories comes from a study done by Schooler and Zahn (24). Using chronic nonparanoid schizophrenics, they found that cooperative social interaction both increased arousal and improved performance on a block-design test. In other words, specific arousal may improve performance. When arousal has been found to be associated with a decrement in schizophrenic performance, it is generally in a situation where the arousal is associated with distracting demands of a sort likely to make programs appropriate to the task under study more vulnerable to interference.

All of the evidence cited against drive-arousal interference may be misleading and simply reflect the fact that increased specific motivation can overcome the deleterious effects of increased arousal. One could imagine motivation acting to preempt more circuits for the dominant program, and so to supply enough excess redundancy to protect against increased interference. This would preserve the intuitively appealing image of a positive feedback loop in acute schizophrenia where interference causes arousal and arousal causes more interference.

ETIOLOGY

Viewed as the result of internal interference with programs, schizophrenia is obviously a syndrome and not a disease of a single etiology. In direct analogy to the "schizophrenic" computer mentioned earlier, we might expect transient pulses in that part of the brain concerned with value judgments to produce just the state of affairs required for schizophrenia. This calls to mind Heath's (25) observations on septal spikes which have recently been confirmed by Hanley et al. (26), as well as those temporal lobe seizures that can mimic schizophrenia (27).

Gross lesions that interfere with specific input and output operations (i.e., operate sections of TOTEs) would produce disorders quite distinct from schizophrenia. Examples of these would be palsies, aphasias, agnosias, etc. Such gross lesions could also intrude on part of *Test* circuits, and this may account for the similarities that Goldstein (28) found between patients with schizophrenia and patients with gross brain damage. Interference with *Tests* could also occur if certain biochemical abnormalities interfered with the functioning of higher level *Test* operations.

We have been using the word "schizophrenia" as a kind of shorthand for the "thought-process disorder characteristic of schizophrenia." It goes without saying that the self-same thought-process disorder may not be called schizophrenic if more specific etiological diagnoses are available (i.e., myxedematous madness, paresis, porphyria, amphetamine abuse, etc.).

This theory is also compatible with learning as a factor in schizophrenia. Some years ago, Rashevsky (29) proposed a model for schizophrenia based on two Landahl-type neurons operating as choice elements. This would serve very nicely as a simplified model of a *Test*. He conceived of these elements as choosing between internal and external stimuli, but this restriction seems unnecessary. With this model, he then shows how defective choices could be learned and why schizophrenia should make its appearance at the time of life that it usually does.

Since organization can afford a degree of protection against interruption and since all of us must cope with internal interference, it is conceivable that early training in disoranized, diffused thinking as described by Wynne and Singer (30) could lead to the development of programs with a high vulnerability to interference. On the other hand, some happy families may take a child with a schizophrenic genotype and teach him programs that work even with a high level of internal interference. This fortunate person might then be able to use his "noise" to evolve novel ideas, yet operate reliably enough to meet the demands of reality. An individual like this might be a creative genius. Thus, a spicing of schizophrenogenic genes might have adaptive value for the group by furnishing a few individuals as reservoirs of novel plans for those times when changing circumstances invalidate the laws of tradition. Huxley (31) suggested that since schizophrenia occurs with almost the same frequency in culturally and genetically diverse populations, the trait probably has some adaptive function.

PSYCHOTHERAPY

When a computer program goes bad, we like to find a single hardware defect, for when it is repaired, things will go again. In a man with schizophrenic symptoms, we are equally delighted to find a simple cause like a toxic state, for then a return to normal function can be anticipated.

When such a happy discovery cannot be made, we turn to other solutions. In the case of the computer, we may have to revise our programming. Some schizophrenics may learn to be nonschizophrenic, and retraining of the schizophrenic is analogous to reprogramming a faulty computer. Wagner (32) found that both attending and abstracting responses in schizophrenics could be rapidly improved by training. It would seem that the skills existed (i.e., the programs were available) but needed rewards to bring them into play, and practice to make them less vulnerable to interference. The defective computer may be also usable if we can be content with running only simple programs. Likewise, simplifying the environment may help the schizophrenic by allowing him to adopt simpler, less vulnerable programs. On the other hand, in schizophrenia "one can certainly conceive of a toxic dose of environmental stimulation" (33).

Sensory deprivation may cause striking deterioration in normals. Schizophrenics tolerate it very well, and may even show improvement after periods of drastically reduced sensory stimulation. Harris (34) tried perceptual isolation in order to decide whether schizophrenics suffer from excessive internal mental activity (in which case, he reasoned, perceptual isolation should make them worse) or whether schizophrenics are overwhelmed by incoming stimuli (in which perceptual isolation should help). Although he used no controls, he found that schizophrenics either were not disturbed by isolation or else were actually benefitted by the experience. Recent controlled studies by Mehl and Cromwell (35) were somewhat equivocal, but their review of the literature indicates that most studies have confirmed Harris' findings. Perhaps some schizophrenics are able to reduce the complexity of their programs during a brief retreat and then, for a time afterwards, are less vulnerable to interference and interruption.

Sensory deprivation was, however, not included when Shakow (2) listed the following seven normalizing factors: (1) repetition, (2) passage of time, (3) cooperation, (4) time for preparation, (5) social influence, (6) stress (task related), and (7) shock (e.g., such as electric and insulin shock which presumably disrupt recently acquired maladaptive programs). All of the psychological maneuvers would, among other things, minimize interference with programs.

PHARMACOLOGICAL THERAPY OF SCHIZOPHRENIA

Without undervaluing psychological treatment of schizophrenia, available evidence (36) indicates that phenothiazines are currently the most potent therapeutic tools, and any model of schizophrenia must make some attempt to account for this.

Chlorpromazine (CPZ) is a good representative phenothiazine for our purposes. If, for argument's sake, we assume that CPZ protects the programs of the schizophrenic from interference, we generate some apparent paradoxes for, in normals, CPZ increases vulnerability to interference. Sedatives, such as a barbiturate, tend to interfere primarily with cognitive or coding tasks, such as the digit symbol substitution task, whereas CPZ in doses that have very little effect on the coding task interferes markedly with a continuous performance task where one must watch for an occasional meaningful sequence in a repetitive series of stimuli paced by the experimenter. After CPZ, attention seems interfered with, since the subject misses cues embedded in the presentations (17, 37). The paradox is illustrated by the observation that schizophrenia also impairs performance on the continuous performance task, yet as CPZ-treated schizophrenics improve, continuous performance task scores also improve, and the correlation is much better than the correlation between clinical improvement and coding task performance (38).

CPZ and schizophrenia both also seem to increase vulnerability to visual noise. Stilson and Kopell (39) originally found schizophrenics to be particularly vulnerable to visual noise when attempting to discriminate a stable but dim background figure. Their studies left unclear what role drugs might be playing in this observation. To study this, Kopell and Wittner (40) tested psychiatric patients (including some exschizophrenics) who were recovered and awaiting discharge. In a careful dose-response study designed to determine the effects of CPZ on the ability to recognize figures embedded in visual noise, they found that CPZ produced a marked impairment of performance. Finally, Rappaport (41) studied a task that required recognition of voice messages under conditions of auditory distractions. Acute schizophrenics did poorly and showed "periodic defocusing of attention." Nonacute, but yet nonchronic, schizophrenics did as well as normals and CPZ had no discernible effect.

In short, it would seem that CPZ is not simply decreasing the sensitivity of psychiatric patients to all interfering stimuli.

A resolution of the paradox is suggested by the observation that CPZ is highly specific in reducing drive for positively reinforcing midbrain (septal, etc.) stimulation. In addition, the faster the rate of self-stimulation, the more impressive are the effects of CPZ. A relation between this and schizophrenia was suggested by Olds and Travis (42), who wrote "counteraction of positive feedback processes subserving positive reinforcement mechanisms may be a key to the control of certain psychiatric episodes."

Returning to the TOTE model, the transition from *Test* to *Exit* must be controlled by something akin to the positive reinforcement mechanism. In anthropomorphic terms, something must say, "Good and now for the next step," when enough *Operates* have been done to satisfy the *Test*. If CPZ put a damper on these positive reinforcement or *Exit* signals, then CPZ might impair the performances of normals by making the subject dwell too long on each *Test*. In the schizophrenic, however, if the trouble is primarily due to premature *Exits,* the damping effect of CPZ might improve performance. Delaying *Exits* would slow down information processing, and this would allow increased redundancy and hence decrease sensitivity to interference. Finally, when given to episodic lapses of bad judgment, the slower one acts, the less likely one will be to get into trouble. Thus, although CPZ may reduce the fundamental problem in schizophrenia by putting a damper on *Tests,* it may also make these individuals more acceptable to the society in which they must function. Studies by Ray et al. (43) would support such an interpretation. They found that ward behavior of chronic women schizophrenics improved most when the patients were put on CPZ and deteriorated fastest when patients were taken off the drug. Cognitive tasks, on the other hand, improved significantly, yet less than ward behavior, on drugs, and did not deteriorate after removal of drugs.

A recent experiment in our laboratory (44) is compatible with this model. CPZ was found to prolong the availability of visual short-term memory.

The experiment employed the well-known Sperling (45) procedure. A 3×3 matrix of nine letters is flashed tachistoscopically. A cue tone (high, middle, or low pitch) signals the subject to recall either the top, middle, or lower line of letters. The longer the tone comes after the visual display, the fewer letters are recalled. CPZ improved recall when the cue tone was delayed for 200 msec. CPZ could protect visual trace by increasing filtering of subsequent stimuli. Alternatively, the visual trace could decay as a function of an active coding and transfer process (46). In this case, CPZ might protect the visual trace by delaying this processing.

These alternatives are not exclusive. It seems reasonable to consider that in man the operation of any program tends to inhibit the running of other programs that may be ready for possible next steps. Since even the storing of a short-term visual trace represents some coding (i.e., the operation of a program), then input of new data to the short-term visual memory would call on new programs. Thus, delay in processing (persistence of a program) would, in effect, be a sort of filter (inhibition of other input programs). In this case, the first of a series of stimuli would act with full force, but subsequent stimuli would show habituation (47, 48); this is quite in line with electrophysiological evidence reported by Killam (49).

CPZ tends to suppress avoidance behavior (50). Low et al. (51) give evidence that this is not just due to delayed motor responses, as suggested by Posluns (52), but that it is also due to decreased attention (i.e., increased filtering of) to cues needed for timing behavior.

In summary, if we postulate that CPZ delays the *Exit* from a program (TOTE), we then have an increased sensory filtering since a persisting input program inhibits other data-input programs. Inhibition of positive feedback from reinforcement mechanisms seems a good candidate for the mechanism by which this *Exit*-delay is accomplished. With the postulate of an optimum *Exit*-sensitivity, we have a mechanism whereby CPZ could move both normals and schizophrenics towards lesser *Exit*-sensitivity, with improvement in function for the schizophrenic and impairment in function for the normal. However, it is only fair to point out that if one substitutes the word "arousal" for *Exit*-sensitivity, then differences between the present model and the Mirsky-Kornetsky model (37) all but vanish.

EVIDENCE FROM EEG EVOKED RESPONSES

Since verbal associations are disordered in schizophrenia, there has long been a search for some technique which might bypass language. The averaged evoked response (AER) is such a technique, and research on schizophrenia using AERs supports the notion that schizophrenia is related to an instability of cognitive processes which might result from interference with programs.

To study evoked responses, stimuli are given, the brain wave is sampled, and various computations are made on these samples. By properly designing the stimulus presentation and the data analysis, such things as attention deployment, distractibility, and even intelligence can be probed—all with little demand for voluntary responses from the subject.

In both auditory and visual AERs, schizophrenics show more variability than normals. Early work on auditory AERs in schizophrenia arose from Shakow's concept of segmental set. It was hypothesized that schizophrenics would continue to make a distinction between two physically distinct signals even though these signals carried no particular psychological meaning. If 600 cycles per second and 1,000 cycles per second tones are sounded repeatedly in a haphazard order to a normal, then the AER to all of the 1,000 cycles per second tones appears almost identical with the AER to the 600 cycles per second tones. Normals given some valid reason to distinguish between the tones on the basis of pitch showed increased differences between the two AERs. Schizophrenics tended to show greater differences between AERs, even when they were instructed to ignore the tones (53).

A series of studies, demonstrating the degree of difference between AERs to the two tones, distinguished between schizophrenics and non-schizophrenic psychiatric patients who were all on relatively equivalent drug dosage. As schizophrenic patients showed fluctuations in their clinical course, the AER difference correlated with thought disorder while it did not correlate with disturbances of affect or with coopera-tiveness (54, 55).

Unfortunately, the measurement of the difference between AERs used in these studies did not distinguish between consistently different re-sponses dependent on pitch on one hand and generally variable responses independent of the pitch of the evoking tones on othe other. When finally the statistics necessary to make such a distinction were worked out, the variability of the evoked response was found to distinguish schizophrenics from normals and to account for the dissimilar two tone AERs.

The hypothesis that the schizophrenics' dissimilar two tone AERs re-sulted from a consistent distinction between the psychologically trivial tones had to be discarded. This was best demonstrated in a study: tones of a single pitch were used and two AERs were arbitrarily drawn from the set of brain wave samples time-locked to the stimulating tones. In this situation, schizophrenics still showed more dissimilarity between their pairs of AERs. Only variability could have been a factor since there was no physical difference between the tones (56).

More direct measures of variability supported this interpretation. Fur-thermore, this sort of observation is not confined to auditory AERs. Thus, both Speck et al. (57) and Lifshitz (58) have demonstrated increased variability in the visual AERs of schizophrenics. In addition, evidence to date indicates that background electroencephalograph activity is not responsible for the difference between schizophrenics and normals. How-ever, schizophrenics have been reported to have choppy EEGs (59).

SECONDARY SYMPTOMS OF SCHIZOPHRENIA

The model presented so far is concerned with the primary symptoms of schizophrenia, but it also forms a useful basis for considering a number of the secondary symptoms. Various methods of organizing one's response patterns might reduce one's vulnerability to this internal interference. The simple, all-encompassing paranoid scheme would afford a degree of protection. Arieti (60) has remarked on how schizophrenics can use concrete thinking to simplify the problems they face. Thus, the man who considers himself "a stinking, rotten mess" may simplify things greatly if he develops a delusional system about his offensive body odors in place of the complex consideration he needed to deal with a global feeling of rottenness.

If this line of defense fails, the individual may give in to interruptions when they occur. Then, instead of responding with anxiety in an attempt to cope, the schizophrenic may find comfort in the child-like responses of the hebephrenic. One charming hebephrenic girl was being given some standard test questions. When asked, "What would you do if you were lost in a forest," she quickly said, "I'd change my clothes. . . ." Then, catching herself, she gave a silly laugh and continued ". . . to make it more dramatic. Then I'd make a trail from torn up paper and follow it out of the forest."

Withdrawal would seem to be the least effective technique and would be expected to result in the most disorganization and the most chronic visceral arousal. This is what is observed (24).

Julian Silverman (61, 62) has described a cognitive characteristic which he calls "scanning." By "scanning," he refers to the extensiveness with which an individual searches his environment for information. Chronic process nonparanoid schizophrenics scan less than normals while acute reactive paranoid schizophrenics scan more. Cromwell (63) confirmed Silverman's observations but challenged the conceptualization on the basis of additional experimental data. Cromwell proposed that instead of "scanning" vs. "non-scanning," the concept of "participatory" vs. "preparatory" fits more data. These terms are drawn from more recent works on "plans" published by Pribram (64). Cromwell's paper merits careful study as it deals with a complex subject. To oversimplify things, Table 1 gives the main features of participatory and preparatory states, along with pertinent references.

A participatory set may represent a last ditch defense against the disrupting effects of unstable *Tests*. The participatory, non-scanning long latency, high amplitude, long duration, high redundancy mode of operation would result in a maladaptive behavior in an environment that was shifting and changing (i.e., that demanded a preparatory mode). However, a participatory mode would avoid the use of *Tests* as much as possible and, if all else failed, it would, in the face of a high level of

TABLE 1

PARTICIPATORY AND PREPARATORY STATES

State	Preparatory Scanning Habituating	Participatory Nonscanning Orienting
Typical input (63)	Brief Noisy background Low redundancy	Prolonged Homogeneous background High redundancy
Information Processing	High rate High redundancy	Low rate Low redundancy
Typical output	Fast low amplitude Quick recovery	Slow high amplitude Slow recovery
Size match (62)	Underestimate Standard (near)	Overestimate Standard (near)
Saccadic rate	High in normals	High in schizophrenic
Muller Lyer Illusion (63)	Large illusion	Small illusion
Schizophrenia (61)	Good premorbid Paranoid	Poor premorbid Nonparanoid
Focus of attention (65) Produced by (66)	Broad Atropine	Narrow Amphetamine Anti-cholinesterase Cold-pressor procedure LSD-25
Neurophysiology (64)	Self-inhibition	Collateral inhibition

Neuroanatomy
  Suppressed by
  Excited by
	
	Hippocampus
	Sensory-motor
	  Association cortex
		
		Amygdala
		Temporal isocortex

internal interference, minimize the number of interruptions in plans. This would reduce unpleasant visceral arousal, particularly in a monotonous hospital setting, therefore it should be a rewarding strategy for a chronic patient.

The scheme sketch in the Table is highly speculative and quite baroque considering its slender base of supporting data. It is obviously too unstable to serve as a support for the *Test*-interference model, and is simply one illustration of how the *Test*-interference model can support future developments by suggesting a potentially fruitful approach to secondary symptoms in schizophrenia.

Miller et al. (13) take a different approach and suggest that the non-paranoid schizophrenic hangs on to strategic programs (plans) to the point of calling on ineffective tactical programs. This contrast between defective strategic programs and defective tactical subprograms seems useful in considering neurotic behavior, in studying secondary symptoms of schizophrenia, and in classifying the results of certain gross brain lesions. Thus, the character disorder has learned poor strategies, the neurotic repeats maladaptive tactics over and over, and the frontal lobotomized patient has unstable and evanescent strategies.

For contrast, consider the classic nonparanoid acute patient with a moderate illness. He may have reasonable general goals (i.e., strategic programs) and individual tactical maneuvers. The defect lies in the interference that occurs in the operation of the otherwise reasonable programs. For example, "subroutines" for word recognition may fail so that the patient codes the meaning of a word prematurely. The word reported as heard is related to the word spoken by phonetic similarity rather than by symbolic links, as though the patient had jumped to a conclusion without considering all the phonetic information (67). Schizophrenics are also reported (68) to prematurely (and erroneously) recognize blurred photographs presented in order of increasing clarity, although more recent evidence (69) raises some questions about that report. Similarly, on the strategic level, it seems as though tactical programs are put into play prematurely. As one patient put it, "There should be a filter between all the things deep in one's mind, and the part of the mind that does things. My filter seems broken and the things in the doing part of my mind get mixed up."

THE FORMAL MODEL

Schizophrenia is diagnosed when a person shows signs of interference with his more organized and goal-directed functions (i.e., when the ego is disordered). Like Miller et al., we postulate a system of programs behind all goal-directed behavior, including perceptual as well as motor activity. Schizophrenia then becomes, by definition, a disorder involving interference with programs. At this stage, we have an indestructible, tautological, or flexible model.

We have considered that the interference occurring in the schizophrenic might be similar to the blocks or lapses of attention during sleep loss, but decided that such blocks are different from the interference found in schizophrenia.

Using the Miller et al. model, we considered that interference could act on the *Test* portion of a program or on the *Operate* portion. *Operate* defects would include thought-content disorder, lesions of input-output systems such as paresis and agnosia, and data storage defects such as the aphasias. *Operate* disorders of the thought-content variety, of course, occur in schizophrenia but are also a factor in any neurotic disturbance. In other words, maladaptive programs and idiosyncratic images of the world are found in schizophrenia but do not set schizophrenia off from the rest of psychopathology. In contrast, thought-process disorder, the "sine qua non" of schizophrenia, is diagnosed on the basis of performance variability rather than on the basis of the performance repertory itself, and this corresponds to interference with *Test* portions of programs.

In computer programs, it is useful to distinguish between samplings of incoming data made at times selected by the program, and so-called hardware interruptions which allow incoming information to interrupt an ongoing program and institute another program to handle this unplanned-for information. Thus, schizophrenia might be conceptualized as a specific disorder of such unplanned interruptions.

Unexpected external stimuli fail to account for the results of a study done by Moon et al. (67). They found that schizophrenics made more errors than normals in trying to repeat words as they heard them. These authors further claim that the disordered association of the schizophrenic can be accounted for almost entirely on the basis of reasonable association to misheard words. In this situation, the words were presented in a regular sequence to the subject, thus they were not unexpected stimuli nor did they call for unexpected shifting of plans or sets.

Unreliable *Tests* might occur principally in certain input or output systems. Clinical evidence would suggest that in schizophrenia auditory perception is more vulnerable than are other senses (70). However, evidence from evoked responses would indicate that variability or instability can be observed in visual responses as well as auditory (57). During a discussion held in December 1968, Margaret T. Singer remarked how, on a ward of disturbed adolescents, the psychopaths move with preternatural cat-like grace and offer a particularly marked contrast to the gawky, uncoordinated schizophrenics. Thus, even at the simple motor level, the programs of the schizophrenic seem to suffer from interference.

In spite of evidence for diffuse interference certain schizophrenics may show defects predominantly in one area. Auditory functions usually seem most affected in schizophrenia, but perhaps this is simply because auditory perception is most involved in language and interpersonal communication and these are the most complex, and hence most vulnerable, of human programs. Are there any schizophrenics with interruption most apparent in visual functioning?

Does the apparent interference at the *Test* portion of the program represent interference with the decision mechanism, or is it a secondary effect of some defect in the storage and retrieval of memories needed for adequate *Test* functioning? Is schizophrenia simply one type of response to extreme sensory sensitivity? The list of questions could continue, but let us turn to some of the ways we might get answers to questions already raised.

TESTS SUGGESTED BY THE MODEL

One of the simplest tests suggested by the model concerns the possibility that there may be individual differences in the sorts of programs exhibiting the most marked effects of interference. An easy approach to this could be made using evoked response techniques. We could determine whether some people show differences in the index of variability of the evoked response depending on whether the response is evoked by auditory or visual stimuli. If consistent individual differences were found, it would be of interest to determine the correlation between such differences and the clinical state. This is an example of how, at the simple analogical level, the model suggests areas where further exploration might be rewarding.

The best alternative to the elaborate *Test* interference model is a memory defect model. Of course, memory is required for adequate *Tests,* and defective *Tests* due to memory problems confined to *Tests* would be quite compatible with the *Test*-interference model. There are two, not mutually exclusive, more general memory defect models that are legitimate alternatives to the *Test*-interference model. These are: (1) a fast short-term memory decay model and (2) a slow memory retrieval model.

A study suggesting fast short-term memory decay has been reported by Neale (71). He found that schizophrenics did as well as normals and nonschizophrenic control patients in recognizing tachistoscopically presented letters. However, when they were required to detect a specific letter in a matrix of noise letters, the schizophrenic group did worse than the control subjects. Neal entertained several hypotheses. For example, he considered that excessive perceptual variability could have been a factor, but two measures of performance variability were calculated and neither was strongly related to the schizophrenics' poor performance. Vulnerability to interference from irrelevant signals was considered, but detailed analysis of the trials indicated that the specific number of noise letters surrounding the target had little effect on the performance. Unplanned stimuli were not a factor. In this task, the subjects were well practiced, and there were no unexpected signals. Furthermore, the normal thresholds of the schizophrenics indicate that the difficulty did not lie in coping with unplanned events.

Two alternative explanations for Neale's results remain. Perhaps the schizophrenics were unable to scan the display rapidly enough, or alternatively, the display trace decays too rapidly from memory.

According to the *Test*-interference theory, schizophrenics should have trouble scanning rapidly. A normal can adapt a loose, diffuse strategy and accept limited criteria for recognizing the target when he tries to search an array that is too large for complete recognition. The schizophrenic, on the other hand, might have to use a well-practiced complete recognition strategy, for if he attempted to relinquish the redundancy afforded by the standard recognition plan, his internal interference might make him unable to capitalize on the possible advantages of this less organized strategy.

Alternatively, perhaps the schizophrenic has difficulty in scanning the array for a target letter because the memory trace decays too rapidly.

Neale has suggested that instead of drawing "noise" letters for the array from the whole alphabet, only the letter "U" might be used. With practice, the schizophrenic should be able to develop a simple search plan as good as that of the normal. Although the all "U" matrix might be searched faster by the normal, the schizophrenic should show a much greater speed. On the other hand, if the schizophrenic has only a fast decaying trace, the simple all "U" display should be scanned faster by both schizophrenics and normals and both should do better but the difference in performance between schizophrenics and normals should remain the same. Although the *Test*-interference model predicts both slow scan and fast decay, performance of normals and schizophrenics would have to be more similar with an all "U" matrix than with the regular matrix if the *Test*-interference model is to be supported.

Another study suggests that the *Test*-interference model may be entirely wrong, and long-term memory retrieval may be the principal problem. Court and Garwoli (72) found that as task complexity increased the reaction time of both schizophrenics and normals increased, but the increases were parallel. If complexity made the schizophrenic deteriorate, the performance difference between schizophrenics and normals should have been progressively greater as complexity increased. In this study, complexity was increased by simply increasing the number of possible signals in a disjunctive reaction time task. Now responses are slower the larger the number of signal lights and associated response buttons that must be considered. However, this type of increase in complexity may not increase in the number of *Tests* but rather increase time required for visual search and hand response. A series of tasks is being designed to require increasing numbers of *Test* operations. If, again, the performances of schizophrenics and normals are slowed only proportionately with increasing *Tests,* the *Test*-interference model will have to be abandoned. Various alternative explanations for such an outcome would have to be entertained, but the best alternative would seem to be that schizophrenics perform *Tests* adequately but call up the requisite motor response plans from memory more slowly than normals.

There are still other alternatives to the *Test*-interference model, but one final example would seem sufficient. Silverman (62) has implied that the schizophrenic suffers interference because he is hypersensitive to low level stimuli. There is indeed evidence that normal introverts have low sensory threshold (73), and Silverman argues that failure to find low thresholds in schizophrenics may be due to problems of attention and motivation. This is again a problem for the laboratory. Given an adequate measure of sensory sensitivity and a measure of thought-process disorder, if no schizophrenics are found with thought-process disorder unless they also have low thresholds, then the elaborate *Test*-interference model would be quite superfluous.

SUMMARY

There are certain similarities between human minds and programmable computers constructed of unreliable components. Reliability of operation can be improved by duplicating operations and by simultaneously running several versions of the same program. Nevertheless, the risk of interference and interruption is ever present, and this risk can be increased either by an increase in internal noise, or by an increase in the vulnerability of the programs themselves. Time pressure, task irrelevant stress, complexity, and novelty—all reduce the resistance to interference by reducing the redundancy of operations. In humans, interruption of ongoing programs produces visceral arousal, and this may, in some cases, add to the disruption of function. Schizophrenic thought disorder can be usefully modeled as the results of interference with the running of programs in the human computer.

It is hardly necessary to add that any human suffering from schizophrenia is far more than a "noisy computer." Nevertheless, this model organizes past observations and suggests new areas for inquiry. Using this parallel between human thought and computer operation, we can clarify some things by simply imagining how one of the simpler nonhuman computers might malfunction like a human with schizophrenia. This model takes account of the growing corpus of work on computer models of human thought (74). Finally, if such a model eventually becomes complex enough to make simple thought experiments chancy yet remains valuable enough to merit further use, then actual computer simulation may provide a feasible technique for future explorations.

NONPROPRIETARY AND TRADE NAMES OF DRUG

Chlorpromazine—*Thorazine*.

This work was supported by the Office of Naval Research Contract NONR 2931 (00).

REFERENCES

1. McGhie, A.: "Studies of Cognitive Disorder in Schizophrenia," in Coppen, A., and Walk, A. (eds.): *Recent Developments in Schizophrenia (Brit. J. Psychiat.* special publication No. 1, Royal Medico-Psychological Association), Ashford, Kent: Headley Brothers Ltd., 1967, pp. 69-78.
2. Shakow, D.: Psychological Deficit in Schizophrenia, *Behav. Sci.* 8:275-305 (Oct.) 1963.
3. Broen, W. E., Jr., & Storms, L. H.: Lawful Disorganization: The Process Underlying a Schizophrenic Syndrome, *Psychol. Rev.* 73:265-279 (July) 1966.
4. Cromwell, R. L., & Dokecki, P. R.: "Schizophrenic Language: A Disattention Interpretation," in Rosenberg, S., and Koplis, J. H. (eds.): *Developments in Applied Psycholinguistics Research,* New York: Macmillan Co., 1968, pp. 209-261.
5. Ornitz, E. M., & Ritvo, E. R.: Perceptual Inconstancy in Early Infantile Autism, *Arch. Gen. Psychiat.* 18:76-98 (Jan.) 1968.
6. Winograd, S., & Cowan, J. D.: *Reliable Computation in the Presence of Noise,* Cambridge, Mass.: M.I.T. Press, 1963.
7. Buss, A. H., & Lang, P. J.: Psychological Deficit in Schizophrenia: I. Affect, Reinforcement, and Concept Attainment, *J. Abnorm. Psychol.* 70:2-24 (Feb.) 1965.
8. Lang, P. J., & Buss, A. H.: Psychological Deficit in Schizophrenia: II. Interference and Activation, *J. Abnorm. Psychol.* 70:77-106 (April) 1965.
9. Kristofferson, M. W.: Shifting Attention Between Modalities: A Comparison of Schizophrenics and Normals, *J. Abnorm. Psychol.* 72:388-394 (Oct.) 1967.
10. Cromwell, R. L., et al: Reaction Time, Locus of Control, Choice Behavior, and Descriptions of Parental Behavior in Schizophrenic and Normal Subjects, *J. Personality* 29:363-379 (Dec.) 1961.
11. Foulds, G. A., et al: Cognitive Disorder Among the Schizophrenias: I. The Validity of Some Tests of Thought-Process Disorder, *Brit. J. Psychiat.* 113:1361-1368 (Dec.) 1967.
12. Bannister, D., & Fransella, F.: A Grid Test of Schizophrenic Thought Disorder, *Brit. J. Soc. Clin. Psychol.* 5:95-102 (June) 1966.

13. MILLER, B. A.; GALANTER, E.; & PRIBRAM, K. H.: *Plans and the Structure of Behavior*, New York: Henry Holt & Co., Inc., 1960.

14. NEISSER, U.: *Cognitive Psychology*, New York: Appleton-Century-Crofts, Inc., 1967.

15. LURIA, A. R.: *The Role of Speech in the Regulation of Normal and Abnormal Behavior*, New York: Pergamon Press, Inc., 1961.

16. McCULLOCH, W. S.: *Embodiements of Mind*, Cambridge, Mass.: M.I.T. Press, 1965.

17. MANDLER, G.: "The Interruption of Behavior," in Levine, D. (ed.): *Nebraska Symposium on Motivation, 1964*, Lincoln, Neb.: University of Nebraska Press, 1964, pp. 163-219.

18. VENABLES, P. H., & WING, J. K.: Level of Arousal and the Subclassification of Schizophrenia, *Arch. Gen. Psychiat.* 7:114-119 (Aug.) 1962.

19. KORNETSKY, C., & MIRSKY, A. F.: On Certain Psychopharmacological and Physiological Differences Between Schizophrenic and Normal Persons, *Psychopharmacologia* 8:309-318 (Dec. 30) 1965.

20. YERKES, R. M., & DODSON, J. D.: The Relation of Strength of Stimulus to Rapidity of Habit-Formation, *J. Comp. Neurol.* 18:459-482 (Nov.) 1908.

21. STORMS, L. H., & BROEN, W. E.: A Theory of Schizophrenic Behavioral Disorganization, *Arch. Gen. Psychiat.* 20:129-144 (Feb.) 1969.

22. ROSENBAUM, G.: Reaction Time Indices of Schizophrenic Motivation: A Cross Cultural Replication, *Brit. J. Psychiat.* 113:537-541 (May) 1967.

23. LANG, P. J.: The Effect of Aversive Stimuli on Reaction Time in Schizophrenia, *J. Abnorm. Soc. Psychol.* 59:263-268 (Sept.) 1959.

24. SCHOOLER, C., & ZAHN, T. P.: The Effect of Closeness of Social Interaction on Task Performance and Arousal in Chronic Schizophrenia, *J. Nerv. Ment. Dis.* 147:394-401 (Oct.) 1968.

25. HEATH, R. G.: Schizophrenia: Biochemical and Physiologic Aberrations, *Int. J. Neuropsychiat.* 2:597-610 (Dec.) 1966.

26. HANLEY, J., et al: Spectral Characteristics of EEG Activity Accompanying Deep Spiking in a Patient With Schizophrenia, read before the annual meeting of the American EEG Society, San Francisco, Sept. 12-15, 1968.

27. MONROE, R. R., & MICKLE, W. A.: Alpha Chloralose-Activated Electroencephalograms in Psychiatric Patients, *J. Nerv. Ment. Dis.* 144:59-68 (Jan.) 1967.

28. GOLDSTEIN, K.: The Significance of Psychological Research in Schizophrenia, *J. Nerv. Ment. Dis.* 97:261-279 (March) 1943.

29. RASHEVSKY, N.: Some Possible Quantitative Aspects of a Neurophysiological Model of Schizophrenias, *Bull. Math. Biophys.* 27:21-26 (March) 1965.

30. WYNNE, L. C., & SINGER, M. T.: Thought Disorder and Family Relations in Schizophrenics: II. A Classification of Forms of Thinking, *Arch. Gen. Psychiat.* 9:199-206 (Sept.) 1963.

31. HUXLEY, J.: Psychometabolism, *J. Neuropsychiat.* 3 (suppl. 1):S1-S14 (Aug.) 1962.

32. WAGNER, B. R.: The Training of Attending and Abstracting Responses in Chronic Schizophrenics, *J. Exp. Res. Personality* 3:77-88 (June) 1968.

33. COLE, J. O.: A Lack of Controls, *Int. J. Psychiat.* 4:129-130 (Aug.) 1967.

34. HARRIS, A.: Sensory Deprivation and Schizophrenia, *J. Ment. Sci.* 105:235-237 (Jan.) 1959.

35. MEHL, M. M., & CROMWELL, R. L.: The Effect of Brief Sensory Deprivation and Sensory Stimulation on the Cognitive Functioning of Chronic Schizophrenics, *J. Nerv. Ment. Dis.* 148:586-596 (June) 1969.

36. MAY, P. R. A.: *Treatment of Schizophrenia*, New York: Science House, 1968.

37. MIRSKY, A. F.: "Neuropsychological Bases of Schizophrenia," in Mussen, P. H., and Rosenzweig, M. R. (eds.): *Annual Review of Psychology*, Palo Alto, Calif.: Annual Reviews, Inc., 1969, vol. 20, pp. 321-348.

38. ORZACK, M. H.; KORNETSKY, C.; FREEMAN, H.: The Effects of Daily Administra-

tion of Carphenazine on Attention in the Schizophrenic Patient, *Psychopharmacologia* 11:31-38 (April) 1967.

39. STILSON, D. W., & KOPELL, B. S.: The Recognition of Visual Signals in the Presence of Visual Noise by Psychiatric Patients, *J. Nerv. Ment. Dis.* 139:209-221 (Sept.) 1964.

40. KOPELL, B. S., & WITTNER, W. K.: The Effects of Chlorpromazine and Methamphetamine on Visual Signal-from-Noise Detection, *J. Nerv. Ment. Dis.* 147:418-424 (Oct.) 1968.

41. RAPPAPORT, M.: Attention to Competing Voice Messages by Nonacute Schizophrenic Patients, *J. Nerv. Ment. Dis.* 146:404-411 (May) 1968.

42. OLDS, J., & TRAVIS, R. P.: Effects of Chlorpromazine, Meprobamate, Pentobarbital and Morphine on Self-Stimulation, *J. Pharmacol. Exp. Ther.* 128:397-404 (April) 1960.

43. RAY, T. S.; RAGLAND, R. E.; & CLARK, M. L.: Chlorpromazine in Chronic Schizophrenic Women: Comparison of Differential Effects on Various Psychological Modalities During and After Treatment, *J. Nerv. Ment. Dis.* 138:348-353 (April) 1964.

44. STONE, G. C., et al.: Chlorpromazine Slows Decay of Visual Short-Term Memory, Perception and Psychophysics, *Psychonomic Sci.* 16:229-230, 1969.

45. SPERLING, G.: The Information Available in Brief Visual Presentations, *Psychol. Monogr.* 74: (No. 11) 1960.

46. LAWRENCE, C. M., & ROSS, J.: Information Available From Brief Visual Presentations Using Two Types of Report, *Psychonomic Sci.* 13:199-200 (Dec. 5) 1968.

47. GLASER, E. M.: *The Physiological Basis of Habituation,* London: Oxford University Press, 1966.

48. KEY, B. J.: The Effects of Chlorpromazine and Lysergic Acid Diethylamide on the Rate of Habituation of the Arousal Response, *Nature* 190:275-277 (April 15) 1961.

49. KILLAM, E. K.: "Pharmacology of the Reticular Formation," in Efron, D. H., et al. (eds.): "Psychopharmacology: A Review of Progress 1957-1967," in the *Proceedings of the Sixth Annual Meeting of the American College of Neuropsychopharmacology, Dec. 12-15,* 1967, PHS publication No. 1836, 1968, pp. 411-446.

50. COOK, L., & CATANIA, A. C.: Effects of Drugs on Avoidance and Escape Behavior, *Fed. Proc.* 23:818-835 (July-Aug.) 1964.

51. LOW, L. A.; ELIASSON, M.; & KORNETSKY, C.: Effect of Chlorpromazine on Avoidance Acquisition as a Function of CS-US Interval Length, *Psychopharmacologia* 10:148-154 (Oct. 31) 1966.

52. POSLUNS, D.: An Analysis of Chlorpromazine Induced Suppression of the Avoidance Response, *Psychopharmacologia* 3:361-373 (Oct. 31) 1962.

53. CALLAWAY, E.; JONES, R. T.; & LAYNE, R. S.: Evoked Responses and Segmental Set of Schizophrenia, *Arch. Gen. Psychiat.* 12:83-89 (Jan.) 1965.

54. JONES, R. T., et al.: The Auditory Evoked Response as a Diagnostic and Prognostic Measure in Schizophrenia, *Amer. J. Psychiat.* 122:33-41 (July) 1965.

55. JONES, R. T.; BLACKER, K. H.; & CALLAWAY, E.: Perceptual Dysfunction in Schizophrenia: Clinical and Auditory Evoked Response Findings, *Amer. J. Psychiat.* 123:639-645 (Dec.) 1966.

56. CALLAWAY, E.; JONES, R. T.; & DONCHIN, E.: AER Variability in Schizophrenia, to be published.

57. SPECK, L. B.; DIM, B.; & MERCER, M.: Visual Evoked Responses of Psychiatric Patients, *Arch. Gen. Psychiat.* 15:59-63 (July) 1966.

58. LIFSHITZ, K.: Information Handling Indicated by the AER in Normals and Schizophrenics, read before the American Psychiatric Association, Boston, May 13-17, 1968.

59. DAVIS, P. A.: Comparative Study of the EEGs of Schizophrenic and Manic-Depressive Patients, *Amer. J. Psychiat.* 99:210-217 (Sept.) 1942.

60. ARIETI, S.: "Schizophrenia: The Manifest Symptomatology, the Psychodynamic and Formal Mechanisms," in Arieti, S. (ed.): *American Handbook of Psychiatry*, New York: Basic Books, Inc., Publishers, 1959, vol. 1, pp. 455-484.

61. SILVERMAN, J.: Variations in Cognitive Control and Psychophysiological Defense in the Schizophrenias, *Psychosom. Med.* 29:225-251 (May-June) 1967.

62. SILVERMAN, J.: A Paradigm for the Study of Altered States of Consciousness, *Brit. J. Psychiat.* 114:1201-1218 (Oct.) 1968.

63. CROMWELL, R. L.: Stimulus Redundancy and Schizophrenia, *J. Nerv. Ment. Dis.* 146:360-375 (May) 1968.

64. PRIBRAM, K. H.: "Emotion: Steps toward a Neuropsychological Theory," in Glass, D. C. (ed.): *Neurophysiology and Emotion*, New York: Rockefeller University Press, 1967, pp. 3-40.

65. WACHTEL, P. L.: Conceptions of Broad and Narrow Attention, *Psychol. Bull.* 68: 417-429 (Dec.) 1967.

66. CALLAWAY, E., & STONE, G.: "Re-evaluating Focus of Attention," in Uhr, V. M., and Miller, J. G. (eds.): *Drugs and Behavior*, New York: John Wiley & Sons, Inc., 1960, pp. 393-398.

67. MOON, A. F., et al: Perceptual Dysfunction as a Determinant of Schizophrenic Word Associations, *J. Nerv. Ment. Dis.* 146:80-84 (Jan.) 1968.

68. DRAGUNS, J. G.: Responses to Cognitive and Perceptual Ambiguity in Chronic and Acute Schizophrenics, *J. Abnorm. Soc. Psychol.* 66:24-30 (Jan.) 1963.

69. EBNER, E., & RITZLER, B.: Perceptual Recognition in Chronic and Acute Schizophrenics, *J. Consult. Clin. Psychol.* 33:200-206 (April) 1969.

70. LAWSON, J. S.; McGHIE, A.; & CHAPMAN, J.: Distractibility in Schizophrenia and Organic Cerebral Disease, *Brit. J. Psychiat.* 113:527-535 (May) 1967.

71. NEALE, J. M.: *Perceptual Span in Schizophrenia*, thesis, Vanderbilt University, Nashville, 1968.

72. COURT, J. H., & GARWOLI, E.: Schizophrenic Performance on a Reaction-Time Task With Increasing Levels of Complexity, *Brit. J. Soc. Clin. Psychol.* 7:216-223 (Sept.) 1968.

73. SMITH, S. L.: Extraversion and Sensory Threshold, *Psychophysiology* 5:293-299 (Nov.) 1968.

74. LOEHLIN, J. C.: *Computer Models of Personality*, New York: Random House, Inc., 1968.

36

PSYCHOLOGICAL DIFFERENTIATION
AND PROCESS-REACTIVE
SCHIZOPHRENIA

Robert Cancro and A. Arthur Sugerman

Fifty-one consecutive male admissions to a psychiatric receiving hospital
who had a staff diagnosis of schizophrenia were kept drug free for a period of testing. The rod-and-frame test (RFT) showed a curvilinear correlation coefficient of .28 with the Phillips Prognostic Rating Scale (PRS).
The midrange on the RFT showed a good prognosis, with the process
cases being at the extremes of the RFT scores. There was a significant
relationship between RFT and duration of hospital stay at 1 and 2 yr. but
not after 3 yr. of follow-up. The readmission pattern suggested that intermediate cases on the RFT leave the hospital sooner but return more frequently. The data failed to demonstrate a relationship between RFT and
measures of conceptual plasticity, abstract attitude, severity of schizophrenic thought disorder, and severity of reality disruption.

The persistent problems in diagnosis of schizophrenia necessitated an
improvement in classification. The concept of process-reactive schizophrenia was just such an effort to improve the nomenclature. The empirical finding that this distinction was useful has led to the attempt to
clarify the underlying basis for the distinction. Many authors (Becker,
1956; Fine and Zimet, 1959; Herron, 1962; Kantor and Herron, 1965;
Kantor and Winder, 1959; and Zimet and Fine, 1965) have suggested
that classification is an expression of differences in the degree of psycho-

Initial data collection was done at the State University of New York, Downstate
Medical Center, with grant support from the Commonwealth Fund. The authors wish
to thank Grant Dahlstrom and Herbert E. Spohn for their helpful comments and
suggestions.

Requests for reprints should be sent to Robert Cancro, U. of Conn. Health Center,
Hartford, Conn. 06112.

Reprinted, by permission of author and editor, from: *Journal of Abnormal Psychology*, 74:415-419, 1969.

logical differentiation between schizophrenics. The process cases are viewed as less differentiated than the reactive cases.

There are no more reliable or better validated experimental measures of differentiation than those developed by Witkin, Dyk, Faterson, Goodenough, and Karp (1962). These measures have been subjected to rigorous use in a theoretical framework of differentiation for a number of years. Two efforts (Bryant, 1961; Gibeau, 1965) to examine the process-reactive dimension in schizophrenia with these measures have produced slightly different results. A major source of variance has been the use of drugged, as well as chronically institutionalized patients. Differences reported between process and reactive cases could easily be related to group differences in types, dosage, duration, or action of drugs. The effect of differences in the length of hospitalization between process and reactive patients could also account for some findings. Recognizing the essential need to control for the effects of drugs and duration of current hospital stay, the authors obtained a population that fulfilled these requirements. The attempts to demonstrate a linear relationship between position on the process-reactive continuum and the rod-and-frame test (Sugerman, 1962) and the sophistication of body concept test (Cancro, 1962) were unsuccessful.

An increasing number of reports by various investigators suggest that a linear relationship is not to be expected between these variables (Silverman, 1964; Voth, 1947; Witkin, 1965; Witkin, Lewis, Hertzman, Machover, Meissner and Wapner, 1954). These reports stimulated the present reexamination of this drug-free population for the presence of a nonlinear relationship between psychological differentiation and the process-reactive classification. The secondary purpose was to seek out possible relationships between psychological differentiation, duration of hospitalization, and certain signs of the illness, specifically, ability to shift conceptual set, abstract attitude, severity of thought disorder, and degree of reality disruption.

METHOD

Subjects

Fifty-one consecutive male admissions to the wards of a large city psychiatric observation hospital, who had a senior staff diagnosis of schizophrenia, ranged in age from 18 to 44, and were fluent in English were admitted to this study.* While the use of the staff diagnosis introduced an indeterminate amount of variability, it was chosen over the authors' diagnosis in order to avoid the problem of unconscious bias in the selection of cases. The age range was selected in order to screen out early adolescent reactions, involutional states, and premature senility. The patients whose clinical picture was complicated by organic, neurological, or extraneous factors such as alcoholism, were rejected. An important methodological feature of this study was that patients received no tranquilizers or long-acting sedatives until after the period of testing and examinations, so that the clinical picture would not be contaminated by drug effect.

Procedure

Toward the end of the first week of hospitalization the patient received the rod-and-frame test (RFT, body erect), in Witkin's laboratory, without the technician knowing the patient's clinical history or mental status findings. The RFT score was used as the measure of psychological differentiation.

The patients were interviewed, and the material obtained was used to fill out the Prognostic Rating Scale (PRS, Phillips, 1953), which served to classify the patients on the process-reactive dimension. The patients were not divided into nominal categories on the basis of the PRS, but rather assigned their actual numerical score.

Patients were followed for a period of 3 years, and the outcome measure was the total number of nights spent in any mental institution during the specific time period under examination. The patients were sent to state and veterans' hospitals for treatment, without the treating hospitals being informed of their research status. There were no significant interinstitutional differences in duration of hospital stay for this sample.

The Metalog Test (Zubin and Windle, 1951) was used as the measure of ability to shift conceptual set and was scored blindly and independently. A Proverb List (Benjamin, 1944) was admiinstered and inde-

---

* The age range of the population was 18-44, $M=29.5$, $SD=7.4$. The mean number of years of education was 11.3, $SD=2.3$. The mean scaled WAIS vocabulary score was 9.3, $SD=3$. Twenty-eight patients (55%) had no prior psychiatric hospitalization. Of the 23 patients (45%) who were previously hospitalized, the mean duration of total prior hospitalization was 15.9 mo. with only 2 cases being hospitalized for a lifetime total of more than 36 mo. and no case for over 5 yr. Twelve patients with a history of previous hospitalization were classified as reactive so that patients with prior hospitalization were represented more highly in the reactive group (60%) than in the process group (40%). Thirty-four patients (66.7%) were in Hollingshead's Group V; 12 (23.5%) were in Group IV; 4 (7.8%) were in Group III; and only 1 patient was in Group I. There was no significant relationship between social class and the process-reactive classification in this sample.

pendently scored for abstraction, using a scale developed by Meadow (Meadow, Greenblatt, Funkenstein and Solomon, 1953). The severity of the thought disorder was clinically quantified by two separate and independently scored measures. The first of these was a rating of the severity of the formal signs on a 4-point scale. A score of 0 was given if no thought disorder was manifested during a 1-hour, mental status interview, done during the first few days of hospitalization. A rating of 1 was assigned if the patient showed circumstantiality, literalness, or concreteness. A rating of 2 was given if the patient showed autistic intrusions, predicative identifications, or loosening of associations. A rating of 3 was assigned if the patient showed perseverations, echolalia, blocking, neologisms, or incoherence. The patient was given the score of the most severe formal sign demonstrated. For example, if he showed loosening of associations and echolalia he was given a rating of 3. The second measure was the frequency of intrusions of formal signs of schizophrenic thought disorder in the proverb responses.

A clinical measure, designed to measure the degree of reality disruption on a 7-point ordinal scale of severity, was used (Cancro, 1962). Curvilinear correlation coefficients were used so that nonlinear relationships would be allowed to emerge. The RFT was treated as the nominal variable with the 51 cases divided into three equal groups of 17 each, representing the low, middle, and high range of differentiation. Pearson correlations were also calculated and F tests were done on the basis of the difference between the curvilinear and the Pearson correlations.

RESULTS

The RFT correlated with the PRS at .28, $F=4.0816$, $p<.05$. The intermediate group on the RFT consisted primarily of reactive cases as determined by the PRS. The most differentiated cases included most of the process patients and a very few reactives. The most undifferentiated group contained both process and reactive cases. In summary, the process cases tended to be at the RFT extremes, although more often at the highly differentiated rather than at the undifferentiated end, while the reactive cases were mostly in the midrage and to a lesser degree in the undifferentiated end of the continuum.

The duration of hospital stay was correlated with RFT at four specific times during the 3-year follow-up period—6, 12, 24, and 36 months. The RFT correlated with 6-month duration at .24, $p<.20$; with 12-month duration at .33, $p<.05$; with 24-month duration at .30, $p<.05$; and with 36-month duration at .22, $p<.20$. At all four of these points it was the midrange group on the RFT that had the shortest duration of hospital stay. The least differentiated cases had an intermediate duration, and the most differentiated cases had the longest duration of hospital treatment. The susceptibility of the curvilinear correlation coefficient to variations in the manner of grouping patients into low, medium, and high RFT scores suggested the wisdom of grouping the patients by other criteria to confirm the relationship between RFT and outcome. Taking those 13 patients whose RFT score was within plus or minus .5 sigma from the mean as the midrange group produced a second grouping with 14 patients in the least differentiated and 24 patients in the most differ-

TABLE 1

CURVILINEAR CORRELATIONS BETWEEN RFT AND DURATION OF HOSPITAL STAY

Grouping	Month			
	6	12	24	36
First	.24	.33*	.30*	.22
Second	.19	.32*	.29*	.23
Third	.28*	.40**	.32*	.22

Note.—$N = 51$.
* $p < .05$.
** $p < .01$.

entiated groups. This second grouping of the RFT correlated with 6-month duration at .19; with 12-month duration at .32, $p < .05$; with 24-month duration at .29, $p < .05$; and with 36-month duration at .23, $p < .20$. Witkin and associates (Witkin, Lewis, Hertzman, Machover, Meissner and Wapner, 1954) reported in a study drawn from the same observation hospital that only 20% of their cases represented the midrange and that the remainder were equally split between high and low scores on the RFT. Grouping this patient population in a similar manner with the middle 20% ($n = 11$) representing the intermediate cases still gave essentially similar results. The third grouping of the RFT correlated with 6-month duration at .28, $p < .05$; with 12-month duration at .40, $p < .01$; with 24-month duration at .32, $p < .05$; and with 36-month duration at .22, $p < .20$.

The Metalog Test correlated with the RFT at .32 but the curvilinearity was not significant. The Pearson correlation between the Metalog Test and the RFT was .27 with the most differentiated patients showing the most conceptual plasticity. There was a strong linear correlation between the Metalog Test and Wechsler Adult Intelligence Scale (WAIS) Vocabulary score of .46 in this sample. There was a marginal linear correlation between RFT and WAIS Vocabulary score and when the effect of the Vocabulary score was removed, the correlation between the RFT and the Metalog Test became nonsignificant.

There were no significant correlations between the RFT and the measures of abstract attitude, severity of thought disorder, and degree of reality disruption.

DISCUSSION

The importance of performing perceptual tests on a drug-free population cannot be overemphasized. Differences between patient groups, such as process and reactive, on a variety of psychological measures can be solely an expression of degree of tranquilization. It is also essential to control for length of hospitalization, especially since the process patients in any given study are likely to have been hospitalized longer than the reactive group to which they are compared.

The tendency to see process cases as sicker and more primitive than reactive cases, coupled with the tendency to see less differentiated people as more primitive and less stable, may have contributed to the establishment of a mental set that the relationship between these variables must be linear.

The finding that the midrange of differentiation, as measured on the RFT, consisted almost exclusively of reactive schizophrenics suggests that an intermediate degree of differentiation was correlated with good prognosis. The relationship between RFT and duration of hospital stay tended to support the conclusion that differentiation contributes to the predictive power of the PRS. The cognitive stance and defensive preference of the extreme groups on the RFT differed sharply. Both extremes of differentiation were seen as overly committed to a particular ego style and lacking in the flexibility to shift according to the demands of the situation. From this point of view, patients in the midrange of differentiation would have a better prognosis, since they are less firmly committed to a particular style and can change more readily (Haronian and Sugerman, 1967). While this change may signal a true improvement it may only reflect the ability of the patient to comply with what the treating institution expects. One cannot help but be reminded of the warning about patients who improve rapidly only to lose their gains just as easily (Freud, 1964). This admonition, coupled with the failure of the RFT to significantly correlate with 6- and 36-month duration, suggested an examination of admission and discharge patterns over the 3 years of follow-up.

The curvilinear correlation between RFT and total number of admissions was .24, $p < .20$, while that between RFT and the total number of discharges was .23, $p < .20$. While not significant, the results were in the direction of the midrange on the RFT, having a higher number of readmissions, with the most differentiated cases having the fewest readmissions and the least differentiated cases an intermediate number. This was the same pattern that emerged with the discharges as well. The difference in duration of hospital stay between various RFT groups becomes nonsignificant because the higher readmission rate of the midrange and least differentiated patients begins to compensate for the longer initial hospital stay of the most differentiated patients at about 36 months. This pattern of hospitalization suggests the long-term predictive elements of the PRS are not those that are related to psychological differentiation.

The failure of the RFT to correlate with any of the clinical variables studied suggests that these measures are not related to psychological differentiation. The restricted range of the Ss tested leaves open the possibility that a relationship between various clinical signs and differentiation may exist in other types of patient samples. The clinical measures used in this study were affected to varying degrees by the severity of the schizophrenic process, and the failure to demonstrate a relationship to the RFT was consistent with the observation that psychological differentiation contributes to the form of the pathology and not its severity.

REFERENCES

BECKER, W. C. A genetic approach to the interpretation and evaluation of the process-reactive distinction in schizophrenia. *Journal of Abnormal and Social Psychology,* 1956, 53:229-236.

BENJAMIN, J. D. A method for distinguishing and evaluating formal thinking disorders in schizophrenia. In J. S. Kasanin (Ed.), *Language and thought in schizophrenia.* Los Angeles: University of California, 1944.

BRYANT, A. R. P. An investigation of process-reactive schizophrenia with relation to perception of visual space. Unpublished doctoral dissertation, University of Utah, 1961.

CANCRO, R. *A comparison of process and reactive schizophrenia.* (Doctoral dissertation, State University of New York, Brooklyn) Ann Arbor, Mich.: University Microfilms, 1962. No. 5166.

FINE, H. J., & ZIMET, C. N. Process-reactive schizophrenia and genetic levels of perception. *Journal of Abnormal and Social Psychology,* 1959, 59:83-86.

FREUD, S. Analysis terminable and interminable. In, *Complete psychological works of Sigmund Freud.* Vol. 23. London: Hogarth Press, 1964.

GIBEAU, P. J. Field dependency and the process-reactive dimension in schizophrenia. Unpublished doctoral dissertation, Purdue University, 1965.

HARONIAN, F., & SUGERMAN, A. A. Fixed and mobile field independence: Review of studies relevant to Werner's dimension. *Psychological Reports,* 1967, 21:41-57.

HERRON, W. G. The evidence for the unconscious. *Psychoanalytic Review,* 1962, 49:70-92.

KANTOR, R. E., & HERRON, W. G. Perceptual learning in the reactive-process schizophrenias. *Journal of Projective Techniques and Personality Assessment,* 1965, 29:58-70.

KANTOR, R. E., & WINDER, C. L. Process-reactive continuum: A theoretical proposal. *Journal of Nervous and Mental Disease,* 1959, 129:429-434.

MEADOW, A., GREENBLATT, M., FUNKENSTEIN, D., & SOLOMON, H. Relationship between capacity for abstraction in schizophrenia and physiologic response to autonomic drugs. *Journal of Nervous and Mental Disease,* 1953, 118:332-338.

PHILLIPS, L. Case history data and prognosis in schizophrenia. *Journal of Nervous and Mental Disease,* 1953, 117:515-525.

SILVERMAN, J. The problem of attention in research and theory in schizophrenia. *Psychological Review,* 1964, 71:352-379.

SUGERMAN, A. A. Prognostic factors in schizophrenia: A developmental approach. Unpublished doctoral dissertation, State University of New York, Brooklyn, 1962.

VOTH, A. C. An experimental study of mental patients through the autokinetic phenomenon. *American Journal of Psychiatry,* 1947, 103:793-805.

WITKIN, H. A. Psychological differentiation and forms of pathology. *Journal of Abnormal Psychology,* 1965, 70:317-336.

WITKIN, H. A., DYK, R. B.. FATERSON, H. F., GOODENOUGH, D. R., & KARP, S. A. *Psychological differentiation.* New York: Wiley, 1962.

WITKIN, H. A., LEWIS. H. B., HERTZMAN, M., MACHOVER, K., MEISSNER, P. B., & WAPNER, S. *Personality through perception.* New York: Harper, 1954.

ZIMET, C. N., & FINE, H. J. Primary and secondary process thinking in two types of schizophrenia. *Projective Techniques and Personality Assessment,* 1965, 29:93-99.

ZUBIN, J., & WINDLE, C. The prognostic value of the Metenym Test in a follow-up study of psychosurgery patients and their controls. *Journal of Clinical Psychology,* 1951, 7:221-223.

37

PREDICTION OF CHANGES IN SEVERITY OF THE SCHIZOPHRENIC SYNDROME WITH DISCONTINUATION AND ADMINISTRATION OF PHENOTHIAZINES IN CHRONIC SCHIZOPHRENIC PATIENTS:

Language as a Predictor and Measure of Change in Schizophrenia

Louis A. Gottschalk, Goldine C. Gleser, John M. Cleghorn, Walter N. Stone, and Carolyn N. Winget

The purpose of this investigation was to explore possible predictors of change in the severity of the schizophrenic syndrome among chronic schizophrenic patients with cessation and administration of phenothiazine chemotherapy. A special feature of this study was the use of five-minute samples of schizophrenic speech to serve as predictor scores and

Supported in part by Grant T 57-74 from the Foundations Fund for Research in Psychiatry; National Institute of Mental Health Grants MH-08282 and MH-K3-14, 665; and a grant from the Robert Stern Fund.

Louis A. Gottschalk, M.D.: Chairman and Professor, Department of Psychiatry and Human Behavior, College of Medicine, University of California at Irvine, Irvine, Calif. Goldine C. Gleser, Ph.D.: Professor of Psychology and Director, Psychology Division, Department of Psychiatry, College of Medicine, University of Cincinnati, Cincinnati, Ohio. John M. Cleghorn, M.D.: Associate Professor of Psychiatry, Department of Psychiatry, McMaster University Medical School, Hamilton, Ontario, Canada. Walter N. Stone, M.D.: Assistant Professor of Psychiatry, Department of Psychiatry, College of Medicine, University of Cincinnati, Cincinnati, Ohio. Carolyn N. Winget, M.A.: Research Associate, Department of Psychiatry, College of Medicine, University of Cincinnati, Cincinnati, Ohio.

Reprinted, by permission of author and publisher, from: *Comprehensive Psychiatry*, 11: 123-140, 1970.

change scores of the schizophrenic symptom complex (16-18, 20, 22). An independent set of change scores and predictor scores was provided by the use of the Mental Status Schedule of Spitzer et al. (29-32) and of predictor scores alone by the 16 PF test of Cattell and Eber (3).

MATERIALS AND METHODS

A group of 74 chronic schizophrenic patients, 35 males and 39 females, was selected from the schizophrenic inpatient population at Longview State Hospital in Cincinnati, Ohio, on the following bases: the patients had no complicating medical or neurological illness other than chronic schizophrenia; they were receiving a phenothiazine derivative and no anti-depressant medicament of any kind; they were not mute and were capable of cooperating with the procedures used in the measurements of change. They had the following other characteristics: they had been hospitalized from 6 months to 25 years on the present admission, with a median of 11 years; those hospitalized for the shortest periods had had one to four previous admissions; all patients had been on one of the phenothiazine drugs continually for at least six months (approximately 37% were on trifluoperazine, 19% on fluphenazine, 19% on perphenazine, and the remaining 25% on such drugs as chlorpromazine, thioridazine, or triflupromazine); the patients were all Caucasians and in the age range from 24 to 54, with an average age of 42.9 years.

For the initial assessment of these patients, several procedures were carried out while they were still receiving their phenothiazine medication. Tape-recorded, five-minute verbal samples were obtained from each patient two or three times in the initial week, using the Gottschalk-Gleser method of asking each patient to tell an interesting or dramatic life experience (15, 22).

Each patient was then seen by a psychiatrist or a third-year psychiatric resident who conducted a standardized interview from which he filled out the Mental Status Schedule (29-32). The 16 PF test, Form A (3), was administered by a psychologist and research assistant to groups of 6 to 12 patients at any one session. Directions were read aloud and repeated when necessary to make sure that each patient knew what he was to do. Individual attention was given to each person at some point during the time he was answering the test to make sure that he was recording answers correctly and in some cases items were read to him if he was having difficulty reading or understanding the statements. By these means, complete test results were obtained on 35 females and 34 males, or 69 of the 74 patients. The findings from the 16 PF test have been reported elsewhere (11) and will not be presented in detail at this time.

On completion of initial psychological evaluations, all patients had their phenothiazine medication changed, ostensibly, to a new drug, which was actually a placebo of identical appearance to thioridazine. None of the hospital personnel (doctors, nurses, or attendants) was told that a placebo was substituted for the psychoactive drug.

Five-minute speech samples were obtained twice weekly, by the same interviewer whenever possible, from each patient throughout the next eight weeks of the study.

Four weeks after the patients had been taking the placebo, one-half of the group, selected according to Mental Status scores to equate groups, was started on thioridazine in doses comparable to the amount they had been individually receiving in the form of this or any other phenothiazine derivative at the onset of this study (300-1000 mg./day). The other half of the group of patients was continued on the placebo. At this four-week point of the study, all patients were re-evaluated on the Spitzer et al. Mental Status Schedule, and a third evaluation by this measure was done at the end of the eighth week of the study. Different raters were used each time.

Thus, half of the patients were on a placebo for eight weeks and the other half received a placebo for four weeks and then were given the phenothiazine derivative, thioridazine, for four weeks. During the course of this study, if patients became disturbed, they were administered only chloral hydrate (8 cc.) or a placebo by mouth or sodium phenobarbital (0.1 Gm.) intramuscularly. Four patients became difficult to manage during the first four weeks, and had to be dropped from the study.

Typescripts of the five-minute verbal samples were scored independently and blindly by two content analysis technicians for anxiety, hostility outward, hostility inward, ambivalent hostility and social alienation-personal disorganization, following the Gottschalk-Gleser scales. These scales provide an objective procedure for measuring psychological states through the content analysis of small samples of verbal behavior. This method of content analysis, which considers the grammatical clause as the unit of communication of meaning, consists of sets of categories of content, meaning or themes, organized and weighted according to various scaled psychological dimensions. Reliability and validity studies have been reported on scales for measuring, by this method, anxiety (10, 18), three kinds of hostility (19), social alienation-personal disorganization (16, 17, 20, 22), and other psychological states (22).

The Mental Status Schedule, which was completed on each patient during the initial, fourth, and eighth weeks, contains a set of 248 items describing symptoms and behavior to which the psychiatrist responds true or false on the basis of a structured interview with the patient. The authors of this schedule have collected data on over 2000 patients throughout the United States and, at the time of this study, were in the process of determining subscales by means of factor analysis (29-32). A verimax rotation of the first three principal component factors yielded subscores for neuroticism (feelings and concerns), psychoticism (delusions, hallucinations, grandiosity), and disorientation (confusion, retardation). Forty-two subscales have been derived on more specific and circumscribed symptom clusters.

The 16 PF test claims to measure "functionally unitary and psychologically significant dimensions" (3) as determined by factor analytic and construct validation methods. Standardization tables (1964) provide norms for males in general population based on a substantial number of cases.

All measurements on all patients were computer-analyzed for intercorrelations, means, standard deviations, and other relevant mathematical assessments.

RESULTS

Group Trends in Social Alienation-Personal Disorganization Scores

Of the 74 patients placed on placebo at the beginning of the study, only four (two males and two females) were discontinued at the end of the first four weeks because of clinical considerations for their well being. These four had required sedatives and had become assaultive or suicidal about the third week on placebo so that it was considered unwise to expose them to the risk of continuing another four weeks on placebo should they happen to be assigned to that group. All four patients decreased steadily in the average number of words they spoke in the five minute sessions, and all but one was mute throughout the third or fourth week. Their scores on the scale for social alienation-personal disorganization increased steadily, with a total average rise of about 10 points in the four weeks. These data, which corroborate the clinical observations, add additional evidence to the validity of the verbal scale for assessing the severity of schizophrenic disorder.

There were a number of occasions for which verbal scores were not available. In some cases data were missing because patients were working or out on pass at the time of some of their scheduled sessions. More often scores were missing because the patient refused to speak or spoke less than the minimum of 45 words needed to obtain a reliable score on the "schizophrenic scale." (At least 70 words are needed to score the affect scales with even a minimum of reliability.) From a previous study validating the verbal measure of social alienation-personal disorganization (20, 22), it was possible to make an estimate of the average score on social alienation-personal disorganization that would be obtained by patients equally disturbed clinically but who spoke little or not at all. On the basis of extrapolations from rating scale scores used as criterion

TABLE 1

AVERAGE WEEKLY SOCIAL ALIENATION-PERSONAL DISORGANIZATION
SCORES AND NUMBER OF WORDS (PER VERBAL SAMPLE) FROM
CHRONIC SCHIZOPHRENIC PATIENTS

Time of Five-Minute Verbal Sample	Group A (Placebo for eight weeks, N = 32)				Group B (Thioridazine last four weeks, N = 32)			
	Average Number of Words (per verbal sample)		Average Social Alienation-Personal Disorganization Scores		Average Number of Words (per verbal sample)		Average Social Alienation-Personal Disorganization Scores	
	X	s.d.	X	s.d.	X	s.d.	X	s.d.
Pre-placebo	502.0	258.7	1.9	3.5	526.0	223.6	2.0	4.0
Week 1	407.4	247.7	1.4	4.6	438.6	221.8	2.9	4.8
2	411.2	258.8	2.4	5.0	429.9	243.6	2.6	5.4
3	416.3	282.4	2.5	4.8	392.7	189.0	4.6	7.4
4	410.3	282.3	3.7	5.0	364.8	238.6	3.7	7.7
Slope (Wks. 0-4)	— 17.6	53.0	0.48	1.10	— 36.6	47.3	0.50	1.41
5	405.5	288.5	3.6	5.7	394.3	246.5	4.3	6.1
6	404.0	287.2	3.4	5.6	437.8	261.2	3.5	5.8
7	437.8	301.0	3.7	5.6	450.9	268.1	3.2	6.6
8	436.4	294.0	3.9	5.6	459.6	258.5	3.6	6.1
Slope (Wks. 4-8)	6.2	18.7	0.07	0.68	25.5	34.0	—0.14	1.19

measures against which "schizophrenic" scores from speech samples were compared in this previous study, a score of 8.0 was assigned to verbal samples of up to 45 words and a score of 11.6 to verbal samples in which the subject was completely mute. These estimates helped considerably in obtaining more regular trends. However, six patients spoke so seldom after the first week or two that they were dropped from consideration in analyzing overall longitudinal trends.

The average weekly social alienation-personal disorganization scores of the 64 patients who were followed throughout the study are given in Table 1. Separate averages are provided for those patients who were maintained on placebo throughout the eight weeks and those who re-

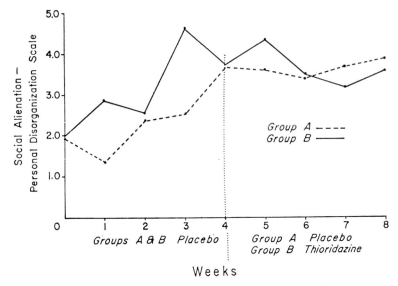

Fig. 1.—Average weekly scores on social alienation-personal disorganization scale for two groups of chronic schizophrenic subjects on two different experimental regimens.

ceived thioridazines the last four weeks. The slopes of the best-fitting linear trend lines for the first and second four-week periods were calculated and the average slopes are indicated in Table 1. These slopes can be interpreted as average weekly rates of change. The average slopes for the first four-week placebo period do not differ significantly between the two groups. The combined average slope of 0.49 for social alienation-personal disorganization scores during the first four weeks is significantly different from a zero slope at the .01 level, indicating an increase in severity of symptomatology during this four-week placebo period.

In the second four-week period for those on placebo, the average scores on the social alienation-personal disorganization scale continued to increase, but at a much slower rate. In fact, almost as many of the patients improved as regressed, so that the average slope of .07 was not significant. Clinically there were no further patients who, because of severely disturbed behavior, had to be dropped from the study. The patients who were placed in thioridazine showed some improvement on the average, but again, the average slope of —0.14 was not significantly different from zero. Neither was the difference significant between this average slope and that for patients on placebo. These results are illustrated graphically in Fig. 1.

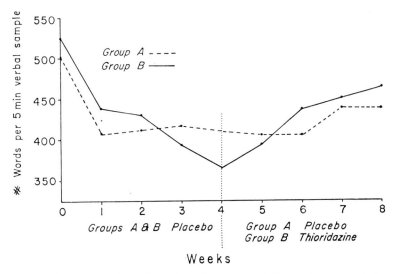

F<small>IG</small>. 2.—Average number of words spoken per verbal sample per week by two groups of chronic schizophrenics.

Group Trends in Quantity of Speech

The number of words spoken each week, on the average, is also given in Table 1 and graphically in Fig. 2. The decrease with placebo during the first four weeks (slope = —27.1 words/week) is very significant (p<.001). The difference in slope for the two groups (group A and B) during the placebo period is not significant. In the second four-week period, the patients receiving the active drug (group B) increased their speech at the average rate of 25.5 words per week, a highly significant increase. The placebo group (A) also showed a small rise, but this increase was not significant. The difference in slope for the two treatment groups was highly significant (t = 2.68, p<.01).

Intercorrelations Among Content Analysis Scores of Speech of Chronic Schizophrenics

Before examining the prediction of individual differences among chronic schizophrenics in response to changes in phenothiazine administration, it is instructive to look briefly at the intercorrelations among various content analysis scores of the speech of these patients obtained in the week prior to the experimental regimen. Table 2 shows the means, standard deviation, and intercorrelations among verbal behavior measures for the 69 chronic schizophrenic patients who were able to cooperate at the beginning of the study. These numbers were obtained by averaging such scores from the two or three verbal samples given by the patient within the week's interval while the patient was on one of the phenothiazine pharmacological agents. Scores for social alienation-personal disorganization correlated significantly ($p<.05$) with *hostility outward,* especially *overt hostility outward* ($r = .52$) (composed of statements of the self being hostile to others) and *ambivalent hostility* ($r = .32$) (com-

TABLE 2

INTERCORRELATIONS AMONG VERBAL BEHAVIOR MEASURES*
FOR SAMPLE OF CHRONIC SCHIZOPHRENICS (N = 69)

Variable	Mean	s.d.	2	3	4	5	6	7	8
						Correlation with variable			
1. Number of Words	508.8	235.2	—.12	.15	.18	.32	—.06	.22	.01
2. Anxiety	1.55	0.58		.44	.36	.51	.51	.62	.35
3. Overt Hostility Out	0.72	0.34			.23	.84	.48	.69	.52
4. Covert Hostility Out	0.67	0.23				.67	.10	.25	.06
5. Total Hostility Out	0.95	0.39					.37	.64	.40
6. Hostility In	0.80	0.35						.42	.10
7. Ambivalent Hostility	0.80	0.42							.32
8. Social Alienation-Personal Disorganization	2.04	3.89							

* Average of scores on two or three verbal samples taken within interval of one week while patients were on phenothiazine pharmacologic agent.

posed of statements of others being hostile to the self) and *anxiety* ($r = .35$). Covert hostility outward scores (composed of statements of others being hostile to others or hostility inferred from events involving inanimate objects) and *hostility inward* scores (composed of statements about the self being hostile to the self) were not significantly correlated with social alienation-personal disorganization scores. All content analysis scales, except, possibly, total hostility outward, were independent of the number of words spoken.

Predictive Aspects of Content Analysis Scores and Changes in Severity of Schizophrenic Syndrome

Table 3 presents summary data on the principal factor scores (*neuroticism, psychoticism, disorientation*) obtained from the Mental Status Schedule examinations performed initially and after the patients had

been on placebo for four weeks. All three factor scores increased significantly after four weeks on placebo relative to the initial values.

Let us examine the correlations between these Mental Status Schedule
scores and the verbal behavior measures obtained during the initial week.
Here an interesting pattern emerges. The initial scores for social alienation-personal disorganization are not only very significantly correlated

TABLE 3

CORRELATIONS BETWEEN VERBAL BEHAVIOR SCORES AND MENTAL STATUS
SCHEDULE FACTOR SCORES OBTAINED FROM CHRONIC SCHIZOPHRENICS
(N = 69) INITIALLY WHILE ON PHENOTHIAZINES
AND AFTER FOUR WEEKS OF PLACEBO

	Mental Status Schedule Scores					
	Neuroticism (feelings, concerns)		Psychoticism (delusions, hallucinations)		Disorientation (confusion, retardation)	
	T_1*	T_2*	T_1*	T_2*	T_1*	T_2*
Mean	6.4	9.6	5.6	7.3	4.1	5.7
Standard Deviation	4.9	6.8	4.5	5.3	5.1	4.9
Verbal Behavior Scores	*Correlations*					
No. of Words	—.17	—.03	—.05	.17	—.33	—.27
Social Alienation-Personal Disorganization	.19	.29	.41	.52	.43	.33
Anxiety	.19	.14	.17	.16	.17	.14
Overt Hostility Out	.13	.34	.22	.31	.09	.00
Covert Hostility Out	—.09	.02	—.15	.06	—.25	—.28
Hostility In	.06	.30	.03	.08	.04	.09
Ambivalent Hostility	.16	.20	.24	.26	.03	—.01

* T_1 = Initial period while patients were on phenothiazines. T_2 = Four weeks after withdrawal of
phenothiazine drugs. Italicized correlations are all significant at $p < .05$.

($p<.01$) with *psychoticism* ($r = .41$) and *disorientation* ($r = .43$)
scores in the initial period, but they are also correlated ($p<.05$) with
all three Mental Status factor scales in the follow-up period four weeks
later (*psychoticism, $r = .52$; disorientation, $r = .33$; neuroticism, $r =$
.29*). Initial overt hostility outward scores (but not covert hostility outwards) obtained while the patients were still on phenothiazine drugs,
correlated with and predictive of neurotic (*neuroticism*, $r = .34$, $p<.01$)
and psychotic phenomena (*psychoticism*, $r = .31$, $p<.05$) as assessed by
subscales of the Mental Status Schedule four weeks after discontinuation
of phenothiazine drug therapy. Initial hostility inward scores correlated
with *neurotic symptoms* ($r = .30$, $p<.05$) as assessed by the Mental

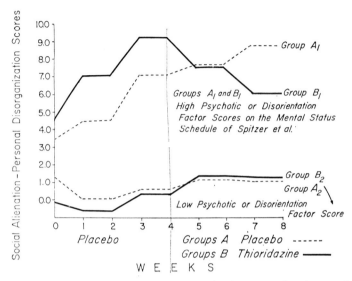

FIG. 3.—Social alienation-personal disorganization scores for drug and placebo groups classified on basis of initial mental status factor scores.

Status Schedule after four weeks off phenothiazine drugs. In contrast to these correlations, initial covert hostility outwards scores, obtained while the chronic schizophrenic patients were still on phenothiazines, correlated *negatively* with the *disorientation* ($r = -.28$, $p < .05$) subscale of the Mental Status Schedule four weeks after drug therapy was terminated.

It is evident that, on the average, patients became increasingly disturbed during the first four weeks that they were on placebo as judged by both the amount and content of their speech samples (Figs. 1 and 2) and from Mental Status Schedule Ratings (Table 3). However, some patients showed almost no deterioration in their behavior, and, if anything, seemed to improve during the first four weeks on placebo. Even after eight weeks of placebo these patients seemed as well or better off than when they started (Fig. 3).

One of the major interests in this study was trying to find some indicators in the initial data by which one could predict which patients would do well when taken off phenothiazines and which would not. In order to find predictors of response to phenothiazine withdrawal it was necessary to derive some measure to characterize the general trend of scores on the scale of social alienation-personal disorganization for each individual. For this purpose the slopes of the linear trend-line for the first four weeks and for the second four weeks were computed separately for each individual. This method of computing the rate of increase or decrease resulted in a more reliable rate of change measure than would simple difference scores.

Table 4 presents the correlations between the personality factor scores of the 16 PF, and the initial score on social alienation-personal disorgan-

TABLE 4

CORRELATIONS OF 16 PF FACTORS WITH INITIAL SCORES AND AVERAGE RATE OF CHANGE IN SOCIAL ALIENATION-PERSONAL DISORGANIZATION

16 PF Scale	Initial Score	First 4 weeks	Average Rates of Change Last 4 weeks	
	(N=69)	(N=69)	placebo (N=30)	drug (N=28)
A. Warmth	—.10	—.20	—.22	.00
B. Intelligence	—.25	—.04	—.01	.20
C. Emotional Stability	—.17	—.21	.37	.24
E. Assertiveness	.08	.04	—.10	—.28
F. Enthusiasm	—.16	—.22	.04	—.17
G. Conscientiousness	—.39	—.17	.04	.22
H. Venturesomeness	—.10	—.10	.10	.22
I. Sensitivity	—.10	.04	—.07	.21
L. Distrustfulness	.01	—.05	.25	—.01
M. Autism	.30	.10	—.22	—.01
N. Sophistication	—.30	—.18	—.08	.42
O. Insecurity	.08	.21	.08	—.37
Q_1 Free-thinking	—.02	.15	—.21	.25
Q_2 Self-sufficiency	.07	—.10	.29	.12
Q_3 Self-sentiment	—.32	—.01	.06	.31
Q_4 Drive Tension	.11	.11	—.32	—.06
Rate of change first four weeks.			—.18	—.55

ization, and the algebraic slope of the trend-line for social alienation-personal disorganization scores during the first four weeks. For completeness, correlations between 16 PF scores and social alienation-personal disorganization slopes in the last four weeks for patients given placebo and separately for those on thioridazine are also included. (For additional information on 16 PF scores in this study see reference 11.) From the correlations it appears that patients with emotional warmth (A), high emotional stability (C), enthusiasm (F), conscientiousness (G), and shrewdness-sophistication (N), and those who are not particularly insecure (0-) or free thinking (Q-), tend to have the least increment in social alienation-personal disorganization scores over the four weeks after phenothiazine withdrawal. However, none of these zero-order correlations reaches significance at the .05 level. A multiple regression equation was obtained which maximized the multiple correlation using a minimum number of predictors according to the technique suggested by DuBois (62). Using the six scales, A, C, F, N, O, and Q_1 from the 16 PF, a multiple correlation of .389 was obtained. The weights ranged from .08 for

TABLE 5

INTERRELATIONS AMONG INITIAL PRINCIPAL FACTOR AND SELECTED SUBSCALE
SCORES DERIVED FROM MENTAL STATUS SCHEDULE AND INITIAL SCORES
AND AVERAGE RATE OF CHANGE IN FIRST FOUR WEEKS FOR
SOCIAL ALIENATION-PERSONAL DISORGANIZATION (N = 74)

	b.	c.	d.	e.	f.	g.	h.	i.	Rate of Change
a. Neuroticism	.39	.22	.38	.02	.32	.08	.16	.19	.01
b. Psychoticism		.12	.80	.17	.07	.37	.52	.41	.19
c. Disorientation (primary)			.04	.77	.85	.22	.29	.43	.31
d. Delusions-Hallucinations				.12	—.06	.33	.34	.31	.20
e. Disorientation					.39	.17	.17	.35	.30
f. Apathy-Retardation						.07	.20	.31	.23
g. Silly Disorganization							.55	.38	.31
h. Elated Excitement								.36	.18
i. Initial Score Social Alienation-Personal Disorganization									.11

insecurity (O) to —.17 for enthusiasm (F). (Note that the predictor scores are such that a high value corresponds to a high rate of increase in social alienation-personal disorganization after phenothiazine withdrawal.)

Intercorrelations among the three principal factor scores and selected factor analytically-derived cluster scores from the Mental Status Schedule, initial scores on social alienation-personal disorganization, and rate of change of these scores over the first four weeks are shown in Table 5. *Disorientation* was the only one of the three principal component Mental Status factors that was significantly correlated with rate of change of social alienation-personal disorganization scores. Among the cluster scores *disorientation, apathy-retardation,* and *silly disorganization,* each significantly predicted rate of change scores. The first two of these are highly correlated with the primary disorientation scale, however, and hence are simply giving more specific symptom information.

Using the principal factors, a multiple R of .350 was obtained for the weighted sum of *psychoticism* and *disorientation* factor scores. The cluster scores yielded a multiple correlation of .422 for the weighted sum of scores for *disorientation, apathy-retardation, silly disorganization,* and *delusions-hallucinations.* Thus, the more specific symptom scores appeared to be considerably better predictors than the factor scores. It should be remembered that these scores are probably not as reliable as the more general factor scores and also that there is more opportunity for error to inflate the multiple.

The correlation was obtained between the two sets of predictor scores, i.e., the one from the 16 PF and the one from the Mental Status Schedule symptom clusters, to determine the extent to which they overlapped. The correlation between them was only .33, which, while significant, indicated considerable independence of prediction. The two scores, combined, predicted the average rate of change in social alienation-personal disorganization scores with an R of .497.

Looking again at Table 4, it is evident that individual differences in response to placebo during the second four-week period are not generally predictable from the same set of 16 PF factors as are individual differences in the first four weeks after drug withdrawal. The correlation between rates of change for the two periods is —.18, which is not significantly different from zero. Furthermore, many of the zero-order correlations between the 16 PF scales and rate of change are markedly different for the two periods. For example, the more emotionally stable (C) and self-sufficient (Q_2) patient became increasingly socially alienated during the second four weeks, whereas patients who were more free-thinking (Q_1) and tense (Q_4) in the baseline period showed some improvement.

The correlations between rates of change of social alienation-personal disorganization scores in the first four weeks and those in the last four weeks for subjects on drug was —.55, which is highly significant and indicates that these may be complementary processes. Subjects who showed the greatest increase in social alienation-personal disorganization when they were taken off phenothiazines tended to show the greatest improvement when given an active drug whereas those who did well on placebo tended to lose any gains they had made when they were put back on drugs. This is further borne out by the fact that the linear equation from the combined Mental Status and 16 PF predictors of social alienation-personal disorganization slope for the first period was also correlated

—.22 with the slope in the second period for those on thioridazine. (The corresponding correlation for the placebo group is .002).

On examination, the multiple regression equations from the Mental Status Scales, the 16 PF, or the two combined sets of scores appeared to be yielding inflated multiple correlations as the result of the correspondence of a few extreme values. Many intermediate sized changes were being missed and the regression equations did not seem to select those persons who continued to deteriorate with placebo during the second four weeks. Since it was hoped that a simple rule could be found for possible use in decisions to terminate drug therapy, and such a decision does not entail a continuous variable, it was decided to examine the possibility of making the prediction by the use of cut-off scores on the principal Mental Status Schedule factors. By trial and error it was determined that a score of less than seven on both the *psychoticism* and *disorientation* factors selected patients who did not get worse over the eight week period when the drug was withdrawn. On the other hand, a score of seven or greater on either scale indicated a poor prognosis for drug withdrawal. This decision rule actually provided a better separation of patients who did and did not deteriorate with placebo than did the linear regression predictor as measured by a phi coefficient.

Figure 3 shows the scores on the social alienation-personal disorganization scale averaged over successive two-week periods for patients classified according to the multiple cut-off criterion for their assignment to drug or placebo group at the end of the fourth week. Those patients who became mute are not included in these averages. Some interesting features are evident in this figure. The patients who had high *psychoticism* or *disorientation* scores on the initial Mental Status score (N = 29) tended to be somewhat more socially alienated to begin with and remained so throughout the study. This might have been anticipated from the fact that *psychoticism* and *disorientation* scores are positively correlated with scores on social alienation-personal disorganization in the base period (22). Using a cut-off criterion of 2.0 on the initial social alienation-personal disorganization scores from five-minute verbal samples also divided the chronic schizophrenic patients into those who reacted adversely to discontinuation of phenothiazine medication (scores above 2.0) and those who were relatively unreactive to phenothiazine withdrawal (or administration) during the period of observation.

The average rate of change of scores on the social alienation-personal disorganization scale during the first four weeks was 1.0. Those patients who had low scores on the *psychoticism* and *disorientation* scales of the Mental Status Schedule (N = 35) had low average social alienation-personal disorganization scores on their verbal samples, and they continued to have low scores over the entire eight weeks of the study provided they were in the placebo group. If they were put back on drug (N = 17) at the end of four weeks, they actually showed a slight (non-significant) increase in social alienation-personal disorganization. Another point of interest is the dip in scores in the first two weeks after drug withdrawal for the low symptom group. This drop has a p value of .10 by a sign test. It will be remembered that over the total duration of this study there was no difference in rate of change scores in the second four-week period for those on drug as compared to placebo. The trend scores in the second period for patients who had scores of seven or higher in *psychoticism* or *disorientation* differ more markedly depending on whether they were given drug or placebo, although the difference still has a probability of approximately .12 of arising by chance.

Since the average number of words spoken in a verbal sample had been noted to decrease when patients were on placebo and increase when they were again given a psychoactive drug, the question arose as to whether individual differences in these trends were also related to the dichotomy of high versus low *psychoticism* and *disorientation* Mental Status Schedule scores. The high symptom group showed an average decrease in the first four weeks of —42.3 words per week, whereas the decrease for the low symptom group was only —15.2 words per week, a difference significant at the .05 level. Those having high scores who were given psychoactive drugs the second four weeks, increased an average of 31.2 words per week as compared to only 0.4 words per week for the placebo group, again a significant difference. For the low symptom groups the corresponding values were 17.5 for those on drug and 11.3 for those on placebo the last four weeks, a non-significant difference.

DISCUSSION

The intercorrelations among content analysis scores of the speech of schizophrenics indicate that anxiety, overt hostility outward, and ambivalent hostility (but not covert hostility nor hostility inward) are associated with high social alienation-personal disorganization scores. These common variances are not due to occasional scoring of the same content categories in the different scales. Rather, we take those correlations to signify that the sicker schizophrenics are more likely to manifest their disorder in open, destructive aggression, in paranoid ideation, or in higher anxiety. The lack of correlation of social alienation-personal disorganization scores with hostility inward scores indicates that, in our sample of chronic schizophrenics, self-criticism and self-hate, though present, does not contribute to the dimension of severity of the schizophrenic syndrome. Other studies have indicated that our hostility inward scores are associated with various measures of depression (19). It seems fitting that the social alienation-personal disorganization scale is, hence, not directly concerned with the dimension of hostility inward or, by extension, the dimension of depression. It is of some relevance that hostility inward scores significantly predict (Table 3, r — .30) those individuals who will show four weeks later, after withdrawal of phenothiazine drugs, higher scores on the factor of *neuroticism* on the Mental Status Schedule, but these same hostility inward scores will not be predictive of the *psychoticism* or *disorientation* factor scores.

The covert hostility outward scale shows evidence, in this study and with these patients, of being more a measure of relative health than sickness. The covert hostility outward scores (that is, statements of others being hostile to others) do not correlate with scores of social alienation-personal disorganization; rather, the baseline covert hostility outward scores tend to be predictive of those individuals who will not be disoriented later as evaluated on the Mental Status Schedule, four weeks after their tranquilizing pharmacologic agent has been stopped (r = —.28, p<.05). This finding suggests that the more the schizophrenic patient verbalizes about the hostility among and between others, the more likely is this a sign of relative alertness to external events and, hence, one index of the capacity to test reality. It is noteworthy to consider the ability of the pre-phenothiazine withdrawal scores of social alienation-personal disorganization and overt hostility outward to predict the degree of psychotic exacerbation as assessed by the Mental Status Schedule four weeks after withdrawal of phenothiazine. Elsewhere, with nonpsychotic psychiatric outpatients coming to a brief psychotherapy clinic, Gottschalk et al. observed that high scores on this same "schizophrenic" scale is predictive of those patients who remain the most maladjusted after treatment (21).

In general, the verbal sample technique for assessing behavior appears to offer a fruitful method for following longitudinal changes in the magnitude of the schizophrenic syndrome and in finding predictors of trend with various types of therapy. The many kinds of problems involved when assessing change in psychiatry and the behavioral sciences have been well documented (24, 34). The use of repeated measures through which one can pass a best-fitting trend line and determine its slope for each subject offers an improved technique for dealing with change, provided the measurement procedure involved is one that can be performed frequently without carry-over effects. Verbal samples are well suited to this requirement.

Considerable evidence that the therapeutic effects of phenothiazines are not maintained following drug withdrawal has been reported in the literature (1, 6). These studies have been reviewed recently by Kamano who points out the need to find an effective method of predicting which patients can tolerate long periods without drugs and which cannot (25). The present study is a contribution in this direction. Our findings indicate that, on the average, chronic schizophrenic patients speak progressively fewer words and obtain higher social alienation-personal disorganization scores in the first four weeks after the phenothiazines they are taking are replaced by a placebo. Looking further, we find that if the psychoactive drug on which the chronic psychotic patient has been maintained has not succeeded in eliminating the more florid schizophrenic symptoms such as delusions and hallucinations or the symptoms of disorientation, apathy, and retardation, then drug treatment should be continued. Chronic patients who are relatively free of such symptoms while on tranquilizing drugs can go at least eight weeks without such medication with no exacerbation of schizophrenic symptoms. They may actually show some symptomatic improvement, possibly because of a decrease of undesirable side-effects. Social alienation-personal disorganization scores over 2 or low covert hostility outward or hostility inward scores on the Gottschalk-Gleser content analysis scales, as well as high *psychoticism* or *disorientation* scores in the Spitzer et al. Mental Status Schedule, are predictive of an adverse response to phenothiazine drug discontinuation.

It is interesting that the number of words spoken in the five-minute interview is also sensitive to pharmacological intervention. A significant difference was found in average rate of change in the number of words spoken for patients on thioridazine as compared to placebo. One reason for the sensitivity of this measure may lie in its objectivity and reliability and in its availability for all subjects. Psychologically, its importance lies in the fact that a low rate of speech is one of the "withdrawal" signs that Goldberg et al. have noted to be among the first symptoms to disappear when patients are treated with phenothiazines (12). These speech rate symptoms usually improve maximally by the end of five weeks on phenothiazine drugs. We found that at the end of four weeks on thioridazine, speech returned almost to the baseline rate, a finding which is consistent with those of Goldberg and his colleagues. The speech content measure of social alienation-personal disorganization is not only related to evidence (from the Mental Status Schedule) of disorientation and social withdrawal, but also to other schizophrenic symptoms, such as delusions, hallucinations, belligerence, and memory deficit, all of which Goldberg et al. found continued to abate up to 13 weeks after the start of pheno- thiazine treatment. In this respect, it is unfortunate that our patients were not followed for a longer period of time.

Several other investigators have looked for predictors of the kinds of reactions that chronic patients may have with the discontinuation of phenothiazine medication. Denber and Bird reported that relapse fol- lowing withdrawal of chlorpromazine in 1523 patients was related to severity of illness, duration of illness, or length of hospitalization before treatment, but not to duration of hospitalization itself or to clinical diagnosis (4, 5). Others have concluded that there is no realtionship between duration of previous chlorpromazine treatment and tendency to regress when chlorpromazine is withdrawn (14). Freeman and Olson stated that their study of chlorpromazine withdrawal in 96 chronic, hos- pitalized male psychotics did not provide useful clinical criteria for iden- tifying those patients who require uninterrupted drug treatment (9). They mentioned, however, that "sicker patients, particularly those who are confused or show little interest in their environment, tend to be poorer risks for drug discontinuation. . . ." In their study of the with- drawal of perphenazine in 39 male chronic schizophrenics, Whittaker and Hoy reported that it was impossible for them to predict which pa- tients would relapse (33). Collaborating in a Veterans Administration cooperative study on discontinuing or reducing chemotherapy in chronic schizophrenics, Caffey et al. found no evidence that the probability of relapse was related to diagnosis, length or amount of previous medica- tion, length of hospitalization or age (2). They also could not substanti- ate that prestudy psychiatric ratings, using the Inpatient Multidimen- sional Psychiatric Scale (IMPS) (27) and the Psychotic Reaction Profile (PRP) (26) enabled them to predict which patient would relapse if drugs were discontinued.

We believe that the lack of consistent findings of other investigators, with respect to predictors of which patients will relapse if psychophar- macological agents are discontinued, is due in part to the nature of the change measures previously used and the unreliability involved in de- ciding when a patient has relapsed. The fact that hospitalized chronic schizophrenics, by definition, are already in a hospital before their phenothiazine medication had been discontinued, makes somewhat in- definite the point at which one decides they have relapsed. In our study of phenothiazine withdrawal, the criteria of change were our objective social alienation-personal disorganization measure and the Mental Status

Schedule of Spitzer et al., and the research design did not involve the clinical decision as to whether or not the patient had relapsed.

The present study reemphasizes the difficulty of using chronic schizophrenic patients in large hospitals for the evaluation of new drugs, unless a long washout period from previous drug administration has been allowed. Almost all such patients are on some kind of phenothiazine medication. If they are not, it is very likely they constitute a different population with regard to drug response than those who are continuously maintained on drugs. The latter, again, consists of two types: those who become more floridly psychotic after discontinuing medication and those who remain unchanged or even improve slightly. If such patients were used indiscriminately for new drug studies, experimental results would vary according to the relative proportions of each type of patient in the sample, and the length of time elapsing between medications.

Many further questions are stimulated by the results of this investigation. It would be interesting to know how long the patients characterized as having a good prognosis with drug withdrawal could function reasonably adequately without drugs. Are such patients those who have always functioned marginally with or without drugs or have they had symptoms of disorientation and psychoticism at some prior time which were reduced when a drug was administered, and, most crucially, what accounts for the differential responses of these patients to phenothiazine withdrawal? In this respect, does a difference in metabolic turnover of phenothiazines account for the difference? It may be that the high and low symptom groups are characterized by differences in the metabolic handling of phenothiazine drugs which would be reflected in differences in the blood levels and/or excretion rates of the phenothiazines. Caffey et al. examined the hypothesis that differential relapse with phenothiazine withdrawal in chronic schizophrenics might be related to some aspects of urine metabolite excretion (2). Using the Forrest test (8) for urinary metabolite excretion, they could not confirm this hypothesis on their patients. Previously, Forrest and Forrest claimed a correlation of drug excretion rate and relapse pattern could be established in 70 percent of 20 chronic mental patients in their drug discontinuation (7). We believe further studies of this relationship are warranted, using other criteria of change of the schizophrenic syndrome, such as our verbal behavior measure.

Another possible explanation of the differential response to phenothiazine withdrawal is that the chronic schizophrenic patients differ with respect to the prior course of the disease process, in their premorbid personality characteristics, and/or in their previous treatment. Aside from the work of Denber and Bird as indicated previously (4, 5), there has been no substantiation of these hypotheses. In this respect, there is some suggestive evidence to support one or more of these explanations from the 16 PF scores, although the differences are not very great (11). The patients with the more severe symptoms had been hospitalized slightly longer (12.5 versus 9.5 years) but the lengths of stay overlap greatly so that this does not appear to be a crucial factor.

This study raises the possibility that different phenothiazines might be compared fruitfully with respect to the length of time they remain effective after medication is discontinued. While no contrasting effects among phenothiazines were evident for the groups studied here, the number of patients in each group who had been taking any one phenothiazine derivative was rather small. Obviously, further research studies are needed to account for the underlying mechanisms among chronic schizophrenics of the differential response to phenothiazine withdrawal.

SUMMARY

Seventy-four hospitalized chronic schizophrenic patients, who were able to cooperate with testing and interview procedures, were studied for eight weeks to sequentially evaluate the effect of withdrawal and readministration of phenothiazine medication. The patients, Caucasians of both sexes, in the age range 24-54, had been on some one phenothiazine derivative for at least the previous six months. For the first four weeks all patients were on placebo, while during the next four weeks half were on placebo and half were on thioridazine.

Patients were assessed initially using the standardized Spitzer et al. Mental Status Schedule and the Cattell 16 PF test. In addition, two or three five-minute verbal samples were obtained from each patient in the initial pre-drug withdrawal week to assess the level of social alienation-personal disorganization, hostility, and anxiety by the Gottschalk-Gleser method. Additional verbal samples were obtained twice weekly for the next eight weeks and Mental Status Schedule interviews were obtained at the end of four and eight weeks.

The following results were obtained: (1) Average scores for social alienation-personal disorganization increased significantly over the first four weeks, indicating increased psychopathology. (2) Those patients who continued on placebo showed little further increase in social alienation-personal disorganization scores in the second four weeks; whereas, those patients who were given thioridazine showed a small, nonsignificant decrease in such scores. (3) The average number of words spoken in a verbal sample decreased significantly for the first four weeks while patients were on placebo. Patients having thioridazine drug the second period showed a significant increase in the number of words spoken. (4) Using multiple correlation techniques with scores obtained during the initial testing period it was possible to predict individual differences in response to phenothiazine withdrawal. A multiple correlation of .39 was obtained using six of the 16 PF factor scales. A multiple correlation of .42 was obtained using four "narrow" factor scales of the Mental Status Schedule. Using both sets of predictors the correlation was .50. (5) Using the general principal factor scores of *psychoticism* and *disorientation* from the Mental Status Schedule, a multiple cut-off criterion of 7 or more in either scale divided the patients into those who gave verbal samples with increasingly high scores in social alienation-personal disorganization when on placebo from those who showed practically no change on this verbal score measure. The same multiple cut-off differentiated those who showed a significant decrease in the number of words spoken in the first period. (6) A cut-off criterion of 2 on the initial social alienation-personal disorganization (content analysis) scores from five minute verbal samples, was also predictive of the chronic schizophrenic patients who were unreactive to phenothiazine drug withdrawal or administration (less than two) and those who reacted with an exacerbation of the schizophrenic syndrome to phenothiazine drug withdrawal or with a decrease in the schizophrenic symptom complex with phenothiazine drug administration (more than two). This cut-off criterion also differentiated those patients who showed a significant decrease in the number of words spoken during the first four week placebo period. (7) The theoretical and practical implications of these findings are discussed.

ACKNOWLEDGMENTS

We wish to express our appreciation to Dr. John Toppen, Superintendent, for his permission to use the facilities of Longview State Hospital; to the resident psychiatrists and research technicians who assisted in gathering and processing the data; and to the technicians who scored the verbal samples. We thank Drs. Richard Bibb, Mansell Pattison, Eric Hanson, Anthony Gottlieb, Henry Udelmann and Eugene Woods for conducting standardized interviews and afterward filling out the Mental Status Schedule.

REFERENCES

1. BLACKBURN, H. L., & ALLEN, J. L.: Behavioral effects of interrupting and resuming tranquilizing medicine among schizophrenics. *J. Nerv. Ment. Dis.* 133:303-308, 1961.
2. CAFFEY, E., JR., DIAMOND, L. S., FRANK, T. V., GRASBERGER, J. C., HERMAN, L., KLETT, C. J., & ROTHSTEIN, C.: Discontinuation or reduction of chemotherapy in chronic schizophrenics. *J. Chron. Dis.* 17:347-358, 1964.

3. CATTELL, R. B., & EBER, H. W.: Handbook for the Sixteen Personality Factor Questionnaire. Champaign, Ill., Institute for Personality and Ability Testing, 1957 (1964 Supplementation).

4. DENBER, H. D. B., & BIRD, E. G.: Chlorpromazine in the treatment of mental illness. II. Side effects and relapse rates. Amer. J. Psychiat. 112:465, 1955.

5. ——, & ——: Chlorpromazine in the treatment of mental illness. IV. Final results with analysis of data on 1523 patients. Amer. J. Psychiat. 113:972-978, 1957.

6. DIAMOND, L. S., & MARKS, J. B.: Discontinuance of tranquilizers among chronic schizophrenic patients receiving maintenance dosage. J. Nerv. Ment. Dis. 131:247-251, 1960.

6a. DUBOIS, P. H.: Multivariate Correlation Analysis. New York, Harper, 1957.

7. FORREST, F. M. & FORREST, I. S.: Urine tests for the detection of the newer phenothiazine compounds, drug excretion rates, clinical implications and recent developments in research on phenothiazine drugs. Trans. 4th Veterans Admin. Res. Conf. Chemotherapy in Psychiatry, p. 245, 1960.

8. ——, FORREST, I. S., & MASON, A. S.: Review of rapid urine tests for phenothiazine and related drugs. Amer. J. Psychiat. 118:300-307, 1961.

9. FREEMAN, L. S., & ALSON, E.: Prolonged withdrawal of chlorpromazine in chronic patients. Dis. Nerv. Syst. 23:522-525, 1962.

10. GLESER, G. C., GOTTSCHALK, L. A., & SPRINGER, K. J.: An anxiety measure applicable to verbal samples. Arch. Gen. Psychiat. 5:593-605, 1961.

11. ——, & GOTTSCHALK, L. A.: Personality characteristics of chronic schizophrenics in relationship to sex and current functioning. J. Clin. Psychol. 23:349-354, 1967.

12. GOLDBERG, S. C., SCHOOLER, N. R., & MATTSSON, N. B.: Paranoid and withdrawal symptoms in schizophrenia: differential symptom reduction over time. J. Nerv. Ment. Dis. 145:158-162, 1967.

13. ——, & MATTSSON, N. B.: Schizophrenic subtypes defined by response to drugs and placebo. Dis. Nerv. Syst. 29:153-158, 1968.

14. GOOD, W. W., STERLING, M., & HOLTZMAN, W. H.: Termination of chlorpromazine with schizophrenic patients. Amer. J. Psychiat. 115:443-448, 1958.

15. GOTTSCHALK, L. A., & HAMBRIDGE, G., JR.: Verbal behavior analysis: a systematic approach to the problem of quantifying psychologic processes. J. Proj. Techn. 19:387-409, 1955.

16. ——, GLESER, G. C., DANIELS, R. S., & BLOCK, S.: The speech patterns of schizophrenic patients: a method of assessing relative degree of personal disorganization and social alienation. J. Nerv. Ment. Dis. 127:153-166, 1958.

17. ——, ——, MAGLIOCCO, B., & D'ZMURA, T. L.: Further studies on the speech patterns of schizophrenic patients: Measuring interindividual differences in relative degree of personal disorganization and social alienation. J. Nerv. Ment. Dis. 132:101-113, 1961.

18. ——, SPRINGER, K. J., & GLESER, G. C.: Experiments with a method of assessing the variations in intensity of certain psychologic states occurring during two psychotherapeutic interviews. In Gottschalk, L. A., (Ed.). Comparative Psycholinguistic Analysis of Two Psychotherapeutic Interviews. New York, International Universities Press, 1961.

19. ——, GLESER, G. C., & SPRINGER, K. J.: Three hostility scales applicable to verbal samples. Arch. Gen. Psychiat. 9:254-279, 1963.

20. ——, & GLESER, G. C.: Distinguishing characteristics of the verbal communications of schizophrenic patients. In: Disorders of Communication A.R.N.M.D. Vol. 42, pp. 401-413. Baltimore, Williams and Wilkins, 1964.

21. ——, MAYERSON, P., & GOTTLIEB, A.: The prediction and evaluation of outcome in an emergency brief psychotherapy clinic. J. Nerv. Ment. Dis. 144:77-96, 1967.

22. ——, & GLESER, G. C.: The Measurement of Psychological States Through the Content Analysis of Verbal Behavior. Berkeley, University of California Press, 1969.

23. GREEN, D. E., FORREST, I. S., FORREST, F. M., & SERRA, M. T.: Interpatient variation in chlorpromazine metabolism. *Exp. Med. Surg.* 23:278-287, 1965.

24. Group for the Advancement of Psychiatry, Committee on Research: Psychiatric Research and the Assessment of Change. Vol. VI, Report No. 63. New York, Group for the Advancement of Psychiatry, pp. 357-478, 1966.

25. KAMANO, D. K.: Selective review of effects of discontinuation of drug treatment: Some implications and problems. *Psychol. Rep.* 19:743-749, 1966.

26. LORR, M., O'CONNOR, J. P., & STAFFORD, J. W.: The psychotic reaction profile. *J. Clin. Psychol.* 16:241-245, 1960.

27. ——, KLETT, C. J., McNAIR, D. M., & LASKY, J. J.: The Manual of the Inpatient Multidimensional Psychiatric Scale, Palo Alto, Calif., Consulting Psychologists' Press, 1963.

28. OVERALL, J. E., & GORHAM, D. P.: The brief psychiatric rating scale (BPRS). *Psychol. Rep.* 10:799-812, 1962.

29. SPITZER, R. L., FLEISS, J. L., BURDOCK, E. I., & HARDESTY, A. S.: The mental status schedule; rationale. reliability and validity. *Compr. Psychiat.* 5:384-395, 1964.

30. ——, ——, KERNOHAN, W., LEE, J. D., & BALDWIN, I. T.: Mental status schedule. *Arch. Gen. Psychiat.* 13:448-455, 1965.

31. ——: Immediate available record of mental status examination. *Arch. Gen. Psychiat.* 13:76-78, 1965.

32. ——, FLEISS, J. L., ENDICOTT, J., & COHEN, J.: Mental status schedule: Properties of factor analytically derived scales. *Arch. Gen. Psychiat.* 16:479-493, 1967.

33. WHITTAKER, C. B., & HOY, R. M.: Withdrawal of Perphenazine in chronic schizophrenia. *Brit. J. Psychiat.* 109:422-427, 1963.

34. WORCHEL, P., & BYRNE, D. (Eds.): Personality Change. New York, Wiley, 1964.

38

WORD ASSOCIATIONS IN SCHIZOPHRENICS:
A Ten-Year Follow Up

K. Flekkoy, C. Astrup, and T. Hartmann

INTRODUCTION

In a review of the literature from 1939 to 1955, Yates (1956) concluded that the performance of schizophrenics on verbal tests declines with increasing hospitalization time.

Higgins et al. (1965), presented a free association test to male schizophrenics, and found a significant correlation between length of hospitalization time (age held constant) and reduction in the number of associations shared with the norm-group.

Wynne (1963), in a cross-section study, matched two groups of male schizophrenics on a number of factors. The two groups were hospitalized 2.5 years and 14.4 years respectively. Presenting a free association test, he obtained a significant decrease of primary responses and increase of individual responses in the long time group compared to the short time cases.

Moran et al. (1960), retested 30 chronic schizophrenics after a period of 6 years. The responses on a free association test were scored on conceptual relatedness to the stimulus words. Comparison of test and retest gave no significant difference in performance, nor was there any significant difference between the number of patients doing better and worse on the retest, compared to their own performance on the first test.

The present work is a longitudinal study of changes in associative behavior of 47 chronic schizophrenics over a period of ten years. Based on the literature, we shall expect a deterioration or no significant change in performance.

Reprinted, by permission of author and editor, from *Acta Psychiatrica Scandanavica*, 45:209-216, 1969.

Ten years ago Astrup examined schizophrenic patients with a free association test. 54 of them are staying at Gaustad Hospital at present. Six
of the patients refused to be tested again, and one had developed senile
dementia. Thus 47 patients completed the retest; 28 males, 19 females.
Flekkoy carried out the retests assisted by Hartmann.

Present age, age at first admission, total time of hospitalization and
years of education are presented in Table 1.

The group includes 31 paranoid cases (13 females), 10 hebephrenics
(4 females) and 6 catatonics (2 females). The material should thus be

TABLE 1

PRESENT AGE, AGE AT FIRST ADMISSION, TIME OF HOSPITALIZATION AND EDUCATION IN YEARS (N = 47)

	Present age	Age at first admission	Time of hospitalization	Years of education
Mean	56.8 ± 13.5	33.0 ± 12.0	17.9 ± 10.9	8.4 ± 2.4
Median	58.0	30.0	11.8	8.0
Range	31 — 83	19 — 65	2.6 — 40	7 — 16

representative of a chronic schizophrenic population attainable for
testing.

On the first examination, 30 percent of the patients received psychotropic drugs, while 92 percent get such treatment now. None of them
are treated with ECT in conjunction with testing. The mean time between test and retest is 10.7 years (median: 10.7 years, range: 9.5-11.6
years). Of this 9.1 years is mean time of hospitalization (median: 10.3
years, range: 3.3-11.6 years). The mean hospitalization time before the
first testing is 8.5 years, with a range from 0 to 30 years. 55 percent were
hospitalized 0 to 5 years, with the rest falling mainly between 5 and 10
years.

METHOD

Fifty nouns were presented orally to the patients, with the instruction
to say the first word that occurred to them as quickly as possible. They
were told to answer with only one word. If necessary, they were reminded
of this in the first few trials. Having finished the list, the stimulus words
were presented again, and the patients were asked to recall their associations.

Wrong reproductions were noted. Reaction time is registered with a stop-watch, measuring in units of .1 second, and gives the time from the presentation of the stimulus word to the first word of the response. For each person, mean and median reaction time for all of the 50 stimulus words are used.

The quality of responses was coded according to the same principles at test and retest (Astrup (1962)). "Higher verbal associations" are one word responses, corresponding to the common and normal responses in the Kent-Rosanoff test. "Primitive associations" are for instance only sound resembling, repetitions or derivatives of the stimulus word. "Incoherent associations" are reactions with no understandable, or only remote, connections to the stimulus words. "Echolalia responses" are "yes," "no" or mere repetitions of the stimulus words. "Multiword responses" are reactions containing more than one word.

Astrup scored the first test, while Flekkoy scored the retest without knowledge of previous performance. With independent scoring of the retest, the correlation (Pearson r) between Flekkoy and Astrup was .99 for the higher, .89 for the primitive and .99 for the incoherent associations. The coefficients of reliability are thus high, and the other measures give no scoring problems. As there is a ten years interval between the tests, we cannot expect "improvement" due to practice. "Improvement in performance" means an increase in the number of higher associations, a decrease of primitive, incoherent and multiword responses, wrong reproductions and reaction times.

A parametric mean test, corrected for correlation, is used in computing the significance of the differences between performance on test and retest; and a t-test is used in analyzing the relationship between performance and a) diagnostic category, b) education, and c) sex. The first- and second-order partial correlation coefficients are computed by means of formulas presented in Guilford (1965). Differences from the null-hypothesis on and beyond the 5 percent level are considered significant.

RESULTS

Table 2 shows that the performance tends to improve from test to retest: reaction times are shorter, the number of higher associations increases, and primitive, incoherent and echolalic responses and wrong reproductions decrease. An exception is the category of multiword responses, where the level of performance is the same as before. On three of the categories the improvement is significant: Higher association (p<.03, echolalia (p<.03) and wrong reproduction (p<.002). If the patients are grouped in "improved" and "not improved" in comparison to their former performance, a chi-square analysis shows that a significantly higher number have improved in the categories higher association (p<.02) and median reaction time (p<.02). The tendency to improve is also the rule for the rest of the categories, except for multiword, where the number of improved and not improved cases is exactly the same. Consequently, the differences between test and retest cannot be due to an improvement of a small part of the sample, but must be a general tendency. For the same individual, improvement on one measure can be correlated with improvement on another. A person who produces more higher associations also tends to respond faster (p<.05).

TABLE 2

RESULTS ON TEST AND RETEST (N = 47)

Categories	Test	Retest
Reaction time (mean)	5.7 + 3.4	5.0 + 2.7
Reaction time (median)	4.6 + 4.2	3.9 + 2.3
Higher ass. (mean)	24.4 + 15.3	29.1 + 14.8
Primitive ass. (mean)	12.1 + 15.2	10.5 + 11.7
Echolalia (mean)	16.8 + 16.6	12.3 + 13.5
Multiword (mean)	11.4 + 14.1	11.8 + 14.2
Wrong reproduction (mean)	3.5 + 22.8	2.3 + 21.6
Incoherent (mean)	18.6 + 14.5	13.3 + 27.4

In order to find variables which are relevant for the present performance, a second order partial correlation analysis was carried out between the individual measures and the following variables: a) time of hospitalization, b) present age, and c) age at first admission.

The following results were obtained: neither hospitalization time nor age at first admission is significantly correlated with the individual measures.

Age, however, is positively and significantly correlated with echolalia ($r = .3921$, $p<.001$), and with an increase in mean reaction time ($r = .3268$, $p<.009$). The correlations with the remaining categories are not significant.

As a more direct test of the relationship between hospitalization time and performance, a first order partial correlation analysis was carried out between the change in performance between test and retest and the length of hospitalization time between test and retest. The age factor cannot be included, because *all* the patients are about 10 years older than they were at the first examination. A correlation between change of performance and increase of age could only demonstrate the relationship within each ten-year of age-span. No significant effect of time in hospital could be demonstrated in relation to associative performance. Correlations of age at first admission and change of performance on each of the measures were all near zero.

Because of the small number of cases in each of the catatonic (10) and hebephrenic (6) groups, these groups were combined, and the total material divided into paranoid (31) and non-paranoid (16) cases. The performance of the two groups is presented in Table 3.

TABLE 3

PERFORMANCE ON TEST AND RETEST OF THE PARANOID (N = 31) AND NON-PARANOID SCHIZOPHRENICS (N = 16)

Categories	Paranoid		Non-paranoid	
	Test	Retest	Test	Retest
Reaction time (mean)	6.0	4.9	5.0	5.3
Reaction time (median)	4.9	3.7	3.6	3.9
Higher ass. (mean)	24.7	30.3	23.9	26.8
Primitive ass. (mean)	9.9	10.5	16.3	10.4
Echolalia (mean)	17.4	10.5	16.0	15.7
Multiword (mean)	12.3	11.3	9.8	13.3
Incoherent (mean)	3.6	3.9	3.3	0.9
Wrong reproduction (mean)	16.3	13.5	23.1	13.1

For paranoid schizophrenics, the improvement of performance is significant for higher association ($p < .01$) and echolalic responses ($p < .001$). For non-paranoid cases, only the number of wrong reproductions is significantly lower in the retest ($p < .01$). The paranoid cases are contributing most to the general improvement. But also for the non-paranoid group the tendency towards improvement is predominant.

If the paranoid schizophrenics have improved more than the non-paranoid cases, they should show significantly greater change in performance on the individual measures. The general tendency does show that the paranoids improve most. For reproduction only, is the difference between paranoids and non-paranoids significant ($p < .05$), but in this case in favor of the non-paranoid schizophrenics.

Comparisons of the two groups on the individual measures on test and retest show no significant difference, but the paranoids tend to perform best. Thus, the general tendency is that the best performance is found among the paranoid cases, which also show most improvement.

The effect of education on the present performance and on change in performance was examined by dividing the total material into patients with up to 9 years of school and patients with further education, and comparing their performance on the individual measures.

Only one significant difference was found on the present performance: patients of the first group produced a mean of 13.2 primitive responses, while the other group gave only 4.4. The difference is significant beyond the 5 percent level. The general tendency is a lower level of performance (reaction times included) among patients of the first group compared to the other.

Comparison of these groups on change in performance gives a few more details: the decline in mean number of wrong reproductions is 1.9 for the first group, and 13.4 for the second $(p<.01)$. For the first group, the increase in mean number of higher associations is 1.4, while it is 11.8 for the second $(p<.02)$. Comparisons of the other measures demonstrate no significant differences, but the tendency is always towards greater improvement of performance in patients with education beyond the level of 9 years.

An examination of the relationship between sex, present performance and change in performance, gives the following results: males have 11.1 (mean), wrong reproductions on the retest, females 16.6 $(p<.05)$. This is the only measure revealing a significant difference. There is a general tendency for men to improve their performance more than females do, but on no point do the differences reach a level of significance.

DISCUSSION

The expectations based on the literature were not confirmed, presumably because of the following points of discrepancy between the present work and the studies quoted: a) method, b) patient material, and c) scoring of performance.

Only Moran et al. use the same longitudinal method as employed in the present study. The other researchers utilize cross-section methods. Presumably, their long time patients are a more pathological group than their short time cases; and because of this, they demonstrate a reduced performance-level.

Scoring of performance is qualitative in the work of Moran et al., and partly so in the present work, while the other two cited studies relate the performance quantitatively to norm samples. The discrepancy be-

tween Moran et al. and the present study must be attributed to differences in patient material and scoring of performance.

The two most outstanding findings of this study are a) a rise in performance-level on almost every measure, and b) a positive and significant
partial correlation between age, number of echolalic responses and mean
reaction time.

The first result indicates a tendency to improvement over time, while
the second means that the older patients produce more echolalic responses
and react more slowly than the young ones. In spite of increasing age,
the group as a whole gives fewer echolalic reactions and shorter RT's on
the retest.

We calculated correlations between hospitalization time and present
performance, and hospitalization time between test and retest and change
in performance during the same period of time. The partial correlations
are all close to zero. This indicates that hospitalization is not related to
improvement of performance.

The paranoid group was found to perform best on test and retest, and
to have the most marked improvement. A comparison shows that the
paranoids are the oldest: mean age 59 years for paranoid and 52 years for
non-paranoids. Age at first admission is 36 years for the paranoids, 32
years for the others. The figures for total time in hospital are 17 and 20
years, respectively. None of the differences are significant.

Mean number of years in school is almost alike: 8.4 years for paranoids
and 8.7 years for non-paranoids. The males of this material tended to
improve most, but this factor does not make any difference: 58 percent
of the paranoid and 63 percent of the non-paranoid cases are males. Consequently the only essential difference left is the diagnosis. The findings
seem to support the clinical experience that the paranoid schizophrenics
tend to resist general deterioration better than catatonic and hebephrenic
cases.

The relatively higher level of performance of patients with education
beyond 9 years, may be an effect of more verbal experience among these
cases. The marked tendency towards improvement also seems to indicate
better resources of personality and a higher ability to profit from modern
hospital treatment.

The improvement of males compared to females presumably reflects the
positive correlation between increase of age and decrease of performance,
as the females are generally older than the males.

The most plausible cause of the rise in performance-level is the increased use of psychopharmaca: 30 percent received such treatment 10
years ago as compared to 92 percent at the present time. All patients have

been under prolonged treatment with psychotropic drugs. This has probably counteracted deterioration and even improved many patients.

SUMMARY

The present work is a longitudinal study of changes in associative performance of 47 chronic schizophrenics in a 10-year period.

At test and retest, they were given a free association test. Their performance is scored as 1) associations of good quality (higher associations), 2) primitive associations, 3) incoherent associations, 4) echolalia, 5) multiword responses, 6) wrong reproductions, and 7) reaction time (mean and median).

The main results are: a) significant increase in number of higher associations and decrease in echolalic responses and wrong reproductions. On the other categories there is a tendency towards improvement, except for multiword responses, where the result now is about the same as before. b) Hospitalization time and age at first admission do not correlate with the individual measures of performance. Chronological age is positively and significantly correlated with increase in number of echolalic responses and increase in mean reaction time. c) Improvement is most marked for the paranoid schizophrenics, but there is a general tendency towards improvement within the catatonic and hebephrenic group as well. d) Patients with more than 9 years of school improve more than patients who ended their education on that level. The improvement of performance is related to extensive use of psychopharmaca in the test-retest period.

ACKNOWLEDGMENTS

This investigation received financial support from the World Health Organization and the Scottish Rite Committee on Research in Schizophrenia.

REFERENCES

ASTRUP, C. (1962): Schizophrenia: Conditional reflex studies. Springfield, Ill.

GUILFORD, J. P. (1965): Fundamental statistics in psychology and education, 4th ed. New York.

HIGGINS, J., MEDNICK, S. A., & PHILIP, F. J. (1965): Associative disturbance as a function of chronicity in schizophrenia. J. Abnorm. Soc. Psychol. 70, 451-452.

MORAN, L. J., GORHAM, D. R., & HOLTZMAN, W. H. (1960): Vocabulary knowledge and usage of schizophrenic subjects: a six-year follow up. J. Abnorm. Soc. Psychol. 61, 246-254.

WYNNE, R. D. (1963): The influence of hospitalization on the verbal behavior of chronic schizophrenics. Brit. J. Psychiat. 109, 380-389.

YATES, A. J. (1956): The use of vocabulary in the measurement of intellectual deterioration—a review. J. Ment. Sci. 102, 409-440.

39

STUDIES IN SPEECH DISORDER IN SCHIZOPHRENIA

A. D. Forrest, A. J. Hay, and A. W. Kushner

PART I

INTRODUCTION

Most clinical psychiatrists would agree that many but not all schizophrenic subjects show abnormalities in the field of language. Many use neologisms, i.e. new words for old referents, and some chronic patients talk in a more or less private language which at times degenerates into a word salad. The following features have been noted in the schizophrenic's verbal productions—alliteration, condensation, over-inclusiveness and the personal distortion of the symbol—referent tie. Stuart Chase said: "The point of every discussion is to find the referent. When it is found emotional factors dissolve in mutual understanding." Psychiatrists often assume that they have identified the referent which ties in with the symbol the patient is using, but sometimes the patient uses new symbols, as "Bill" did the other week when he astonished the other group members by announcing that he was "troubled by warpations and distressed by ignorances."

This has been the focus of our research—the examination of the symbol-referent connection in our schizophrenic patients. We have been concerned with semantics, and we have not considered syntactics nor the more philosophical problem of whether disorder of speech merely reflects a more basic disorder of thinking.

From a research analytic viewpoint, Davie and Freeman (1961) seem to regard the perceptual defect leading to the disordered thinking as the primary mechanism. They emphasize that the patterning of perception is an ego function, and quote a patient whose thought processes seemed

Reprinted, by permission of author and editor, from: *The British Journal of Psychiatry*, 115:833-841, 1969.

to be unprotected from the effect of incoming sensory signals. Davie and Freeman suggest that Freud's (1900) concepts can illuminate the two main varieties of thought disorder: (*i*) the failure to sustain logical thought for more than a few seconds, and (*ii*) the sustained but unintelligible flow of thought (as expressed in words). The first variety depends on a failure of the perceptual process, whilst the latter depends on a failure of the representational process, i.e. a failure to use verbal symbols in relation to their normal referents.

Bleuler (1950) also seemed to consider the defect in thinking as the primary defect; he postulated a weakness of association, in consequence of which fears and wishes rather than logical connection control the trend of thought.

Freeman et al. (1965), in their *Studies on Psychosis* remark (p. 97) that psychoanalytic studies in general confirm the views of Bleuler, but they remind us that it is only through the defects in verbalization that we gain insight into the state of the thought processes.

The present authors wish to evade this controversy about thought and speech. Thinking occurs without spoken speech, though many people do "talk to themselves" when concentrating. Thinking can also occur without reference to verbal symbols, i.e. mathematical or problem-solving thinking. There is, in fact, evidence that thinking involving visual symbols is also disturbed in schizophrenia (Weckowicz, 1957; Johannsen et al., 1964) so the problem becomes more complex as soon as one looks at it. Thinking, therefore, whether based on the manipulation of visual or verbal symbols, may be disturbed in schizophrenia. Our research interest has focused on spoken speech, since it has such clear reference for the clinical practice of psychiatry. Like other orthodox British psychiatrists, we ask the patient to explain proverbs, or to interpret the "donkey story" or the "cowboy and dog story." Sometimes these stratagems work. Some time ago one of us asked a fairly chronic patient the meaning of "A rolling stone gathers no moss" and got this answer: "A rolling stone is a new moon which is other side and blue on the far side where are the Russians." Harry Stack Sullivan (1953) always maintained that schizophrenic comment was not stupid but simply rather oblique—and that adjective fits. At this clinical level, then, the fact of disturbed speech in many schizophrenic subjects needs no elaboration.

The following dialogue is a transcript of a taped interview with a fifty-eight-year-old male ex school teacher:

Q. "What does the word winter mean to you?"
A. "Well, in winter we win the T.R., the tell-tale notes where there was discord in Ayr re erring, I suppose, but I wouldn't like to say, but there

was that tendency for error and we had to be going down and out helping to record poverty."

Q. "If what you have just said is winter, what does summer mean to you?"

A. "Well, the winter is coming round to be the summer and everything is improving, and winning T.R. will mean setting prize competitions with tartan glove governments and that will make us ready when we can make up our minds about the winter, about the winning of news we will be able to sum the m-e-r and put that to the culmination of the winter to better information than the summer."

Q. "What are these things?"

A. "Keys."

Q. "What are they used for?"

A. "For opening doors more or less, lids maybe, but mostly doors."

Q. "What is this?"

A. "A cigarette."

Q. "What does one do with a cigarette?"

A. "One puts it in the mouth, lights it up and smokes it" (pause) "and it gets in key with thought."

Q. "What is a shop?"

A. (Pause) "Well, I suppose a shop was where somebody who couldn't get past the bank examiners who had to come down through the banks and shown a shop at some borderline examination shopping bar. However, somebody had broken down the manifold and over-claimed in somebody's life and had got in a muddle and we think scouts should be called in to organize their sorts of imposition bar migraines as in connection with the shops."

The problem of speech dysfunction in schizophrenia has received attention from other psychoanalytic writers (Ferreira, 1960; Szasz, 1957) and researchers interested in the possible basis of the illness in faulty or anomalous communicational systems within families (Haley, 1959; Bateson, Jackson, Haley and Weakland, 1956). Szasz (1957) is interested in the acquisition of Goldstein's "abstract attitude" and the failure to develop this attitude in schizophrenic subjects. Deriving from Fairbairn (1952) regarding the internalization of early objects, the association of objects and the later process of learning how to relinquish them and acquire new ones, Szasz suggests that without secure relationships the child cannot "acquire objects." One of the central problems for the schizophrenic is that he is deficient in internal objects, and the loss of external objects by bereavement or separation is liable to provoke a crisis. Szasz suggests that there is a parallelism in the growing child between the development of object relations and the increasing capacity for abstraction. The formation of internal objects favors the process of symbol formation, and allows the ego to deal with external objects not only as "immediate objects" but also as abstractions, represented by symbols. To quote Szasz regarding schizophrenic patients: "They do not treat symbols as abstractions but rather regard them as concrete, real objects." And again: "Not only do internal objects potentiate the acquisition of symbols but the learning of symbols further facilitates the ego's relationship." (Cf. Cherry (1966) *On Human Communication*.) Ferreira (1960) propounds the theory that the peculiarities of the schizophrenic language attain a high degree of comprehensibility if apprehended in the context of the basic relationship to the mother-figure. He suggests that we must consider the semantics of the language and the context of human relationship in which the language is used, i.e. the pragmatics. Semantics is the discipline concerned with the study of the meaning of words. Ferreira suggests that schizophrenics alter the usual relationships between the symbol, i.e. the word, and the referent, i.e. the object; they invent personal words (neologisms) or use ordinary words to relate to extraordinary referents (technical neologisms). He suggests that they do this because of the uneven and asymmetrical relationship with the mother-figure, within which relationship and about which relationship the schizophrenic is for ever speaking. Unable to comment assertively on the situation, or alternatively to leave the situation, the schizophrenic must carefully censor his messages so that no element of his wish for autonomy or his anger at the superintendent of his destiny is revealed. The schizophrenic creates a language foreign enough not to be understood and private enough to allow him the expression of some feelings, if not loudly at least safely.

The following dialogue is from a taped interview with a 27-year-old male patient who seems to show both loss of abstract attitude and the intrusion of perceptual referents.

Q. "Can you tell me what is winter?"
A. "Well, that has something to do with those are just dirty isometrics and this something to be done with eager abilities. Winter is something to do with the frost, snows, seasons of the year. It's acutely cold and very benefacting to wintertimes with cold eh noses and the usual things we look at the street windows eh, sort of sickening waste of time, cold rain coming down past the window, eh cold impact coming off the window, the cold glass being glittered with sort of harvest combine thanksgiving going on round about the trees."
Q. "If this is winter, what is summer?"
A. "Summer is boiling hot harsh days, dry days, perspiring skin, damp, burning, binding, blending, providing hot amoebic conditions for visions of eh disapparelment or what is thought to be observed and musical symbols of trees and that becoming depleted with em hot outstanding reasonatogen tones."

Q. "What are these things?"

A. "That's a keyring surmounted by a special lockproof keyring with metal and brass keys for different face plate locks."

Q. "What does one do with the key?"

A. "You can get at obtainable places like eh drawers and sheds. That's usually what you can get at obtainable with. You can get at obtainable things in drawers, like knives and cutlery and cabbage knives."

Q. "And what is this thing?"

A. "That's a cigarette."

Q. "What are cigarettes used for?"

A. "They are usually used, you can use them for trade with natives, so I believe, or um in this country you can use them for smoking."

Q. "What is a shop?"

A. "A shop is a place where things are sold over the counter, guaranteed they're in the shop to be sold for use by the public for fixed prices as seen in the window, as an apple and an orange. Beyond the fixed price is what's thought as a controlled politic and that might be something that costs practically nothing, and that is something to do presents, metal bodies, and that is something like cars or something like that, and imagine getting an electric train for millionaire in America and see what happens and write to him or something like that."

DISCUSSION

The justification for publishing these transcripts is perhaps to convince the sceptics about the "reality" of schizophrenic speech disorder. The qualities in such speech that seem most obviously different from normal speech are, (a) the "wandering" quality—open-ended questions result in free-associative, over-inclusive monologue, and (b) the personalized use of symbols so that the usual symbol-referent tie is distorted. Ferreira (1960) has suggested that this obscurity in the schizophrenic's speech may have a purposive, defensive function. If the object is to achieve the maximum of emotional expression with the minimum risk of being understood, then mothers should not understand their schizophrenic sons, etc. In fact, our experience is that they often talk in rather the same way. We propose to examine this aspect in more detail by organizing a mothers' and sons' group and tape-recording the discourse. Sommer et al. (1960) investigating whether there was a speech form common to all schizophrenics drew a negative conclusion, and commented that schizophrenics have just as much difficulty in understanding each other as do their doctors.

PART II

INTRODUCTION

In the first part of this paper we reviewed some of the analytic views on disordered speech in schizophrenia. In this part we wish to make brief reference to the "organic" hypotheses and report two studies of our own.

The first hypothesis is that the schizophrenic subject has an unstable perceptual organization which can easily be overloaded by incoming signals because of a relative failure to monitor out irrelevant signals. From the point of view of psychological research such a hypothesis is supported by the work of Johannsen et al. (1964), Weckowicz (1957) and Bannister (1963). In a clinical paper, McGhie and Chapman (1961) described the difficulties reported by their patients in the perception of spoken speech. Thus, patient 19 said: "I can concentrate quite well on what people are saying if they talk simply. It's when they go on with long sentences that I lose the meanings. It just becomes a lot of words that I would need to string together to make sense." A patient of ours spent almost the whole cocktail party sitting in the cloak-room—he said that when he went in to the main room he kept getting confused by fragments of the other speakers' conversations and could not "take in" what was being said to him.

The capacity to listen to and to recall spoken speech seems to depend on the capacity of the subject to monitor out irrelevant signals and to use contextual clues to provide an anticipatory set. In 1950, Miller and Selfridge reported an experiment involving normal (student) volunteers on the effect of contextual constraint on the recall of spoken speech. They used different degrees of contextual constraint from nonsense assemblies to full text, and also different lengths of word lists, from ten to forty. They found, perhaps not surprisingly, that the recall varied with the list length and also with the degree of approximation to full text. Lawson et al. (1964) repeated this on normal and schizophrenic subjects and found that the latter showed relatively little improvement in recall with increasing degrees of contextual constraint. We repeated the work of Lawson et al., using a randomized presentation procedure (Kushner et al., 1967), and found that even with the nonsense assemblies the schizophrenics did much worse than the "normals," and that while both improved with increasing degrees of contextual constraint the "normals" did not improve significantly more than the schizophrenics. We think that our failure to repeat the work of Lawson et al. may lie in the different relationship of the patients to the experimenters. Lawson's subjects had all had a good deal of interviewing, and one imagines that they had established a relationship with the experimenters. Our subjects were taken from the admission wards, and many had had no prior contact with the experimenters. However, Raeburn and Tong (1968) have likewise been unable to replicate the work of Lawson et al.

A different hypothesis is one which emphasizes the overlap between organic and schizophrenic speech disorder and uses Goldstein's (1948) concept of the loss of "abstract attitude" as the bridging mechanism. Thus, Stengel (1947, 1964) has commented on the similarities between the speech of some schizophrenic patients and some non-aphasic organic subjects. Allison (1962) noted the personalized element in the speech of some subjects with senile dementia. For example: "Occasionally those patients would produce the correct names but add some personal reference. For instance, I showed a patient a purse—instead of naming it, he said, 'not mine'; a coin—'it's money, it's not mine'; a tie—'your tie,' etc. . . . This kind of response can be regarded as a manifestation of what Goldstein (1948) described as concrete behavior. These patients are excessively tied to the situation." Again, Stengel (1964) quotes Curran and Schilder (1935) as noting the similarities between the speech disorder of dementia and schizophrenic as well as dysphagic language disorders. Paterson (1944) emphasized the dysphasic characteristics of the speech of the demented subject. Clarke et al. (1958) observed a similar type of language disorder in a case of Korsakov's syndrome, and described it as a kind of confabulation in the sphere of language. It should perhaps be mentioned that a similar nominal dysphagia has often been reported in patients having E.C.T. (Rochford and Williams, 1962). There is, in fact, a real overlap in the speech pathology of organic illness (senile, presenile and other dementias) and schizophrenia. Zangwill (1964) in a paper in the symposium on "Psychopathology of Dementia" took the view that non-aphasic speech disorder in dementia probably did reflect focal lesions. Zangwill questions Goldstein's view (1939, 1948) that there is a fundamental disorder in all dementias, namely a loss of "abstract attitude." Zangwill interprets this as "an incapacity to deal with objects at the conceptual level and an undue dependence on their immediate, concrete attributes." Clinical experience suggests that those schizophrenics who show speech disorder very often also manifest this loss of "abtsract attitude." We decided to explore this factor of the "abstract attitude" in "normal" and schizophrenic subjects.

MATERIALS AND METHODS

We constructed a list of thirteen paired questions; the first member of each pair is supposed to evoke a concrete response, while the second requires the use of abstractions or concepts for an adequate answer (see Appendix I). As a preliminary, the subject was given instructions to try and answer the questions to his or her own satisfaction, and to raise a hand when finished. An example was given: (1) What is a ship? (1a) What is the Royal Navy? The experimenter supplied the answer and explained it where necessary. Then the whole test was tape-recorded so that the answers could be scored later. The subjects were not required to write anything down. Immediately after the test, the subjects were asked to complete Raven's Matrices and the Mill Hill Vocabulary Test.

The subjects were 25 "normals" working in or associated with the Royal Edinburgh Hospital. They comprised nurses, cleaners, orderlies, medical students and secretaries. The patients were all schizophrenics; for this purpose defined as an illness characterized by passivity feelings, auditory hallucinations, disorders in the possession and content of thought. Not all patients showed all these symptoms at the time of testing, but all had at one time experienced at least two of the four symptom-categories.

Scoring was performed by a panel of three psychiatrists and one psychologist. Each answer was scored as concrete, abstract, or wrong (see Appendix II). On the protocols, we tried to note irrelevancies and the intrusion of personalized material. The results have been organized to show the concrete and abstract replies as percentages of the total number of answers given and are shown in Tables 1-4.

DISCUSSION

When we constructed our list of paired questions, we thought that we could answer them all, and we have been astonished at the difficulty most of our normal subjects had to evoke abstract replies with the questions scheduled. We have since read in *Studies in Communication* (1955) a passage by Professor Ayer in which he comments that the question "What is time?" would be likely to evoke the most extreme difficulty in the person questioned. It is also clear the verbal skill as measured by the Mill Hill Vocabulary Test is more closely related to the percentage of abstract responses than is the IQ from Raven's Matrices. This might be construed to mean that if you can talk well then you can answer difficult questions. We think that our questions have some bearing on Goldstein's "abstract attitude," and that results on this test are as much tied to intelligence as they are to whether the subject happens to be a hospial orderly or a hospitalized schizophrenic.

Two other points of interest emerge. Patients actually showing schizophrenic speech disturbance at the time of testing were virtually untestable. They made some sort of showing on the concrete questions, but on

TABLE 1

MANN-WHITNEY U TEST: EFFECT OF INTELLIGENCE ON PERCENTAGE ABSTRACT RESPONSES IN NORMAL SUBJECTS

Above-average IQ		Below-average IQ	
% Abstract Responses	Rank Order	% Abstract Responses	Rank Order
69.2	23	8.0	4
53.9	21	19.2	9.5
53.9	21	23.1	14
38.4	19	11.5	6
40.0	20	4.2	2
26.9	15	8.4	5
53.9	21	19.2	9.5
20.0	12.5	20.0	12.5
29.1	17	4.0	1
19.2	9.5	4.3	2
19.2	9.5	16.0	8
28.6	16	12.0	7
34.6	18		

$n_2 = 13$ $R_2 = 222.5$ $n_1 = 12$ $R_1 = 81.5$

The hypothesis is that normal subjects above the 50th percentile will not perform significantly be:ter than those below it in the percentage abstract responses.

$$U = n_1 n_2 + \frac{n_1(n_1 + 1)}{2} - R_1 = 24.5$$

Therefore $p < 0.01$ (one-tailed test) and we must reject the hypothesis.

the abstract they rambled off on to a personalized monologue. And even subjects who at the time were speaking more or less normally revealed themselves by the number of oblique answers. Here are two examples: (1) "A clock is a component of an object used for telling the time." (1a) "Time is the stated earth factor or factors—you would use it to devise time limits to a person's whole life." (4) "A garage is an object of protection used by the public for protection of cars." (4a) "To reach by scientific research a method to reach decisions into the factors for exploring space."

GENERAL DISCUSSION OF PARTS I AND II

Our study in this field has, over a period of three years, involved taped interviews with organic patients (6), "normals" (33) and schizophrenics (39). Patients who were excited or ecstatic were usually overinclusive (in Payne's sense), but the most overinclusive tape in the verbal test of

TABLE 2

MANN-WHITNEY U TEST: EFFECT OF INTELLIGENCE ON PERCENTAGE
ABSTRACT RESPONSES IN SCHIZOPHRENIC SUBJECTS

Above-average IQ		Below-average IQ	
% Abstract Responses	Rank Order	% Abstract Responses	Rank Order
50.0	21	30.8	18
46.1	20	16.0	8
38.5	18	30.0	17
43.1	19	4.5	1
23.1	12.5	23.1	12.5
21.7	11	20.0	10
		28.0	14
		28.8	15
		29.3	16
		8.4	5
		15.3	7
		8.0	4
		4.7	2
		5.8	3
		18.8	9
		10.0	6

$n_1 = 6$ $R_1 = 105.5$ $n_2 = 16$ $R_2 = 147.5$

The hypothesis is that schizophrenic subjects above the 50th percentile will not perform significantly better than those below it in the percentage abstract responses.

$$U = n_1 n_2 + \frac{n_1(n_1 + 1)}{2} - R_1 = 11.5$$

Therefore $p < 0.01$ (one-tailed test) and we must reject the hypothesis.

abstracting function was one recorded by a male nurse. By contrast, some of the most negative and monosyllabic tapes were those recorded from normal subjects with modest intelligence. Some organic patients, especially those showing subacute dysmnestic syndromes, do "confabulate in the field of language" (Clarke et al., 1958).

This study has convinced us that the use of proverb interpretation to demonstrate thought disorder or loss of the abstracting function is of little value unless corrections are made for intelligence (cf. Gorham,

TABLE 3

MANN-WITHNEY U TEST: COMPARISON OF PERCENTAGE ABSTRACT
RESPONSES BETWEEN ALL NORMAL AND ALL SCHIZOPHRENIC SUBJECTS

Schizophrenics		Normals	
% Abstract Responses	Rank Order	% Abstract Responses	Rank Order
50.0	43	69.2	47
46.1	42	53.9	45
38.5	39	53.9	45
43.1	41	38.4	38
23.1	27	40.0	40
21.7	25	26.9	29
30.8	36	53.9	45
16.0	15.5	20.0	23
30.0	35	29.1	33
4.5	4	19.2	19.5
23.1	27	19.2	19.5
20.0	23	28.6	31
28.0	30	34.6	37
28.8	32	8.0	7.5
29.3	34	19.2	19.5
8.4	9.5	23.1	27
15.3	14	11.5	12
8.0	7.5	4.2	2
4.7	5	8.4	9.5
5.8	6	19.2	19.5
18.8	17	20.0	23
10.0	11	4.0	1
		4.3	3
		16.0	15.5
		12.0	13

$n_1 = 22$ $R_1 = 523.5$ $n_2 = 25$ $R_2 = 604.5$

The hypothesis is that schizophrenic subjects will not perform significantly different from normals in the percentage of abstract responses.

$$U = n_1 n_2 + \frac{n_1(n_1 + 1)}{2} - R_1 = 279.5$$

$$U^1 = n_1 n_2 + \frac{n_2(n_2 + 1)}{2} - R_2 = 270.5$$

$$Z = U^1 - \frac{n_1 n_2}{2} \Bigg/ \sqrt{\frac{(n_1 n_2)(n_1 + n_2 + 1)}{12}} = -0.09574$$

Therefore $p = .4641$ (one-tailed test) and we must accept the hypothesis.

1956; Shimkunas et al., 1967). We also wonder whether the central meaning of a proverb is not more "culture-bound" than psychiatrists realize. Here in Edinburgh, the proverb "People who live in glass houses should not throw stones" is definitely an import from the south, whereas "It's a case of the pot calling the kettle back" is rooted in the local culture. A patient from the West Indies told us on admission, when she was in a very disturbed state, that she was "the fifth wheel of the wagon." When partially recovered from her acute paranoid schizophrenic episode, she said that this related to a local proverb which her grandmother had taught her.

TABLE 4

Comparison of Percentage Abstract Responses for Different Groups Expresed as p Values

Description of Groups	p value— Mann-Whitney Non-Parametric Statistics*
Normal and schizophrenic subjects above 50th percentile	$p < 0.01$
Normal and schizophrenic subjects at or below 50th percentile	$p < 0.01$
All normal and schizophrenic subjects...	$p = .4641$
* One-tailed test.	

Another aspect which impressed us throughout is the difference in responses to "closed, concrete" questions and "open, abstract" questions. This applied least to "normals," more to organics, and most of all to schizophrenic subjects.

The overlap in phenomenology between schizophrenics and organics is quite real, but is perhaps just another example of a "common end path," analogous to the presence of auditory hallucinations in schizophrenic and organic states. The biological question whether, as Ferreira (1960) suggests, the schizophrenic masks his utterances in a defensive way so as not to be too clearly understood cannot yet be answered.

The clinical impression that patients and relatives share a common idiosyncrasy of language was not borne out entirely in our experience with a group of mothers and sons extending over five months. The majority (three out of five) of the mothers were protective, and the relationship was a restrictive, symbiotic one. The mothers therefore "spoke for" their sons, and these sons mostly kept quiet. Eric Berne in his book *Games*

People Play (1966) suggests that if one were living in such a family the only game left is that of playing schizophrenic.

Our tentative conclusions might be stated thus: (1) the disturbed speech of adult schizophrenics is somehow related to abnormal learning experience in families where communication is often devious and contradictory; (2) the disturbed speech has a defensive, personalized quality (cf. Ferreira, 1960); it often also has an overinclusive quality (cf. Payne, 1962), and it is also associated, we believe, with a relative deficiency in the abstracting function (cf. Szasz, 1957); (3) patients with mental subnormality and organic defects also show a loss of abstracting function; we think that the degree of ego organization may be the intermediate mechanism which underlies the defect in abstracting function shown by the schizophrenic (Szasz refers to the number and quality of relationships to internal objects—a statement about the same area but from a Fairbairnian viewpoint); if the capacity to abstract is related to "ego strength" one should expect such a deficiency in psychopathic personality disorders; (4) we feel that schizophrenic speech disturbance is psychogenic in origin and not evidence of organic deterioration, and base our view largely on the observation that it can, to some extent, be switched on or off, depending on the questions and the context.

SUMMARY

1. Some of the literature on schizophrenic speech disorder has been reviewed, and the question whether this phenomenon should be viewed as an organic defect or a biological defense has been discussed.

2. Transcripts from interviews with two schizophrenic patients have been presented to illuminate the differential response to "closed, concrete" questions and "open, abstract" questions.

3. The results of our attempt to replicate the work of Lawson et al. (1964) on ten "normal" and ten schizophrenic subjects have been reported. There was no significant difference as regards the effect of greater degrees of contextual constraint.

4. A verbal test aimed at discriminating between concrete and abstract responses was given to 25 "normals" and twenty-two schizophrenic subjects. The results suggested that the capacity to respond abstractly was related to intelligence, not to diagnostic category.

ACKNOWLEDGMENTS

We should like to express our thanks to colleagues who allowed us access to patients; to Miss K. Bruce, Matron, and Miss C. Tracey, Domestic Supervisor, who were of such great help to us in arranging interviews with staff members; to Miss N. McDonald, who helped us with the statistics; and to Miss A. Guise, who has transcribed the manuscript.

REFERENCES

ALLISON, R. S. (1962). *The Senile Brain.* London: Edward Arnold.

AYER, A. J. (1955). *Studies in Communication.* London: Secker and Warburg.

BANNISTER, D. (1963). "The genesis of schizophrenic thought disorder: a serial invalidation hypothesis." *Brit. J. Psychiat.,* 109, 680.

BATESON, G., JACKSON, D. D., HALEY, J., & WEAKLAND, J. H. (1956). "Toward a theory of schizophrenia." *Behav. Sci.,* 1, 251.

BERNE, E. (1966). *Games People Play.* London: Deutsch.

BLEULER, E. (1911). *Dementia Praecox or the Group of Schizophrenias.* (Trans. Ziskin, T., 1950). New York: I.U.P.

CHERRY, C. (1966). *On Human Communication.* New York: Wiley.

CLARKE, P. R. F., WYKE, M., & ZANGWILL, O. L. (1958). "Language disorder in a case of Korsakow's syndrome." *J. Neuropsychiat.,* 21, 190.

CURRAN, F. J., & SCHILDER, P. (1935). "Paraphasic signs in diffuse lesions of the brain." *J. Nerv. Ment. Dis.,* 82, 613.

DAVIE, J., & FREEMAN, T. (1961). "Disturbance of perception and consciousness in schizophrenic states." *Brit. J. Med. Psychol.,* 34, 33.

FAIRBAIRN, W. R. D. (1952). *Psychoanalytic Studies of the Personality.* London: Tavistock.

FERREIRA, A. J. (1960). "The semantics and the context of the schizophrenic language." *Arch. Gen. Psychiat.,* 3, 128.

FREEMAN, T., CAMERON, J. L., & McGHIE, A. (1965). *Studies on Psychosis.* London: Tavistock.

FREUD, S. (1900). *The Interpretation of Dreams.* London: Allen and Unwin.

GOLDSTEIN, K. (1939). *The Organism.* New York: Beacon Press Inc.

—— (1948). *Language and Language Disturbances.* New York: Grune and Stratton Inc.

GORHAM, D. R. (1956). "The use of the proverbs test for differentiating schizophrenics from normals." *J. Cons. Psychol.,* 20, 435.

HALEY, J. (1959). "An interactional description of schizophrenia." *Psychiatry: Journal for the Study of Interpersonal Processes,* 22 (4), 321.

JOHANNSEN, W. J., FRIEDMAN, S. H., & LICCIONE, J. V. (1964). "Visual perception as a function of chronicity in schizophrenia." *Brit. J. Psychiat.,* 110, 561.

KUSHNER, A. W., HAY, A. J., & FORREST, A. D. (1967). "The effect of contextual constraint on verbal recall in normals and schizophrenics." Paper given at Scottish Psychiatric Research Society.

LAWSON, J. S., McGHIE, A., & CHAPMAN, J. (1964). "Perception of speech in schizophrenia." *Brit. J. Psychiat.,* 110, 375.

McGHIE, A., & CHAPMAN, J. (1961). "Disorders of attention and perception in early schizophrenia." *Brit. J. Med. Psychol.,* 34, 103.

MILLER, G. A., & SELFRIDGE, J. A. (1950). "Verbal context and the recall of meaningful material." *Amer. J. Psychol.,* 63, 177.

PATERSON, A. (1944). "Discussion on disorders of personality after head injury." *Proc. Roy. Soc. Med.,* 37, 556.

PAYNE, R. W. (1962). "An object-identification test as a measure of overinclusive thinking in schizophrenic patients." *Brit. J. Soc. Clin. Psychol.,* 1, 213.

RAEBURN, J. M., & TONG, J. W. (1968). "Experiments on contextual constraint in schizophrenia." *Brit. J. Psychiat.*, 114, 43.

ROCHFORD, G., & WILLIAMS, M. (1962). "Studies in the development and breakdown in the use of names." *J. Neurol. Neurosurg. Psychiat.*, 25, 222.

SHIMKUNAS, A. M., GYNTHER, M. D., & SMITH, K. (1967). "Schizophrenic responses to the proverbs test: abstract, concrete, or autistic?" *J. Abnor. Soc. Psychol.*, 72 (2), 128.

SOMMER, R., DEWAR, R., & OSMOND, H. (1960). "Is there a schizophrenic language?" *Arch. Gen. Psychiat.*, 3, 113.

STENGEL, E. (1947). "A clinical and psychological study of echo-reactions." *J. Ment. Sci.*, 93, 598.

—— (1964). "Psychopathology of dementia." *Proc. Roy. Soc. Med.*, 57, 911.

SULLIVAN, H. S. (1953). *An Interpersonal Theory of Psychiatry*. London: Tavistock.

SZASZ, T. S. (1957). "A contribution to the psychology of schizophrenia." *Arch. Neurol. Psychiat.*, 77, 420.

WECKOWICZ, T. E. (1957). "Size constancy in schizophrenic patients." *J. Ment. Sci.*, 103, 425.

ZANGWILL, O. L. (1964). "Psychopathology of dementia." *Proc. Roy. Soc. Med.*, 57, 914.

APPENDIX I

Our test of the ability to use abstract concepts in speech comprised the following thirteen pairs of questions:

1. What is a clock?
1a. What is time?
2. What do you do with a key?
2a. What is security?
3. What is a book?
3a. What is literature?
4. What is a garage?
4a. What is the object of exploring space?
5. Why do we wear shoes?
5a. What is fashion?
6. What does a flag look like?
6a. What is patriotism?
7. Where can I find a church?
7a. What is religion?
8. What is a bed?
8a. What are dreams?
9. What is a hospital?
9a. What is illness?
10. What is food?
10a. Man cannot live by bread alone—what does this saying mean?
11. What is a camera?
11a. What is the difference between a painting and a photograph?
12. Where is Holyrood House?
12a. What do we mean by a monarchy?
13. What is a pen?
13a. What is communication?

APPENDIX II

CRITERIA FOR SCORING

The four judges listened to the taped answers of the subjects and classed each response, on the basis of a majority decision, as concrete, abstract, or wrong. Sometimes a tape had to be played several times before a decision was reached. It was decided that the dominant quality of the answer was to be the concern of the judges, i.e. some answers were both wrong and concrete—if the answer was more wrong than concrete, then the response was classed as wrong.

1. *Concrete.* When another object from the same logical category was quoted, or a description in terms of that category, or an instrumental answer provided, then the response was classed as concrete, i.e.
   Q. "What is a pen?"
   A. "An instrument for writing."
   Q. "Man does not live by bread alone?"
   A. "No, he needs water."

2. *Abstract.* An answer involving a concept or concepts or invoking logical categories of a higher order, i.e.

   Q. "What is time?"
   A. "Time is the fourth dimension, the continuum on which are suspended the notes of a melody, the course on which our lives are run."

3. *Wrong.* An answer simply unrelated to the question, usually due to either not knowing the word, or, in the case of some schizophrenic subjects, excessive intrusion of personalized material.

   Sometimes answers were difficult to rate because they were compounded of clichés, i.e.
   Q. "What is religion?"
   A. "Belief in God."
This was a very common response, and at first we were inclined not to accept it as an abstract response, but after reference to the dictionary it seemed that we must do so, and the general decision was made that this response would be acceptable. The concrete answer for this question would have to be rather more concrete, i.e. "Well, it's going to church, the Bible, that sort of thing." Some answers contained both abstract and concrete replies, and again it was the dominant quality or theme of the answer which determined the classification.

40

DISORDERS OF PERCEPTION COMMON TO EARLY INFANTILE AUTISM AND SCHIZOPHRENIA

Edward M. Ornitz

In a previous publication Ornitz and Ritvo described a syndrome of perceptual inconstancy occurring in autistic children (1). It was suggested that both the natural history and examination of the behavior of the autistic child revealed disturbances of perception fundamental to the other major symptomatology of this disease. The perceptual disturbances are of the type wherein there is inadequate modulation or homeostatic regulation of sensory input so that the autistic child either gets too much or too little afferent stimulation. When autistic children are observed over the long course of their illness, periods of hyperreactivity (hypersensitivity) are seen to alternate with periods of hyporeactivity (hyposensitivity) to stimuli. Frequently, however, these periods are short and at times there may be day to day, hour to hour, or even moment to moment shifts from states of over-responsiveness to non-responsiveness. These fluctuating behavioral states are manifestations of underlying perceptual inconstancy. This faulty modulation of sensory input involves all sensory modalities (1).

Whereas classical paranoid ideation, hallucinations, and delusions are not regularly observed in autistic children (2, 3), the symptoms suggestive of fluctuating sensory overload and underload occur at one time or another in the histories of nearly all autistic children. These perceptual disturbances are the basic symptoms of early infantile autism (1).

Although some authors have regarded early infantile autism as a

This work was supported by USPHS Grant MH 13517 and the McGregor Fund.

Edward M. Ornitz, M.D.: Assistant Professor of Psychiatry, University of California at Los Angeles Medical School, Los Angeles, Calif.

Reprinted, by permission of author and publisher, from: *Comprehensive Psychiatry*, 10:259-274, 1969.

syndrome distinct from either the childhood or adult form of schizophrenia (3, 4), there is a developmental relationship between the two conditions with merging of the clinical syndromes. Thus, the clinical differences between early infantile autism and its variants and schizophrenia need not be fundamental differences but rather may reflect the influence of maturational level on the overt expression of a single disease process (1). However, a more basic and positive relationship between early infantile autism and schizophrenia can be established because the symptoms of perceptual dysfunction which are basic to the development of childhood autism appear on detailed observation to be the basic symptoms of adult schizophrenia and to antedate the more elaborate hallucinatory and delusional phenomena of the schizophrenic psychosis. While in the young autistic child, the symptoms of disordered perception are found in non-verbal behavior, in the adult schizophrenic, the same symptoms are found in the subjective experience of the patient. After a brilliant detailed study of the early symptoms of schizophrenia, Chapman concluded that "at one moment the patient's consciousness may be flooded with an excess of sensory data . . ." and ". . . then, within a brief space of time, the same patient may find himself almost completely cut off from sensory experience" (5).

The hypothesis of a perceptual disorder in schizophrenia derives from both clinical and psychological, psychophysiological, and neurophysiological investigations. It is the purpose of this paper to review and evaluate the evidence for a basic disturbance of the modulation of sensory input in both the adult and childhood forms of schizophrenia, including early infantile autism, and to demonstrate the equivalence of the basic symptomatology in these conditions.

While there has been a recent increase in interest in the perceptual basis of the thought and affect disorder found in schizophrenia (5-14), symptoms suggestive of alterations in sensory input have been commented upon by both schizophrenic patients and their physicians for over one hundred years. Useful reviews of autobiographical material and classical psychiatric description have brought much of this literature together (9, 10, 15, 16). However, many of these accounts do not make the point that their reviewers intend because the form in which the schizophrenic patient's symptoms are expressed or described leaves it unclear as to whether we are dealing with a primary change in the quality of sensory input or a more complex secondary distortion of perception induced by fantasy and intense emotion. Perceval's account of his illness in 1830 and Conolly's descriptions of his patients in 1849 are cases in point (9, 17). The question which has come down to us today from such accounts remains unanswered: Does disturbed reality testing distort that which is perceived or does the disordered reality testing derive from a primary distortion of perception? The view will be developed in this paper that the latter is true both for the earliest developmental expression of schizophrenia, the autistic child, and for the adult patient.

CLINICAL STUDIES

To demonstrate the *primacy* of faulty modulation or inadequate homeostatic regulation of sensory input in schizophrenia, it is necessary to show that sensory changes precede other symptoms in the development of the psychosis, that these sensory changes are elemental, involving the basic units of sensory experience, e.g., light intensity, color, depth perception, sound intensity, pitch, or equilibrium, that more than one sensory modality is involved, and that subsequent hallucinatory and delusional phenomena are rooted in the preceding sensory changes. The evidence that meets these criteria can be found in certain of the descriptions of schizophrenic patients' subjective experiences of the onset of psychosis and their physicians' painstaking and unelaborated accounts of these early symptoms.

An early and famous autobiographic account of a patient's schizophrenic illness is that of Daniel Paul Schreber (18). Immeshed in this laborious recounting of his delusional world, we find occasional episodes suggestive of primary changes in sensation. The following account early in the course of Schreber's illness is particularly instructive.

> The first really bad, that is to say almost sleepless night, occurred in the last days of October or the first days of November. It was then that an extraordinary event occurred. During several nights when I could not get to sleep, a recurrent crackling noise in the wall of our bedroom became noticeable at shorter or longer intervals; time and again it woke me as I was about to go to sleep. Naturally we thought of a mouse although it was very extraordinary that a mouse should have found its way to the first floor of such a solidly built house. But having heard similar noises innumerable times since then, and still hearing them around me every day in daytime and at night, I have come to recognize them as undoubted divine miracles—they are called "interferences" by the voices talking to me—and I must at least suspect, without being too definite about it, that even then it was already a matter of such a miracle; *in other words that right from the beginning the more or less definite intention existed to prevent my sleep and later my recovery from the illness resulting from the insomnia for a purpose which cannot at this stage be further specified.*

Here we see the characteristic onset of schizophrenia with the accompanying sleep disturbance associated with a heightened awareness of auditory stimuli. At first there is an attempt to rationalize the experience ("We thought of a mouse") but soon the hyperacusia becomes the basis of a complex delusional system with typical ideas of reference. The main consideration is that the patient has described an increased awareness (hypersensitivity) of sound which preceded the delusional system which was rooted in the perceptual distortion. Dr. Weber's expert report to the Superior County Court of Dresden in 1902 is a clear statement of his observations of the onset of Schreber's illness.

> . . . I have in no way assumed *a priori* the pathological nature of these ideas, but rather tried to show from the history of the patient's illness how the appellant first suffered from severe hyperaesthesia, hypersensitivity to light and noise; how to this were added massive hallucinations and particularly disturbances of common sensation which falsified his conception of things, how on the basis of these hallucinations he at first developed fantastic ideas of influence which ruled him to such an extent that he was driven to suicidal attempts and how from these pathological events, at last the system of ideas was formed which the appellant has recounted in such detail and so vividly in his memoirs. . . .

In the sequence of symptoms described, the hypersensitivities to light and sound precede and then participate in the development of hallucinations and delusions.

In contrast to Schreber's auditory and visual symptoms, Angyal's patient experienced tactile, kinesthetic, and vestibular distortions (19). He complained of impressions that the ground seemed to swing up and down under his feet and that it seemed to become soft, unsteady, or wavy. He stated that "as long as I stand on a spot it is all right, but when I start to go, the whole thing [the spot] moves." There were also sensations of falling through space, floating up into the air, and spinning around. Of particular interest is the following sequence.

> . . . then he was requested to place his palm against the wall and to report what he felt. After a few seconds he said: "Something is coming out of the wall. It goes back and forth, back and forth." Then he continued to interpret his experience in a delusional manner: "The horse comes out of the wall. Some animal flesh. . . ."

Again, the delusion is derived from and preceded by the perceptual distortion.

MacDonald's description of her schizophrenic illness reiterates the same sequence of events (20).

> There has been so much written about acute schizophrenic illnesses, and there is so much material available on delusions and hallucinations, that I won't go further into those. What I do want to explain, if I can, is the exaggerated state of awareness in which I lived before, during, and after my acute illness. . . . By the time I was admitted to hospital I had reached a stage of "wakefulness" when the brilliance of light on a window sill or the color of blue in the sky would be so important it could make me cry. . . . Noises can be tiring too, and colors. . . .

The patients of Bower and Freedman stated that the earliest subjective experience of change in the normal mental state was that sights and sounds suddenly took on a greater "keenness," "intensity," and "sharpness" (10).

The most detailed documentation of the symptomatology of the onset of schizophrenia is found in the work of McGhie and Chapman (12) and Chapman (5). In the first study, 26 early schizophrenic patients were interviewed. The patients stated: "I just can't shut things out." "I listen to sounds all the time. I let all the sounds come in that are there." "Things are coming in too fast. I lose my grip of it and get lost. I am attending to everything at once. . . ." "I have noticed that noises all seem to be louder to me than they were before . . . background noises . . . seem to be just as loud and sometimes louder than the main noises that are going on. . . ." "Colours seem to be brighter now, almost as if they are luminous." "Everything's brighter and louder and noisier." ". . . all sorts of little things like markings in the surface, pick up my attention too."

The authors note that along with the heightening of sensory vividness there is an overloading of the perceptual system. The symptoms suggest that consciousness is so flooded with sensory data that discrimination and significance are lost. Chapman studied 40 schizophrenics and found that 40 percent of this group of patients experienced a breakdown in visual perceptual stability (5):

> ". . . suddenly the other person became smaller and then larger and then he seemed to get smaller again . . . with another person, I felt he was getting taller and taller. There is a brightness and clarity of outline of things around me." "I see things flat. Whenever there is a sudden change I see it flat."

Other patients complained of "taking in too much of my surroundings" or "I can't shut things out of my mind." Extraneous and irrelevant stimuli intruded into the patient's awareness. Chapman observed that at one moment the patient's consciousness is flooded with sensory data while at another moment the patient seems cut off from sensory experience. Sensory intake is either more or less than the optimum required for utilization. These disturbances of perceptual constancy occurred before the patients became noticeably ill, and alterations in color or sensory quality preceded more complex disturbances of visual perception. Earlier pleasant experiences of objects standing out unusually vividly in contrast to background preceded dissolution of perception accompanied by intense anxiety. As this prodromal phase of the illness unfolded, object and background became undistinguishable and the patients "were looking at many irrelevant aspects of the environment." Withdrawal was then attempted to avoid over-stimulation, and when delusions developed, they could be traced to the disturbances of perception. Chapman concluded that many though not all delusions in schizophrenia develop insidiously and are preceded by profound disturbances in perception.

PSYCHOLOGICAL AND PSYCHOPHYSIOLOGICAL STUDIES

The clinical evidence of primary perceptual dysfunction in schizophrenia has stimulated a considerable number of experimental studies of disturbed perception utilizing psychological variables. The procedures have included card sorting tests, word association tests, tasks involving distractions, figural after effect tasks, and matching of stimulus parameters. In general, the results of these studies have supported the concept of faulty modulation of perception in schizophrenia in that there has been either increased variability of response to stimuli or evidence of either deficient or excessive function of inhibitory mechanisms.

The card sorting test of Hoffer and Osmond is closest to the clinical studies which have been reviewed (9). Subjects judged a series of statements reflecting perceptual changes as being true or false for themselves. A sample card stated that "people's faces sometimes pulsate as I watch them." Depending on sensory modality, schizophrenics judged 19.2-25.8 percent of such cards to be true for themselves as opposed to 7.0-13.6 percent for neurotics.

A number of studies suggest that schizophrenics are unable to maintain a state of readiness for response to a coming stimulus because of distraction by irrelevancies in the stimulus situation, the environment, or the subject himself. The patient cannot maintain a set freeing his attention from these irrelevant stimuli (21). If schizophrenics are required to observe and report relevant auditory information in the presence of distracting stimuli, they do poorly compared to controls (22). However, when distracting stimuli are deliberately minimized, schizophrenics still misperceive auditory information (6). In a word association test with controls for mishearing, Moon et al. also found that distant associations (disturbance of association) did not differentiate schizophrenics from nonschizophrenics when mishearing of stimulus words was taken into account. An increase in mishearings did, however, distinguish the patients from the controls in spite of normal auditory acuity in all subjects.

The application of figural aftereffect studies to the issue of perceptual dysfunction in schizophrenia has received considerable experimental attention. These studies involve the degree of distortion of perceived shape or pattern or augmentation or reduction of perceived size of test objects after prior relatively prolonged or intense exposure to similar objects which vary in shape, pattern or size. The results of these procedures have not been unambiguous when considered in toto. Depending on the experimental conditions, schizophrenics have shown smaller figural aftereffects and greater figural aftereffects than controls (13, 23-25). In addition to experimental conditions, subject selection has been shown to influence these variations in group differences (26, 27). Of particular interest is the fact that in normals figural aftereffects reveal individual response styles: one-third of normal subjects consistantly overestimate the apparent size of test objects while one-third underestimate (25). Schizophrenics, however, make extreme overestimations or extreme underestimations under the influence of figural aftereffects (27) and they show unusual variation in response from trial to trial, overestimating on one occasion and underestimating on another (25).

This type of perceptual instability or inconstancy has also been demonstrated in experiments based on the matching of stimulus parameters. Chronic but not acute schizophrenics showed greater intraindividual variability than controls while attempting to match the shape of a test object (28). Schizophrenics also had an impaired ability to match the shape (28), distance (29) and size (30) of test objects. These results were interpreted as indicating impaired shape, distance and size constancy in schizophrenics; the findings, however, were that schizophrenics either underestimated or overestimated these parameters.

These psychological experiments have implicated increased lability of response with extremes of both hyperreactivity and hyporeactivity. Psychophysiological studies have implicated either exaggerated inhibition or lack of adaptation in response to stimulation depending on the intensity and the novelty of the stimulus. Galvanic skin responses to repeated noise are reported to drop less in schizophrenics than normals (21), suggesting hyperreactivity. Reaction times tend to be slower in schizophrenics than in normals (21) suggesting hyporeactivity (increased inhibition) to stimulation but the latter findings are clearly dependent on stimulus intensity (27, 31). Pupillary contraction in response to light stimuli occurs earlier in schizophrenics than normals suggesting exaggerated inhibition of light stimuli (32).

The results of all of these psychological and psychophysiological experiments depend on the type of schizophrenic subject selected. In general paranoid and nonparanoid schizophrenics show distinctively different response patterns (11, 21, 27). Interacting with this diagnostic variable is the influence of stimulus intensity. Silverman (27) has concluded that while schizophrenics react more extremely than normals to environmental stimuli, those schizophrenics (nonparanoid, "long-term hospitalized") who appear hypersensitive to low intensity stimulation over-inhibit and therefore appear hyposensitive to high intensity input (27). Paranoid and "early-term hospitalized" schizophrenics who do not tend to appear hypersensitive to low intensity stimuli also do not appear hyposensitive to high intensity stimuli. This does not necessarily imply, however, a fundamental difference between the two patient populations. It should be noted that in most of the psychologic and psychophysiologic experiments, the patients in both groups are studied in a relatively consolidated stage of the disease when secondary factors may have compensated for primary disturbances. Consolidation of secondary defensive mechanisms is more developed in paranoid than in, e.g., hebephrenic schizophrenia and the primary perceptual dysfunction may no longer be accessible to experimental scrutiny. Furthermore, the early symptoms of schizophrenia, which in the clinical studies suggest primary perceptual dysfunction, antedate the onset of the psychosis and are present at a stage of the disease when distinctions between paranoid and other forms of schizophrenia are not relevant. In Chapman's clinical study of perceptual changes in early schizophrenia, 15 out of 40 patients had the presenting complaints of persecutory ideas or ideas of reference and yet had symptoms indicative of primary perceptual dysfunction (5).

While in general the results from the psychological and psychophysiological studies have been compatible with the clinical observations of faulty modulation of sensory input in schizophrenia, they have not further advanced our understanding of the basis of the perceptual disturbance. The inconsistencies in the results of this type of experimentation are neither less nor more than those obtained from clinical studies and perhaps reflect the natural group and individual differences found in schizophrenia. Shakow notes coefficients of variation for groups of schizophrenics to be consistently three times that of normals in psychological studies (21). Many of the questions raised by psychological studies have shed more light on methodologic issues in psychologic experimentation than on perceptual dysfunction in schizophrenia. This stems in part from the necessity to make inferences from complex procedures usually involving the presentation of multiple interacting stimuli to the subject. In the figural aftereffects experiment, for example, the subject is usually confronted with at least three different stimuli and differential instructions for responding to each. Not only do such procedures permit several possible interpretations of results regardless of the direction of differences found between schizophrenic and control groups, but it is often unclear as to whether or not schizophrenic subjects understand the instructions and actually attend to the procedures either as intended by the experimenter or in the same way as control subjects. Even under the most simplified experimental conditions, this "subject option" may remain as an uncontrolled variable (33).

NEUROPHYSIOLOGIC STUDIES

Attempts to confront the problem of perceptual modulation in schizophrenia more directly through neurophysiologic studies have not entirely done away with either the problems of interpretation or subject option. A case in point is the recent finding that both schizophrenic men and normal women who underestimate size of objects as a result of figural aftereffects ("reducers") also have *reduced* average evoked response amplitudes to light flashes when intensity is *increased* (34). In contrast, normal men also selected as "reducers" did not show the same degree of inverse relationship between evoked response amplitude and stimulus intensity. Although the experiment was designed to demonstrate stimulus intensity control* on a neurophysiologic level, the fact that light flashes of different intensities were given in blocks permitted subjects to establish response sets out of the control of the investigator, e.g., possibly to pay more attention to low intensity flashes, perhaps finding them more challenging (33). Or it is possible that what sensitive normal women and sensitive schizophrenic men had in common was not only a tendency to reduce intense input on a cortical level but also to avert the eyes from intense light.

---

* Stimulus intensity control is the tendency for some normals and most schizophrenics to reduce the apparent intensity of sensory input as demonstrated by figural aftereffect experiments (25, 27).

Other averaged cortical evoked response experiments have revealed increased variability of response amplitudes to sound and light in schizophrenics (35, 36). These results are of particular interest because they relate directly to the hypothesis that the homeostatic modulation of sensory input is impaired in schizophrenia; and the procedures do not depend on the set of the subjects to the same extent as does the stimulus intensity control experiment. However, the subject's option to sustain attention or intermittently disregard the repetitive stimuli remains. Therefore it remains an open question as to whether the schizophrenic's disordered attention (12) is due to faulty central nervous system modulation of input, or whether the instability of cortical evoked response amplitude is simply a correlate of faulty attention.

Reduced variability of the waking EEG in schizophrenia suggesting hyperactivation, hyper-arousal or sensory overload is compatible with the notion of faulty modulation (insufficient inhibition) of input, although here the schizophrenic may be over-attending to the recording room situation (37, 38). The attention factor can be minimized during sleep. Ornitz et al. have found that during the ocular motility of REM sleep, young autistic children fail to show the normal depression of the averaged auditory evoked response (39). This finding is relevant to the concept of faulty perceptual modulation because the eye movement burst phase of REM sleep is characterized by strong excitatory and inhibitory activity within the central nervous system (40, 41). Sensory evoked responses are normally inhibited as manifested by reduction of amplitude. The unusually large amplitudes of auditory evoked responses during the eye movement bursts of REM sleep in autistic children suggest a dysequilibrium between facilitation and inhibition of sensory input at a time when subject option is not a factor.*

The response to vestibular stimulation has been studied in schizophrenic adults and children (42, 43). In both studies, the duration of nystagmus was reduced compared to controls following rotation in a Barany chair. Thus, increased inhibition of vestibular input seems to have been demonstrated. Colbert et al. also found increased variability of the response in the schizophrenic children (43). Ritvo et al. recently confirmed the reduced duration of nystagmus in autistic children but found that the inhibition of the response was dependent on a free visual field (44). In the dark, the autistic children showed the same response duration as the normals. It will require further investigation to determine whether

---

* The special significance of a disruption of the normal equilibrium between excitation and inhibition during REM sleep for schizophrenia has been discussed (39, 41).

in the light the schizophrenic subjects fixated differently than the normals, or whether visual and vestibular input interacted on a neurophysiological level to reduce nystagmus. Again the question of subject option intrudes into even a simple experimental design construed to be on a neurophysiologic level.

Having reviewed a number of clinical, psychological, psychophysiological, and neurophysiological studies, how much evidence is there for the theory of a basic dysfunction in the homeostatic modulation of sensory input in schizophrenia? In summary, the clinical evidence seems clearly to suggest that schizophrenics suffer from a primary distortion of the basic elements of perception (light, color, sound intensity, pitch) which precede the classical symptoms of the disease. The latter symptoms, particularly the hallucinations and the delusions, can be shown to be derived from the earlier perceptual changes. The basic perceptual dysfunction is manifested by either too much or too little sensory input. Therefore there is both increased lability of perceptual experience and deficient or excessive inhibition of sensory input. The psychological, psychophysiological, and neurophysiological findings have, despite some inconsistencies probably related to procedural issues, generally been consistent with the clinical observations. However, they have not increased our understanding of the mechanisms underlying the perceptual dysfunction because, with certain exceptions, these studies have not been able to do away with the subject's option to attend in his own way to the experiment. The experimental studies have been carried out during varying secondary stages of the disease process after defensive, restitutive, compensatory or malignant complications of the original breakdown in perceptual modulation have occurred. This is true whether the patient groups have been dichotomized as process-reactive, chronic-acute, long term-short term hospitalized, or nonparanoid-paranoid. However, within these limits, the experimental studies have revealed some significant differences in the direction of perceptual distortion when schizophrenics are dichotomized according to these categories (11, 21, 27). These differences suggest that the breakdown in perceptual modulation proceeds in the direction of excessive inhibition in one type of schizophrenia and deficient inhibition in another. Thus the experimental studies tend to focus on differences between schizophrenic subtypes while the clinical studies of the prodromal and early stages of the disease have emphasized what is common to schizophrenia.

STUDIES IN CHILDREN

The same disturbed modulation of sensory input which has been found in the prodomal and early stages of adult schizophrenia is observed in the behavior of young autistic children (1). In earlier studies the same type of children have been referred to as psychotic children with unusual sensitivities and schizophrenic children (45-48). The children described by Bergman and Escalona related in the same disturbed way as did those cases of early infantile autism described by Kanner (45, 49). At the same time, or earlier in their development, these children showed a striking intolerance for noises, bright lights, certain textures, odors, tastes, changes in temperature, and sudden change in position. Some of the schizophrenic children described by Goldfarb lacked speech, were disinterested in persons or objects, and did not discriminate between familiar persons and strangers (48). Yet they showed "extreme receptor hypersensitivity manifested either in reactions of excruciating discomfort (hypersensitivity) or a total defensive exclusion (hyposensitivity) when an intense sensory stimulus is presented." In an auditory startle experiment, the most marked extremes of hypersensitivity and hyposensitivity to a sudden loud sound were found in those schizophrenic children with the greatest impairments in perceptual, conceptual, and psychomotor functions (46, 48). Clinical expressions of discomfort often appeared unrelated to intensity of stimulation. "Thus a schizophrenic child may cover his ears and go into a shuddering panic on hearing a whisper or the rustling of leaves, or he may be completely unconcerned when surrounded with shattering noise. . . . Receptor hypersensitivity and hyposensitivity are ordinarily found in the same child, even during a single day . . . one frequently sees a hyposensitive child with an earlier history of hypersensitivity" (47). Two aspects of faulty perceptual modulation appear in these descriptions of schizophrenic (autistic) children which have been observed in schizophrenic adults. The striking fluctuation between hypersensitivity and hyposensitivity is also found in Chapman's patients who at one moment "may be flooded with an excess of sensory data" and then may be "almost completely cut off from sensory experience" (5). The apparent lack of relationship between expressions of discomfort and intensity of stimulation and the later substitution of hyposensitivity for earlier hypersensitivity are paralleled and explained by the finding that adult schizophrenics who are hypersensitive to low intensity stimulation over-inhibit and appear hyposensitive to high intensity stimulation (27). In another study (50) a group of children closely similar to those with early infantile autism as described by Kanner (49) showed both a marked lack of response to sounds and, paradoxically, distress in relation to sounds. Both types of response occurred in a significantly greater number of the psychotic children than in the controls.

Ornitz and Ritvo described a group of symptoms in autistic children indicative of disturbed perception in auditory, visual, tactile, olfactory, gustatory, vestibular and pain modalities (1). The distortions of perception common to all sensory modalities included: (1) heightened awareness of stimuli in the environment, (2) heightened sensitivity to stimulation, and (3) nonresponsiveness. These three types of perceptual dysfunction found in autistic children are strikingly similar to the disturbances of perception observed in a number of clinical and experimental studies of adult schizophrenics. Silverman has summarized these findings in schizophrenia: they include (1) unusually acute awareness of sensory stimulation; (2) a hyper-reactivity to irrelevant stimuli; and (3) reduction of the intensity of sensory input (27). As is the case in adult schizophrenia (5), the perceptual distortions in autistic children can often be shown to precede or at least to coincide with the onset of other symptomatology (1). While the onset of early infantile autism can be retrospectively traced to the neonatal period or the early months of life, the diagnosis cannot be made with certainty until after two or three years of age. Specific questions concerning the symptoms of heightened awareness and heightened sensitivity must be directed to the parents of autistic children in the course of taking developmental histories. Just as the early symptoms of perceptual dysfunction in adult schizophrenia may disappear with the full development of delusional thinking or catatonic withdrawal, so may the marked hypersensitivities of the autistic child tend to abate while the disturbances of relating, language, and communication persist.

Chapman observed that the social withdrawal of his patients seemed to be a voluntary attempt to reduce the intake of sensory stimulation from the environment (5). As the psychosis became more florid, the patients used more concrete methods such as plugging their ears. Young autistic children also protect themselves from auditory stimuli by covering their ears. Other behaviors in schizophrenics not directly related to sensory phenomena have noteworthy parallels in autistic children. The posturing of autistic children is quite similar to the catatonic immobility exhibited by Chapman's patients.* These patients also occasionally spoke about themselves in the third person and frequently used echolalic speech; both peculiarities of speech are frequently observed in autistic children (1). Ornitz and Ritvo presented case histories of autistic chil-

---

* Actually the episodes of immobility in the schizophrenics were related to the "breakdown in visual perceptual constancy" (5). Both catatonic immobility and the posturing of autistic children may serve to minimize visual input by reducing the changes in the visual field.

dren who later developed a characteristic schizophrenic thought disorder (1).** This longitudinal demonstration of a schizophrenic outcome in some autistic children coupled with the present demonstration of equivalent disturbances of perception in both the autistic child and the schizophrenic adult argues for a fundamental relationship between the two conditions.

THEORETICAL CONSIDERATIONS

The observations of hypersensitivity and hyposensitivity to stimuli in autistic children and schizophrenic adults have evoked several related interpretations.

Data obtained from electroencephalographic studies in autistic children (51) and chronic schizophrenic adults (37) have suggested that the patients are in a sustained state of hyperarousal. Such a state might influence the process of attention to incoming stimuli or might result from a more fundamental alteration of the normal impact of sensory input upon the central nervous system. The results of a number of psychological studies have been compatible with a state of narrowed attention in chronic schizophrenics. Conversely, "the acute (and possibly the reactive and paranoid) patient is characterized by an inability to restrict the range of his attention . . ." (11).

Several authors have emphasized disturbances in the direction of attention. Failure to attend *selectively* to environmental stimuli (12, 22), inability to *shift* attention from one source of sensory input to another (14), and inability to maintain a major set or state of readiness for response to a particular stimulus in the presence of competing stimuli (21) have been suggested as explanations of the perceptual disturbances. However, as the subjective experiences of the older patients (5), the behavior of the younger patients (1), and the experimental demonstration of paradoxical hyposensitivity to high intensity stimulation (27) suggest that the patients are overwhelmed by environmental stimuli, the inability to direct attention or maintain sets against distracting or irrelevant stimuli could be a concomitant rather than an explanation of the basic pathology.

Other workers have offered a more direct explanation of the hypersensitivity to stimuli observed in autistic children (45, 52), and schizo-

---

** Case 5 who had been followed to 11 years old in the previous report had exhibited persistent hypersensitivities to sound since 3 months old and developed somatic delusions between 6 and 11 years. At 12½ years with the onset of puberty he suffered an acute paranoid schizophrenic episode with concerns that other children were talking about him and influencing him.

phrenic adults (8, 13) in terms of a defective stimulus barrier or filtering function. Thus the full impact of unattenuated stimuli would impinge directly upon the nervous system. The "filter" need not conform to a passive inorganic model but could be an active inhibitory function. It is often worth while to listen to patients. One schizophrenic patient came to this conclusion about her illness (20):

> Each of us is capable of coping with a large number of stimuli, invading our being through any one of the senses. We could hear every sound within earshot and see every object, line and color within the field of vision, and so on. It's obvious that we would be incapable of carrying on any of our daily activities if even one-hundredth of all these available stimuli invaded us at once. So the mind must have a filter which functions without our conscious thought, sorting stimuli and allowing only those which are relevant to the situation in hand to disturb consciousness. And this filter must be working at maximum efficiency at all times, particularly when we require a high degree of concentration. What had happened to me in Toronto was a breakdown in the filter, and a hodgepodge of unrelated stimuli were distracting me from things which should have had my undivided attention.

Closely related to the concept of a defective filtering mechanism is the notion of a fundamental perceptual inconstancy from which disorders of attention and thought are derived. This hypothesis is implicit in clinical (5) and neurophysiologic (35) investigations of schizophrenic adults and has been stated explicitly in studies of autistic children (1, 39, 41). The inconstancy of perception results from a defective modulation of sensory input related to dissociated states of excitation and inhibition which are part of the disease process and which are manifest in the behavior of young autistic children (1). This concept depends on the observed tendency of schizophrenic adults and autistic children to be flooded with sensory stimuli in the early stages of the disease; a breakdown of inhibitory functions is implied. An example of the failure of an inhibitory function in autistic children is the overriding of the normal phasic inhibition of auditory evoked responses during the ocular activity of REM sleep (39).

The concept of perceptual inconstancy in early infantile autism and schizophrenia should be construed to imply certain characteristics of the patient's responses to stimuli: (1) The occurrence of increased variability of response to sensory stimuli; (2) both deficient and excessive inhibition of response to sensory stimuli; and (3) alternation of response from hyperreactivity to hyporeactivity depending on clinical state, i.e., diagnostic subgroup, and stimulus intensity. These characteristics of response to stimulation are found in the clinical and experimental studies of schizophrenic adults and autistic children reviewed in this paper.

As the emphasis in this paper has been on a special type of perceptual dysfunction common to and underlying the psychopathology of autistic children and schizophrenic adults, consideration must be given to the very disparate and diverging clinical types which occur. There are indeed major differences between a mute or echolalic and completely detached autistic child who spends hours switching lights on and off or watching the water swirl in the toilet bowl and an actively hallucinating delusional schizophrenic adult. The argument of this paper is that these differences represent secondary manifestations of the disease process and are determined in part by the developmental and maturational level of the patient during the time that the breakdown in homeostatic regulation of sensory input is active. The manner in which the perceptual disturbances precede and then determine the subsequent development of psychopathology has been described for schizophrenic adults (5) and autistic children (1). Here we will be concerned with the interaction of maturational level and the breakdown of perceptual modulation.

The failure of autistic children to relate from the beginning of life has been contrasted with the later withdrawal of schizophrenics, and the adult form of schizophrenia has not been observed by some investigators prior to eight years of age (53). The reason for these differences is that in the young autistic child the state of perceptual inconstancy occurs prior to and during the time that self is normally distinguished from nonself and that the capacity for imitative responses which are fundamental to later identification and identity formation normally occur. Consequently, both these processes and the development of thought, language, communication, and fantasy which depend on the successful development of self-nonself differentiation are aborted, stunted or distorted depending on the severity of the pathologic process. In contrast, the psychotic response to the breakdown of sensory regulation in schizophrenia occurs in an individual whose social, cognitive, and affective life has developed relatively intact prior to the perceptual dissolution. Finally transitional states between the two types of development are observed (1).

The diagnosis of early infantile autism depends on four distinctive features: (1) inability to relate in the ordinary way to people and situations from the beginning of life; (2) failure to use language for communication; (3) an anxious desire to maintain sameness in the environment; and (4) a fascination with and awareness of the fine details of the arrangement of objects (53, 54). These characteristics were described in children with good intellectual potential (53). To minimize diagnostic confusion, it is emphasized that the term "autistic child" used in this report refers to children who show these same four features. However, good intellectual potential is often more apparent than real. Rutter and Lockyer (50) have also observed a lack of relationship with intelligence. In addition to showing the four specific features described by Kanner (54), and Eisenberg (53), the autistic children we have observed have had specific hypersensitivities to environmental stimuli. Many of the children have also had disturbances of motility (1). Considering the four diagnostic features specified by Kanner and Eisenberg for the autistic child, the inability to relate and the failure to communicate stem from the stunting of self-nonself differentiation due to the inconstancy of sensory experience. The anxious desire to maintain sameness seems to be a secondary defensive attempt to reduce the intensity of sensory input by minimizing novelty in the environment. Similar reactions are seen in adult schizophrenia (5). Finally, the overawareness of the detailed arrangements of objects is a direct manifestation of the perceptual hypersensitivity. The flooding of the sensorium with irrelevant background stimuli is the same process in schizophrenia (5).

The emphasis in this paper on postulated underlying pathologic mechanisms common to early infantile autism and schizophrenia is not to be interpreted as a desire to ignore clinical differences in these and related conditions. Eisenberg is quite right in saying that differential diagnosis "is the very stuff of medicine" (53).* However, as both early infantile autism and schizophrenia continue to be diseases of unknown etiology, the differential diagnosis is as likely to be based on secondary manifestations or complications of an underlying unitary pathology as it is to relate to diseases with differing pathology. For purposes of prognosis and therapeutic planning, it is undoubtedly best to consider these clinical states separately. It has been the purpose of this paper to bring together certain common aspects of these conditions that might relate to a common underlying etiologic factor.

---

* Historically, advances in medicine have actually been the product of a dynamic alternation between efforts to isolate specific clinical syndromes and efforts to unify them under more fundamental concepts of pathology. With diseases of unknown etiology such as those under consideration here, there are usually some periods when "splitting" is in style and other periods which favor "lumping." It is hoped that the "lumping" which has been attempted here will have some heuristic value in promoting further investigation into the etiology of these conditions.

SUMMARY

The results of clinical, psychological, psychophysiological, and neurophysiological investigations have suggested that a break-down of the homeostatic regulation of sensory input occurs in early infantile autism and in schizophrenia. These investigations are reviewed and evaluated. It is concluded that a profound disturbance of perception is found in both autistic children and schizophrenic adults, and that this perceptual dysfunction may be common to and underlie the divergent clinical pathology present in these conditions.

REFERENCES

1. ORNITZ, E., & RITVO, E.: Perceptual inconstancy in early infantile autism. *Arch. Gen. Psychiat.* 18:76-98, 1968.

2. EISENBERG, L.: The autistic child in adolescence. *Amer. J. Psychiat.* 112:607-612, 1956.

3. RUTTER, M.: The influence of organic and emotional factors on the origins, nature and outcome of childhood psychosis. *Develop. Med. Child. Neurol.* 7:518-528, 1965.

4. RIMLAND, B.: Infantile Autism, the Syndrome and Its Implications for a Neural Theory of Behavior. New York, Appleton-Century-Crofts, 1964.

5. CHAPMAN, J.: The early symptoms of schizophrenia. *Brit. J. Psychiat.* 112:225-251, 1966.

6. MOON, A. F., et al.: Perceptual dysfunction as a determinant of schizophrenic word associations. *J. Nerv. Ment. Dis.* 146:80-84, 1968.

7. WIENER, H.: External chemical messengers II. Natural history of schizophrenia. *New York State J. Med.* 67:1144-1165, 1967.

8. LEHMANN, H. E.: Pharmacotherapy of schizophrenia. *In* Hoch, P., and Zubin, J. (Eds.): Psychopathology of Schizophrenia. New York, Lippincott, 1966, pp. 388-411.

9. HOFFER, A., & OSMOND, H.: Some psychological consequences of perceptual disorder and schizophrenia. *Int. J. Neuropsychiat.* 2:1-19, 1966.

10. BOWERS, M. B., JR., & FREEDMAN, D. X.: "Psychedelic" experiences in acute psychoses. *Arch. Gen. Psychiat.* 15:240-248, 1966.

11. VENABLES, P. H.: Input dysfunction in schizophrenia. *In* Maher, B. (Ed.): Progress in Experimental Personality Research. New York, Academic Press, 1964, pp. 1-47.

12. McGHIE, A., & CHAPMAN, J.: Disorders of attention and perception in early schizophrenia. *Brit. J. Med. Psychol.* 34:103-116, 1961.

13. PAYNE, R. W., MATTUSSEK, P., & GEORGE, E. I.: An experimental study of schizophrenic thought disorder. *J. Ment. Sci.* 105:627-652, 1959.

14. METTLER, F. A.: Perceptual capacity, functions of the corpus striatum and schizophrenia. *Psychiat. Quart.* 29:89-111, 1955.

15. SOMMER, R., & OSMOND, H.: Autobiographies of former mental patients. *J. Ment. Sci.* 106:648-662, 1960.

16. WIENER, H.: External chemical messengers III. Mind and body in schizophrenia. *New York State J. Med.* 67:1287-1310, 1967.

17. BATESON, G.: Perceval's Narrative. Stanford, Stanford University Press, 1961.

18. MACALPINE, I., & HUNTER, R.: Daniel Paul Schreber. Memoirs of My Nervous Illness. London, Dawes and Sons, 1955.

19. ANGYAL, A.: The perceptual basis of somatic delusions in a case of schizophrenia. *Arch. Neurol. Psychiat.* 34:270-279, 1935.

20. MacDONALD, N.: The other side. Living with schizophrenia. *Canad. Med. Ass. J.* 82:218-221, 1960.

21. SHAKOW, D.: Segmental set. A theory of the formal psychological deficit in schizophrenia. *Arch. Gen. Psychiat.* 6:1-17, 1962.

22. McGHIE, A., CHAPMAN, J., & LAWSON, J. S.: Disturbances in selective attention in schizophrenia. *Proc. Roy. Soc. Med.* 57:419-422, 1964.

23. WERTHEIMER, M.: The differential satiability of schizophrenic and normal subjects: A test of a deduction from the theory of figural after-effects. *J. Gen. Psychol.* 51:291, 1964.

24. ——, & JACKSON, C. W.: Figural after-effects, "brain modifiability" and schizophrenia: A further study. *J. Gen. Psychol.* 57:45-54, 1957.

25. PETRIE, A., HOLLAND, T., & WOLK, I.: Sensory stimulation causing subdued experience: Audioanalgesia and perceptual augmentation and reduction. *J. Nerv. Ment. Dis.* 137:312-321, 1963.

26. SILVERMAN, J.: Perceptual control of stimulus intensity in paranoid and nonparanoid schizophrenia. *J. Nerv. Ment. Dis.* 139:545-549, 1964.

27. ——: Variations in cognitive control and psychophysiological defense in the schizophrenias. *Psychosom. Med.* 29:225-251, 1967.

28. WECKOWICZ, T. C.: Shape constancy in schizophrenic patients. *J. Abnorm. Soc. Psychol.* 68:117-183, 1964.

29. ——, SOMMER, R., & HALL, R.: Distance constancy in schizophrenic patients. *J. Ment. Sci.* 104:1174-1182, 1958.

30. ——: Size constancy in schizophrenic patients. *J. Ment. Sci.* 103:475-486, 1957.

31. KRIEGEL, J., & SUTTON, S.: Effect of modality shift on reaction time in schizophrenia. Paper presented at Objective Indicators in Psychopathology, Sterling Forest, N. Y., Feb. 15, 1968.

32. HAKEREM, G., SUTTON, S., & ZUBIN, J.: Pupillary reactions to light in schizophrenic patients and normals. *Ann. N. Y. Acad. Sci.* 105:820-831, 1964.

33. SUTTON, S.: The definition and measurement of "psychological" independent variables in an averaged evoked potential experiment. Paper presented at Current Research Problems in the Study of Averaged Evoked Potentials, San Francisco, September 10-12, 1968.

34. BUCHSBAUM, M., & SILVERMAN, J.: Stimulus intensity control and the cortical evoked response. *Psychosom. Med.* 30:12-22, 1968.

35. LIFSHITZ. K.: Averaged evoked responses and information processing in normal and schizophrenic subjects. Paper presented at A.P.A. meeting, Boston, 1968.

36. CALLAWAY, E.: Diagnostic uses of the averaged evoked potentials. Paper presented at Current Research Problems in the Study of Average Evoked Potentials, San Francisco, September 10-12, 1968.

37. GOLDSTEIN, L., et al.: Electro-cerebral activity in schizophrenics and non-psychotic subjects: Quantitative EEG amplitude analysis. *Electroenceph. Clin. Neurophysiol.* 19:350-361, 1965.

38. MARJERRISON, G., KRAUSE, A. E., & KEOGH, R. P.: Variability of the EEG in schizophrenia: Quantitative analysis with a modulus voltage integrator. *Electroenceph. Clin. Neurophysiol.* 24:35-41, 1968.

39. ORNITZ, E. M., et al.: The auditory evoked response in normal and autistic children during sleep. *Electroenceph. Clin. Neurophysiol.* 25:221-230, 1968.

40. ——, et al.: The variability of the auditory averaged evoked response during sleep and dreaming in children and adults. *Electroenceph. Clin. Neurophysiol.* 22:514-524, 1967.

41. ——, & RITVO, E. R.: Neurophysiologic mechanisms underlying perceptual inconstancy in autistic and schizophrenic children. *Arch. Gen. Psychiat.* 19:22-27, 1968.

42. ANGYAL, A., & BLACKMAN, N.: Vestibular reactivity in schizophrenia. *Arch. Neurol. Psychiat.* 44:611-620, 1940.

43. COLBERT, E. G., KOEGLER, R. R., & MARKHAM, C. H.: Vestibular dysfunction in childhood schizophrenia. *Arch. Gen. Psychiat.* 1:600-617, 1959.

44. RITVO, E. R. et al.: Decreased post-rotatory nystagmus in early infantile autism. *Neurology* (in press).

45. BERGMAN, P., & ESCALONA, S. K.: Unusual sensitivities in very young children. *Psychoanal. Stud. Child.* 3-4:333-352, 1949.

46. GOLDFARB, W.: Childhood Schizophrenia. Cambridge, Mass., Harvard University Press, 1961.

47. ——: Self-awareness in schizophrenic children. *Arch. Gen. Psychiat.* 8:47-60, 1963.

48. ——: An investigation of childhood schizophrenia. *Arch. Gen. Psychiat.* 11:620-634, 1964.

49. KANNER, L.: Early Infantile Autism. *J. Pediat.* 25:211-217, 1944.

50. RUTTER, M., & LOCKYER, L.: A five- to fifteen-year follow-up study of infantile psychosis. I. Description of sample. *Brit. J. Psychiat.* 113:1169-1182, 1967.

51. HUTT, S. J., et al.: A behavioral and electroencephalographic study of autistic children. *J. Psychiat. Res.* 3:181-197, 1965.

52. ANTHONY, J.: An experimental approach to the psychopathology of childhood: Autism. *Brit. J. Med. Psychol.* 31:211-225, 1958.

53. EISENBERG, L.: Psychotic disorders in childhood. *In* Cooke, R. (Ed.): The Biologic Basis of Pediatric Practice. New York, Blakiston, 1968.

54. KANNER, L.: Autistic disturbances of affective contact. *Nerv. Child.* 2:217-250, 1943.

Section VII

PROGNOSIS

41

SHORT-TERM PROGNOSIS OF SCHIZOPHRENIC PATIENTS

Martin Harrow, Gary J. Tucker, and Evelyn Bromet

In the past decade there has been an increase in interest concerning factors which relate to or predict the prognosis of hospitalized schizophrenic patients. One aspect of their prognosis is posthospital adjustment, and it has received extensive attention in the recent literature. Another aspect of the prognosis of schizophrenic patients which has received far less attention is length of hospitalization. Detailed information on what variables predict length of hospitalization would be of both theoretical and practical importance.

In relation to theory, data concerning the prognosis of schizophrenics, based on their posthospital adjustment, have been of value in increasing our understanding of schizophrenia. Formulations about good and poor premorbid schizophrenics (1, 2), and related (but not identical) ones about process and reactive schizophrenics (3) are based in part on research on such prognostic factors.

In addition, research on prognosis which has been used to support formulations about the importance of premorbid social competence in the schizophrenic patient has been placed into the framework of a developmental theory of psychopathology (4, 5). The developmental theory views pathology as being a consequence of failure to cope with the developmental tasks which confront every person. Immature people who have not reached a high developmental level are more likely to break down or exhibit psychopathology at early stages of social chal-

Submitted for publication Jan. 23, 1969.

From the Department of Psychiatry, School of Medicine, Yale University, New Haven, Conn.

Reprint requests to Department of Psychiatry, Yale University, New Haven, Conn. 06510 (Dr. Harrow).

Reprinted, by permission of author and editor, from: *Archives of General Psychiatry,* 21:195-202, 1969.

lenge. Since these people have acquired relatively few skills or resources, their prognosis is likely to be poorer than patients who break down later and thus have developed more personal resources to cope with problem areas.

Much of the data on prognosis which forms a basis for the developmental theory has been collected in relation to posthospital adjustment. It would seem important to extend the above theories and evaluate their applicability to other aspects of prognosis, such as length of hospitalization. Thus, the current study was designed to determine whether factors which predict posthospital adjustment (such as premorbid social competence) are also predictors of length of hospitalization in schizophrenic patients.

From a practical standpoint further information on factors predicting length of hospitalization would seem extremely important due to the increasing emphasis on short-term community based psychiatric hospitals (6). One of the goals behind this movement is the attempt to discharge patients back into the community as rapidly as improvement in their condition allows (7, 8). Further knowledge concerning what factors predict length of hospitalization in schizophrenic patients would be of help in formulating admission policies for these institutions and might also help in overall planning concerning such patients.

The specific questions which the present research attempts to answer are.

1. Do demographic and sociologic variables related to premorbid social competence predict length of hospitalization of schizophrenic patients?

2. Do variables assessing childhood events and prehospital functioning predict length of hospitalization?

3. Do variables assessing schizophrenics' functioning at the time of hospitalization predict length of hospitalization?

METHODS

Setting.—The research was carried out on schizophrenic patients from the Psychiatric Inpatient Division of the Yale-New Haven Hospital (9). The patient population of this service includes the major types of psychiatric disorders necessitating hospitalization (primarily depressives, schizophrenics, and character disorders). The unit emphasizes milieu, group, and family treatment, with frequent use of ataractic medications (10-12). The primary therapeutic goal of the ward is the rapid return of the patient to the community with a reduction in symptomatology and the restoration of ability to function in the family, with peers, and at work (13, 14). The criteria for discharge involve a patient's being able to resume these functions successfully without recurrence of florid symptoms. When patients seem to be approaching discharge they are given short passes to their home and work situations to allow them to demonstrate their ability to function again, with discharge following shortly afterwards.

Subjects.—The sample was composed of 125 successive schizophrenic patients admitted to the service. Demographically the patient sample was typical of the population of many short-term private psychiatric hospitals, with the major deviation from the usual population norms being a greater proportion of upper middle class and female patients. A complete description of the patient sample is presented in Table 1. Most previous studies on prognosis have been conducted in state and federal mental hospitals. The present setting offered the chance to assess variables which relate to length of hospitalization for a different population, one that clusters within the middle and upper classes.

In regard to the patients' use of medication, prior to hospital admission, 20.5% of the patients had been on some type of phenothiazine, 43.8% had not been on phenothiazines but had been on some other type of medication (including sedatives), and 35.6% of the population had not been on any medication. The relationship between having been on medication prior to hospitalization and length of hospitalization was not significant ($r = 0.09$). After the patient was in the hospital, medications (usually phenothiazines) were used extensively; 93.7% of the patients were put on phenothiazines at some point during hospitalization, with only 6.3% not being treated with phenothiazines. Concerning the extent of treatment with *any* medication while the patients were in the hospital, 78.7% received medications continually or almost continually, another 12.6% received medications over half of the time, 5.5% received medications during less than half of their hospitalization and 3.1% received no regular medications at any time. There was no significant relationship between length of hospitalization and (1) in-hospital treatment with phenothiazines ($r = 0.03$), or (2) extent of treatment with any medications ($r = 0.01$). One factor which may have influenced these two low correlations is that the few patients not put on any medication may represent a different type of patient (e.g., they were less "psychotic" at admission than the others, in the sense of being significantly less delusional and exhibiting significantly less bizarre behavior).

Data Collection and Analysis.—The major results used in this study are correlations between the length of hospitalization and a wide range of data relating to demographic and sociologic factors, childhood events and prehospital functioning, and functioning during the morbid period just prior to and after hospitalization. Most of these data were gathered from a standardized research interview schedule administered to the patients within the first few weeks of hospitalization, and from other standardized research schedules administered by the social workers to the patients' immediate relatives. Ratings of the patients' symptoms and behavior were obtained from psychiatric residents who filled out standardized rating forms on admission and then weekly, and from nurses who filled out the standardized rating forms daily (15). Satisfactory reliability had previously been obtained for these rating scales and they have been used successfully in other studies (16-18). Since some sections of the research interview schedules administered to the patients and their relatives were completed after the study began, information on some variables in the later sections of the research schedules are not available for all patients. Thus, the final N varies somewhat for a number of the variables.

In addition to examining the correlation between each variable and length of hospitalization, we also divided the sample studied, arbitrarily, into two groups of schizophrenics according to length of hospital stay. Those patients who stayed for more than 90 days ($N = 72$) were classified as "long-stay" patients. Those who stayed for less than 90 days ($N = 53$) were classified as belonging to the "short-stay" group. These two groups were then compared on each variable.

RESULTS AND COMMENTS

Since the developmental theory of psychopathology is one of the prominent theories addressing itself to issues concerning the prognosis of schizophrenic patients, much of the following sections will be discussed in relation to this formulation. The developmental theory emphasizes the importance of premorbid social competence as an index of the level of maturity attained by an individual, and hence as an indicator of prognosis (4, 5).

Demographic and Sociologic Variables.—Table 2 presents an analysis of the data collected on demographic and sociologic variables. This includes variables assessing age, marital status, sex, education, student status, social class, intelligence, and number of previous hospitalizations.

Age was found to be an important discriminator between the long-stay and short-stay groups of patients. Other research has also indicated that the younger the patient is at the time of the break, the poorer is his prognosis (4, 19). In this case the younger patients tended to stay

TABLE 1

CHARACTERISTICS OF PATIENT SAMPLE

	% (N=125)
A. Age	
13 to 19 yr.	30.7
20 to 29 yr.	47.2
30 to 39 yr.	10.2
40 yr. or over	11.8
B. Sex	
Male	46.5
Female	53.5
C. Marital Status	
Never married	69.3
Ever married	30.8
D. Educational Level	
No high school	2.4
Some high school	21.4
High school graduate	17.5
Some education beyond high school	30.2
College graduate	7.1
Some education beyond college	21.4
E. Schizophrenic Subtype	
Borderline or pseudoneurotic	31.0
Acute or catatonic	33.3
Schizoaffective	5.6
Paranoid	19.8
Chronic	10.3
F. Length of Illness	
Less than 3 mo.	32.1
3 to 6 mo.	15.1
6 to 12 mo.	17.0
1 to 2 yr.	15.1
2 to 5 yr.	5.7
More than 5 yr.	15.1
G. No. of Previous Hospitalizations	
None	59.5
1	25.0
2	10.7
3 or more	4.8
H. Length of Current Hospitalization	
Less than one mo.	8.0
31 to 60 days	12.0
61 to 90 days	22.4
91 to 120 days	24.8
121 to 150 days	12.8
More than 5 mo.	20.0

in the hospital for a longer period of time. These results fit in with previous hypotheses that the older patient has developed a backlog of conflict resolutions to fall back on during treatment and after discharge, in contrast to the younger patient who is less well equipped to deal with conflict situations. It is also possible that problems in disposition (i.e., negative staff feelings about sending the younger patients back into conflict-laden parental homes) might have tended to lengthen their hospitalization.

TABLE 2

RELATIONSHIP OF DEMOGRAPHIC AND SOCIOLOGIC VARIABLES
TO LENGTH OF HOSPITALIZATION (LOH)

Variable	Correlation With LOH (N=125)	χ^2vs LOH (N=125)	P
Age	—0.22		<0.05
Marital status		7.18	<0.01
Sex		0.19	ns
Education	0.03		ns
Student status		5.27	<0.05
Social class (head of household)	—0.13		ns
Intelligence	—0.13		ns
Previous hospitalizations	0.01		ns

Marriage has also been used in the past as an index of social competence (20, 21), and in the present study marital status distinguished between the long and short-stay groups. Patients who had been married stayed in the hospital for a shorter period of time as compared to patients who had never been married. When the sample was analyzed for marital status, while controlling for age, the results were similar with married patients staying for shorter periods independently of age. Similarly, younger patients stayed in the hospital longer than older patients independently of marital status.

Sex and years of education were not related to length of hospitalization. There was, however, a strong trend (P <0.05) for students to stay in the hospital longer than nonstudents. When student status was analyzed while controlling for age and marital status, however, this trend diminished sharply, although it was still present to a slight extent. Thus, the apparent statistical relationship between being a student and staying in the hospital longer was due primarily to the confounding effect of the student's being younger and unmarried.

Neither social class (assessed by using the educational level of the head of the household) (22) nor intelligence was a good predictor for this population. It should be noted that the range of scores for intelligence and for social class is more narrow than that found in the general population; this tends to diminish the prospects of finding significant differences, even when such do exist in the general population.

No relationship was found between previous hospitalizations and length of stay in the hospital. Previous hospitalizations in this sample, however, had occurred for a minority of both the short and long-stay patients. It is possible that a relationship between these two variables might be found in a sample with a larger percentage of chronic patients.

Overall, we find our data in general support of a developmental theory of psychopathology (4, 5) as applied to schizophrenic patients. More of the older and married patients, who in a sense are more responsible for themselves and a family or both stayed for a significantly shorter period of time and both of these variables have been linked by others to social competence. Thus, the more socially competent the patient, the better is his prognosis in terms of length of hospitalization. The relationship, however, was far from a perfect one and several variables in this area did not relate to length of hospitalization.

Childhood Events and Prehospital Functioning.—Table 3 reports the results concerning premorbid factors. Three of these variables relate to childhood events and four others to prehospital functioning.

The three variables related to childhood events are: whether the patient was closer to the same-sexed parent or the opposite-sexed parent as a child (which can be utilized as a rough index of adequate sexual identification) (23), special problems the patient may have had as a child (e.g., environmental or personal difficulties), and whether there were any major family problems while the patient was a child. All three of these variables have been discussed extensively in regard to schizophrenia by other workers (23-25), and they have all been related to prognosis. The data did not indicate significant relationships between any of these three variables and length of hospitalization for the present sample.

The four other variables, which were assessed as predictors of length of hospitalization, are associated with prehospital functioning. These variables include two estimates of premorbid social functioning, an additional one assessing the presence of a clear precipitating event for the current illness, and also one on the length of the current illness prior to hospitalization. Each of these factors also has been reported to be related to prognosis by other investigators (21, 26, 27).

The two estimates of *premorbid* social functioning are the age patient first started dating and amount of comfort with the opposite sex as a teen-ager. Two other variables were assessed which relate to social functioning *during the morbid period,* and these are discussed in the succeeding section. Those patients who felt uncomfortable with the opposite sex as teen-agers tended to stay in the hospital longer. This is consonant with Phillips' and Zigler's theory concerning premorbid social adequacy and is especially important because the variable utilized to assess this factor is related to one of the items used in his scale (item 1B, Phillips Scale). One way of conceptualizing this result is that schizophrenics who are socially competent prior to their formal illness are more likely to be socially competent (and to adjust better to new hospital surroundings) during their period of acute illness, and probably after their period of acute illness.

With regard to a clear precipitating event for the illness there was no significant difference between the long-stay and short-stay groups.

Patients who were ill for a longer period of time prior to entering the hospital remained in the hospital for a longer period ($P < 0.05$). It is possible that the longer the period of time after the onset of a schizophrenic episode the more fixed the thought and behavior patterns, and hence the more difficult they are to dislodge. Thus, the longer the process, the more difficult the psychiatric treatment becomes.

Functioning at the Time of Hospitalization.—Table 4 presents the data on functioning at the time of hospitalization. Included among these variables are two assessing social functioning, two assessing the patient's in-hospital functioning as perceived by other patients, four assessing neurotic type symptomatology, five assessing psychotic and other severe symptomatology, and two assessing depressive features.

The two indicators of social functioning apply to the morbid period just before and just after hospitalization. The first of these ratings, time spent socializing with other patients, is derived from nurses' observations during the patient's first week in the hospital, and was rated daily by the nursing staff. The long and short-stay groups of schizophrenics were not significantly different, but there was a slight tendency for more of the long-stay group to spend less time socializing. The second rating assesses the amount of isolation which the patient displayed during the week just prior to hospitalization (and for the first day or two in the hospital) and was noted by the patient's psychiatrist on the second or third day after hospital admission on a standardized rating form. The scores the psychiatrist assigned for isolation and for all of the remaining eleven symptoms discussed in this section were based on their observations, and on reports they gathered during their interviews of the patients and their immediate relatives. There was no significant difference on isolation between the short and long-stay schizophrenics. Overall, while the results on *premorbid* social functioning tended to be in harmony with the findings on prognostic factors by others, and with Phillips' theories about social adequacy, the results on social functioning *during the morbid period* are more mixed, with only some mild support for the theory.

TABLE 3

RELATIONSHIP OF CHILDHOOD EVENTS AND PREHOSPITAL FUNCTIONING TO LENGTH OF HOSPITALIZATION (LOH)

Variable	*Correlation With LOH* (N=75)	χ^2 *vs LOH* (N=75)	P
Closer to same-sexed parent as child		0.99	ns
Special problems as child	0.05		ns
Major problems in family when child	—0.14		ns
Age started dating	0.09		ns
Comfort with opposite sex as teen-ager	0.29		<0.05
Clear precipitating event for illness	0.10		ns
Length of present illness	0.31		<0.05

In line with theories about the importance of the level of social functioning, two important variables were studied which assess the patients' functioning on the hospital unit. A "ladder" of patient status operates. At the lower end of this ladder, patients are placed on "staff specials" (a staff member watches and accompanies a patient at all times). Near the upper end of this ladder the patient is placed on the "buddy system" (the patient is able to leave the ward with a fellow patient for a walk, or to go shopping, with both patients being responsible for each other). What is of interest for the present research is that the patients themselves make the decisions about who is moved up or down the ladder. These decisions are usually based, in part, on the adequacy of the patient's social functioning and on his ability to assume responsibility. Although the staff has the power to veto the patients' decisions, approximately

91% of these decisions are accepted (28). In this ladder system, as patients improve they are placed by their peers in a "monitor pool" with patients on this status helping the nurses to deal with other disturbed patients and also helping to manage the ward in general. Likewise, a patient is placed on the buddy system by other patients after he has demonstrated to his peers an ability to socialize and to assume responsibility on the unit.

TABLE 4

RELATIONSHIP OF FUNCTIONING AT TIME OF HOSPITALIZATION
TO LENGTH OF HOSPITALIZATION (LOH)

Variable	Correlation With LOH ($N = 123$)	P
Isolation	0.07	ns
Time spent socializing	0.15	ns
Time to achieve monitor pool status	0.37	<0.01
Time to achieve buddy system status	0.40	<0.01
Overt anxiety	—0.13	ns
Phobias	—0.20	<0.05
Compulsivity or obsessions	—0.04	ns
Hypochondriasis or somatization	—0.16	ns
Paranoid thoughts	—0.04	ns
Bizarre speech or behavior	0.03	ns
Delusions	—0.07	ns
Hallucinations	—0.27	<0.01
Confusion	—0.20	<0.05
Depression	—0.08	ns
Guilt	—0.17	ns

The short-stay group of schizophrenic patients attained both monitor pool and buddy system faster than did those who stayed for a longer period of time. The salient aspect of these data is that the outcome variables which are based in part on staff decisions, are in agreement with decisions by the patients' peers.

The four variables assessing the relationship between neurotic-type symptomatology at the time of hospital admission and prognosis showed a weak, but consistent, trend for patients with these symptoms to have shorter hospitalizations. Thus patients with phobic symptoms spent significantly (P <0.05) less time in the hospital, and there was some trend (nonsignificant) for patients with hypochondriacal features and with more overt anxiety to have shorter hospitalizations.

In regard to the results on psychotic and other severe symptomatology the findings were mixed. Length of hospitalization was not related, significantly, to the extent of paranoid thoughts, of bizarre behavior, or of delusions. The presence of hallucinations and of confusion were related, significantly, to outcome, in the direction of confused and hallucinating schizophrenics staying in the hospital for a shorter period of time. The results on confusion are consonant with the findings of Vaillant (29) and of Stephens *et al.* (30) that the presence of this feature in schizophrenics is a good prognostic indicator.

Neither depression nor guilt was a strong indicator of prognosis for our schizophrenic sample, although the results on guilt did show a trend (P <0.10) in the direction reported by other investigators. Thus, there was a tendency for more members of the short-stay group to give some indications of guilt than did members of the long-stay group. According to the developmental theory of Zigler and Phillips (4, 31), the more mature individual is more likely to have incorporated the values of society and display some guilt when he fails to meet these values. If this is the reason for the trend towards greater guilt among the short-stay schizophrenics, then one might expect it to apply to other non-schizophrenic psychiatric patients. Thus, according to this formulation, guiltier character disorders and guiltier depressives would also be expected to be more mature and to be discharged quicker (4, 5). Preliminary indications of ours on a sample of depressive patients and on a sample of character disorders do not confirm this formulation. Further work in this area is needed.

CONCLUSIONS

The data tend to support the hypothesis that factors indicative of good posthospital prognosis in schizophrenia are also predictive of shorter hospitalization. The general theory enhanced by the data is that the level of premorbid functioning is directly related to outcome and length of hospitalization. The findings in all three areas indicate that those patients who are considered mature, according to Phillips' and Zigler's definition, who do not have a premorbid schizoid personality adjustment, and who were able to assume ward responsibilities earlier, had, in general, a shorter hospital stay. Early hospital symptoms discriminated to a lesser degree; nevertheless, the general direction of the results was consonant with the data in other areas.

It should be noted that while the results are in general support of the developmental theory, based on early social competence, proposed by

Phillips and others, alternate interpretations of the data are possible. Thus, on the basis of the present data it is equally possible that extent of "illness" is the important factor determining prognosis, and that early social competence is one indicator of the length and severity of the disorder for *schizophrenic* patients (with patients with inadequate premorbid functioning having earlier traces of the disorder and also being more severely ill). Either general hypothesis (one based on developmental level and one based on severity of illness) might predict the present results (that schizophrenics with poorer premorbid functioning take longer to recover when hospitalized).

While the predictions from either formulation are the same for schizophrenics, this may not be the case for other disorders. Thus, according to the developmental theory one would predict that depressives (or character disorders) with poorer premorbid functioning would also have poorer prognoses, but a severity of illness hypothesis would not necessarily predict that depressives with poorer premorbid functioning have early traces of their later depression, or are more severely ill later when they become depressed. We are currently attempting to study this problem and contrast factors associated with length of hospitalization for non-schizophrenic psychiatric patients versus those for schizophrenics.

The present study attempted to determine whether the short-term prognosis of 125 hospitalized schizophrenics could be predicted by variables assessing: (1) demographic and sociologic factors, (2) childhood events and prehospital functioning, and (3) symptoms and functioning, at the time of hospitalization.

Data on demographic and sociologic variables indicated that older patients and married patients were hospitalized for a significantly shorter period of time. Variables assessing childhood events did not relate to patients' length of hospitalization. Patients with better premorbid functioning and those who were ill for a shorter period of time had a significantly better prognosis. In regard to functioning at the time of hospitalization, patients whose social functioning was assessed more favorably by other patients tended to be discharged quicker. Schizophrenic patients with additional neurotic symptomatology were hospitalized for a shorter period of time. Patients with confusion and hallucinations also had a significantly better short-term prognosis. There was a slight trend for guilty patients to be discharged quicker.

The overall results indicate that factors such as (premorbid) social competence, which are indicative of good posthospital prognosis for schizophrenics, are also predictive of a shorter hospitalization. This fits in with a developmental theory which emphasizes the importance of premorbid social competence as an index of the level of maturity attained and hence as an indicator of prognosis in schizophrenia. An alternate theory, however, based on the extent and severity of illness would also explain the present data.

A copy of the interview schedules used in the research may be obtained from Martin Harrow, Ph.D., Department of Psychiatry, Yale University School of Medicine, New Haven, Conn. 06510.

REFERENCES

1. FARINA, A., et al.: Premorbid Behavior and Prognosis in Female Schizophrenic Patients, *J. Consult. Psychol.* 76:56-60 (Feb.) 1962.
2. RODNICK, E. H., & GARMEZY, N.: "An Experimental Approach to the Study of Motivation in Schizophrenia," in Jones, M. R. (ed.): *Nebraska Symposium on Motivation, 1957,* Lincoln, Neb.: University of Nebraska Press, 1967, pp. 109-184.
3. BELLAK, L. (ed.): *Schizophrenia: A Review of the Syndrome,* New York: Logos, 1958.
4. ZIGLER, E., & PHILLIPS, L.: Social Competence and Outcome in Psychiatric Disorders, *J. Abnor. Soc. Psychol.* 63:264-271 (Sept.) 1961.
5. ZIGLER, E., & PHILLIPS, L.: Social Competence and the Process-Reactive Distinction in Psychopathology, *J. Abnor. Soc. Psychol.* 65:215-222 (Oct.) 1962.
6. The Joint Commission on Mental Illness and Health: *Action for Mental Health,* New York: Basic Books, Inc., Publishers, 1961.
7. DETRE, T. P., KESSLER, D., & SAYERS, J.: "A Socio-Adaptive Approach to Treatment of Acutely Disturbed Psychiatric Inpatients," in the *Proceedings, Third World Congress of Psychiatry,* Toronto: University of Toronto Press, 1961, pp. 501-506.
8. SOSKIS, D. A., HARROW, M., & DETRE, T. P.: Long-Term Follow-up of Schizophrenics Admitted to a General Hospital Psychiatric Ward, *Psychiat. Quart.,* to be published.
9. NORTON, N. M.. DETRE, T. P., & JARECKI, H. G.: Psychiatric Services in General Hospitals: A Family-Oriented Redefinition, *J. Nerv. Ment. Dis.* 136:475-484 (May) 1963.
10. ASTRACHAN, B. M., et al.: The Unled Group as a Therapeutic Tool, *Int. J. Group Psychother.* 17:178-191 (April) 1967.
11. HARROW, M., et al.: An Investigation Into the Nature of the Patient-Family Therapy Group, *Amer. J. Orthopsychiat.* 37:888-899 (Oct.) 1967.
12. HARROW, M., et al.: Influence of the Psychotherapist on the Emotional Climate in Group Therapy, *Hum. Relations* 20:49-64 (Feb.) 1967.
13. DETRE, T. P., KESSLER, D. R., & JARECKI, H. G.: The Role of the General Hospital in Modern Community Psychiatry, *Amer. J. Orthopsychiat.* 33:690-700 (July) 1963.
14. HARROW, M., & FERRANTE, A.: Locus of Control in Psychiatric Patients, *J. Consult. Psychol.,* to be published.
15. TUCKER, G.. et al.: Perceptual Experiences in Schizophrenic and Non-Schizophrenic Patients, *Arch. Gen. Psychiat.* 20:159-166 (Feb.) 1969.
16. AMDUR, M. J., et al.: Anorexia Nervosa: An International Study, *J. Nerv. Ment. Dis.,* to be published.
17. HARROW, M., et al.: Changes in Adolescents' Self-Concepts and Their Parents' Perceptions During Psychiatric Hospitalization, *J. Nerv. Ment. Dis.* 147:252-259 (Sept.) 1968.

18. KUPFER, D. J., DETRE, T. P., & HARROW, M.: Relationship Between Sleep Disorders and Symptomatology, *Arch. Gen. Psychiat.* 17:710-716 (Dec.) 1967.

19. ROSEN, B., et al.: Social Competence and Posthospital Outcome, *Arch. Gen. Psychiat.* 19:165-170 (Aug.) 1968.

20. FARINA, A., GARMEZY, N., & BARRY, H.: Relationship of Marital Status to Incidence and Prognosis of Schizophrenia, *J. Abnor. Psychol.* 67:624-630 (Dec.) 1963.

21. PHILLIPS, L.: Case History Data and Prognosis in Schizophrenia, *J. Nerv. Ment. Dis.* 117:515-525 (June) 1953.

22. HOLLINGSHEAD, A. B., & REDLICH, F. C.: *Social Class and Mental Illness,* New York: John Wiley & Sons, Inc., 1958.

23. LIDZ, T., & FLECK, S.: Schizophrenia, Human Integration, and the Role of the Family, in Jackson, D. (ed.): *Etiology of Schizophrenia,* New York: Basic Books, Inc., Publishers, 1959, pp. 323-345.

24. FARINA, A.: Patterns of the Dominance and Conflict in Parents of Schizophrenic Patients, *J. Abnor. Psychol.* 61:31-38 (July) 1960.

25. FLECK, S., LIDZ, T., & CORNELISON, A.: Comparison of Parent-Child Relationships of Male and Female Schizophrenic Patients, *Arch. Gen. Psychiat.* 8:1-7 (Jan.) 1963.

26. VAILLANT, G. E.: The Prediction of Recovery in Schizophrenia, *J. Nerv. Ment. Dis.* 135:534-543 (Dec.) 1962.

27. VAILLANT, G. E.: An Historical Review of the Remitting Schizophrenica, *J. Nerv. Ment. Dis.* 138:48-56 (Jan.) 1964.

28. ASTRACHAN, B. M., HARROW, M., & FLYNN, H. R.: Influence of the Value-System of a Psychiatric Setting on Behavior in Group Therapy Meetings, *Soc. Psychiat.* 3:165-172 (Oct.) 1968.

29. VAILLANT, G. E.: Prospective Prediction of Schizophrenic Remission, *Arch. Gen. Psychiat.* 11:509-518 (Nov.) 1964.

30. STEPHENS, J. H., ASTRUP, C., & MANGRUM, J. C.: Prognostic Factors in Recovered and Deteriorated Schizophrenics, *Amer. J. Psychiat.* 122:1116-1121 (April) 1966.

31. ZIGLER, E., & PHILLIPS, L.: Social Effectiveness and Symptomatic Behaviors, *J. Abnor. Psychol.* 61:231-238 (Sept.) 1960.

42

SCHIZOPHRENIA: DIAGNOSIS AND PROGNOSIS

Gabriel Langfeldt

The Stanley R. Dean Research Award was established by the Fund for the Behavioral Sciences and is presented jointly with the American College of Psychiatrists to emphasize the importance of basic research toward an understanding of schizophrenia; each year, a scientist who has made an important contribution in this area is honored.

Following is the text of a lecture delivered by Dr. Gabriel Langfeldt on the occasion of his receiving the seventh annual award of $2,000 at a seminar held in New Orleans, Louisiana, February 1, 1969, by the American College of Psychiatrists. Dr. Langfeldt, a pioneer in diagnostic criteria for schizophrenia, outlines the procedures which led to the recognition of schizophreniform, or schizophrenia-like, psychosis, an important step toward isolating the "true" schizophrenias.

My interest in a clearcut and circumscribed diagnosis of schizophrenia disorders began during the years 1923-26, when I was studying the effect of these illnesses (called "dementia praecox" at that time in Norway) on the functioning of the endocrine and vegetative systems. With methods at that time considered the best available for the detection of endocrine anomalies and functional disturbances of the vegetative nervous system, I investigated forty cases with a typical clinical symptomatology. The methods at hand were a general clinical investigation, which included x-ray examination of the Sella turcica (the depression in the skull containing the pituitary gland) and the epiphyses (the cartilaginous lines at which growth occurs in the long bones of the young) and determination of the blood picture and basal metabolism as well as a study of subcutaneous adrenalin injection and peroral administration of sexual gland extracts and thyroid tablets upon basal metabolic levels, which are abnormally low in some schizophrenics. In all cases an examination

Reprinted from *Behavioral Science*, Volume 14, No. 3, 1969 by permission of James G. Miller, M.D., Ph.D., Editor, and the American College of Psychiatrists, Sponsors of the Stanley R. Dean Research Award. Copyright 1969, *Behavioral Science*.

of the carbohydrate metabolism was also performed. The autonomic nervous system was examined clinically as well as with intravenously applied adrenalin, atropine, and pilocarpin.

Although I found none of the well-known endocrine disorders, I did find, as a result of my examinations, metabolic anomalies well known to the endocrine clinic. A leading idea in my procedure was that possible physiological anomalies should be correlated not only with the type of schizophrenic disorder in question, but also with the dominating mental picture and stage of development. The results of my findings were collected in a monograph entitled "The endocrine glands and autonomic system in dementia praecox."

In my opinion the most interesting result of this study was the conclusion that Kraepelin's three types of dementia praecox—catatonic, hebephrenic, and paranoid—were characterized by different physiological anomalies, varying, in addition, with whether the stage of development was quiescent or chronic. While there is no point in my dwelling on my 1926 findings here, I merely mention that I showed, then, for the first time that one distinction between catatonic cases, on the one hand, and hebephrenic and paranoid cases, on the other, was that the former were, at times, immune to intravenously injected adrenalin, in that no elevation of blood pressure was demonstrated. Because some normal persons, as I also discovered then, show a similar negative reaction to adrenalin, I could not use this test to help diagnose schizophrenia, or to differentiate between catatonic and other types of the disorder.

Another observation was that basal metabolism is reduced predominantly in acute, withdrawn cases of catatonia (in 6 out of 8 cases). Of 13 cases of hebephrenia, only one was characterized by a reduction in basal metabolism—about 22 percent. I also found that such reduced basal metabolism could not be raised by the administration of thyroid hormone and that there were essential differences in the blood picture and the condition of the autonomic nervous systems, especially between the catatonic and hebephrenic cases. These led me to feel strongly that future research on schizophrenia needed to correlate possible somatic findings, type of disorder, and stage of development with the actual symptomatology.

I would like to cite the following lines from my 1926 monograph: "On the basis of these [1926] studies, it must be emphasized here that the tendency which at present prevails among a great number of psychiatrists to let the whole dementia praecox idea be absorbed by the collective designation 'schizophrenia,' is extremely detrimental to the further progress of psychiatry. 'Schizophrenia' is a symptom complex, not a diagnosis. On the other hand, when we speak of catatonia, every psychiatrist and most physicians know what picture of disease we have before us. The same is the case with hebephrenia, which—we have learned from our experiments—is also somatically well correlated." As is well known, since my investigation with the rather simple methods of 45 years ago, intensive research has taken place for the purpose of detecting somatic and psychological factors related to the etiology of schizophrenia. Imposing work has been performed with the help of methods from the natural sciences, experimental and clinical psychology, psychoanalysis, and even existential philosophy. However, in spite of the thousands of investigations, thus far no conclusion has been borne to the point of universal authority by further investigation. This circumstance is, in part, due to the fact that there is no agreement on the characteristics of the schizophrenic disorders.

During the last 25 years I have been visiting many psychiatric hospitals and clinics in Scandinavia, Germany, Austria, Switzerland, Great Britain, and the United States, discussing, among other things, the concept of schizophrenia. The diagnostic term "schizophrenia" differs, unfortunately, not only from country to country, but even from hospital to hospital within a country. While in some places the term was reserved for a group with a quite typical history, symptomatology, and course, this term was in other places a rather comprehensive one including psychoses with a widely varying symptomatology. If researchers on schizophrenia, in reporting their findings, had always indicated the special type and mental state of the disorder instead of merely using the term "schizophrenia," the progress in research on these sorts of disorders would probably have been much greater.

The prognosis for dementia praecox was viewed differently from today in the years before Bleuler proposed, in 1911, that "dementia praecox" be replaced by "schizophrenia," at the same time extending the latter term to include psychoses of a widely varying origin. At the time of Kraepelin, psychiatrists were interested in follow-up investigations of dementia praecox cases. Researchers of the day were in agreement that the prognosis of this disorder was poor, and the results of follow-up investigations corresponded fairly well to the reports of Kraepelin: in long-term studies, 12.6 percent of the group diagnosed as dementia praecox recovered immediately. Because most of these suffered a relapse within two or three years, the number of *lasting* recoveries amounted to only 2.6 percent. While 17 percent showed a social remission, the rest deteriorated. (Kraepelin cites in his textbook several reports from other experienced psychiatrists who, like Albrecht, Mattouschech, Schmidt, Stern, and Zabloha, had achieved similar results.)

If the percentage of recovery varied a little, it was generally felt before the time of the appearance of the schizophrenia concept that a real cure for dementia praecox was an exception. Most research workers reported that 30-40 percent of the socialized group were more or less able to work, while the rest steadily deteriorated to a degree which made permanent hospitalization or other support necessary. The content of the schizophrenia group, as described by Bleuler, is in no way identical with that of the dementia praecox group. The latter—and many other psychoses which we now consider to have quite another etiology and symptomatology—were described by Bleuler as belonging to the schizophrenia group. Thus he writes that "in the term 'schizophrenia' are included atypical melancholias and manias of other schools, most of the hallucinatoric confusions, a great deal of what other psychiatrists diagnose as amentia, some types of psychoses described as acute delirium, Wernickes disease, the primary and secondary dementias without any typical picture, most cases of paranoia from other schools, and almost all cases of hypochondriasis with poor prognosis as well as certain nervous, obsessional, and compulsive neuroses. In addition, the diseases described as juvenile and masturbatory as well as the great number of psychoses described by Magnan as degenerative psychoses associated with puberty are included."

Little by little the term "schizophrenia" replaced the term "dementia praecox" all over the world. Because of the diffuse description of its content, however, it is no wonder that the diagnosis has differed tremendously from hospital to hospital. Consequently since 1911, when the term was introduced, most researchers have found the prognosis for schizophrenia to be better than that for dementia praecox. Bellak, for instance, discovered that before shock treatment, improvement rates ranged from 8.8 to 44 percent. Subsequently, Sakel found an 88 percent rate of improvement in cases of schizophrenia treated with insulin comas. There can be no doubt that one of the principal causes of the difference between the course of dementia praecox cases, on the one hand, and the schizophrenias, on the other, is that the schizophrenia group included different syndromes. The reasons for this difference are many, and I shall return to them later.

SCHIZOPHRENIFORM PSYCHOSES

I became more interested in the diagnosis and prognosis of schizophrenia when Sakel announced in 1935 that, through the use of insulin-coma therapy, he had been able to bring about a satisfactory social remission in 88 percent of what, at the Vienna clinic, had been diagnosed as schizophrenia. I was at that time senior psychiatrist at the University Psychiatric Clinic of Oslo. I had the opportunity to make a trip to Vienna, where I was able to study the records of many of the patients treated. From this inspection I concluded rather quickly that a large proportion of the patients who were "schizophrenic" in Vienna would, in Norway, have been diagnosed under other categories: psychogenic psychoses, reactive psychoses, toxic and infective reaction types, as well as psychoses in individuals with organic brain disorders. I also noticed that while patients with such psychoses—which since 1937 I have grouped as "schizophreniform"—as a rule reacted favorably to the treatment, the cases which did not improve corresponded to the cases which at the Oslo clinic were diagnosed as true schizophrenias. Meduna, at the same time, drew a similar conclusion: cases which reacted favorably to metrazole treatment did not belong to the dementia praecox group. I decided upon my return to Oslo to treat ten cases of typical schizophrenia of short duration with insulin-coma therapy in the manner of Sakel. Two of these had a brief remission but relapsed, and all of them had to be transferred to a mental hospital. Follow-up investigation indicated that all had deteriorated severely.

During the following years, the results of more and more investigations of the treatment of schizophrenia with metrazole and insulin shock appeared. All of them, however, had two essential drawbacks: they merely used the term "schizophrenia," without indicating type, symptomatology, or phase of disorder. As a rule, control material was also completely lacking. Thus, I became more and more convinced that most of the cases which recovered after such treatment were those which had a tendency to spontaneous remission, and that they could be helped by other, less dangerous therapy. To prove this, it was necessary, in the first place to get a thorough knowledge of the spontaneous course of the psychoses diagnosed as schizophrenic. As I've said, by then there was a rather comprehensive body of knowledge indicating the course of dementia praecox cases, but statistics relating to the more extensive group of the schizophrenias were rather scanty. Certainly, some interest in this question had been shown, but most of the statistics presented were based only on written reports from either the patients themselves or their relatives. In my book *The Prognosis of Schizophrenia and the Course of the Disease* (1937), I showed how unreliable such reports can be. Comparison of a report like this with a follow-up study of the patient would indicate often that the patient was, for example, severely demented even though according to the report he was well-adjusted. There is not necessarily any contradiction here: the patient's adjustment in the nonstressful home situation may have been adequate or his "queerness" may have become accepted by the family and not noticed by them. In the years after that, therefore, I considered determination of the spontaneous course of those psychoses usually diagnosed as schizophrenic, including individual follow-up investigation, to be an important topic for research. Only with such material at hand would it be possible to estimate, among other things, the value of the different types of shock treatment.

Next, my experiences with the highly variable content of the concept of schizophrenia had made it quite clear to me that the enormous number of papers on the effects of treatment could never be helpful in deciding the question of whether the real schizophrenic disorder had been influenced by the treatment. Conditions seemed to indicate that a therapist who had included many of the typical dementia praecox cases in his concept of schizophrenia would get far fewer remissions than would his colleague whose concept consisted mainly of schizophrenialike cases belonging to other groups of psychoses regularly connected with a tendency to spontaneous remission. In my opinion, then, this is the principal cause of an 85 percent variation in remission rates: from 3-4 percent to 50-60 percent (as mentioned by Sakel), and on up to as much as 88 percent.

THE DICHOTOMY

It would have been an easy matter to determine the effect of the shock treatment on the true schizophrenias if, at that time—34 years ago—generally accepted diagnostic criteria of the genuine schizophrenias had existed. But this was not the case. On the contrary, the different psychiatric schools defined schizophrenia in very different ways, a fact which was the natural consequence of Bleuler's broad concept of the psychic pictures included in the term. As already mentioned, in later decades researchers have searched eagerly for a specific cause of schizophrenia and for clues to its diagnosis and prognosis. Thousands of investigations have been performed with methods from the fields of genetics, biochemistry, immunology, physiology, and others. Also, experimental psychology and experiments with model psychoses as well as psychoanalytic and existential philosophical approaches have been directed to the establishment of valid diagnostic criteria. There can be no doubt that some of these investigations have led to interesting results. We must, however, bear in mind that these findings, no matter how interesting, have not yet been adequately verified.

In addition, we must also remember that there has not been agreement as to whether the results mentioned are primarily connected with the schizophrenic disorder as such, or if they can be explained more reasonably as secondary or parallel to emotional or other psychic disturbances. One must also assume that if schizophrenia is not a single disease but a conglomerate of different psychotic disorders, it is not reasonable that a single cause of the disorder will be detected. Although the great body of data on the schizophrenic disorders is most interesting, it is impossible to consider it here. Let me, on this point, merely conclude that it is at present of little practical significance to the task of providing clues to diagnosis and prognosis which might be easy to teach medical students and could also be useful in international comparative psychiatry. We must never forget that a principal aim of psychiatric research is to produce information about the psychiatric disorders which will help the practicing physician as well as the psychiatric specialist. I assume that, among other things, psychoanalytical and existential philosophical concepts revolving about this question are of more theoretical than practical significance. It would be hopeless, for example, to diagnose schizophrenia on the basis of "the way of life" of the patient. Neither can the capacity for social adjustment be helpful. On the whole, a single aspect of behavior or a single symptom is not a usable basis for diagnosis or prognosis. Most psychiatrists, I assume, now agree that schizophrenia is a multiform disorder in which individually varying, inborn, and exogenic psychic and somatic factors play roles in the production of symptoms and final outcome of the disorder.

Since my somatic studies of schizophrenia in the twenties, I have stressed the significance of restricting the diagnosis of schizophrenia to the group of disorders which, as proven by individual follow-up investigation, have a poor prognosis. The initial advantage of such a diagnostic method is that in reports on schizophrenia research we can compare the same type of disorder internationally. It is also easy to teach students the symptoms related to this diagnosis. By reserving the diagnosis of schizophrenia to the cases which empirically are connected with a poor prognosis, we will, I believe, also have much greater chances of detecting possible metabolic and psychological changes characteristic of the group.

My proposal in 1937 was that this central group should be termed typical or genuine schizophrenias, while psychoses whose relation to the group was doubtful should be termed schizophreniform psychoses. This dichotomy embraced the advantages outlined above.

CONTRIBUTIONS

I should like now to summarize my own contributions to the diagnosis and prognosis of schizophrenia as well as some comparable, individual follow-up investigations. I had a good starting point because two sorts of "schizophrenia" had already been distinguished at the University Psychiatric Clinic of Oslo, when it opened in 1926. The great influence in Scandinavia of the Kraepelin school led Dr. Vogt, the director of the Oslo Clinic at that time, to stress whether or not a case of schizophrenia belonged to the central dementia praecox group. If so, the diagnosis at discharge was "schizophrenia." If at discharge there was any doubt, one, two, or three question marks were added to the diagnosis. (The more doubt, the more question marks.) In addition, the type of disorder (hebephrenic, catatonic, paranoid) was noted as a subdiagnosis. In the cases with question marks, the other possible diagnoses were added: paranoid-hallucinatory psychosis in an alcoholic, sensitive self-reference psychosis, or confusional psychosis in a feebleminded personality, for example.

Following the Course of Spontaneous Remission

To produce material illustrating the spontaneous course of schizophrenia, I decided, in 1936, to follow up each of 200 schizophrenics who had been hospitalized during the years 1926-29—that is, during a period before shock treatment. One hundred of these had at their discharge been diagnosed as schizophrenias belonging to the central dementia praecox group, while the other hundred had received one or more question marks. These last cases, which in a 1937 monograph I described as schizophreniform psychoses, were—because they involved hallucinations, delusions, and special personality traits, among other things—reminiscent of the true schizophrenias, even though they lacked the central, primary symptoms typical of the classic dementia praecox cases. Many interesting facts were revealed through my follow-up investigations in 1936, a comparison of diagnosis at discharge with information about the mental status of the patient gained at his home, 7-10 years later. Sixty-six of the cases diagnosed as typical schizophrenics at discharge were unchanged or worse, while 17 had completely recovered, and 17 others were improved.

Because a change in the concept of the content of schizophrenic disorders had taken place during the seven to ten years which elapsed between the hospitalization of these patients and re-examination in 1936, I decided to revise the diagnosis of the cases followed up. After such revision it became apparent that out of the 100 cases considered schizophrenia at discharge in 1926-29, 13 were lacking the symptoms which I considered essential to this group in 1936. The final result of this follow-up of the typical schizophrenias—then consisting of 87 cases—was that by 1936, only 6 had recovered completely, while 11 of the 13 cases which were considered schizophreniform had recovered completely, and 2 had improved. Of the group of 100 schizophrenics considered doubtful at discharge in 1926-29, 32 cases had recovered at the follow-up in 1936. Twenty-five had improved, and 43 were unchanged or worse. After the latter revision of the diagnosis, however, it appeared that of the 100 schizophrenia-like or schizophreniform psychoses, 45 had revealed a history and symptomatology which—in 1936—was considered characteristic of the central group. Of these 45 cases only one had recovered and 8 improved by the follow-up in 1936. Of the 55 schizophreniform cases still diagnosed as such at the re-examination, 31 had recovered and 17 improved, while only 7 were unchanged or worse.

If we summarize the outcome of the total number of psychoses, we find—taking into account the diagnosis at the follow-up in 1936—that of 132 typical cases of schizophrenia, 102 had remained unchanged or worse, 7 had recovered, and the remainder, 23, had improved. On the other hand, of the total number of schizophreniform psychoses—68 cases—only 17 were worse or unchanged, while 42 had recovered and 19 had improved. These results seem to indicate convincingly that by dividing the large schizophrenia group into typical and schizophreniform cases, we had succeeded in differentiating between two prognostically widely varying groups of the psychotic disorders regularly diagnosed as schizophrenia. We can learn from this follow-up that the best clue to a valid prognostication is a demonstration of the presence of central symptoms which empirically indicate a poor prognosis. If such symptoms are not present in the initial stages, the course cannot be predicted with the same accuracy.

In this connection I must mention, however, what Strömgren has stressed in a special paper on the schizophreniform psychoses, that although the term "schizophreniform" has now certainly been widespread through the literature, different meanings have been assigned to it. The term "schizophreniform psychoses" should only indicate that we have to do with a psychosis which is characterized by a schizophrenia-like picture, but without such symptoms of schizophrenia as regularly are connected with a poor prognosis. In the early stages of such psychoses it may be difficult to detect the typical schizophrenic symptoms, and as a consequence of this several cases of schizophreniform psychoses may develop in the direction of schizophrenic deterioration. Most cases of schizophreniform psychoses, however, belong to other types of psychoses. This term does not represent—as some writers assume—a distinct diagnostic entity.

It need only be added that from my studies it emerged that in addition to the symptomatology in the initial stages, several other factors—such as bodily constitution and temperament type, age of outbreak and duration of the psychosis from outbreak until admission to the hospital, precipitating external factors, and whether there was acute or gradual onset—might in the single case have some prognostic significance. It was proven statistically that acute onset and external precipitating factors were prognostically favorable factors, but in the single case it is the constellation of the different signs and symptoms which indicates the further course.

Diagnosis

Initial changes in the personality and the acute mental symptomatology are, in my experience, the most general and best clues to a diagnosis of the genuine schizophrenic type regularly connected with a poor prognosis. Changes in the personality, which are rather characteristic in many of the typical cases of schizophrenia, manifest themselves as a special type of emotional blunting followed by lack of initiative and altered, frequently peculiar behavior. In hebephrenia especially these changes are quite characteristic and are a principal clue to the diagnosis. The changes which take place are frequently more difficult to describe than to recognize, but the experienced psychiatrist regularly feels intuitively that he is confronted with a morbid personality of the genuine schizophrenic type. In catatonic types, the history as well as the typical signs in periods of restlessness and stupor (with negativism, oily facies, catalepsy, special vegetative symptoms, and so on) are frequently so characteristic that no doubt can exist that the case belongs to the typical schizophrenia type.

The greatest difficulty arises in connection with the diagnosis of paranoid cases of schizophrenia. Especially as described by Retterstöl in his monograph on paranoid and paranoiac psychoses, the paranoid syndrome appears in most types of psychoses, and—as a whole—the prognosis for these disorders does not seem to be unfavorable. Consequently, it is important in the initial stages of a paranoid disorder to be able to decide whether it is a case belonging to the prognostically unfavorable central group of schizophrenias, or whether it is a psychosis with a more favorable course. Even in recent times, a psychosis characterized by paranoid ideas and hallucinations is in many hospitals diagnosed as schizophrenia, even if none of the symptoms which indicate a progressive course with deterioration are present. In my follow-up investigations, it was proved that the paranoid psychoses which regularly were associated with a poor prognosis were characterized by essential symptoms of split personality (or "depersonalization symptoms") and a loss of reality feeling ("derealization symptoms"). In addition, Kraepelin's cases of dementia praecox characterized by primary—in contrast to secondary—delusions had an unfavorable course. I cannot here describe in detail the symptoms characteristic of the depersonalization and derealization states. I shall only stress the fact that for the typical signs of schizophrenia it is not enough that the patient talk about being influenced by forces from the outer world, or that he entertain strange ideas about his surroundings. He must—as stressed by Mauz—really experience these influences. It should be emphasized that mild depersonalization and derealization symptoms may occur as transient symptoms in neuroses and in some psychoses, especially those connected with confusional states. If no sign of organic brain disorder, infection, or intoxication can be demonstrated, however, a mental picture dominated by what I have described as depersonalization and derealization is characteristic of the genuine cases of paranoid schizophrenia associated with a poor prognosis.

Thus, the significant clues to a diagnosis of the genuine types of schizophrenic disorder are a typical break in personality development, emotional blunting, and catatonic restlessness and stupor, as well as the symptoms of depersonalization and derealization. If we restrict the diagnosis "schizophrenia" to these groups, we can, with high probability, predict an unfavorable course. According to my proposal all psychoses which—because they involve hallucinations and delusions—may have a superficial similarity with the genuine schizophrenias but are lacking the essential symptoms of these, should be diagnosed as schizophreniform psychoses. The question of confusional or emotionally abnormal states and many paranoid psychoses will be important here. Many psychoses in feebleminded, hysterical, obsessional, and hypersensitive individuals are characterized by delusions and hallucinations, but they lack other symptoms of the true schizophrenias as defined above. In international literature, cases which should be considered belonging to the group of schizophreniform psychoses have different names such as oneiro-phrenia, schizoaffective states, acute confusional states, ambulatoric schizophrenia, sensitive delusions, pseudoneurotic or pseudopsychopathic schizophrenias, and others. The reason these cases are often diagnosed as schizophrenia is probably that the personality types in question con-tribute to the subjective symptomatology. Some features—schizoid traits, emotional flattening, ideas of reference, for example—can resemble genu-ine schizophrenic symptoms. The further course of these cases, however, have been proven by many researchers to be much more favorable than are true cases of genuine schizophrenia.

Second Follow-Up: The Course of Spontaneous Remission

I arrived at the above conclusions by studying the spontaneous course of cases of schizophrenia which had been submitted to only the usual types of therapy during the years 1926-29. As it was of interest to make a similar follow-up of cases treated with one or another type of shock treatment, or with lobotomy, my senior psychiatrists, L. Eitinger and C. L. Laane at the University Psychiatric Clinic of Oslo, and I agreed to carry out such a comparison. The follow-up was carried through the year 1955. It dealt with 783 patients hospitalized during the years 1940-49. Every patient was re-examined by questionnaire, and also 154 of these patients were re-examined individually by Drs. Eitinger and Laane. In my discussion here I shall limit my remarks only to the 154 individually examined patients. My assistants and I had agreed that in this follow-up I would confine myself to diagnosis and prediction on the basis of the records of hospitalization, while they would actually travel around and perform the re-examinations. Thus, I made up my mind as to whether the case should be considered a typical schizophrenia or a schizophreni-form psychosis and, at the same time, indicated whether recovery, im-provement, or lack of change was the most probable outcome. After the cases were followed up, my prognostication was compared to the actual results 5 to 15 years after discharge had taken place.

We found that for those treated with electrical shock, insulin coma, or lobotomy, the outcome was much better in the schizophreniform cases than in the genuine schizophrenias. The correspondence between my prognostication and the real facts as determined independently by my assistants was good. Of the 110 cases diagnosed by me as typical schizo-phrenias, 105 had, according to the statements of my assistants, developed as such—101 of them had deteriorated, while 4 had recovered or were improved. On the other hand, of 39 schizophreniform psychoses, 14 were essentially unchanged, while the rest had recovered or were much improved. It seems reasonable, therefore, to draw the conclusion that cases of typical schizophrenia treated differently in the long run do not have a more favorable course than untreated cases. On the other hand, many schizophreniform psychoses seem to recover after different treatment.

CORROBORATING RESEARCH

Little by little, the dichotomy into genuine schizophrenias and schizophreniform psychoses attracted interest, especially among Scandinavian psychiatrists. Several papers and some monographs have been published in which the results of different kinds of therapy and follow-up investigations have been related to the two groups. In a 1962 monograph by Astrup, Fossum, and Holmboe, the result of a follow-up of 1,102 patients during the years 1955-60 is reported. The patients had been hospitalized during the years 1938-50 and had been subjected to the usual shock treatment. From this publication I would like to quote the following: "Whereas the primary symptoms of Bleuler are rather vaguely defined, the process-symptoms of Langfeldt are as a rule so clear-cut that they can be established when present. In our previous publication we could show, like Langfeldt, that when process-symptoms are not present, the risk of a schizophrenic deterioration is very small. One could therefore agree with Langfeldt that psychoses without process symptoms should not be diagnosed as schizophrenias. When process symptoms were present, there was always a considerable risk of schizophrenic deterioration." In this study, of the schizophreniform cases without classical schizophrenic symptoms, 78 percent recovered, while of the nuclear group of schizophrenia, only 13 to 20 percent recovered.

Retterstöl (1966), reporting his follow-up of different types of psychoses, has stated that only in two out of 31 cases of schizophrenia was the diagnosis changed. He concluded therefore that on the basis of the process-symptoms it should be possible to differentiate between process-schizophrenia and schizophreniform psychoses 90 to 95 percent of the time.

In 1961 Achte published a monograph on the course of schizophrenia and the schizophreniform psychoses from Lapinlahti Hospital in Finland. His population consisted of 100 patients who had been hospitalized in 1930 and 100 patients hospitalized in 1950. During the years 1950-60 he followed up on the 132 cases which could at that time be traced. He writes that "The criteria conform by and large to Langfeldt's [1953] concept of the primary symptoms of schizophrenia. On the other hand, if the patient had displayed none of them, the case is regarded as schizophreniform psychosis." It is further stated that the classification was carried out by relying upon the entries in the case records and without any knowledge of the post-hospital progress of the patient. According to the classification, 70 percent of the 1930 patients belonged to the group of schizophrenias; the corresponding figure for the 1950 material was 54 percent.

I cannot go into the details of the result of the follow-up of these cases four years after the discharge, but Achte states: "If account is taken of all the patients who had social remissions within four years, on the one hand, the prognosis of the patients with schizophreniform disease pictures was significantly better (0.1 percent) than the diagnosis of those affected by typical schizophrenias. This holds good for the materials of both decades." And further: "It can accordingly be concluded that typical schizophrenia is rarely cured even by methods which are in use at our clinic today." The author adds, however, that if the typical signs of schizophrenia are not present in the initial stages of the disorder, it is difficult to make a dependable prognosis regarding the course of the psychosis in question.

Eva Johanson (1958) has carried through a similar follow-up investigation in Sweden of 100 cases of typical schizophrenias, 27 patients with uncertain schizophrenias, and 11 cases in which the psychoses had not been considered as schizophrenic at all. The prognosis of the typical cases was highly unfavorable, for only one case could be considered "recovered" and eight additional cases were considered predominantly favorable. The prognosis in the uncertain or schizophreniform psychoses was significantly better, and the author concludes that the differences between the two groups are so large that "there seems to be good reason for a separation."

Strömgren and Welner have described in a 1958 paper a genetic and clinical study of a benign group of schizophreniform psychoses differentiated from the main group of more or less malignant schizophrenias by means of clinical criteria. Seventy-two patients carefully diagnosed as schizophreniform psychoses were observed from 1.5 to 20 years, 8.8 years on the average. The follow-up showed that the cases were either cured or suffered from nonschizophrenic psychopathology. The conclusion of this study is that "the family picture indicates that the psychoses concerned are not manifestations of a specific genetic factor. From a genetic point of view, there seems, therefore, to be good reason to keep the typical schizophrenias in a separate group."

Finally, it should be pointed out that in England a comprehensive follow-up investigation of schizophrenic and schizophreniform psychoses has been carried through by Roth and his associates. Over three years they followed up 1,100 cases classified as schizophrenic and 72 as schizophreniform psychoses: "In a survey of the results of treatment in all patients admitted to hospitals in the northeast of England, it was found that schizophreniform psychoses, differentiated by criteria similar to those of Langfeldt, responded to some forms of treatment including a combination of *ECT* and tranquilizing drugs more favorable than schizophrenic cases, as judged by status on discharge and length of span in hospital. Readmission rates were also substantially lower for schizophreniform cases, although the differences are not statistically significant."

CONCLUSION

Psychiatrists in different countries have been able to differentiate between the typical or genuine schizophrenias and the schizophrenia-like psychoses I have called schizophreniform. Researchers have arrived at the conclusion that the typical schizophrenias have a much poorer prognosis, with or without treatments, than is the case with schizophreniform psychoses. I am personally convinced that if researchers in the field of psychiatry, in the teaching of students, in research, and in practical clinical psychiatry would always adhere to the dichotomy I proposed, psychiatry would profit much from it. In all types of schizophrenia research the findings must be correlated with the special symptomatology in the two groups, schizophrenia and schizophreniform psychoses.

To avoid misunderstandings, I would like to close by stressing that the poor prognosis of typical cases of schizophrenia should not result in a pessimistic attitude toward the possibility of rehabilitation and a better social adjustment for these patients. Occupational therapy, psychotherapy, and pharmacotherapy are certainly useful in this regard. Scientific evidence that the basic schizophrenic disorders can be effectively and lastingly cured is still lacking, however. The great hope is that metabolic disorders, possibly different in various types of genuine schizophrenia, will be detected and that treatment of these disorders will return the patient to complete health.

REFERENCES

ACHTÉ, K. A. Der Verlauf der Schizophrenien und der Schizopreniformen Psychosen. *Acta Psych. Scand.*, Suppl. 155, 1961.

ASTRUP, C., FOSSUM, A., & HOLMBOE, R. *Prognosis in Functional Psychosis. Clinical, Social and Genetic Aspects.* Springfield, Ill.: Charles C Thomas, 1962.

BELLAK, L. *Schizophrenia.* New York: Logos Press, 1958.

Johanson, Eva. A study of schizophrenia in the male. A psychiatric and social study based on 138 cases with follow-up. *Acta Psych. Scand.*, Suppl. 125, 1958.

Langfeldt, G. The endocrine glands and the autonomic systems in dementia praecox. Bergen, Norway: J. W. Eide, 1926.

Langfeldt, G. Clinical and experimental investigations on the relation between internal secretions and dem. praecox. *Acta Medica Scand.* Suppl. XVI, 1926.

Langfeldt, G. Die Insulin-Schockbehandlung der Schizophrenie. Psych-Neurol. Wochenschrift. nr. 38, 1936.

Langfeldt, G. The prognosis in schizophrenia and the factors influencing the course of the disease. Monograph. London: Humphrey Melford, 1937.

Langfeldt, G. Neue Gesichtspunkte zur Bewertung der Insulinschock Therapie bei Schizophrenie. Monatschr. fur Psych. und Neurol. Ed. 98. P. 352, 1938.

Langfeldt, G. The schizophreniform states. Monograph. London: Humphrey Melford, 1939.

Langfeldt, G. Zur Frage der spontanen Remissionen der Schizophreniformen Psychosen mit besonderer Berücksichtigung der Frage nach der Dauer dieser Remissionen. Zeitschr. f. d. g. Neurol. und Psych. 164 Bd. 4 H, 1939.

Langfeldt, G. The clinical subdivision of the schizophrenia group. Premiér Congrès Mondial de Psychiatrie. Compt. rendues des séances. Paris: Hermann & Cie, 1950.

Langfeldt, G. The diagnosis of schizophrenia. *Americ. J. Psych.*, 1951, 108.

Langfeldt, G. Modern viewpoints on the symptomatology and diagnostics of schizophrenia. *Acta Psych. et Neurol. Scand.*, Suppl. 80, 1953.

Langfeldt, G., Ford, L., Mazzitelli, Helen, Rohan, Anne Marie. Comparative diagnostic considerations and prognostic evaluations of electro-shock and insulin coma treatments. A Norwegian-American psychiatric-psychological teamwork. *Amer. J. Psych.*, 1955.

Langfeldt, G. La portée d'une dichotomie du groupe des schizophrénies. L'Evolution Psychiatrique No. 2, 1966.

Retterstöl, N. *Paranoid and paranoiac psychoses.* Springfield, Ill.: Charles C Thomas, 1966.

Strömgren, E. Schizophreniform psychoses. Celebration volume for Gabriel Langfeldt. *Act. Psych. Scand.* Vol. 41, fasc. 3, 1965.

Welner, J., & Strömgren, E. Clinical and genetic studies on benign schizophreniform psychoses based on a follow-up. *Act. Psych. Scand.* 33:377-399, 1958.

43

SOCIAL AND CLINICAL FACTORS IN THE OUTCOME OF SCHIZOPHRENIA

B. M. Mandelbrote and K. L. K. Trick

The present study was carried out on patients admitted to the "A" division of Littlemore Hospital Oxford during a 12-month period from August 1963. Patients in this part of the hospital are under the care of two consultants. The wards are organized on the principle of "therapeutic communities," (Mandelbrote (1965)). Within this organization considerable effort is used to exploit all methods of social and occupational rehabilitation. The patients are drawn from a large geographical area comprising the county and City of Oxford, with parts of Berkshire and Gloucestershire.

The cohort studied was selected by considering all patients admitted in a twelve-month period to the "A" division in whom "schizophrenia" was mentioned in the provisional diagnosis. All cases labelled depression or hypomania were also reconsidered. Applying the more stringent diagnostic criteria of the study (appendix I) seventy-four (74) patients were selected. Of these, two were eliminated as admission during this period was purely administrative maneuver, three Polish patients were excluded on the grounds that their almost total lack of English made assessment very difficult and was also a major factor in their continued hospitalization. The remaining sixty-nine (69) patients formed the subject of the study. Three of these died before the two-year follow-up period was completed. Six patients left the district and adequate details could not be obtained. Thus the final number of patients on whom full information was obtained was sixty-three (63). The follow-up interview was carried out two years from the date of discharge. In patients who had remained in hospital the follow-up was three years after the date of admission.

Reprinted, by permission of author and editor, from: *Acta Psychiatrica Scandanavica,* 46:24-34, 1970.

The data was obtained by interview with the patient, and where possible, a relative. This information was checked and supplemented by reference to case notes, hospital records, General Practitioners and Mental Welfare Officers reports. The details were recorded on a standard form which covered 54 items, plus a symptom rating scale. The data was coded and transferred to punch cards.

The present cohort did not differ significantly from the national figures for admission of schizophrenics in regard to sex distribution, mean age, or ratio of first to subsequent admissions. With regard to marital status, two factors which have been noted in previous studies were again found.

(1) The much lower proportion of married men in the cohort compared to the general population.
(2) The higher incidence of divorce/separation than in the general population.

The cohort could be divided on the basis of outcome into three groups.

1. Those who after key admission were discharged and remained out of hospital continuously for the 2-year period following discharge.
2. Those who were discharged and readmitted.
3. Those who remained in hospital throughout a 3-year period.

A wide range of personal and social factors have been considered to affect the short-term prognosis of schizophrenia. In the present study no one factor played an obviously overwhelming part in determining the outcome.

Social Factors

The lower incidence of married people in G.3 is probably related to the length of time that most of these patients have spent in hospital. While groups 1 and 2 show little difference, there is a marked difference between G.1, G.2 and G.3.

G. W. Brown (1962) suggested that the degree of emotional involvement between the patient and the people with whom he lived as an important prognostic factor. In this study no specific measures of the

TABLE 1

	M.	F.	Total	
G.1. (remained out) 13	13	16	29*	(not including 1 patient who died while still out of hospital)
G.2. (readmitted)	12	14	26	(including 1 dead)
G.3. (remained in hospital)....	7	3	10	(including 1 dead)

TABLE 2

MARITAL STATE

		G.1.	G.2.	G.3.
Married	M	1	4	0
	F	8	8	1
Single	M	11	7	7
	F	2	4	0
Widow	M	1	0	0
	F	3	0	1
Separated or Divorced	M	0	2	0
	F	3	1	1

TABLE 3

HOUSEHOLD COMPOSITION PRIOR TO KEY ADMISSION

	G.1.	G.2.	G.3.
Living alone	1	1	3
With wife/husband	6	10	1
Parents	8	8	—
In-Laws	—	1	—
Grown up child	1	0	—
Other relatives	4	1	—
Non relatives	5	5	6

All Group 3 patients, at time of admission, had no family ties or fixed living place.

TABLE 4

HOUSEHOLD COMPOSITION AT TIME OF DISCHARGE

	G.1.	G.2.
Living alone	0	2
With wife/husband	8	9
Parents	7	7
In-Laws	—	—
Grown up child	2	—
Other relatives	3	2
Nonrelatives	6	5

Return to relatives did not influence outcome.

degree of "emotional involvement" were made, as it was felt that such estimates were incapable of objective assessment. On a priori grounds it might be considered that in living siutations involving blood relatives or married partners, there would be a greater emotional loading than in situations involving nonrelatives. On this basis 65% of G.1 patients returned to an "emotionally charged" living situation and 73% of G.2 patients returned to a similar environment. Patients in G.3 without exception had no family ties and no fixed living place.

In G.1 65% living in situation in which emotional involvement probable.

In G.2 73% living in situation in which emotional involvement probable.

FACTORS RELATING TO ILLNESS

TABLE 5

LENGTH OF HISTORY OF ILLNESS

	Less than 1 year	1-2 years	2-5	5+
G.1.	9	—	9	11
G.2.	7	7	3	9
G.3.	—	4	1	5

This period was taken as the time prior to their first referral to their General Practitioner or one of the Mental Health Services with symptoms considered to be schizophrenic.

The persistence of certain symptoms or symptom complexes might be expected to influence the prognosis. Patients were rated at interview for the presence and severity of the following symptoms. (Degree of severity was based on a four-point scale).

Withdrawal, passivity, thought disorder, incongruity of affect, depression, elation, delusions, hallucinations and catatonic symptoms. On the basis of their scores on this rating the patients were divided into those with a mild, moderate and severe degree of persistent symptomatology. These categories were distributed between the three outcome groups as below.

TABLE 6

PERSISTENT SYMPTOMS

	G.1.	G.2.	G.3.
Mild	20	9	6
Moderate	8	10	2
Severe	1	6	2

The distribution of particular symptoms between groups as shown in Table 7.

The presence of each symptom type is more frequent in G.2 than G.1 as might be expected. A striking feature, however, is the lower frequency of symptoms in the continuously hospitalized group. This may reflect the fact that control of symptoms by supervised medication is relatively easy. The continued stay of these patients is due to factors not directly related to the nature of their illness.

Disturbed Behavior

Any of the following forms of behavior occurring other than as isolated events were rated as "disturbed behavior,"—self-neglect, noisy and abusive behavior, wandering from home, threats of suicide, suicidal attempts, threats of violence and acts of violence.

TABLE 7

	G.1.		G.2.		G.3.	
Avoidance of social contacts......	19	57%	8	32%	4	40%
Thought disorder	20	60%	23	92%	5	50%
Flattening of affect	20	60%	19	76%	5	50%
Delusions	19	57%	16	64%	4	40%
Hallucinations	11	33%	11	44%	2	20%

TABLE 8

	G.1.		G.2.		G.3.	
Present	12	38%	13	50%	8	80%

More important than the presence or absence of symptoms is the recurrence of disturbed behavior on the patient's part, irrespective of the underlying cause.

Such episodes are a frequent cause of readmission to hospital. The percentage of patients with disturbed behavior is shown in Table 8. It will be noted that Group 3 shows a high percentage of disturbed behavior in comparison with their low level of persistent symptomatology. It would seem that episodes of acting-out behavior in this group are a major contributory cause to their prolonged hospitalization. Such behavior may reflect an under-lying personality disorder unrelated to the schizophrenic illness. It is possible, however, that the disturbed behavior reflects the prolonged period of their hospitalization rather than being

a cause of it. Consideration of Group 1 patients who demonstrated disturbed behavior, revealed that these patients formed a small sub-group
constituting about 20% of the total of Group 1. Members of the subgroup showed a wide range of disturbed behavior, including threats of
violence, restlessness and wandering, in addition to refusing to work and
neglecting personal hygiene. They avoided all arrangements made for
their follow-up at discharge and stopped taking medication shortly after
leaving hospital. A high proportion of this sub-group were readmitted to
hospital or other institution in the period following the two-year study
period. Members of this sub-group appeared to remain out of hospital
because of their ability to avoid mental health service follow-up, rather
than any return to normality on their part.

Factors Relating to Treatment

TABLE 9

PREVIOUS ADMISSIONS

	None	%	One	%	Two	%	Three	%	More	%
G.1.	9	31	5	16	5	16	4	13	6	20
G.2.	5	19	9	34	5	19	—		7	37
G.3.	0		3	30	2	20	1	1	4	40

In G.1. almost half had no—or 1 previous admission, though 20% had
    3+ admissions
   G.2. half had 1 or less.   37% had 3+
   G.3. 30% had 1 or less.   40% had 3+

64% of first admissions remained out of hospital for at least 2 years
after discharge, a further 36% of first admissions were discharged but
readmitted within the 2-year period.

No first admission remained in hospital throughout the whole period
of the survey.

Group 3 contained double the percentage of 3+ admissions as
Group 1.

The amount of time that the patient had spent in hospital in the two
years prior to the start of the follow-up study is shown in Table (10).

TABLE 10

TIME SPENT IN HOSPITAL IN PREVIOUS TWO YEARS

	None	3/12	3-6/12	6/12-1 yr.	More than 1 yr.
G.1.	19	4	5	1	0
G.2.	11	5	5	3	2
G.3.	1	0	1	3	5

It will be seen that the majority of Group 3 patients had spent long periods of this time in hospital and in this group their key admission represented one of many such events in a long history.

The Use of Drugs

All the patients in the study received some form of drug treatment during their time in hospital and in almost all cases were recommended to remain on drug treatment at the time of discharge. Prescribing responsibility was then usually given to their General Practitioner, but in some instances prescribing was carried out from the out-patient department and occasionally Mental Welfare Officers were asked to supervise patients' medication. It had been hoped to check whether patients were taking their drugs by means of urine testing, but this proved impracticable. The tests available were not sufficiently sensitive to detect the drugs in the dose range which some were given. Many patients, particularly those visited at home, were reluctant to co-operate in this part of the investigation. Comments on medication are based on the statement of patients, confirmed wherever possible by reference to relatives and to their General Practitioner.

The proportion of patients taking drugs in each of the three groups is shown in Table 11.

TABLE 11

DRUGS BEING TAKEN AT INTERVIEW

	M.	F.	T.	
G.1.	10	9	19	65%
G.2.	9	11	20	76%
G.3.	7	3	10	100%

Amongst Group 1 patients, a number said that they had stopped their tablets because they had felt free of symptoms for a long period and decided that they no longer required medication. In some instances the drugs had been stopped on advice of their General Practitioner. Other patients had given up their tablets because of side effects which they considered undesirable. Similar reasons were expressed by patients in Group 2.

The design of this study does not permit of any firm conclusion being drawn about the effects of continued medication in preventing relapse.

There appeared to be no marked difference between the results obtained for different methods of follow-up, though the numbers involved are too small to form any firm conclusion. Also the form of follow-up was decided on a variety of factors and patients were not allocated at

TABLE 12

FOLLOW-UP ARRANGEMENTS

	G.1.	G.2.	G.3.
Day Hospital	4	2	—
Out-patient Clinic	13	10	—
Mental Welfare Officer	4	7	—
General Practitioner only	4	2	—
Hospital Socials	2	2	—
No Services	2	2	—

random, so that it is not possible to know that the patients in the various categories share similar characteristics. Sheldon (1964) reported a study in which patients were randomly allocated to follow-up by the psychiatric services or by their General Practitioner. He found that psychiatric after-care was associated with a significantly lower readmission rate.

DISCUSSION

The prognosis of schizophrenia in the light of recent developments in treatment and the emphasis on social care has been discussed by Brown, Bone, Dalison & Wing in their Maudsley Monograph (1966). They point out that schizophrenia was a diagnosis which carried a high probability that the patient would stay in hospital until he died. They further comment that most papers published before 1945 did not make any attempt to distinguish between the primary disabilities due to the disease, and those consequent upon prolonged stay in hospital. This makes it difficult to compare earlier studies with more recent ones.

Most early studies revealed that about 60% of first admitted schizophrenics were still in hospital five years after admission. This contrasts markedly with the present portion in which 64% of first admissions were discharged and remained out of hospital for at least the next two years. The remaining 36% of first admissions were also discharged, but were readmitted for at least some time during the subsequent two years. Thus, as far as short-term social prognosis is concerned, there seems to have been a marked improvement. With respect to their symptomatic state, more than half of those who remained out of hospital for two years showed no evidence of disturbed behavior and had only mild persistent symptoms. From the present study it is not possible to say to what extent this change in prognosis is due to the effects of physical and other treatment, or whether it is determined by the basically remitting nature of the illness. It might be that the more liberal and optimistic attitude towards discharge allows patients to return and live at home, who previously would have been detained long enough during the first admission for them to acquire the handicaps of institutionalization. Though this group contained a higher percentage of patients who cooperated diligently in taking maintenance medication, and attending for follow-up interviews, it cannot be assumed that such factors contributed to their favorable outcome. If these patients have a form of schizophrenia in which good remissions occur, they might well attribute their improvement to their drugs—a view likely to be shared by their doctors—and thus continue to take them. Patients whose symptoms do not remit may well abandon drugs as useless, or even as being actively harmful.

A number of studies have been carried out in an attempt to demonstrate the effect of continuing medication, but the results are inconclusive, and the methodology often questionable. One of the better designed studies (F. R. Scarpitti (1964)) showed that of patients receiving either a phenothiazine drug or a placebo, within 18 months 82% of those on the active drug were still at home, while only 32% of the "placebo" group were still out of hospital.

In patients with established illness, the prognosis is considered to be less good. Thus in a study by J. K. Wing (1964) of male schizophrenics, 49% were readmitted within a year, and a substantial percentage were considered to be a severe burden on their relatives. In the present cohort 60% of patients had a history of illness in excess of 2 years and 50% had more than 3 previous admissions to hospital. Half of these patients were discharged and remained out for two years. A further one-third were discharged but readmitted, and the remainder were still in hospital three years later.

A large number of studies have been concerned with the effects of social factors in the prognosis of schizophrenia. Occupation and social class has been considered. Cooper (1961) in a five-year follow-up of all schizophrenic admissions in Bristol concluded that social class did affect the total length of time a patient spent in hospital, but not the number of readmissions. In the present study the vast majority of patients came from social class IV, V. Thus it was not possible to compare outcome for different social groups.

Marital state has often been reported as having no relationship with outcome, though other studies have shown that married people had fewer readmissions. It is obvious that it cannot be considered in isolation, but has to be related to a variety of clinical factors. (Malamud, W. (1939), Renton, G. A. (1963), Williams, M. (1965), Schooler, N. R. (1967)).

The present study did not reveal any social factor which seemed to play a major part in determining outcome, except that lack of social ties and prolonged hospitalization mitigated against discharge.

There is some support for the idea that the prognosis of schizophrenia remains largely determined by the nature of the disorder. The differences in outcome could be explained on the basis of three different types of illness.

(1) A remitting illness in which the length of remission exceeds two years.

(2) A relapsing illness in which episodes of remission are rarely complete and last for less than two years.

(3) A rare form in which progressive deterioration seems to occur in spite of determined treatment, both physical and psychological.

SUMMARY

1. 46% of patients admitted with a diagnosis of schizophrenia were discharged within twelve months and not readmitted during the subsequent two years.

2. 41% were discharged within 12 months, but were readmitted during the subsequent two-year period.

3. 13% remained in hospital for three years from the time of their "key" admission.

4. 64% of first admissions were discharged and remained out of hospital for two years. A further 26% were discharged and readmitted during the following two-year period. Thus the majority of first admissions have an excellent short term prognosis, both in terms of symptomatic and social recovery. However, a few such patients, even with a short previous history seem to pursue a gradually deteriorating course. In

the small numbers involved and the short follow-up period it was not possible to define the characteristics of this type of patient.

5. 20% of those patients who remained out of hospital had a high level of persistent symptomatology, with episodes of disturbed behavior. They constituted a considerable burden on the community in general and their families in particular.

6. Those patients who were discharged but readmitted had a greater frequency of persistent symptoms than the patients who remained out of hospital.

7. The length of history of illness, the length of time spent in hospital prior to key admission, the lack of established social contact and occupation, and the occurrence of episodes of disturbed behavior, seem to play a major part in prolonged hospitalization, rather than any intrinsic feature of the illness.

ADDENDUM

Since the study was carried out, of those who had remained continuously in hospital, a further seven have been discharged. Two of these are in full time employment. One woman has been out of hospital for almost two years as a result of the establishment of a "group house" on a local estate. This illustrates that some of even the most difficult long stay patients can be maintained in the community if a sufficiently diverse range of supporting services exist.

ACKNOWLEDGMENTS

The authors would like to express their thanks to the Oxford Regional Hospital Board for their financial support for this project. During the period of this investigation K. L. Trick was employed as a Research Senior Registrar.

REFERENCES

Brown, G. W., Bone, M., Dalison, B., & Wing, J. K. (1966): Schizophrenia and social care. Maudsley Monograph 17, Oxford University Press.

Brown, G. W., Monk, E. M., Carstairs, G. M., & Wing, J. K. (1962): The influence of family life on the course of schizophrenic illness. *Brit. J. Prev. Soc. Med.* 16:55.

Cooper, B. (1961): Social class and prognosis in schizophrenia. *Brit. J. Prev. Soc. Med.* 15:17-41.

Malamud, W., & Render, I. N. (1939): Course and prognosis in schizophrenia. *Amer. J. Psychiat.* 95:1039.

Mandelbrote, B. M. (1965): The use of psychodynamic and sociodynamic principles in the treatment of psychotics. A change from ward unit concepts to grouped communities. *Comprehens. Psychiat.* 6:381-7.

RENTON, C. A., AFFLECK, J. W., CARSTAIRS, G. M., & FORREST, A. D. (1963): A follow-up study of schizophrenic patients in Edinburgh. *Acta Psychiat. Scand.* 39:548.

SCARPITTI, F. R., LEFTON, M., DINITZ, S., & PASAMANICK, B. (1964): Problems in a home care study for schizophrenics. *Arch. Gen. Psychiat.* 10:143-154.

SCHOOLER, N. R., GOLDBERG, S. C., BOOTHE, H., & COLE, J. O. (1967): One year after discharge: Community adjustment of schizophrenic patients. *Amer. J. Psychiat.* 123: 986-996.

SHELDON, A. (1964): An evaluation of psychiatric after care. *Brit. J. Psychiat.* 110:662-7.

WILLIAMS, M., KRUPINSKI, J., & STOLLER, A. (1965): Factors influencing community adjustment of discharged long term schizophrenic patients. *Med. J. Aust.* 52: (11), 821-825.

WING, J. K., MONK, E., BROWN, G. W., & CARSTAIRS, G. M. (1964): Morbidity in the community of schizophrenic patients discharged from London mental hospitals in 1959. *Brit. J. Psychiat.* 110:10-21.

44

A PROGNOSTIC INVESTIGATION OF FEMALE SCHIZOPHRENIC PATIENTS DISCHARGED FROM SCT. HANS HOS-PITAL, DEPARTMENT D, DURING THE DECADE 1951-1960

E. Röder

INTRODUCTION

The object of this study has been to gain an impression of the prognosis for female schizophrenic patients discharged during the decade 1951-1960, particularly with reference to the duration and the frequency of the admissions of these patients, in order that an evaluation of the effect of medication instigated by the introduction of the neuroleptic agents in 1954 may be attempted.

The fact that a change in the hospitalization of psychiatric patients in Denmark has occurred in recent years has been demonstrated by the surveys of Arentsen & Strömgren (1957) and Juel-Nielsen & Strömgren (1963). It came out in these reports that the greatest change was due to a reduction in the number of hospitalized schizophrenic patients, particularly middle-aged women.

REVIEW OF LITERATURE

Boje-Rasmussen (1966) finds in an investigation of the admissions and discharges of male schizophrenic patients at Sct. Hans Hospital in the decade 1950-1960 a modest reduction in the number of hospital beds occupied by these patients. He further finds that the number of admissions increased during the last years of the period and states that the

Reprinted, by permission of author and editor, from: *Acta Psychiatrica Scandanivica,* 46:50-63, 1970.

serious and alarming *symptoms* of these patients may be controlled and the patients easily discharged, but the severity of their *illness* makes them easily readmitted.

It was not until 1958-59 that there was an increase in the number of patients who were able to avoid a readmission within 3 years of discharge. With regard to the duration of these readmissions, Boje-Rasmussen finds a slight increase in the number of protracted admissions from 1950 to 1959 (readmissions of 2 to 3 years' duration within a period of 3 years of discharge) while readmissions of briefer duration (particularly of under 6 months) had increased considerably in 1958 and 1959.

Apo & Achté (1966) have compared two groups of schizophrenic patients treated at the Central Mental Hospital in South-East Finland, in 1950-1952 (series 1) and 1957-1959 (series 2) respectively, for duration of admissions and frequency of readmissions. They find no significant difference in the duration of admissions in the two series if the patients are grouped according to admissions of under two years' and over five years' duration. But with reference to readmissions of patients discharged for the first time, they find 39% in series 1 and 47% in series 2 were readmitted within an observation period of from 3 to 5 years. In series 1 there was an average period of 18.5 months before readmission, as compared with 15.9 months in series 2.

It may be seen from a study of the average duration of admission for those patients whose first admission lasted under two years that, in series 1, the admission was for 106 days and in series 2 for 162 days, the *treatment period* thus being briefer in 1950-1952 than in 1957-1959. But if the patients receiving electroshock therapy in 1957-1959 are studied, it appears that the average duration of admission for this group is briefer than for that of patients treated in 1950-1952. Apo & Achté come to the conclusion that the therapeutical development of recent years cannot be ascribed to tranquillizers alone, but that the treatment of schizophrenics is not effective unless medication is prescribed in conjunction with psychotherapy, occupational therapy and rehabilitation *as well as* electroshock therapy in certain cases, especially in those cases where the number of medical staff in the department is insufficient for active psychotherapy.

Odegard (1965) has investigated discharge patterns in Norwegian psychiatric hospitals prior and subsequent to the "drug era," especially in patients admitted from 1948 until 1952 compared with patients admitted from 1955 until 1959. If these patients are followed up until the end of 1953 and 1960, respectively, it appears that there is no statistically significant difference for all diagnostic groups, i.e. including schizophrenia, regarding the number of first discharged and non-readmitted patients in the two periods. On the other hand, there is a certain, albeit slight, tendency for more rapid discharge during the "drug era." The conclusion to be drawn, therefore, is that the new drugs have brought about no revolution in the discharge pattern. The discharge percentage is increased but so, simultaneously, are the readmissions, with the result that the net gain is barely statistically significant. Odegard states that the clinician's immediate impression of therapeutical progress is probably correct, but that this, in the first place, is due not to the intensity of discharge but to the quieter and more congenial atmosphere at the hospital. In the second place, most of the progress in Norway had taken place prior to the new drug era (Odegard (1961)), partly very probably, in consequence of the somatic therapy introduced about 1936, and partly very probably, in connection with the easier working conditions that have facilitated the social rehabilitation of psychiatric patients.

Strömgren (1965) states that there seems to be a certain difference between developments in Norway and in Denmark. There is no doubt that the introduction of electroshock therapy, at the end of the 1930's in both countries, produced a change in the picture indicating that many hospitalized patients are able to manage on briefer admissions. While, however, the development in Norway has been more even, it is clear that, in Denmark, pharmacotherapy plus rehabilitation have produced a further break in the curve, possibly because the supervision of patients under medication and of their rehabilitation is simpler in Denmark, the average distance between the hospital and the patients' homes being less than in Norway.

Auch (1963), in an investigation of the duration of stay in hospital and of recurrences for schizophrenic patients prior and subsequent to the introduction of the new psychopharmacological agents, respectively, came to the following conclusion: No significant change in the duration of admission for patients in 1946-51 and 1955-60, respectively. On the other hand, compared with the former period, a considerably greater number of the female patients suffered recurrences subsequent to the discharge period 1955-60. The frequency of recurrence for discharged patients in 1946-51 was 50% for both men and women and in 1955-60 it was still 50% for men but had risen to 67% for women. The course of the chronic cases with an admission duration of over $1\frac{1}{2}$ years showed no significant difference in the two periods.

Several writers (Boardman et al (1956), Childers (1964), Fink et al. (1958) and Langsley et al (1959)) have compared groups of patients either treated with insulin and electroshock therapy or with neuroleptic agents. The results do not entirely concord with one another, but Cornu

(1963) in his survey of the literature, notes that several experts are of the opinion that neuroleptic agents influence the reduction of the duration of admissions, even though this is due to several other factors as well.

Out-patient after-care also pertains to the new drug era. There is much disagreement as to the significance of this after-care in respect of hospital admissions as is apparent in a survey of the appropriate literature made by Orlinsky & D'ella (1964). According to several writers, out-patient after-care has had no significance for the frequency of recurrences or readmissions. The result arrived at by Orlinsky & D'ella from their own investigations was that of 1336 schizophrenic patients attending out-patient after-care, 25.7% were readmitted within 1 year of discharge, and of 796 schizophrenic patients who did not attend out-patient after-care, 45.5% were readmitted within 1 year of discharge. They further noted a significant connection between the frequency of after-care during the first 6 months of discharge and the number of readmissions. Their patients attended the out-patients clinic approximately once a month. On the basis of their investigation, these writers come to the conclusion that "their results suggest that *motivation* to attend an after-care clinic may be as important as the care actually received in predicting how long the patient remains in the community after hospital discharge."

MATERIAL AND METHODS

Sct. Hans Hospital receives patients from Copenhagen, primarily from psychiatric reception departments, i.e. patients requiring prolonged hospital care. In recent years the number of patients directly admitted to Sct. Hans Hospital has shown a tendency to increase. These direct admissions are, for the most part, readmissions from the out-patients clinic.

The material comprises 310 schizophrenic women, 64 of whom died during their first admission in the period under investigation. The remaining 246 patients comprise the total number of schizophrenic women discharged from Sct. Hans Hospital, Department D (SHH/D) during the decade 1951-1960. Patients who have been transferred to another hospital or other institution have not been considered as discharged and have hence not been included in the material (except, however, 8 patients discharged to "De gamles By," the main geriatric institution in Copenhagen).

Information on the patients has been obtained from the files and case histories at Sct. Hans Hospital and at the psychiatric departments in Copenhagen (Bispebjerg Hospital, Frederiksberg Hospital, Copenhagen

Municipal Hospital and The University Clinic of Copenhagen). In cases where the patients had been admitted to other psychiatric departments, their case histories have been lent to me, every admission to psychiatric institutions thus being registered. Beyond this, information has been obtained from the national registers and also, for deceased patients, from the central files of dead persons of the Public Health Board.

A transfer of a patient from a reception department or other department to SHH has been counted as one total admission.

TABLE 1

Diagnostic Description of 310 Schizophrenic Women Discharged from Sct. Hans Hospital, Department D, 1951-60

Psychiatric diagnoses:
  277 schizophrenia
  33 schizophrenia obs. pro

Secondary psychiatric diagnoses:
  13 borderline mental retardation
  3 psychopathy
  6 drug addiction and alcoholism
  44 lobotomy sequela

Somatic diagnoses:
  34 patients with a serious somatic disease affecting
       duration of admission
  2 cryptogenic epilepsy
  14 tuberculosis
  11 syphilis sequela

The diagnostic selection has been based on the diagnosis made at SHH/D. No amendment of the diagnosis was made at the time of the investigation. Previous admissions under another diagnosis, provided these have occurred within the investigation period, have been included, thus, it is believed, giving a truer picture of the course of the disease.

The diagnoses of the patients appear in Table 1 and show that 33 of the 310 patients were "only" diagnosed as "observation for schizophrenia" as their final diagnosis at SHH/D. Somatic secondary diagnoses have been included in order to provide a further characterization of the patients, because, among other reasons, somatic disorders, at times, considerably affect the discharge possibilities. 34 of the patients were thus suffering from a somatic disorder that is considered either to have prolonged the admission or to have directly precluded discharge. These are chiefly arteriosclerotic diseases of the circulation or of the heart or serious disorders of the heart in general. Not included in Table 1, however, is dementia or general debility on account of age, as this is hard to assess, but the significance of age in the material is seen in Tables 2 and 9.

The relatively high number of tuberculosis patients is explained by the fact that every female schizophrenic patient from Copenhagen suffering from tuberculosis is admitted to SHH/D.

A factor that has a bearing upon admissions without having direct relation to the course, is the legal status of the patients. This, however, plays no great part in the present material, inasmuch as only 4 of the patients had been committed one or several times to the hospital on account of criminal offences. These include one who had attempted

TABLE 2

AGE OF 310 SCHIZOPHRENIC WOMEN ON THEIR FIRST DISCHARGE (OR DEATH) DURING THE DECADE 1951-1960

20 years or under	4	50-59 years	60
20-29 years	21	60-69 years	46
30-39 years	60	70 years or over	41
40-49 years	78		

homicide, and mention may here be made of one patient who effectuated the homicide of her children, committing suicide at the same time.

The age distribution of the material is seen in Table 2, the age given being that at the first discharge (or at death) in the course of the decade. The age of the majority (64%) is seen to be between 30 and 59 years.

Table 3 gives a survey of the social conditions, partly at the first discharge and partly at the last, or at the time of the investigation (September, 1966). The discrepancy between the numbers of patients at these two times is due to the fact that 64 patients died during their first admission.

Table 3a gives information of the civil status. Compared with the figures obtained from other writers, e.g. Apo & Achté (1966), the number of divorced persons in the present material is considerably higher.

Table 3b illustrates housing conditions, grouped according to whether the patients were, or were not, enjoying some form of support, in order to get an idea of the possible effect of this on the prognosis. Thus, patients grouped as not living alone are in receipt of some form of assistance, inasmuch as they live either with their husband, their parents, cohabitor or friend, grown-up children or other relatives. The chief difference in the course of the decade is that several patients had gone to live at an institution, presumably, mainly on account of increasing age. The employment and working capacity of the patients appears in Table 3c. As is to be expected, the chief difference between the two times investigated is that, in the course of the years, far fewer patients

TABLE 3

Social Conditions of 310 Schizophrenic Women Discharged from 1951-1960 from SHH/D at their First Admission During the Period and at their Last (or at the Time of the Investigation, September 1966) Respectively

Table 3a
Civil status:

married	87	(28%)	52	(21%)
unmarried	139	(45%)	105	(43%)
formerly married	64	(21%)	66	(27%)
widowed	20	(6%)	23	(9%)

Table 3b
Housing conditions:

alone	139	(45%)	83	(34%)
at an institution	11	(3%)	39	(16%)
not alone	153	(50%)	121	(49%)
no fixed abode	7	(2%)	3	(1%)

Table 3c
Employment:

housewife	79	(25%)	44	(18%)
regular employment	81	(26%)	21	(9%)
no regular employment	150	(49%)	181	(73%)
disability pension	94	(33%)	157	(64%)
skilled	67	(21%)		

have become capable of steady, sustained effort, and, in consequence, have had to be granted a disability pension. 64% of the surviving patients during the period, i.e. about one half of the total received disability pensions. In this case, too, the high average age must be taken into account.

In Table 3c may, moreover, also be seen the number of patients who, at some time or other, had been capable of some form of skilled employment (21%). This being taken in the broadest sense, including patients employed as shop assistants or machinists not requiring any real training. To these social particulars must be added the fact that practically speaking all these patients belonged to the financially poorest category in Copenhagen.

Every patient admitted after 1954-55 has been given neuroleptic agents with the appearance of these drugs.

After-care of discharged patients is a feature of the new drug era. The after-care clinic of Sct. Hans Hospital, situated in Copenhagen, was opened on 1.11.1954. To begin with few patients only were under this control and the work was far more loosely organized than it is today. In recent years it has been considerably increased and is run on firm lines. During the first years of the clinic's existence, the case histories contain no exact notes of attendance, with the result that information of the first years for the purpose of this study, has been hard to come by. This has, therefore, entailed a curtailment in the registration to a division of the patients into two groups, viz. one comprising patients with a total attendance, either continuous or interrupted by admissions, at the after-care clinic of over 1 year during the registered period, the other comprising patients who have either had no after-care at all or who have attended a psychiatric clinic for less than 1 year. Not included in either of these groups are patients who since 1955 in one admission have been hospitalized for more than 3 years, which is one of the reasons why the figures for the registered patients are comparatively small.

RESULTS

An attempt will be made in the following to make a prognostic evaluation of patients discharged during the decade 1951-60 with particular reference to variations in their forms of admission prior to and subsequent to the introduction of the new drugs in 1954-55.

Table 4 shows the duration of admissions for patients discharged for the first time in the decade from SHH/D. It will be seen that there are relatively fewer admissions of brief duration (under 3 months) in the first years (1951-55) amounting to 28% of admissions of under 2 years in this period, whereas there were relatively more admissions of brief duration in the last years (58%). This difference is statistically significant ($\chi^2 = 15.9$, df: 1, p$<$0.001).

A reference to admissions of over two years shows that it was possible in 1955 and 1956 to discharge more patients who had been admitted from 2 to 10 years than in other years, i.e. at a time when these patients had been under neuroleptic medication for the previous 1 to 2 years prior to discharge, which fact must be considered essential. It should also be noted that from 1955 to 1960 it was possible to discharge 18 patients

TABLE 4

DURATION OF ADMISSION FOR THOSE PATIENTS WHO, DURING THE DECADE
1951-1960 WERE DISCHARGED FOR THE FIRST TIME FROM SCT. HANS
HOSPITAL, DEPARTMENT D. (310 PATIENTS MINUS 64 DECEASED
DURING 1ST ADMISSION DURING THE PERIOD)

	1951	1952	1953	1954	1955	1956	1957	1958	1959	1960
Under 1 month	1	2	2	1	0	1	2	2	1	2
1-3 months	6	4	4	2	8	11	6	6	8	8
3-6 months	9	3	12	9	9	5	1	1	5	5
6-12 months	4	6	2	7	2	3	3	3	2	3
1-2 years	2	3	3	4	2	0	0	2	0	1
	22	18	23	23	21	20	12	14	16	19
2-5 years	2	4	2	0	10	1	3	1	0	0
5-10 years	0	0	1	1	1	7	2	2	2	1
Over 10 years	0	0	0	0	4	2	2	4	1	5

whose duration of admission had been over 10 years, whereas previous to
1955 it had not been possible to discharge patients after such prolonged
admissions.

The following tables pertain to circumstances of readmissions and they
include all admissions to psychiatric departments.

Table 5 shows the distribution of patients into those who had not
been readmitted after their first discharge from a psychiatric department
during the period, and into those who thereafter had been readmitted
for up till 6 months, from $\frac{1}{2}$ to 2 years and from 2 to 3 years respectively
subsequent to their first discharge within the period and followed up for
3 years. In this period there is no statistically significant difference in the
number of readmitted patients. There is, however, a significant difference
between the duration of readmissions in these years, inasmuch as briefer
readmissions (under $\frac{1}{2}$ year) dominate the last part of the period, whereas readmissions of longer duration dominate the first year ($\chi^2 = 21.5$,
df:8, $p < 0.01$).

Similarly, Table 6 gives a survey of the 3 years prognosis, but in contrast to Table 5, which comprises patients discharged for the first time
within the period, this table comprises all discharged patients within the
period. The table shows the number of these patients who were not
readmitted within 3 years of discharge. It will be seen that a relatively
greater number of patients after 1955 than before 1955 avoided readmission. The difference is statistically significant ($\chi^2 = 13.19$, f:1,
$p < 0.001$).

TABLE 5

THREE YEARS PROGNOSIS FOR PATIENTS DISCHARGED FROM A PSYCHIATRIC
DEPARTMENT FOR THE FIRST TIME DURING THE PERIOD 1951-1960 STATED
BY THE TOTAL DURATION OF READMISSIONS. (THE FIGURES IN BRACKETS
INDICATE THE PERCENTAGE OF DISCHARGED PATIENTS IN THE RESPECTIVE
YEARS, EXCLUSIVE OF THOSE WHO DIED DURING THE 1ST ADMISSION OR
DURING THE 3 YEARS PERIOD)

	No. of discharged patients	Dead	Not readmitted	Under 6 mo.	Readmitted 1/2-2 yrs.	2-3 yrs.
1951-52	79	12	16 (24)	17	21	13
1953-54	62	9	14 (27)	16	20	3
1955-56	66	11	17 (30)	23	14	1
1957-58	59	20	14 (36)	14	8	3
1959-60	44	14	15 (50)	8	2	5

TABLE 6

THREE YEARS PROGNOSIS FOR PATIENTS DISCHARGED FROM A PSYCHIATRIC
DEPARTMENT DURING THE PERIOD 1951-1960 STATED BY THE NUMBER OF
PATIENTS (EXCLUSIVE OF THE DEAD), WHO WERE NOT READMITTED
WITHIN 3 YEARS OF DISCHARGE

	No. of discharged patients	Not readmitted
1951-52	77	16 (20.8%)
1953-54	103	25 (24.3%)
1955-56	139	54 (38.2%)
1957-58	105	33 (31.4%)
1959-60	133	59 (44.4%)

The prognosis for patients who, taken all together, have attended the
after-care clinic for over 1 year and for those who have not done so may
be seen in Table 7. Owing to the fact that in the first years of the clinic's
existence the patients attending for control were primarily such as had
had prolonged admissions or readmissions thus demonstrating that their
prognosis was poor, the groups registered scarcely lend themselves to
comparison with reference to the prognosis, and for this reason I have not
ventured to draw any conclusion from this survey with regard to the
possible prognostic significance of out-patient after-care, particularly, as
has already been mentioned, as the registration of out-patient after-care
in the first years was not entirely satisfactory.

TABLE 7

THE PROGNOSIS, RESPECTIVELY FOR THOSE PATIENTS WHO HAVE, AND FOR THOSE WHO HAVE NOT ATTENDED THE AFTER-CARE CLINIC FOR ALTOGETHER OVER 1 YEAR STATED BY THE AVERAGE NUMBER OF DAYS OF READMISSION FOR EACH PATIENT AFTER THE FIRST DISCHARGE DURING THE 5 YEARS PERIOD 1955-1959 UNTIL SEPTEMBER, 1966

	After-care out-patient for more than 1 year (42 patients)	Not after-care out-patient for more than 1 year (92 patients)
1955	295 days/patient	157 days/patient
1956	296 days/patient	143 days/patient
1957	331 days/patient	36 days/patient
1958	340 days/patient	68 days/patient
1959	243 days/patient	52 days/patient

TABLE 8

THE PROGNOSIS FOR PATIENTS LIVING ALONE AND FOR THOSE NOT DOING SO AFTER THE 1ST DISCHARGE DURING THE PERIOD 1951-1960 STATED BY THE CONDITIONS OF READMISSION WITHIN 3 YEARS OF DISCHARGE

Living alone:

      (139 admitted patients—36 dead during admission=103 pts.)

Not readmitted or readmitted for up to 1/2 year:	Readmitted from 1/2-2 yrs.	2-3 yrs.
68 (66%)	28 (27%)	7 (7%)

Not living alone:

      (153 admitted patients—24 dead during admission=129 pts.)

Not readmitted or readmitted for up to 1/2 year:	Readmitted from 1/2-2 yrs.	2-3 yrs.
81 (63%)	35 (27%)	13 (10%)

With the object of assessing the possible effect on the prognosis of some social factor it was decided to test it on patients living alone and on patients not living alone on discharge, as the latter might be presumed to possess some social support that would favor the prognosis. It will be seen, however, from Table 8 that this is not the case. There is thus no significant difference between the frequency of readmissions of those who live alone and of those who do not. Neither is there any significant difference between the duration of the readmissions of these two categories of patients. In this connection it may be assumed that several social factors influence admission to hospital. Odegard (1961), for instance,

TABLE 9

THE PROGNOSIS FOR THE VARIOUS AGE GROUPS STATED BY CONDITIONS OF
READMISSION AFTER THE 1ST DISCHARGE DURING THE PERIOD 1951-1960
AND 3 YEARS HENCE. (THE FIGURES IN BRACKETS INDICATE THE PERCENTAGE
OF DISCHARGED PATIENTS MINUS THE DECEASED)

	No. of patients	Dead	Not readmitted or readmitted up to 1/2 yr.	Readmitted for 1/2-? yrs.	2-3 yrs.
20-29 years	21	1	10 (50)	7 (35)	3 (15)
30-39 years	60	1	39 (66)	18 (31)	2 (3)
40-49 years	78	2	44 (58)	23 (30)	9 (12)
50-59 years	60	7	42 (79)	10 (19)	1 (2)
60-69 years	46	18	17 (61)	6 (22)	5 (17)
Over 70 years	41	35	2 (33)	0 (0)	4 (67)

TABLE 10

CAUSES OF DEATH FOR THE 115 DECEASED SCHIZOPHRENIC WOMEN IN THE
MATERIAL (DYING FROM 1951 TO SEPTEMBER, 1966)

Infectious diseases (including pneumonia 12)	15
Neoplasms	30
Cerebral hemorrhage	11
Morbus cordis	30
Pyelonephritis and Uremia	6
Hepatic insufficiency	3
Pernicious anemia	1
Incarcerated hernia	1
Senile atrophy	4
Multiple fractures	1
Suicide	13

mentions the fact that patients not only receive social support from their
surroundings but are also under a social pressure impelling them to
submit to medical attention.

Finally, Table 9 gives a survey of readmissions with respect to age.
Those aged 50-59 years seem to manage best, inasmuch as readmissions
for this group are fewer and briefer. Apart from this no certain trend
with age is seen.

The causes of death in the 115 deceased patients of this material (until
September, 1966) appear in Table 10. It will be seen that 13 of the
patients committed suicide, i.e.c. 4% of the total number and c. 11% of
the deceased. Two of these suicides occurred during admission (by sub-
mersion) the remainder after discharge (by drug or carbon monoxide

poisoning). Of these 11, 5 were under after-care, whereas the 6 had either not been put under after-care, or had not yet put in their first attendance at the clinic, the suicide in every case having been committed within a month of discharge. 12 of the suicides were committed after 1954 and one only before that year which might be indicative of a greater risk in the psychopharmacological era, when a greater number of schizophrenic patients are out of hospital than was formerly the case.

In addition, a further 25 of the 310 patients attempted suicide at some time or another.

DISCUSSION AND CONCLUSION

The most important of the above-mentioned results of the investigation are that the duration of admissions for female schizophrenic patients, both for those discharged for the first time during the period under investigation and also for those readmitted, has become briefer since 1954-1955 and that more patients avoid readmission during the "drug era," excepting, however, patients discharged for the first time during the period.

When such a significant change in the prognosis for schizophrenic patients in the "drug era" may thus be demonstrated, it would be reasonable to relate this development to the appearance and development of pharmaco-therapy, while bearing in mind that statistical analysis can only be a supplement to intensive studies of individual patients or groups of patients. It must, furthermore, be said that to elucidate the prognosis from the forms of admission and readmission of the patients is one-sided and can only form a supplement to the total evaluation of each individual patient's social, psychic and somatic conditions.

Several factors of prognostic significance have followed in the wake of the development of the new drugs.

The rehabilitation of schizophrenic patients has thus been extended in recent years. This may be judged to be not only an indirect effect of better treatment but also, subsequently, a direct result of those measures for rehabilitation instituted by society in recent years. As has been pointed out by Strömgren (1965) the rehabilitation measures required for maintaining pharmaco-therapeutical results did not really develop until after the instigation of psychopharmaco-therapy.

Fairly similar conditions apply to the out-patient after-care of schizophrenics. This is a direct consequence of the development of pharmaco-therapy, but its organization has lagged, which, as already mentioned, is one of the obstacles impeding a retrospective study of the prognostic significance of out-patient after-care and which it has not been possible to elucidate in this study.

Another prognostic factor to which an attempt has been made to draw attention in this study is the somatic diseases of the patients. It appears that 34 patients (11%) suffered from a somatic disease which is thought to have prolonged admission or, in some cases, actually to have prevented discharge. Better treatment of these diseases during the decade might well have affected the prognosis with regard to admission. Such a factor, independent of psychopharmacological therapy has not been found elucidated in similar published studies and whether it may have produced the suggested possible shift in the prognosis during the decade cannot be determined in the present investigation.

SUMMARY

An account is given of some studies of the prognosis regarding the duration of admissions and readmissions of schizophrenic patients prior to and subsequent to the introduction of the neuroleptic agents in 1954. The results of these studies do not concur. Danish surveys show that fewer schizophrenic patients were admitted after 1954. Reference is also made to a study of the significance for the hospitalization of schizophrenics of out-patient after-care.

The present material comprises 310 schizophrenic women, 64 of whom died during their first admission during the period investigated. The remaining 246 patients comprise the total number of schizophrenic women discharged from Sct. Hans Hospital, Department D during the decade 1951-1960.

Diagnostically, the patients are described by their secondary psychiatric and somatic diagnoses. 34 (11%) of the patients suffered from somatic diseases affecting the duration of admission.

The age of the majority (64%) of the patients was between 30 and 59 years (on their first discharge during the period).

For the surviving 246 patients, the duration of admission is registered at the first discharge from Sct. Hans Hospital, Department D during the decade under investigation. The result arrived at is that treatment time (admissions of less than 2 years) has become briefer in the psychopharmacological era. The number of discharges after prolonged admission (over 2 years) is significantly greater after 1955, with a clear increase appearing in 1955-1956.

The number of readmissions within 3 years of *the first discharge* during the period remained unchanged, but readmissions of under 6 months were more frequent during the "drug era," while readmissions of more than 6 months were more frequent before 1954. For *the total number* of discharged patients p. a., it appears that the 3 years prognosis is better in the second half of the period, inasmuch as a relatively greater number of patients avoided readmission after 1955.

An attempt has been made to estimate the significance for admission to hospital for out-patient after-care. As, however, a change has taken place in the selection of patients for after-care during these years, one cannot venture to draw any conclusion from the attempted survey.

There is, furthermore, a survey of the social conditions of the patients (civil status, housing and employment) partly at the first discharge during the period, partly at the last or at the time of investigation. It is specially to be noted that 64% of the patients were, at the latter time, in receipt of disability pensions. The 3 years prognosis for patients living alone and for patients not doing so is the same.

The 3 years prognosis has also been studied in respect of age groups. The 50-59 year olds seem to manage best inasmuch as readmissions here are fewer and briefer.

Finally, a survey is given of the causes of death of the 115 deceased patients in the material. 4% of the sum total of patients and c. 11% of the deceased committed suicide. Only 1 suicide occurred before 1954, the remainder after, which might be indicative of a greater risk during the psychopharmacological era, when fewer schizophrenics are admitted to hospital.

In conclusion, the various prognostic factors, dependent on or independent of the development of psychopharmaco-therapy are discussed.

REFERENCES

Apo, M., & Achté, K. A. (1966): Schizofreniundersökning 1950-1952 och 1957-1959. *Nord. Psykiat. T.* 20:125-140.

Arentsen, K., & Strömgren, E. (1957): Patients in Danish Psychiatric Hospitals. Result of a Census in 1957. *Acta Jutlandica* 31.

Auch, W. (1963): Beeinflusst die Psychopharmakotherapie. *Fortschr. Neurol. Psychiat.* 31:548-565.

Boardman, R. H., Lomas, J., & Markone, M. (1956): Insulin and Chlorpromazin in Schizophrenia. *Lancet* 2:487.

Boje-Rasmussen, E. (1966): Admission and Discharge of Schizophrenic Male Patients 1950-1960. *Acta Psychiat. Scand.*: Sct. Hans Hosp. 1816-1966, suppl., 216-231.

Childers, L. B. (1964): Comparison of Four Regimens in Newly Admitted Female Schizophrenics. *Amer. J. Psychiat.* 120:1010-1011.

Cornu, F. (1963): Psychiatrie der Gegenwart. Springer. Berlin Göttingen Heidelberg. 1/2, 495.

Fink, M., Shaw, R., Gross, G. E., & Coleman, F. S. (1958): Comparative Study of Chlorpromazin and Insulin Coma in the Therapy of Psychosis. *J.A.M.A.* 166:1846-1850.

JUEL-NIELSEN, N., & STRÖMGREN, E. (1963): Five Years Later. A comparison between Census Studies of Patients in Psychiatric Institutions in Denmark in 1957 and 1962. *Acta Jutlandica* 35.

LANGSLEY, D. G., ENTERLINE, J. D., & HICKERSON, G. X. (1959): Comparison of Chlorpromazin and EST in Treatment of Acute Schizophrenic and Manic Reactions. *Arch. Neurol. Psychiat.* 81:384-391.

ORLINSKY, N., & D'ELLA, E. (1964): Rehospitalization of the Schizophrenic Patient. *Arch. Gen. Psychiat.* 10:47-54.

STRÖMGREN, E. (1965): De danske Tvaersnitsundersogelser og Psykofarmaka. *Nord. Psychiat. T.* 19:101-114.

ODEGARD, O. (1965): Utskrivningsmonstret fra norske psykiatriske sykehus for og etter den moderne medikamentbehandling. *Nord. Med.* 70:961-965.

ODEGARD, O. (1961): Pattern of Discharge and Readmission in Psychiatric Hospitals in Norway, 1926 to 1955. *Ment. Hyg.* (N. Y.) 45:185-193.

ODEGARD, O. (1962): Psychiatric Epidemiology. *Proc. Roy. Soc. Med.* 55:831-837.

Section VIII

THERAPY

45

DRUG WITHDRAWAL IN MALE AND FEMALE CHRONIC SCHIZOPHRENICS

M. H. Abenson

Although the value of phenothiazines is without question in the treatment of acute schizophrenia, their value in chronic schizophrenia is questionable. Cawley (1) states that social and environmental factors become more prominent for symptom relief and social adjustment with increasing chronicity. Both Ekblom and Lassenius (2) and Simon *et al.* (7), who did long-term follow-up studies on drug-treated schizophrenics, found only slight improvement when compared with control groups. Letemendia and Harris (4) found no significant improvement on phenothiazine treatment of previously untreated chronic schizophrenics when compared with a control group. On the other hand Kelly and Sargant (3) found a distinct improvement after two years in a group of phenothiazine-treated patients, who were compared with earlier admissions to the same hospital before the introduction of drugs. However, whilst Pritchard (6) found the short term prognosis was better for phenothiazine-treated schizophrenics when compared with patients admitted prior to introduction of these drugs, he found the three-year follow-up produced little difference.

Although the value of phenothiazines in chronic schizophrenia is in doubt the effects of drug withdrawal have not been studied to any great extent. This appears particularly important when the side effects of long-term administration of phenothiazines are taken into account.

METHOD

Drugs were withdrawn for a period of three months from 161 chronic schizophrenics (105 males and 56 females, mean length of illness = 22.3 years). These patients were between 28 and 59 years old. Most pa-

Reprinted, by permission of author and editor, from: *The British Journal of Psychiatry,* 115:961-962, 1969.

tients were on large doses of phenothiazines; 44 percent were on trifluo-perazine (range 10-90 mgs. daily), 27 percent on thioridazine 100-1,200 mgs. daily), 16 percent on chlorpromazine (75-1,100 mgs. daily) and 13 percent on other phenothiazines.

Wing's (8) rating scale and the Psychotic Reaction Profile (PRP) (5) were completed by the nursing staff at the beginning (initial scores) and end (final scores) of the withdrawal period. High scores indicate more abnormality and low scores less abnormality. All patients with moderate to large increases in their scores, i.e. an increase of 25 percent

TABLE 1

NUMBER OF PATIENTS BETTER (B) OR WORSE (W) AFTER 3
MONTHS WITHOUT DRUGS

Sex			P.R.P.				Wing's scale			
	W. scale		P.B. scale		T.D. scale		S.W. scale		S.E. scale	
	B	W	B	W	B	W	B	W	B	W
Females (n=56)	24	16	18	22	19	22	13	24	11	14
Males (n=105)	36	53	21	55	11	74	29	42	11	56

W Scale = Withdrawal
PB Scale = Paranoid belligerence
TD Scale = Thinking disorganization
SW = Social withdrawal
SE = Social embarrassing behavior

of the maximum possible score, in any two of the five scales, of the two tests used, were noted. All patients were under constant supervision and any deterioration immediately treated. As the trial was not blind the two sexes were compared.

RESULTS

The females had significantly high initial scores (p<.01) using the chi-squared test on all three scales of the PRP. The males had signif-icantly higher initial scores (p<.01) on the Social Withdrawal Scale of Wing's Scale. The final scores on the rating scales did not show any significant differences between the sexes.

There was no correlation between drug dosage and patients with moderate to large changes on the rating scales. Moderate to large changes were seen in 3 females and 32 males (p<.01).

The initial (on-drug scores) and final scores (off-drug scores) on the rating scales were compared. If the final score was higher than the initial score, the patient was worse and vice versa. Unaltered scores were disregarded. The comparisons are shown in the following table.

Application of the sign test to the comparison of scores in this table shows the following significant changes after drug withdrawal.

(1) Females become more socially withdrawn $(p<.05)$.
(2) Males have an increase in paranoid belligerence $(p<.01)$.
(3) Males have an increase in thinking disorganization $(p<.01)$.
(4) Males have an increase in socially embarrassing behavior $(p<.01)$.

DISCUSSION

The comparison of scores of the sexes on the rating scales shows that where the males had significantly lower initial scores on the rating scales they deteriorated more significantly than the females after drug withdrawal, and that the same occurred for the females. These changes appear to indicate that the amount the males and females deteriorated was determined by their initial scores.

The lack of correlation between drug dosage (usually high) and moderate to large changes in the rating scales is against the use of excessive amounts of phenothiazines as maintenance therapy.

The moderate to large changes and comparisons of the rating scale scores show that phenothiazines help in the control of male patients. The relatively small deterioration of the females shows that in certain circumstances drugs can be withdrawn without gross changes. This lesser change is related to the initial scores of the females, which suggests that they were initially more hostile and belligerent and supports the contention that careful handling of psychotic patients without drugs can often be effective. This and other environmental factors may be responsible for some recent studies (1, 2, 4, 6, 7) showing minimal effects of phenothiazines on long term prognosis of chronic schizophrenia. Whether drugs are nevertheless helpful requires a double-blind study with a constant environment. The present report suggests that many chronic schizophrenics, especially females, should be tried without drugs for a trial period.

REFERENCES

1. Cawley, R. H. (1967). The present status of physical methods of treatment of schizophrenia. In *Recent Advances in Schizophrenia*. p. 97. (Ed. Coppen, A., and Walk, A.) Headley Brothers: Ashford, Kent.

2. EKBLOM, B., & LASSENIUS, B. (1964). A follow up examination of patients with chronic schizophrenia, who were treated during a long period with psychopharmacological drugs. *Acta Psychiat. Scand.*, 40:249.

3. KELLY, D. H. W., & SARGANT, W. (1965). Present treatment of schizophrenia—a controlled follow up study. *Brit. Med. J.*, ii:147.

4. LETEMENDIA, F. J. J., & HARRIS, A. D. (1967). Chlorpromazine and the untreated chronic schizophrenic. *Brit. J. Psychiat.*, 113:950.

5. LORR, M., O'CONNOR, J. P., & STAFFORD, W. J. (1960). The psychotic reaction profile. *J. Clin. Psychol.*, 16:241.

6. PRITCHARD, M. (1967). Prognosis of schizophrenia before and after pharmacotherapy. I: Short term outcome. II: Three year follow-up. *Brit. J. Psychiat.*, 113:1345.

7. SIMON, W., WIRT, A. L., & HALLORAN, W. V. (1965). Long term follow up study of schizophrenia patients. *Arch. Gen. Psychiat. (Chic.)*, 12:510.

8. WING, J. K. (1963). A simple and reliable subclassification of chronic schizophrenia. *J. Ment. Sci.*, 107:862.

46

EXPERIENCE, MEDICATION, AND THE EFFECTIVENESS OF PSYCHOTHERAPY WITH SCHIZOPHRENICS

Bertram P. Karon and Gary R. Vandenbos

In their article published in this Journal in 1965, May and Tuma (1) suggested that only the use of medication made a difference in the outcome with schizophrenics, and that psychotherapy, whether or not combined with medication, made essentially no difference. Their data, however, as in so many psychotherapy projects, referred only to patients treated by inexperienced therapists, namely psychiatric hospital residents under supervision.

In the two experimental groups of the Michigan State Psychotherapy Project patients were assigned for treatment to experienced therapists as well as to the inexperienced therapists supervised by them. Thirty-six schizophrenic patients were randomly assigned to three treatment groups. The control group underwent routine treatment (medication and supportive therapy) at a good public hospital where the patient/resident ratio is eight to one, with transfer, if necessary, after a few weeks to the intensive treatment service (patient/doctor ratio of 30 to one) of a state hospital. Experimental group A received psychoanalytic therapy of an "active" variety (2) *without* medication. Four patients were treated by the supervisor, eight patients by five inexperienced therapists (one patient died of an embolism and another was found to be organic). Experimental group B received psychoanalytic therapy of an "ego-analytic" variety, employing medication adjunctively. Four patients were treated by the supervisor and eight patients by five inexperienced therapists. One supervisor (B) was a psychiatrist, one a clinical psychologist (A), and each group of therapists under supervision included both profes-

---

Reprinted, by permission of author and editor, from: *The British Journal of Psychiatry*, 116:427-428, 1970.

sions. Patients in the experimental groups averaged approximately 60 hours per year of psychoanalytic psychotherapy.

Before assignment to treatment groups, all patients were evaluated by personnel not connected with the treatment service. The evaluations were repeated at six and at twelve months. Intellectual tests included Thorn-dike-Gallup Vocabulary, Porteus Mazes, Wechsler, and the Feldman-Drasgow (3) Visual-Verbal test (VVT), a concept formation task in the Kasanin, Cameron, Goldstein tradition designed to be specifically susceptible to the schizophrenic thought disorder. A thorough clinical status

TABLE 1

Corrected Outcome Measures After Twelve Months of Treatment

	n	Days hos-pitalized	T-G	PM	VVT	WAIS	TAT	ROR	CSI
Control	12	116.7	8.7	9.4	19.8	85.3	1.00	1.07	.92
Experimental (pooled)	22	71.0	8.7	8.6	13.4	86.7	1.01	1.05	1.07
Significance level (E *vs.* C)		p<.05	ns	ns	p<.001	ns	ns	ns	p<.05
Supervisor A	4	84.6	7.7	7.8	7.0	84.7	.98	.97	1.06
A trainees	6	126.0	11.1	9.6	12.2	89.0	1.08	1.06	1.10
Supervisor B	4	91.6	10.6	11.9	14.0	90.3	1.05	1.17	1.14
B trainees	8	12.6	6.7	7.8	18.0	84.2	1.00	1.02	1.02
Significance level (5 groups)		p<.01	ns	ns	p<.01	ns	ns	ns	ns

interview (CSI) by an experienced psychiatrist was recorded on tape, so that clues to differential treatment could be deleted and ratings made blindly by two raters. Similarly, Rorschach and TAT tests were administered and the transcribed protocols rated blindly by two judges. Number of days hospitalized during the first six months and the first year were also examined.

With respect to each measure of illness, analysis of covariance procedures were utilized to compare treatments, correcting for initial performance on that measure and any background characteristics or other test performances which were significantly related. These procedures are described in detail in Karon and O'Grady (4). The results are shown in Table 1.

Additional hours of psychotherapy (averaging all patients in both experimental groups without respect to experience of the therapist, difference in technique, or use of medication) led to significantly shorter periods of hospitalization (approximately 46 days less in the first year), significantly less thought disorder as measured by the VVT, and significantly higher ratings of overall functioning on the basis of the information elicited in the clinical status interview, as compared to the hospital control group.

One of the most striking findings was the relevance of the experience of the therapist, and its interaction with the effects of medication. Patients treated by the experienced therapists were hospitalized for a shorter length of time, showed less psychotic thought disorder (on the Visual-Verbal test), and were viewed as functioning at healthier levels (clinical status interview rating) than control patients. Surprisingly differences in theoretical rationale, technique, and the use of medication did not make much difference in the effectiveness of the supervisors.

For the inexperienced therapists, the use of medication was critical. Patients treated by inexperienced therapists not utilizing medication were hospitalized longer than the hospital control group, but showed dramatic improvement in their underlying thought disorder. Patients treated by inexperienced therapists utilizing medication were hospitalized for very short periods of time (less even than the patients of their supervisor), but showed little or no greater improvement than the controls in their thought disorder. Thus the experienced therapists tend to produce more balanced change, while inexperienced therapists concentrate on one or another aspect of improvement, that aspect easiest to obtain with their treatment modality.

There were significant individual differences in effectiveness among the inexperienced therapists; these were not a function of profession or supervisor but seemed to be related to general maturity and the degree to which suprvision was effectively utilized.

Thus our findings suggest that May and Tuma's conclusions that psychotherapy has little to offer the schizophrenic patient needs to be restricted to inexperienced therapists.

ACKNOWLEDGMENTS

This research was supported by the Michigan State Psychotherapy Project, NIMH Grant †MH-08790. We should like to thank Kenneth Pitts, M.D., and the staff of Detroit Psychiatric Institute for their cooperation.

REFERENCES

1. MAY, P. R. A., & TUMA, A. H. (1965). Treatment of schizophrenics: an experimental study of five treatment methods. *British Journal of Psychiatry*, 111:503-10.

2. KARON, B. P. (1963). The resolution of acute schizophrenic reactions: a contribution to the development of non-classical psychotherapeutic techniques. *Psychotherapy: Theory, Research, and Practice*, 1:27-43.

3. FELDMAN, M. J., & DRASGOW, J. (1951). A visual-verbal test for schizophrenia. *Psychiatric Quarterly Supplement*, 25:55-64.

4. KARON, B. P., & O'GRADY, P. (1969). Intellectual test changes in schizophrenic patients in the first six months of treatment. *Psychotherapy: Theory, Research, and Practice*, 6:88-96.

47

FOLLOWUP EVALUATION OF FAMILY CRISIS THERAPY

Donald G. Langsley, Kalman Flomenhaft, and Pavel Machotka

Six-month followup evaluations of 150 family crisis therapy cases and 150 hospital treatment cases demonstrate that those treated as outpatients do as well as the hospital cases. Social functioning is maintained equally in both groups. Patients are less likely to be rehospitalized if admission was avoided initially.

Crisis therapy has evolved from increased attention to the ego and its decompensation in the face of external stress. The techniques focus on coping style and ego support rather than on insight into unconscious conflict. The goal of crisis therapy is integration and recompensation.

The brief therapies have also evolved in a changing political arena, which declares that health services are a right of all citizens rather than the privilege of a few. To some, the brief therapies represent an expedient distribution of services, so that everyone gets a little rather than a few getting a lot. To other professionals, crisis therapy is seen in a more positive light as an opportunity for mastery rather than regression.

Crisis therapy has received more attention at a time when the role of the mental hospital is being questioned. Repeatedly it is found that institutional testings encourage disability rather than overcoming it. To remove a patient from his home and job to a distant hospital adds problems to the existing disability. Hospitalizing one member of a family

Presented at the 1969 annual meeting of the American Orthopsychiatric Association, New York, N. Y.

Dr. Langsley is now professor and chairman of the department of psychiatry of the School of Medicine, University of California, Davis.

This research was supported by USPHS Grants MH-1577 and MH-16286.

Reprinted by permission of author and editor, from: *American Journal of Orthopsychiatry,* 39:753-759, 1969. Copyright, The American Orthopsychiatric Association, Inc.

gives credence to the disease model and suggests that the problem is entirely within the patient's biology or psyche.

The focus on crisis therapy and community mental health has been accompanied by many claims of efficacy and success, but few have been based on followup studies. The federal legislation encouraging community mental health centers has given great impetus to program development but there is a dearth of evaluative research. Outcome studies used to focus on personality change; brief therapy is not designed to seek change in long-term behavioral patterns. Instead it attends to functioning, adaptation, symptom reduction and the avoidance of hospitalization. In this study of family crisis therapy (FCT) the design of the project included systematic evaluation from its inception. This paper will report the results of a comparison of FCT and hospital treatment for two groups, each consisting of 150 patients randomly selected from a population which would ordinarily be treated by immediate admission to a mental hospital. Six-month followup data are reported for both groups. Eighteen-month data are presently being collected and analyzed.

PROCEDURES

From 1965 to 1968 the Family Treatment Unit at Colorado Psychiatric Hospital (a University of Colorado psychiatric treatment center) selected and treated a random sample of those patients ordinarily immediately admitted to the hospital. These patients all lived in a family within an hour's travel from the hospital. An equal-sized sample of control patients was drawn from the same population. The control patients were all hospitalized. Baseline measures of social adaptation, functioning, crisis management, and other clinical schedules were obtained from FCT and hospital cases. Treatment of the FCT cases was carried on by a full-time clinical team from the Family Treatment Unit. Control cases were admitted to the hospital and treated by the inpatient service professional staff.

The techniques of FCT are reported in a book recently published by this group (2). Treatment for the FCT cases consisted of an average of 4.2 office visits, 1.3 home visits, 5.4 telephone calls, and 1.2 collateral contacts with social agencies. The treatment was carried on over a mean period of 24.2 days from admission to termination. All 150 FCT cases were treated without admission to the hospital. Despite the fact that this group consisted of a sample of patients ordinarily hospitalized immediately (including acutely disturbed schizophrenics, suicidal depressive and other dramatic behavioral disturbances), it was possible to effect recompensation and remission using the treatment described above.

Patients admitted to the hospital were treated with individual and group psychotherapy, milieu therapy, pharmacotherapy, and the varied approaches of a modern psychiatric hospital. The average length of stay for hospital cases was 28.6 days.

Followup studies were done six months after discharge from treatment and annually thereafter. The evaluations were done by professional social workers employed on a part-time basis. These clinicians had no other connection with the project. The baseline scales and measures were repeated in addition to a clinical interview in the family home of each patient.

FINDINGS

Although the randomness of sample selection procedures gives confidence that the groups are comparable, further examination confirms this. FCT and hospital cases are compared on 15 characteristics and 10 additional features of family composition (see Table 1). It will be apparent that the groups are similar in terms of the patients (age, sex, race, marital status, social class, religion), the area of residence, the types of families, previous mental hospital admissions, and diagnosis. Indeed, the only significant difference is due to the time of day admitted, a factor due to the increased number of hospital cases admitted during the night hours. Since the FCT and hospital groups are indistinguishable by chi^2, the groups comparisons are valid undertakings.

One measure of outcome is the fact that all FCT cases were treated without admission to a mental hospital. Was hospitalization truly avoided or merely postponed? It is no problem to keep patients out of a hospital; one merely has to close the door. For this reason careful records were kept of subsequent hospital histories for both groups. Table 2 presents these data for both groups during the six months immediately following treatment. It should be emphasized that the hospitalizations listed are readmissions for the control group and initial hospitalization for the FCT cases. The data makes it clear that treating an acute regressive episode by admission to a mental hospital increases the probability of readmission. 29% of the hospital cases are readmitted within six months, while only 13% of the FCT cases are hospitalized during that period. When it is necessary to hospitalize from either group, the length of stay is also affected by the previous treatment. If previous treatment of-commission in a mental hospital by the group previously hospitalized. was hospital admission, the re-hospitalization is nearly three times as long for the group. More than 1,700 additional man-days were spent out-

TABLE 1

COMPARISON OF 149 FCT AND 150 HOSPITAL PATIENTS

Area of Comparison	CHI²	Degrees Freedom
Sex	.61	1
Age	6.74	7
Marital Status	8.14	4
Race	2.03	3
Religion	8.14	4
Social Class	7.54	4
Geographic Residence	0	3
Brought to Hospital By	6.29	5
Voluntariness of Admission	1.00	1
Day of Week Admitted	7.73	6
Time of Day Admitted	14.33[a]	3
Number of Previous Psychiatric Hospitalizations	.09	1
Suicidal Attempt or Ideation	7.95	6
Diagnosis	3.79	5
Number of Previous Nonhospital Psychiatric Contacts	10.87	7
Presence of Spouse in Household	1.61	2
Presence of I.P.'s Father in Household	.07	2
Presence of I.P.'s Mother in Household	3.08	2
Presence of Father-in-Law in Household	5.06	2
Presence of Mother-in-Law in Household	3.94	2
Presence of Grandparents in Household	3.50	2
Number of Marriages of I.P.	5.14	4
Number of Marriages of I.P.'s Spouse	3.59	4
Number of Marriages of I.P.'s Father	2.11	4
Number of Marriages of I.P.'s Mother	1.16	4

[a] $p < .01$.

TABLE 2

HOSPITALIZATION OF 150 FCT AND 150 HOSPITAL CASES

	Cumulative No. of Patients Hospitalized		Cumulative No. of Hospital Days		Percent of Potential Hospital Days		Percent of Sample Not Hospitalized	
	FCT	Hosp.	FCT	Hosp.	FCT	Hosp.	FCT	Hosp.
Acute Treatment Period	None	150	None	4,284	None	100%	100%	None
1st Posttreatment Month	5	28	70	417	1.6%	9.3%	96.7%	81.3%
2nd Month	10	29	178	834	2.0	9.3	93.3	80.7
3rd Month	12	33	307	1,191	2.3	8.8	92.0	78.0
4th Month	14	36	433	1,602	2.4	8.9	90.7	76.0
5th Month	18	38	521	2,013	2.3	8.9	88.0	74.7
6th Month	19[a]	41[a]	609	2,335	2.3	8.6	87.3	70.7

[a] $\chi^2 = 10.06$.
$p < .001$.

TABLE 3

Social Adjustment Inventory Group Mean Scores

	Social & Family Relations		Social Productivity		Self-Management		Antisocial Behavior		Totals	
	FCT	Hosp.	FCT	Hosp.	FCT	Hosp.	FCT	Hosp.	FCT	Hosp.
Baseline	3.14	3.15	2.89	2.79	2.43	2.47	2.01	2.01	10.46	10.44
3 months	2.89	2.92	2.34	2.44	2.23	2.28	1.98	1.88	9.43	9.54
6 months	2.73	2.91	2.13	2.18	2.20	2.27	1.97	1.89	9.03	9.67

	N			Significant Differences		
	FCT	Hosp.		t	P	
Base	142	150	FCT Base vs. 3 mo.	1.98	$<.05$	Social & Family Relations
3 mo.	112	114	FCT Base vs. 6 mo.	3.46	$<.001$	"
6 mo.	132	135				
			FCT Base vs. 3 mo.	3.51	$<.001$	Social Productivity
			FCT Base vs. 6 mo.	4.97	$<.001$	"
			Hosp. Base vs. 3 mo.	2.29	$<.05$	"
			Hosp. Base vs. 6 mo.	4.29	$<.001$	"
			FCT Base vs. 3 mo.	1.98	$<.05$	Self-Management
			FCT Base vs. 6 mo.	2.31	$<.05$	"
			Hosp. Base vs. 6 mo.	1.98	$<.05$	"
			FCT Base vs. 3 mo.	3.47	$<.001$	Totals
			FCT Base vs. 6 mo.	4.88	$<.001$	"
			Hosp. Base vs. 3 mo.	2.73	$<.01$	"

Another measure of comparison centers on the adjustment of the patient before and after treatment. Since the goal of FCT (as well as that of hospitalization) is to effect recompensation and readjustment to the usual environment and usual role performance, instruments were chosen to focus on this area. The Social Adjustment Inventory (SAI) taps information under the headings of Social and Family Relations, Social Productivity, Self-Management and Antisocial Behavior (1). These four scores are combined to make a total SAI score. On this measure, lower scores indicate "better" social adjustment. This scale was administered at baseline, and at three and six months after treatment for both FCT and hospital cases. In some instances three-month measures were not obtained, but the six-month measures are available for 90% of both groups. Group mean scores are listed in Table 3. Comparisons between FCT and hospital cases at baseline, three months, and six months were tested by significance by a matrix of t tests. No differences between groups were found on any of the subtests or total scores at baseline, three months, or six months. The measures of difference from baseline to three months and six months are significant in Family and Social Relations, Social Productivity, Self-Management, and Total Scores for the FCT group. The hospital group shows significant improvement from baseline to three and six months in Social Productivity. Self-Management improves from baseline to six months for the hospital cases, and the Total Score for this group improves significantly at three months, but not at six. Although the differences between FCT and hospital groups do not reach significance, the trend is in the direction of better role

TABLE 4

Personal Functioning Scale Group Means

	Functioning		Health		Psychiatric Symptoms		Totals	
	FCT	Hosp.	FCT	Hosp.	FCT	Hosp.	FCT	Hosp.
Baseline	2.49	2.56	2.31	2.23	3.04	3.08	7.80	7.87
6 months	2.05	2.08	2.00	1.85	2.44	2.42	6.45	6.35

	N		Significant Differences			
	FCT	Hosp.		t	p	
Base	132	150	FCT Base vs. 6 mo.	3.98	<.001	Functioning
6 mo.	141	131	Hosp. Base vs. 6 mo.	5.12	<.001	"
			FCT Base vs. 6 mo.	3.71	<.001	Health
			Hosp. Base vs. 6 mo.	5.04	<.001	"
			FCT Base vs. 6 mo.	8.16	<.001	Psychiatric Symptoms
			Hosp. Base vs. 6 mo.	8.71	<.001	"
			FCT Base vs. 6 mo.	7.09	<.001	Totals
			Hosp. Base vs. 6 mo.	8.62	<.001	"

performance by the FCT patients. It is of interest that so little change takes place in Antisocial Behavior, a fact probably due to the chronicity of these patterns. Neither short-term FCT or hospitalization changes long-term maladaptive behavior.

Another instrument was developed to measure role performance at work, school, or household, as well as health and presence or absence of psychiatric symptoms. This Personal Functioning Scale (PFS) was administered at baseline and at the six months evaluation. As with the SAI, lower scores indicate "healthier" functioning. The findings (Table 4) are similar to those seen with the SAI. There is improvement from baseline to six months which is highly significant for both FCT and hospital cases. The groups do not differ from each other either at baseline or at six months. The major change is in the area of Psychiatric Symptoms.

Symptoms usually associated with psychiatric illness are not necessarily deleterious to family life. These symptoms are found in significant proportions of people who are not hospitalized. They are labeled eccentricity unless the symptomatic individual has been hospitalized and then become labeled "mental illness." The amount of time lost from work, school, or homemaking does affect the family, however. The breadwinner out of commission in a mental hospital, or the homemaker similarly treated, does affect the family and community in substantial fashion. Table 5 summarizes days lost from functioning at the usual role assign-

TABLE 5

Days Lost from Functioning During Treatment

	FCT (N=140)	Hosp. (N=138)
Mean	10.0	32.4
Median	5	23
S.D.	13.8	28.1

Days Lost After Termination Before Return to Functioning

	FCT (N=139)	Hosp. (N=126)
Mean	26.0	47.8
Median	0	3
S.D.	50.4	70.0

ment during treatment. It also reports days after treatment before resumption of usual functioning. Data is available on 90% or more of both samples. The median number of days is probably a more accurate representation since the mean could be skewed by a few disproportionate values. The hospital cases are "out of commission" for 23 days as compared with five for the FCT cases. The difference represents nearly two weeks per patient. Similarly, the median case lost no time before resumption of usual role functioning when treated by FCT, but lost another three days following termination if treated by hospitalization.

DISCUSSION

It is apparent that patients treated by FCT instead of admission to a mental hospital are functioning as well six months later, and are less likely to have spent part of that six months in a mental hospital. The average FCT patient will have gained two weeks of role functioning. Cost estimates, presented in another report (3), also demonstrate that FCT is far less expensive (one-sixth or less) than the cost of hospital treatment. Throughout the nation, discussions of health care services focus on the dramatic increases in cost. These are mostly attributed to the expense of hospital treatment rather than to outpatient costs. Increased cost is true for mental hospitals as well as general medical hospitals. Mental health professionals cannot ignore cost in organizing mental health services for large populations.

The deleterious effects of unnecessary hospitalization are well documented. Any hospital admission involves regression and disruption of individual and family life. Admission to a mental hospital still carries significant social stigma and may influence subsequent employment, admission to college, the ability to obtain a driver's license, or other real life factors. Unnecessary hospitalization is also an unnecessary expense to someone. It is incumbent on all of us to seek alternatives to hospitalization and to avoid unnecessary admissions. The findings of this project, with its systematic efforts to do careful sampling and followup evaluation with minimal bias, are that most patients admitted to a mental hospital can be treated by FCT if they live in a family and are reasonably close to a treatment center. Of the total population admitted to Colorado Psychiatric Hospital for 1967, 53% met these criteria.

Why family? The choice of conjoint family crisis therapy rather than individual crisis therapy focuses on two factors: (1) family or interactional tensions are often the precipitant of psychotic regression in a susceptible patient; (2) the family is a source of strength, support, and aid, as well as of problems. The family has always been the first arena of help for crises. To remove a patient from the family (by hospitalization) removes him from a potential source of psychological support. The goal of FCT is not to blame the family but to help the entire group resolve current difficulties. The patient who lives alone presents a more difficult problem. He can often be treated by individual crisis therapy, but it is doubtful that all cases in this series could have been managed without a family.

Do these findings suggest that we ought to close all the mental hospitals? That is not the interpretation or suggestion of this report. It is easier to avoid hospitalization for those who live in a family, but not all patients do. A certain proportion of patients seen in mental health centers will require specialized treatment available only in a hospital. A certain population of individuals accustomed to using the mental hospital to solve problems will make it difficult to avoid hospitalization.

Nevertheless, it is apparent that most patients from an acute psychiatric hospital can be treated with FCT with results equal to those achieved by hospitalization.

REFERENCES

1. BERGER, D., RICE, C., SEWALL, L., & LEMKAU, P. (1964). Post-hospital evaluation of psychiatric patients: the Social Adjustment Inventory method. APA Psychiatric Studies and Projects #15.
2. LANGSLEY, D., KAPLAN, D., PITTMAN, F., MACHOTKA, P., FLOMENHAFT, K., & DE YOUNG, C. (1968). The Treatment of Families in Crisis. Grune & Stratton, New York.
3. LANGSLEY, D., PITTMAN, F., MACHOTKA, P., & FLOMENHAFT, K. (1968). Family crisis therapy—results and implications. *Family Process,* 7 (2):145-158.

48

THE INFLUENCE OF FAMILY STUDIES ON THE TREATMENT OF SCHIZOPHRENIA

Theodore Lidz

The honor of being invited to present this lecture has particular meaning for me through again linking me to the memory of Dr. Fromm-Reichmann, who was a friend and mentor as well as a teacher. Some persons are revered most by those who knew them only through their writings and reputation: not so with Frieda Fromm-Reichmann, who was not only respected and admired, but loved by those close to her. She played an important part in my life, and she remains very much with me as a guiding ideal. I give at least fleeting thought to her each evening as I enter our study and see the painting of the hills of Jerusalem by her friend Gertrud Jacob that for many years hung in Frieda's study, and when I enter my office, where the sole certificate is that of the first Frieda Fromm-Reichmann award for research in schizophrenia.

Dr. Fromm-Reichmann's life as a psychiatrist was primarily devoted to analytically oriented psychotherapy with schizophrenic patients and to demonstrating that such persons, even when their condition had become chronic, were not beyond the reach of the persistent and devoted therapist. With the extraordinary determination and persistence that permeated her kindly small body she proceeded to demonstrate this potentiality to her colleagues and to the world. The treatment of schizophrenic patients has altered markedly since her death and I wish she could have lived to see the change. I cannot match the inspiring testament to her

Dr. Lidz (M.D. Columbia 36) is Professor in the Yale University Department of Psychiatry.

The Twelfth Annual Frieda Fromm-Reichmann Memorial Lecture, given on November 15, 1968, at the Department of Interior, Washington, D.C., under the auspices of the Washington School of Psychiatry.

lifework given in Hannah Green's *I Never Promised You a Rose Garden,* but I shall attempt tonight to link her work with the therapeutic advances that have resulted from the studies of the family environments in which schizophrenic patients grow up and that together with the tranquilizing drugs and the new concepts of milieu therapy have vastly altered the future lives of schizophrenic patients.

Nowhere in medicine has it been so apparent that the hypotheses held concerning the nature and etiology of a condition influence treatment as in the case of schizophrenia. Belief in demonic possession led to exorcisms and burnings. The conviction that these patients suffered from a somatic disorder was, in large measure, responsible for the relegation of generations of patients to neglect in custodial institutions. The hypothesis, accepted as fact, that the brain or its metabolism was at fault provoked the damaging of countless brains by insulin, metrazol, electricity, and lobotomy. Jung's and Bleuler's beliefs that the psychological disturbances they described were secondary to a toxic disorder, and Freud's idea that the schizophrenic patient's narcissistic fiixation and regression made a transference relationship impossible convinced psychoanalysts that these patients were beyond their approach. Indeed, when Sullivan, Fromm-Reichmann, and Hill demonstrated that transference relationships could be established, many other analysts were skeptical and even derogatory because the fact ran counter to accepted tenets. The theory that schizophrenic reactions, as the most profound regressions, are due to fixations during the oral phase, led to the focus on maternal rejection during infancy—a period beyond conscious recollection; this orientation has led some therapists to believe that supplying the nurture and love the patient lacked during infancy forms the cornerstone of treatment.

It is essential to have hypotheses to guide therapy, but science progresses when hypotheses are based upon ascertained data rather than primarily upon theoretic assumptions. For many years, I have, together with various colleagues, been engaged in an intensive scrutiny of the family settings in which schizophrenic patients had grown up (Lidz et al., 1965). We started from the clinical observation that schizophrenic patients seemed always to have emerged from seriously disturbed families; and from the hypothesis that because the foundations of language and thought are laid down within the family, the thought disorder that forms the distinctive feature of schizophrenia might well be related to these disturbed family environments. We hoped to find something specific within the radius of the family circle that was related to the etiology of schizophrenia; but the global nature of the family pathology created difficulties. Something was seriously amiss with each aspect of the family and its transactions that we examined. Whereas some of the mothers had been unable properly to invest the patient as an infant, others had serious difficulties in establishing boundaries between themselves and the children who became schizophrenic. Most but not all of the mothers were strange if not seriously disturbed, but the fathers just as frequently displayed severe psychopathology. Many of the families were rent by serious schisms between the parents, but others were distorted by a skewed parental relationship in which an apparent harmony or pseudo-mutuality was maintained because the aberrant ideas and ways of child-rearing of one parent were not countered by the passive spouse. The failures of parents to maintain boundaries between generations and to adhere to their gender-linked roles led to incestuous problems, gender identity confusions, and homosexual tendencies in both parents and offspring. The peculiarities of communication and the distortions of reality within the family fostered a proclivity toward irrationality in the children. The extrafamilial socialization of the child had been impeded by a variety of asocial influences in these families. I cannot review the nature of these difficulties but wish to emphasize that the serious problems found in virtually all areas in all of these families had started prior to the birth of the patient and were continuing when the patient became overtly psychotic in adolescence or early adult life. We described our findings as objectively as we could; and many others have published similar findings and amplified them. When the protocols of family studies carried out in Bethesda,[1] in Paris,[2] in Finland,[3] or in Palo Alto[4] are reviewed, they reveal essentially the same difficulties, even though sometimes differing in emphasis concerning what is considered most salient. It has become apparent by now that whatever else may enter into the genesis of schizophrenia, the family problems have major pertinence (Lidz, 1967a).

Focusing upon the etiology and understanding of schizophrenic reactions, I have written relatively little about their treatment in recent years. However, our explorations of the families were carried out in a therapeutic setting and included analytically oriented therapy of the patients. In looking back over the past twenty years I realize that my own treatment of schizophrenic patients, and that of some of my colleagues as well, has been profoundly influenced by the data and the conceptualiza-

---

[1] See Bowen, 1957, 1960; Bowen, Dysinger, and Basamania; Wynne et al. 1957; Wynne et al. 1958.

[2] See Delay et al., 1957, 1960, 1962.

[3] See Alanen, 1958, 1960a, 1960b.

[4] See Bateson et al.; Jackson; Jackson and Weakland.

tions derived from these studies. I shall discuss some of these influences and effects.

The first consequence that I wish to note may seem almost trivial but I believe it has had great therapeutic moment. It is the assurance the therapist can have that he will find ample and tangible material for psychotherapeutic work. He can set aside concerns that he is confronted by some mysterious ailment of metabolic origin and that he is struggling with useless epiphenomena, doubts fostered by the weight of tradition and bolstered by the constant flow of articles announcing the discovery of some new metabolic defect, none of which is subsequently verified—doubts to which the therapist may be vulnerable because of the discouraging turns that are an inevitable part of the work with schizophrenic patients. He can also feel assured that the problems are not beyond the reach of a psychotherapeutic approach, or that they may only become accessible after prolonged analysis. Assurance is essential because the therapist must arouse glimmers of hope in a person who has abandoned hope of coping with the world and those who people it; and the schizophrenic patient is unusually sensitive to pretense of conviction.

Further, the therapist can feel assured that the material he needs to establish a meaningful relationship is not cryptic, for some guides are usually fairly obvious to one who can but observe and hear them.

Let us consider a 17-year-old high school student whom I saw on the day I wrote these paragraphs. He had been flown to the hospital from a preparatory school where he had started behaving strangely, expressing delusions and talking almost incoherently. When I asked what brought him to the hospital, he responded, "My mother." "Your mother?" I asked. "My mother is a witch!—A seductive witch—No, she's a wonderful person—She won't let me do anything I want—No one is good enough for me—She controls me and my father is a weak man who does what she wants—He's a strong man—He was a West Pointer—He beat the hell out of me when I was little." He slipped back and forth, talking of the preparatory school and the nursery school he had once attended, but through it ran themes of ambivalence to his two unhappy parents and their conflicts, and his inability to be free from his mother's needs and demands. Yet, not so many years ago much of what he said about his witch mother, who seduced and controlled, would have been disregarded as but a reflection of his schizophrenic illness.

Even when the patient is out of contact, highly pertinent directives may be inadvertently provided by the parents.

For example, a college girl was admitted to the hospital after having been removed from a train bewildered and acutely delusional. I interviewed her parents when they arrived. In terms of the history alone, the girl's desperate condition sounded much like a bolt out of the blue. She had been a fine student who was interested in writing, somewhat shy but sociable and well liked by her friends and roommates. However, the session itself was replete with material familiar to those who work with parents of schizophrenic patients. The mother did all of the talking, while the father, a wealthy art dealer, remained silent. When I directed remarks at him, I gained a response from his wife. Even when I turned my back on the mother and pointedly placed a question to the father, she intruded before he completed a sentence. It was difficult to learn much about the patient for the mother told about herself, her Pilgrim ancestry, and her ambitions as a writer. When I finally interrupted and asked about the daughter's college career and her interests, I learned that the girl's whole life revolved about becoming a novelist; she had a passion for Virginia Woolf. The mother became enthusiastic; she prayed that her daughter would become another Virginia Woolf. I hesitated, and then commented, "But Virginia Woolf had psychotic episodes and committed suicide." The mother did not hesitate when she replied, "It would be worth it."

I could form a working hypothesis that in this family the parents' marriage was skewed, with the mother dominating the family transactions, preempting roles usually filled by the husband and unable properly to fill the maternal expressive-affectional role, at least toward this daughter. The father, no matter how competent in his career, did not occupy much of the masculine, instrumental role in the family. The mother's interest in the patient was egocentric, seeking to raise a daughter who would carry out her own frustrated ambitions, and she was likely to be intrusive but impervious to the girl's own desires and needs. The girl probably felt accepted only insofar as she could salvage her mother's own frustrated ambitions.

While making rounds some weeks later I noted several novels by Virginia Woolf in the patient's room and asked about them. She replied in a flat voice, "Mother sent them—she has a thing about Virginia Woolf." Over the next months the patient talked of her despair over her inadequacies as a writer, her desires for a marriage in which she could help a husband assert himself, and her resentments over her obligation to live out her mother's aspirations for her. I had some difficulty in believing that she was complying to the extent of becoming psychotic like Virginia Woolf, which proved a serious error, a fatal error. When the patient emerged from her psychosis, her mother insisted she continue her treatment on the west coast where they lived. At home, caught up in her mother's control, she relapsed, and then followed the fate foisted upon her by committing suicide.

The therapist can not only feel secure that meaningful material for psychotherapy will be available, but he can anticipate the nature of the problems upon which the therapeutic transactions will usually focus. As I have noted, difficulties exist in virtually all aspects of the family transactions throughout the patient's life, and we have set down our findings elsewhere. I would now like to extrapolate from this abundant material those difficulties that I currently believe are essentially schizophrenogenic.

When we began our studies, we considered that the patient's dependency and symbiotic needs followed upon the mother's inability to establish boundaries between herself and her child (Lidz and Lidz, 1951). Needing the patient to complete her own life, often to live out the life that was closed to her because she was a woman, she failed to differentiate her own needs and feelings from those of her offspring, who then could not develop as a separate individual. His energies and attention went primarily into giving meaning to his mother's life and supporting her tenuous emotional equilibrium, rather than into his own development. The child could not clearly distinguish his needs, feelings, and wishes from those of his mother. I believe that these observations, which had also been made by Reichard and Tillman and which were elaborated by Hill, were on the right track. However, it is not always the mother's inability to differentiate from the child that leads to the patient's failure properly to establish boundaries between himself and others and attain a distinct identity. The father may be the prime source of such difficulties, particularly with daughters, or with sons when the father has strong homosexual tendencies (Fleck et al., 1958; Raybin). Then, too, when the parents' marriage is markedly schismatic, the child may be caught in the conflict so that his major investment lies in seeking to bridge the gap between the parents, perhaps even by serving as a scapegoat upon whom the burden of the parental difficulties can be placed. The result is much the same in that his own emergence as a person is thwarted and sacrificed to preserve one or both parents. He is prematurely burdened by a task that stifles his development. Study reveals that one parent—or both—is profoundly egocentric; that is to say, the parent is seriously handicapped in being able to understand others only in terms of his own life. Not only is the child understood merely as an extension of the parents' existence, but the spouse is also treated egocentrically; and events are perceived only in terms of the parent's life and needs, and are often distorted to fit into an extremely egocentric view of the world.

Now, whereas the parent is limited, at least he or she has an egocentric orientation and strives to preserve his integration. The patient, however, is not as fortunate, for his orientation is mother-centered or parent-centered; he views the world according to the parent's feelings, needs, and defenses, and lives to protect the persons from whom he has not properly differentiated (Lidz, 1967b).

Fortunately, this statement of the situation is something of an exaggeration. Most patients who become schizophrenic in late adolescence or adult life have been able to try to differentiate and live their own lives, but because they are poorly prepared to understand others and to relate to them, they become enmeshed in difficulties and give up. Successful regression is impossible, for it leads back to dependency upon the engulfing parent, who arouses homicidal impulses or provokes incestuous fears. The questions of how the patient solves this dilemma and where he seeks refuge lead us to consider the thought disorder that forms the essence of schizophrenia.

As various investigators have pointed out, the patient's foundations in the meaning system and logic of his culture had been faulty. My colleagues and I described the transmission of irrationality within the family because of the parents' proclivities to distort reality in order to maintain their own precarious emotional equilibria. Commonly patients had been placed in a "double bind" (Bateson et al.) in seeking to fill a parent's mutually exclusive demands in order to feel loved or accepted; or had become perplexed about the utility of verbal communication because of the discrepancies between what parents said and what they conveyed by their behavior, or because of "the mystification" (Laing), in their contradictory communications. As Wynne and Singer (1963a, 1963b; Singer and Wynne, 1965a, 1965b) have amply demonstrated, there is a strange amorphous or fragmented quality in the parents' communications. The patient who is parent-centered tends to perceive in terms of a parent's needs rather than in terms of how perception and communication help him master his environment and how others in his community perceive and understand. Those patients who had been caught between irreconcilable parents try to maintain irreconcilable versions of the world that can only be brought together and resolved paralogically.

There is another aspect of the problem of the schizophrenic thought disorder that is difficult to explain succinctly. In order to perceive, think, or communicate, one must divide the ceaseless flow of experience into categories. By and large the vocabulary of a language is a catalogue of the categories a culture uses in dividing experience. In learning the language the child learns what his society considers essential or useful in understanding the world, and also what can be neglected and what must be ignored. This division of experience into categories requires the separation of what is actually a continuity. Experience is continuous—categories are discrete. Each culture teaches its members to ignore what would blur boundaries between essential categories. A fundamental step in establishing categories that must occur in each child's life concerns the differentiation of the self from the non-self. Every culture places a taboo on things that had been self and become non-self, such as secretions and excretions (Leach) ; and upon fusions of the self and the mother, as in nursing and the oedipal ties; and also upon other blurrings of essential divisions, such as the attributes of the two sexes. In persons who become schizophrenic, such boundaries have never been clearly established—between the self and the mother, between what is masculine and feminine—and these failures affect subsequent category formation and conceptualization. It is in the hiatus, in the nebulous region that lies between categories that the schizophrenic finds refuge. Often he returns to fantasies of a vague union with the mother in which boundaries are obliterated, a union that is now sexualized in a polymorphous perverse manner; and to a state where he is neither clearly male nor female, and where the burdens of being an individual self have vanished (Lidz, 1968). Others, perhaps less able to regress in this fashion, but still with poor boundaries between the self and others, attribute their own impulses to others in what we term projection, or seek to control forbidden impulses by extrojecting poorly internalized parental prohibitions as hallucinations and delusions.

I believe that this explication of what I currently consider to be the crux of the schizophrenic situation provides the therapist with guidelines through the maze of data and the perplexing contradictions of the patient's communication and behavior; it permits the therapist to gain and retain perspective despite the booby traps that the patient can so adroitly set for him, and despite the inevitable flights from reinvolvement with the world and the unreliable, egocentric individuals who people it.

The therapist can know that the basic therapeutic task lies in releasing the patient from the bondage of completing a parent's life or of bridging the divisiveness between his parents, and in enabling the patient to become a person in his own right, investing his energies in his own development rather than remaining tied to the problems of the preceding generation. The therapist persistently fosters the patient's latent desires for individuation that he has given up as hopeless, and counters his fears of rejection and abandonment if he asserts his own needs and desires and his terror that self-assertion and expression of his ambivalent hostilities will destroy his parents. The patient must become capable of perceiving his parents, their behavior, and the interpersonal environment differently from the way his parents need to see these matters and from the way his parents require him to see them, and he must learn to trust his own feelings and perceptions.

Now, such therapeutic tasks require an approach that differs in many ways from conventional psychoanalytically oriented therapy. Our emphasis is *not* on analysis of distortions of understanding arising from mechanisms of defense that are utilized to buttress the ego, but is rather on analysis of distortions that have been imposed by significant others to defend their egos. Rather than raise doubts in the patient concerning his perceptions and motives, we often seek to imbue him with trust in his own feelings and ideas, accepting them while questioning ideas and feelings that are essentially his parents' offered as his own. The patient constantly tests the therapist's ability to differentiate the two. We do not foster anxiety to achieve proper therapeutic movement, for anxiety is apt to disorganize further, but rather we convey respect and trust of the patient's ideas and feelings to foster the patient's expression of what he has long been taught to distrust. We do not evoke free association, for the patient needs to be guided into sharper conceptualizations and common modes of communication. Thus, waiting and long silences have little use; the patient is weaned from his autistic world and idiosyncratic communication by the therapist's ability to hear what the patient seeks to express even as he seeks to conceal in terms of metaphor and cryptic associations. Our knowledge of the common dilemmas and life situations of schizophrenic patients, knowledge gained from direct family studies, has particular importance in permitting us to be alert to what the patient is saying in his strange ways. The schizophrenic must come to trust verbal communication, and he does so by learning that the therapist listens to what the patient says and means what he says, but is not imposing his ideas upon the patient. Thus, the therapist does not interpret so much as seek clarification of nebulous material from the patient. Then, too, whereas a therapist commonly questions why a neurotic patient blames his parents, and interprets in terms of distortions created by oedipal conflicts, he encourages the schizophrenic patient to express feelings about parents even if those feelings contain projective elements—for only then can the patient begin to sort out his confusions about his parents and properly question their attitudes and demands.

The schizophrenic patient develops a transference relationship when he can trust, and he trusts when he feels understood and when he begins to dare believe that the therapist will not use him or abandon him because he is understood. But the therapeutic relationship is long a tenuous thread before it becomes a means of reliving and reevaluating childhood experiences. It is fraught with the actual dangers of the patient's childhood intrafamilial relationships. A therapist's interest, concern, care, and affection are apt to be equated with parents' intrusiveness and envelopment, and with their imperviousness to the patient's own needs and feelings. In brief, a major requirement for the therapist concerns the ability to care and refuse to give up while not needing the patient or his devotion. The therapist seeks to convey that even though he wants very much for the patient to improve and will go a long way and make personal sacrifices to foster such improvement, he pursues this goal neither for the parents' sake nor because of his own need for a therapeutic success.

Then, too, because the patient has learned to disregard what is said, the unspoken signals are of great importance. "I long ago learned to stop listening and note how mother was feeling," said one young woman. Much has been written about the schizophrenic patient's intuitive capacities. They have learned to base their interactions with parents on indications and to become skilled in responding to feelings. However, despite such abilities or because such abilities are based upon relationships with peculiar parents, schizophrenic patients often misinterpret. Similarly, it is often difficult to know what a remark will mean to the patient, who can plunge into inchoate blackness of despair because of an imagined rebuff. It is important to counter a patient's tendency to consider the therapist as omniscient, for errors and misunderstandings are bound to occur; and many schizophrenic patients have learned that they must accept the parent's views or be rebuffed. The relationship can also be threatened by the common practice of considering as projections the patient's concerns that the therapist will seduce, or that the therapist wishes to be rid of him. A woman who seems to believe firmly that her analysis will lead to an affair with her analyst may be projecting her wishes to some extent, but, basically, she is transferring to the therapist her hope and fear that if she shows affection, he will seduce her, even as her father had started masturbating her when she became pubescent.

As many schizophrenic patients were raised by parents who had vacillated between intrusive closeness and inattentive withdrawal into their own fantasies or problems, establishing a proper working distance in therapy presents difficulties. A patient's feelings that I was withdrawn in some sessions and oppressively intrusive in others depended upon inadvertent changes of two or three inches in the customary placement of her chair. In general, schizophrenic patients have been burned by having been seduced into involvement with their engulfing parents, and because of the pain have renounced forever hopes of any meaningful relationships. They are wary and must be wary. When they find their resistances to the therapist melting they are very likely to flee . . . flee the hospital, flee into panic, or flee into withdrawn states. The therapist who has properly been encouraged by the developing relationship can become profoundly discouraged and even give up. This is a critical moment in treatment that must be anticipated even though it does not always occur. Now the therapist is being tested and if he persists and surmounts the rebuff, theraeputic movement can gain momentum, for a less tentative relationship will follow.

I have, perhaps, dwelt too long on how certain core problems in establishing and maintaining a useful therapeutic relationship gain meaning in the light of the family studies. Knowledge of the types of settings from which schizophrenic patients emerge provides guidance in many other ways. I shall offer a few examples rather than endeavor to be comprehensive.

Let us consider the common preoccupatiens of schizophrenic patients with homosexuality and with fears of undergoing a change of gender. An appreciation of the parents' confused gender identities and failures to maintain the gender-linked roles provides a therapeutic approach that is more useful than ideas about innate bisexuality. A firm sexual identity forms a foundation of a stable ego identity. In these families a child does not have a suitable model for identification in the parent of the same sex, whose worth is further undercut by the parent of the opposite sex whose love the child seeks. Sometimes the parents have virtually reversed gender roles and in other cases a parent's homosexual tendencies are apparent. A schizophrenic youth with many effeminate traits and homosexual and masochistic preoccupations had an alcoholic father who had been an eminent football player. The father was contemptuous of his effete, artistic son, whereas the mother had fostered his esthetic development, conveying the idea that he must not become like his crass father. Eventually, the youth began to speak of his notions that his father had homosexual tendencies. They were not projections. His mother abreacted with a social worker the anguish she had experienced when her husband had admitted that his attraction to athletics involved his fascination with nude male bodies, and when his impotence and his intense attachment to a fellow athlete had marred the early years of their marriage. The homosexual concerns of the patient could be approached meaningfully in terms of his perceptions of his father, who represented the type of man attractive to his mother, and in terms of the unacceptability of masculinity when it meant the callousness he and his mother had experienced from his father—and later through attention to his unresolved identification with his mother.

Fears of incest, which create panic because the patient fears proximity to the parent he needs, are not simply regressions and projections but reflect both the parents' own incestuous tendencies and the pathological family structure. A young man who had brought a girl friend into the home to sleep with him after his father left his mother was incoherent when hospitalized, but his mother begged, "You must cure him—he is all of my life—when he started to become sick I slept with him just like man and wife." A young woman who had been hospitalized because of her confusion and public promiscuity had her genitalia examined by her physician father each time she returned home from a date to make certain she was still a virgin.

We learn, too, that not all of the poor habits and sloppiness of the patient are evidence of schizophrenic dilapidation; some are reflections of the failure of parents to inculcate basic social behavior and essential adaptive techniques. A young male patient befriended a schizophrenic young woman and took her out to dinner. He reported to his psychiatrist that he could not continue the friendship for he could scarcely eat because of his disgust with the girl's sloppiness. She not only spilled food all over herself but blew her nose in the napkin. When the matter was broached with the young woman, she wanted to know what was wrong—her father, an eminent professor, blew his nose in his napkin. Another young woman always appeared untidy, and the nurses observed that she did not know how to put her nylons on properly nor how to adjust her brassiere. At the age of 26 she would not go to buy a properly fitting bra; she did not know how, for her mother had always brought them home for her. Such lack of education concerning social amenities can, in turn, interfere with socialization with peers, from whom the adolescent must learn so much about interpersonal relationships. We have come to appreciate that many schizophrenic patients require guidance in techniques of living and need group experiences which promote interchange about personal behavior to supplement or offset the intrafamilial experiences.

Along similar lines, the patient's thought disorder requires specific attention. It is not simply a regression or an intrusion of autistic primary process material, but a complex resultant of the parents' amorphous or fragmented styles of communicating, of poor training in categorizing, of having been taught paranoid mistrust within the home, of the paralogical thinking that results from trying to elude the "double bind," of thinking irrationally to suit the parents' egocentric needs. The topic is too large to pursue here. However, a major function of the special high school for adolescents in the Yale Psychiatric Institute lies in providing a type of instruction that counters the schizophrenic patient's overinclusive thinking and enhances focal attention and clear conceptualization. The therapist can promote such changes by fostering clear boundaries between the patient and others, and by clarifying conflicting feelings and attitudes. Increasingly, however. I have focused specifically on freeing the patient from the need to distort his perceptions and meanings to fit into his parents' aberrant version of the world. It is a difficult passage, but when accomplished, the patient is out of the mire and on more solid ground. Conjoint family therapy when used as an adjunct to individual therapy can be particularly helpful. In the family sessions the patient may be unable to avoid realizing that one or both of his parents distort reality to their own needs, that they will reject the patient if he challenges their defenses, and that their remarks are untrustworthy. The patient may have become capable of assessing what his parents say through his experiences in therapeutic groups where participants challenge others and comment on defensive maneuvers. The patient finds it easier to cope with the actual parent with a therapist present than with the parent as a malignant introject. The woman who had not known how to purchase a brassiere had made little progress until conjoint family sessions were started. She had considered her mother as a perfect woman who had long sacrificed herself to keep the family solvent after the father had become depressed and ineffectual. In the family sessions, whenever the patient sought to discuss problems in the home that had troubled her childhood and adolescence, the mother consistently shifted to talking about the patient's difficulties as a child, intimating that no parent could have been successful with an inherently disturbed child. Yet, at other times, she would insist that the patient had been a normal but highly gifted child. With but slight help from the therapist, the inconsistencies came into focus. Then, in a crucial session, the patient saw her mother in a new light. The mother persistently asked to have the patient at home for a weekend, but in these meetings it became apparent that whenever the patient could make the trip, the mother found the occasion unsuitable. Eventually, the visit home could not be sidestepped. During the subsequent session the father criticized the patient for various trivial short-comings during the weekend. The patient finally said that although it had been good to be home she would have enjoyed it more if her father had not nagged so much. The mother immediately snapped, "Your father never nags." The patient was silent, but later remarked, "You know, Mother, I am just realizing that I often feel ill at ease with you." To this the mother replied, "If you are, you are the only person I know who is." The bind had been placed, but it was too apparent. There was no argument, no blow-up, but the patient now began to express her own feelings and her own ideas.

The priority I have given to discussing how knowledge of the patient's family milieu can serve to guide psychotherapy does not indicate a disinterest in direct work with the family. Indeed, I believe that neglect of the family has been a major cause of therapeutic failure. Particularly with youthful patients efforts must be made to modify parental attitudes toward the patient as well as the patient's attitudes toward his parents. All too often when a patient is hospitalized a member of the staff elicits a history from the parents, notes that they are difficult or even troublesome, and lets them know that they have handed over their offspring to competent surrogates. Of course, it seems simpler if the staff can focus on the patient without the family's interference—but the family problems cannot be avoided through avoidance of the family. The opposite extreme—of hospitalizing the family with the patient, as carried out experimentally by Bowen and his colleagues (1957)—does not permit the patient the disengagement that is a major purpose of hospitalization.

If the parents were not difficult or peculiar, it is unlikely that the patient would be schizophrenic, but this does not mean that they are not intensely involved with their child, whose hospitalization is one of the unhappiest experiences in their lives. They require support lest one of them or the marriage collapse under the strain. They also need to face the family problems rather than believe that their child's illness is the major source of their unhappiness and difficulties. Commonly, therapists who know that months or years of intensive work will be required with a patient, somehow expect the parents to change simply because they are told to do so.

The premature removal of the youthful schizophrenic patient just as a good therapeutic relationship is being established is often a major frustration in hospital treatment (Fleck et al., 1957). The parents are likely to remove their child for several reasons. The mother cannot believe that her son or daughter can survive without her, a concern that earlier had caused the school phobia from which many of these patients had suffered, and which had blocked their socialization with peers. Only a person who has worked with such mothers after their children have been hospitalized can appreciate the almost unbearable anxiety they suffer. The mother must control the treatment because no one can understand or really care for her unique child. The parent may also dread the patient's growing attachment to the therapist, experiencing it as total abandonment. Then, when as part of his improvement the patient displays hostility to the parents, they know that he has become sicker and find reasons to remove him from the hospital. If the staff members have been hostile to the parents or have neglected them, they can more readily believe that the hospital is turning the patient against them. Such crises must be anticipated and headed off. When someone on the staff understands the parents' problems, keeps them informed, and works with them to modify their concerns about the patient and their fears of losing their offspring, they are less likely to disrupt the therapy.

The removal of the patient from the family commonly creates an intrafamilial crisis. The difficulties with the patient had served to mask the incompatibilities of the parents; or the mother becomes anxious and depressed, deprived of the major focus of her life; or recriminations flare into the open, with each parent blaming the other for their child's illness; or another child now feels the brunt of the family difficulties. The hospital cannot fully shelter the patient from the aggravated family problems. Sometimes, the family establishes a new equilibrium without the patient, particularly when the parents have been excluded from the hospital. The family closes ranks, leaving no room for the patient, and despite protests to the contrary, will resist resuming any responsibility for him—a common cause of abandonment of patients in state hospitals.

Stanton and Schwartz made a major contribution to the understanding of the treatment process when they pointed out that flare-ups of disorganized behavior often occurred in response to disagreements among the staff members about the patient. The patient had become sensitized by being the focal point of the family schisms and sometimes had been a master at provoking them in his role as a scapegoat for parental conflicts. In the hospital he is apt to be sensitive to the expressed or covert disagreements about him between parents, or between parents and staff, and caught between his loyalties, he covers the situation by regressive behavior. It is worth a great deal of effort to try to unite the parents concerning the need for hospitalization and the plan of treatment, even if they cannot agree about anything else. Neglect of the parents, hostile exclusion of them, or condescension toward them often leads to aggravation of the patient's condition even though the psychiatrist may believe he is protecting the patient from their malignant influence.

Indeed, it has now become apparent—how had it been overlooked?—that the acute onset of many schizophrenic reactions, or the exacerbation that leads to hospitalization, follows upon the patient's being placed in an insoluble bind by his parents' impending separation. The patient is pulled in two directions by the competing parents—condition reflected in the ideation of the catatonic excitement or stupor. A few days ago I listened to an interview with a graduate student who had suffered several catatonic episodes. She told of her delusions during the first episode, when she believed that everyone in the world loved her but she was responsible for their well being. At the time, her parents had finally decided to end their unhappy marriage. Both used the patient, their oldest child, as a confidant and sought her as an ally. Her mother told the patient that she feared the father would seduce the patient's pubescent sister, with whom he frequently slept. The father confided that the mother was a Lesbian and a menace to the three daughters.

When one realizes that an acutely disturbed patient is responding to an approaching break-up of his parents' marriage in which he is torn between them or knows that he will be left irrevocably tied to the task of salvaging a parent's life, one can accomplish considerable therapeutic work even when the patient is inaccessible. A 16-year-old youth was admitted in an extreme state of excitation, believing that an atom bomb had destroyed the city, that he alone remained alive, and that no one else was real. During the several months during which he remained out of contact, it was possible to modify his parents' relationship so that they no longer planned to separate. At first, the mother, who claimed she had only remained with her highly eccentric husband for the children's sake, had become even more determined to leave him, blaming him for their son's psychosis. However, as discussions continued, she realized that they had both been at fault: Their marriage had never led to a proper family life because both were pathologically tied to their families of origin, each of which undercut the worth of the other. The patient, who had long sought to bridge this schism, had become terrified at the prospect of being the mother's major support in the absence of his grandiose father. Receiving emotional support from the hospital staff during the crisis, the parents stopped blaming one another and began to face their shortcomings as spouses and parents. They supported one another sufficiently to give up their stranglehold on their son and later to accept the advice to send their son to a preparatory school. Their difficulties were far from resolved—the father's severe pathology precluded any easy solution—but they managed to have their son remain away from home and from further involvement in their problems.

At present the current flows strongly in the direction of brief hospitalization for schizophrenic patients lest the hospital foster regression or increased withdrawal from socialization. A hospital that is a therapeutic community does not promote regression but provides a retreat from living situations that have overwhelmed the patient, and fosters the socializing experiences with peers he had lacked at home. The pathology of the family is extensive and can be changed only under fortunate circumstances and with prolonged and intensive therapeutic work with the family. It forms a pathogenic environment, particularly for the patient who has become sensitized to it. Even after a prolonged hospital stay, it is usually unwise for the patient to return to his family. It requires considerable work with the parents as well as the patient to make such separation possible, but it is often vital for any definitive and lasting change in the patient's life.

We would like to believe that we can alter the family transactions and modify the parents' attitudes sufficiently to permit the patient to return to more normal ways and resume his development. This is the goal of conjoint family therapy, which some psychiatrists now believe is the treatment of choice for schizophrenic patients. Undoing the influences that had been throttling or distorting the patient's development throughout his formative years is scarcely possible without intensive psychotherapeutic work with the patient. It is a very different matter from eliciting changes in the family when the child is still very young. Moreover, the parents are no longer youthful and their personalities and patterns of interaction are set. Still it is worth the effort for when inroads are made, changes in the family are followed by significant changes in the patient. Although conjoint family therapy has much to offer in clarifying family problems to the family members, and can open the way for profound changes in attitudes, my own experience leads me to doubt its effectiveness as the sole approach rather than as part of a more total program of treatment for both the patient and the family. Another highly useful form of family therapy is carried out in open-ended parents' groups. In these groups parents not only relate to others with similar problems and can together try to work out some solutions, but also may be able to see in others what they had been unable to see in themselves.

I have sought to present some of the influences upon the treatment of schizophrenic patients that have been emerging with the realization that these patients have grown up in seriously disturbed and distorting family environments, and with our increasing knowledge of what these families are like and just how they have failed to provide certain requisites for the patient's integrated development. I have considered some of the ways in which such knowledge provides directives for psychotherapy with the patient, and also for effecting changes in the family situation, in the parents' relationships with each other, and in their attitudes toward the patient. We cannot always change the situation and we cannot often change it profoundly. We can seek to make it possible for the patient to escape from it into a different way of living rather than into irrationality and delusion. Occasionally, the patient gains sufficient independence, rationality, and perspective to appreciate that his parents had been so deprived in their own childhoods, so caught up in a net created by their parents' difficulties, that they could not have been different than they were, and that he, the patient, cannot salvage their lives for them, but rather has all he can do to make something of his own and break the pathological chain that has extended from generation to generation. Then, the ambivalent animosities toward his parents and his fears of them can dissolve into compassion for them. It was such compassionate resolution that Tennessee Williams sought in writing *The Glass Menagerie* long after he had fled his home and that Eugene O'Neill strove to work out in the series of plays that culminated in *Long Day's Journey into Night*. The patient is unlikely to achieve such understanding if his therapist regards the parents as villains and feels hostile to them, rather than grasping the tragedy of the parents' lives even as he seeks to understand and empathize with the patient.

REFERENCES

ALANEN, YRJÖ O. "The Mothers of Schizophrenic Patients," *Acta Psychiatrica Neurologica Scand.* (1958) 33: Suppl. No. 124.

ALANEN, YRJÖ O. "Some Thoughts of Schizophrenia and Ego Development in the Light of Family Investigations," *Arch. Gen. Psychiatry* (1960) 3:650-656. (a)

ALANEN, YRJÖ O. Über die Familiensituation der Schizophrenie-Patienten," *Acta Psychotherapeutica et Psychosomatica* (Basel) (1960) 8:89-104. (b)

BATESON, GREGORY, et al. "Towards a Theory of Schizophrenia," *Behavioral Science* (1958) 1:251-264.

BLEULER, EUGEN. *Dementia Praecox or the Group of Schizophrenias* [1911]; Internat. Univ. Press, 1950.

BOWEN, MURRAY. "Family Participation in Schizophrenia," paper presented at meeting of American Psychiatric Assn., 1957.

BOWEN, MURRAY. "A Family Concept of Schizophrenia," in Don D. Jackson (Ed.), *The Etiology of Schizophrenia;* Basic Books, 1960.

BOWEN, MURRAY, DYSINGER, ROBERT H., & BASAMANIA, BETTY. "The Role of the Father in Families with a Schizophrenic Patient," *Amer. J. Psychiatry* (1959) 115:1017-1020.

BOWEN, MURRAY, et al. "Study and Treatment of Five Hospitalized Families Each with a Psychotic Member," paper presented at meeting of Amer. Orthopsychiatric Assn., 1957.

DELAY, J., DENIKER, P., & GREEN, A. "Le Milieu Familial des Schizophrènes: I. Proposition du Probleme," *Encephale* (1957) 46:189-232.

DELAY, J., DENIKER, P., & GREEN, A. "Le Milieu Familial des Schizophrènes: II. Méthodes d'Approche," *Encephale* (1960) 49:1-21.

DELAY, J., DENIKER, P., & GREEN, A. "Le Milieu Familial des Schizophrènes: III. Résultats et Hypothèses," *Encephale* (1962) 51:5-73.

FLECK, STEPHEN, et al. "The Intrafamilial Environment of the Schizophrenic Patient: II. Interaction Between Hospital Staff and Families" [1957], in Theodore Lidz, Stephen Fleck, and Alice R. Cornelison, *Schizophrenia and the Family;* Internat. Univ. Press, 1965.

FLECK, STEPHEN, et al. "The Intrafamilial Environment of the Schizophrenic Patient: Incestuous and Homosexual Problems" [1958], in Theodore Lidz, Stephen Fleck, and Alice R. Cornelison, *Schizophrenia and the Family;* Internat. Univ. Press, 1965.

FROMM-REICHMANN, FRIEDA. "Transference Problems in Schizophrenia," *Psychoanal. Quart.* (1939) 8:412-426.

GREEN, HANNAH. *I Never Promised You a Rose Garden;* Holt, Rinehart & Winston, 1964.

HILL, LEWIS. *Psychotherapeutic Intervention in Schizophrenia;* Univ. of Chicago Press, 1955.

JACKSON, DON D. "The Family and Sexuality," in Carl A. Whitaker (Ed.), *Psychotherapy of Chronic Schizophrenic Patients;* Little, Brown, 1958.

JACKSON, DON D., & WEAKLAND, JOHN H. "Schizophrenic Symptoms and Family Interaction." *Arch. Gen. Psychiatry* (1959) 1:618-621.

JUNG, CARL. *The Psychology of Dementia Praecox;* New York, J. Nervous and Mental Diseases Publ. Co., 1909.

LAING, RONALD D. *The Self and Others: Further Studies in Sanity and Madness;* London, Tavistock Publ., 1962.

LEACH, EDMUND. "Anthropological Aspects of Language: Animal Categories and Verbal Abuse," in Eric Lenneberg (Ed.), *New Directions in the Study of Language;* M.I.T. Press, 1966.

LIDZ, RUTH WILMANN, & LIDZ, THEODORE. "Therapeutic Considerations Arising from the Intense Symbiotic Needs of Schizophrenic Patients" [1951], in Eugene B. Brody and Fredrick C. Redlich (Eds.), *Psychotherapy with Schizophrenics;* Internat. Univ. Press, 1952.

LIDZ, THEODORE. "The Family, Personality Development and Schizophrenia," in John Romano (Ed.), *The Origins of Schizophrenia;* The Hague, Excerpta Medica Foundation, 1967. (a)

LIDZ, THEODORE. Salmon Lectures, 1967, to be published. (b)

LIDZ, THEODORE. "Familie, Sprache und Schizophrenie," *Psyche* (1968) 22:701-719.

LIDZ, THEODORE, FLECK, STEPHEN, & CORNELISON, ALICE. *Schizophrenia and the Family;* Internat. Univ. Press, 1965.

O'NEILL, EUGENE. *Long Day's Journey Into Night;* Yale Univ. Press, 1956.

RAYBIN, JAMES. "Homosexual Incest," *J. Nervous and Mental Disease,* in press.

REICHARD, SUZANNE, & TILLMAN, CARL. "Patterns of Parent-Child Relationships in Schizophrenia," *Psychiatry* (1950) 13:247-257.

ROSENTHAL, DAVID (Ed.). *The Genain Quadruplets;* Basic Books, 1963.

SINGER, MARGARET T., & WYNNE, LYMAN C. "Thought Disorder and Family Relations of Schizophrenics: III. Methodology Using Projective Techniques," *Arch. Gen. Psychiatry* (1965) 12:187-200. (a)

SINGER, MARGARET T., & WYNNE, LYMAN C. "Thought Disorder and Family Relations of Schizophrenics: IV. Results and Implications," *Arch. Gen. Psychiatry* (1965) 12:201-212. (b)

STANTON, ALFRED H., & SCHWARTZ, MORRIS S. *The Mental Hospital;* Basic Books, 1954.

SULLIVAN, HARRY STACK. "Conceptions of Modern Psychiatry: Therapeutic Conceptions," *Psychiatry* (1940) 3:87-117.

WILLIAMS, TENNESSEE. *The Glass Menagerie;* New Directions, 1945.

WYNNE, LYMAN C., et al. "The Family Relations of a Set of Monozygotic Quadruplet Schizophrenics," in *Congress Report of the 2nd. Internat. Congress of Psychiatry,* Zurich (1957) 2:43-49.

WYNNE, LYMAN C., et al. "Pseudo-Mutuality in the Family Relations of Schizophrenics," *Psychiatry* (1958) 21:205-220.

WYNNE, LYMAN C., & SINGER, MARGARET T. "Thought Disorder and Family Relations of Schizophrenics: I. A Research Strategy," *Arch. Gen. Psychiatry* (1963) 9:191-198. (a)

WYNNE, LYMAN C., & SINGER, MARGARET T. "Thought Disorder and Family Relations of Schizophrenics: II. A Classification of Forms of Thinking," *Arch. Gen. Psychiatry* (1963) 9:199-206. (b)

49

A FOLLOW-UP STUDY OF INTEN-
SIVELY TREATED CHRONIC
SCHIZOPHRENIC PATIENTS

Michel Messier, Richard Finnerty, Constance S. Botvin,
and Lester Grinspoon

Two groups of chronic schizophrenic patients were treated with intensive psychotherapy for a period of two years, starting in 1962 and 1964.
Half of the patients also took phenothiazines. Control groups at a local
state hospital received phenothiazines but no psychotherapy. A follow-up
of the groups on three tests of adjustment, administered at the end of
1967, indicated some trends toward better adjustment by patients who had
received psychotherapy but there were no statistically significant differences among the groups.

This paper is a follow-up of a study conducted in the Clinical Research Center at the Massachusetts Mental Health Center by Drs. Grinspoon, Ewalt, and Shader on the long-term treatment of chronic schizophrenia (1). The study focused on the relationship between long-term
pharmacotherapy with phenothiazines and long-term intensive psycho-

Based on a paper read at the 124th annual meeting of the American Psychiatric
Association, Boston, Mass., May 13-17, 1968.

Dr. Messier is a psychiatrist at the Service de Hospitalization Domicile, Paris,
France; Mr. Finnerty is unit psychologist, Boston State Hospital; Miss Botvin and Dr.
Grinspoon are at the Massachusetts Mental Health Center, 74 Fenwood Rd., Boston,
Mass. 02115, where Miss Botvin is research assistant and Dr. Grinspoon is director of
psychiatry (research). Dr. Grinspoon is also associate clinical professor of psychiatry,
Harvard Medical School. Requests for reprints should be addressed to Dr. Grinspoon.

This work was supported by Public Health Service grants MH-12556 from the National Institute of Mental Health and FR-05555 from the Division of Research Facilities and Resources.

The authors wish to thank Drs. Milton Greenblatt, Jonathan O. Cole, and Jack R.
Ewalt for their important contributions to this paper, and Gerald Hogarty, M.S.W.,
and Douglas Zahn for their assistance with statistical analysis.

therapy conducted by experienced psychotherapists in an active therapeutic milieu.

All of the patients in the study were male, between the ages of 18 and 35, unmarried, free of organic disease, and hospitalized as schizophrenic for three or more years in a large state hospital in Boston. The diagnosis of schizophrenia was agreed upon by three senior psychiatrists, who arrived independently at this diagnosis. Of the patients who satisfied these criteria, ten were chosen and transferred to a small, specially built research ward at the Massachusetts Mental Health Center for two years of study. Two years later a second group of ten was chosen and studied in an identical fashion.

All of the study patients were exposed to an active therapeutic milieu. A nursing staff of 25 people, an occupational therapist, and a social worker involved the patients and their families in an intensive program for the entire two-year period. Among the various facets of the milieu program were diverse activities ranging from therapeutic community meetings and other group or individual ward functions to frequent beach outings, museum visits, and the like. In addition, each of the patients had intensive individual psychotherapy at least twice a week with senior staff psychiatrists, all of whom were psychoanalysts or psychoanalytically oriented and all of whom had had considerable experience in the psychotherapy of schizophrenics.

After an initial "drying out" period of several weeks, during which all patients received an inert placebo, half of the patients were randomly selected to receive thioridazine while the others continued to receive a placebo for the remainder of the study.

Grinspoon, Ewalt, and Shader's main finding (1) was that phenothiazine treatment is perhaps one of the most powerful tools now available for the treatment of chronic schizophrenia. While two years of psychotherapy alone did little or nothing for the chronic schizophrenic patients, there was ample evidence that the combination of drugs and psychotherapy had beneficial effects. It was not possible, however, to make any statement regarding the therapeutic effects of drugs without concomitant psychotherapy, since both experimental groups received psychotherapy.

It is to this question that we wish to direct our attention. In this follow-up study the remaining comparison (that between treatment using drugs with psychotherapy and using drugs without psychotherapy) can perhaps be made since chronic patients at the Boston State Hospital generally receive high dosages of phenothiazines and since individual psychotherapy is rarely given to patients as chronic as those in this study. Too, the atmosphere of the state hospital chronic ward lacks the richness and variety of experience found at the Clinical Research Center, although various occupational and vocational rehabilitation services, including paid employment, are now available at the state hospital. It is the purpose of this paper to determine whether those patients treated at the Clinical Research Center, either with or without drugs, did in fact improve clinically or make an adjustment to the community to a greater extent than those who remained at the Boston State Hospital.

METHOD

The subjects for the follow-up study were 41 patients selected from among chronic patients at the Boston State Hospital according to the criteria outlined above. In 1962, 21 patients were selected; ten were transferred to the Clinical Research Center (CRC) for a period of two years, and 11 remained in the continuous treatment services of the Boston State Hospital. The participation of the latter group in this project was unknown to the Boston State Hospital staff. In 1964, 20 other patients were selected; half were transferred to the CRC for two years, and half stayed at the hospital under the same conditions. Subjects who opposed transfer or whose families were unable to participate in the study remained at Boston State Hospital. Because of this distinction a bias in the otherwise random selection of subjects may have been introduced.

Table 1 indicates that there were no significant differences among any of the groups of patients in age, education, or length of previous hospitalization—a result confirmed by the F-test in a one-way analysis of variance on each characteristic.

The treatment of the two groups transferred to the CRC has been described above. It should be noted that three of the 20 CRC patients had changes of therapists during the two-year period; the remaining 17 were treated by just one therapist for the entire time. Generally all patients who remained at the Boston State Hospital received high doses of various phenothiazines and none were exposed to formal psychotherapy. The hospital milieu included limited recreational and gradually improving occupational facilities.

The instruments used for this study were:

1. Modified General Adjustment Planning Scale (GAPS) (4). This is an objective scale measuring the patient's (or former patient's) adjustment in four dimensions. Of these, we have chosen to use three: employment status, recreational status, and living status. The fourth, mental status, we have eliminated in favor of the Quantified Mental Status, which we found more reliable and discriminating. Each dimension of

the GAPS is divided into six levels along a continuum; living status, for example, ranges from independent community living to restriction to a closed hospital ward.

2. Quantified Mental Status (QMS) (3). The QMS measures the extent of pathology along several continua and arrives at a total score indicative of the general level of "psychoticness" observable to the experienced interviewer.

3. Discharge Readiness Inventory (DRI) (2). The DRI attempts to assess the degree to which a patient is ready to be discharged from the

TABLE 1

Demographic Data

Characteristics	BSH I	BSH II	Study Groups[1] CRC ID	CRC IP	CRC IID	CRC IIP
Age						
Mean	27.0	28.3	27.2	26.4	29.4	24.8
Standard deviation	3.70	5.57	3.96	6.96	7.52	3.96
Education						
Mean	11.0	9.7	11.0	10.0	11.6	11.8
Standard deviation	1.60	1.93	2.00	1.27	1.95	2.95
Months since first hospitalization						
Mean	116.0	101.8	92.6	77.8	73.2	131.2
Standard deviation	55.2	46.0	54.3	21.4	35.8	58.3
Total months in hospital						
Mean	97.4	85.9	78.8	68.0	63.8	108.6
Standard deviation	42.8	49.1	50.3	24.3	25.9	37.4

[1]BSH=Boston State Hospital, CRC=Clinical Research Center, I=Study group 1, II=Study group 2, D=on drugs, P=on placebo.

hospital, regardless of whether there are facilities to accommodate him. Using information obtained from the patient, ward personnel, and other staff members, items of information covering areas such as social effectiveness, community involvement, and presence of belligerence or bizarre behavior are completed.

The QMS was completed by the senior author on 38 of the 41 patients. One patient committed suicide while on escape, and two refused to meet with the interviewer. The DRI was administered only to subjects who were still inpatients as of December 15, 1967. This questionnaire was completed by staff members caring for the patients with the assistance of the authors. The modified GAPS was completed on all subjects by the authors with the help of ward personnel and families.

Figure 1 presents the means of the three dimensions used in the GAPS and the QMS for four patient groupings: all BSH patients (BSH I and BSH II combined), all CRC patients (CRC I and CRC II combined), and the same CRC patients divided into drug and placebo subgroups (CRC-D and CRC-P). The appropriate F- or t-tests revealed that there were no statistically significant differences among the groups on any of the indices measured.

Fig. 1.—Group differences on adjustment scores.

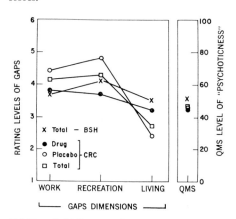

GAPS and QMS on patients divided into hospital groups. On both scales, lower scores indicate better adjustment.

There is, however, a trend indicating that patients in the CRC groups scored consistently lower in psychotic symptomatology on the QMS than the patients in the BSH groups. Also, the living status of the CRC patients is generally better than that of the BSH patients. Sixty-five percent of the CRC patients and 37 percent of the BSH patients are living out of the hospital environment. These trends are not significant but are consistent for both time periods.

Another trend is that the CRC drug groups generally scored worse than the placebo groups in living arrangements but better in work and recreational status. This apparent contradiction will be discussed. Also, the CRC drug groups follow closely the profile of the BSH groups on the three dimensions of the GAPS. Figure 2 presents the means of the same indices as figure 1 but for different groupings of patients. The first grouping includes all the patients started in 1962 (BSH I and CRC I); the second includes all patients started in 1964 (BSH II and CRC II). On all four indices the more recent groups have scores indicating better adjustment than the earlier groups.

Finally, in all four dimensions of the DRI—Psychosocial Adequacy, Belligerence, Community Adjustment Potential, and Manifest Psychopathology—there are no significant differences among the groups.

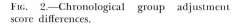

Fig.   2.—Chronological   group   adjustment score differences.

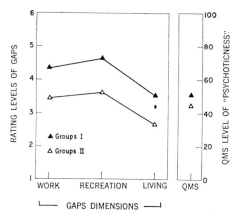

GAPS and QMS on patients divided into time periods. On both scales, lower scores indicate better adjustment.

DISCUSSION

It would appear from these results that, even though the 41 subjects were offered quite different treatment programs for two years, their overall adjustment after one or three years of follow-up was generally similar. On none of the indices did we find differences that were significant at conventional significance levels. This may be due to the small size of the samples rather than to a complete lack of difference among the groups. There is an indication that differences do exist when we consider certain nontrivial differences or trends in the data.

It seems that the first groups, started in 1962, are making a less satisfactory adjustment than the groups started two years later. Unfortunately, since the design of the original study did not include a standardized clinical assessment of all patients at the beginning and the end of the study period, we cannot tell whether the difference noted above represents some deterioration over time or a basic difference between the groups.

The finding indicating a better living status for CRC patients might be explained by the fact that their families were interested in their transfer and were more involved in the treatment process, perhaps because of the intervention of social workers from the CRC.

It is also interesting to note that the QMS scores of the patients transferred to the CRC indicate a lesser degree of psychotic symptomatology. We are unable at this time to determine whether this is due to the active therapeutic milieu, the intensive psychotherapy, or other unknown variables. Too, those patients who agreed to take part in the study may have been less psychotic than those who refused to be transferred.

There is no consistent correlation between work and recreational statuses on the one hand and living status on the other. Our personal observations suggest that of the patients living out of the hospital, those living at home are particularly inactive. They are generally unemployed and usually stay indoors, watch television, and have little or no interaction outside the extended family. It would appear that the lack of stimulation in the environment, as well as the absence of consistent, firm pressure to engage in activities and to take on responsibilities, results in a much more impoverished existence than that of comparable patients who remain in the hospital. This finding is borne out by the second trend noticed in figure 1, which shows the CRC placebo group living out of the hospital but not working or engaging in recreational activities. We have no explanation at this time for the fact that the living status of the placebo group has improved more than the drug group; we tend to view that as an artifact of the small samples involved.

Since 23 of the 40 living patients were still hospitalized on part- or full-time programs, we used the DRI to determine whether there would be some differences among the groups as illustrated by a greater readiness to be discharged. In this way we hoped to account in part for the bias introduced in the selection of study subjects. No statistically significant differences were found among the groups, however, on any of the four dimensions. The trends found on the other indices were not supported by the DRI.

SUMMARY

This is a follow-up study of 41 patients diagnosed as chronic schizophrenics, 20 of whom underwent intensive long-term psychotherapy conducted by experienced psychotherapists in an active therapeutic milieu. Half of these patients also received pharmacotherapy with phenothiazines. The remaining 21 patients remained at a local state hospital and received no special treatment other than the regular ward milieu and pharmacotherapy with phenothiazines.

The results as indicated by the indices of evaluation used here suggest that there were no significant differences between those patients treated at the CRC and those treated at BSH. There were trends on some test variables, but none of them reached statistical significance.

REFERENCES

1. GRINSPOON, L., EWALT, J., & SHADER, R.: Psychotherapy and Pharmacotherapy in Chronic Schizophrenia, *Amer. J. Psychiat.* 124:1645-1652, 1968.
2. HOGARTY, G.: The Discharge Readiness Inventory: Validity as an Outcome Measure in the Treatment of Chronic Schizophrenia, read at the fith annual meeting of the American College of Neuropsychopharmacology, San Juan, Puerto Rico, December 1966, in press.
3. ROCKLAND, L. H., & POLLIN, W.: Quantification of Psychiatric Mental Status, *Arch. Gen. Psychiat.* 12:23-28, 1965.
4. WALKER, R., FROST, E., & ASCI, M.: Habilitative Flash: Rehabilitative Changes Among Long-Stay Hospitalized Psychiatric Patients, in preparation.

50

RELAPSE IN CHRONIC SCHIZO-PHRENICS FOLLOWING ABRUPT WITHDRAWAL OF TRANQUILIZING MEDICATION

Robert F. Prien†, Jonathan O. Cole‡, and
Naomi F. Belkin§

Physicians are often faced with the problem of determining whether long-stay schizophrenics require continuous treatment with tranquilizers. Prolonged ingestion of ataractics has both physical and economic disadvantages. Recent reports on oculo-cutaneous changes (3, 13, 20, 27, 28), persistent dyskinesia (6, 18) and sudden deaths (16, 25) have focused attention on the potential dangers of prolonged use of tranquilizing medication. On the other hand, discontinuation of medication may lead to recurrence of acute psychotic behavior. The literature on drug withdrawal provides no solution to the dilemma. The results from drug discontinuation studies are complex and contradictory. Some investigators report extremely high relapse rates while others report little deterioration even when drugs are withdrawn for long periods of time. A brief review of the literature will give some indication of the contradictory nature of results.

Most drug withdrawal studies were patterned after a study of Good,

Supported by NIMH grants numbered, MH-10292, MH-11384, MH-10496, MH-10989, MH-11046, MH-11047, MH-10332 and USPHS Contract SA-43-ph-3064.

† Formerly Project Co-ordinator, NIMH-PRB Collaborative Studies on Chronic Schizophrenia, Biometric Laboratory, The George Washington University. Currently Research Psychologist, Central NP Research Laboratory, V.A. Hospital, Perry Point, Maryland.

‡ Superintendent, Boston State Hospital, Boston, Massachusetts.

§ Research Scientist, Biometric Laboratory, The George Washington University.

Reprinted, by permission of author and editor, from: *The British Journal of Psychiatry,* 115:679-686, 1969.

Sterling, and Holzman (12). Active medication was abruptly withdrawn and a placebo was substituted, usually for a period of three to six months. A few studies deviated from this model. Caffey *et al.* (5) and Garfield *et al.* (10) gradually reduced dosage before withdrawing active medication. Caffey reported a high incidence of deteriorated behavior and Garfield a low incidence over a four-month period. Olson and Peterson (22) and Judah, Josephs, and Murphee (19) did not substitute placebo after withdrawing medication. Both reported substantially higher relapse rates than most of the investigators using placebo. However, Whitaker and Hoy (29) used both placebo and complete withdrawal of all pills in the same study and found no difference between the two treatments.

The least favorable report on drug discontinuation was that of Olson and Peterson (22) who withdrew phenothiazines from 127 chronic schizophrenics. By the end of six months, 74 percent of the patients had deteriorated to a point requiring resumption of medication. Judah *et al.* (19) removed medication from 519 chronic schizophrenics for 90 days; during this period 72 percent of the patients had to be returned to medication because of regressed behavior. Zeller (31) interrupted chlorpromazine and reserpine treatment for one month in 40 psychotic patients, and found that 68 percent relapsed. Whitaker and Hoy (29) withdrew perphenazine from 39 long-stay schizophrenics. Approximately 40 percent required the drug within 10 weeks. Caffey *et al.* (5) found that 45 percent of 171 male chronic schizophrenics on placebo had to be returned to active medication during a 16 week study period. Blackburn and Allen (2) reported a similar relapse rate, 43 percent, over a four-month period. Brooks (4) reported significant regression within a month following withdrawal of medication.

In contrast, five investigators report relatively little regression resulting from phenothiazine withdrawal. Freeman and Alson (9) removed medication from 48 chronic male psychotics for a period of six months and found that only 27 percent required resumption of medication. At the end of three months, only 13 percent of the patients had relapsed. Garfield *et al.* (10) administered placebo to 18 female chronic schizophrenics. Only 22 percent had to be returned to active medication during a five-month study period. Good *et al.* (12), using a sample of 112 chronic schizophrenics, concluded that chlorpromazine could be withdrawn for a period of three months without any noticeable regression in behavior; though withdrawal for longer periods produced a significant increase in pathology. Rothstein (26) also reported that medication could be withdrawn for three months without significant increase in pathology. Finally, Hughes and Little (17) withdrew chlorpromazine from 21 female psychotics and found that only 19 percent had to be returned to medication during an 18-month period.

Efforts to identify patients who can tolerate long periods off medication have not been very successful. Denber and Bird (7) found that probability of relapse was related to severity of illness but not to length of hospitalization or clinical diagnosis. Winkleman (30) suggested that patients on medication long enough to achieve ego reorganization were less likely to relapse when drugs were discontinued. Freeman and Alson (9) found that sicker patients, particularly those who were confused or apathetic, were poorer risks for discontinuation. Diamond and Marks (8) also reported that withdrawn patients seemed to require tranquilizers more than patients in whom thinking disorders predominated. On the other hand, Caffey et al. (5) found no evidence to show that probability of relapse was related to clinical diagnosis, duration of illness, length of hospitalization, or length and amount of previous medication. Judah et al. (19) reported that clinical diagnosis, length of illness, and duration, dosage or type of drug were not factors affecting relapse. Finally, Good et al. (12) and Brooks (4) found no relationship between relapse and dose or type of previous tranquilizing medication.

In summary, the studies on drug withdrawal provide widely differing results. Even where the study designs appear quite similar, results are often strikingly different. Judah et al. (19) and Rothstein (26) suggest that part of this difference may be due to environmental effects. In particular, tolerance for deterioration may vary considerably from hospital to hospital and conceivably from ward to ward. A study by Rathod (24) comparing two wards on which discontinuation was carried out appears to support this view. Studies by Hamilton et al. (14, 15), Barrett et al. (1), Goldsmith and Drye (11) and Meszaros and Gallagher (21) also suggest that drug effect is related to treatment milieu.

The present study will investigate the effects of withdrawing ataractic medication from long-stay schizophrenics at a number of hospitals. One purpose of this investigation was to determine whether hospital setting is an important variable affecting probability of relapse. A second purpose is to determine whether probability of relapse is related to patient and medication variables, such as length of hospitalization, age, severity of illness, and type and dose of previous medication.

METHOD

This investigation of drug discontinuation was part of a multi-hospital collaborative study on the relative effectiveness of various dose levels of phenothiazines in the treatment of chronic schizophrenic patients. The collaborative study was developed under the National Institute of Mental Health (NIMH) psychopharmacology program. The general background of the project, the details of the research design, and the characteristics of the samples are presented elsewhere (23). A summary of the research design is provided here for orientation.

Seven public mental hospitals participated in this study: Boston State Hospital, Boston, Massachusetts; Broughton State Hospital, Morganton, North Carolina; Dorothea Dix State Hospital, Raleigh, North Carolina; Kentucky State Hospital, Danville, Kentucky; Manhattan State Hospital, New York, New York; St. Louis State Hospital, St. Louis, Missouri; and Springfield State Hospital, Sykesville, Maryland. These hospitals were selected to represent the entire urban-rural continuum. Three hospitals admitted patients exclusively from large urban centers, two hospitals served both urban and rural communities, and two hospitals served almost exclusively rural areas.

Approximately 120 chronic schizophrenics, half male and half female, were selected at each of the seven hospitals by the following criteria:

(1) A primary diagnosis of schizophrenia.
(2) Age between 19 and 55.
(3) Continuous hospitalization of at least two years.
(4) No evidence of organic brain disease, lobotomy, mental deficiency (IQ below 70), or medical conditions contra-indicating the use of high doses.

The mean age of the patient sample was 41.6 years, 61 percent being over 40 years of age. Length of hospitalization ranged from 2 to 34 years, with a mean of 14.5 years; 54 percent of the patients had been hospitalized over ten years.

Patients were randomly assigned to one of four groups: (1) high dose —2,000 mg. of chlorpromazine per day; (2) low dose—300 mg. of chlorpromazine per day; (3) placebo; and (4) physician's choice, consisting of whatever medication or dose the hospital chose to administer. Each treatment group consisted of approximately 210 patients, 30 from each hospital.

Patients were observed on their normal hospital medication for eight weeks. At the end of this eight-week baseline period, patients who had been assigned to high dose, and placebo were shifted to study medication. All medication was administered in liquid form under double-blind conditions. Patients were maintained on their assigned treatment for 24 weeks.

A patient was considered relapsed if he regressed and had to be re-turned to known medication before the end of the 24-week period. The decision to terminate study medication was usually made jointly by the principal investigator and the treatment physician. When returned to known medication patients were treated at the discretion of the responsi-ble physician.

The clinical status of the patient was assessed in two ways. First, doc-tors made overall clinical judgments of severity of illness and degree of improvement. Second, specific psychopathology was rated by doctors, nurses, and social workers. All patients were evaluated just before the study and at eight-week intervals during the study period. Patients ter-minated before the end of 24 weeks were evaluated at the time they left the study.

RESULTS

The placebo group had a significantly higher relapse rate than the groups receiving active medication. Forty percent of the placebo patients relapsed, compared to only 13 percent of the low-dose patients and 6 percent of the high-dose patients. Chi square analyses showed that the differences between placebo and each of the groups were significant at the .01 level. The remainder of this paper will deal primarily with placebo results. Detailed results for the other treatment groups are presented elsewhere (23).

Figure 1 shows the cumulative percentage of placebo patients who relapsed at various periods during the study. It may be seen that very few relapses occurred during the first six weeks on placebo. Most relapses, 72 percent, occurred between week 6 and week 16. Relapse was generally characterized by the return of hallucinations, delusions, and confusion, or by disrupting symptoms such as extreme hostility, excitement, and threatening or destructive behavior.

Probability of relapse was significantly related to the dose of tranquil-izing medication the patient was receiving before he was put on placebo—the higher the dose the greater the probability of relapse. Fig. 2 shows the cumulative percentage of relapses for patients on three dose levels of pre-study tranquilizing medication, "low" (under 300 mg./day), "mode-rate" (300 to 500 mg./day), and "high" (over 500 mg./day).* Only 18 percent of the 65 patients on low doses of pre-study medication relapsed when medication was withdrawn. In contrast, 47 percent of the 60 pa-

---

* All doses of pre-study tranquilizing medication were converted to equivalent doses of chlorpromazine.

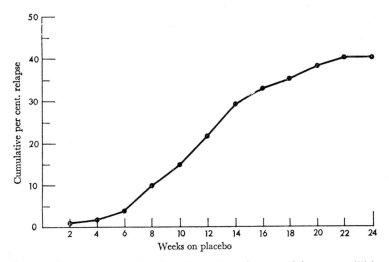

FIG. 1.—Relapses on placebo (includes only patients receiving tranquillizing medication before the study).

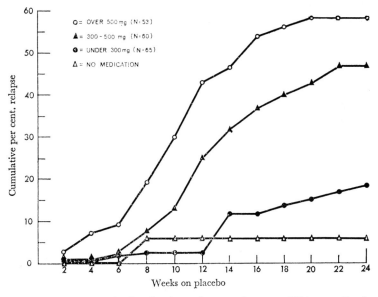

FIG. 2.—Relapses on placebo: by dose of pre-study tranquillizing medication (all doses were converted to equivalent doses of chlorpromazine).

tients on moderate doses and 58 percent of the 53 on high doses relapsed when drugs were withdrawn. Chi square analyses showed that the difference in relapse rate between low dose and each of the other dose levels was highly significant (p<.01). There was no significant difference between moderate and high dose (p>.05). Fig. 2 also gives the relapse rate for patients who received no tranquilizing medication prior to the study. Only one of the 18 patients, 6 percent, failed to complete the full 24 weeks on placebo.

TABLE 1

Relapses on Placebo: By age and Dose of Pre-Study Tranquilizing Medication

Daily dose of pre-study medication*		Age in years		
		Under 40	40-49	Over 50
Under 300 mg.	Total N	10	35	20
	N relapsed	2	5	5
	% relapsed	20	14	25
300 mg. and over	Total N	49	48	16
	N relapsed	28	22	8
	% relapsed	57	46	50
All doses	Total N	59	83	36
	N relapsed	30	27	13
	% relapsed	51	33	36

* All doses were converted to equivalent doses of chlorpromazine.

Younger patients (i.e. patients under 40) had a higher relapse rate than older patients. However, this was due to the fact that younger patients were receiving higher doses of tranquilizing medication before the study. Table 1 shows the relationship between dose of pre-study medication and age. There was no significant difference in relapse rate between the various age groups within each dose level. This indicates that dose, not age, was the critical factor affecting relapse.

Table 2 gives the number and percentage of relapsed patients at each hospital. It may be seen that relapse rate varied considerably among hospitals, ranging from 12 percent to 68 percent (the probability is less than .01 that this distribution of relapse rates could have occurred by chance alone). The greatest difference between hospitals occurred with patients receiving moderate or high doses of pre-study medication. The relapse rate for patients on low doses of pre-study medication was relatively low at each hospital.

TABLE 2

RELAPSES ON PLACEBO: BY HOSPITAL AND DOSE OF PRE-STUDY TRANQUILIZING MEDICATION

Daily dose of pre-study medication*		A	B	C	Hospitals D	E	F	G	Total
No medication	Total N	2	2	4	2	2	2	4	18
	N relapsed	0	0	1	0	0	0	0	1
	% relapsed	0	0	25	0	0	0	0	6
Under 300 mg.	Total N	4	8	7	11	8	12	15	65
	N relapsed	1	2	1	2	2	2	2	12
	% relapsed	25	25	14	18	25	17	13	18
300-500 mg.	Total N	11	10	7	7	10	8	7	60
	N relapsed	8	6	4	3	3	3	1	28
	% relapsed	73	60	57	43	30	38	14	47
Over 500 mg.	Total N	10	10	9	9	6	6	3	53
	N relapsed	8	6	6	6	3	2	0	31
	% relapsed	80	60	67	67	50	33	0	58
All doses	Total N	25	28	23	27	24	26	25	
	N relapsed	17	14	11	11	8	7	3	
	% relapsed	68	50	48	41	33	27	12	

* All doses were converted to equivalent doses of chlorpromazine.

TABLE 3

PATIENTS COMPLETING 24 WEEKS ON PLACEBO WITH NO DETERIORATION IN GLOBAL PSYCHIATRIC STATE: BY HOSPITAL AND DOSE OF PRE-STUDY TRANQUILIZING MEDICATION*

Daily dose of pre-study medication†		A	B	C	Hospitals D	E	F	G	Total
No medication	Total N	2	2	4	2	2	2	4	18
	N not worse	2	2	3	2	2	2	4	17
	% not worse	100	100	75	100	100	100	100	94
Under 300 mg.	Total N	4	8	7	11	8	12	15	65
	N not worse	3	5	4	8	5	9	12	46
	% not worse	75	63	57	73	63	75	80	71
300 mg. and over	Total N	21	20	16	16	16	14	10	113
	N not worse	0	6	4	7	7	8	6	38
	% not worse	0	30	25	44	44	57	60	34
All doses	Total N	25	28	23	27	24	26	25	
	N not worse	3	11	8	15	12	17	18	
	% not worse	12	39	35	56	50	65	72	

* Change in global psychiatric state was determined from the Global Change Scale comparing the patient's clinical condition at week 24 with his clinical condition prior to the study.
† All doses were converted to equivalent doses of chlorpromazine.

Patients classified as "relapsed" were not the only patients to show clinical deterioration. Approximately 20 percent of the patients who completed the full 24 weeks on placebo also regressed,* though not severely enough to warrant resumption of medication. It is doubtful whether the behavior of some of these patients would have been tolerated had the patient not been involved in a study. Table 3 shows the number and percentage of patients at each hospital who were able to complete 24 weeks on placebo without showing signs of clinical deterioration. Again, the difference between hospitals was quite pronounced. For example, 72 percent of the patients at Hospital G were able to remain off medication without showing signs of clinical deterioration, compared to only 12 percent of the patients at Hospital A.

DISCUSSION

The results show that the large majority of patients on low doses of tranquilizers are able to remain off drugs for six months without significant deleterious effects. This suggests that drug discontinuation is a feasible treatment policy for patients currently receiving low doses of ataractic medication at public mental hospitals. Patients receiving moderate to high doses of medication, on the other hand, show relatively high relapse rates when drugs are discontinued. Probability of relapse appears too high to commend long term drug withdrawal as a treatment policy for this group of patients.

Some investigators advocate treatment programs for chronic patients which involve periodic short-term withdrawal of phenothiazines (12, 22, 26). This study was not designed to evaluate the effectiveness of these "intermittent chemotherapy" programs. However, our results do indicate that when such programs are used with patients on moderate to high doses of tranquilizing medication, the drug-free period should not exceed six weeks. After this period, the probability of relapse and deterioration sharply increases.

The results also show that relapse rates vary considerably among hospitals. There are a number of possible explanations for this finding. First, it is possible that patients at high-relapse hospitals (e.g. hospital A) were initially more severely ill than patients at low-relapse hospitals (e.g. hospital G). This would explain why fewer patients at high-relapse hospitals were able to remain off medication. There is one drawback to this explanation. On the symptom rating scales, there was no significant difference in pre-study symptomatology between high- and low-relapse hos-

---

* The criterion for regression was the Global Change Scale (23) which compared the patient's clinical condition at week 24 with his condition before treatment.

pitals. However, this does not necessarily mean that differences did not exist. Tranquilizing medication may have effectively controlled the symptoms of patients at high-relapse hospitals so that they appeared no more ill than patients at low-relapse hospitals. Only when medication was withdrawn did the greater severity of illness of patients at high-relapse hospitals become apparent. This explanation also assumes that a large proportion of patients receiving tranquilizing medication at low-relapse hospitals were really in no need of ataractic drugs.

A second possible explanation should not be overlooked. The criteria for relapse may have differed significantly between high-relapse and low-relapse hospitals. As was explained previously, a patient was considered "relapsed" if he deteriorated to the point where he was unable to remain on placebo for the full 24 weeks. It is possible that high-relapse hospitals showed less tolerance for deteriorated behavior than low-relapse hospitals. High-relapse hospitals may have terminated the experiment at the first sign of deterioration, while low-relapse hospitals may have resumed medication only for severely disturbed behavior. If this were true, it would account for the difference in relapse rate between hospitals. Evidence from the rating scales indicates that this was not the case. There was no significant difference in degree of deterioration between "terminated" patients at high-relapse hospitals and those at low-relapse hospitals. Also, patients at high-relapse hospitals were not put back on medication any earlier in the study than patients at low-relapse hospitals.

These findings on hospital differences have important implications for research on drug withdrawal. If the study had been conducted only at Hospital G (relapse rate 12 percent), we might have concluded, as some investigators have, that drug withdrawal is a feasible treatment policy for all long-stay patients. Conversely, if the study had been conducted only at Hospital A (relapse rate 68 percent), the conclusions would have been very different. If hospitals using the same study design show widely differing relapse rates, what agreement can be expected among single hospital studies using different selection criteria, evaluation instruments and methods of analysis? Hospital differences may well explain a good proportion of the contradictions noted in the drug withdrawal literature. More important, these findings indicate that considerable caution should be observed in generalizing from studies involving a single hospital or ward.

SUMMARY

In a seven-hospital collaborative study, 210 chronic schizophrenics were assigned to a placebo for a 24-week period. During that time, 40 percent of the patients relapsed and had to be returned to active medication. Probability of relapse was related to two variables: (1) the hospital conducting the study and (2) the dose of tranquilizing medication the patient was receiving before being put on placebo. Patients receiving low doses of tranquillizing medication before the study were less likely to relapse than patients receiving moderate to high doses. The practical and theoretical implications of these findings are discussed.

REFERENCES

1. BARRETT, W. W., ELLSWORTH, R. B., CLARK, L. D., & ENNISS, J. (1957). "Study of the differential behavioral effects of reserpine, chlorpromazine and a combination of these drugs in chronic schizophrenics." *Dis. Nerv. Syst.*, 18:209-215.
2. BLACKBURN, H., & ALLEN, J. (1961). "Behavioral effects of interrupting and resuming tranquilizing medication among schizophrenics." *J. nerv. ment. Dis.*, 133: 303-307.
3. BOCK, R., & SWAIN, J. (1962). "Ophthalmological findings in patients on long-term chlorpromazine therapy." *Amer. J. Ophthal.*, 56:808-810.
4. BROOKS, G. W. (1959). "Withdrawal from neuroleptic drugs." *Amer. J. Psychiat.*, 115:931-932.
5. CAFFEY, E. M., DIAMOND, L. S., FRANK, T. V., GRASBERGER, J. C., HERMAN, L., KLETT, C. J., & ROTHSTEIN, C. (1964). "Discontinuation or reduction of chemotherapy in chronic schizophrenics." *J. Chron. Dis.*, 17:347-358.
6. CRANE, G., & PAULSON, G. (1967). "Involuntary movements in a sample of chronic mental patients and their relation to the treatment with neuroleptics." *Int. J. Neuropsychiat.*, 3:286-291.
7. DENBER, H. D., & BIRD, E. G. (1955). "Chlorpromazine in the treatment of mental illness. II. side effects and relapse rates." *Amer. J. Psychiat.*, 112:465-468.
8. DIAMOND, L. S., & MARKS, J. D. (1960). "Discontinuance of tranquilizers among chronic schizophrenic patients receiving maintenance dosage." *J. Nerv. Ment. Dis.*, 131:247-251.
9. FREEMAN, L. S., & ALSON, E. (1962). "Prolonged withdrawal of chlorpromazine in chronic patients." *Dis. Nerv. Syst.*, 23:522-525.
10. GARFIELD, S., GERSHON, S., SLETTEN, I., NEUBAUER, H., & FERREL, E. (1966). "Withdrawal of ataractic medication in schizophrenic patients." *Ibid.*, 27:321-325.
11. GOLDSMITH, J, & DRYE, R. (1963). "Milieu as a variable in clinical drug research." *Ibid.*, 24:742-745.
12. GOOD, W. W., STERLING, M., & HOLZMAN, W. H. (1958). "Termination of chlorpromazine with schizophrenic patients." *Amer. J. Psychiat.*, 115:443-448.
13. GREINER, A. C., & NICOLSON, G. A. (1964). "Pigment deposition in viscera associated with prolonged chlorpromazine therapy." *Canad. Med. Ass. J.*, 91:627-635.
14. HAMILTON, M., HORDERN, A., WALDROP, F. N., & LOFFT, J. (1963). "A controlled trial on the value of prochlorperazine, trifluoperazine and intensive group treatment." *Brit. J. Psychiat.*, 109:510-522.
15. ———, SMITH, A. L., LAPIDUS, H. E., & CADOGEN, E. P. (1960). "A controlled trial of thiopropazate dihydrochloride, chlorpromazine and occupational therapy in chronic schizophrenics." *J. Ment. Sci.*, 106:40-55.
16. HOLLISTER, L. E., & KOSEK, J. C. (1965). "Sudden death during treatment with phenothiazine derivatives." *J. Amer. Med. Ass.*, 192:1035-1038.
17. HUGHES, J. S., & LITTLE, J. C. (1967). "An appraisal of the continuing practice of prescribing tranquilizing drugs for long-stay psychiatric patients." *Brit. J. Psychiat.*, 113:867-873.

18. HUNTER, R., EARL, C. J., & THORNICROFT, S. (1964). "An apparently irreversible syndrome of abnormal movements following phenothiazine medication." *Proc. Roy. Soc. Med.*, 57:758-762.

19. JUDAH, L. N., JOSEPHS, Z. M., & MURPHEE, O. D. (1961). "Results of simultaneous withdrawal of ataraxics in 500 chronic psychotic patients." *Amer. J. Psychiat.*, 118:156-158.

20. MARGOLIS, L., & GOBLE, J. (1965). "Lenticular opacities with prolonged phenothiazine therapy." *J. Amer. Med. Ass.*, 193:95-97.

21. MESZAROS, A. F., & GALLAGHER, D. L. (1958). "Measuring indirect effects of treatment on chronic wards." *Dis. Nerv. Syst.*, 19:167-172.

22. OLSON, G. W., & PETERSON, D. B. (1960). "Sudden removal of tranquilizing drugs from chronic psychiatric patients." *J. Nerv. Ment. Dis.*, 131:252-255.

23. PRIEN, R. F., & COLE, J. O. (1968). "High dose chlorpromazine therapy in chronic schizophrenia." *Arch. Gen. Psychiat.*, 18:482-495.

24. RATHOD, N. H. (1958). "Tranquilizers and patients' environment." *Lancet, i*, 611-613.

25. RICHARDSON, H. L.. GRAUPNER, K. I., & RICHARDSON, M. E. (1966). "Intramyocardial lesions in patients dying suddenly and unexpectedly." *J. Amer. Med. Ass.*, 195: 254-260.

26. ROTHSTEIN, C. (1960). "An evaluation of the effects of discontinuation of chlorpromazine." *New Eng. J. Med.*, 262:67-69.

27. SIDDALL, J. (1965). "The ocular toxic findings with prolonged and high dosage chlorpromazine intake." *Amer. Med. Ass., Arch. Ophthal.*, 74:460-464.

28. WETTERHOLM, D., SNOW, H., & WINTER, F. (1965). "A clinical study of pigmentary change in cornea and lens in chronic chlorpromazine therapy." *Ibid.*, 74:55-56.

29. WHITAKER, C. B., & HOY, R. M. (1963). "Withdrawal of perphenazine in chronic schizophrenia." *Brit. J. Psychiat.*, 109:422-427.

30. WINKLEMAN, N. M. (1957). "An appraisal of chlorpromazine." *Amer. J. Psychiat.*, 113:961.

31. ZELLER, W. W. (1956). "Use of chlorpromazine and reserpine in the treatment of emotional disorders." *J. Amer. Med. Ass.*, 160:179-185.